SOURCES OF DEMOCRACY

ALSO BY SAUL K. PADOVER

THE REVOLUTIONARY EMPEROR: JOSEPH II

SECRET DIPLOMACY AND ESPIONAGE
(with James Westfall Thompson)

THE LIFE AND DEATH OF LOUIS XVI

JEFFERSON *(a biography)*

EXPERIMENT IN GERMANY

LA VIE POLITIQUE DES ÉTATS-UNIS

FRENCH INSTITUTIONS: VALUES AND POLITICS

THE GENIUS OF AMERICA

UNDERSTANDING FOREIGN POLICY

THE MEANING OF DEMOCRACY

THOMAS JEFFERSON AND THE FOUNDATIONS OF AMERICAN FREEDOM

Edited by Saul K. Padover

THE KARL MARX LIBRARY

VOL. I: KARL MARX ON REVOLUTION

VOL. II: KARL MARX ON AMERICA AND THE CIVIL WAR

VOL. III: KARL MARX ON THE FIRST INTERNATIONAL

(other volumes in preparation)

THOMAS JEFFERSON ON DEMOCRACY

THE COMPLETE JEFFERSON

THOMAS JEFFERSON AND THE NATIONAL CAPITAL

A JEFFERSON PROFILE

THE WRITINGS OF THOMAS JEFFERSON

THE COMPLETE MADISON (also titled: THE FORGING OF AMERICAN FEDERALISM)

THE WASHINGTON PAPERS

THE MIND OF ALEXANDER HAMILTON

WILSON'S IDEALS

THE LIVING UNITED STATES CONSTITUTION

CONFESSIONS AND SELF-PORTRAITS

THE WORLD OF THE FOUNDING FATHERS

NEHRU ON WORLD HISTORY

TO SECURE THESE BLESSINGS

SOURCES OF DEMOCRACY

VOICES OF FREEDOM HOPE AND JUSTICE

Selected with commentary by

Saul K. Padover

Distinguished Service Professor, Graduate Faculty,
New School for Social Research

McGRAW-HILL BOOK COMPANY
New York   St. Louis   San Francisco
Düsseldorf   London   Mexico   Sydney   Toronto

123456789DODO79876543

The Editor gratefully acknowledges the following for permission to reprint selections in this volume:

Appleton-Century-Crofts, Educational Division, Meredith Corporation, for BENEDICT DE SPINOZA, *Writings on Political Philosophy,* ed. by A. G. A. Balz.

Basil Blackwell, for THOMAS AQUINAS, *Selected Political Writings,* transl. by A. P. D'Entrèves.

Clarendon Press, Oxford, for SAMUEL PUFENDORF, *De Jure Natural et Gentium Libri Octo,* Vol. II, transl. by C. H. Oldfather and W. A. Oldfather. "The Classics of International Law," No. 17, ed. by James Brown Scott. Oxford: at the Clarendon Press; London, Humphrey Milford, 1934.

Columbia University Press, for MARSILIUS OF PADUA, *The Defender of Peace,* Vol. II: The *Defensor Pacis,* transl. by Alan Gewirth. "The Records of Civilization, Sources and Studies," No. XLVI; ed. under the auspices of the Department of History, Columbia University. 1956.

Estate of Martin Luther King, Jr., and Joan Daves, for DR. MARTIN LUTHER KING, JR., "How Long, Not Long," speech in Montgomery, Alabama, © March 25, 1965.

Harvard University Press, for POLYBIUS, *The Histories,* transl. by W. R. Patton, The Loeb Classical Library, 1923.

Oxford University Press, for THUCYDIDES, *The History of the Peloponnesian War,* ed. in transl. by Sir R. W. Livingstone.

School and Society, for an address by JOHN DEWEY, titled "Democracy and Educational Administration," April 3, 1937.

Library of Congress Cataloging in Publication Data
Padover, Saul Kussiel, date
The sources of democracy.

Bibliography: p.
1. Democracy—Addresses, essays, lectures.
2. Political science—History—Addresses, essays,
lectures. 3. Political science—History—United
States—Addresses, essays, lectures. I. Title.
JC421.P33   320.5'1   72-10247
ISBN 0-07-048073-7

As always,
TO PEGGY,
Who knows and loves
what is best in America

CONTENTS

No definition of democracy can adequately comprise the vast history which the concept connotes. To some it is a form of government, to others a way of social life. Men have found its essence in the character of the electorate, the relation between government and the people, the absence of wide economic differences between citizens, the refusal to recognize privileges built on birth or wealth, race or creed. Inevitably it has changed its substance in terms of time and place."

From "Democracy," in *Encyclopedia of the Social Sciences*, III, 1931.

INTRODUCTION REFLECTIONS ON DEMOCRACY

The word democracy is older than the political system which it connotes nowadays and which prevails, in one form or another, in many parts of the world. The term is of Greek origin (a combination of *demos,* the people, and *kratein,*[1] rule) and was first used in Greece about twenty-four hundred years ago. The earliest reference to it is found in the *History of the Peloponnesian War,* by the Greek historian Thucydides, who quotes Pericles as saying that his Athens was a model democracy:

"Our constitution is named a democracy, because it is in the hands not of the few but of the many."

This is perhaps the first known definition of democracy. The Periclean system contained two essentially democratic ingredients. One was the concept of equality, the other the assumption of community wisdom.

Equality, however, was not of universal applicability. It was limited to citizens. In Periclean Athens women, slaves, and aliens were excluded from the political process. Of a total population of about 300,000, only around 50,000—or approximately 16 percent—had the privileges of citizenship. But within that relatively small group political equality did prevail.

The second Periclean premise, that wisdom resided in the many, underlay democracy as a practical system of government. From it flowed two consequences. In the first place, it stimulated the citizens to active participation, on the ground that they, the rich as well as the poor, in their totality were capable of making wiser decisions than any single individual or any small group of individuals could. In the second place, it followed that the community as a whole was entitled to select its rulers and officials, since it was the best judge of what was good for its own welfare.

In this respect, too, the Athenian system had basic democratic elements, although it differed from modern democracy in that it was direct, rather than representative. In the Athenian democracy, the citizens met—in one recorded instance, their

---

[1] Another possible combination is *demos* and *kratos,* meaning "authority." Thus democracy can be defined as "government [authority] of the people."

number was 3,616—in the popular assembly, known as *Ekklesia,* and proposed legislation, which was then passed by a committee called the *Boule* or the *Council of Five Hundred.* The *Boule,* composed of fifty men from the ten tribal districts that made up the Athenian city state, was chosen by lot.

Executive power was in the hands of a committee of ten generals, known as the *strategoi.* They were elected by the citizens and were eligible for indefinite reelection. The most famous of these *strategos* was Pericles, who was in power most of the time for about a third of a century, between the years 461 and 429 B.C. According to Thucydides, Pericles' rule was in reality "an aristocratical government that went by the name of a democracy." Plutarch writes that Pericles' natural bent was "far from democratical." Nevertheless, Pericles, a rich man and a general, exercised his power democratically, through persuasion rather than by violence. Plutarch says of Pericles' leadership:

> . . . he was able generally to lead the people along, with their own wills and consents, by persuading and showing them what was to be done; and sometimes, too, urging and pressing them forward extremely against their will, he made them, whether they would or no, yield submission to what was for their advantage. In which, to say the truth, he did but like a skillful physician. . . .

In a world of monarchies, oligarchies, and tyrannies, the Greek democratic system was indeed a unique venture in government. "Our government," Pericles said, "is not copied from those of our neighbors: we are an example to them rather than they to us." Greeks were rightly proud of what they had invented. Euripides, in his *Medea* (*ca.* 431 B.C.), has Jason exclaim: "A good Greek land has been thy lasting home, not barbary. Thou hast seen our ordered life, and justice, and the long still grasp of law not changing with the strong man's pleasure."

More than two millennia later, Thomas Jefferson, a connoisseur of democracy, was to pay great tribute to that ancient model. Greece, he wrote, was the first civilized nation to "present examples of what man should be."

But these governmental examples found few imitators. In the civilizations that followed Greece's Golden Age, it was "barbary" rather than democracy that dominated political life. The small democracies of the Hellenistic world gave way to tyrannies. The Roman Republic, an early experiment in freedom *(libertas)* and self-government, succumbed to Caesarism. Everywhere else, for centuries thereafter, the established forms of government were not democracies either in conception or in practice. By whatever names they went—monarchy, aristocracy, theocracy, feudalism, autocracy—they were fundamentally political systems built on and around "the strong man's pleasure." In those polities, the people were not the masters; they were mastered.

The meaning of the words "democracy" and "republic" (or "republicanism"), and the difference between them, will be further developed later on in this book. Here, "democracy" is used as a general term referring to government exercised by the people directly, and "republic" (or "republicanism") connotes any self-government that is not monarchical. In this sense, a republic may be aristocratic or autocratic. It may also be democratic, but not necessarily so.

Why did the ancient democracies fail to survive? An analysis of the reasons for their extinction helps to understand the essence of democracy today, and perhaps also its future. One answer to the question is that, at the stage of history when democracy first appeared, man was not ready for it, hence its continuity was not possible. Neither psychologically nor politically was the society of antiquity prepared for so arduous an enterprise as self-government, exercised by the people, within a framework of consistent and orderly freedom. Woodrow Wilson was undoubtedly right when he said that "democracy is the most difficult form of government." Such a political system requires for its successful functioning and continuity a steady awareness of the self as an independent entity, combined with similar individual entities, all together seeking to achieve, through a sense of civic obligation, the requirements and expectations of each person.

The early experiments in democracy broke down because they were erected on fragile foundations, that is to say, on societies in which true individualism had not yet developed. There existed, of course, outstanding individuals in antiquity—men like Pericles and Cicero come easily to mind—but the ancient communities as a whole did not put a premium on the importance of the self, particularly on self-realization through political identification, civic responsibility, and democratic action. The people of antiquity were more group-conscious and group-affiliated than individualistic. There are, for example, no autobiographies in ancient Greece and virtually no Roman ones, unless one wants to stretch the meaning of the word to include Caesar's *Commentaries.*[2] The ties of the ancients were with a family, a tribe, a city, or a religion, within the circle of which they worked, found fulfillment, and attained whatever feeling of security was possible. The people as such—that is to say, the aggregation of members of the community—lacking a developed sense of self and an identification with an enlarged civic entity, did not determine or shape the larger decisions in the realm of politics and public affairs. Government was left in the hands of a chief or a council of headmen, whose authority generally derived from selection by a small body of people or from automatic transmission through heredity.

In the absence of self-propelling individualism, there developed no theory of self-government to give strength and direction to practical institutions. This explanation can, of course, also be stated in reverse: that the lack of a theory of self-government mitigated against the development of the idea of individualism.

The Roman Republic did have democratic or partly democratic features in such institutions as the Tribunate and, although less so, in the Senate. But there was too much caprice in their selection and insufficient orderly restraint in the exercise of their power. On the one hand, the rulers were not hedged by a consistent system of constitutional laws; on the other hand, the people were not able to bind their rulers, because they were not educated enough to know what their rights and duties were. As Jefferson once put it, the Romans "had no ideas of

government" or of the real meaning of liberty. They were thus vulnerable to appeals made by ambitious athletes of the larynx—orators who held sway through the emotions. When that happened, judgment and rationality fled; blunders and conspiracies reigned; and ultimately dictatorships took over. To this day, it may be said that mindless oratory has been a recurrent danger to republics, especially democratic ones, with low levels of education and weak institutionalized safeguards.

The ancient republics succumbed because they did not build their liberties on sound institutional bases. Perhaps they did not know how, but it is clear that they failed to create the proper machinery for the perpetuation of self-government and orderly liberty. From their experience, modern republics, especially those of the developing nations, can learn helpful lessons.

The ancients were deficient in at least three areas of political operation without which, as modern experience has shown, republicanism, above all democratic self-government, is not possible and cannot survive. One was an independent judicial structure; another, free and competing political parties; a third, a universal public school system. In a democratic polity each of these is a necessity, and all of them together go far toward providing its security and continuity.

Independent courts of justice serve a triple function. On the level of individual relationships they adjudicate differences with objectivity and impartiality. If they perform their functions properly, they mete out justice in a way that conforms to the average man's sense of right and wrong. This nourishes the idea of equality and strengthens the citizens' identification with government—in other words, it promotes democracy. A second function of an independent judiciary is that of clarification of the rules by which the community lives—it provides for a government of laws and not of capricious men. Third, such a judiciary imposes legal restraints on the arbitrariness of power. By defining the laws and defending the rule of law, independent courts can put a damper on willful personal power and overweening political ambition.

The emphasis here is on the word independence.

---

[2] See Saul K. Padover, *Confessions and Self-Portraits: 4,600 Years of Autobiography* (1957), pp. xiii–xiv.

To carry out their functions as guardians of justice and liberty, courts must be independent of political and other pressures. They must not be the creatures of any class or special interest. They must not only be free but feel free—from threat, intimidation, or reprisal. Such independence and freedom can be achieved and secured only by the community. And the community can best do so if it acknowledges the importance of an independent judiciary and cherishes it as a basic safeguard of its liberties.

Political parties, another mechanism for the maintenance of self-government, were not known as such in antiquity. They are, in fact, a relatively modern invention. Antiquity did witness, and suffer from, political (as well as social and economic) conflict, often in harsh terms, but such struggles were not as a rule organized under law or canalized into orderly processes. They were, rather, factions, which James Madison, a profound student of political history, defined (and sharply rejected) as "a number of citizens . . . who are united and actuated by some common impulse of passion, or of interest, adverse to the rights of other citizens, or to the permanent and aggregate interests of the community."

The factions tended to revolve around, or be incited by, some individual, not infrequently a persuasive demagogue. They battled for selfish or narrowly partisan aims, often with a passion that blinded them to the general welfare. So fierce was the factionalism of the early republics—including the city states in the Hanseatic League of the Middle Ages and the Italian city states of the Renaissance—that it helped further to discredit republicanism in the eyes of succeeding generations.

The dread of factionalism, considered a concomitant of democracy, probably slowed up the development of proper political parties which, even as late as the eighteenth century, were widely identified with, and viewed as, factions. This was true even in America after the founding of the United States as a Federal Republic. In his *Farewell Address,* for example, George Washington solemnly warned his countrymen against the "danger of Parties" and their "baneful effects." He pointed out that even in self-governing republics, parties led to excesses, and hence were "not to be encouraged."

Once a political party comes into existence, Washington cautioned, it becomes "a fire not to be quenched; it demands a uniform vigilance to prevent its bursting into a flame, lest, instead of warming, it should consume."

The modern political party, however, is not a faction as defined by Madison and feared by Washington. Actually it is, as Thomas Jefferson (who founded the Republican-Democratic Party in the 1790s) was one of the first to realize, a necessary instrument for self-government and an indispensable agency for the maintenance of freedom. This is especially true in democracies where the population is reasonably large, as in Great Britain, or where it is both large and scattered over an extensive territory, as in the United States.

A political party differs from a faction in several respects. Unlike a faction, a political party is not built around the selfish or self-seeking interests of an ambitious few, but is, rather, in the words of Edmund Burke, an aggregation of men "united for promoting by their joint endeavours the national interest, upon some particular principle in which they are all engaged." Where the premises of self-government are accepted and the processes of democracy are understood and honored, the political party performs functions that cannot be accomplished by any other institution.

To begin with, the modern political party provides an opportunity for like-minded people to express their needs and voice their demands. The party furnishes the leadership, the candidates, the mechanism, and the program for the achievement of the wishes, felt or known, of its members. Indeed, a numerous citizenry could not possibly do anything effective for itself without some party machinery. This is true not only on a national scale but also on local levels, particularly in the big cities. A successful New York political "boss," Edward J. Flynn, once explained the reasons for the necessity of party "machines," the role of which is often misunderstood:

. . . suppose you do away with machines. Without them you . . . would have to devise some alternative means of discovering, before each election, the men and women best qualified for public office. Could you, out of your present knowledge, choose a city-wide slate on which your neighbors could agree? Obviously you would have to talk things over with your neighbors. But since every New Yorker has eight million "neighbors" . . . doesn't this suggest some system of representation? . . . Would you be willing to drop your business every two years to devote full time to attending meetings, canvassing potential candidates, canvassing voters from door to door, raising the indispensable campaign funds? . . . One evening of it would convince you that politics is a full-time job, not a hobby.

Second, where the political party functions freely —where it is not misused by some dictatorship or special-interest group—it attains public consent and consensus by legitimate means, through discussion and persuasion. In this sense, democracy may, in fact, be called government by discussion. Insofar as the party is successful in achieving this objective, it goes far toward reducing those nagging uncertainties and festering frustrations that, under different political systems, often result in chronic turmoil or hopeless apathy.

Even when the party—in this context, its chosen slate of candidates—is defeated in its bid for power, it still performs services vital to the democratic process. For one thing, in defeat it canalizes potentially active discontent into rightful expectation. Where periodic elections are fixed by law, the defeated party holds out the promise of future victory, of which there is always a reasonable chance. In any well-functioning party government, the loser of today is likely to be the victor of tomorrow.

For another thing, the party that is out of power expects, and is expected by its followers, to serve as critic of the actions and program of the party holding office. In Great Britain this role, amounting in effect to a systematized watchdog attitude, is called "His [or Her] Majesty's loyal opposition." The emphasis here is on the word *loyal,* understood as meaning that it operates within the framework of the existing rules and that it accepts the prevailing democratic principles. Provided, therefore, that the opposition criticism is loyal and not aimed at the subversion of the whole established system of freedom, it promotes the vigor of self-government in at least two ways. It exposes, or threatens to expose, corrupt officials and inefficient practices, and thus helps to improve government. It also brings issues to sharp or sharper focus, and thus helps to educate public opinion in regard to the prevailing men and measures.

In sum, the modern political party performs functions supremely essential to democracy. It regulates conflict, which exists in every dynamic society that contains numerous interest groups. It legalizes the operations of such competitive interests. It provides the electorate with an acceptable and stable instrument to express its views and attain its objectives. Finally, it furnishes society with an outlet for accumulated aggressions generated by the pressures and vicissitudes of life. Without the vent of a political party, the temptation to use violence might not be easily resisted. James Fenimore Cooper put it with felicity: "The man who can right himself by a vote will seldom resort to a musket."

The third deficiency in antiquity, insofar as the survival of democracy was concerned, was the absence of a universal public school system. As throughout most of history, so also in the early republics, learning was confined to a limited number of persons, although not necessarily always to the upper classes. A knowledge of reading and writing was to be found among priests, scribes, professional men, and occasionally among rulers, but rarely among the common people. Up to modern times, illiteracy has been a virtually universal condition of mankind.

Given a state of general illiteracy, it proved to be impossible for free and self-governing polities to survive. A benevolent ruler or group might on occasion set up a more or less democratic system, but without an informed citizenry it was built on quicksand. For freedom requires constant alertness based on knowledge, and especially a knowledge of the conditions of freedom. The ignorant cannot long sustain institutions that call for decisions based upon a measure of reasonably informed judgment. Such information can be steadily supplied only in societies where schools are not merely available but also compulsory for all youth, at least in elementary forms. Universal compulsory education, supported by public taxation, is an absolute condition for democratic functioning and continuance. As Jefferson said, "If a nation expects to be ignorant and free, in a state of civilization, it expects what never was and never will be."

This does not mean that education and literacy are in themselves sufficient to guarantee a democratic polity. Literate citizens, in fact, have been known to support and even glorify unfree political systems. In recent years mankind has witnessed the phenomenon of important countries with high levels of literacy being ruled in a totalitarian, sometimes boastfully antidemocratic fashion. Widespread elementary education has been no obstacle to dictatorship. Obviously other ingredients than a nation-wide public school system are needed to constitute and preserve a democracy.

The point is that although it is possible to have education without democracy, it is not possible to have democracy without a considerable measure of education. This is even more true today than in the past. Educational expectation has become broader and higher. In Jefferson's day schools were expected to buttress freedom and to provide "happiness." Nowadays, notably in democratic countries such as the United States, citizens have come to put almost illimitable trust in the promises of education. They assume, as a fundamental democratic right, not only that schools must be made available to all, but also that educational institutions will serve as training centers for the attainment of virtually all the aspirations that move modern man. On November 8, 1965, when he signed the Higher Education Act, providing $2.3 billions for scholarships and loans, President Lyndon B. Johnson told a student audience at his own alma mater, Southwest Texas State College:

Here the seeds were planted from which grew my firm conviction that for the individual, education is the path to achievement and fulfillment; for the nation, it is a path to a society that is not only free but civilized; and for the world, it is the path to peace.

For about eighteen hundred years after the end of the Roman republic (which contained democratic features), democracy, both as a desirable idea and as a practical system, more or less disappeared from Western civilization. It had few advocates. If democracy was discussed at all, it was either as an irrelevancy or as a bad example. At best it was misunderstood; at worst it was spurned and maligned.

The presumed irrelevance of democracy derived from the widespread opinion that, at most, it was applicable only to small communities. This was asserted as a doctrine by leading writers, including Montesquieu and Voltaire. Even such a well-wisher of democracy as Jean Jacques Rousseau restated in his *Social Contract* the belief that it could work only in "a very small state where the people can be readily assembled and where each citizen can with ease know all the others." From this assumption it followed that democracy (or any self-governing republic) could not possibly be considered as a practical polity for a sizable nation.

The idea that a self-governing republic could work only on a very small geographic scale was effectively exploded by Americans in the late eighteenth century. The founders of our republic were, of course, familiar with this theory, but rejected it on the ground that the political writers who had popularized it, including such illustrious ones as Montesquieu, had confused democracy with republicanism. Jefferson considered it a "brilliant fallacy."

The American founders believed that, while the objectives of democracy and republicanism—justice and freedom—might well be the same, there was a great difference between the two systems.

In essence, the difference may be said to be operational and functional. The classic conception of democracy, often referred to as "pure" democracy, is that of a system involving direct citizen participation in public affairs. As James Madison put it, in a democracy "the people meet and exercise the government in person." Under this definition a democracy must necessarily be limited in numbers and spatial range. Madison said: "The natural limit of a democracy is that distance from the central point which will just permit the most remote citizens to assemble as often as their public functions demand, and will include no greater number than can join in those functions."

A republic, on the other hand, is a government in which decisions are made, not by the citizens assembling and legislating directly, but by their representatives. They act as the people's agents in some political center that may be remote from the homes of the voters. Hence a republic, unlike a democracy, need not be confined to a limited number of citizens or restricted to a small geographic area: it is representation and not size that characterizes a republic.

Two conditions must underlie a republic. One is the recognition that power derives from the great body of the people, and not from a favored few. According to John Adams, a republic is a government in which "the people have collectively, or by representation, an essential share in the sovereignty." The other condition is that the representatives must be chosen, directly or indirectly, for limited periods of service, and not for undefined terms. These conditions are, of course, democratic in essence if not necessarily in name.

Having clarified what Madison called a "confusion of names" in regard to democracy and republicanism, the Americans, in 1789, proceeded to establish a republic which had two unprecedented features. First, it included a vast territory, extending a thousand miles north and south, from the borders of Maine to those of Florida, and running some five hundred miles deep. Second, it was constructed on a federal basis, with power decentralized and systematically distributed throughout the land—in component states, counties, and cities. Among the many objectives of the federal structure, self-government and freedom were perhaps foremost. The federal system secured the citizens in their rights to govern themselves locally and regionally, and at the same time it helped to guarantee their liberties. Federalism, in fact, has made it possible for the United States to function both as a republic and as a democracy on a large scale. At base the United States is a

democratic republic, and has been so for about a century and a half.

In this context the words "democracy" and "republicanism" can be used as interchangeable terms.

One of the lessons the American experience with federal republicanism teaches is that an extensive territory can be a help rather than a hindrance to the functioning of self-government. In small republics, as the historic record shows, struggles and changes tended to have a total impact. They could not be confined to the limits of a locality. Its very smallness insured that the whole community would be affected whenever there was serious internal conflict. This may indeed have been a major cause for the extinction of ancient republics.

Large republics, on the other hand, could experience convulsions and hysteria or violations of rights in one section without the whole country's being drawn in. On more than one occasion an area of the United States has succumbed to a temporary dictatorship while the rest of the country remained normally democratic. The very bigness of the nation provided it with a necessary margin of safety. While one state or region was in derangement, the remaining ones, substantial enough in size and power to cushion the shocks coming from the disturbed and undemocratic part, could bide their time until the situation was corrected.

Size, the American experience has shown, has still another advantage in a federal republic. Where the component states enjoy a large measure of autonomy, as in the United States, it is possible for them to try out political and social experiments on a local scale without heavy cost to the whole nation. If successful in one state, such experiments may be adopted by other states or by the country at large. If unsuccessful, they serve as an object lesson for the other states. Pointing to these advantages of a democratic (self-governing) federal system, Justice Louis Brandeis called the states "detached laboratories"— a view of federalism shared by other democratic leaders, including Franklin D. Roosevelt.

Size in itself, of course, does not guarantee democracy. If it did, then colossal countries like China (Imperial or Communist) and Russia (Czarist or

Soviet) would have been democracies long ago. Obviously other ingredients are necessary. Here it is merely pointed out that the long-prevailing tenet that bigness and democracy were incompatible—a belief that helped slow up the development and establishment of democracy for centuries—is no longer valid. The fallacy has been destroyed in practice by the United States, which set the first example—for all the world to see and imitate if it wished—that bigness and democracy are not mutually exclusive. We know today that any big country can be ruled democratically if its leaders and citizens so desire. Democracy, as we shall see, has its problems, but size is not necessarily one of them.

Another effective charge, which for centuries weighed heavily against its acceptability to the educated classes, was that democracy was simply an undesirable form of government. The authority of the classic philosophers, whose influence on Western thought was overriding, was cited in proving the case against democracy. "A kingdom," Aristotle stated in his *Politics,* "may degenerate into a tyranny, an aristocracy into an oligarchy, and a state into a democracy." Plato was almost as devastating when he remarked in *The Republic,* perhaps with a trace of irony, that democracy was "a charming form of government, full of variety and disorder, dispensing a sort of equality to equals and unequals alike."

The traditional European distrust of democracy was carried over to America. With a few rare exceptions, of whom Roger Williams was probably the foremost, the early settlers of America shared this virtually universal antipathy for democracy. It was against the will of God and contrary to nature; it was ignoble in conception and scandalous in execution. John Winthrop, first governor of Massachusetts Bay (1631), called "Democratie" the "meanest and worst of all formes of Government." His friend John Cotton, a Boston clergyman famous in his day for his fervid and influential sermons, averred in 1636 that he did not "conceyve that ever God did ordeyne [democracy] as a fitt government eyther for church or commonwealth." Dominant Puritan thought generally favored rule by the select, preferably a theocracy.

Such views had long echoes. In the period of the American Revolution, when democratic aspirations, though still inchoate, were struggling to come to the surface, many a distinguished leader expressed horror of democracy. There was no great sympathy for monarchy or hereditary aristocracy, but both were regarded as less evil than democracy. Typical of influential conservative opinion was that of John Adams. In his book, *Defense of the Constitutions of Government of the United States of America,* published the year the Federal Constitutional Convention met in Philadelphia (1787), Adams wrote: "Democracy never has been and never can be so desirable as aristocracy or monarchy, but while it lasts, is more bloody than either . . . It soon wastes, exhausts, and murders itself." Alexander Hamilton, speaking in the New York State Constitutional Ratification Convention (June 21, 1788), said:

> The ancient democracies, in which the people themselves deliberated, never possessed one feature of good government. Their very character was tyranny; their figure, deformity. When they assembled, the field of debate presented an ungovernable mob, not only incapable of deliberation, but prepared for every enormity.

This kind of criticism drew justification from the prevalent belief that democracy must necessarily always be "pure," that is, direct. It was fortunate that Americans of the late eighteenth century did not permit themselves to be permanently bound by rigid doctrine. Many leaders had deep misgivings about popular government, but they were willing to experiment with new forms.

More basic apprehensions revolved around the question of whether the common people had sufficient wisdom and self-restraint to be entrusted with any substantial amount of political power. Historical experience, as enemies of democracy never tired of pointing out, proved the contrary. The extent of the misgivings about popular government, the qualms shared by even such moderates as Benjamin Franklin and James Madison, are clear in the extraordinary debates of the Philadelphia Constitutional Convention in 1787,[3] as well as the ones that followed in the State Ratification Conventions.[4] Those debates, together with *The Federalist,* which has become a widely translated classic,[5] are unmatched in the literature on republicanism and, less directly, on democracy. For political realism and penetration, these analyses of the problems of self-government are easily among the world's foremost works on politics.

As the constitutional debates and *The Federalist* papers show, the American leaders and thinkers were troubled by the age-old dilemma posed by the desire for liberty and the imperatives of order. Primarily concerned with freedom, they were hard-headed enough to know that a mere proclamation in favor of it had no practical meaning. Rhetoric and invocation served, no doubt, to satisfy the emotions, but was of limited utility in an arena where power was paramount. The founders of the American republic, most of them experienced lawyers and practicing politicians, were keenly aware that politics always involved power—power in use or in abuse, in execution or in restraint. For them, therefore, the fundamental question was: How, in a system of self-government, do you harness power and control it institutionally so as to safeguard liberty?

The Americans of 1787–89 came up with what proved to be brilliant solutions to the problem. They did so with a number of delicate political contrivances that were designed to check and balance— Montesquieu, whose thought was deeply influential

in this area, had used the term "ballast"—political power at all levels. To assure as large a measure of self-government as possible, they provided for a federal republic in which the bulk of political activities was left in the hands of the individual states, while at the same time prohibiting the latter from operating in certain vital areas—foreign policy and coinage, for example. To prevent tyranny in the central government, they followed the teachings of Montesquieu by decentralizing it. They separated its powers into three independent, yet at some crucial points interdependent, elements, so arranged that none could legally domineer over the others. For, as James Madison, echoing Montesquieu, pointed out in *The Federalist* (No. 47), a concentration of legislative, executive, and judiciary powers in the same hands, whether of an individual or a group, "may justly be pronounced the very definition of tyranny."

So much for the institutional safeguards. What about the rights of the citizens in this delicately contrived republican machine? Was democracy lost in the process? In long-term consequences, it was actually secured, and stoutly secured.

To be sure, dubieties about democracy persisted, and continued to persist well into the nineteenth century, as can be seen in the provisions of the Constitution, which also served as model and guide for subsequent state constitutions. Distrusting the "imprudence of democracy," to use Hamilton's phrase, the founders of the republic did not give the people direct access to power or decision making. The republic was established in the name of "We, the People," who were considered to be the ultimate source of all political power. But in that republican government everything was to be done by indirection, in the name of the people, for the people, but not by them.

Thus the chief executive was to be elected, but indirectly, through electors, who were, however, agents of the majority of the voters in their respective states. Thus federal judges were to be appointed by the chief executive, but the nominations required the consent of the Senate before they could take effect. Thus the senators were to be appointed by

---

[3] They are fully recorded in Max Farrand's *Records of the Federal Convention of 1787,* 4 vols. (1937). For a condensed but thematically complete one-volume record of the debates, see Saul K. Padover, *To Secure These Blessings* (1962).

[4] See Jonathan Elliot's *Debates in the Several State Conventions on the Adoption of the Federal Constitution,* 4 vols. (1827–1830); 5 vols. (1906).

[5] *The Federalist* essays, written in defense of the United States Constitution, were first published in the New York press in the winter of 1787–88, and in book form in 1788. Since then there have been numerous editions, including a number in paperback. The authors of the eighty-five essays were John Jay (five), Alexander Hamilton (at least forty-one), and James Madison (about twenty-four). Three of the essays were the combined work of Hamilton and Madison, and the rest (twelve) were by either one or the other. See E. G. Bourne, "The Authorship of *The Federalist,*" in *American Historical Review,* vol. II (1897), pp. 443–60 and 675–87. See also D. Adair in *William and Mary Quarterly,* April and July, 1944; and A. T. Mason in *American Historical Review,* April, 1952, pp. 625–43.

the state legislatures,[6] whose members, however, were elected by the local voters. Only the House of Representatives was to be chosen by the people directly, every two years—but in most states at that time the suffrage was limited to certain males, primarily white property owners and taxpayers.

But these circuitous arrangements may have helped the development of democracy in America. The federal system, with its indirect contrivances, probably gave the republic the precious time needed to take root and establish itself firmly in the habits of the nation. By keeping the people out of direct participation in national affairs, the republic avoided the risk of possible disruption at a time when the electorate still had insufficient experience, education, or maturity in politics to give intelligent support to a large-scale, nation-wide democracy. At the same time the people were free to continue and develop the practice of local self-government. This was an invaluable school for training in the politics of freedom, as Jefferson pointed out in a conversation with an English visitor in 1817:

> Another cause [of successful American self-government], Mr. Jefferson observed, might be discovered in the many court and county meetings, which brought men frequently together on public business, and thus gave them habits, both of thinking and of expressing their thoughts on subjects, which in other countries are confined to the . . . privileged few.[7]

It is to be noted that nowhere in the area of its institutionalized ambagiousness did the American system aim to deprive the people of personal rights or liberties. The one early serious attempt made in that direction—the Alien and Sedition Acts of 1798 —ended in swift and disastrous defeat for the Federalist party, which had sponsored the repressive legislation. The Federalists had underestimated the democratic spirit that underlies any genuinely functioning republican government.

Insofar as the American people in general were

concerned, avenues to national power and decision were not hermetically closed to them, but merely circumvented, and that, as it turned out, only temporarily. For, it is clear upon analysis, the main features of the American republic—government of the people, regular elections, liberty under law— were democratic in essence, that is, democratic in everything but name. The name was to come later, beginning in the 1820s, when the Republican Party, founded by Jefferson and Madison some thirty years earlier, changed its name to become the Democratic Party. That was a point in history of which Alexis de Tocqueville wrote prophetically in 1833: "The century is primarily democratic. Democracy is like a rising tide; it only recoils to come back with greater force, and soon one sees that for all its fluctuations it is always gaining ground."

The "rising tide" of democracy, which de Tocqueville so clearly discerned in the first half of the nineteenth century, was particularly powerful in America, where the establishment of the federal republic in 1789 was not the end of the matter, but only the beginning. "Conceived in liberty," as Lincoln said, the republic was a landmark, rather than a consummation. Under the overarching umbrella of the Constitution, the American people proceeded—"rushed" would be a better word, perhaps—to build, in Lincoln's unforgettable words, a new nation "dedicated to the proposition that all men are created equal."

The American democracy, so conceived, has developed steadily and has continuously widened its horizons both as to meaning and as to goals, but it would be a mistake to assume that this growth has been either automatic or guaranteed by some special fate. In truth, it took effort, struggle, thought, and dedication to create and sustain free government in America. It still does, and probably always will. "It is a terrible truth," Simón Bolívar once wrote, "that it costs more strength to maintain freedom than to endure the weight of tyranny." For this in itself is one of the essential elements in the democratic philosophy: it requires constant effort and renewal.

A proper understanding of the whole development makes it necessary to call to mind that the

---

[6] This practice was abolished by the Seventeenth Amendment (1913), which provided for the direct election of senators.

[7] Francis Hall, *Travels in Canada and the United States in 1816 and 1817* (1818).

American democracy was favored and also flavored by certain special conditions. Of these, at least two were crucial. One was immigration; another, availability of land and, at a later period, jobs. These interacted to create potent motives for behavior and action on the part of those who came to America and became Americans.

The motives behind immigration did not vary essentially from generation to generation. They may be described in two words: freedom and opportunity. In the early period in New England, the idea of freedom centered on religion. Puritans and other settlers sought a haven where they could worship God (or, as with Roger Williams in his later years, not worship) according to their own conceptions, without coercion by national ecclesiastical authority supported by government. Subsequently the concept of freedom, and the struggle for its maintenance, became increasingly political. The early Americans, as well as the later ones, developed the habit of looking at governmental restraint with strong distaste. They wanted to be as free as was compatible with an orderly existence, which, until well into the twentieth century, meant a minimum of government. Ralph Waldo Emerson, the offspring of generations of New England Protestants, encapsulated this idea in his essay "Politics" (1842): "The less government . . . the better."

The other motive, opportunity, has also been ever present. From the earliest days immigrants were impelled by the need and desire for material betterment, and attracted to America which held out the hope for its attainment. This was a natural human drive, as that astute Maine legislator and sometime Speaker of the House of Representatives, Thomas B. Reed, reminded his countrymen when he said in 1894: "It would be a sight hitherto unknown on earth if men forsook their home without being either pushed or pulled." Another New Englander, whose name, alas, is unrecorded, once reacted to sanctimonious claims to purely idealistic motivations by blurting out: "Our ancestors came here to catch fish." This pull and push of immigration had a lasting effect on the development of self-government and the shaping of democracy in America.

During the first centuries of immigration economic self-improvement was based on the soil. It was a time when land was the primary source of livelihood and the ownership of it coveted as a means of achieving not only security but also self-respect, and what is called "status" today. More than that, ownership of land was considered to be a mainstay of public virtue, and hence of republicanism, which, according to the widely accepted analysis of Montesquieu, was the essential element in that form of government. Jefferson, himself a farmer and a descendant of farmers, believed that the agrarian population, as contrasted with that of big cities, was the safest repository of freedom and its institutions. "Cultivators of the earth," he wrote to John Jay in 1785, "are the most vigorous, the most independent, the most virtuous, and they are tied to their country, and wedded to its liberty and interests, by the most lasting bonds." In his *Notes on Virginia* (Query 19) he developed this idea at greater length.

This particular facet of the democratic theory held that such permanent bonds to one's country, a vital necessity in self-rule, could come only from the possession of property. Those who owned nothing—for example, the hungry rural as well as urban proletariat, such as that of ancient Rome or eighteenth-century Paris—obviously had no "stake in the land," and hence no personal pride in, no individual interest in, no desire for participation in, and no real commitment to a society that condemned them to live on the lowest level of existence and without hope. To make them good citizens, it was necessary to provide them with a measure of economic well-being or, at the very least, the prospect of achieving it.

In this respect Jefferson's view is still relevant today, when land is no longer the exclusive base of property or prosperity. Twentieth-century jobless and hopeless slum dwellers have no more incentive to good citizenship than did eighteenth-century proletarians. In modern American cities many American blacks feel themselves rotting in slums without economic opportunities or a decent future. Alienated from the main stream of the society, they are hardly good material for a healthy democracy. After the race riots in Watts, the black ghetto of Los Angeles, in August, 1965, one young unemployed Negro, on the verge of being drafted into the army, said with characteristic bitterness: "Why go over to Vietnam and get shot and 'fight for your country'? What country? I don't have a country." Clearly, a democratic society cannot afford to tolerate such alienation; it must supply its citizens, even and perhaps especially the humblest ones, with opportunities, respect, and hope for the future.

In the seventeenth and eighteenth centuries many propertyless and landless Europeans felt toward their native countries as alienated moderns do. In the Europe of the period of the founding of America land was tightly held by the ruling classes, and its acquisition all but impossible for those who labored on it. Well into the nineteenth century, Europe's class system and aristocratic rule were rooted largely in land ownership (this was true also in Asia, including Japan), of which the elite, both civilian and military, had a monopoly. Under such conditions—and they did not begin to change in Europe until the age of the French Revolution—genuinely democratic institutions and practices were hardly possible.

In America, however, land was known to be available and could be obtained by those who had the ambition and the hardihood to brave the wilderness. Thus land-hungry Europeans emigrated to the New World, in many instances as indentured servants, in the hope of achieving ultimately the cherished goals of possession and the independence that derives from ownership of property, even though it be small in amount. Not all the immigrants became land or property owners, but a considerable number did, and their proportion was larger by far than anything to be found among the common people of Britain. They formed a sizable yeomanry which became the sturdy underpinning of American self-government and individualism.

In a later period, when America was developing an urban and industrial civilization, the dream of material self-improvement still beckoned to millions, more so, indeed, than ever before. In the first two decades of the twentieth century alone—before mass immigration was stopped by Act of Congress in 1921—more than 14,000,000 immigrants, most-

ly Europeans, entered the United States. Just as the earlier immigrants were attracted by land, so the later ones were drawn to America by the hopes of jobs and other opportunities, such as education, to be found in the cities. "So at last," Mary Antin wrote in her immigrant classic, *The Promised Land* (1912), "I was going to America! Really, really going, at last! The boundaries burst. The arch of heaven soared. A million suns shone out for every star. The winds rushed in from outer space roaring in my ears, 'America! America!'"

Altogether, in the three centuries of relatively free immigration, about 40,000,000 immigrants reached American shores. The effect of this unprecedented movement of humanity has been deep and continuous, resulting in what Woodrow Wilson, himself an offspring of immigrants ("My ancestors were troublesome Scotsmen"), called "a process of constant re-creation" of American life. It was a re-creation on many levels, always involving the central motivations of self-improvement and self-realization through economic opportunity in an atmosphere of freedom.

The immigrants of the industrial age differed in origin and religion from their predecessors, and unavoidably they added a different dimension to the American democracy. They were no longer mainly British or Protestant, but primarily German, Irish, Italian, Jewish, Scandinavian, and Slavic, as well as Latin American and Asian. As an illustration, one can take 1912, the year *The Promised Land* was published. In that year, which may be regarded as fairly typical of the new immigration, about 718,000 newcomers entered the United States, of whom only around 57,000 were British. This was hardly more than 8 percent of the total. The origin of the rest (given here in round figures, on the basis of the U.S. Census[8]) was:

26,000	Irish
27,000	Scandinavian
28,000	German
157,000	Italian
162,000	Russian
179,000	Central European

[8] See *Historical Statistics of the United States: Colonial Times to 1957* (1960), p.56.

21,000	"other Eastern" European
23,000	"other Northwestern" European
38,000	"other Southern" European

In many significant ways the immigrants of the industrial age differed from those of the agricultural era. Large numbers of them brought with them political and religious traditions either hostile to the democratic spirit or ignorant of it. Millions came from societies where autocracy prevailed in both religion and politics. Unlike the earlier British immigrants, few of the newcomers had had experience in freedom, orderly liberty, the rule of law, or self-government. Nevertheless, and this is a tribute to the soundness of America's democratic foundations, the newer immigrants and their descendants, coming here in search of a better life, became permeated with the spirit of freedom that reigned in America and not only embraced it vigorously but added new dimensions to it.

Up to and through the Second World War, newer Americans of the industrial age, especially those concentrated in the cities, were largely instrumental in widening the conceptions and meaning of democracy as it needed to be adjusted to an increasingly complex urban society. This was notably true in regard to the role of the state. Under the pressure and influence of the industrial cities, the view of government gradually shifted from the traditional American emphasis on individual freedom to a stress on social welfare. This has meant a systematic enlargement of the function of government in ways and areas—labor legislation and social welfare, for example—often distasteful to the earlier Americans, particularly those living in rural areas and small towns.

The contributions of those earlier Americans, the founders of this country, have been absolutely indispensable. It is, in fact, doubtful whether a self-governing republic, and still less a democracy, would ever have been established durably in America without them. If they had been different people, the United States, if indeed there could have been a United States, would have been a polity of another sort than it is today. One need only look at Latin America, colonized roughly at about the same time as North America, to see the startling political contrast between the two halves of the Western Hemisphere.

The nations of Latin America, founded by the Spanish and Portuguese, have always reflected the political ideas and institutions of their mother countries, that is to say, hardly mitigated oppression, tyranny, and inequality. The Iberian founders of Latin America had no tradition of self-government either in state or in church, and they carried with them no ideal of freedom under law. For generations Latin American democrats, often men with high ideals, have tried to establish and stabilize institutions of freedom, but with limited success. When Senator Robert F. Kennedy, on his visit to dictator-ridden Brazil in November, 1965, made the simple democratic point, "I believe in all individuals being able to participate in the political life of a nation," a startled local congressman replied: "If you were a Brazilian, Mr. Kennedy, you would be considered a subversive or a leftist."

As far back as a century and a half ago, observing with sympathy ("God send them a safe deliverance") the struggle of the Latin Americans for independence from Spain, Jefferson concluded pessimistically that their background was such as to make any genuine self-government, let alone democracy, impossible. His reasons, which derived from his democratic philosophy, were as sound as his prognosis turned out to be:

"I join you sincerely," he wrote to Lafayette on November 30, 1813,

> in wishes for the emancipation of South America. That they will be liberated from foreign subjection I have little doubt. But the result of my enquiries does not authorize me to hope they are capable of maintaining a free government. Their people are immersed in the darkest ignorance, and brutalized by bigotry & superstition. Their priests make of them what they please, and though they may have some capable leaders, yet nothing but intelligence in the people themselves can keep these faithful to their charge. Their efforts, I fear, will end in establishing military despotisms.

Not so North America. Fortunately for the United States and for democracy in general, the English settlers did not bring with them a tradition of blind subjection or a practice of absolute obedience to chieftains or ecclesiarchs. Quite the contrary. As Englishmen, they came to America with historic memories of the long struggle for parliamentary rule, and with ideas, no matter how imperfect as yet, of self-government. As dissenting Protestants, they carried with them a sense of hostility to a politically dominated church. It was this "great struggle" against the Church of England, John Adams wrote in his *Dissertation on the Canon and Feudal Law* (1765), "that peopled America."

These English Protestants brought to America ideas of personal judgment in all matters of the spirit, including a personal reading and interpretation of the Holy Book. Similarly, their view of God was that of an omnipresent reality that could be understood without the need of centrally prescribed dogmas, and worshiped without hierarchic intermediaries. On both counts, in politics as well as in religion, the English Protestants were oriented, not toward a powerfully organized state or highly centralized ecclesiarchy, but in the direction of the individual soul and its strivings. It was this sense of the self, with all its crotchets and not infrequently excessive individualism and personal intolerance, that went into the marrow of America's institutions of freedom and democracy.

The earliest political instruments of those sturdy, self-assertive Britons in America offer eloquent testimony to their character and purposes. The very first document which might be called truly American, the Mayflower Compact, signed by forty-one adult males on board ship at Cape Cod on November 11, 1620, was symbolic: "We . . . solemnly and mutually in the presence of God, and one of another, covenant and combine our selves together into a civill body politick, for our better ordering and preservation." Thus also the "Fundamental Orders" for the government of Connecticut, drafted in January, 1639, provided for self-rule by the inhabitants and residents along the "Conectecotte" River: "We . . . doe therefore assotiate and conioyne our

selves to be as one Publike State or Commonwelth . . . to be guided and governed according to such Lawes, Rule, Orders and decrees as shall be made."

Thanks to Roger Williams, Rhode Island, in the decree of its General Court (March 16, 1641), went a step further. It not only unanimously agreed to form a self-governing body politic but a democracy, using that very word for the first time in America, and defining it as a "body of freemen, orderly assembled, or major part of them, to make or constitute just laws." And Pennsylvania, after William Penn's "Frame of Government" of 1683 proved to be unworkable, drafted a "Charter of Privileges" (October 28, 1701), which was a regular constitution that continued in force until the Revolution. The Charter provided for an assembly chosen yearly by the freemen of the colony and for a government based on "the Rights of the free-born Subjects of England."

None of those early polities was a democracy in the modern sense of the term. They were flawed politically by a narrowly limited suffrage and tainted morally by the existence of servitude (white) and slavery (black). Involuntary servitude was not confined to the South. It was a blemish on all of British America. Southerners made permanent slaves out of black men. Northerners made money from the slave trade. In Massachusetts, for example, slavery was given legal sanction as early as 1641. It should be noted, however, that from the very beginning slavery and its modern concomitant, the struggle for Negro rights, have been simultaneously both a blot upon and a challenge to the American conscience. Let us recall the protest issued by a group of Quakers in Germantown, Pennsylvania, in April 1688:

. . . most part of such Negars are brought hither against their will and consent, and . . . many of them are stollen. Now tho' they are black, we cannot conceive there is more liberty to have them slaves, as it is to have other white ones. There is a saying, that we shall doe to all men licke as we will be done ourselves: macking no difference of what generation, descent, or colour they are . . . In Europe there are many oppressed for Conscience sacke; and here there are those oppressed who are of a black Colour.

Despite such limitations, the colonial governments did contain features which were residually democratic, among them the assertion of the right to self-rule (by freemen) and its incorporation in legal forms. They furnished invaluable experience in and habits of self-government, as well as the rule of law. They prepared the ground for the subsequent expansion of republican institutions and democratic practices.

The founders of free government in America established and perpetuated a philosophy of politics that is still, to a considerable degree, to be found in the United States today. That view may be characterized as a distrust of political power and politicians, especially centralized power. "All power in human hands," James Madison, the archetype of eighteenth-century American republicanism,[9] was fond of saying, "is liable to be abused." Hence it must never be allowed to exist without extensive curbs. Even the best conceivable government, a free republic for example, was not to be fully trusted but always viewed as a potential enemy of freedom.

To the founders of America, as also, it is clear, to modern Americans, freedom was not a rhetorical or metaphysical conception. Despite references to "natural rights," a claim that had great polemical appeal, they viewed freedom as something quite practical, to be incorporated in political institutions. Reduced to its simplest terms, freedom, as they saw it, meant the absence of coercion by organized bodies, be they political or religious. In this context freedom had two facets, individual and governmental. On the one hand, the individual had an "inalienable" right to think, speak, and act freely. On the other, he was to be free from fear of domination or punishment or undue intervention by some political tyranny. This attitude toward freedom obviously required a special kind of government both to respect it and to safeguard it.

[9] See Saul K. Padover, ed., *The Forging of American Federalism: Selected Writings of James Madison* (Harper Torchbooks, 1965).

At all levels, therefore, political power was to be restricted and fenced in with as much ingenuity as possible. This explains why the founders of America insisted upon limitations on power through "checks and balances," legal restraints on the rulers (politicians), and political functions carefully restricted to absolute public necessity, such as national defense and the maintenance of law and order. This explains not only the national Bill of Rights, which is a set of prohibitions put on government, but also the state constitutions, which Chief Justice John Marshall, in *Barron v. Baltimore* (1833), referred to as providing "limitations and restrictions" on the local governments. In fact, in *The Federalist,* No. 84, Hamilton pointed out that the national Constitution itself was "in every rational sense, and to every useful purpose, A BILL OF RIGHTS." In other words, the federal government was designed to be a structure of self-limitations.

This view of power—that government must be strictly limited in all spheres not immediately or urgently political—also helps to explain the provisions for separation of church and state which are incorporated in the various American constitutions. They were meant to make doubly sure that there would be no political domination over the most crucial of all human activities, those of the mind and the spirit. The founders of America, in fact, considered separation of religion from politics the keystone of American liberties.

Even so, they remained skeptical of government and distrustful of those who operated the political machinery, including those elected. Here, once again, Jefferson offers wise and, indeed, timely comment. In the Kentucky Resolutions, which he wrote in 1798 as a protest against the oppressive Alien and Sedition Acts, he stated a principle that no believer in democracy and freedom may take lightly:

It would be a dangerous illusion, were a confidence in the men of our choice to silence our fears for the safety of our rights: . . . confidence is everywhere the parent of despotism—free government is founded in jealousy, and not in confidence; it is jealousy and not confidence which prescribes limited constitutions, to bind down those whom we are obliged to trust with power.

The basic principles of free government, constantly redefined and adapted by federal courts and political thinkers, still continue in force in the United States. Within the democratic framework, America's free government—here used in a generic sense, to include local and national polities, which share a common spirit—has functioned and expanded.

The promises inherent in the democratic polity— equality, freedom, happiness, among others—have carried their own dynamism. Under their impetus the people have used their government for their own betterment, and always in the direction of more democracy. Among the earliest moves to implement the democratic philosophy were the founding of primary schools, supported by local taxation, in order to provide the common people with elementary education. This was followed by tax-financed and tax-maintained secondary schools, and finally by state-supported colleges, many of them based on federal land grants and made accessible to all who cared to acquire an education. In the United States education ceased to be a privilege of the elite, as it had been traditionally nearly everywhere in the world, and became democratic.

Similarly, in the name of equality, a basic component of the democratic creed, limitations on the suffrage, which prevailed in most of the states at the beginning of the history of the republic, were gradually whittled down. By the middle of the nineteenth century voting had become universal for white males, and so was officeholding, which for a long time had been restricted to those who possessed property or had other special qualifications. It took another four generations for women to win the vote, and another century for Negroes to do so. Struggle for the rights of Negroes and other minority groups, in the name of democracy and the idea of equality inherent in it, still goes on, as can be seen from the Reports of the U.S. Commission on Civil Rights and the Supreme Court decisions included in this volume.

As the country grew in numbers and size, so did the promises implicit in democracy. Indeed, the American people, in solid control of their own government, came to embrace it as a national ideal. By 1871, Walt Whitman, perhaps the nation's greatest poet, could exclaim: "I shall use the words America and Democracy as convertible terms" *(Democratic Vistas)*. And less than half a century later, Woodrow Wilson, who was inclined to a Whitmanesque laudation of democracy in prose, took America into the First World War and engaged in international politics in the name of that ideal. His avowed purpose was to "make the world safe for democracy." Even discounting much of the political rhetoric as propaganda, as one must, the ideal of a democratic world, which the post-Wilsonian United States still proclaims, remains a valid element in the country's foreign policy today.

In the twentieth century the horizons of democracy have necessarily expanded to keep step with the revolutionary changes that have taken place in American civilization. The needs of an industrial society have compelled government to move away from its traditional position of nonintervention through self-limitation to a positive role of regulation in innumerable areas of life. Immense metropolitan aggregations with tens of millions of people whose livelihood is totally dependent upon an intricate nexus of interwoven businesses, gigantic industries, and impersonal corporations, call for a network of governmental regulations and public services undreamt of in Jefferson's day. As Woodrow Wilson reminded his countrymen during the campaign of 1912, when he pleaded for more, rather than less, government in the name of Jeffersonian democracy: "In these great beehives, where in every corridor swarm men of flesh and blood, it is the privilege of government . . . to see that human life is protected."

In essence, this has been the democratic philosophy of our own day. The emphasis is no longer on fear of tyranny but on a demand for security. The New Deal and the Fair Deal, and also the Great Society, were predicated on the assumption that government must assume large-scale responsibility for human welfare on all fronts. This enlarged dimension of democracy has brought governmental assistance, guidance, protection, and controls into the daily lives of all the people. It should be stressed that the reforms and institutions thus brought about —in fields such as labor legislation, public housing, social security, health insurance—have been enacted democratically, that is, by freely elected representatives legislating with the support and approval of public opinion. And the great problems of modern life, including the recurrent one involving the limits of personal freedom in an interdependent society, have been continuous subjects of reexamination and adjudication by the judiciary. This too is an essential part of the democratic process.

In the light of these radical changes, and given the ever widening role of government, we may ask what the meaning of democracy is and what is still applicable in its philosophy today. To answer, we can review briefly its rock-bottom elements.

Philosophically, two ideas are basic to democracy:

1. Equality.
2. Freedom.

Equality, in this context, is a political concept. It does not mean psychological or economic or social equality. It means the "natural" right to equal participation in the government and to equal opportunity in public affairs. In a radio address of June 11, 1963, John F. Kennedy, speaking of education for all children, thus summarized this kind of equality: "Not every child has an equal talent or an equal ability or equal motivation. But they [sic] should have the equal right to develop their talent and their ability and their motivation to make something of themselves."

Freedom is perhaps the most fundamental of all "natural" rights. In regard to democracy, it has two consequences. One is that the individual is free from governmental arbitrariness. As John Locke put it, "natural freedom" means that a person is not to be "subjected to the will or authority of any other man." Hence in a democratic society the citizen enjoys freedom from highhanded police action and intimidation. Where democracy functions properly, he has recourse to the courts or to public opinion

against the arbitrariness of authority. He is protected by basic law of the kind incorporated in the Bill of Rights.

The other consequence is that the individual has the freedom to establish and control his own government. By implication this means that the citizen has a right to criticize those who govern him in his name. More than that, he has an obligation to do so, if he wishes to keep control over his government and to have it truly represent him, as Jefferson pointed out in the Kentucky Resolutions. Once the citizen loses the right to criticize freely, or is not interested in using it, he loses his freedom.

Operationally, there are at least half a dozen irreducible ingredients that make up a democracy:

1. Periodic election of policy-making officials (members of Congress, governors, mayors, etc.).
2. Fixed terms of office.
3. Guaranteed rights of political minorities.
4. Independent political parties, free from governmental coercion, control, or intimidation.
5. Free communications media (press, radio, television, book publishing, etc.).
6. An independent judiciary.

There may be more to democracy, but there can never be less. A democracy that lacks those ingredients is either flawed or no democracy at all. The current fashion in many parts of the world of referring to dictatorships as "people's democracy," "basic democracy," or "guided democracy" is a libel on democracy. It is a fraud perpetrated by dictators to mislead the people. For any nation that wishes to live in freedom—or to put it differently, to retain a measure of control over its rulers—there is, in fact, no known or effective substitute for these six ingredients. Being basic, they are timeless, and as necessary today as when they were formulated and established by earlier generations of democrats.

As for the larger meanings of democracy, it is clear that they are still evolving. In its promises and implications democracy has, indeed, already gone far beyond its original conceptions, which were mainly of a political nature—control over, and restrictions on, power. Nowadays democracy tends to embrace the totality of man's hopes, including his sense of dignity and identity and purpose. Democracy is becoming a general philosophy of life through which man seeks to achieve, as Walt Whitman foresaw, his highest aspirations. It shapes outlooks, institutions, and daily attitudes.

This is what John Dewey, speaking on his eightieth birthday in 1939, called "creative democracy." He visualized it as "a way of life controlled by a working faith in the possibilities of human nature" as exhibited in every human being regardless of "race, color, sex, birth, and family, of material or cultural wealth." From this viewpoint democracy has endless possibilities.

It also has heavy responsibilities. Democracy is not a mechanical process. Institutionalized contrivances, no matter how ingenious or elaborate, will not, by themselves, guarantee its proper functioning, or even its survival. There must be faith in its workings and morality at its heart. For democracy is rooted in moral values: moderation, reason, justice, compassion, faith in man, human dignity—what Professor Harold D. Lasswell calls "a commonwealth of mutual respect."

And always at the heart of democracy there must lie a feeling of obligation to the community. A citizen must give of himself to the community before he can make moral claims on it. Claims without appropriate duties corrupt the democratic fabric. As its founders, formulators, and champions have repeatedly reminded us, democracy requires not only constant vigilance but also active participation. Democracy can never afford to recognize "rights" without concomitant responsibilities.

SOURCES OF DEMOCRACY

PART I

DEMOCRACY AND REPUBLICANISM— WHAT THEY ARE AND ARE NOT

Democracy and republicanism may be synonymous, but are not always or necessarily so. It is possible to have democracy without a republic, as in Great Britain and Scandinavia. It is also possible to have a republic without democracy, as in Spain, Portugal, and most of Latin America. In the world today one finds democratic monarchies and nondemocratic republics.

The difference, in brief, is this: Democracy is government elected and controlled by the people; republicanism is government by nonhereditary and nonmonarchical rulers. Where the elements of democracy are added to those of republicanism the result is a democratic republic, such as the United States.

Democracy first emerged in ancient Greece some twenty-five hundred years ago, in the days of Pericles, but for a variety of historical and cultural reasons it did not survive. Democracy as an ideal and an institution did not reemerge until relatively recent times, with the coming of the American and French revolutions in the latter part of the eighteenth century.

The Americans of the Revolutionary period rarely used the word "democracy" in their political thinking or writing. As the reader will see, they preferred words like "republicanism," "self-government," "popular government," and "freedom," to describe their political ideas. This was true even of such ardent champions of democracy as Thomas Jefferson.

In the United States, the ideal of democracy—including the word itself—began to come to the fore in the period of Andrew Jackson. It was then that the name of the oldest American political party, the Republican, was changed to the *Democratic* party. The 1830s also saw the appearance of books using the word and some of the concepts, foremost among them Alexis de Tocqueville's classic work, *Democracy in America* (1835), and James Fenimore Cooper's *The American Democrat* (1838). Thereafter the idea of democracy, the word as well as the practice, grew steadily. In the nineteenth century Walt Whitman gave it inspired form in poetry and prose. In the twentieth century Woodrow Wilson introduced "democracy" into foreign affairs; and Franklin D. Roosevelt applied it to all mankind.

Today democracy has become a key word in the world's political language. It is often misunderstood and misinterpreted, but what is significant is that most of the world's peoples pay tribute to it as an ideal to be attained.

1

OPINIONS OF ANTIQUITY

Pericles
Athenagoras
Aristotle
Polybius

• PERICLES

For our government is not copied from those of our neighbors: we are an example to them rather than they to us. Our constitution is named a democracy, because it is in the hands not of the few but of the many. But our laws secure equal justice for all in their private disputes, and our public opinion welcomes and honors talent in every branch of achievement, not for any sectional reason but on grounds of excellence alone. And as we give free play to all in our public life, so we carry the same spirit into our daily relations with one another. We have no black looks or angry words for our neighbor if he enjoys himself in his own way, and we abstain from the little acts of churlishness which, though they leave no mark, yet cause annoyance to whoso notes them. Open and friendly in our private intercourse, in our public acts we keep strictly within the control of law. We acknowledge the restraint of reverence; we are obedient to whomsoever is set in authority, and to the laws, more especially to those which offer protection to the oppressed and those unwritten ordinances whose transgression brings admitted shame.

Yet ours is no work-a-day city only. No other provides so many recreations for the spirit—contests and sacrifices all the year round, and beauty in our public buildings to cheer the heart and delight the eye day by day. Moreover, the city is so large and powerful that all the wealth of all the world flows in to her, so that our own Attic products seem no more homelike to us than the fruits of the labors of other nations.

Our military training too is different from our opponents'. The gates of our city are flung open to the world. We practice no periodical deportations, nor do we prevent our visitors from observing or discovering what an enemy might usefully apply to his own purposes. For our trust is not in the devices of material equipment, but in our own good spirits for battle.

So too with education. They toil from early boyhood in a laborious pursuit after courage, while we, free to live and wander as we please, march out none the less to face the self-same dangers. Here is the proof of my words. When the Spartans advance into our country, they do not come alone but with all their allies; but when we invade our neighbors we have little difficulty as a rule, even on foreign soil, in defeating men who are fighting for their own homes . . . Here as elsewhere, then, the city sets an example which is deserving of admiration.

We are lovers of beauty without extravagance, and lovers of wisdom without unmanliness. Wealth to us is not mere material for vainglory but an opportunity for achievement; and poverty we think it no disgrace to acknowledge but a real degradation to make no effort to overcome. Our citizens attend both to public and private duties, and do not allow absorption in their own various affairs to interfere with their knowledge of the city's. We differ from other states in regarding the man who holds aloof from public life not as "quiet" but as useless; we decide or debate, carefully and in person, all matters of policy, holding not that words and deeds go ill together, but that acts are foredoomed to failure when undertaken undiscussed. For we are noted for being at once most adventurous in action and most reflective beforehand. Other men are bold in ignorance, while reflection will stop their onset. But the bravest are surely those who have the clearest vision of what is before them, glory and danger alike, and yet notwithstanding go out to meet it. In doing good, too, we are the exact opposite of the rest of mankind. We secure our friends not by accepting favors but by doing them. And so we are naturally more firm in our attachments; for we are anxious, as creditors, to cement by kind offices our relation toward our friends. If they do not respond with the same warmness it is because they feel that their services will not be given spontaneously but only as the repayment of a debt. We are alone among mankind in doing men benefits, not on calculations of self-interest, but in the fearless confidence of freedom.

In a word I claim that our city as a whole is an education to Greece, and that her members yield to none, man by man, for the independence of spirit, many-sidedness of attainment, and complete self-reliance in limbs and brain. ∎

From Funeral oration at Athens, *431* B.C., *as reported in Thucydides,* The History of The Peloponnesian War, *Book II, Paragraphs 37–41.*

• ATHENAGORAS

It will be said, perhaps, that democracy is neither wise nor equitable, but that the holders of property are also the best fitted to rule. I say, on the contrary, first, that the word *demos,* or people, includes the whole state, oligarchy only a part; next, that if the best guardians of property are the rich, and the best counselors the wise, none can hear and decide so well as the many; and that all these talents, severally and collectively, have their just place in a democracy. But under an oligarchy, while the masses take their share of dangers, the few claim not merely the largest share, but the whole, of the profits; this is what the powerful and young among you aspire to, but in a great city cannot possibly obtain. ∎

From speech quoted in Thucydides, The History of the Peloponnesian War, *Book VI, Paragraph 39.*

• ARISTOTLE

Having answered these questions [what is the essence of a citizen], we must next consider whether there is one form of government or many, and if many, what they are and how many, and what are the differences between them.

A constitution is the organization of a state with regard to its offices, especially to that which is supreme in all matters. The civic body is everywhere sovereign in the state, and the civic body is in fact the constitution. In democracies, for example, the people are supreme, but in oligarchies the few; therefore we say that these two forms of government differ from one another, and so in other cases.

We must ascertain (1) the end for which the state exists, and (2) by how many forms of government human society is regulated.

(1) As I explained in Book I, when discussing household management and the control of slaves, man is by nature a political animal. Thus men feel a natural urge to live together, even when they do not require one another's help. But a common interest also brings them together as each one attains some degree of the good life, which is indeed the principal end, both of individuals and of states. Again, men coalesce and strive to maintain the political society for the sake of *mere* life, in which, I think you will agree, there is a noble element, so long as the evils of existence do not outweigh the good. We see men clinging to life even at the cost of great suffering, which goes to show that they find in life a natural sweetness and happiness.

(2) It is easy to distinguish the forms of rule commonly recognized; they have been often defined in works not peculiar to this school. Although the natural slave and the natural master have in fact a common interest, the master's rule is exercised chiefly for his own benefit, and only incidentally for that of the slave, whose extinction terminates the rule itself. But the rule over a wife and children, and over the household generally, which we call household management, is exercised mainly for the benefit of the ruler and ruled alike. Essentially it is exercised for that of the ruled, as we see to be the case with other arts, e. g., medicine and gymnastic, although an art may be concerned incidentally with the good of the artist himself. . . .

The foregoing discussion leads us to consider next the number and nature of the various constitutions. In the first place we must ask what are the *right* forms; once they are recognized the deviations from them will be apparent. The terms "constitution" and "the government" mean the same thing; and the government, which is the supreme authority in every state, must be in the hands of one, or of the few, or of the many. Therefore, the right forms of government must be those in which (a) an individual, (b) a minority, or (c) a majority govern for the common benefit of all; but governments which rule with an eye to the private interest either of (a), (b), or (c) above are deviation forms, for the members of a state, if they are to be called true citizens, must share in its advantages. The rule of an individual, when it looks to the common good, is known as kingship; the rule of a few, when it fulfills the same condition, is called aristocracy; but when the citizens as a whole govern the state for the common benefit of all alike, we describe this form of government by the generic name "polity." There is good reason for using the generic term. One man or a few may excel in virtue, but as the number increases it becomes proportionately difficult for them to attain perfection in every virtue, though they may do so in military virtue, which is by no means rare among the masses. Hence in a polity the fighting men have supreme power, and those who possess arms are the citizens.

The deviation forms of the above are as follows: of kingship, tyranny; of aristocracy, oligarchy; of polity, democracy. For tyranny is the rule of a monarch who has only his own interest at heart; oligarchy has in view the interest of the well-to-do; democracy, of the have-nots. None of them looks to the common good of all.

These forms of government give rise to a number of problems, and it is therefore necessary to dwell a little longer on their respective natures. When one intends making a philosophical study of any science, with an eye to something more than practical considerations, one ought not to overlook or omit the slightest detail—one must uncover the whole truth.

Now tyranny, as I have said, is monarchy ruling a political association in the way that a master rules his slaves. There is oligarchy where the reins of government are held by men of property, and conversely there is democracy where power is in the hands of the poorer classes rather than of the well-to-do. Our first problem, then, concerns the distinction between democracy and oligarchy. You have democracy when the many are supreme; but what if those many are rich? Likewise, you have oligarchy when the few are in power; but what if the poor, though *fewer* than the rich, control the state because they are *stronger?* In such cases our distinction between these forms of government would appear to be unsatisfactory.

Suppose, then, we associate wealth with the few and poverty with the many, and name the two constitutions accordingly—defining an oligarchy as that in which the wealthy few, and a democracy as that in which the many poor, are supreme. But here again there is a difficulty. If there are no forms of oligarchy and democracy other than those just defined, how describe the forms imagined above, in which there is a majority of rich men and a minority or poor, and each is supreme in its respective state?

The argument seems to demonstrate that the small number of the sovereign body in an oligarchy, or its large number in a democracy, is an accident due to the fact that the rich are generally few, and the poor generally numerous. But if that is so, the causes underlying the differences between oligarchy and democracy have been misrepresented; the true difference between them is poverty and wealth.

Wherever men rule by virtue of their wealth, be they few or many, there you have oligarchy; and where the poor rule, there you have democracy. But it so happens, as I have said, that the rich are few and the poor numerous. Few men are well off, whereas all have a share in freedom; and it is upon the grounds of wealth and freedom respectively that the oligarchical and democratic parties lay claim to power.

We must next ascertain what are the marks of oligarchy and democracy as generally recognized by their respective advocates, and what are the oligarchical and democratic notions of justice. Both sides cling to justice of one kind or another, but their conceptions are inadequate and fail to express the idea in all its fullness. For example, justice is thought by the democrats to mean equality; so it does, but only for equals—not for all. Oligarchs, on the other hand, believe that justice means inequality; so it does, but only for unequals—not for all. Both sides overlook the relation of justice to persons, and thereby go astray; they are passing judgment upon themselves, and men are notoriously bad judges in

their own case. Justice is relative to persons as well as to things; and a just distribution, as I have explained in the *Ethics,* implies the same ratio between the persons receiving as between the things given. Now the advocates both of democracy and of oligarchy agree as to what constitutes equality among *things,* but differ as to what constitutes *personal* equality. This is mainly due to the fact mentioned above, that they are poor judges in their own case, but also to the fact that both sides are referring to a limited and partial form of justice. The oligarchs believe that superior wealth gives them absolute superiority; while the democrats hold that equality in a single respect—e.g., of free birth—implies absolute equality. Both sides, however, ignore the crucial point—the purpose of the state. If men formed themselves into associations *for the sake of wealth alone,* their share in civic rights would be determined by the amount of their property, and the oligarchical theory would then appear the most tenable. But the state exists for the sake of the *good* life, and not for that of life *as such;* otherwise slaves and brute beasts might constitute a state—which they cannot in fact do, because they have no share in true felicity and the exercise of free will. Nor does the state exist for the sake of mutual defense against all and sundry, nor yet for the sake of commercial intercourse; otherwise peoples who, like the Etruscans and Carthaginians, are bound to one another by trade agreements, would be citizens of a single state. Certainly they have covenants regulating imports, concordats providing for the settlement of disputes without recourse to arms, and nonaggression pacts. There are, however, no magistracies common to the contracting parties; different states have each their own magistracies. Again, neither of the contracting parties is concerned with the moral welfare of the other; neither is interested in making sure that the other commits no crime or misdemeanor *of any sort,* but only in seeing that it suffers no injustice at the other's hands. Those, on the contrary, who have good government at heart look to the internal virtues and vices of the state. It is evident therefore that any state deserving of the name must concern itself with the promotion of virtue. Otherwise, the political association becomes a mere alliance differing only in respect of place from those alliances whose members live at some distance from one another; and the law becomes mere convention, "a guarantor of mutual justice," as the sophist Lycophron said, powerless to make the citizens into good and just men. . . .

Clearly, then, a state is not merely an association living on one site, established for the purpose of mutual defense and for the promotion of trade. These are admittedly conditions without which there can be no state; but they do not actually *constitute* a state. The state is an association of families and groups of families in a good life, for the sake of a perfect and self-suffixing existence, although this cannot be achieved unless the members dwell in a single place and intermarry. It was in order to provide those conditions that there arose in cities such institutions as fraternities, clubs, common sacrifices, and social entertainments. But these are the *business of friendship* [as distinct from that of a state], i.e., of the will to live together; the *end or purpose of the state* is the good life, and they are the means thereto. The state itself is an association of families and villages in a perfect and self-suffixing existence, i.e., a life of true felicity and goodness.

We conclude, therefore, that political associations exist for the sake of good actions, and not of mere social life. Whence it follows that those who contribute most to an association of this kind have a greater share in the state than those who are equal (or even superior) to them in freedom or nobility of birth, but inferior as regards civic virtue, or than those who surpass them in wealth but are outstripped by them in virtue.

It is sufficiently clear from what I have said that, in advocating different forms of government, both democrats and oligarchs put forward an incomplete notion of justice.

Next we ask: What *should* be the sovereign body in the state? The masses? The wealth? The better sort of men? The one best man? Or a tyrant? Each of these alternatives appears to involve unacceptable consequences.

(1) Surely it is unjust for the poor, on the strength of mere numbers, to divide among themselves the possessions of the rich. "Of course not," you may say; "the supreme authority wills it and therefore it is just." To which I reply, that if this is not the acme of injustice, what is? Again, taking men as a whole, irrespective of wealth and poverty, if the majority divide among themselves the possessions of the minority, the state will inevitably be ruined. But virtue does not ruin its possessor, nor is justice destructive of the state; and therefore such a law is beyond question unjust. Otherwise every act of a tyrant must be just; for he uses his superior strength only to oppress others, in the same way as the masses would oppress the wealthy.

(2) Is it just that a wealthy minority should rule? Suppose they behave in like manner, robbing and plundering the masses: what then? Is that just? If so, then the former case will be likwise just. No; all such arrangements are manifestly wrong and unjust.

(3) Ought the better sort of men to enjoy supreme authority? If they do, everyone else will be excluded from office and thereby dishonored. The offices of state are recognized as honors, and if they are permanently held by the same group of men, the rest will be deprived of them.

(4) Is it better, perhaps, that the one best man should rule? Well, this is even more oligarchical; for still more persons are thus without honors. It may be urged that, since every man is subject to the accidents of human passion, it is wrong that an individual, rather than the law, should hold supreme power. Yes, but suppose the law be oligarchical or democratic, how will that solve our difficulties? Indeed it will not; the same results will follow.

Postponing further discussion of (2), (3), and (4) above, let us go back to the first alternative, viz., that sovereignty should lie with the people at large rather than with a few persons of very high quality. This view, although it involves some difficulty, is by no means indefensible, and seems to contain an element of truth. The many, when taken *individually* may be quite ordinary fellows; but when they meet together they may well be found *collectively* better than the few. A feast to which many have contributed is better than one provided from a single

purse. In the same way, each of those numerous individuals has some degree of virtue and moral prudence; and all of them met together may become as
it were a single person combining many good qualities of character and intelligence, just as they form
a unit having many hands, many feet, and many
senses. This is why the many are better judges of
music and poetry than the few; some appreciate one
part, others another, so that all together can assess
the true worth of the whole. There is a similar combination of qualities in good men, who differ from
the common run of their fellows; in them otherwise
scattered elements are brought together. It is not
clear, however, that this principle holds good of
any and every group of men. Of some it definitely
cannot; for if it did, it would apply equally to brutes,
between whom and certain classes of men there is
little or no difference. Our statement may nevertheless be true of *some* popular bodies; in which
case we have solved the original problem,[1] and are
on the way to solving another closely akin to it—
viz., What *extent* of sovereignty should be assigned
to freemen, or the general body of citizens, who are
not rich and have no claim to the reward of personal
merit? It is dangerous for such persons to share in
the highest offices of state, for their folly may lead
them into error, and their dishonesty into crime. On
the other hand, it is risky to exclude them from such
positions: a state in which many poor men are debarred from office cannot but have numerous enemies in its midst. The only alternative is to allow
them deliberative and judicial functions; and it was
on these grounds that Solon and other legislators assigned to them the power of electing magistrates
and calling them to account, but *not* the right of
holding office individually. When they all meet together their discrimination is sufficiently reliable,
and combined with the better class they are useful
to the state; but each individual on his own is lacking in judgment.

Popular government of this kind, however, involves a number of difficulties. (a) It might be argued that the best judge of whom to employ as a

doctor is one who can himself here and now cure a
man of disease and restore him to health—in other
words a doctor . . . The same principle would seem
to hold good in the matter of elections, for a sound
choice can be made only by those having the requisite knowledge. Looking at the question from this
angle, we must conclude that the masses should not
be entrusted either with the election of magistrates
or with the scrutiny of their administration. Perhaps, on the other hand, some of these objections
may appear groundless in the light of our former
thesis, that so long as the people are not utterly
degraded, although individually they may be worse
judges than those with special knowledge, collectively they are as good, if not better. Furthermore,
there are certain arts in which the artists themselves
are not the best, let alone the only, judges. Such are
those whose products can be appreciated even by
men who lack the skill to produce them. For instance, the builder is not the only one who can
perceive the merits or demerits of a house; its user
(i.e., the householder) will be a better judge, just
as a pilot will be a better judge of a rudder than the
carpenter, and a diner will estimate the quality of a
meal better than the cook.

I think we may now claim to have disposed of this
problem; but it leads directly to another.

(b) It is surely unreasonable that inferior persons
should enjoy supreme authority in affairs of greater
moment than those entrusted to men of outstanding
merit. Now to elect magistrates and to audit their
accounts are the most important duties; and yet
these, as I said above, are assigned under some constitutions to the popular assembly, which has plena-
ry powers in all such matters. Furthermore, the
assembly, whose members are entitled to deliberate
and to exercise judicial functions, includes men of
any age and of little property; but a high qualification is attached to such great offices of state as those
of treasurer and General. This difficulty may be
overcome in the same way as the preceding, and the
existing practice of democracies shown to be justified. It is not in individual members of the court, the
council, or the assembly that authority resides, but
in the court as a whole, the council as a whole, or

---

[1] What *persons* are to form the sovereign body?

the assembly as a whole; and each individual member is only a part of the particular whole. On these grounds the people can rightly claim sovereignty in affairs of greater moment than those entrusted to a more distinguished minority; for the popular assembly and the council and the courts consist of many individuals, and their property is collectively greater than the property of one or of a few persons holding high office. So much for that question. ■

From Politics, *Book III, "State and Citizen."*

• POLYBIUS

Similarly that is no true democracy in which the whole crowd of citizens is free to do whatever they wish or purpose, but when, in a community where it is traditional and customary to reverence the gods, to honor our parents, to respect our elders, and to obey the laws, the will of the greater number prevails, this is to be called a democracy. We should therefore assert that there are six kinds of governments, the three above mentioned which are on everyone's mouth and the three which are naturally allied to them, I mean monarchy, oligarchy, and mob rule. Now the first of these to come into being is monarchy, its growth being natural and unaided; and next arises kingship derived from monarchy by the aid of art and by the correction of defects. Monarchy first changes into its vicious allied form, tyranny; and next, the abolishment of both gives birth to aristocracy. Aristocracy by its very nature degenerates into oligarchy; and when the commons inflamed by anger take vengeance on this government for its unjust rule, democracy comes into being; and in due course the licence and lawlessness of this form of government produces mob rule to complete the series. The truth of what I have just said will be quite clear to anyone who pays due attention to such beginnings, origins, and changes as are in each case natural. For he alone who has seen how each form naturally arises and develops, will be able to see when, how, and where the growth, perfection, change, and end of each are likely to occur again. And it is to the Roman constitution above all that this method, I think, may be successfully applied, since from the outset its formation and growth have been due to natural causes.

5. Perhaps this theory of the natural transformations into each other of the different forms of government is more elaborately set forth by Plato and certain other philosophers; but as the arguments are subtle and are stated at great length, they are beyond the reach of all but a few. I therefore will attempt to give a short summary of the theory, as far as I consider it to apply to the actual history of facts and to appeal to the common intelligence of mankind. For if there appear to be certain omissions in my general exposition of it, the detailed discussion which follows will afford the reader ample compensation for any difficulties now left unsolved.

What then are the beginnings I speak of and what is the first origin of political societies? When owing to floods, famines, failure of crops, or other such causes there occurs such a destruction of the human race as tradition tells us has more than once happened, and as we must believe will often happen again, all arts and crafts perishing at the same time, then in the course of time, when springing from the survivors as from seeds men have again increased in numbers and just like other animals form herds—it being a matter of course that they too should herd together with those of their kind owing to their natural weakness—it is a necessary consequence that the man who excels in bodily strength and in courage will lead and rule over the rest. ■

From The Histories, *Book VI, Part II,*

2
THE SOURCE OF POWER: MONARCHY VERSUS PEOPLE

The Prophet Samuel
Thomas Aquinas
Marsilius of Padua
John Milton
Jacques Bénigne Bossuet
Thomas Jefferson

• THE PROPHET SAMUEL

Then all the elders of Israel gathered themselves together, and came to Samuel unto Ramah. And they said unto him: "Behold, thou art old, and thy sons walk not in thy ways; now make us a king to judge us like all the nations." But the thing displeased Samuel, when they said: "Give us a king to judge us." And Samuel prayed unto the Lord. And the Lord said unto Samuel: "Hearken unto the voice of the people in all that they say unto thee; for they have not rejected thee, but they have rejected Me, that I should not be king over them. According to all the works which they have done since the day I brought them up out of Egypt even unto this day, in that they have forsaken Me, and served other gods, so do they also unto thee. Now therefore hearken unto their voice; howbeit thou shalt earnestly forewarn them, and shalt declare unto them the manner of the king that shall reign over them."

And Samuel told all the words of the Lord unto the people that asked of him a king. And he said: "This will be the manner of the king that shall reign over you: he will take your sons, and appoint them unto him, for his chariots, and to be his horsemen; and they shall run before his chariots. And he will appoint them unto him for captains of thousands, and captains of fifties; and to plow his ground, and to reap his harvest, and to make his instruments of war, and the instruments of his chariots. And he will take your daughters to be perfumers, and to be cooks, and to be bakers. And he will take your fields, and your vineyards, and your olive yards, even the best of them, and give them to his servants. And he will take the tenth of your seed, and of your vineyards, and give to his officers, and to his servants. And he will take your men-servants, and your maidservants, and your goodliest young men, and your asses, and put them to his work. He will take the tenth of your flocks; and ye shall be his servants. And ye shall cry out in that day because of your king whom ye shall have chosen you; and the Lord will not answer you in that day." But the people refused to hearken unto the voice of Samuel. ■

From 1 Samuel, *Chapter 8.*

• THOMAS AQUINAS

Having introduced our question it is now our further task to inquire whether it is better for a realm or a city to be ruled by one person or by many: and this question is best approached by considering the object of government.

The aim of any ruler should be to secure the well-being of the realm whose government he undertakes; just as it is the task of the helmsman to steer the ship through perilous seas to a safe harborage. But the welfare and prosperity of a community lies in the preservation of its unity; or, more simply, in peace. For without peace a communal life loses all advantage; and, because of discord, becomes instead a burden. So the most important task for the ruler of any community is the establishment of peaceful unity. Nor has he the right to question whether or no he will so promote the peace of the community, any more than a doctor has the right to question whether he will cure the sick or not. For no one ought to deliberate about the ends for which he must act, but only about the means to those ends. Thus the Apostle, when stressing the unity of the faithful, adds (Ephesians, IV:3) "Be ye solicitous for the unity of the Spirit in the bond of peace." So, therefore, government is the more useful to the extent that it more effectively attains peaceful unity. For that is more fruitful which better attains its object. Now it is clear that that which is itself a unity can more easily produce unity than that which is a plurality: just as that which is itself hot is best adapted to heating things. So government by one person is more likely to be successful than government by many.

Furthermore. It is clear that many persons will never succeed in producing unity in the community if they differ among themselves. So a plurality of individuals will already require some bond of unity before they can even begin to rule in any way whatsoever. Just as the whole crew of a ship would never succeed in sailing it on any course unless they were in agreement among themselves. But many may be said to be united in so far as they approach a unity. So it is better for one to rule rather than many who must first reach agreement.

Again. That is best which most nearly approaches a natural process, since nature always works in the best way. But in nature, government is always by one. Among members of the body there is one which moves all the rest, namely, the heart: in the soul there is one faculty which is pre-eminent, namely reason. The bees have one king, and in the whole universe there is one God, Creator and Lord of all. And this is quite according to reason: for all plurality derives from unity. So, since the product of art is but an imitation of the work of nature, and since a work of art is better for being a faithful representation if its natural pattern, it follows of necessity that the best form of government in human society is that which is exercised by one person.

This conclusion is also borne out by experience. For cities or provinces which are not ruled by one person are torn by dissensions, and strive without peace. . . On the other hand, cities and provinces which are governed by one king enjoy peace, flourish in justice and are made glad by an abundance of riches. ■

From De Regimine Principum, *Book I, Chapter II.*

• MARSILIUS OF PADUA

We must next discuss that efficient cause of the laws which is capable of demonstration. For I do not intend to deal here with that method of establishing laws which can be effected by the immediate act or oracle of God apart from the human will, or which has been so effected in the past. It was by this latter method, as we have said, that the Mosaic law was established; but I shall not deal with it here even insofar as it contains commands with regard to civil acts for the status of the present world. I shall discuss the establishment of only those laws and governments which emerge immediately from the human mind.

2. Let us say, to begin with, that it can pertain to any citizen to discover the law taken materially and in its third sense, as the science of civil justice and and benefit. Such inquiry, however, can be carried on more appropriately and be completed better by those men who are able to have leisure, who are

older and experienced in practical affairs, and who are called "prudent men," than by the mechanics who must bend all their efforts to acquiring the necessities of life. But it must be remembered that the true knowledge or discovery of the just and the beneficial, and of their opposites, is not law taken in its last and most proper sense, whereby it is the measure of human civil acts, unless there is given a coercive command as to its observance, or it is made by way of such a command, by someone through whose authority its transgressors must and can be punished. Hence, we must now say to whom belongs the authority to make such a command and to punish its transgressors. This, indeed, is to inquire into the legislator or the maker of the law.

3. Let us say, then, in accordance with the truth and the counsel of Aristotle in the *Politics,* Book III, Chapter 6, that the legislator, or the primary and proper efficient cause of the law, is the people or the whole body of citizens, or the weightier part thereof, through its election or will expressed by words in the general assembly of the citizens, commanding or determining that something be done or omitted with regard to human civil acts, under a temporal pain or punishment. By the "weightier part" I mean to take into consideration the quantity and the quality of the persons in that community over which the law is made. The aforesaid whole body of citizens or the weightier part thereof is·the legislator regardless of whether it makes the law directly by itself or entrusts the making of it to some person or persons, who are not and cannot be the legislator in the absolute sense, but only in a relative sense and for a particular time and in accordance with the authority of the primary legislator. And I say further that the laws and anything else established through election must receive their necessary approval by that same primary authority and no other, whatever be the case with regard to certain ceremonies or solemnities, which are required not for the being of the matters elected but for their well-being, since the election would be no less valid even if these ceremonies were not performed. Moreover, by the same authority must the laws and other things established through election

undergo addition, subtraction, complete change, interpretation, or suspension, insofar as the exigencies of time or place or other circumstances make any such action opportune for the common benefit. And by the same authority, also, must the laws be promulgated or proclaimed after their enactment, so that no citizen or alien who is delinquent in observing them may be excused because of ignorance.

4. A citizen I define in accordance with Aristotle in the *Politics,* Book III, Chapters 1, 3, and 7, as one who participates in the civil community in the government or the deliberative or judicial function according to his rank. By this definition, children, slaves, aliens, and women are distinguished from citizens, although in different ways. For the sons of citizens are citizens in proximate potentiality, lacking only in years. The weightier part of the citizens should be viewed in accordance with the honorable custom of polities, or else it should be determined in accordance with the doctrine of Aristotle in the *Politics,* Book VI Chapter 2.

5. Having thus defined the citizen and the weightier part of the citizens, let us return to our proposed objective, namely, to demonstrate that the human authority to make laws belongs only to the whole body of the citizens or to the weightier part thereof. Our first proof is as follows. The absolutely primary human authority to make or establish human laws belongs only to those men from whom alone the best laws can emerge. But these are the whole body of the citizens, or the weightier part thereof, which represents the whole body; since it is difficult or impossible for all persons to agree upon one decision, because some men have a deformed nature, disagreeing with the common decision through singular malice or ignorance. The common benefit should not, however, be impeded or neglected because of the unreasonable protest or opposition of these men. The authority to make or establish laws, therefore, belongs only to the whole body of the citizens or to the weightier part thereof.

The first proposition of this demonstration is very close to self-evident, although its force and its ultimate certainty can be grasped from Chapter V of this discourse. The second proposition, that the best law is made only through the hearing and command of the entire multitude, I prove by assuming with Aristotle in the *Politics,* Book III, Chapter 7, that the best law is that which is made for the common benefit of the citizens. As Aristotle said: "That is presumably right," that is, in the laws, "which is for the common benefit of the state and the citizens." But that this is best achieved only by the whole body of the citizens or by the weightier part thereof, which is assumed to be the same thing, I show as follows: That at which the entire body of the citizens aims intellectually and emotionally is more certainly judged as to its truth and more diligently noted as to its common utility. For a defect in some proposed law can be better noted by the greater number than by any part thereof, since every whole, or at least every corporeal whole, is greater in mass and in virtue than any part of it taken separately. Moreover, the common utility of a law is better noted by the entire multitude, because no one knowingly harms himself. Anyone can look to see whether a proposed law leans toward the benefit of one or a few persons more than of the others or of the community, and can protest against it. Such, however, would not be the case were the law made by one or a few persons, considering their own private benefit rather than that of the community. ■

From Defensor Pacis, *Discourse One, Chapter XIII, 1324; published 1522.*

• JOHN MILTON

Indeed, if the race of kings were eminently the best of men, as the breed of Tutbury is of horses, it would in reason then be their part only to command, ours always to obey. But kings by generation no way excelling others, and most commonly not being the wisest or the worthiest by far of whom they claim to have the governing; that we should yield them subjection to our own ruin, or hold of them the right of our common safety . . . we may be sure was never the intent of God, whose ways are just and equal; never the intent of nature, whose works

are also regular; never of any people not wholly barbarous, whom prudence, or no more but human sense, would have better guided when they first created kings, than so to nullify and tread to dirt the rest of mankind, by exalting one person and his lineage without other merit looked after, but the mere contingency of a begetting, into an absolute and uncontrollable dominion over them and their posterity. ■

From Eikonoklastes, *1649.*

• JACQUES BÉNIGNE BOSSUET

Seventh Proposition: Monarchy is the most common, the oldest, and the most natural form of government. The people of Israel subjected themselves to monarchy as being the universally accepted government. "Make us a king to judge us like all the nations" (1 Samuel 8:4). If God was irritated it was because up till then He had governed this people himself, and that He was their true king. That is why He said to Samuel: ". . . for they have not rejected thee, but Me, that I should not reign over them."

Indeed this form of government is so natural that one finds it first of all with all peoples. . . .

If it is the most natural, it is consequently the most durable, and thus also the strongest. ■

From "Politics Drawn from the Holy Scriptures,"
in Oeuvres complètes de Bossuet, *Vol. XVI,*
1838 ed.

• THOMAS JEFFERSON

And above all things I am astonished at some people's considering a kingly government as a refuge. Advise such to read the fable of the frogs who solicited Jupiter for a king. If that does not put them to rights, send them to Europe to see something of the trappings of monarchy, and I will undertake that every man shall go back thoroughly cured. If all the evils which can arise among us from the republican form of our government from this day to the day of judgment could be put into a scale against what this country [France] suffers from its monarchical form in a week, or England in a month, the latter would preponderate. Consider the contents of the Red Book in England, or the Almanac Royale of France, and say what a people gain by monarchy. No race of kings has ever presented above one man of common sense in twenty generations. The best they can do is to leave things to their ministers, & what are their ministers but a committee, badly chosen? If the king ever meddles it is to do harm. ■

From letter to Benjamin Hawkins, Paris, August 4, 1787.

● THOMAS JEFFERSON

When I observed, however, that the King of England was a cipher, I did not mean to confine the observation to the mere individual now on that throne. The practice of kings marrying only in the families of kings has been that of Europe for some centuries. Now, take any race of animals, confine them in idleness and inaction, whether in a sty, a stable or a state room, pamper them with high diet, gratify all their sexual appetites, immerse them in sensualities, nourish their passions, let everything bend before them, and banish whatever might lead them to think, and in a few generations they become all body and no mind; and this, too, by a law of nature, by that very law by which we are in the constant practice of changing the characters and propensities of the animals we raise for our own purposes. Such is the regimen in raising kings, and in this way they have gone on for centuries.

While in Europe, I often amused myself with contemplating the characters of the then reigning sovereigns of Europe. Louis the XVI was a fool, of my own knowledge, and in despite of the answers made for him at his trial.[1] The King of Spain was a fool, and of Naples the same. They passed their lives in hunting, and dispatched two couriers a week, one thousand miles, to let each other know what game they had killed the preceding days. The King of Sardinia was a fool. All these were Bourbons. The Queen of Portugal, a Braganza, was an idiot by nature. And so was the King of Denmark. Their sons, as regents, exercised the powers of government. The King of Prussia, successor to the great Frederick, was a mere hog in body as well as in mind. Gustavus of Sweden and Joseph of Austria[2] were really crazy, and George of England, you know, was in a strait waistcoat. There remained, then, none but old Catherine, who had been too lately picked up to have lost her common sense. In this state Bonaparte found Europe; and it was this state of its rulers which lost it with scarce a struggle. These animals had become without mind and powerless; and so will every hereditary monarch be after a few generations. Alexander, the grandson of Catherine, is as yet an exception. He is able to hold his own. But he is only the third generation. His race is not yet worn out. And so endeth the book of kings, from all of whom the Lord deliver us, and have you, my friend, and all such good men and true, in his holy keeping. ■

From letter to John Langdon, Monticello, March 5, 1810.

---

[1] See Saul K. Padover, *The Life and Death of Louis XVI* (1939; rev. ed., 1963).

[2] See Saul K. Padover, *The Revolutionary Emperor: Joseph II* (1934, 1967).

3

MODERN EUROPEAN VIEWS

Jean Jacques Rousseau
Voltaire
Edmund Burke
Walter Bagehot
John Stuart Mill
Karl Marx and Michael Bakunin
Sir Henry Maine

• JEAN JACQUES ROUSSEAU

He who makes the laws knows better than anyone how they should be executed and interpreted. It would seem, then, that there could be no better constitution than one in which the executive power is united with the legislative; but it is that very circumstance which makes a democratic government inadequate in certain respects, because things which ought to be distinguished are not, and because the prince and the sovereign, being the same person, only form as it were a government without government.

It is not expedient that he who makes the laws should execute them, nor that the body of the people should divert its attention from general considerations in order to bestow it on particular objects. Nothing is more dangerous than the influence of private interests on public affairs; and the abuse of the laws by the government is a less evil than the corruption of the legislator, which is the infallible result of the pursuit of private interests. For when the state is changed in its substance all reform becomes impossible. A people which would never abuse the government would likewise never abuse its independence; a people which always governed well would not need to be governed.

Taking the term in its strict sense, there never has existed, and never will exist, any true democracy. It is contrary to the natural order that the majority should govern and that the minority should be governed. It is impossible to imagine that the people should remain in perpetual assembly to attend to public affairs, and it is easily apparent that commissions could not be established for that purpose without the form of administration being changed.

In fact, I think I can lay down as a principle that when the functions of government are shared among several magistracies, the least numerous acquire, sooner or later, the greatest authority, if only on account of the facility in transacting business which naturally leads them on to that.

Moreover, how many things difficult to combine does not this government presuppose! First, a very small state, in which the people may be readily assembled, and in which every citizen can easily know all the rest; secondly, the greatest simplicity of manners, which prevents a multiplicity of affairs and thorny discussions; next, considerable equality in rank and fortune, without which equality in rights and authority could not long subsist; lastly, little or no luxury, for luxury is either the effect of wealth or renders it necessary; it corrupts both the rich and the poor, the former by possession, the latter by covetousness; it betrays the country to effeminacy and vanity; it deprives the state of all its citizens in order to subject them one to another, and all to opinion.

That is why a famous author has assigned virtue as the principle of a republic, for all these conditions could not subsist without virtue; but through not making the necessary distinctions, this brilliant genius has often lacked precision and sometimes clearness, and has not seen that the sovereign authority being everywhere the same, the same principle ought to have a place in every well-constituted state, in a greater or less degree, it is true, according to the form of government.

Let us add that there is no government so subject to civil wars and internal agitation as the democratic or popular, because there is none which tends so strongly and so constantly to change its form, none which demands more vigilance and courage to be maintained in its own form. It is especially in this constitution that the citizen should arm himself with strength and steadfastness, and say every day of his life from the bottom of his heart what a virtuous Palatine said in the Diet of Poland: *Malo periculosam libertatem quam quietum servitium*. [Better the perils of liberty than the quietude of servility].

If there were a nation of gods, it would be governed democratically. So perfect a government is unsuited to men. ■

From Social Contract *Book III, Chapter 4, 1762.*

Chapter 4.

• VOLTAIRE

Democracy seems suitable only to a very little country . . . Small though it be, it will make many mistakes, because it will be composed of human beings.

Discord will reign there as in a monastery; but there will be no St. Bartholomew,[1] no Irish massacres,[2] no Sicilian Vespers,[3] no Inquisition, no condemnation to the galleys for having taken some water from the sea without paying for it. ■

From Philosophical Dictionary, *1764.*

• EDMUND BURKE

But where popular authority is absolute and unrestrained, the people have an infinitely greater, because a far better founded confidence in their own power. They are themselves, in a great measure, their own instruments. They are nearer to their objects. Besides, they are less under responsibility to one of the greatest controlling powers on earth, the sense of fame and estimation. The share of infamy that is likely to fall to the lot of each individual in public acts, is small indeed; the operation of opinion being in the inverse ratio to the number of those who abuse power. Their own approbation of their own acts has to them the appearance of a public judgment in their favour. A perfect democracy is therefore the most shameless thing in the world. As it is the most shameless, it is also the most fearless. No man apprehends in his person he can be made subject to punishment. Certainly the people at large never ought: for as all punishments are for example towards the conservation of the people at large, the people at large can never become the subject of punishment by any human hand.[4] It is therefore of infinite importance that they should not be suffered to imagine that their will, any more than that of kinds, is the standard of right and wrong. They ought to be persuaded that they are full as little entitled, and far less qualified, with safety to themselves, to use any arbitrary power whatsoever. . . .

I reprobate no form of government merely upon

---

[1] A massacre of French Protestants, on August 24, 1572; more than 2,000 were killed in Paris alone.

[2] In 1649 Oliver Cromwell's armies massacred Irish Catholic garrisons in Ireland.

[3] In 1282 Sicily revolted against French domination and slaughtered Frenchman, 8,000 of them in Palermo alone.

[4] *Quicquid multis peccatur inultum* (Whatever the transgressions of the many, they are unpunished). — Author's note.

abstract principles. There may be situations in which the purely democratic form will become necessary. There may be some (very few, and very particularly circumstanced) where it would be clearly desirable. This I do not take to be case of France, or of any other great country. Until now, we have seen no examples of considerable democracies. The ancients were better acquainted with them. Not being wholly unread in the authors, who had seen the most of those constitutions, and who best understood them, I cannot help concurring with their opinion, that an absolute democracy, no more than absolute monarchy, is to be reckoned among the legitimate forms of government. They think it rather the corruption of degeneracy, than the sound constitution of a republic. If I recollect rightly, Aristotle observes, that a democracy has many striking points of resemblance with a tyranny.[1] Of this I am certain, that in a democracy, the majority of the citizens is capable of exercising the most cruel oppressions upon the minority, whenever strong divisions prevail in that kind of polity, as they often must; and that oppression of the minority will extend to far greater numbers, and will be carried on with much greater fury, than can almost ever be apprehended from the dominion of a single sceptre. In such a popular persecution, individual sufferers are in a much more deplorable condition than in any other. Under a cruel prince they have the balmy compassion of mankind to assuage the smart of their wounds; they have the plaudits of the people to animate their generous constancy under their sufferings; but those who are subjected to wrong under multitudes, are deprived of all external consolation. They seem deserted by mankind; overpowered by a conspiracy of their whole species. ∎

From Reflections on the Revolution in France, *1790.*

[1] When I wrote this I quoted from memory, after many years had elapsed from my reading the passage. A learned friend has found it, and it is as follows: "The ethical character is the same; both exercise despotism over the better class of citizens; and decrees are in the one, what ordiances and decrees are in the other: the demagogue too, and the court favorite, are not unfrequently the same identical men, always bear a close analogy; and these have the principal power, each in their respective forms of government, favorites with the absolute monarch, and demagogues with a people such as I have described." Aristotle, *Politics*, Liber IV, Chap. 4.—Author's note.

• WALTER BAGEHOT

We are indeed disposed to believe, in spite of much direct assertion to the contrary, that the democratic theory still rests not so much on reason as on a kind of sentiment—on an obscure conception of abstract rights. The animation of its advocates is an indication of it; they think they are contending for the "rights" of the people, and they endeavour to induce the people to believe so too . . . We find it impossible to believe that all the struggles of men for liberty, all the enthusiasm it has called forth, all the passionate emotions it has caused in the very highest minds, all the glow of thought and rustle of obscure feeling which the very name [democracy] excites in the whole mass of men, have their origin in calculations of advantage and a belief that such and such arrangements would be beneficial. The masses of men are very difficult to excite on bare ground of self-interest; most easy, if a bold orator tells them confidently they are *wronged.* The foundation of government upon simple utility is but the fiction of philosophers; it has never been acceptable to natural feelings of mankind. . . .

Fitness to govern—for that is the real meaning of exercising the franchise which elects a *ruling* assembly—is not absolute quality of any individual; that fitness is relative and comparative—it must depend on the community to be governed and on the merits of other persons who may be capable of governing that community. . . . The true principle is, that every person has a right to *so much political power as he can exercise without impeding any other person who would more fitly exercise such power.* If we apply this to the lower orders of society, we see the reason why, notwithstanding their numbers, they must always be subject—always at least be comparatively uninfluential: whatever their capacity may be, it must be less than that of the higher classes, whose occupations are more instructive and whose education is more prolonged. Any such measure for enfranchising the lower orders as would overpower and consequently disenfranchise the higher should be resisted on the ground of "abstract right": you are proposing to take power from those who have the superior capacity, and to vest it in those who have but an inferior capacity, or in many cases no capacity at all. If we probe the subject to the bottom, we shall find that justice is on the side of a graduated rule, in which all persons should have an influence proportioned to their political capacity: and it is at this graduation that the true maxims of representative government really aim; they wish that the fairly intelligent persons, who create public opinion ... should rule in the state, which is the authorised means of carrying that opinion into action. This is the body which has the greater right to rule; this is the *felt intelligence* of the nation. ...

We may say that political intelligence will in general exist rather in the educated classes than in the less educated, rather in the rich than the poor; and not only that it will exist, but that it will in the absence of misleading feelings be *felt* by both parties to exist. ...

As the higher orders are felt by the lower to be more capable of governing, they will be chosen by the lower if the latter are left free to choose; that therefore no matter how democratic the government—in fact, the more democratic the government the surer are the upper classes to lead. But experience shows that this is an error. If the acquisition of power is left to the unconscious working of the natural influences of society, the rich and the cultivated will certainly acquire it; they obtain it insensibly, gradually, and without the poorer orders knowing that they are obtaining it: but the result is different when, by the operation of a purely democratic constitution, the selection of rulers is submitted to the direct vote of the populace. The lower orders are then told that they are perfectly able to judge; demagogues assert it to them without ceasing; the constitution itself is appealed to as an incontrovertible witness to the fact—as it has placed the supreme power in the hands of the lower and more numerous classes, it would be contravening it to suppose that the real superiority was in the higher and fewer. Moreover, when men are expressly asked to acknowledge their superiors, they are by no means always inclined to do so; they do not object to yield a mute observance, but they refuse a definite act of homage; they will obey, but they will not *say* that they will obey. In consequence, history teaches us that under a democratic government, those who speak the feelings of the majority themselves have a greater chance of being chosen to rule than any of the higher orders, who under another form of government would be admitted to be the better judges. The natural effect of such a government is to mislead the poor. ■

From The English Constitution, *1867.*

• KARL MARX AND MICHAEL BAKUNIN

MICHAEL BAKUNIN

We have already expressed our repugnance for the theory of Lassalle and Marx, which recommends to the workers, if not as a final ideal, at least as the next best objective, the founding of a *people's state,* which, to use their expression, would be *organized* with the *proletariat as the ruling class.* One asks: If the proletariat is to be the ruling class, over whom would it rule? This means that still another proletariat would remain behind as subjects of this new domination, this new state.

KARL MARX (comment)

This means that so long as other classes, especially the capitalist one, still exist and the proletariat struggles with them (for the capitalist governments are its enemy and the old organization of society has not yet disappeared), the proletariat must use *forcible* means, hence governmental means. So long as it still remains a class, and the economic conditions on which the class struggle rests still exist, and the other classes have not yet disappeared, and have to be cleared out of the way by force or transformed, the process of transformation is to be hastened by force.

MICHAEL BAKUNIN

For example, the common peasantry, the peasant mob, which, as is well known, does not enjoy the benevolence of the Marxists, and which finds itself at the lowest level of the culture, will in all probability be ruled by the city and factory proletariat.

KARL MARX (comment)

This means that where the peasant exists in the mass as private property owner, where he even forms a more or less substantial majority, as he does in all the states of the West European continent, where he has not disappeared and been replaced by agricultural day laborers, as in England, the following cases develop: Either he prevents or frustrates every workers' revolution, as he has hitherto done in France; or the proletariat (for the property-owning peasant does not belong to the proletariat, and even where he belongs to it according to his condition, he does not believe that he does) must take governmental measures directly to improve the peasant's condition, so as to win him over to the revolution; measures, however, that in their germ facilitate the transition from private land ownership to collective ownership. . . .

MICHAEL BAKUNIN

Where there is a state, there is unavoidable domination, consequently also [slavery]; domination without slavery, hidden or masked, is unthinkable—hence we are enemies of the state.

What does it mean, the proletariat (organized as a ruling class)?

KARL MARX (comment)

It means that the proletariat, instead of fighting singly against the economically privileged classes, has attained sufficient strength and organization to be able to apply general means of coercion against them; but it can apply only the economic means that will abolish its own character as *salariat* [wage worker], and hence as class; with its complete victory, therefore, its rule comes to an end, because its class character had disappeared.

MICHAEL BAKUNIN

Will the whole proletariat perhaps be at the head of the government?

KARL MARX (comment)

In a trade union, does the whole union make up its executive committee? In the factory, will all division of labor, as well as the various functions arising therefrom, cease? And in the Bakuninist structure (from the bottom up), will everybody be up? In which case, there is no bottom. Will all members of the community administer the common interests of the domain at the same time? In which case, there is no difference between community and domain.

MICHAEL BAKUNIN

The Germans amount to approximately 40,000,000. Will, for example, all the 40,000,000 be members of the government?

KARL MARX (comment)

Certainly! Since the matter begins with the self-government of the community.

MICHAEL BAKUNIN

The whole people will govern, and there will be no governed.

KARL MARX (comment)

When a man is his own master, he does not, by this principle, rule over himself; for he is, after all, himself and no other.

MICHAEL BAKUNIN

Then there will be no government, no state, but if there is a state, there will be also the governed and slaves.

KARL MARX (comment)

This merely means: when class rule has disappeared there will be no state in the present political sense.

MICHAEL BAKUNIN

This dilemma in the theory of the Marxists is explained simply. Under people's government, they understand government of the people through a small number of representatives, selected by the people.

KARL MARX (comment)

Jackass! This is democratic twaddle, political drivel. Election—political form, that found in the smallest

Russian commune and artel. The character of the election does not depend on those labels, but on the economic basis, the economic interconnection of the voters. The moment these functions have ceased to be political, (1) there exists no governmental function; (2) the division of the general functions has become merely a technical business, which does not result in domination; (3) election has nothing of the present-day political character. ■

From comments written by Marx between 1874 and 1875 on Bakunin's book State and Anarchy *(Geneva), 1873. See Karl Marx:* On the First International *(McGraw-Hill, N.Y., 1973).*

• JOHN STUART MILL

It has long . . . been a common saying, that if a good despot could be ensured, despotic monarchy would be the best form of government. I look upon this as a radical and most pernicious misconception of what good government is. . . .

The supposition is, that absolute power, in the hands of an eminent individual, would ensure a virtuous and intelligent performance of all the duties of government . . . What should we then have? One man of superhuman mental activity managing the entire affairs of a mentally passive people. Their passivity is implied in the very idea of absolute power. The nation as a whole, and every individual composing it, are without any potential voice in their own destiny. They exercise no will in respect to their collective interests. All is decided for them by a will not their own, which is legally a crime for them to disobey. What sort of human beings can be formed under such a regimen? . . .

A person must have a very unusual taste for intellectual exercise in and for itself, who will put himself to the trouble of thought when it is to have no outward effect, or qualify himself for functions which he has no chance of being allowed to exercise. The only sufficient incitement to mental exertion, in any but a few minds in a generation, is the prospect of some practical use to be made of its results. It does not follow that the nation will be wholly destitute of intellectual power. The common business of life, which must necessarily be performed by each individual or family for themselves, will call forth some amount of intelligence and practical ability, within a certain narrow range of ideas. There may be a select class of savants, who cultivate science with a view to its physical uses, or for the pleasure of pursuit. There will be a bureaucracy, and persons in training for the bureaucracy, who will be taught at least some empirical maxims of government and public administration. There may be, and often has been, a systematic organization of the best mental power in the country in some special direction (commonly military) to promote the grandeur of the despot. But the public at large remain without information and without interest on all the greater matters of practice; or, if they have any knowledge of them, it is but a dilettante knowledge. . . .

Nor is it only in their intelligence that they suffer. Their moral capacities are equally stunted. Wherever the sphere of action of human beings is artificially circumscribed, their sentiments are narrowed and dwarfed in the same proportion. The food of feeling is action: even domestic affection lives upon voluntary good offices. Let a person have nothing to do for his country, and he will not care fot it. It has been said of old, that in a depotism there is at most but one patriot, the despot himself. . . .

But (setting aside the fact, that for one despot who now and then reforms an abuse, there are ninety-nine who do nothing but create them) those who look in any such direction (as despotism) for the realization of their hopes leave out of the idea of good government its principal element, the improvement of the people themselves.

One of the benefits of freedom is that under it the ruler cannot pass by the people's minds, and amend their affairs for them without amending them . . . It is true, a despot may educate the people; and to do so really, would be the best apology for his despotism. But any education which aims at making human beings other than machines, in the long run makes them claim to have the control of their own actions . . . Whatever invigorates the faculties, in however small a measure, creates an increased desire for their more unimpeded exercise. . . .

There is no difficulty in showing that the ideally best form of government is that in which the sovereignty, or supreme controlling power in the last resort, is vested in the entire aggregate of the community; every citizen not only having a voice in the exercise of that ultimate sovereignty, but being, at least occasionally, called on to take an actual part in the government, by the personal discharge of some public function, local or general. . . .

The ideally best form of government . . . does not mean one which is practicable or eligible in all states of civilization, but the one which, in the circumstances in which it is practicable and eligible, is attended with the greatest amount of beneficial consequences, immediate and prospective. A completely popular government is the only policy which can make out any claim to this character. . . .

Its superiority . . . rests upon two principles, of as universal truth and applicability as any general propositions which can be laid down respecting human affairs. The first is, that the rights and interests of every or any person are only secure from being disregarded when the person interested is himself able, and habitually disposed, to stand up for them. The second is, that the general prosperity attains a greater height, and is more widely diffused, in proportion to the amount and variety of the personal energies enlisted in promoting it. . . .

From these accumulated considerations it is evident that the only government which can fully satisfy all the exigencies of the social state is one in which the whole people participate; that any participation, even in the smallest public function, is useful; that the participation should everywhere be as great as the general degree of improvement of the community will allow; and that nothing less can be ultimately desirable than the admission of all to a share in the sovereign power of the state. But since all cannot, in a community exceeding a single small town, participate personally in any but some very minor portions of the public business, it follows that the ideal of a perfect government must be representative. ■

From Considerations on Representative Government, *Chapter III, 1875.*

• SIR HENRY MAINE

Political liberty, said Hobbes, is political power. When a man burns to be free, he is not longing for the "desolate freedom of the wild ass"; what he wants is a share of political government. But in wide democracies, political power is minced into morsels, and each man's portion of it is almost infinitesmally small. One of the first results of this political comminution . . . is that two of the historical watchwords of Democracy exclude one another, and that, where there is political liberty, there can be no equality. . . .

There is no doubt that, in popular governments resting on a wide suffrage, either without an army or having little reason to fear it, the leader, whether or not he be cunning, or eloquent, or well provided with commonplaces, will be the Wire-puller. The process of cutting up political power into petty fragments has in him its most remarkable product. The morsels of power are so small that men, if left to themselves, would not care to employ them. . . .

The wire-pulling system when fully developed, will infallibly lead to the constant enlargement of the area of the suffrage. What is called universal suffrage has greatly declined in the estimation, not only of philosophers who follow Bentham, but of the *à priori* theorists who assumed that it was the inseparable accompaniment of a Republic, but who found that in practice it was the natural basis of a tyranny. But extensions of the suffrage, though no longer believed to be good in themselves, have now a permanent place in the armory of parties and are sure to be a favourite weapon of the Wirepuller. . . .

But one of the strangest of vulgar ideas is that a very wide suffrage could or would promote progress, new ideas, new discoveries and inventions, new arts of life. Such a suffrage is commonly associated with Radicalism; and no doubt amid its most certain effects would be the extensive destruction of existing institutions. . . .

A moment's reflection will satisfy any competently instructed person that this is not too broad a proposition. Let him turn over in his mind the great epochs of scientific invention and social change during the last two centuries, and consider what would have occurred if universal suffrage had been established at any one of them. . . .

There are possibly many persons who, without denying these conclusions in the past, tacitly assume that no such mistakes will be committed in the future, because the community is already too enlightened for them, and will become more enlightened through popular education. But without questioning the advantages of popular education under certain aspects, its manifest tendency is to diffuse popular commonplaces, to fasten them on the mind at the time when it is most easily impressed, and thus to stereotype average opinion. It is of course possible that universal suffrage would not now force on governments the same legislation which it would infallibly have dictated a hundred years ago; but then we are necessarily ignorant what germs of social and material improvement there may be in the womb of time, and how far they may conflict with the popular prejudice which hereafter will be omnipotent. . . .

It is perfectly possible, I think, as Mr. Herbert Spencer has shown . . . to revive even in our day the fiscal tyranny which once left even European populations in doubt whether it was worth while preserving life by thrift and toil . . . You have only to take the heart out of those who would willingly labour and save, by taxing them *ad misericordiam* for the most laudable philanthropic objects. For it makes not the smallest difference to the motives of the thrifty and industrious part of mankind whether their fiscal oppressor be an Eastern despot, or a feudal baron, or a democratic legislature . . . Here then is the great question about democratic legislation, when carried to more than a moderate length. How will it affect human motives? What motives will it substitute for those now acting on men? The motives, which at present impel mankind to the labour and pain which produce the resuscitation of wealth in ever increasing quantities, are such as infallibly to entail inequality in the distribution of wealth. They are the springs of action called into activity by the strenuous and never ending struggle for

existence, the beneficent private war which makes one man strive to climb on the shoulders of another and remain there through the law of the survival of the fittest.

These truths are best exemplified in the part of the world to which the superficial thinker would perhaps look for the triumph of the opposite principle. The United States have justly been called the home of the disinherited of the earth; but, if those vanquished under one sky in the struggle for existence had not continued under another the same battle in which they had been once worsted, there would have been no such exploit performed as the cultivation of the vast American territory from end to end and from side to side. There could be no grosser delusion than to suppose this result to have been attained by democratic legislation. It has really been obtained through the sifting out of the strongest by natural selection. The government of the United States . . . now rests on universal suffrage, but then it is only a political government. It is a government under which coercive restraint, except in politics, is reduced to a minimum. There has hardly ever before been a community in which the weak have been pushed so pitilessly to the wall, in which those who have succeeded have so uniformly been the strong, and in which in so short a time there has arisen so great an inequality of private fortune and domestic luxury. And at the same time, there has never been a country in which, on the whole, the persons distanced in the race have suffered so little from their ill-success . . . It all reposes on the sacredness of contract and the stability of private property, the first the implement, and the last the reward, of success in the universal competition . . . The Americans are still of the opinion that more is to be got for human happiness by private energy than by public legislation. . . .

I have thus shown that popular governments of the modern type have not hitherto proved stable as compared with other forms of political rule, and that they include certain sources of weakness which do not promise security for them in the near or remote future . . . There is not at present sufficient evidence to warrant the common belief, that these gov-

ernments are likely to be of indefinitely long duration. . . .

The imitations [of the British type of popular gov-
ernment] have not been generally happy. One nation
alone, consisting of Englishmen, has practised a
modification of it successfully, amidst abounding
material plenty. It is not too much to say, that the
only evidence worth mentioning for the duration
of popular government is to be found in the success
of the British Constitution during two centuries
under special conditions, and in the success of the
American Constitution during one century under
conditions still more peculiar and more unlikely to
recur.　■

From Popular Government, *1886.*

4

AMERICAN VIEWS

James Madison
Alexander Hamilton
John Adams
Thomas Jefferson
James Monroe
James Fenimore Cooper
Ralph Waldo Emerson
Parke Godwin
Theodore Parker
Abraham Lincoln
Walt Whitman
Woodrow Wilson
John Dewey
Franklin D. Roosevelt
Harry S. Truman

• JAMES MADISON

I will state some of the ideas which have occurred to me on the subject. Those who contend for a simple Democracy, or a pure republic, actuated by the sense of the majority, and operating within narrow limits, assume or suppose a case which is altogether fictitious. They found their reasoning on the idea, that the people composing the Society, enjoy not only an equality of political rights; but that they have all precisely the same interests, and the same feelings in every respect. Were this in reality the case, their reasoning would be conclusive. The interest of the majority would be that of the minority also; the decisions could only turn on mere opinion concerning the good of the whole, of which the major voice would be the safest criterion; and within a small sphere, this voice could be most easily collected, and the public affairs most accurately managed. We know however that no society ever did or can consist of so homogeneous a mass of Citizens. In the savage state indeed, an approach is made towards it; but in that state little or no Government is necessary. In all civilized societies distinctions are various and unavoidable. A distinction of property results from that very protection which a free Government gives to unequal faculties of acquiring it. There will be rich and poor; creditors and debtors; a landlord interest, a monied interest, a mercantile interest, a manufacturing interest. These classes may again be subdivided according to the different productions of different situations and soils, and according to different branches of commerce and of manufactures. In addition to these natural distinctions, artificial ones will be founded, on accidental differences in political, religious, or other opinions, or an attachment to the persons of leading individuals. However erroneous or ridiculous these grounds of dissension and faction may appear to the enlightened Statesman or the benevolent philosopher, the bulk of mankind who are neither Statesmen nor Philosophers, will continue to view them in a different light. It remains then to be enquired whether a majority having any common interest, or feeling any common passion, will find sufficient motives to restrain them from oppressing the minority. An individual is never allowed to be a judge or even a witness, in his own cause. If two individuals are under the bias of interest or enmity against a third, the rights of the latter could never be safely referred to the majority of the three. Will two thousand individuals be less apt to oppress one thousand or two hundred thousand one hundred thousand? Three motives only can restrain in such cases: 1. A prudent regard to private or partial good, as essentially involved in the general and permanent good of the Whole. This ought no doubt to be sufficient of itself. Experience however shows that it has little effect on individuals, and perhaps still less on a collection of individuals, and least of all on a majority with the public authority in their hands. If the former are ready to forget that honesty is the best policy, the last do more. They often proceed on the converse of the maxim, that whatever is politic is honest. 2. Respect for character. This motive is not found sufficient to restrain individuals from injustice. And loses its efficacy in proportion to the number which is to divide the pain or the blame. Besides, as it has reference to public opinion, which is that of the majority, the standard is fixed by those whose conduct is to be measured by it. 3. Religion. The inefficacy of this restraint on individuals is well known. The conduct of every popular Assembly, acting on oath, the strongest of religious ties, shews that individuals join without remorse in acts against which their consciences would revolt, if proposed to them separately in their closets. When indeed Religion is kindled into enthusiasm, its force like that of other passions is increased by the sympathy of a multitude. But enthusiasm is only a temporary state of Religion, and whilst it lasts will hardly be seen with pleasure at the helm. Even in its coolest state, it has been much oftener a motive to oppression than a restraint from it. If then there must be different interests and parties in society; and a majority when united by a common interest or passion cannot be restrained from oppressing the minority, what remedy can be found in a republican Government, where the majority must ultimately decide, but that of giving such an extent to its sphere, that no common

interest or passion will be likely to unite a majority of the whole number in an unjust pursuit. In a large Society, the people are broken into so many interests and parties, that a common sentiment is less likely to be formed, by a majority of the whole. The same security seems requisite for the civil as for the religious rights of individuals. If the same sect form a majority and have the power, other sects will be sure to be depressed. *Divide et impera,* the reprobated axiom of tyranny, is under certain qualifications, the only policy, by which a republic can be administered on just principles. It must be observed however that this doctrine can only hold within a sphere of a mean extent. As in too small a sphere oppressive combinations may be too easily formed against the weaker party; so in too extensive a one, a defensive concert may be rendered too difficult against the oppression of those entrusted with the administration.

The great desideratum in Government is, so to modify the sovereignty as that it may be sufficiently neutral between different parts of the Society to controul one part from invading the rights of another, and at the same time sufficiently controuled itself, from setting up an interest adverse to that of the entire Society.

In absolute monarchies, the Prince may be tolerably neutral towards different classes of his subjects but may sacrifice the happiness of all to his personal ambition or avarice. In small republics, the sovereign will is controuled from such a sacrifice of the entire Society, but is not sufficiently neutral towards the parts composing it. ∎

From letter to Thomas Jefferson, October 24, 1787.

• JAMES MADISON

From this view of the subject it may be concluded that a pure democracy, by which I mean a society consisting of a small number of citizens, who assemble and administer the government in person, can admit of no cure for the mischiefs of faction. A common passion or interest will, in almost every case, be felt by a majority of the whole; a communication and concert result from the form of government itself; and there is nothing to check the inducements to sacrifice the weaker party or an obnoxious individual. Hence it is that such democracies have ever been spectacles of turbulence and contention; have ever been found incompatible with personal security or the rights of property; and have in general been as short in their lives as they have been violent in their deaths. Theoretic politicians, who have patronized this species of government, have erroneously supposed that by reducing mankind to a perfect equality in their political rights, they would, at the same time, be perfectly equalized and assimilated in their possessions, their opinions, and their passions.

A republic, by which I mean a government in which the scheme of representation takes place, opens a different prospect, and promises the cure for which we are seeking. Let us examine the points in which it varies from pure democracy, and we shall comprehend both the nature and cure and the efficacy which it must derive from the Union.

The two great points of difference between a democracy and a republic are: first, the delegation of the government, in the latter, to a small number of citizens elected by the rest; secondly, the greater number of citizens, and greater sphere of country, over which the latter may be extended.

The effect of the first difference is, on the one hand, to refine and enlarge the public views, by passing them through the medium of a chosen body of citizens, whose wisdom may best discern the true interest of their country, and whose patriotism and love of justice will be least likely to sacrifice it to temporary or partial considerations. Under such regulation, it may well happen that the public voice, pronounced by the representatives of the people, will be more consonant to the public good than if pronounced by the people themselves, convened for the purpose. On the other hand, the effect may be inverted. Men of factious tempers, of local prejudices, or of sinister designs, may, by intrigue, by corruption or by other means, first obtain the suffrages, and then betray the interests, of the people.

The question resulting is, whether small or extensive republics are more favorable to the election of proper guardians of the public weal; and it is clearly decided in favor of the latter by two obvious considerations:

In the first place, it is to be remarked that, however small the republic may be, the representatives must be raised to a certain number, in order to guard against the cabals of a few; and that, however large it may be, they must be limited to a certain number, in order to guard against the confusion of a multitude. Hence, the number of representatives in the two cases not being in proportion to that of the two constituents, and being proportionally greater in the small republic, it follows that, if the proportion of fit characters be not less in the large than in the small republic, the former will present a greater option, and consequently a greater probability of a fit choice.

In the next place, as each representative will be chosen by a greater number of citizens in the large than in the small republic, it will be more difficult for unworthy candidates to practice with success the vicious arts by which elections are too often carried; and the suffrages of the people being more free, will be more like to center in men who possess the most attractive merit and the most diffusive and established characters.

It must be confessed that in this, as in most other cases, there is a mean, on both sides of which inconveniences will be found to lie. By enlarging too much the number of electors, you render the representative too little acquainted with all their local circumstances and lesser interests; as by reducing it too much, you render him unduly attached to these, and too little fit to comprehend and pursue great and national objects. The Federal Constitution forms a happy combination in this respect; the great and aggregate interests being referred to the national, the local and particular to the State legislatures.

The other point of difference is, the great number of citizens and extent of territory which may be brought within the compass of republican than of democratic government; and it is this circumstance principally which renders factious combinations less to be dreaded in the former than in the latter. The smaller the society, the fewer probably will be the distinct parties and interests composing it; the fewer the distinct parties and interests, the more frequently will a majority be found of the same party; and the smaller the number of individuals composing a majority, and the smaller the compass within which they are placed, the more easily will they concert and execute their plans of oppression. Extend the sphere, and you take in a greater variety of parties and interests; you make it less probable that a majority of the whole will have a common motive to invade the rights of other citizens; or if such a common motive exists, it will be more difficult for all who feel it to discover their own strength, and to act in unison with each other. Besides other impediments, it may be remarked that, where there is a consciousness of unjust or dishonorable purposes, communication is always checked by distrust in proportion to the number whose concurrence is necessary.

Hence, it clearly appears, that the same advantage which a republic has over a democracy, in controlling the effects of faction, is enjoyed by a large over a small republic—is enjoyed by the Union over the States composing it. Does the advantage consist in the substitution of representatives whose enlightened views and virtuous sentiments render them superior to local prejudices and to schemes of injustice? It will not be denied that the representation of the Union will be most likely to possess these requisite endowments. Does it consist in the greater security afforded by a greater variety of parties, against the event of any one party being able to outnumber and oppress the rest? In an equal degree does the increased variety of parties comprised within the Union, increase this security? Does it, in fine, consist in the greater obstacles opposed to the concern and accomplishment of the secret wishes of an unjust and interested majority? Here, again, the extent of the Union gives it the most palpable advantage.

The influence of factious leaders may kindle a flame within their particular States, but will be unable to spread a general conflagration through the other States. A religious sect may degenerate into a political faction in a part of the Confederacy; but the variety of sects dispersed over the entire face of it must secure the national councils against any danger from that source. A rage for paper money, for an abolition of debts, for an equal division of property, or for any other improper or wicked project, will be less apt to pervade the whole body of the Union than a particular member of it; in the same proportion as such a malady is more likely to taint a particular county or district, than an entire State.

In the extent and proper structure of the Union, therefore, we behold a republican remedy for the diseases most incident to republican government. ∎

From The Federalist, *No. 10, November 23, 1787.*

• ALEXANDER HAMILTON

It has been observed that a pure democracy, if it were practicable, would be the most perfect government. Experience has proved, that no position in politics is more false than this. The ancient democracies, in which the people themselves deliberated, never possessed one feature of good government. Their very character was tyranny; their figure deformity. When they assembled, the field of debate presented an ungovernable mob, not only incapable of deliberation, but prepared for every enormity. In these assemblies the enemies of the people brought forward their plans of ambition systematically. They were opposed by their enemies of another party; and it became a matter of contingency, whether the people subjected themselves to be led blindly by one tyrant or by another. . . .

After all, Sir, we must submit to this idea, that the true principle of a republic is that the people should choose whom they please to govern them. Representation is imperfect, in proportion as the current of popular favor is checked. This great source of free government, popular election, should be perfectly pure, and the most unbounded liberty allowed. Where this principle is adhered to; where, in the organization of the government, the legislative, executive, and judicial branches are rendered distinct;

where, again, the legislative is divided into separate houses, and the operations of each are controlled by various checks and balances, and above all by the vigilance and weight of the State governments, to talk of tyranny and the subversion of our liberties, is to speak the language of enthusiasm. ■

From speech at New York State Ratification Convention, June 21, 1788.

• JAMES MADISON

Republican—The people themselves. The sacred trust can be nowhere so safe as in the hands most interested in preserving it.

Anti-republican—The people are stupid, suspicious, licentious. They cannot safely trust themselves. When they have established government they should think of nothing but obedience, leaving the care of their liberties to their wiser rulers.

Republican—Although all men are born free, and all nations might be so, yet too true it is, that slavery has been the general lot of the human race. Ignorant —they have been cheated; asleep—they have been surprised; divided—the yoke has been forced upon them. But what is the lesson? that because the people may betray themselves, they ought to give themselves up, blindfold, to those who have an interest in betraying them? Rather conclude that the people ought to be enlightened, to be awakened, to be united, that after establishing a government they should watch over it, as well as obey it.

Anti-republican—You look at the surface only, where errors float, instead of fathoming the depths where truth lies hid. It is not the government that is disposed to fly off from the people; but the people that are ever ready to fly off from the government. Rather say then, enlighten the government, warn it to be vigilant, enrich it with influence, arm it with force, and to the people never pronounce but two words—Submission and Confidence.

Republican—The centrifugal tendency then is in the people, not in the government, and the secret art lies in restraining the tendency, by augmenting the attractive principle of the government with all the weight that can be added to it. What a perversion of the natural order of things! to make power the primary and central object of the social system, and Liberty but its satellite.

Anti-republican—The science of the stars can never instruct you in the mysteries of government. Wonderful as it may seem, the more you increase the attractive force of power, the more you enlarge the sphere of liberty; the more you make government independent and hostile towards the people, the better security you provide for their rights and interests. Hence the wisdom of the theory, which, after limiting the share of the people to a third of the government . . . establishes two grand hereditary orders . . . inveterately hostile to the rights and interests of the people, yet by a *mysterious* operation all combining to fortify the people in both.

Republican—Mysterious indeed! But mysteries belong to religion, not to government; to the ways of the Almighty, not to the works of man. And in religion itself there is nothing mysterious to its author; the mystery lies in the dimness of the human sight. So in the institutions of man let there be no mystery, unless for those inferior beings endowed with a ray perhaps of the twilight vouchsafed to the first order of terrestial creation.

Anti-republican—You are destitute, I perceive, of every quality of a good citizen, or rather of a good *subject*. You have neither the light of faith nor the spirit of obedience. I denounce you to the government as an accomplice of atheism and anarchy.

Republican—And I forbear to denounce you to the people, though a blasphemer of their rights and an idolater of tyranny. Liberty disdains to persecute. ■

From article in the National Gazette, *December 20, 1792.*

• JOHN ADAMS

It is a fixed principle with me that all good government is and must be republican. But, at the same time, your candor will agree with me that there is not in lexicography a more fraudulent word.[1] Whenever I use the word *republic* with approbation, I mean a government in which the people have collectively, or by representation, an essential share in the sovereignty.

With you, I have also the honor most perfectly to harmonize in your sentiments of the humanity and wisdom of promoting education in knowledge, virtue, and benevolence. But I think that these will confirm mankind in the opinion of the necessity of preserving and strengthening the dikes against the ocean, its tides and storms. Human appetites, passions, prejudices, and self-love will never be conquered by benevolence and knowledge alone, introduced by human means. . . .

"These [nobles] have waged everlasting war against the common rights of men." True . . . So have the plebeians; so have the people; so have the kings; so has human nature, in every shape and combination, and so it ever will be . . . It would not be true, but it would not be more egregiously false, to say that the people have waged everlasting war against the rights of men.

"The love of liberty," you say, "is interwoven in the soul of man." So it is, according to La Fontaine, in that of a wolf; and I doubt whether it be much more rational, generous, or social in one than in the other, until in man it is enlightened by experience, reflection, education, and civil and political institutions, which are at first produced and constantly supported and improved by a few; that is, by the nobility. The wolf, in the fable, who preferred running in the forest, lean and hungry, to the sleek, plump, and round sides of the dog, because he found the latter was sometimes restrained, had more love of liberty than most men. The numbers of men in all ages have preferred ease, slumber, and good cheer to liberty . . . We must not, then, depend alone upon the love of liberty in the soul of man for its preservation. Some political institutions must be prepared, to assist this love against its enemies. Without these, the struggle will ever end only in a change of impostors. When the people who have no property feel the power in their own hands to determine all questions by a majority, they ever attack those who have property, till the injured men of property lose all patience, and recur to finesse, trick, and stratagem to outwit those who have too much strength, because they have too many hands to be resisted any other way. Let us be impartial, then, and speak the whole truth. ◼

From letter to Samuel Adams, October 18, 1790.

• THOMAS JEFFERSON

To you, then, gentlemen, who are charged with the sovereign functions of legislation, and to those associated with you, I look with encouragement for that guidance and support which may enable us to steer with safety the vessel in which we are all embarked amidst the conflicting elements of a troubled world.

During the contest of opinion through which we have passed [the presidential election campaign of 1800] the animation of discussions and of exertions has sometimes worn an aspect which might impose on strangers unused to think freely and to speak and to write what they think; but this being now decided by the voice of the nation, announced according to the rules of the Constitution, all will, of course, arrange themselves under the will of the law, and unite in common efforts for the common good. All, too, will bear in mind this sacred principle, that though the will of the majority is in all cases to prevail, that will to be rightful must be reasonable; that the minority possess their equal rights, which equal law must protect, and to violate would be oppression. Let us restore to social intercourse that harmony and affection without which liberty and even life itself are but dreary things. And let us reflect that, having banished from our land that reli-

---

[1] Adams' ambivalence in regard to a republic (as against monarchy) can also be seen in his letter to Mercy Warren, January 8, 1776: "For my own part I am so tasteless as to prefer a republic . . . But a republic, although it will infallibly beggar me and my children, will produce strength, hardiness, activity, courage, fortitude, and enterprise, the manly, noble, and sublime qualities in human nature, in abundance. A monarchy would probably, somehow or other make me rich, but it would produce so much taste and politeness, so much elegance in dress, furniture, equipages, so much music and dancing, so much fencing and skating, so much cards and backgammon, so much horse racing and cockfighting, so many balls and assemblies, so many plays and concerts that the very imagination of them makes me feel vain, light, frivolous, and insignificant."

gious intolerance under which mankind so long bled and suffered, we have yet gained little if we countenance a political intolerance as despotic, as wicked, and capable of as bitter and bloody persecutions . . . But every difference of opinion is not a difference of principle. We have called by different names brethren of the same principle. We are all Republicans, we are all Federalists. If there be any among us who would wish to dissolve this Union or to change its republican form, let them stand undisturbed as monuments of the safety to combat it. I know, indeed, that some honest men fear that a republican government can not be strong, that this Government is not strong enough; but would the honest patriot, in the full tide of successful experiment, abandon a government which has so far kept us free and firm on the theoretic and visionary fear that this Government, the world's best hope, may by possibility want energy to preserve itself? I trust not. I believe this, on the contrary, the strongest Government on earth. I believe it the only one where every man, at the call of the law, would fly to the standard of the law, and would meet invasions of the public order as his own personal concern. Sometimes it is said that man cannot be trusted with the government of himself. Can he, then, be trusted with the government of others? Or have we found angels in the forms of kings to govern him? Let history answer this question.

Let us, then, with courage and confidence pursue our own Federal and Republican principles, our attachment to union and representative government. Kindly separated by nature and a wide ocean from the exterminating havoc of one quarter of the globe; too high-minded to endure the degradations of the others; possessing a chosen country, with room enough for our descendants to the thousandth and thousandth generation; entertaining a due sense of our equal right to the use of our own faculties, to the acquisitions of our own industry, to honor and confidence from our fellow-citizens, resulting not from birth, but from our actions and their sense of them; enlightened by a benign religion, professed, indeed, and practiced in various forms, yet all of them inculcating honesty, truth, temperance, gratitude, and the love of man; acknowledging and

adoring an overruling Providence, which by all its dispensations proves that it delights in the happiness of man here and his greater happiness hereafter— with all these blessings, what more is necessary to make us a happy and a prosperous people? Still one thing more, fellow-citizens—a wise and frugal Government, which shall restrain men from injuring one another, shall leave them otherwise free to regulate their own pursuits of industry and improvement, and shall not take from the mouth of labor the bread it has earned. This is the sum of good government, and this is necessary to close the circle of our felicities.

About to enter, fellow-citizens, on the exercise of duties which comprehend everything dear and valuable to you, it is proper you should understand what I deem the essential principles of our Government, and consequently those which ought to shape its Administration. I will compress them within the narrowest compass they will bear, stating the general principle, but not all its limitations. Equal and exact justice to all men, of whatever state or persuasion, religious or political; peace, commerce, and honest friendship with all nations, entangling alliances with none; the support of the State governments in all their rights, as the most competent administrations for our domestic concerns and the surest bulwarks against antirepublican tendencies; the preservation of the General Government in its whole constitutional vigor, as the sheet anchor of our peace at home and safety abroad; a jealous care of the right of election by the people—a mild and safe corrective of abuses which are lopped by the sword of revolution where peaceable remedies are unprovided; absolute acquiescence in the decisions of the majority, the vital principle of republics, from which is no appeal but to force, the vital principle and immediate parent of despotism; a well-disciplined militia, our best reliance in peace and for the first moments of war, till regulars may relieve them; the supremacy of the civil over the military authority; economy in the public expense, that labor may be lightly burthened; the honest payment of our debts and sacred preservation of the public faith; encouragement of agriculture, and of commerce as its handmaid; the diffusion of information and arraignment of all abuses at the bar of the public reason; freedom of religion; freedom of the press, and freedom of person under the protection of the habeas corpus, and trial by jury impartially selected. These principles form the bright constellation which has gone before us and guided our steps through an age of revolution and reformation. The wisdom of our sages and blood of our heroes have been devoted to their attainment. They should be the creed of our political faith, the text of civic instruction, the touchstone by which to try the services of those we trust; and should we wander from them in moments of error or of alarm, let us hasten to retrace our steps and to regain the road which alone leads to peace, liberty, and safety. ∎

From First Inaugural Address, March 4, 1801.

• THOMAS JEFFERSON

Indeed, it must be acknowledged that the term *republic* is of very vague application in every language. Witness the self-styled republics of Holland, Switzerland, Genoa, Venice, Poland. Were I to assign to this term a precise and definite idea, I would say, purely and simply, it means a government by its citizens in mass, acting directly and personally, according to rules established by the majority; and that every other government is more or less republican, in proportion as it has in its composition more or less of this ingredient of the direct action of the citizens. Such a government is evidently restrained to very narrow limits of space and population. I doubt if it would be practicable beyond the extent of a New England township.

The first shade from this pure element, which, like that of pure vital air, cannot sustain life of itself, would be where the powers of the government, being divided, should be exercised each by representatives chosen either *pro hac vice,* or for such short terms as should render secure the duty of expressing the will of their constituents. This I should consider as the nearest approach to a pure republic, which is practicable on a large scale of country or population. And we have examples of it in some of our State constitutions, which, if not poisoned by priestcraft,

would prove its excellence over all mixtures with other elements; and, with only equal doses of poison, would still be the best. Other shades of republicanism may be found in other forms of government, where the executive, judiciary and legislative functions, and the different branches of the latter, are chosen by the people more or less directly, for longer terms of years, or for life, or made hereditary; or where there are mixtures of authorities, some dependent on, and others independent of the people. The further the departure from direct and constant control by the citizens, the less has the government of the ingredient of republicanism; evidently none where the authorities are hereditary, as in France, Venice . . . or self-chosen, as in Holland; and little, where for life. . . .

The purest republican feature in the government of our own State, is the House of Representatives. The Senate is equally so the first year, less the second, and so on. The executive still less, because not chosen by the people directly. The judiciary seriously antirepublican, because for life; and the national arm wielded, as you observe, by military leaders, irresponsible but to themselves. Add to this the vicious constitution of our county courts (to whom the justice, the executive administration, the taxation, police, the military appointments of the county, and nearly all our daily concerns are confided), self-appointed, self-continued, holding their authorities for life, and with an impossibility of breaking in on the perpetual succession of any faction once possessed of the bench. They are in truth, the executive, the judiciary, and the military of their respective counties, and the sum of the counties makes the State. And add, also, that one half of our brethren who fight and pay taxes, are excluded, like helots, from the rights of representation, as if society were instituted for the soil, and not for the men inhabiting it; or one half of these could dispose of the rights and the will of the other half, without their consent.

What constitutes a State?
Not high-raised battlements, or labor'd mound,
Thick wall, or moated gate;
Not cities proud, with spires and turrets crown'd;
No: men, high minded men;

Men, who their duties know;
But know their rights; and knowing, dare maintain,
These constitute a State.[1]

In the general government, the House of Representatives is mainly republican; the Senate scarcely so at all, as not elected by the people directly, and so long secured even against those who do elect them; the executive more republican than the Senate, from its shorter term, its election by the people, in *practice* (for they vote for A only on an assurance that he will vote for B), and because, *in practice also,* a principle of rotation seems to be in course of establishment; the judiciary independent of the nation, their coercion by impeachment being found nugatory.

If, then, the control of the people over the organs of their government be the measure of its republicanism, and I confess I know no other measure, it must be agreed that our governments have much less of republicanism than ought to have been expected; in other words, that the people have less regular control over their agents than their rights and their interests require. And this I ascribe, not to any want of republican dispositions in those who formed these constitutions, but to a submission of true principle to European authorities, to speculators on government, whose fears of the people have been inspired by the populace of their own great cities, and were unjustly entertained against the independent, the happy, and therefore orderly citizens of the United States. Much I apprehend that the golden moment is past for reforming these heresies. The functionaries of public power rarely strengthen in their dispositions to abridge it, and an unorganized call for timely amendment is not likely to prevail against an organized opposition to it. We are always told that things are going on well; why change them? *"Chi sta bene non si muove,"* said the Italian, "let him who stands well, stand still." This is true; and I verily believe they would go on well with us under an absolute monarch, while our present character remains, of order, industry and love of peace, and restrained, as he would be, by

[1] From "Ode in Imitation of Alcaeus," by Sir William Jones (1746–94).

the proper spirit of the people. But it is while it remains such, we should provide against the consequences of its deterioration. And let us rest in the hope that it will yet be done, and spare ourselves the pain of evils which may never happen.

On this view of the import of the term *republic,* instead of saying, as has been said, "that it may mean anything or nothing," we may say with truth and meaning, that governments are more or less republican, as they have more or less of the element of popular election and control in their composition; and believing, as I do, that the mass of the citizens is the safest depository of their own rights, and especially, that the evils flowing from the duperies of the people, are less injurious than those from the egoism of their agents. ■

From letter to John Taylor, May 28, 1816.

• JAMES MONROE

In our whole system, national and State, we have shunned all the defects which unceasingly preyed on the vitals and destroyed the ancient Republics. In them there were distinct orders, a nobility and a people, or the people governed in one assembly. Thus, in the one instance there was a perpetual conflict between the orders in society for the ascendancy, in which the victory of either terminated in the overthrow of the government and the ruin of the state; in the other, in which the people governed in a body, and whose dominions seldom exceeded the dimensions of a county in one of our States, a tumultuous and disorderly movement permitted only a transitory existence. In this great nation there is but one order, that of the people, whose power, by a peculiarly happy improvement of the representative principle, is transferred from them, without impairing in the slightest degree their sovereignty, to bodies of their own creation, and to persons elected by themselves, in the full extent necessary for all the purposes of free, enlightened, and efficient government. The whole system is elective, the complete sovereignty being in the people, and every officer in every department deriving his authority from and being responsible to them for his conduct. . . .

By steadily pursuing this course in this spirit there is every reason to believe that our system will soon attain the highest degree of perfection of which human institutions are capable. ▪

From Second Inaugural Address, March 5, 1821.

• JAMES FENIMORE COOPER

We live in an age, when the words aristocrat and democrat are much used, without regard to the real significations. An aristocrat is one of a few, who possess the political power of a country; a democrat, one of the many. The words are also properly applied to those who entertain notions favorable to aristocratical, or democratical forms of government. Such persons are not, necessarily, either aristocrats, or democrats in fact, but merely so in opinion. Thus a member of a democratical government may have an aristocratical bias, and vice versa. . . .

Some men fancy that a democrat can only be one who seeks the level, social, mental and moral, of the majority, a rule that would at once exclude all men of refinement, education and taste from the class. These persons are enemies of democracy, as they at once render it impracticable . . . They are, in truth, aristocrats in principle, though assuming a contrary pretension; the ground work of all their feelings and arguments being self . . . [The aim of liberty] is to leave every man to be the master of his own acts; denying hereditary honors, it is true, as unjust and unnecessary, but not denying the inevitable consequences of civilization.

The law of God is the only rule of conduct, in this, as in other matters. Each man should do as he would be done by. . . .

All that democracy means, is as equal a participation in rights as is practicable; and to pretend that social equality is a condition of popular institutions, is to assume that the latter are destructive of civilization, for, as nothing is more self-evident than the impossibility of raising all men to the highest standard of tastes and refinement, the alternative would

be to reduce the entire community to the lowest. The whole embarrassment on this point exists in the difficulty of making men comprehend qualities they do not themselves possess. We can all perceive the difference between us and our inferiors, but when it comes to a question of the difference between us and our superiors, we fail to appreciate merits of which we have no proper conceptions. In face of this obvious difficulty, there is the safe and just governing rule . . . of permitting everyone to be the undisturbed judge of his own habits and associations, so long as they are innocent, and do not impair the rights of others to be equally judges for themselves. . . .

In a democracy, men are just as free to aim at the highest attainable places in society, as to obtain the largest fortunes; and it would be clearly unworthy of all noble sentiment to say, that the grovelling competition for money shall alone be free, while that which enlists all the liberal acquirements and elevated sentiments of the race, is denied the democrat. . . .

The democratic gentleman must differ in many essential particulars, from the aristocratical gentleman, though in their ordinary habits and tastes they are virtually identical. Their principles vary . . . The democrat, recognizing the right of all to participate in power, will be more liberal in his general sentiments, a quality of superiority in itself; but, in conceding this much to his fellow man, he will proudly maintain his own independence of vulgar domination, as indispensable to his personal habits. The same principles and manliness that would induce him to depose a royal despot, would induce him to resist a vulgar tyrant.

There is no more capital . . . error than to suppose him an aristocrat who maintains his independence of habits; for democracy asserts the control of the majority only in matters of law, and not in matters of custom. The very object of the institution is the utmost practicable personal liberty. . . .

An aristocrat, therefore, is merely one who fortifies his exclusive privileges by positive institutions, and a democrat, one who is willing to admit of a free competition, in all things. ▪

From The American Democrat, *1838.*

• RALPH WALDO EMERSON

In dealing with the State, we ought to remember that its institutions are not aboriginal, though they existed before we were born: that they are not superior to the citizen: that every one of them was once the act of a single man: every law and usage was a man's expedient to meet a particular case: that they all are imitable, all alterable; we may make as good; we may make better. . . .

The same necessity which secures the rights of person and property against the malignity or folly of the magistrate, determines the form and methods of governing, which are proper to each nation, and to its habit of thought, and nowise transferable to other states of society. In this country, we are very vain of our political institutions, which are singular in this, that they sprung, within the memory of living men, from the character and condition of the people, which they still express with sufficient fidelity —and we ostentatiously prefer them to any other in history. They are not better, but only fitter for us. We may be wise in asserting the advantage in modern times of the democratic form, but to other states of society, in which religion consecrated the monarchical, that and not this was expedient. Democracy is better for us, because the religious sentiment of the present time accords better with it. Born democrats, we are nowise qualified to judge of monarchy, which, to our fathers living in the monarchical idea, was also relatively right. But our institutions, though in coincidence with the spirit of the age, have not any exemption from the practical defects which have discredited other forms. Every actual State is corrupt. Good men must not obey the laws too well. What satire on government can equal the severity of censure conveyed in the word *politic,* which now for ages has signified *cunning,* intimating that the State is a trick? ∎

From Politics, *1842.*

• PARKE GODWIN

This is what we mean by true democracy—a state in which the highest rights and interests of man shall be the means and appliances of a full development; and this democracy, constructive and pacific in its character, becomes the object for which every benevolent and conscientious man should labor. . . .

It is because we believe that an organization, according to our principles, would secure these ends [comfortable subsistence, opportunities for education, easy social intercourse], that we have ventured to speak of Democracy. Never was there a word more abused—never was there a word more profoundly significant. It does not mean that ferocious spirit of levelling, which, in the French Revolution, crumbled the entire Past, and even plucked God from his throne; nor yet the wild, dirty, and turbulent mobism, which, in this country, covers with the slime of its filthiness, every character that is purer and nobler than itself . . . It means a social state, where the whole of life, for nine-tenths of the people, shall not be a suicidal struggle for life—where the finer essences of the soul shall not be ground out to furnish bare nutriment for the body—where none of its families shall esteem it a curse to have children born to them—where honesty and diligence, not impudence and falsehood, shall be the measures of success, and where noble thoughts and generous emotions shall not b ampled out . . . But the great fact of the Brotherhood of Man shall be recognized—that Humanity is a living organism, of which every individual is a member—each in his sphere, bound to his fellows and the whole, as the arm or the foot is bound to the body . . . Then, in the arrangements of the State, the reconciling maxims of distributive equity shall take the place of the insane and destructive doctrines of positive equality—the slavery of pauperism and vice shall be succeeded by rational freedom. ∎

From Democracy, Constructive and Pacific, *1844.*

• THEODORE PARKER

This democratic idea is founded in human nature, and comes from the nature of God, who made human nature. To carry it out politically is to execute justice, which is the will of God. This idea, in its realization, leads to a democracy, a government of all, for all, by all. Such a government aims to give every man all his natural rights; it desires to have political power in all hands, property in all hands, wisdom in all heads, goodness in all hearts, religion in all souls. I mean the religion that makes a man self-respectful . . . which is piety within you, and goodness in the manifestation. Such a government has laws, and the aim thereof is to give justice to all men . . . Such a government founds schools for all; looks after those most who are most in need; defends and protects the feeblest as well as the richest and most powerful. The state is for the individual, and for all the individuals, and so it reverences justice, where the rights of all, and the interests of all, exactly balance. It demands free speech; everything is open to examination, discussion, "agitation," if you will. Thought is to be free, speech to be free, work to be free, and worship to be free. Such is the democratic idea. ■

From sermon, November 28, 1850.

• ABRAHAM LINCOLN

And this issue [secession of the Southern states] embraces more than the fate of these United States. It presents to the whole family of man the question whether a constitutional republic, or democracy—a government of the people by the same people—can or cannot maintain its territorial integrity against its own domestic foes. It presents the question whether discontented individuals, too few in numbers to control administration according to organic law in any case, can always, upon the pretenses made in this case, or in any other pretenses, or arbitrarily without any pretense, break up their government, and thus practically put an end to free government upon the earth. It forces us to ask, Is there in all re-publics this inherent and fatal weakness? Must a government of necessity be too *strong* for the liberties of its own peòple, or too *weak* to maintain its own existence? ■

From Special Message to Congress, July 4, 1861.

• WALT WHITMAN

Did you, too, O friend, suppose democracy was only for selections, for politics, and for a party name? I say democracy is only of use there that it may pass on and come to its flower and fruits in manners, in the highest forms of interaction between men, and their beliefs—in religion, literature, colleges, and schools—democracy in all public and private life, and in the army and navy.[1] I have intimated that, as a paramount scheme, it has yet few or no full realizers and believers. I do not see, either, that it owes any serious thanks to noted propagandists or champions, or has been essentially help'd, though often harm'd, by them. It has been and is carried on by all the moral forces, and by trade, finance, machinery, intercommunications, and, in fact, by all the developments of history, and can no more be stopp'd than the tides, or the earth in its orbit. Doubtless, also, it resides, crude and latent, well down in the hearts of the fair average of the American-born people, mainly in the agricultural regions. But it is not yet, there or anywhere, the fully-receiv'd, the fervid, the absolute faith.

I submit, therefore, that the fruition of democracy, on aught like a grand scale, resides altogether in the future. As, under any profound and comprehensive view of the gorgeous-composite feudal world, we see in it, through the long ages and cycles of ages, the results of a deep, integral, human and divine principle, or fountain, from which issued laws, ecclesia, manners, institutes, costumes,

---

[1] The whole present system of the officering and personnel of the army and navy of these States, and the spirit and letter of their trebly-aristocratic rules and regulations, is a monstrous exotic, a nuisance and revolt, and belong here just as much as orders of nobility, or the Pope's council of cardinals. I say if the present theory of our army and navy is sensible and true, then the rest of America is an unmitigated fraud.—Author's note.

personalities, poems (hitherto unequall'd) faithfully partaking of their source, and indeed only arising either to betoken it, or to furnish parts of that varied-flowing display, whose centre was one and absolute—so, long ages hence, shall the due historian or critic make at least an equal retrospect, an equal history for the democratic principle. It too must be adorn'd, credited with its results—then, when it, with imperial power, through amplest time, has dominated mankind—has been the source and test of all the moral, esthetic, social, political, and religious expressions and institutes of the civilized world—has begotten them in spirit and in form, and has carried them to its own unprecedented heights —has had (it is possible) monastics and ascetics, more numerous, more devout than the monks and priests of all previous creeds—has sway'd the ages with a breadth and rectitude tallying Nature's own —has fashion'd, systematized, and triumphantly finish'd and carried out, in its own interest, and with unparallel'd success, a new earth and a new man. ∎

From Democratic Vistas, *1871.*

• WALT WHITMAN

Democracy most of all affiliates with the open air, is sunny and hardy and sane only with Nature— just as much as Art is. Something is required to temper both—to check them, restrain them from excess, morbidity. I have wanted, before departure, to bear special testimony to a very old lesson and requisite. American Democracy, in its myriad personalities, in factories, workshops, stores, offices— through the dense streets and houses of cities, and all their manifold sophisticated life—must either be fibred, vitalized, by regular contact with out-door light and air and growths, farm-scenes, animals, fields, trees, birds, sun-warmth and free skies, or it will certainly dwindle and pale. We cannot have grand races of mechanics, work people, and commonalty, (the only specific purpose of America,) on any less terms. I conceive of no flourishing and heroic elements of Democracy in the United States,

or of Democracy maintaining itself at all, without the Nature-element forming a main part—to be its health-element and beauty-element—to really underlie the whole politics, sanity, religion and art of the New World.

Finally, the morality: "Virtue," said Marcus Aurelius, "what is it, only a living and enthusiastic sympathy with Nature?" Perhaps indeed the efforts of the true poets, founders, religions, literatures, all ages, have been, and ever will be, our time and times to come, essentially the same—to bring people back from their persistent strayings and sickly abstractions, to the costless average, divine, original concrete. ∎

From Specimen Days in America, *1881-83.*

• WOODROW WILSON

It is for this that we love democracy: for the emphasis it puts on character; for its tendency to exalt the purposes of the average man to some high level of endeavor; for its just principles of common assent in matters in which all are concerned; for its ideals of duty and its sense of brotherhood. Its forms and institutions are meant to be subservient to these things. Democracy is merely the most radical form of "constitutional" government. A "constitutional" government is one in which there is definite understanding as to the sphere and powers of government; one in which individual liberty is defined and guaranteed by specific safeguards, in which the authority and the functions of those who rule are limited and determined by unmistakable custom or explicit fundamental law. It is a government in which these understandings are kept up, alike in the making and in the execution of law, by frequent conferences between those who govern and those who are governed. ∎

From "Democracy and Efficiency," in
Atlantic Monthly, *March, 1901.*

• WOODROW WILSON

How eloquent this little house within this shrine [the log-cabin birthplace of Lincoln near Hodgenville, Kentucky] is of the vigor of democracy! There is nowhere in the land any home so remote, so humble, that it may not contain the power of mind and heart and conscience to which nations yield and history submits its processes. Nature pays no tribute to aristocracy, subscribes to no creed of caste, renders fealty to no monarch or master . . . Here is proof of it. This little hut was the cradle of one of the great sons of men . . . No man can explain this, but every man can see how it demonstrates the vigor of democracy, where every door is open, in every hamlet and countryside, in city and wilderness alike, for the ruler to emerge when he will . . . claim his leadership in the free life. Such are the authentic proofs of the validity and vitality of democracy.

Here, no less, hides the mystery of democracy. Who shall guess this secret of nature and providence and a free polity? Whatever the vigor and vitality of the stock from which he sprang, its mere vigor and soundness do not explain where this man got his great heart that seemed to comprehend all mankind . . . This is the sacred mystery of democracy, that its richest fruits spring up out of soils which no man has prepared and in circumstances amidst which they are the least expected. . . . ∎

From address at Hodgenville, Ky., September 4,
1916.

• JOHN DEWEY

Democracy is much broader than a special political form, a method of conducting government, of making laws and carrying on governmental administration by means of popular suffrage and elected officers. It is that, of course. But it is something broader and deeper than that. The political and governmental phase of democracy is a means, the best means so far found, of realizing ends that lie in the wide domain of human relationships and the development of human personality. It is, as we often say, though perhaps without appreciating all that is involved in the saying, a way of life, social and individual. The keynote of democracy as a way of life may be expressed, it seems to me, as the necessity for the participation of every mature human being in formation of the values that regulate the living of men together: which is necessary from the standpoint of both the general social welfare and the full development of human beings as individuals.

Universal suffrage, recurring elections, responsibility of those who are in political power to the voters, and the other factors of democratic government are means that have been found expedient for realizing democracy as the truly human way of living. They are not a final end and a final value. They are to be judged on the basis of their contribution to an end. . . .

It is a form of idolatry to erect means into the end which they serve. Democratic political forms are simply the best means that human wit has devised up to a special time in history. But they rest back upon the idea that no man or limited set of men is wise enough or good enough to rule others without their consent; the positive meaning of this statement is that all those who are affected by social institutions must have a share in producing and managing them. The two facts that each is influenced in what he does and enjoys and in what he becomes by the institutions under which he lives, and that therefore he shall have, in a democracy, a voice in shaping them, are the passive and active sides of the same fact.

The development of political democracy came about through substitution of the method of mutual consultation and voluntary agreement for the method of subordination of the many to the few enforced from above. Social arrangements which involve fixed subordination are maintained by coercion. The coercion need not be physical. There have existed, for short periods, benevolent despotisms. But coercion of some sort there has been; perhaps economic, certainly psychological and moral. The very fact of exclusion from participation is a subtle form of suppression. It gives individuals no opportunity to reflect and decide what is good for them. Others who are supposed to be wiser and who in any case have more power decide the question for them and also decide the methods and means by which subjects may arrive at the enjoyment of what is good for them. This form of coercion and suppression is more subtle and more effective than are overt intimidation and restraint. When it is habitual and embodied in social institutions, it seems the normal and natural state of affairs. The mass usually become unaware that they have a claim to the development of their own powers. Their experience is so restricted that they are not conscious of restriction. It is part of the democratic conception that they as individuals are not the only sufferers, but that the whole social body is deprived of the potential resources that should be at its service. The individuals of the submerged mass may not be very wise. But there is one thing they are wiser about than anyone else can be, and that is where the shoe pinches, the troubles they suffer from.

The foundation of democracy is faith in the capacities of human nature; faith in human intelligence and in the power of pooled and cooperative experience. It is not belief that these things are complete but that if given a show they will grow and be able to generate progressively the knowledge and wisdom needed to guide collective action. Every autocractic and authoritarian scheme of social action rests on a belief that the needed intelligence is confined to a superior few, who because of inherent natural gifts are endowed with the ability and right to control the conduct of others; laying down principles and rules and directing the ways in which they are carried out. It would be foolish to deny that much can be said for this point of view. It is that which controlled human relations in social groups for much the greater part of human history. The democratic faith has emerged very, very recently in the history of mankind. Even where democracies now exist, men's minds and feelings are still permeated with ideas about leadership imposed from above, ideas that developed in the long early history of mankind. After democratic political institutions were nominally established, beliefs and ways of looking at life and of acting that originated when men were externally controlled and

subjected to arbitrary power, persisted in the family, the church, business and the school, and experience shows that as long as they persist there, political democracy is not secure.

Belief in equality is an element of the democratic credo. It is not, however, belief in equality of natural endowments. Those who proclaimed the idea of equality did not suppose they were enunciating a psychological doctrine, but a legal and political one. All individuals are entitled to equality of treatment by law and in its administration. Each one is affected equally in quality if not in quantity by the institutions under which he lives and has an equal right to express his judgment, although the weight of his judgment may not be equal in amount, when it enters into the pooled result, to that of others. In short, each one is equally an individual and entitled to equal opportunity of development of his own capacities, be they large or small in range. Moreover, each has needs of his own, as significant to him as those of others are to them. The very fact of natural and psychological inequality is all the more reason for establishment by law of equality of opportunity, since otherwise the former becomes a means of oppression of the less gifted.

While what we call intelligence may be distributed in unequal amounts, it is the democratic faith that it is sufficiently general so that each individual has something to contribute, and the value of each contribution can be assessed only as it enters into the final pooled intelligence constituted by the contributions of all. Every authoritarian scheme, on the contrary, assumes that its value may be assessed by some *prior* principle, if not of family and birth or race and color or possession of material wealth, then by the position and rank a person occupies in the existing social scheme. The democratic faith in equality is the faith that each individual shall have the chance and opportunity to contribute whatever he is capable of contributing and that the value of his contribution be decided by its place and function in the organized total of similar contributions, not on the basis of prior status of any kind whatever.

I have emphasized in what precedes the importance of the effective release of intelligence in connection with personal experience in the democratic way of living. I have done so purposely because democracy is so often and so naturally associated in our minds with freedom of *action,* forgetting the importance of freed intelligence which is necessary to direct and to warrant freedom of action. Unless freedom of action has intelligence and informed conviction back of it, its manifestation is almost sure to result in confusion and disorder. The democratic idea of freedom is not the right of each individual to *do* as he pleases, even if it is qualified by adding "provided he does not interfere with the same freedom on the part of others." While the idea is not always, not often enough, expressed in words, the basic freedom is that of freedom of *mind* and of whatever degree of freedom of action and experience is necessary to produce freedom of intelligence. The modes of freedom guaranteed by the Bill of Rights are all of this nature: Freedom of belief and conscience, of expression of opinion, of assembly for discussion and conference, of the press as an organ of communication. They are guaranteed because without them individuals are not free to develop and society is deprived of what they might contribute. ■

From "Democracy and Educational Administration," address published in School and Society, *April 3, 1937.*

• FRANKLIN D. ROOSEVELT

There are some men who believe that democracy, as a form of government and a frame of life, is limited or measured by a kind of mystical and artificial fate—that, for some unexplained reason, tyranny and slavery have become the surging wave of the future—and that freedom is an ebbing tide.

But we Americans know that this is not true.

Eight years ago, when the life of this Republic seemed frozen by a fatalistic terror, we proved that this is not true. We were in the midst of shock—but we acted. We acted quickly, boldly, decisively.

These later years have been living years—fruitful years for the people of this democracy. . . .

Most vital to our present and our future is this experience of a democracy which successfully survived crisis at home; put away many evil things; built new structures on enduring lines; and, through it all, maintained the fact of its democracy.

For action has been taken within the three-way framework of the Constitution of the United States. The coordinate branches of the Government continue freely to function. The Bill of Rights remains inviolate. The freedom of elections is wholly maintained. Prophets of the downfall of American democracy have seen their dire predictions come to nought.

Democracy is not dying.

We know it because we have seen it revive—and grow.

We know it cannot die—because it is built on the unhampered initiative of individual men and women joined together in a common enterprise—an enterprise undertaken and carried through by the free expression of a free majority.

We know it because democracy alone, of all forms of government, enlists the full force of men's enlightened will.

We know it because democracy alone has constructed an unlimited civilization capable of infinite progress in the improvement of human life.

We know it because, if we look below the surface, we sense it still spreading on every continent—for it is the most humane, the most advanced, and in the end the most unconquerable of all forms of human society. ■

From Third Inaugural Address, January 20, 1941.

• HARRY S. TRUMAN

Democracy is based on the conviction that man has the moral and intellectual capacity, as well as the inalienable right, to govern himself with reason and justice.

Communism subjects the individual to arrest without lawful cause, punishment without trial, and forced labor as the chattel of the state. It decrees what information he shall receive, what art he shall produce, what leaders he shall follow, and what thoughts he shall think.

Democracy maintains that government is established for the benefit of the individual, and is charged with the responsibility of protecting the rights of the individual and his freedom in the exercise of his abilities.

Communism maintains that social wrongs can be corrected only by violence.

Democracy has proved that social justice can be achieved through peaceful change.

Communism holds that the world is so deeply divided into opposing classes that war is inevitable.

Democracy holds that free nations can settle differences justly and maintain lasting peace. ■

From Inaugural Address, January 20, 1949.

PART II

FREEDOM AND LIBERTY— WHAT THEY ARE AND ARE NOT

The world," Abraham Lincoln said, "has never had a good definition of the word liberty." It is extraordinarily difficult to define because it involves a variety of elements that are both personal-psychological and social-political.

Liberty can be viewed from at least three angles: the human, the individual, and the civil. Man has liberty by virtue of being born a free—and rational—creature. This liberty man has at birth, as his human heritage. The second liberty is that of the self-realization of each individual person. The third liberty— and the one of main concern to this book—is civil liberty.

Civil liberty in the modern sense is of relatively recent origin. It may be dated from the period of the Renaissance and Reformation, when men began to assert their individualism in both art and religion. Civil liberty may be defined as that which man may enjoy as a member of organized society, within limits set by laws and political institutions. "Liberty," Montesquieu pointed out, "is a right to do whatever the laws permit."

In the nature of things, civil liberty, known also as political liberty, is never absolute. It depends upon the existing state of civilization, the interests of the community, and society's need for self-protection. As Justice Oliver Wendell Holmes put it, no man is at liberty to cry "fire" in a theater and cause a panic.

Political liberty in modern times is tied up with the notion of equality. Despite denials by critics of democracy like John C. Calhoun that such a connection exists, it is nevertheless logically clear that political liberty must mean shared liberty, on a basis of equality of rights. Where all citizens do not share the same liberty, there the political system is one of autocracy or aristocracy, in which freedom is confined to one or at most a handful of persons. In that case it makes no sense to talk about "civil liberty," since it is inapplicable to the civic community, that is to say, most members of the society. By any meaningful definition, civil or political liberty cannot be separated from the idea and ideal of equality.

Liberty is, among other things, a faith and a goal rooted in the hearts of men, as Lincoln pointed out. It requires dedication and courageous struggle for its maintenance. Liberty is also rooted in a political system. As such, it is best understood if one looks at it from the point of view of special freedoms—of speech, of religion, of voting, all separate but fundamentally intertwined.

$\overline{1}$

SEVENTEENTH-CENTURY VIEWS

John Winthrop
John Milton
Sir Algernon Sidney

• JOHN WINTHROP

For the other point concerning liberty, I observe a great mistake in the country about that. There is a twofold liberty, natural (I mean as our nature is now corrupt) and civil or federal. The first is common to man with beasts and other creatures. By this, man, as he stands in relation to man simply, hath liberty to do what he lists; it is a liberty to evil as well as to good. This liberty is incompatible and inconsistent with authority, and cannot endure the least restraint of the most just authority. The exercise and maintaining of this liberty makes men grow more evil, and in time to be worse than brute beasts; *omnes sumus licentia deteriores.* This is that great enemy of truth and peace, that wild beast, which all the ordinances of God are bent against, to restrain and subdue it. The other kind of liberty I call civil or federal, it may also be termed moral, in reference to the covenant between God and man, in the moral law, and the politic covenants and constitutions, amongst men themselves. This is the proper end and object of authority, and cannot subsist without it; and it is a liberty to that only which is good, just, and honest. ■

From speech to the General Court of Massachusetts, after being acquitted of the charge of exceeding his authority, July 3, 1645.

• JOHN MILTON

No man who knows aught can be so stupid to deny that all men naturally were born free, being the image and resemblance of God himself[1] and were by privilege above all the creatures born to command and not to obey: and that they lived so, till from the root of Adam's transgression, falling among themselves to do wrong and violence, and foreseeing that such courses must needs tend to the destruction of them all, they agreed by common

---

[1] Milton repeated this phrase in his *Defence of the People of England* (1651): "All men are naturally born free, being the image and resemblance of God Himself."

league to bind each other from mutual injury, and jointly to defend themselves against any that give disturbance or opposition to such agreement. Hence came cities, towns and commonwealths. And because no faith at all was found sufficiently binding, they saw it needful to ordain some authority, that might restrain by force and punishment what was violated against peace and common right.

This authority and power of self-defence and preservation being originally and naturally in every one of them, and unitedly in them all; for ease, for order, and lest each man should be his own partial judge, they communicated and derived either to one, whom for the eminence of his wisdom and integrity they chose above the rest, or to more than one whom they thought of equal deserving: the first was called a king; the other magistrates: not to be their lords and masters (though afterward those names in some places were given voluntarily to such as have been authors of inestimable good to the people) but to be their deputies and commissioners, to execute, by virtue of their entrusted power, that justice which else every man by the bond of nature and of covenant must have executed for himself, and for one another. And to him that shall consider well why among free persons, one man by civil right should bear authority and jurisdiction over another, no other end or reason can be imaginable.

These for a while governed well, and with much equity decided all things at their own arbitrement: till the temptation of such a power left absolute in their hands, perverted them at length to injustice and partiality. Then did they who now by trial had found the danger and inconveniences of committing arbitrary power to any, invent laws either framed, or consented to by all, that should confine and limit the authority of whom they choose to govern them: that so man, of whose failing they had proof, might no more rule over them, but law and reason abstracted as much as might be from personal errors and frailties. While as the magistrate was set above the people, so the law was set above the magistrate. When this would not serve, but that the law was either not executed, or misapplied, they were constrained from that time, the only remedy

left them, to put conditions and take oaths from all kings and magistrates at their first instalment to do impartial justice by law: who upon those terms and no other, received allegiance from the people, that is to say, bond or covenant to obey them in execution of those laws which they the people had themselves made or assented to. And this ofttimes with express warning, that if the king or magistrate proved unfaithful to his trust, the people would be disengaged. . . .

To say kings were accountable to none but God, is the overturning of all law and government. For if they may refuse to give account, then all covenants made with them at coronation, all oaths are in vain and mere mockeries; all laws which they swear to keep, made to no purpose, for if the king fear not God (as how many of them do not?) we hold then our lives and estates by the tenure of his mere grace and mercy, as from a God, not a mortal magistrate; a position that none but court-parasites or men besotted would maintain! Aristotle therefore, whom we commonly allow for one of the best interpreters of nature and morality, writes in the fourth of his politics, chap. X, that "monarchy unaccountable is the worst sort of tyranny; and least of all to be endured by freeborn men." ∎

From The Tenure of Kings and Magistrates,
1649.

• SIR ALGERNON SIDNEY

Man being a rational creature, nothing can be universally natural to him that is not rational. But this liberty without restraint being inconsistent with any government, and the good which man naturally desires for himself, children and friends, we find no place in the world where the inhabitants do not enter into some kind of society or government to restrain it: and to say that all men desire liberty without restraint and yet that all do not restrain it, is ridiculous. The truth is, man is hereunto led by reason which is his nature. Every one sees they cannot well live asunder, nor many together, without some rule to which all must submit. This submission is a restraint of liberty, but could be of no effect as to the good intended, unless it were general; nor general unless it were natural. Where all are born to the same freedom, some will not resign that which is their own unless others do the like. This general consent of all to resign such a part of their liberty as seems to be for the good of all is the voice of nature, and the act of men (according to their natural reason) seeking their own good. . . .

Again, if man were by nature so tenacious of his liberty without restraint, he must be rationally so. The creation of absolute monarchies, which entirely extinguishes it, must necessarily be most contrary to it, though the people were willing; for they thereby adjure their own nature. The usurpation of them can be no less than the most abominable and outrageous violence of the laws of nature that can be imagined: The laws of God must be in the like measure broken; and of all governments, democracy, in which every man's liberty is least restrained, because every man hath an equal part, would certainly prove to be the most just, rational and natural. . . . He that inquires more exactly into the matter may find that reason enjoins every man not to arrogate to himself more than he allows to others, nor to retain that liberty which will prove hurtful to him; nor to expect that others will suffer themselves to be restrained while he, to their prejudice, remains in the exercise of that freedom which nature allows. He who would be exempted from this common rule must shew for what reason he should be raised above his brethren; and if he do not do it, he is an enemy to them. This is not popularity but tyranny; and tyrants are said *exuisse hominem*—to throw off the nature of men—because they do unjustly and unreasonably assume to themselves that which agrees not with the frailty of human nature, and set up an interest in themselves contrary to their equals, which they ought to defend as their own. ■

From Discourse on Government, *1698.*

2

EIGHTEENTH-CENTURY VIEWS

John Wise
Baron de Montesquieu
Jean Jacques Rousseau
Samuel Adams

• JOHN WISE

The second great immunity of man is an Original Liberty instampt upon his rational nature. He. that intrudes upon this Liberty violates the Law of Nature. . . This Liberty does not consist in a loose and ungovernable freedom, or in an unbounded license of acting. Such license is disagreeing with the condition and dignity of man, and would make man of a lower and meaner constitution than brute creatures; who in all their liberties are kept under a better and more rational government by their instincts. Therefore as Plutarch says, "Those persons only who live in obedience to Reason are worthy to be accounted free: they alone live as they will who have learnt what they ought to will.". . .

Man's external personal, Natural Liberty, antecedent to all human parts or alliances must also be considered. And so every man must be conceived to be perfectly in his own power and disposal, and not to be controlled by the authority of any other. And thus every man must be acknowledged equal to every man, since all subjection and all command are equally banished on both sides; and considering all men thus at liberty, every man has a prerogative to judge for himself, viz., what shall be most for his behoof, happiness, and well-being. ■

From A Vindication of the Government of the New-England Churches, *1717.*

• BARON DE MONTESQUIEU

Ch. 3. It is true that in democracies the people seem to act as they please; but political liberty does not consist in doing what one wishes. In a state, that is, in a society, where there are laws, liberty can consist only in the power of doing what one ought to will, and in not being constrained to do what one ought not to will.

We must ever keep in mind the difference between what is independence and what is liberty. Liberty is the right of doing what the laws permit; and if a citizen could do what they forbid, he would no longer have liberty, because all his fellow citizens would have the same power.

Ch. 4. Democratic and aristocratic states are not by their own nature free. Political liberty is found only in moderate governments; but it is not always found even there. It is there only when there is no abuse of power; but constant experience shows that every man who has power is apt to abuse it, and to carry his power to the limit. Is it not strange to say that virtue itself has need of limits!

Ch. 6. The political liberty of a citizen is that tranquillity of mind which arises from the opinion each person has of his safety; and in order to have this liberty, it is requisite that the government be such that one citizen need not fear another.

When the legislative and executive powers are united in the same person, or in the same body of magistrates, there can be no liberty; because fears may arise lest the same monarch or the same senate should enact tyrannical laws, to execute them tyrannically.

Again, there is no liberty if the judiciary power be not separated from the legislative and executive powers. If it were joined with the legislative, the power over life and liberty of the citizens would be arbitrary; for the judge would then be the legislator. If it were joined to the executive power, the judge would have the power of an oppressor.

There would be an end to everything if the same man or the same body, whether of the nobles or of the people, exercised those three powers: that of enacting laws, that of executing the public resolutions, and that of trying the legal cases of individuals. ∎

From The Spirit of the Laws, *Book XI, 1748.*

• JEAN JACQUES ROUSSEAU

Liberty, not being a fruit of all climates, is not within the reach of all peoples. The more we consider this principle established by Montesquieu, the more do we perceive its truth; the more it is contested, the greater opportunity is given to establish it by new proofs.

In all the governments of the world, the public person consumes, but produces nothing. Whence, then, comes the substance it consumes? From the labor of its members. It is the superfluity of individuals that supplies the necessaries of the public. Hence it follows that the civil state can subsist only so long as men's labor produces more than they need.

Now this excess is not the same in all countries of the world. In several it is considerable, in others moderate, in others nothing, in others a minus quantity. This proportion depends on the fertility due to climate, on the kind of labor which the soil requires, on the nature of the products, on the physical strength of its inhabitants, on the greater or less consumption that is necessary to them, and on several other like proportions of which it is composed.

On the other hand, all governments are not of the same nature; there are some more or less wasteful; and the differences are based on this other principle, that the further the public contributions are removed from their source, the more burdensome they are. We must not measure this burden by the amount of the imposts, but by the distance they have to traverse in order to return to the hands from which they have come. When this circulation is prompt and well established, it matters not whether little or much is paid; the people are always rich, and the finances are always prosperous. On the other hand, however little the people may contribute, if this little does not revert to them, they are soon exhausted by constantly giving; the state is never rich and the people are always in beggary.

It follows from this that the more the distance between the people and the government is increased, the more burdensome do the tributes become; therefore, in a democracy the people are least encumbered, in an aristocracy they are more so, and in a monarchy they bear the greatest weight. Monarchy, then, is suited only to wealthy nations; aristocracy, to states moderate both in wealth and size; democracy, to small and poor states.

Indeed, the more we reflect on it, the more do we find in this the difference between free and monarchical states. In the first, everything is used for the common advantage; in the others, public and private resources are reciprocal, and the former are increased by the diminution of the latter; lastly, instead of governing subjects in order to make them happy, despotism renders them miserable in order to govern them.

There are, then, in every climate natural causes by which we can assign the form of government which is adpated to the nature of the climate, and even say what kind of inhabitants the country should have.

Unfruitful and barren places, where the produce does not repay the labor, ought to remain uncultivated and deserted, or should only be peopled by savages; places where men's toil yields only bare necessaries ought to be inhabited by barbarous nations; in them any polity would be an impossibility. Places where the excess of the produce over the labor is moderate are suitable for free nations; those in which abundant and fertile soil yields much produce for little labor are willing to be governed monarchically, in order that the superfluity of the subjects may be consumed by the luxuries of the Prince; for it is better that this excess should be absorbed by the government than squandered by private persons. There are exceptions, I know; but these exceptions themselves confirm the rule, in that, sooner or later, they produce revolutions which restore things to their natural order.

We should always distinguish general laws from the particular causes which may modify their effects. If the whole south should be covered with republics, and the whole north with despotic states, it would not be less true that, through the influence of climate, despotism is suitable to warm countries, barbarism to cold countries, and a good polity to intermediate regions. . . .

To all these different considerations I may add one which springs from, and strengthens, them; it is that warm countries have less need of inhabitants than cold countries, but would be able to maintain a greater number; hence a double surplus is produced, always to the advantage of despotism. The greater the surface occupied by the same number of inhabitants, the more difficult do rebellions become, because measures cannot be concerted promptly and secretly, and because it is always easy for the government to discover the plans and cut off communications. But the more closely packed a nu-

merous population is, the less power has a government to usurp the sovereignty; the chiefs deliberate as securely in their cabinets as the prince in his council, and the multitude assemble in the squares as quickly as the troops in their quarters. The advantage, then, of a tyrannical government lies in this, that it acts at great distances. By help of the points of support which it procures, its power increases with the distance, like that of levers.[1] That of the people, on the other hands, acts only when concentrated; it evaporates and disappears as it extends like the effect of powder scattered on the ground, which takes fire only grain by grain. The least populous countries are thus the best adapted for tyranny, wild beasts reign only in deserts.   ■

From Social Contract, *Book III, Chapter 8,
1762.*

• SAMUEL ADAMS

I believe that no people ever yet groaned under the heavy yoke of slavery but when they deserved it. This may be called a severe censure upon by far the greatest part of the nations in the world who are involved in the misery of servitude; but however they may be thought by some to deserve commiseration, the censure is just. Zwinglius, one of the first reformers, in his friendly admonition to the Republic of the Switzers, discourses much of his countrymen's throwing off the yoke. He says that they who lie under oppression deserve what they suffer and a great deal more; and he bids them perish with their oppressors. The truth is, all might be free if they valued freedom, and defended it as they ought. Is it possible that millions could be enslaved by a few which is a notorious fact, if all possessed the independent spirit of Brutus, who, to his immortal honor, expelled the proud tyrant of Rome and his "royal

---

[1].This does not contract what I said before (Book II, Chapter 9) on the inconveniences of large states; for there it was a question of the authority of the government over its members, and here it is a question of its power against its subjects. Its scattered members serve as points of support to it for operating at a distance upon the people, but it has no point of support for acting on its members themselves. Thus, the length of the lever is the cause of its weakness in the one case, and of its strength in the other.—Author's note.

and rebellious race"? If therefore a people will not be free, if they have not virtue enough to maintain their liberty against a presumptuous invader, they deserve no pity and are to be treated with contempt and ignominy. Had not Caesar seen that Rome was ready to stoop, he would not have dared to make himself the master of that once brave people. He was indeed, as a great writer observes, a smooth and subtle tyrant, who led them gently into slavery "and on his brow, o'er daring vice deluding virtue smiled." By pretending to be the people's greatest friend, he gained the ascendancy over them; by beguiling arts, hypocrisy, and flattery, which are even more fatal then the sword, he obtained that supreme power which his ambitious soul had long thirsted for. The people were finally prevailed upon to consent to their own ruin. ■

From "On Resistance to Tyranny," 1771.

3

NINETEENTH- AND TWENTIETH-CENTURY VIEWS

John C. Calhoun
Abraham Lincoln
Lord Acton
Woodrow Wilson

• JOHN C. CALHOUN

There is another error, not less great and dangerous [than that all people are equally entitled to liberty], usually associated with the one which has just been considered. I refer to the opinion, that liberty and equality are so intimately united, that liberty cannot be perfect without perfect equality.

That they are united to a certain extent—and that equality of citizens, in the eyes of the law, is essential to liberty in a popular government, is conceded. But to go further, and make equality of *condition* essential to liberty, would be to destroy both liberty and progress. The reason is, that inequality of condition, while it is a necessary consequence of liberty, is, at the same time, indispensable to progress. In order to understand why this is so, it is necessary to bear in mind, that the mainspring to progress is, the desire of individuals to better their condition; and that the strongest impulse which can be given to it is, to leave individuals free to exert themselves in the manner they may deem best for that purpose, as far at least as it can be done consistently with the ends for which government is ordained—and to secure to all the fruits of their exertions. Now, as individuals differ greatly from each other, in intelligence, sagacity, energy, perseverance, skill, habits of industry and economy, physical power, position and opportunity—the necessary effect of leaving all free to exert themselves to better their condition, must be a corresponding inequality between those· who may possess these qualities and advantages in a high degree, and those who may be deficient in them. The only means by which this result can be prevented are, either to impose such restrictions on the exertions of those who may possess them in a high degree, as will place them on a level with those who do not; or to deprive them of the fruits of their exertions. But to impose such restrictions on them would be destructive of liberty—while to deprive them of the fruits of their exertions, would be to destroy the desire of bettering their condition. It is, indeed, this inequality of condition between the front and rear ranks, in the march of progress, which gives so strong an impulse to the former to maintain their position, and to the latter to press forward into their files. This gives to progress its greatest impulse. To force the front rank back to the rear, or attempt to push forward the rear into line with the front, by the interposition of government, would put an end to the impulse, and effectually arrest the march of progress.

These great and dangerous errors have their origin in the prevalent opinion that all men are born free and equal—than which nothing can be more unfounded and false. It rests upon the assumption of a fact, which is contrary to universal observation, in whatever light it may be regarded. It is, indeed, difficult to explain how an opinion so destitute of all sound reason, even could be so extensively entertained, unless we regard it as being confounded with another, which has some semblance of truth—but which, when properly understood, is not less false and dangerous. I refer to the assertion, that all men are equal in the state of nature; meaning . . . a state of individuality, supposed to have existed prior to the social and political state; and in which men lived apart and independent of each other. If such a state ever did exist, all men would have been, indeed, free and equal in it; that is, free to do as they pleased, and exempt from the authority or control of others—as, by supposition, it existed anterior to society and government. But such a state is purely hypothetical. It never did, nor can exist; as it is inconsistent with the preservation and perpetuation of the race. It is, therefore, a great misnomer to call it *the state of nature*. Instead of being the natural state of man, it is, of all conceivable states, the most opposed to his nature—most repugnant to his feelings, and most incompatible with his wants. His natural state is, the social and political—the one for which his Creator made him, and the only one in which he can preserve and perfect his race. As, then, there never was such a state as the, so called, state of nature, and never can be, it follows, that men, instead of being born in it, are born in the social and political state; and of course, instead of being free and equal, are born subject, not only to parental authority, but to the laws and institutions of the country where born, and under whose protection they draw their first breath. . . .

Liberty, then, when forced on a people unfit for it, would, instead of a blessing, be a curse; as it would, in its reaction, lead directly to anarchy—the greatest of all curses. No people, indeed, can long enjoy more liberty than that to which their situation and advanced intelligence and morals fairly entitle them. . . .

Liberty, indeed, though among the greatest blessings, is not so great as that of protection; inasmuch, as the end of the former is the progress and improvement of the race—while that of the latter is its preservation and perpetuation. And hence, when the two come into conflict, liberty must, and ever ought, to yield to protection; as the existence of the race is of greater moment than its improvement.

It follows, from what has been stated, that it is a great and dangerous error to suppose that all people are equally entitled to liberty. It is a reward to be earned, not a blessing to be gratuitously lavished on all alike; a reward reserved for the intelligent, the patriotic, the virtuous and deserving—and not a boon to be bestowed on a people too ignorant, degraded and vicious, to be capable either of appreciating or of enjoying it. Nor is it any disparagement to liberty, that such is, and ought to be the case. On the contrary, its greatest praise—its proudest distinction is, that an all-wise Providence has reserved it, as the noblest and highest reward for the development of our faculties, moral and intellectual. A reward more appropriate than liberty could not be conferred on the deserving; nor a punishment inflicted on the undeserving more just, than to be subject to lawless and despotic rule. The dispensation seems to be the result of some fixed law—and every effort to disturb or defeat it, by attempting to elevate a people in the scale of liberty, above the point to which they are entitled to rise, must ever prove abortive, and end in disappointment. The progress of a people rising from a lower to a higher point in the scale of liberty, is necessarily slow—and by attempting to precipitate, we either retard, or permanently defeat it. ■

From A Disquisition on Government, *1851.*

• ABRAHAM LINCOLN

What constitutes the bulwark of our own liberty and independence? It is not our frowning battlements, our bristling sea coasts, our army and our navy. These are not our reliance against tyranny. All of those may be turned against us without making us weaker for the struggle. Our reliance is in the love of liberty which God has planted in us. Our defence is in the spirit which prized liberty as the heritage of all men, in all lands everywhere. Destroy this spirit and you have planted the seeds of despotism at your own doors. Familiarize yourselves with the chains of bondage and you prepare your own limbs to wear them. Accustomed to trample on the rights of others, you have lost the genius of your own independence and become the fit subjects of the first cunning tyrant who rises among you. And let me tell you, that all these things are prepared for you by the teachings of history. ■

From speech at Edwardsville, Ill.,
September 13, 1858.

• ABRAHAM LINCOLN

The world has never had a good definition of the word liberty, and the American people, just now, are much in want of one. We all declare for liberty; but in using the same word we do not all mean the same thing. With some the word liberty may mean for each man to do as he pleases with himself, and the product of his labor; while with others the same word may mean for some men to do as they please with other men, and the product of other men's labor. Here are two, not only different, but incompatible things, called by the same name, liberty. And it follows that each of the things is, by the respective parties, called by two different and incompatible names—liberty and tyranny.

The shepherd drives the wolf from the sheep's throat, for which the sheep thanks the shepherd as his liberator, while the wolf denounces him for the same act, as the destroyer of liberty, especially as the sheep was a black one. Plainly, the sheep and the wolf are not agreed upon a definition of the word

liberty; and precisely the same difference prevails to-day among us human creatures, even in the North, and all professing to love liberty. Hence we behold the process by which thousands are daily passing from under the yoke of bondage hailed by some as the advance of liberty, and bewailed by others as the destruction of all liberty. ■

From speech in Baltimore, April 18, 1864.

• LORD ACTON

Liberty, next to religion, has been the motive of good deeds and the common pretext of crime, from the sowing of the seed of Athens . . . until the ripened harvest was gathered by men of our race. It is the delicate fruit of a mature civilisation; and scarcely a century has passed since nations, that knew the meaning of the term, resolved to be free. In every age its progress has been beset by its natural enemies,[1] by ignorance and superstition, by lust of conquest and by love of ease, by the strong man's craving for power, and the poor man's craving for food . . . At all times sincere friends of freedom have been rare, and its triumphs have been due to minorities, that have prevailed by associating themselves with auxiliaries whose object often differed from their own. ■

From address, February 26, 1877.

• WOODROW WILSON

The liberty of the individual is limited with the greatest sharpness where his actions come into collision with the interests of the community he lives in.

---

[1] This is true. Many of the champions of freedom had met with a sad fate. See, for example, the statement by Bartolomé Mitré, in G. W. Crichfield's *American Supremacy* (1908), vol. I, pp. 219–20: "The fate of the emancipators of South America is tragical. The first revolutionists of La Paz and of Quito died on the scaffold. Miranda, the apostle of liberty, betrayed by his own people to his enemies, died, alone and naked, in a dungeon . . . Hidalgo, the first popular leader of Mexico, was executed as a criminal . . . O'Higgins, the hero of Chili, died in exile . . . Montufar, the leader of the revolution in Quito, and his comrade Villavicencio, the promoter of that of Cartagena, were strangled. . . . Piar, who found the true base for the insurrection in Colombia, was shot by Bolívar . . . Sucre, the conqueror of Ayacucho, was murdered by his own men on a lonely road. Bolívar and San Martín died in banishment."

My liberty consists in a sort of parole. Society says to me, "You may do what you please until you do something that is in violation of the common understanding, of the public interest; then your parole is forfeited. We will take you into custody. We will limit your activities. We will penalize you if you use this thing that you call your liberty against our interest." Business does not want, and ought not to ask for, more liberty than the individual has; and I have always in my own thought summed up individual liberty, and business liberty, and every other kind of liberty, in the phrase that is common in the sporting world, "A free field and no favor." ■

From address to the American Electric Railway Association, Washington, D.C., January 29, 1915.

PART III

EQUALS
AND UNEQUALS

All students of democracy, from Aristotle to our own day, have agreed that its core idea is equality. One writer, Edward Bellamy, called equality the "vital principle of democracy." Without the concept and, indeed, the practice of equality, the democratic philosophy has little meaning in theory and could not survive in practice.

But the notion of equality is a complicated one, involving many facets of human existence—biological, psychological, social, religious, economic, legal, and political. It has, therefore, been both challenged and defended through the ages. Thus John C. Calhoun called equality an "unfounded and false" idea, while Abraham Lincoln considered it basic for "augmenting the happiness" of all people everywhere.

The modern doctrine of equality was first developed in the eighteenth century in connection with the revolutionary struggles for republicanism. Since self-government involved citizens' participation, political equality was obviously a necessary basis for such a system. It is, as we saw in Part One, closely

tied up with the idea of freedom. Among the leading early exponents of equality have been Claude Adrien Helvétius and Jean
Jacques Rousseau in France, and Thomas Jefferson and John
Taylor in the United States. Subsequently others—including
de Tocqueville, Lincoln, and Woodrow Wilson—have contributed to a widening understanding of the notion of equality.

This section, centering on *political* equality and its ramifications, highlights its diverse and conflicting aspects. It includes
an epistolary debate between John Adams and Thomas Jefferson on aristocracy.

1

GENERAL VIEWS

Aristotle
John Calvin
Francis Bacon
Thomas Hobbes
Samuel Pufendorf
Jean Jacques Rousseau
Claude Adrien Helvetius
Benjamin Franklin

• ARISTOTLE

The end or purpose of every art and science is some good. That of the most authoritative, i.e., of political science, is the greatest and most eagerly desired good—justice or, in other words, the common welfare. Now justice is recognized universally as some sort of equality. All men agree to some extent with the philosophical conclusions I have drawn on the subject of ethics; for they admit that just involves an assignment of things to persons, and that equals are entitled to equal things. But here we are met by the important question: Equals and unequals *in what?* This is a difficult problem, and entails philosophical speculation in the field of politics. It may be argued that offices of state should be distributed unequally on the basis of superiority *in any one respect whatsoever,* even though there be no difference between one citizen and the next in any other respect; and this argument may be founded on the assumption that those who differ from one another must have different rights.

But surely, if this is true, (1) a man's complexion, height, or any other such advantage will earn him a greater share of political rights. The error is plain for all to see, and may be illustrated from other arts and sciences. When a number of flautists are equally skillful players, there is no reason why those of them who are nobly born should receive the better flutes; they will play no better. It is the superior artist who deserves the superior instrument. If my point is not yet clear, it will become so by carrying the example a stage further. Take a man who is a first-rate flautist, but of humble extraction and far from handsome. Blue blood and physical beauty may be greater assets than the art of flute playing, and may excel the latter in a higher degree than our flautist excels others in his art; nevertheless, he still has a claim to the best flutes—unless the advantages of wealth and birth enhance the skill of an instrumentalist, which they manifestly do not.

Furthermore, (2) every quality will be commensurable with every other. If a given height is measurable against a given degree of wealth or birth, then

height in general can be measured against wealth
and birth in general. But if we are going to allow
that, in a particular instance, A excels in height
more than B does in goodness, and that, in general,
height excels to a greater degree than does goodness,
then we shall have to allow that all qualities are
commensurable; for if amount P of a certain quality
is better than amount Q of another quality, then an
amount other than P must be equal to it. But since
no such comparison is admissible, there is clearly
good reason why in politics also men should not
base their claim to office on any and every kind of
superiority. Some are slow and others swift, but
that does not entitle the former to little and the
latter to much; it is in athletic contests that such
excellence takes the prize. No, rival claims to office
must be grounded exclusively on the possession of
those elements which go to form the state; and
therefore men of noble descent, free birth, or wealth
may fairly lay claim to office. Those who hold positions of this kind must be freemen and taxpayers:
a state can no more consist entirely of poor men
than of slaves. But if wealth and free birth are
necessary elements, so too are justice and valor;
without the former qualities a state cannot exist
at all, and without the latter there can be no good
life. ■

From Politics, *Book III, "State and Citizen."*

• JOHN CALVIN

Predestination, by which God adopts some to the
hope of life, and adjudges others to eternal death,
no one, desirous of the credit of piety, dares absolutely to deny. But it is involved in many cavils,
especially by those who make foreknowledge the
cause of it. We maintain, that both belong to God;
but it is preposterous to represent one as dependent
on the other. When we attribute foreknowledge to
God, we mean that all things have ever been, and
perpetually remain, before his eyes, so that to his
knowledge nothing is future or past, but all things
are present; and present in such a manner, that he
does not merely conceive of them from ideas formed

in his mind, as things remembered by us appear
present to our minds, but really beholds and sees
them as if actually placed before him. And this
foreknowledge extends to the whole world, and to
all the creatures. Predestination we call the eternal
decree of God, by which he has determined in himself, what he would have to become of every individual of mankind. For they are not all created
with a similar destiny; but eternal life is fore-
ordained for some, and eternal damnation for
others. ■

From Institutes of the Christian Religion,
Book III, Chapter XXI.

• FRANCIS BACON

We will speak of Nobility first as a portion of an
estate, then as a condition of particular persons.
A monarchy where there is no nobility at all, is
ever a pure and absolute tyranny; as that of the
Turks. For nobility attempers sovereignty, and
draws the eyes of the people somewhat aside from
the line royal. But for democracies, they need it
not; and they are commonly more quiet and less
subject to sedition, than where there are stirps of
nobles. For men's eyes are upon the business, and
not upon the persons; or if upon the persons, it is
for the business sake, as fittest, and not for flags
and pedigree. We see the Switzers last well, notwithstanding their diversity of religion and of can-
tons. For utility is their bond, and not respects.
The united provinces of the Low Countries in their
government excel; for where there is an equality,
the consultations are more indifferent, and the payments and tributes more cheerful. A great and
potent nobility addeth majesty to a monarch, but
diminisheth power; and putteth life and spirit into
the people, but presseth their fortune. It is well
when nobles are not too great for sovereignty nor
for justice; and yet maintained in that height, as
the insolency of inferiors may be broken upon them
before it come on too fast upon the majesty of kings.
A numerous nobility causeth poverty and inconvenience in a state; for it is a surcharge of expense;

and besides, it being of necessity that many of the nobility fall in time to be weak in fortune, it maketh a kind of disproportion between honour and means.

As for nobility in particular persons; it is a reverend thing to see an ancient castle or building not in decay; or to see a fair timber tree sound and perfect. How much more to behold an ancient noble family, which hath stood against the waves and weathers of time. For new nobility is but the act of power, but ancient nobility is the act of time. Those that are first raised to nobility are commonly more virtuous, but less innocent, than their descendents; for there is rarely any rising but by a commixture of good and evil arts. But it is reason the memory of their virtues remain to their posterity, and their faults die with themselves. Nobility of birth commonly abateth industry; and he that is not industrious, envieth him that is. Besides, noble persons cannot go much higher: and he that standeth at a stay when others rise, can hardly avoid motions of envy. . . . ■

From Essays, *"Of Nobility," 1625.*

• THOMAS HOBBES

Nature hath made men so equal in the faculties of the body and mind, as that, though there be found one man sometimes manifestly stronger in body or of quicker mind than another, yet when all is reckoned together the difference between man and man is not so considerable as that one man can thereupon claim to himself any benefit to which another may not pretend as well as he. For, as to the strength of body, the weakest has strength enough to kill the strongest, either by secret machination or by confederacy with others that are in the same danger with himself.

And, as to the faculties of the mind, setting aside the arts grounded upon words and especially that skill of proceeding upon general and infallible rules called science, which very few have and but in few things, as being not a native faculty born with us, nor attained, as prudence, while we look after somewhat else, I find yet a greater equality amongst

men than that of strength. For prudence is but experience, which equal time equally bestows on all men in those things they equally apply themselves unto. That which may perhaps make such equality incredible is but a vain conceit of one's own wisdom, which almost all men think they have in a greater degree than the vulgar, that is, than all men but themselves, and a few others whom by fame or for concurring with themselves they approve. For such is the nature of men that, howsoever they may acknowledge many others to be more witty or more eloquent or more learned, yet they will hardly believe there be many so wise as themselves, for they see their own wit at hand and other men's at a distance. But this proveth rather that men are in that point equal than unequal. For there is not ordinarily a greater sign of the equal distribution of anything than that every man is contented with his share.

From this equality of ability ariseth equality of hope in the attaining of our ends. . . . ■

From Leviathan, *Chapter XIII, 1651.*

• SAMUEL PUFENDORF

In addition to that love which every man cherishes for his life, his person, and his possessions, by which he cannot avoid repelling or fleeing before everything that tends to their destruction, there is to be observed, deep-seated in his soul, a most sensitive self-esteem; and if any one undertakes to impair this, he is rarely less and often more disturbed than if an injury were being offered his person and property. Although a number of factors unite to intensify this esteem, its prime source is, apparently, human nature. For indeed the word "man" is felt to have a certain dignity, and the last as well as the most telling reply with which the rude insults of other men is met, is, "I am not a dog or a beast, but as much a man as you are." Statius, *Thebaid,* Book XII

Suffice it, noble Theseus, that with thee
They bore a manly form, a thinking mind,
And all the properties of human kind.

Now since human nature belongs equally to all men, and no one can live a social life with a person by whom he is not rated as at least a fellow man, it follows, as a precept of natural law, that "Every man should esteem and treat another man as his equal by nature, or as much a man as he is himself."

2. That this equality between men may be better understood, it should be observed that Hobbes, *De Cive,* Chapter 1, § 3, confines it to a parity of strength and other human faculties, with which mature men are endowed, and undertakes to show why, therefore, men have reason, because of their nature, to stand in mutual fear of one another. For he can inspire no terror in me whose powers do not extend far enough to do me harm. And yet, although one man may be a bit inferior to another in strength, he may still, by the aid of cunning, agility, and familiarity with weapons, be able to inflict death upon even the most robust of men. . . .

Indeed, just as in well-ordered states, one citizen is above another in position or wealth, but all share equally in liberty, so however much one man may excel others in mental and bodily gifts, he is none the less bound to exercise toward them the duties of natural right, and he may expect the same of others as well, nor, for all his gifts, is he allowed any greater licence to injure others. Thus, however niggardly nature or fortune has been toward a man, he is not condemned on that score to share less fully than others in the benefits of the law. But whatever one man can claim or hope for from another, the same others can claim or hope for from him, other things being equal, and whatever law a man appeals to against another, he must under every circumstance admit against himself. . . .

From this equality as we have posited it, there flow other precepts, the observance of which has the greatest influence in preserving peace and friendly relations among men. Now it is clear at the outset that, if a man wishes to avail himself of the assistance of the other men for his own advantage, he must in his turn lend his own talents to their accommodation. "Hand washes hand" is the old proverb. Surely a man considers others his inferiors if he demands that they labor for him while he him-

self always desires to be independent, and whoever maintains such an attitude cannot avoid offending others, and giving occasion to a breach of peace. It was a hardy reply of Caractacus, in Tacitus, *Annals,* XII: "And if you Romans must needs lord it over the world, does it follow that all welcome your yoke?" Lactantius, *Divine Institutes,* Book III, chapter xxii: "Nothing is done wisely which is useless and evil if it is done by all." And just as surely as it implies a contradiction to draw different conclusions from things which entirely agree, so one cannot lay down different rules in exactly similar cases that concern myself and another. Nay, since every man knows his own nature best and the nature of other men, at least so far as concerns their general inclinations, just as well, it follows that he who decides one way in another man's right, and another way in a similar right of his own, is guilty of a contradiction in the very plainest matter, and this is evidence of a seriously disordered mind. No sufficient proof, indeed, can be advanced why something that I feel to be proper for myself, I should feel to be improper for others who are my equals, other things being equal. Thus, just as those men are best fitted for a social life who are willing to allow the same things to others as to themselves—as Horace, *Satires,* Book I, sat. iii, puts it: "He who expects his friend not to be annoyed at his wens will excuse the other's warts. It is fair play that one who asks indulgence for shortcomings should give it in return"—so those are plainly unsocial who, from a feeling of their own superiority, would have every liberty allowed themselves alone, overlook every fault in themselves, pardon nothing in others, and claim for themselves, although they enjoy no special right above others, honor before all other men, and a special share in things which are the common property of all. For just as in the erection of a building, a stone which, because of its angular and rough shape, takes more space than it fills, cannot be easily cut or shaped because of its hardness, and prevents the completion of the structure, is rejected as useless, so πλεονέκται [greedy men], who, in their miserliness, rob others of the necessities of life by keeping more than they can use, and who cannot be changed in their way, such is the stubbornness of their make-up, constitute a permanent menace and burden upon society. ∎

From De Jure Naturae et Gentium Libri Octo,
Book III, Chapter 2, 1688.

• JEAN JACQUES ROUSSEAU

If the reader thus discovers and retraces the lost and forgotten road, by which man must have passed from the state of nature to the state of society . . . he cannot fail to be struck by the vast distance which separates the two states . . . In a word, he will explain how the soul and the passions of men insensibly change their very nature; why our wants and pleasures in the end seek new objects; and why, the original man having vanished by degrees, society offers to us only an assembly of artificial men and factitious passions, which are the work of all these new relations, and without any real foundation in nature . . . The savage and the civilized man differ so much in the bottom of their hearts and in their inclinations, that what constitutes the supreme happiness of one would reduce the other to despair. The former breathes only peace and liberty; he desires only to live and be free from labor . . . Civilized man, on the other hand, is always moving, sweating, toiling and racking his brains to find still more laborious occupations: he goes on in drudgery to his last moment . . . It is sufficient that I have proved that this [corruptions of civilization] is not by any means the original state of man, but that it is merely the spirit of society, and the inequality which society produces, that thus transform and alter all our natural inclinations.

I have endeavored to trace the origin and progress of inequality, and the institution and abuse of political societies . . . It follows from this survey that, as there is hardly any inequality in the state of nature, all the inequality which now prevails owes its strength and growth to the development of our faculties and the advance of the human mind, and becomes at last permanent and legitimate by the establishment of property and laws. Secondly, it follows

that moral inequality, authorized by positive right alone, clashes with natural right, whenever it is not combined with physical inequality; a distinction which sufficiently determines what we ought to think of that species of inequality which prevails in all civilized countries; since it is plainly contrary to the law of nature, however defined, that children should command old men, fools wise men, and that the privileged few should gorge themselves with superfluities, while the starving multitude are in want of the bare neccessities of life. ∎

From A Discourse on the Origin and Foundations
of Inequality Among Men, *1754.*[1]

• CLAUDE ADRIEN HELVÉTIUS

I have examined, "Whether education, necessarily different in different men, be not the cause of that inequality of understandings hitherto attributed to the unequal perfection of their organs."

To this purpose I have inquired at what age the education of man begins, and who are his instructors.

I see that man is the pupil of every object which surrounds him, of all the positions in which chance has placed him, in short, of every incident that happens to him.

That these objects, positions, and incidents are not exactly the same for any two persons, and consequently no two receive the same instructions.

That if it were possible for two men to have the same objects before their eyes, these objects not striking them at the precise moment when their minds are in the same situation, will not, in consequence, excite in them the same ideas: therefore the pretended uniformity of instruction received, either

---

[1]Voltaire made some witty remarks about this book of Rousseau's: "I have received, sir, your new book against the human species, and I thank you for it. You will please people by your manner of telling them the truth about themselves, but you will not alter them. The horrors of human society . . . have never been painted in more striking colors: no one has ever been so witty as you are in trying to turn us into brutes: to read your book makes one long to go on all fours. Since, however, it is now some sixty years since I gave up the practice, I feel that it is unfortunately impossible for me to resume it: I leave this natural habit to those more fit for it than you and I are."

in the schools or in the paternal house, is one of those suppositions whose impossibility is proved by facts, and by the influence that chance, independent of instructors, has, and always will have, on the education of childhood and youth.

These matters settled, I consider the extreme extent of the power of chance, and I examine,

Whether illustrious men do not frequently owe to it their taste for a particular sort of study, and consequently their talents and their success in that study. . . .

If after these several examinations, and on the supposition that all men have an equal aptitude for understanding, the mere difference in their education ought not to produce a difference in their ideas and their talents. From whence it follows, that the inequality in understanding cannot be regarded, in men commonly well organized, as a demonstrative proof of their unequal aptitude to acquire it. . . .

I . . . demonstrate,

That men commonly well organized are susceptible of the same degree of passion.

That their unequal force is always the effect of the difference of situations in which chance has placed them.

That the original character of each man (as Pascal observes) is nothing more than the product of his first habits: that man is born without ideas, without passions, and without other wants than those of hunger and thirst, and consequently without character: that he often changes it without any change in his organization: that those changes, independent of the greater or less fineness of his senses, operate according to the changes that happen in his situation and ideas.

That the diversity of characters depends solely on the different manners in which the sentiment of self-love is modified in men. . . .[1] ∎

From A Treatise on Man, *1773.*

---

[1] Helvétius' assertion of natural equality was challenged by his contemporary Encyclopedist, Denis Diderot (1713–1784). In his "Refutation de Helvétius," written about 1774, Diderot replied to Helvétius' statement that "All men are born with equality of understanding": "All men are born without understanding; they have it neither false nor just: it is the experience of the things of life that disposes them toward justness or falseness. He who has always made bad use of his senses will have false understanding. He who, mediocrely educated, thinks he knows all, will have false understanding. He who, carried away by self-sufficiency and haste, is hurried in his judgments, will

• BENJAMIN FRANKLIN

My dear child:

Your care in sending me the newspapers is very agreeable to me. I received by Captain Barney those relating to the *Cincinnati.*[1] My opinion of the institution cannot be of much importance. I only wonder that, when the united wisdom of our nation had in the Articles of Confederation, manifested their dislike of establishing ranks of nobility, by authority either of the Congress or of any particular state, a number of private persons should think proper to distinguish themselves and their posterity from their fellow citizens and form an order of *hereditary knights,* in direct opposition to the solemnly declared sense of their country! I imagine it must be likewise contrary to the good sense of most of those drawn into it by the persuasion of its projectors, who have been too much struck with the ribands and crosses they have seen hanging to the button-holes of foreign officers. And I suppose those who disapprove of it have not hitherto given it much opposition, from a principle somewhat like that of your good mother, relating to punctilious persons, who are always exacting little observances of respect: that, *"if people can be pleased with small matters, it is a pity but they should have them."*

In this view, perhaps, I should not myself, if my advice had been asked, have objected to their wearing their ribands and badges themselves according to their fancy, though I certainly should to the entailing it as an honor on their posterity. For honor, worthily obtained (as that, for example, of our officers), is in its nature a *personal* thing, and incommunicable to any but those who had some share in obtaining it. Thus among the Chinese, the most

---

have false understanding. He who attaches too much or too little importance to certain things will have false understanding. He who dares pronounce himself on a question which exceeds the capacity of his natural talent will have false understanding. There is nothing so rare as logic: an infinity of men lack it, almost all women have none at all. He who is subject to prejudices will have false understanding. He who is obstinate out of conceit, out of a desire to be different, or out of inclination for paradoxes, will have false understanding. And he who trusts his reason too much and he who trusts it too little will have false understanding. Thence I conclude that equality of understanding is in every respect a figment of the imagination."

[1] The Society of the Cincinnati was a fraternal organization founded in 1783, after the American Revolution, by officers of the Continental Army.

ancient and from long experience the wisest of nations, honor does not *descend,* but *ascends.* If a man,
from his learning, his wisdom, or his valor, is promoted by the Emperor to the rank of Mandarin, his
parents are immediately entitled to all the same
ceremonies of respect from the people that are
established as due to the Mandarin himself; on the
supposition that it must have been owing to the
education, instruction, and good example afforded
him by his parents that he was rendered capable of
serving the public. ■

From letter to Sarah Franklin Bache,
Paris, January 26, 1784.

THE BURKE-PAINE POLEMIC ON EQUALITY

Edmund Burke
Thomas Paine

• EDMUND BURKE

I readily admit (indeed I should lay it down as a fundamental principle) that in a republican government, which has a democratic basis, the rich do require an additional security above what is necessary to them in monarchies. They are subject to envy, and through envy to oppression . . . The contest between the rich and the poor is not a struggle between corporation and corporation, but a contest between men and men; a competition not between districts but between descriptions. It would answer its purpose better if the scheme were inverted; that the votes of the masses were rendered equal; and that the votes within each mass were proportioned to property.

Let us suppose one man in a district . . . to contribute as much as an hundred of his neighbours. Against these he has but one vote. If there were but one representative for the mass, his poor neighbours would outvote him by an hundred to one for that single representative. Bad enough. But amends are to be made him. How? The district, in virtue of his wealth, is to choose, say, ten members instead of one: that is to say, by paying a very large contribution he has the happiness of being outvoted, an hundred to one, by the poor for ten representatives, instead of being outvoted exactly in the same proportion for a single member. In truth, instead of benefitting by this superior quantity of representation, the rich man is subjected to an additional hardship. The increase of representation within his province sets up nine persons more, and as many more than nine as there may be democratic candidates, to cabal and intrigue, and to flatter the people at his expence and to his oppression. An interest is by this means held out to multitudes of the inferior sort, in obtaining a salary of eighteen livres a day (to them a vast object) besides the pleasure of a residence in Paris and their share in the government of the kingdom. The more the objects of ambition are multiplied and become democratic, just in that proportion the rich are endangered. ■

From Reflections on the Revolution in France, *1790.*

• THOMAS PAINE

The genuine mind of man, thirsting for its native home, society, contemns the gewgaws that separate him from it. Titles are like circles drawn by the magician's wand, to contract the sphere of man's felicity. He lives immured within the Bastille of a word, and surveys at a distance the envied life of man.

Is it then any wonder that titles should fall in France? Is it not a greater wonder they should be kept on anywhere? What are they? What is their worth, and "what is the amount"? When we think or speak of a *judge* or a *general,* we associate with it the ideas of office and character; we think of gravity in the one, and bravery in the other; but when we use a word merely as a title, no ideas associate with it.

Through all the vocabulary of Adam, there is no such an animal as a duke or a count; neither can we connect any idea to the words. Whether they mean strength or weakness, wisdom or folly, a child or a man, or a rider or a horse, is all equivocal. What respect then can be paid to that which describes nothing, and which means nothing? Imagination has given figure and character to centaurs, satyrs, and down to all the fairy tribe; but titles baffle even the powers of fancy, and are a chimerical nondescript.

. . . this makes it necessary to inquire further into the nature and character of aristocracy.

That, then, which is called aristocracy in some countries and nobility in others, arose out of the governments founded upon conquest. It was originally a military order . . . and to keep up a succession of this order for the purpose for which it was established, all the younger branches of those families were disinherited, and the law of primogenitureship set up.

The nature and character of aristocracy shows itself to us in this law. It is a law against every law of nature . . . By the aristocratical law of primogeniture, in a family of six children, five are exposed. Aristocracy has never more than *one* child. The rest are begotten to be devoured. . . .

As everything which is out of nature in man, affects, more or less, the interest of society, so does this. All the children which the aristocracy disowns (which are all, except the eldest) are, in general, cast like orphans on a parish, to be provided for by the public, but at a greater charge. Unnecessary offices and places in governments and courts are created at the expense of the public, to maintain them. . . .

Let us examine the grounds upon which the French Constitution has resolved against having such a House [of Peers] in France.

Because, in the first place, as is already mentioned, aristocracy is kept up by family tyranny and injustice.

Secondly, because there is an unusual unfitness in an aristocracy to be legislators for a nation. Their ideas of distributive justice are corrupted at the very source. They begin life by trampling on all their younger brothers and sisters, and relations of every kind, and are taught and educated so to do. With what ideas of justice or honor can that man enter a house of legislation, who absorbs in his own person the inheritance of a whole family of children, or doles out to them some pitiful portion with the insolence of a gift?

Thirdly, because the idea of hereditary legislators is as inconsistent as that of hereditary judges, or hereditary juries; and as absurd as an hereditary mathematician, or an hereditary wise man; and as ridiculous as an hereditary poet-laureate.

Fourthly, because a body of men holding themselves accountable to nobody, ought not to be trusted by anybody.

Fifthly, because it is continuing the uncivilized principle of the governments founded in conquest, and the base idea of man having property in man, and governing him by personal right.

Sixthly, because aristocracy has a tendency to degenerate the human species. By the universal economy of nature it is known . . . that the human species has a tendency to degenerate, in any small number of persons, when separated from the general stock of society, and intermarrying constantly with each other.

It defeats even its pretended end, and becomes

in time the opposite of what is noble in man. Mr. Burke talks of nobility; let him show what it is. The greatest characters the world has known, have risen on the democratic floor. Aristocracy has not been able to keep a proportionate pace with democracy. ■

From The Rights of Man, *Part I, 1791.*

3

THE ADAMS-JEFFERSON EXCHANGE ON ARISTOCRACY

John Adams
Thomas Jefferson

• JOHN ADAMS

I recollect, near some thirty years ago, to have said carelessly to you that I wished I could find time and means to write something upon aristocracy. You seized upon the idea, and encouraged me to do it with all that friendly warmth that is natural and habitual to you. I soon began, and have been writing upon that subject ever since. . . .

Your *aristoi* are the most difficult animals to manage of anything in the whole theory and practice of government. They will not suffer themselves to be governed. They not only exert all their own subtility, industry, and courage, but they employ the commonalty to knock to pieces every plan and model that the most honest architects in legislation can invent to keep them within bounds. . . .

But who are these *aristoi?* . . . [*In*] a collection of moral sentences from all the most ancient Greek poets . . . I read . . . a couplet, the sense of which was "Nobility in men is worth as much as it is in horses, asses, or rams; but the meanest-blooded puppy in the world, if he gets a little money, is as good a man as the best of them." Yet birth and wealth together have prevailed over virtue and talents in all ages. The many will acknowledge no other *aristoi.* Your experience of this truth will not differ much from that of your old friend. ■

From letter to Thomas Jefferson, July 9, 1813.

• JOHN ADAMS

I should render the Greek [from Theognis] into English thus: "Nor does a woman disdain to be the wife of a bad rich man. But she prefers a man of property before a good man; for riches are honored, and a good man marries from a bad family, and a bad man from a good one. Wealth mingles races." . . .

The five pillars of aristocracy are beauty, wealth, birth, genius, and virtue. Any one of these three first can, at any time, overbear any one of the two last. . . .

And is this great fact in the natural history of man [aristocracy], this unalterable principle of morals, philosophy, policy, domestic felicity, and daily experience from the creation, to be overlooked, forgotten, neglected, or hypocritically waved out of sight, by a legislator, by a professed writer upon civil government, and upon constitutions of civil government? . . .

You may laugh at the introduction of beauty among the pillars of aristocracy. But Madame du Barry says, "*La véritable royauté c'est la beauté,*" and there is not a more certain truth. Beauty, grace, figure, attitude, movement, have in innumerable instances, prevailed over wealth, birth, talents, virtues, and everything else, in men of the highest rank, greatest power, and, sometimes, the most exalted genius, greatest fame, and highest merit. ■

From letter to Thomas Jefferson, September 2, 1813.

• THOMAS JEFFERSON

The passage you quote from Theognis, I think has an ethical rather than a political object. The whole piece is a moral *exhortation . . .* and this passage particularly seems to be a reproof to man, who while with his domestic animals he is curious to improve the race, by employing always the finest male, pays no attention to the improvement of his own race, but intermarries with the vicious, the ugly, or the old, for considerations of wealth or ambition. . . . The selecting the best male for a harem of well-chosen females also, which Theognis seems to recommend from the example of our sheep and asses, would doubtless improve the human, as it does the brute animal, and produce a race of veritable *aristoi.* For experience proves, that the moral and physical qualities of man, whether good or evil, are transmissible in a certain degree from father to son. But I suspect that the equal rights of man would rise up against this privileged Solomon and his harem, and oblige us to . . . content ourselves with the accidental *aristoi* produced by the fortuitous concourse of breeders. For I agree with you that there is a natural aristocracy among men. The grounds of this are virtue and talents. Formerly, bodily powers gave place among the *aristoi.* But

since the invention of gunpowder has armed the weak as well as the strong with missile death, bodily strength, like beauty, good humor, politeness and other accomplishments, has become but an auxiliary ground for distinction. There is also an artificial aristocracy, founded on wealth and birth, without either virtue or talents; for with these it would belong to the first class. The natural aristocracy I consider as the most precious gift of nature, for the instruction, the trusts, and government of society. And indeed, it would have been inconsistent in creation to have formed man for the social state, and not to have provided virtue and wisdom enough to manage the concerns of the society. May we not even say, that that form of government is the best, which provides the most effectually for a pure selection of these natural *aristoi* into the offices of government? The artificial aristocracy is a mischievous ingredient in government, and provision should be made to prevent its ascendency.

On the question, what is the best provision, you and I differ; but we differ as rational friends, using the free exercise of our own reason, and mutually indulging its errors. You think it best to put the pseudo-*aristoi* into a separate chamber of legislation, where they may be hindered from doing mischief by their coordinate branches, and where, also, they may be a protection to wealth against the agrarian and plundering enterprises of the majority of the people. I think that to give them power in order to prevent them from doing mischief, is arming them for it, and increasing instead of remedying the evil. For if the coordinate branches can arrest their action, so may they that of the coordinates. Mischief may be done negatively as well as positively. . . . Nor do I believe them necessary to protect the wealthy; because enough of these will find their way into every branch of the legislation, to protect themselves. . . . I think the best remedy is exactly that provided by all our constitutions, to leave to the citizens the free election and separation of the *aristoi* from the pseudo-*aristoi,* of the wheat from the chaff. In general they will elect the really good and wise. In some instances, wealth may corrupt, and birth blind them; but not in sufficient degree to endanger the society. . . .

With respect to aristocracy, we should further consider, that before the establishment of the American States, nothing was known to history but the man of the old world, crowded within limits either small or overcharged, and steeped in the vices which that situation generates. A government adapted to such men would be one thing; but a very different one, that for the man of these States. Here everyone may have land to labor for himself, if he chooses; or, preferring the exercise of any other industry, may exact for it such compensation as not only to afford a comfortable subsistence, but wherewith to provide for a cessation from labor in old age. Every one, by his property, or by his satisfactory situation, is interested in the support of law and order. And such men may safely and advantageously reserve to themselves a wholesome control over their public affairs. ■

From letter to John Adams, Monticello, October 28, 1813.

• JOHN ADAMS

Your distinction between natural and artificial aristocracy does not appear to me founded. Birth and wealth are conferred upon some men as imperiously by nature as genius, strength, and beauty. The heir to honors, and riches, and power, has often no more merit in procuring these advantages, than he has in obtaining a handsome face, or an elegant figure. When aristocracies are established by human laws, and honor, wealth and power are made hereditary by municipal laws and political institutions, then I acknowledge artificial aristocracy to commence; but this never commences till corruption in elections becomes dominant and uncontrollable. But this artificial aristocracy can never last. The everlasting envies, jealousies, rivalries, and quarrels among them; their cruel rapacity among the poor ignorant people, their followers, compel them to set up a Caesar, a demagogue, to be a monarch, a master; *pour mettre chacun à sa place.* Here you have the origin of all artificial aristocracy, which is the origin of all monarchies. And both artificial aristocracy and monarchy, and civil, military, political, and hierarchical despotism, have all grown out of the natural aristocracy of virtues and talents. . . . ■

From letter to Thomas Jefferson, November 15, 1813.

4

THE TAYLOR-ADAMS EXCHANGE ON ARISTOCRACY

John Taylor
John Adams

• JOHN TAYLOR

It will be an effort of this essay to prove, that the United States have refuted the ancient axiom, "that monarchy, aristocracy and democracy, are the only elements of government," by planting theirs in moral principles, without any reference to those elements; and that by demolishing the barrier hitherto obstructing the progress of political science, they have cleared the way for improvement.

Mr. Adams's system promises nothing.[1] It tells us that human nature is always the same: that the art of government can never change; that it is contracted into three simple principles; as at Athens, Venice, or Constantinople; or those of the same principles compounded, as at London, Rome, or Lacedaemon. And it gravely counts up several victims of democratic rage, as proofs, that democracy is more pernicious than monarchy or aristocracy. Such a computation is a spectre, calculated to arrest our efforts, and appall our hopes, in pursuit of political good. If it be correct, what motives of preference between forms of government remain? On one hand, Mr. Adams calls our attention to hundreds of wise and virtuous patricians, mangled and bleeding victims of popular fury; on the other, he might have exhibited millions of plebeians, sacrificed to the pride, folly and ambition of monarchy and aristocracy; and to complete the picture, he ought to have placed right before us, the effects of these three principles commixed, in the wars, rebellions, persecutions and oppressions of the English form, celebrated by Mr. Adams as the most perfect of the mixed class of governments. Is it possible to convince us, that we are compelled to elect one of these evils? After having discovered principles of government, distinct from monarchy, aristocracy or democracy, in the experience of their efficacy, and the enjoyment of their benefits; can we be persuaded to renounce the discovery, to restore the old principles of political navigation, and to steer the commonwealth into the disasters, against which all

---

[1] John Adams, *A Defence of the Constitutions of Government of the United States of America* (1787–1788) and *Discourses on Davila* (1805).

past ages have pathetically warned us? It is admitted, that man, physically, is "always the same"; but denied that he is so, morally. Upon the truth or error of this distinction, the truth or error of Mr. Adams's mode of reasoning and of this essay, will somewhat depend. . . .

Having apprized the reader, by these general remarks, of the political principles to be vindicated or assailed in this essay; and that an effort will be made to prove, that the policy of the United States is rooted in moral or intellectual principles, and not in orders, class or caste, natural or factitious; this effort must be postponed, until the way is opened to it, by a more particular review of Mr. Adams's system. To this, therefore, I return.

He supposes "that every society must naturally produce an aristocratical order of men, which it will be impossible to confine to an equality of rights with other men." To determine the truth of this position, an inquiry must be made into the mode by which these orders have been produced in those countries, placed before us by Mr. Adams, as objects of terror or imitation.

. . . Superior abilities constitutes one among the enumerated causes of a natural aristocracy. This cause is evidently as fluctuating as knowledge and ignorance: and its capacity to produce aristocracy, must depend upon this fluctuation. The aristocracy of superior abilities will be regulated by the extent of the space, between knowledge and ignorance. As the space contracts or widens, it will be diminished or increased; and if aristocracy may be thus diminished, it follows that it may be thus destroyed.

No certain state of knowledge, is a natural or unavoidable quality of man. As an intellectual or moral quality, it may be created, destroyed and modified by human power. Can that which may be created, destroyed and modified by human power, be a natural and inevitable cause of aristocracy?

It has been modified in an extent, which Mr. Adams does not even compute, by the art of printing, discovered subsequently to almost the whole of the authorities which have convinced Mr. Adams, that knowledge, or as he might have more correctly asserted, ignorance, was a cause of aristocracy.

The peerage of knowledge or abilities, in consequence of its enlargement by the effects of printing, can no longer be collected and controlled in the shape of a noble order or a legislative department. The great body of this peerage must remain scattered throughout every nation, by the enjoyment of the benefit of the press. By endowing a small portion of it with exclusive rights and privileges, the indignation of this main body is excited. If this endowment should enable a nation to watch and control an inconsiderable number of that species of peerage produced by knowledge, it would also purchase the dissatisfaction of its numberless members unjustly excluded; and would be a system for defending a nation against imbecility, and inviting aggression from strength, equivalent to a project for defeating an army, by feasting its vanguard.

If this reasoning is correct, the collection of that species of natural aristocracy (as Mr. Adams calls it) produced by superior abilities, into a legislative department, for the purpose of watching and controlling it, is now rendered impracticable, however useful it might have been, at an era when the proportion between ignorance was essentially different; and this impracticability is a strong indication of the radical inaccuracy of considering aristocracy as an inevitable natural law. The wisdom of uniting exclusive knowledge by exclusive privileges, that it may be controlled by disunited ignorance, is not considered as being an hypothetical question, since this aristocratical knowledge cannot now exist.

Similar reasoning applies still more forcibly to the idea of nature's constituting aristocracy, by means of exclusive virtue. Knowledge and virtue both fluctuate. A steady effect, from fluctuating causes, is morally and physically impossible. And yet Mr. Adams infers a natural aristocracy, from the error, that virtue and knowledge are in an uniform relation to vice and ignorance; sweeps away by it every human faculty, for the attainment of temporal or eternal happiness; and overturns the efficacy of law, to produce private or public moral rectitude.

Had it been true, that knowledge and virtue were natural causes of aristocracy, no fact could more clearly have exploded Mr. Adams's system, or more unequivocally have dissented from the eulogy he bestows on the English form of government. Until knowledge and virtue shall become genealogical they cannot be the causes of an inheritable aristocracy; and its existence, without the aid of superior knowledge and virtue, is a positive refutation of the idea, that nature creates aristocracy with these tools.

Mr. Adams has omitted a cause of aristocracy in the quotation, which he forgets not to urge in other places; namely, exclusive wealth. This, by much the most formidable with which mankind have to contend, is necessarily omitted, whilst he is ascribing aristocracy to nature; and being both artificial and efficacious, it contributes to sustain the opinion, "that as aristocracy is thus artificially created, it may also be artificially destroyed."

Alienation is the remedy for an aristocracy founded on landed wealth; inhibitions upon monopoly and incorporation, for one founded on paper wealth. Knowledge, enlisted by Mr. Adams under the banner of aristocracy, deserted her associate by the invention of alienation, and became its natural enemy. Discovering its hostility to human happiness, like Brutus, she has applied the axe to the neck of what Mr. Adams calls her progeny; and instead of maintaining the exclusiveness of wealth, contributes to its division by inciting competition, and assailing perpetuities. How successfully, let England illustrate. She, no longer relying upon nature for an aristocracy, is perpetually obliged to repair the devastations it sustains from alienation; the weapon invented by knowledge; by resorting to the funds of paper systems, pillage, patronage and hierarchy, for fresh supplies.

. . . In order to illustrate the opinion, that the aristocracy exhibited to us by Mr. Adams, as creating a necessity for his system, is only a ghost, let us turn our eyes for a moment towards its successor.

As the aristocracies of priestcraft and conquest decayed, that of patronage and paper stock grew; not the rival, but the instrument of a king; without rank or title; regardless of honor; of insatiable avarice; and neither conspicuous for virtue and knowledge, or capable of being collected into a legislative chamber. Differing in all its qualities from Mr. Adams's natural aristocracy, and defying his remedy, it is condensed and combined by an interest, exclusive, and inimical to public good.

Why has Mr. Adams written volumes to instruct us how to manage an order of nobles, sons of the Gods, of exclusive virtue, talents, and wealth, and attended by the pomp and fraud of superstition; or one of feudal barons, holding great districts of unalienable country, warlike, high spirited, turbulent and dangerous; now that these orders are no more? Whilst he passes over in silence the aristocracy of paper and patronage, more numerous, more burdensome, unexposed to public jealousy by the badge of title, and not too honorable or high spirited to use and serve executive power, for the sake of pillaging the people. Are these odious vices, to be concealed under apprehensions of ancient aristocracies, which, however natural, are supplanted by this modern one?

. . . For the sake of perspicuity, I shall call the ancient aristocracy, chiefly created and supported by superstition, "the aristocracy of the first age"; that produced by conquest, known by the title of the feudal system, "the aristocracy of the second age"; and that erected on paper and patronage, "the aristocracy of the third or present age."

. . . Having thus conceded to Mr. Adams, that wherever a few possess the mass of the renown, virtue, talents and wealth of a nation, that they will become an aristocracy, and probably ought to do so; it would be a concession, strictly reciprocal, to admit, that wherever no such body is to be found, an aristocracy ought not to be created by legal assignments of wealth and poverty. As the first species of minority will govern, because of the power arising from such monopolies only, so no other species can, without these sources of power. Where its sources are, power will be found; and hence the great mass of wealth, created by the system of paper and patronage, has annihilated the power of the didactick and titled peerage of England; because it has not a sufficient mass of virtue, renown, talents or wealth, to oppose against stock and patronage.

The aristocracies of the first and second ages were indebted for their power to ignorance, fraud and superstition; now reason, sincerity and truth, are demanded by the human mind. It disdains to worship a pageant or fear a phantom, and is only to be guided by views of interest or happiness. This change in the human character indicates an impossibility of reviving the principles which sustained the aristocracies of the first and second age, when mankind believed in the Gods of a pantheon, and in the prophetic powers of convulsed women.

Talents and virtue are now so widely distributed, as to have rendered a monopoly of either, equivalent to that of antiquity, impracticable; and if an aristocracy ought to have existed, whilst it possessed such a monopoly, it ought not also to exist, because this monopoly is irretrievably lost. The distribution of wealth produced by commerce and alienation, is equal to that of knowledge and virtue, produced by printing; but as the first distribution might be artificially counteracted, with a better prospect of success than the latter, aristocracy has abandoned a reliance on a monopoly of virtue, renown and abilities, and resorted wholly to a monopoly of wealth, by the system of paper and patronage. Modern taxes and frauds to collect money, and not ancient authors, will therefore afford the best evidence of its present character.

A distribution of knowledge, virtue and wealth, produced public opinion, which ought now to govern for the reason urged by Mr. Adams in favor of aristocracy. It is the declaration of the mass of national wealth, virtue and talents. Power, in Mr. Adams's opinion, ought to follow this mass in the hands of a few, because it is the ornament of society. It is unimportant whether an aristocracy is a natural, physical or moral effect, if its cause, by means, natural, physical or moral, may be lost or transferred. Whenever the mass of wealth, virtue and talents, is lost by a few and transferred to a great portion of a nation, an aristocracy no longer retains the only sanctions of its claim; and wherever these sanctions deposit themselves, they carry the inter-

woven power. By spreading themselves so generally throughout a nation, as to be no longer compressible into a legislative chamber, or inheritable by the aid of perpetuity and superstition, these ancient sanctions of aristocracy, become the modern sanctions of public opinion. And as its will (now the rightful sovereign upon the selfsame principle, urged in favor of the best founded aristocracy) can no longer be obtained through the medium of an hereditary order, the American invention of applying the doctrine of responsibility to magistrates, is the only one yet discovered for effecting the same object, which was effected by an aristocracy, holding the mass of national virtue, talents and wealth. This mass governed through such an aristocracy. This mass has searched for a new organ, as a medium for exercising the sovereignty, to which it is on all sides allowed to be entitled; and this medium is representation.

When the principles and practice of the American policy come to be considered, one subject of inquiry will be, whether public opinion, or the declaration of the mass of national virtue, talents and wealth, will be able to exercise this its just sovereignty, in union with the system of paper and patronage. If not, it is very remarkable, that this system, denominated the aristocracy of the third age, is equally inimical to Mr. Adams's principles and to mine. We both assign political power to the mass of virtue, talents and wealth in a nation. He only contends for an aristocracy from a supposition that it must possess this mass, and be the only organ of its will; I acknowledge the sovereignty of these qualities, deny their residence in a minority compressible into an aristocracy, and contend for a different organ. ■

From An Inquiry into the Principles and Policy of the Government of the United States, *1814.*

• JOHN ADAMS

I believe that none but Helvétius will affirm that all children are born with equal genius.

None will pretend that all are born of dispositions

exactly alike—of equal weight; equal strength; equal length; equal delicacy of nerves; equal elasticity of muscles; equal complexions; equal figure, grace, or beauty.

I have seen, in the Hospital of Foundlings, the "Enfants Trouvés," at Paris, fifty babes in one room —all under four days old; all in cradles alike, all nursed and attended alike; all dressed alike; all equally neat. I went from one end to the other of the whole row, and attentively observed all their countenances. And I never saw a greater variety, or more striking inequalities, in the streets of Paris or London. Some had every sign of grief, sorrow, and despair; others had joy and gaiety in their faces. Some were sinking in the arms of death; others looked as if they might live to fourscore. Some were as ugly and others as beautiful as children or adults ever are; these were stupid; those sensible. These were all born to equal rights, but to very different fortunes; to very different success and influence in life. . . .

-Will any man say, would Helvétius say, that all men are born equal in strength? Was Hercules no stronger than his neighbors? . . . Will Helvétius or Rousseau say that all men and women are born equal in beauty? . . . That all men are born to equal rights is true. Every being has a right to his own, as clear, as moral, as sacred, as any other being has . . . But to teach that all men are born with equal powers and faculties, to equal influence in society, to equal property and advantages through life, is as gross a fraud, as glaring an imposition on the credulity of the people, as ever was practiced by monks, by Druids, by Brahmins, by priests of the immortal Lama, or by the self-styled philosophers of the French Revolution. For honor's sake, Mr. Taylor, for truth and virtue's sake, let American philosophers and politicians despise it.

Mr. Adams leaves [to others] . . . all their acute speculations about fate, destiny, foreknowledge . . . and predestination . . . He has nothing to do with these interminable controversies. He considers men as free, moral, and accountable agents; and he takes men as God has made them. And will Mr. Taylor deny that God has made some men deaf and some blind, or will he affirm that these will infallibly have as much influence in society, and be able to procure as many votes as any who can see and hear? . . .

Take at random, or select with your utmost prudence, one hundred of your most faithful and capable domestics from your own numerous plantations, and make them a democratical republic. You will immediately perceive the same inequalities, and the same democratical republic, in a very few of the first sessions, transformed into an aristocratical republic; as complete and perfect an aristocracy as the senate of Rome, and much more so. Some will be beloved and followed, others hated and avoided by their fellows. . . .

I give you notice that whenever I use the word *aristocrat,* I mean a citizen who can command or govern two votes or more in society, whether by his virtues, his talents, his learning, his loquacity, his taciturnity, his frankness, his reserve, his face, figure, eloquence, grace, air, attitude, movements, wealth, birth, art, address, intrigue, good fellowship, drunkenness, debauchery, fraud, perjury, violence, treachery, pyrrhonism, deism, or atheism; for by every one of these instruments have votes been obtained and will be obtained. You seem to think aristocracy consists altogether in artificial titles, tinsel decorations of stars, garters, ribbons, golden eagles and golden fleeces, crosses and roses and lilies, exclusive privileges, hereditary descents, established by kings or by positive laws of society. No such thing! Aristocracy was, from the beginning, now is, and ever will be, world without end, independent of all these artificial regulations, as really and as efficaciously as with them!

Let me say a word more. Your democratical republic picked in the streets, and your democratical African republic, or your domestic republic, call it which you will, in its first session will become an aristocratical republic. In the second session it will become an oligarchical republic; because the seventy-four democrats and the twenty-six aristocrats will, by this time, discover that thirteen of the aristocrats can command four votes each; these thirteen will now command the majority, and, consequently, will be sovereign. The thirteen will then be an oligarchy. In the third session, it will be found that among these thirteen oligarchs there are seven, each of whom can command eight votes, equal in all to fifty-six, a decided majority. In the fourth session, it will be found that there are among these seven oligarchs four who can command thirteen votes apiece. The republic then becomes an oligarchy, whose sovereignty is in four individuals. In the fifth session, it will be discovered that two of the four can command six-and-twenty votes each. In the sixth session, there will be a sharp contention between the two which shall have the command of the fifty-two votes. Here will commence the squabble of Danton and Robespierre, of Julius and Pompey, of Anthony and Augustus, of the white rose and the red rose, of Jefferson and Adams, of Burr and Jefferson, of Clinton and Madison, or, if you will, of Napoleon and Alexander.

This, my dear sir, is the history of mankind, past, present, and to come. . . . ■

From letter to John Taylor, April 15, 1814, in reply to Taylor's An Inquiry into the Principles and Policy of the Government of the United States, *1814.*

5

THE PASSION FOR EQUALITY

Alexis de Tocqueville
Woodrow Wilson

• ALEXIS DE TOCQUEVILLE

It cannot be denied that democratic institutions have a very strong tendency to promote the feeling of envy in the human heart; not so much because they afford to every one the means of rising to the level of any of his fellow-citizens, as because those means perpetually disappoint the persons who employ them. Democratic institutions awaken and foster a passion for equality which they can never entirely satisfy. This complete equality eludes the grasp of the people at the very moment when it thinks to hold it fast, and "flies," as Pascal says, "with eternal flight"; the people are excited in the pursuit of an advantage, which is the more precious because it is not sufficiently remote to be unknown, or sufficiently near to be enjoyed. The lower orders are agitated by the chance of success, they are irritated by its uncertainty; and they pass from the enthusiasm of pursuit to the exhaustion of ill-success, and lastly to the acrimony of disappointment. Whatever transcends their own limits appears to be an obstacle to their desires, and there is no kind of superiority, however legitimate it may be, which is not irksome in their sight.

It has been supposed that the secret instinct, which leads the lower orders to remove their superiors as much as possible from the direction of public affairs, is peculiar to France. This, however, is an error; the propensity to which I allude is not inherent in any particular nation, but in democratic institutions in general; and although it may have been heightened by peculiar political circumstances, it owes its origin to a higher cause.

In the United States, the people are not disposed to hate the superior classes of society; but they are not very favorably inclined toward them, and they carefully exclude them from the exercise of authority. They do not entertain any dread of distinguished talents, but they are rarely captivated by them; and they award their approbation very sparingly to such as have risen without the popular support. ■

From Democracy in America, *Part I, Chapter 13, 1835.*

• ALEXIS DE TOCQUEVILLE

Everybody has remarked that in our time . . . this passion for equality is every day gaining ground in the human heart. It has been said a hundred times that our contemporaries are far more ardently and tenaciously attached to equality than to freedom. . . .

Although men cannot become absolutely equal unless they be entirely free, and consequently equality, pushed to its furthest extent, may be confounded with freedom, yet there is good reason for distinguishing the one from the other. The taste which men have for liberty, and that which they feel for equality, are, in fact, two different things; and I am not afraid to add that, among democratic nations, they are two unequal things. . . .

Freedom has appeared in the world at different times and under various forms; it has not been exclusively bound to any social condition, and it is not confined to democracies. Freedom cannot, therefore, form the distinguishing characteristic of democratic ages. The peculiar and preponderating fact which marks those ages as its own is the equality of conditions; the ruling passion of men in those periods is the love of this equality . . . Equality is the distinguishing characteristic of the age they live in; that, of itself, is enough to explain why they prefer it to all the rest.

But independently of this reason there are several others, which will at all times habitually lead men to prefer equality to freedom. . . .

Men . . . not only cling to equality because it is dear to them; they also adhere to it because they think it will last forever.

That political freedom, in its excesses, may compromise the tranquillity, the property, the lives of individuals, is obvious . . . But, on the contrary, none but attentive and clear-sighted men perceive the perils with which equality threatens us, and they commonly avoid pointing them out. They know that the calamities they fear are remote . . . The evils which freedom sometimes brings with it are immediate; they are apparent to all, and all are more or less affected by them. The evils which extreme equality may produce are disclosed slowly; they creep gradually into the social frame. . . .

Political liberty bestows exalted pleasures, from time to time, upon a certain number of citizens. Equality every day confers a number of small enjoyments on every man. The charms of equality are felt every instant, and are within the reach of all: the noblest hearts are not insensible to them, and the most vulgar souls exult in them. The passion which equality engenders must therefore be at once strong and general. Men cannot enjoy political liberty unpurchased by some sacrifices, and they never obtain it without great exertions. But the pleasures of equality are self-proffered; each of the petty incidents of life seems to occasion them, and in order to taste them nothing is required but to live. . . .

I think that democratic communities have a natural taste for freedom: left to themselves, they will seek it, cherish it, and view any privation of it with regret. But for equality, their passion is ardent, insatiable, incessant, invincible: they call for equality in freedom; if they cannot obtain that, they still call for equality in slavery. They will endure poverty, servitude, barbarism—but they will not endure aristocracy.

This is true at all times, and especially true in our own. All men and all powers seeking to cope with this irresistible passion, will be overthrown and destroyed by it. In our age, freedom cannot be established without it, and despotism itself cannot reign without its support. ∎

From Democracy in America, *Part II, Book 2, Chapter 1, 1835.*

• ALEXIS DE TOCQUEVILLE

The principle of equality, which makes men independent of each other, gives them a habit and a taste for following, in their private actions, no other guide but their own will. This complete independence, which they constantly enjoy toward their equals and in the intercourse of private life, tends to make them look upon all authority with a jealous eye, and speedily suggests to them the notion and the love of political freedom. Men living at such times have a natural bias to free institutions. . . .

Of all the political effects produced by the equality of conditions, this love of independence is the first to strike the observing, and to alarm the timid; nor can it be said that their alarm is wholly misplaced, for anarchy has a more formidable aspect in democratic countries than elsewhere . . . I am however persuaded that anarchy is not the principal evil which democratic ages have to fear, but the least. For the principle of equality begets two tendencies; the one leads men straight to independence, and may suddenly drive them into anarchy; the other leads them . . . to servitude. . . .

For myself, I am so far from urging as a reproach to the principle of equality that it renders men intractable, that this very circumstance calls forth my approbation. I admire the fact that it deposits in the mind and heart of man the dim conception and instinctive love of political independence, thus preparing the remedy for the evil which it engenders. ■

From Democracy in America, *Part II, Book 4, Chapter 1, 1835.*

• WOODROW WILSON

The principle of justice, the principle of right, the principle of international amity is this, that there is not only an imaginary but a real equality of standing and right among all the sovereign peoples of the world. I do not care to defend the rights of a people if I must regard them as my inferior, if I must do so with condescension, if I must do so because I am strong and they are weak. You know the men, and the women, too, I dare say, who are respectful only to those whom they regard as their social equals or their industrial equals and of whom they are more or less afraid, who will not exercise the same amenities and the same consideration for those whom they deem beneath them. Such people do not belong in democratic society, for one thing, and, for another, their whole point of view is perverted; they are incapable of justice, because the foundation of justice

is that the weakest has the same rights as the strongest. I must admit, my fellow citizens . . . with a certain profound regret not only but with a touch of shame—that while that is the theory of democratic institutions it is not always the practice. The weak do not always fare as well as the strong, the poor do not always get the same advantage of justice that the rich get; but that is due to the passions and imperfections of human nature. The foundation of the law, the glory of the law, is that the weakest is equal to the strongest in matter of right and privilege, and the goal to which we are constantly though stumblingly and with mistakes striving to go forward is the goal of actual equality, of actual justice, upon the basis of equality of rights. ■

From Address at San Diego, Cal., September 19, 1919.

PART IV

NEGROES AND EQUALITY

In the United States the ideas and ideals of equality and freedom were complicated by the existence of a special minority group. From the beginning of the American Republic, blacks have made up roughly 10 percent of the U.S. population.

The Negro question, as it arose with the full development of slavery, was made complex by doubts, which many whites expressed, about Negroes' inherent abilities. It was argued that a black skin implied natural inferiority. The question, therefore, was: How could presumably "inferior" people be fitted into a commonwealth based on equality and freedom?

Such questions did not die easily, even after Negroes were emancipated more than a century ago. In many parts of the country, not merely the South, blacks were systematically deprived of their rights and opportunities. In recent times science has dispelled the notion of "inherent" racial inferiority; it has also shown the evil effects of institutionalized prejudice. Hence the struggle for the rights of blacks and other minorities has begun to be successful. American opinion, embodied in national as well as state legislation, strengthens the steady movement in the direction of full citizenship for all minority groups.

1

NEGRO ABILITIES

Alexander Hamilton
Thomas Jefferson

• ALEXANDER HAMILTON

Colonel Laurens, who will have the honor of delivering you this letter, is on his way to South Carolina, on a project which I think, in the present situation of affairs there, is a very good one, and deserves every kind of support and encouragement. This is to raise two, three, or four battalions of Negroes. . . .

I have not the least doubt that the Negroes will make very excellent soldiers, with proper management. . . . It is a maxim of some great military judges, that, with sensible officers, soldiers can hardly be too stupid; and, on this principle, it is thought that the Russians would make the best soldiers in the world, if they were under other officers than their own . . . I mention this because I have frequently heard it objected to the scheme of embodying Negroes, that they are too stupid to make soldiers. This is so far from appearing to me a valid objection, that I think their want of cultivation (for their natural faculties are as good as ours), joined to that habit of subordination which they acquire from a life of servitude, will enable them sooner to become soldiers than our white inhabitants. . . .

I foresee that this project will have to combat much opposition from prejudice and self-interest. The contempt we have been taught to entertain for the blacks, makes us fancy many things that are founded neither in reason nor experience; and an unwillingness to part with property of so valuable a kind, will furnish a thousand arguments to show the impracticability, or pernicious tendency, of a scheme which requires such sacrifices. But it should be considered, that if we do not make use of them in this way, the enemy probably will . . . An essential part of the plan is to give them their freedom with their swords. This will secure their fidelity, animate their courage, and, I believe, will have a good influence upon those who remain, by opening a door to their emancipation. This circumstance, I confess, has no small weight in inducing me to wish the success of the project; for the dictates of humanity, and true policy, equally interest me in favor of this unfortunate class of men. ■

From letter to John Jay, President of Congress, March 14, 1779.

• THOMAS JEFFERSON

Comparing them [blacks] by their faculties of memory, reason, and imagination, it appears to me that in memory they are equal to the whites; in reason much inferior, as I think one could scarcely be found capable of tracing and comprehending the investigations of Euclid; and that in imagination they are dull, tasteless, and anomalous. It would be unfair to follow them to Africa for this investigation. We will consider them here, on the same stage with the whites, and where the facts are not apocryphal on which a judgment is to be formed. It will be right to make great allowances for the difference of condition, of education, of conversation, of the sphere in which they move. Many millions of them have been brought to, and born in America. Most of them, indeed, have been confined to tillage, to their own homes, and their own society; yet many have been so situated, that they might have availed themselves of the conversation of their masters; many have been brought up to the handicraft arts, and from that circumstance have always been associated with the whites. Some have been liberally educated, and all have lived in countries where the arts and sciences are cultivated to a considerable degree, and all have had before their eyes samples of the best works from abroad. The Indians, with no advantage of this kind, will often carve figures on their pipes not destitute of design and merit. They will crayon out an animal, a plant, or a country, so as to prove the existence of a germ in their minds which only wants cultivation. They astonish you with strokes of the most sublime oratory; such as prove their reason and sentiment strong, their imagination glowing and elevated. But never yet could I find that a black had uttered a thought above the level of plain narration; never saw even an elementary trait of painting or sculpture. In music they are more generally gifted than the whites with accurate ears for tune and time, and they have been found capable of imagining a small catch. Whether they will be equal to the composition of a more extensive run of melody, or of complicated harmony, is yet to be proved. Misery is often the parent of the most affecting touches in poetry. Among the blacks is misery enough, God knows, but no poetry. Love is the peculiar oestrum [gadfly] of the poet. Their love is ardent, but it kindles the senses only, not the imagination. Religion, indeed, has produced a Phyllis Whately; but it could not produce a poet. The compositions published under her name are below the dignity of criticism. . . .

We know that among the Romans, about the Augustan age especially, the condition of their slaves was much more deplorable than that of the blacks on the continent of America . . . Yet notwithstanding. . . discouraging circumstances among the Romans, their slaves were often their rarest artists. They excelled too in science, insomuch as to be usually employed as tutors to their master's children. Epictetus, Terence, and Phaedrus, were slaves. But they were of the race of whites. It is not their condition then, but nature, which has produced the distinction. Whether further observation will or will not verify the conjecture, that nature has been less bountiful to them in the endowments of the head, I believe that in those of the heart she will be found to have done them justice. That disposition to theft with which they have been branded, must be ascribed to their situation, and not to any depravity of the moral sense. The man in whose favor no laws of property exist, probably feels himself less bound to respect those made in favor of them. When arguing for ourselves, we lay it down as a fundamental, that laws, to be just, must give a reciprocation of right; that, without this, they are mere arbitrary rules of conduct, founded in force, and not conscience; and it is a problem which I give to the master to solve, whether the religious precepts against the violation of property were not framed for him as well as his slave? And whether the slave may not as justifiably take a little from one who has taken all from him, as he may slay one who would slay him? That a change in the relations in which a man is placed should change his ideas of moral right or wrong, is neither new, nor peculiar to the color of the blacks. Homer tells us it was so two thousand six hundred years ago. . . .

But the slaves of which Homer speaks were whites. Notwithstanding these considerations which must weaken their respect for the laws of property, we find among them numerous instances of the most rigid integrity, and as many as among their better instructed masters, of benevolence, gratitude, and unshaken fidelity. The opinion that they are inferior in the faculties of reason and imagination, must be hazarded with great diffidence. To justify a general conclusion, requires many observations, even where the subject may be submitted to the anatomical knife, to optical glasses, to analysis by fire or by solvents. How much more then where it is a faculty, not a substance, we are examining; where it eludes the research of all the senses; where the conditions of its existence are various and variously combined; where the effects of those which are present or absent bid defiance to calculation; let me add too, as a circumstance of great tenderness, where our conclusion would degrade a whole race of men from the rank in the scale of beings which their Creator may perhaps have given them. To our reproach it must be said, that though for a century and a half we have had under our eyes the races of black and of red men, they have never yet been viewed by us as subjects of natural history. I advance it, therefore, as a suspicion only, that the blacks, whether originally a distinct race, or made distinct by time and circumstances, are inferior to the whites in the endowments both of body and mind. It is not against experience to suppose that different species of the same genus, or varieties of the same species, may possess different qualifications. . . . This unfortunate difference of color, and perhaps of faculty, is a powerful obstacle to the emancipation of these people. Many of their advocates, while they wish to vindicate the liberty of human nature, are anxious also to preserve its dignity and beauty. Some of these, embarassed by the question, "What further is to be done with them?" join themselves in opposition with those who are actuated by sordid avarice only. Among the Romans emancipation required but one effort. The slave, when made free, might mix with, without staining the blood of his master. But with us a second is necessary, unknown to history. When freed, he is to be removed beyond the reach of mixture. ■

From Notes on Virginia,
Query XIV, 1782.

• THOMAS JEFFERSON

I have received . . . your . . . volume on the "Literature of Negroes."[1] Be assured that no person living wishes more sincerely than I do, to see a complete refutation of the doubts I have myself entertained and expressed on the grade of understanding allotted to them by nature, and to find that in this respect they are on a par with ourselves. My doubts were the result of personal observation in the limited sphere of my own state, where the opportunities for the development of their genius were not favorable, and those of exercising it still less so. I expressed them therefore with great hesitation; but whatever be their degree of talent it is no measure of their rights. Because Sir Isaac Newton was superior to others in understanding, he was not therefore lord of the person or property of others. On this subject they are gaining daily in the opinions of nations, and hopeful advances are making towards their re-establishment of an equal footing with the other colors of the human family. I pray you therefore to accept my thanks for the many instances you have enabled me to observe of the respectable intelligence in that race of men,[2] which cannot fail to have effect in hastening the day of their relief. ■

*From letter to Henri Grégoire, February 25,
1809.*

---

[1] By Henri Grégoire (1750–1831), a French Revolutionist and bishop who was interested in the emancipation of Negroes and who introduced a motion in the French Constituent Assembly to give them equal rights.

[2] Jefferson expressed a similar sentiment in his letter to the Marquis de Condorcet, August 30, 1791, when he sent him an Almanac composed by Benjamin Banneker, an American Negro: "I am happy to be able to inform you that we have now in the United States a negro, the son of a black man born in Africa, and of a black woman born in the United States, who is a very respectable mathematician . . . I have seen very elegant solutions of Geometrical problems by him. Add to this that he is a very worthy & respectable member of society. He is a free man. I shall be delighted to see these instances of moral eminence so multiplied as to prove that the want of talents observed in them is merely the effect of their degraded condition, and not proceeding from any difference in the structure of the parts on which intellect depends."

$\overline{2}$

SLAVERY

Thomas Jefferson
William Ellery Channing
Abraham Lincoln

• THOMAS JEFFERSON

Dear Sir:

Your favor of July 31 was duly received, and was read with peculiar pleasure. The sentiments breathed through the whole do honor to both the head and heart of the writer. Mine on the subject of slavery of Negroes have long since been in possession of the public, and time has only served to give them stronger root. The love of justice and the love of country plead equally the cause of these people, and it is a moral reproach to us that they should have pleaded it so long in vain, and should have produced not a single effort, nay I fear not much serious willingness to relieve them & ourselves from our present condition of moral & political reprobation. From those of the former generation who were in the fullness of age when I came into public life, which was while our controversy with England was on paper only, I soon saw that nothing was to be hoped. Nursed and educated in the daily habit of seeing the degraded condition, both bodily and mental, of those unfortunate beings, not reflecting that that degradation was very much the work of themselves & their fathers, few minds have yet doubted but that they were as legitimate subjects of property as their horses and cattle. The quiet and monotonous course of colonial life has been disturbed by no alarm, and little reflection on the value of liberty. And when alarm was taken at an enterprise on their own, it was not easy to carry them to the whole length of the principles which they invoked for themselves. In the first or second session of the Legislature after I became a member, I drew to this subject the attention of Col. Bland, one of the oldest, ablest, & most respected members, and he undertook to move for certain moderate extensions of the protection of the laws to these people. I seconded his motion, and, as a younger member, was more spared in the debate; but he was denounced as an enemy of his country, & was treated with the grossest indecorum. From an early stage of our revolution other & more distant duties were assigned to me, so that from that time till my return from Europe in 1789, and I may say till I returned to reside at home in 1809, I had little opportunity of knowing the progress of public sentiment here on this subject. I had always hoped that the younger generation receiving their early impressions after the flame of liberty had been kindled in every breast . . . would have sympathized with oppression wherever found, and proved their love of liberty beyond their own share of it. But my intercourse with them, since my return has not been sufficient to ascertain that they had made towards this point the progress I had hoped. Your solitary but welcome voice is the first which has brought this sound to my ear; and I have considered the general silence which prevails on this subject as indicating an apathy unfavorable to every hope. Yet the hour of emancipation is advancing, in the march of time. It will come; and whether brought on by the generous energy of our own minds; or by the bloody process of St. Domingo . . . is a leaf of our history not yet turned over. As to the method by which this difficult work is to be effected, if permitted to be done by ourselves, I have seen no proposition so expedient on the whole, as that of emancipation of those born after a given day, and of their education and expatriation after a given age. This would give time for a gradual extinction of that species of labor and substitution of another, and lessen the severity of the shock which an operation so fundamental cannot fail to produce. For men probably of any color, but of this color we know, brought up from their infancy without necessity for thought or forecast, are by their habits rendered as incapable as children of taking care of themselves, and are extinguished promptly wherever industry is necessary for raising young. In the meantime they are pests in society by their idleness, and the depredations to which this leads them. Their amalgamation with the other color produces a degradation to which no lover of his country, no lover of excellence in the human character can innocently consent. I am sensible of the partialities with which you have looked towards me as the person who should undertake this salutary but arduous work. But this, my dear sir, is like bidding old Priam to buckle the armor of Hector *"trementibus aequo humeris et*

inutile ferruncingi." No, I have overlived the generation with which mutual labors & perils begat mutual confidence and influence. This enterprise is for the young; for those who can follow it up, and bear it through to its consummation. It shall have all my prayers, & these are the only weapons of an old man. But in the meantime are you right in abandoning this property, and your country with it? I think not. My opinion has ever been that, until more can be done for them, we should endeavor, with those whom fortune has thrown on our hands, to feed and clothe them well, protect them from all ill usage, require such reasonable labor only as is performed voluntarily by freemen, & be led by no repugnancies to abdicate them, and our duties to them. The laws do not permit us to turn them loose, if that were for their good: and to commute them for other property is to commit them to those whose usage of them we cannot control. I hope then, my dear sir, you will reconcile yourself to your country and its unfortunate condition; that you will not lessen its stock of sound disposition by withdrawing your portion from the mass. That, on the contrary you will come forward in the public councils, become the missionary of this doctrine truly Christian; insinuate & inculcate it softly but steadily, through the medium of writing and conversation associate other in your labors, and when the phalanx is formed, bring on and press the proposition perseveringly until its accomplishment. It is an encouraging observation that no good measure was ever proposed, which, if duly pursued, failed to prevail in the end. We have proof of this in the history of the endeavors of the English Parliament to suppress that very trade (slave trade) which brought this evil on us. And you will be supported by the religious precept, "be not weary in well-doing." That your success may be as speedy & complete, as it will be honorable & immortal consolation to yourself, I shall as fervently and sincerely pray as I assure you of my great friendship and respect. ■

From letter to Edward Coles, August 25, 1814.

• WILLIAM ELLERY CHANNING

Free institutions rest on two great political virtues, the love of liberty and the love of order. The slaveholder (I mean the slaveholder by choice) is of necessity more or less wanting in both. How plain is it, that no man can love liberty with a true love, who has the heart to wrest it from others! Attachment to freedom does not consist in spurning indignantly a yoke prepared for our own necks; for this is done even by the savage and the beast of prey. It is a moral sentiment, an impartial desire and choice, that others as well as ourselves may be protected from every wrong, may be exempted from every unjust restraint. Slaveholding . . . is at open war with this generous principle. It is a plain, habitual contempt of human rights, and of course impairs that sense of their sanctity, which is their best protection. It offers, every day and hour, a precedent of usurpation to the ambitious. It creates a caste with despotic powers; and under such guardians is liberty peculiarly secure? It creates a burning zeal for the rights of a privileged class, but not for the Rights of Men. These the voluntary slaveholder casts down by force; and, in the changes of human affairs, the time may not be distant when he will learn, that force, accustomed to triumph over right, is prone to leap every bound, and to make the proud as well as abject stoop to its sway.

Slavery is also hostile to the love of order, which, in union with the love of liberty, is the great support of free institutions. Slaveholding in a republic tends directly to lawlessness. It gives the habit of command, not of obedience. The absolute master is not likely to distinguish himself by subjection to the civil power. The substitution of passion and self-will for law, is nowhere so common as in the slave-holding states.[1] In these it is thought honorable to rely on one's own arm, rather than on the magistrate,

[1] A similar point was made by Thomas Jefferson in his *Notes on Virginia* (1782): "The whole commerce between master and slave is a perpetual exercise of the most boisterous passions, the most unremitting despotism on the one part, and degrading submissions on the other. Our children see this, and learn to imitate it . . . The parent storms, the child looks on, catches the lineaments of wrath, puts on the same airs in the circle of smaller slaves, gives a loose to the worst of passions, and thus nursed, educated, and daily exercised in tyranny, cannot but be stamped by it with odious peculiarities."

for the defence of many rights. In some, perhaps many, districts, the chief peace officer seems to be the weapon worn as part of the common dress; and the multitude seem to be more awed by one another's passions, than by the authority of the state. Such communities have no pledge of stable liberty. Reverence for the laws, as manifestations of the public will, is the very spirit of free institutions. Does this spirit find its best nutriment in the habits and feelings generated by slavery?

Slavery is a strange element to mix with free institutions. It cannot but endanger them. It is a pattern for every kind of wrong. The slave brings insecurity on the free. Whoever holds one human being in bondage, invites others to plant the foot on his own neck. Thanks to God, not one human being can be wronged with impunity. The liberties of a people ought to tremble, until every man is free. . . .

I have endeavored, in these remarks, to show the hostility between slavery and free institutions. If, however, I err, if these institutions cannot stand without slavery for their foundation, then I say, Let them fall. Then they ought to be buried in perpetual ruins. Then the name of republicanism ought to become a by-word and reproach among the nations. Then monarchy, limited as it is in England, is incomparably better and happier than our more popular forms. Then despotism, as it exists in Prussia, where equal laws are in the main administered with impartiality, ought to be preferred. A republican government, bought by the sacrifice of half or more than half of a people, by stripping them of their most sacred rights, by degrading them to a brutal condition, would cost too much. A freedom so tainted with wrong ought to be an abhorrence. . . . ■

From Slavery, *Chapter 4, 1841.*

• ABRAHAM LINCOLN

If A can prove, however conclusively, that he may of right enslave B, why may not B snatch the same argument and prove equally that he may enslave A? You say A is white and B is black. It is color, then; the lighter having the right to enslave the darker? Take care. By this rule you are to be slave to the first man you meet with a fairer skin than your own.

You do not mean color exactly? You mean the whites are intellectually the superiors of the blacks, and therefore have the right to enslave them? Take care again. By this rule you are to be slave to the first man you meet with an intellect superior to your own.

But, say you, it is a question of interest, and if you make it your interest you have the right to enslave another. Very well. And if he can make it his interest he has the right to enslave you. ◼

From "A Fragment on Slavery," July, 1854.

● ABRAHAM LINCOLN

On the occasion corresponding to this four years ago all thoughts were anxiously directed to an impending civil war. All dreaded it, all sought to avert it. . . . Both parties deprecated war, but one of them would *make* war rather than let the nation survive, and the other would *accept* war rather than let it perish, and the war came.

One-eighth of the whole population were colored slaves, not distributed generally over the Union, but localized in the southern part of it. These slaves constituted a peculiar and powerful interest. All knew that this interest was somehow the cause of the war. To strengthen, perpetuate, and extend this interest was the object for which the insurgents would rend the Union forever by war, while the Government claimed no right to do more than to restrict the territorial enlargement of it. Neither party expected for the war the magnitude or the duration which it has already attained. Neither anticipated that the *cause* of the conflict might cease with or even before the conflict itself should cease. Each looked for an easier triumph, and a result less fundamental and astounding. Both read the same Bible and pray to the same God, and each invokes His aid against the other. It may seem strange that any men should dare to ask a just God's

assistance in wringing their bread from the sweat of other men's faces, but let us judge not, that we be not judged. The prayers of both could not be answered. That of neither has been answered fully. The Almighty has his own purposes. "Woe unto the world because of offenses; for it must needs be that offenses come, but woe to that man by whom the offense cometh." If we shall suppose that American slavery is one of those offenses which, in the providence of God, must needs come, but which, having continued through His appointed time, He now wills to remove, and that He gives to both North and South this terrible war as the woe due to those by whom the offense came, shall we discern therein any departure from those divine attributes which the believers in a living God always ascribe to Him? Fondly do we hope, fervently do we pray, that this mighty scourge of war may speedily pass away. Yet, if God wills that it continue until all the wealth piled by the bondsman's two hundred and fifty years of unrequited toil shall be sunk, and until every drop of blood drawn with the lash shall be paid by another drawn with the sword, as was said three thousand years ago, so still it must be said "the judgments of the Lord are true and righteous altogether."

With malice toward none, with charity for all, with firmness in the right as God gives us to see the right, let us strive on to finish the work we are in, to bind up the nation's wounds, to care for him who shall have borne the battle and for his widow and his orphan, to do all which may achieve and cherish a just and lasting peace among ourselves and with all nations. ◼

From Second Inaugural Address, March 4, 1865.

3

RIGHTS

Mr. Townshend
Abraham Lincoln
James A. Garfield
William Howard Taft

• MR. TOWNSHEND

I am opposed, Mr. President to the insertion of the word *white*[1] in this Report. The first reason I have to offer for my opposition is the belief that the intended restriction of the right of suffrage is *unjust.*

Sir, I not only say, but I believe that "*all* men are created equal," that is they are equally endowed by their Creator with certain inherent rights. These rights are essential to our existence, they spring from the necessitites of our being. In order to live we must have a place somewhere, we must have air and food, and each of these and every other necessity imposed on us by our maker, involves a corresponding right whether it pertain to our physical or to our intellectual or moral nature. Some of our rights grow directly out of the relations we sustain, such as husbands or fathers, &, each of these relations imposing certain obligations or duties, and these involving corresponding rights. All men have by nature the same necessities, and may sustain the same or equal relations, consequently all men must have the same natural rights. For the protection of these natural rights governments are instituted among men, and this single purpose of protection is the only legitimate function of government. All the human governments on earth cannot create a right, nor can they take a right away, and the idea that man on entering into jural or civil relations with these, surrenders any part of his natural rights, is only one of the grand but mischievous blunders of the past. Human governments derive all their just authority from the consent of the governed; all persons have the same rights to protect, and are therefore equally interested, and equally entitled to share as principals in government, and the consent of one person is just as necessary as the consent of another person, in order to constitute just authority.

[1] The Ohio Constitutional Convention of 1850–1851 adopted the following article concerning the suffrage (Article V, Sect. 1): "Every white male citizen of the United States, of the age of twenty-one years, who shall have been a resident of the State one year next preceding the election, and of the county, township, or ward, in which he resides, such time as may be provided by law, shall have the qualifications of an elector, and be entitled to vote at all elections." Townshend's speech is a protest by a radical democrat against the inclusion of the word *white,* which meant disfranchisement of Negroes.

To attempt to govern men without seeking their consent is usurpation and tyranny, whether in Ohio or in Austria. There is a portion of the people of this State who have the same right to stand upon this part of God's earth, and to breathe this free air, that you or I have, and yet you seek to impose a government upon them without consulting them. I can only say that they are under no obligation to obey your laws or to submit to your authority. You burthen them with taxation without representation, and thus inflict upon them the identical wrong for which the thirteen United Colonies threw off the yoke of the mother country. To establish a government over them, not based on their consent; to subject them to laws they have had no voice in framing; to tax them while you deny them representation is clearly and manifestly unjust; and I might stop here without urging any further objections to the Report, for with governments there should be really but one enquiry, what is just?

Another objection I have to this limitation of the right of suffrage, I believe it is antidemocratic. I desire to speak on this point with becoming modesty, for I am but a young man, while I see around me many whose hair has grown gray in the study of democratic principles. One of these gentlemen has said with Jefferson that democracy consists in doing "equal and exact justice to all men," another gentleman has said that democracy concedes to others all it demands for itself, and demands for itself all it concedes to others. If the restriction of the elective franchise is tested by either of these rules it will be found antidemocratic. To justify the practice the report recommends, Jefferson's rule should be amended so as to read "equal and exact justice to all white men—or to all men except negroes." If I understand genuine democracy it is neither more nor less than the golden rule of Christianity applied to politics, or to our civil relations—that is doing unto others as we would have others to do unto us, and I see no reason why democracy is not like Christianity, comprehensive enough to embrace the whole family of man. I was looking the other day, Mr. President, into Noah Webster's Dictionary for the meaning of democracy, and I found as I ex-

pected that he defines a democrat to be "one who favors universal suffrage." Now some of our friends here have been busy of late in reading out of the democratic party all who did not come up to their standard of democracy. If they were justified in that proceeding I suppose I shall be equally justified in reading them out if they do not come up to this, the true authoritative standard. I should regret to do it, for some of these gentlemen consider themselves pretty good democrats, although in this particular, they are, as I think, behind the times. Nothing is clearer than that genuine democracy must ever be progressive. The rule "equal and exact justice to all men," perhaps, can never be amended, but in its application our measures will change from year to year. The evils and abuses to which this rule was first applied, have now, many of them, passed away, but every succeeding age develops abuses requiring new applications of the same rule, and he only is a genuine democrat who faithfully applies this good democratic rule to any new species of abuse or injustice that appears, and not he who having used it once or twice throws it away and uses it no further. I believe it to be our duty here to erect a civil platform upon which the foot of every person in the State may stand and on exactly the same level. I have not intentionally given in this body, one vote, nor do I intend to give one vote, to place any man, or set of men, above the common level. I will vote for no franchise, if by that is meant a something which makes one man free to do what may not be done by others. I will vote for no privilege, if by that is meant a private law for the benefit of the few over the many. I will vote for no charters, because I will not by my vote, give to a part by a special grant, what belongs alike to all, and none of these things have any sacredness for me, I will not give the benefit of my vote. I will not give the benefit of holy rood to any hoary abuse, but right the wrong wherever given. But sir, the same sense of justice, which will not permit me to place another man's foot higher than my own, will also prevent me from consenting to place any man a hair's breadth below the common level. If the government of Ohio is to be in the hands of a privileged class, whether that class be large or small, it will be an aristocracy, a form of government for which I have no partiality; this government ought to be democratic—*a government shared by all,* for the *good of all.* Let us then have no limitations of suffrage—for who does not know that all such limitations are antidemocratic?

Another reason for opposing this restriction of what is called the elective franchise, I believe it is impolitic.

We have already stated that the true function *of government* is to protect *rights,* or in other words, to *prevent wrongs.* Experience has taught us that ignorance is one of the most fruitful sources of crime, and it has therefore been found to be good policy to secure the education of the whole people, as a means of preventing crime, which it does at less expense and more effectually than all the jails or penitentiaries, or scaffolds, that were ever erected. I was surprised, when we were considering the subject of education, to hear some gentleman propose to exclude the children of colored persons from the benefits of our common school system. Surely, after what we know of the good influences of education, to provide for keeping one class of our inhabitants in ignorance, would be most miserable policy. But it is not enough that all should have the means of education; we ought to give to all the inhabitants of the State the full benefit of the powerful stimulus of hope and ambition. Let no man feel that the law which ought to be his protector, interposes a barrier to his progress, by saying to him, "thus far shalt thou come, but no farther." Rather let us offer the strongest inducements to the intellectual and moral elevation of every person, of whatever class or condition, by opening the race and offering every prize of wealth, or honor, or usefulness, alike to all. If, on the other hand, we make it impossible for any class of our people to rise—if we consign them to ignorance, and want, and degradation, we ought to consider ourselves responsible for whatever invasion of our rights may be the consequence; we shall reap exactly what we sow. To my view, the political degradation of any portion of our people is in the highest degree impolitic.

I object also to inserting the word *white,* because

for the purpose employed, it is indefinite and ambiguous, and therefore improper.... ■

From Report of the Debates and Proceedings of the Convention for the Revision of the Constitution of the State of Ohio, 1850–51, *Part II, 1851.*

• ABRAHAM LINCOLN

He [Stephen A. Douglas] finds the Republicans insisting that the Declaration of Independence includes *all* men, black as well as white; and forthwith he boldly denies that it includes Negroes at all, and proceeds to argue gravely that all who contend it does, do so only because they want to vote, and eat, and sleep, and marry with Negroes! . . . Now I protest against the counterfeit logic which concludes that because I do not want a black woman for a slave, I must necessarily want her for a wife. I need not have her for either. I can just leave her alone. In some respects she certainly is not my equal; but in her natural right to eat the bread she earns with her own hands without asking leave of anyone else, she is my equal, and the equal of all others.

Chief Justice Taney, in his opinion in the Dred Scott case, admits that the language of the Declaration [of Independence] is broad enough to include the whole human family; but he and Judge Douglas argue that the authors of that instrument did not intend to include Negroes, by the fact that they did not at once actually place them on an equality with whites. Now this grave argument comes to just nothing at all, by the other fact that they did not at once, nor ever afterward, actually place all white people on an equality with one another. And this is the staple argument of both the Chief Justice and the Senator, for doing this obvious violence to the plain, unmistakable language of the Declaration.

I think the authors of that notable instrument intended to include *all* men, but did not intend to declare all men equal *in all respects.* They did not mean to say that all were equal in color, size, intellect, moral developments, or social capacity. They defined with tolerable distinctness in what respects they did consider all men created equal—equal with "certain inalienable rights, among which are life, liberty, and the pursuit of happiness." This they said, and this they meant. They did not mean to assert the obvious untruth that all were then actually enjoying that equality, nor yet that they were about to confer it immediately upon them. In fact, they had no power to confer such a boon. They meant simply to declare the right, so that the enforcement of it might follow as fast as circumstances should permit.

They meant to set up a standard maxim for free society, which should be familiar to all and revered by all—constantly looked to, constantly labored for, and, even though never perfectly attained, constantly approximated, and thereby constantly spreading and deepening its influence, and augmenting the happiness and value of life to all people of all colors everywhere. The assertion that "all men are created equal," was of no practical use in effecting our separation from Great Britain; and it was placed in the Declaration, not for that, but for future use. Its authors meant it to be as, thank God, it is now proving itself, a stumbling-block to all those who in after times might seeks to turn a free people into the hateful paths of despotism. They knew the proneness of prosperity to breed tyrants, and they meant, when such should reappear in this fair land . . . that they should find . . . at least one hard nut to crack. ∎

From speech in Springfield, Ill., June 26, 1857.

• ABRAHAM LINCOLN

Those arguments that are made, that the inferior race are to be treated with as much allowance as they are capable of enjoying; that as much is to be done for them as their condition will allow—what are these arguments? They are the arguments that kings have made for enslaving the people in all ages of the world. You will find that all the arguments in favor of kingcraft were of this class; they always bestrode the necks of the people—not that they wanted to do it, but because the people were better off for being ridden. That is their argument, and

this argument of the Judge [Stephen A. Douglas] is the same old serpent that says, You work and I eat, you toil and I will enjoy the fruits of it. Turn in whatever way you will—whether it come from the mouth of a king, an excuse for enslaving the people of his country, or from the mouth of men of another race, it is all the same old serpent, and I hold if that course of argumentation that is made for the purpose of convincing the public mind that we should not care about this should be granted, it does not stop with the Negro. I should like to know, taking this old Declaration of Independence, which declares that all men are equal upon principle, and making exceptions to it—where will it stop? If one man says it does not mean a Negro, why not another say it does not mean some other man? If that Declaration is not the truth, let us get the statute book in which we find it, and tear it out! Who is so bold as to do it? If it is not true, let us tear it out [cries of "No," "No"]. Let us stick to it, then; let us stick firmly by it, then. . . .

My friends, I have detained you about as long as I desired to do, and I have only to say, let us discard all this quibbling about this man and the other man, this race and that race and the other race being inferior, and therefore they must be placed in an inferior position. Let us discard all these things, and unite as one people throughout this land, until we shall once more stand up declaring that all men are created equal. ∎

From speech in Chicago, Ill., July 10, 1858.

• JAMES A. GARFIELD

The free enjoyment of equal suffrage is still in question, and a frank statement of the issue may aid its solution. It is alleged that in many communities Negro citizens are practically denied the freedom of the ballot. In so far as the truth of this allegation is admitted, it is answered that in many places honest local government is impossible if the mass of uneducated Negroes are allowed to vote. These are grave allegations. So far as the latter is true, it is the only palliation that can be offered for opposing the freedom of the ballot. Bad local government is certainly a great evil, which ought to be prevented; but to violate the freedom and sanctities of suffrage is more than an evil. It is a crime which, if persisted in, will destroy the Government itself. Suicide is not a remedy. If in other lands it be high treason to compass the death of the king, it shall be counted no less a crime here to strangle our sovereign power and stifle its voice. . . .

The danger which arises from ignorance in the voter cannot be denied. It covers a field far wider than that of Negro suffrage and the present condition of the race. It is a danger that lurks and hides in the sources and fountains of power in every state. We have no standard by which to measure the disaster that may be brought upon us by ignorance and vice in the citizens when joined to corruption and fraud in the suffrage.

The voters of the Union, who make and unmake constitutions, and upon whose will hang the destinies of our governments, can transmit their supreme authority to no successors save the coming generation of voters, who are the sole heirs of sovereign power. If that generation comes to its inheritance blinded by ignorance and corrupted by vice, the fall of the Republic will be certain and remedyless. . . .

It is the high privilege and sacred duty of those now living to educate their successors and fit them, by intelligence and virture, for the inheritance which awaits them.

In this beneficent work sections and races should be forgotten and partisanship should be unknown. Let our people find a new meaning in the divine oracle which declares that "a little child shall lead them" for our own little children will soon control the destinies of the Republic. ■

From Inaugural Address, March 4, 1881.

• WILLIAM HOWARD TAFT

The Negroes are now Americans. Their ancestors came here years ago against their will, and this is their only country and their only flag. They have shown themselves anxious to live for it and to die for it. Encountering the race feeling against them, subjected at times to cruel injustice growing out of it, they may well have our profound sympathy and aid in the struggle they are making. We are charged with the sacred duty of making their path as smooth and easy as we can. Any recognition of their distinguished men, any appointment to office from among their number, is properly taken as an encouragement and an appreciation of their progress, and this just policy should be pursued when suitable occasion offers.

But it may well admit of doubt whether, in the case of any race, an appointment of one of their number to a local office in a community in which the race feeling is so widespread and acute as to interfere with the ease and facility with which the local government business can be done by the appointee is of sufficient benefit by way of encouragement to the race to outweigh the recurrence and increase of race feeling which such an appointment is likely to engender. Therefore the Executive, in recognizing the Negro race by appointments, must exercise a careful discretion not thereby to do it more harm than good. On the other hand, we must be careful not to encourage the mere pretense of race feeling manufactured in the interest of individual political ambition.

Personally, I have not the slightest race prejudice or feeling, and recognition of its existence only awakens in my heart a deeper sympathy for those who have to bear it or suffer from it, and I question the wisdom of a policy which is likely to increase it. Meantime, if nothing is done to prevent it, a better feeling between the Negroes and the whites in the South will continue to grow, and more and more of the white people will come to realize that the future of the South is to be much benefited by the industrial and intellectual progress of the Negro. The exercise of political franchises by those of this race will be acquiesced in, and the right to vote will be withheld only from the ignorant and irresponsible of both races. ■

From Inaugural Address, March 4, 1909.

4
THE SUPREME COURT ON NEGRO RIGHTS

• EDITOR'S NOTE

The systematic and widely institutionalized segregation of Negroes, particularly in the South, was given constitutional sanction in the famous "separate but equal" doctrine which the Supreme Court enunciated in *Plessy* v. *Ferguson* in 1896. This doctrine, based on the assumption that the law could not change the fact that Negroes and white were racially different, interpreted the Fourteenth Amendment to mean that States could practice segregation so long as they provided "equal" facilities (schools and transportation, for example) to each race. The *Plessy* v. *Ferguson* opinion, given below, was overthrown half a century later, in *Brown* v. *Board of Education.*[1]

• JUSTICE HENRY B. BROWN

This case turns upon the constitutionality of an act of the General Assembly of the State of Louisiana, passed in 1890, providing for separate railway carriages for the white and colored races. . . .

The first section of the statute enacts "that all railway companies carrying passengers in their coaches in this State, shall provide equal but separate accommodations for the white, and colored races, by providing two or more passenger coaches for each passenger train, or by dividing the passenger coaches by a partition so as to secure separate accommodations: *Provided.* That this section shall not be construed to apply to street railroads. No person or persons, shall be admitted to occupy seats in coaches, other than, the ones assigned, to them on account of the race they belong to."

By the second section it was enacted "that the officers of such passenger trains shall have power and are hereby required to assign each passenger to the coach or compartment used for the race to which such passenger belongs; any passenger insisting on going into a coach or compartment to which by race he does not belong, shall be liable to a fine of twenty-five dollars, or in lieu thereof to imprisonment for a period of not more than

[1] See page 97.

twenty days in the parish prison, and any officer of any railroad insisting on assigning a passenger to a coach or compartment other than the one set aside for the race to which said passenger belongs, shall be liable to a fine of twenty-five dollars, or in lieu thereof to imprisonment for a period of not more than twenty days in the parish prison; and should any passenger refuse to occupy the coach or compartment to which he or she is assigned by the officer of such railway, said officer shall have power to refuse to carry such passenger on his train, and for such refusal neither he nor the railway company which he represents shall be liable for damages in any of the courts of this State."

The third section provides penalties for the refusal or neglect of the officers, directors, conductors and employes of railway companies to comply with the act, with a proviso that "nothing in this act shall be construed as applying to nurses attending children of the other race." The fourth section is immaterial.

The information filed in the criminal District Court charged in substance that Plessy, being a passenger between two stations within the State of Louisiana, was assigned by officers of the company to the coach used for the race to which he belonged, but he insisted upon going into a coach used by the race to which he did not belong. Neither in the information nor plea was his particular race or color averred.

The petition for the writ of prohibition averred that petitioner was seven eights Caucasian and one eighth African blood; that the mixture of colored blood was not discernible in him, and that he was entitled to every right, privilege and immunity secured to citizens of the United States of the white race; and that, upon such theory, he took possession of a vacant seat in a coach where passengers of the white race were accommodated, and was ordered by the conductor to vacate said coach and take a seat in another assigned to persons of the colored race, and having refused to comply with such demand he was forcibly ejected with the aid of a police officer, and imprisoned in the parish jail to answer a charge of having violated the above act.

The constitutionality of this act is attacked upon the ground that it conflicts both with the Thirteenth Amendment of the Constitution, abolishing slavery, and the Fourteenth Amendment, which prohibits certain restrictive legislation on the part of the States. . . .

The object of the amendment was undoubtedly to enforce the absolute equality of the two races before the law, but in the nature of things it could not have been intended to abolish distinctions based upon color, or to enforce social, as distinguished from political equality, or a commingling of the two races upon terms satisfactory to either. Laws permitting, and even requiring, their separation in places where they are liable to be brought into contact do not necessarily imply the inferiority of either race to the other, and have been generally, if not universally recognized as within the competency of the State legislatures in the exercise of their police power. The most common instance of this is connected with the establishment of separate schools for white and colored children, which has been held to be a valid exercise of the legislative power even by courts of States where the political rights of the colored race have been longest and most earnestly enforced. . . .

So far, then, as a conflict with the Fourteenth Amendment is concerned, the case reduces itself to the question whether the statute of Louisiana is a reasonable regulation, and with respect to this there must necessarily be a large discretion on the part of the legislature. In determining the question of reasonableness it is at liberty to act with reference to the established usages, customs and traditions of the people, and with a view to the promotion of their comfort, and the preservation of the public peace and good order. Gauged by this standard, we cannot say that a law which authorizes or even requires the separation of the two races in public conveyances is unreasonable, or more obnoxious to the Fourteenth Amendment than the acts of Congress requiring separate schools for colored children in the District of Columbia, the constitutionality of which does not seem to have been questioned, or the corresponding acts of State legislatures.

We consider the underlying fallacy of the plaintiff's argument to consist in the assumption that the enforced separation of the two races stamps the colored race with a badge of inferiority. If this be so, it is not by reason of anything found in the act, but solely because the colored race chooses to put that construction upon it. The argument necessarily assumes that if, as has been more than once the case, and is not unlikely to be so again, the colored race should become the dominant power in the State legislature, and should enact a law in precisely similar terms, it would thereby relegate the white race to an inferior position. We imagine that the white race, at least, would not acquiesce in this assumption. The argument also assumes that social prejudices may be overcome by legislation, and that equal rights cannot be secured to the Negro except by an enforced commingling of the two races. We cannot accept this proposition. If the two races are to meet upon terms of social equality, it must be the result of natural affinities, a mutual appreciation of each other's merits and a voluntary consent of individuals . . . Legislation is powerless to eradicate racial instincts or to abolish distinctions based upon physical differences, and the attempt to do so can only result in accentuating the difficulties of the present situation. If the civil and political rights of both races be equal one cannot be inferior to the other civilly or politically. If one race be inferior to the other socially, the Constitution of the United States cannot put them upon the same plane.

The judgment of the court below is, therefore, *affirmed.* ■

From Opinion of the Court, Plessy *v.* Ferguson, *1896.*

• EDITOR'S NOTE

P*lessy* v. *Ferguson* undoubtedly perpetuated the existing disabilities from which Negroes suffered in the United States. The "separate but equal" idea in practice always meant "separate" but rarely "equal." Discrimination against Negroes was widely entrenched, legally enforced by state and local legislation. It was not until the 1930s that the "equal pro-

tection" clause of the Fourteenth Amendment began to be invoked in cases involving Negro discrimination. In 1938, for example, in the case of Missouri, ex rel. *Gaines* v. *Canada,* the Court upheld the "equal" aspect of the doctrine by declaring that a Negro had the right to claim a legal education "substantially equal to those which the state there afforded for persons of the white race." Other anti-discrimination decisions followed, among them *Shelley* v. *Kraemer* (1948), impairing enforcement of restrictive covenants in real estate; and *Sweatt* v. *Painter* (1954), invalidating segregation in higher education. The three Supreme Court Opinions given in the following pages—*Chambers* v. *Florida,* historic *Brown* v. *Board of Education of Topeka,* and the *Virginia Voters Cases*—are illuminating examples of the evolution of court decisions from discrimination to equality.

• JUSTICE HUGO L. BLACK

The grave question presented by the petition for certiorari, granted in forma pauperis, is whether proceedings in which confessions were utilized, and which culminated in sentences of death upon four young Negro men in the State of Florida, failed to afford the safeguard of that due process of law guaranteed by the Fourteenth Amendment.

The record shows—

About nine o'clock on the night of Saturday, May 13, 1933, Robert Darcy, an elderly white man, was robbed and murdered in Pompano, Florida. . . The opinion of the Supreme Court of Florida affirming petitioners' conviction for this crime stated that "It was one of those crimes that induced an enraged community. . . ."

Between 9:30 and 10 o'clock after the murder, petitioner Charlie Davis was arrested, and within the next twenty-four hours from twenty-five to forty Negroes living in the community, including petitioners Williamson, Chambers and Woodward, were arrested without warrants and confined in the Broward County jail, at Fort Lauderdale. . . .

It is clear from the evidence of both the State and petitioners that from Sunday, May 14, to Saturday,

May 20, the thirty to forty Negro suspects were subjected to questioning and cross questioning. . . .

The prisoners at no time during the week were permitted to see or confer with counsel or a single friend or relative. When carried singly from his cell and subjected to questioning, each found himself, a single prisoner, surrounded in a fourth floor jail room by four to ten men, the county sheriff, his deputies, a convict guard, and other white officers and citizens of the community. . . .

After one week's constant denial of all guilt, petitioners "broke." . . . No formal charges had been brought before the confession. Two days thereafter, petitioners were indicted, were arraigned and Williamson and Woodward pleaded guilty . . . Later . . . Davis pleaded guilty. When Chambers was tried, his conviction rested upon his confession and testimony of the other three confessors . . . And from arrest until sentenced to death, petitioners were never—either in jail or in court—wholly removed from the constant observation, influence, custody and control of those whose persistent pressure brought about the sunrise confessions.

The scope and operation of the Fourteenth Amendment have been fruitful sources of controversy in our constitutional history. However, in view of its historical setting and the wrongs which called it into being, the due process provision of the Fourteenth Amendment—just as that in the Fifth—had led few to doubt that it was intended to guarantee procedural standards adequate and appropriate, then and thereafter, to protect, at all times, people charged with or suspected of crime by those holding positions of power and authority. Tyrannical governments had immemorially utilized dictatorial criminal procedure and punishment to make scapegoats of the weak, or of helpless political, religious, or racial minorities and those who differed, who would not conform and who resisted tyranny . . . Thus, as assurance against ancient evils, our country, in order to preserve "the blessings of liberty," wrote into its basic law the requirement, among others, that the forfeiture of the lives, liberties or property of people accused of crime can only follow if procedural safeguards of due process have been obeyed.

The determination to preserve an accused's right to procedural due process sprang in large part from knowledge of the historical truth that the rights and liberties of people accused of crime could not be safely entrusted to secret inquisitorial processes. The testimony of centuries, in governments of varying kinds over populations of different races and beliefs, stood as proof that physical and mental torture and coercion had brought about the tragically unjust sacrifices of some who were the noblest and most useful of their generations. The rack, the thumbscrew, the wheel, solitary confinement, protracted questioning and cross questioning, and other ingenious forms of entrapment of the helpless or unpopular had left their wake of mutilated bodies and shattered minds along the way to the cross, the guillotine, the stake and the hangman's noose. And they who have suffered most from secret and dictatorial proceedings have almost always been the poor, the ignorant, the numerically weak, the friendless, and the powerless.

This requirement—of conforming to fundamental standards of procedure in criminal trials—was made operative against the States by the Fourteenth Amendment. . . .

Here, the record develops a sharp conflict upon the issue of physical violence and mistreatment, but shows, without conflict, the drag net methods of arrest on suspicion without warrant, and the protracted questioning and cross questioning of these ignorant young colored tenant farmers by State officers and other white citizens, in a fourth floor jail room, where as prisoners they were without friends, advisers or counselors, and under circumstances calculated to break the strongest nerves and the stoutest resistance. . . .

For five days petitioners were subjected to interrogations culminating in Saturday's (May 20th) all night examinations. Over a period of five days they steadily refused to confess and disclaimed any guilt. The very circumstances surrounding their confinement and their questioning without any formal charges having been brought, were such as to fill petitioners with terror and frightful misgivings. Some were practical strangers in the community; three were arrested in a one-room farm tenant house which was their home; the haunting fear of mob violence was around them in an atmosphere charged with excitement and public indignation. From virtually the moment of their arrest until their eventual confessions, they never knew just when any one would be called back to the fourth floor room, and there, surrounded by his accusers and others, interrogated by men who held their very lives—so far as these ignorant petitioners could know—in the balance. . . . To permit human lives to be forfeited upon confessions thus obtained would make of the constitutional requirement of due process of law a meaningless symbol.

We are not impressed by the argument that law enforcement methods such as those under review are necessary to uphold our laws. The Constitution proscribes such lawless means irrespective of the end. And this argument flouts the basic principle that all people must stand on an equality before the bar of justice in every American court. Today, as in ages past, we are not without tragic proof that the exalted power of some governments to punish manufactured crime dictatorially is the handmaid of tyranny. Under our constitutional system, courts stand against any winds that blow as havens of refuge for those who might otherwise suffer because they are helpless, weak, outnumbered, or because they are non-conforming victims of prejudice and public excitement. Due process of law, preserved for all by our Constitution, commands that no such practice as that disclosed by this record shall send any accused to his death. No higher duty, no more solemn responsibility, rests upon this court, than that of translating into living law and maintaining this constitutional shield deliberately planned and inscribed for the benefit of every human being subject to our Constitution—of whatever race, creed or persuasion.

The Supreme Court of Florida was in error and its judgment is *Reversed.* ■

From Unanimous Opinion,
Chambers *v.* Florida, *1940.*

• CHIEF JUSTICE EARL WARREN

These cases come to us from the States of Kansas, South Carolina, Virginia and Delaware. They are premised on different facts and different local conditions, but a common legal question justifies their consideration together in this consolidated opinion.

In each of the cases, minors of the Negro race, through their legal representatives, seek the aid of the courts in obtaining admission to the public schools of their community on a nonsegregated basis. In each instance, they had been denied admission to schools attended by white children under laws requiring or permitting segregation according to race. This segregation was alleged to deprive the plaintiffs of the equal protection of the laws under the Fourteenth Amendment. In each of the cases other than the Delaware case, a three-judge federal district court denied relief to the plaintiffs on the so-called "separate but equal" doctrine announced by this Court in *Plessy* v. *Ferguson* . . . Under that doctrine, equality of treatment is accorded when the races are provided substantially equal facilities, even though these facilities be separate. In the Delaware case, the Supreme Court of Delaware adhered to that doctrine, but ordered that the plaintiffs be admitted to the white schools because of their superiority to the Negro schools.

The plaintiffs contend that segregated public schools are not "equal" and cannot be made "equal" and that hence they are deprived of the equal protection of the laws. Because of the obvious importance of the question presented, the Court took jurisdiction. Argument was heard in the 1952 Term, and reargument was heard this Term on certain questions propounded by the Court.

Reargument was largely devoted to the circumstances surrounding the adoption of the Fourteenth Amendment in 1868. It covered exhaustively consideration of the Amendment in Congress, ratification by the states, then existing practices in racial segregation, and the views of proponents and opponents of the Amendment. This discussion and our own investigation convince us that, although these sources cast some light, it is not enough to resolve the problem with which we are faced. At best, they are inconclusive. The most avid proponents of the post-War Amendments undoubtedly intended them to remove all legal distinctions among "all persons born or naturalized in the United States." Their opponents, just as certainly, were antagonistic to both the letter and the spirit of the Amendments and wished them to have the most limited effect. What others in Congress and the state legislatures had in mind cannot be determined with any degree of certainty.

An additional reason for the inconclusive nature of the Amendment's history, with respect to segregated schools, is the status of public education at that time. In the South, the movement toward free common schools, supported by general taxation, had not yet taken hold. Education of white children was largely in the hands of private groups. Education of Negroes was almost nonexistent, and practically all of the race was illiterate. In fact, any education of Negroes was forbidden by law in some states. Today, in contrast, many Negroes have achieved outstanding success in the arts and sciences as well as in the business and professional world. It is true that public school education at the time of the Amendment had advanced further in the North, but the effect of the Amendment on Northern States was generally ignored in the congressional debates. Even in the North, the conditions of public education did not approximate those existing today. The curriculum was usually rudimentary; ungraded schools were common in rural areas; the school term was but three months a year in many states; and compulsory school attendance was virtually unknown. As a consequence, it is not surprising that there should be so little in the history of the Fourteenth Amendment relating to its intended effect on public education.

In the first cases in this Court construing the Fourteenth Amendment, decided shortly after its adoption, the Court interpreted it as proscribing all state-imposed discriminations against the Negro race. The doctrine of "separate but equal" did not make its appearance in this Court until 1896 in the case of *Plessy* v. *Ferguson* . . . involving not education but transportation. American courts have since

labored with the doctrine for over half a century. In this Court, there have been six cases involving the "separate but equal" doctrine in the field of public education. . . .

Here . . . there are findings below that the Negro and white schools have been equalized, or are being equalized, with respect to buildings, curricula, qualifications and salaries of teachers, and other "tangible" factors. Our decision, therefore, cannot turn on merely a comparison of these tangible factors in the Negro and white schools involved in each of the cases. We must look instead to the effect of segregation itself on public education.

In approaching this problem, we cannot turn the clock back to 1868 when the Amendment was adopted, or even to 1896 when *Plessy* v. *Ferguson* was written. We must consider public education in the light of its full development and its present place in American life throughout the Nation. Only in this way can it be determined if segregation in public schools deprives these plaintiffs of the equal protection of the laws.

Today, education is perhaps the most important function of state and local governments. Compulsory school attendance laws and the great expenditures for education both demonstrate our recognition of the importance of education to our democratic society. It is required in the performance of our most basic public responsibilities, even service in the armed forces. It is the very foundation of good citizenship. Today it is a principal instrument in awakening the child to cultural values, in preparing him for later professional training, and in helping him to adjust normally to his environment. In these days, it is doubtful that any child may reasonably be expected to succeed in life if he is denied the opportunity of an education. Such an opportunity, where the state has undertaken to provide it, is a right which must be made available to all on equal terms.

We come then to the question presented: Does segregation of children in public schools solely on the basis of race, even though the physical facilities and other "tangible" factors may be equal, deprive the children of the minority group of equal educational opportunities? We believe that it does.

In *Sweatt* v. *Painter* (1954) . . . in finding that a segregated law school for Negroes could not provide them equal educational opportunities, this Court relied in large part on "those qualities which are incapable of objective measurement but which make for greatness in a law school." In *McLaurin* v. *Oklahoma State Regents* . . . the Court, in requiring that a Negro admitted to a white graduate school be treated like all other students, again resorted to intangible considerations; " . . . his ability to study, to engage in discussions and exchange views with other students, and, in general, to learn his profession." Such considerations apply with added force to children in grade and high schools. To separate them from others of similar age and qualifications solely because of their race generates a feeling of inferiority as to their status in the community that may affect their hearts and minds in a way unlikely ever to be undone. The effect of this separation on their educational opportunities was well stated by a finding in the Kansas case by a court which nevertheless felt compelled to rule against the Negro plaintiffs:

"Segregation of white and colored children in public schools has a detrimental effect upon the colored children. The impact is greater when it has the sanction of the law; for the policy of separating the races is usually interpreted as denoting the inferiority of the Negro group. A sense of inferiority affects the motivation of a child to learn. Segregation with the sanction of law, therefore, has a tendency to (retard) the educational and mental development of Negro children and to deprive them of some of the benefits they would receive in a racial(ly) integrated school system."

Whatever may have been the extent of psychological knowledge at the time of *Plessy* v. *Ferguson,* this finding is amply supported by modern authority. Any language in *Plessy* v. *Ferguson* contrary to this finding is rejected.

We conclude that in the field of public education the doctrine of "separate but equal" has no place. Separate educational facilities are inherently unequal. Therefore, we hold that the plaintiffs and others similarly situated for whom the actions have been brought are, by reason of the segregation complained of, deprived of the equal protection of the laws guaranteed by the Fourteenth Amendment. This disposition makes unnecessary any discussion whether such segregation also violates the Due Process Clause of the Fourteenth Amendment.

Because these are class actions, because of the wide applicability of this decision, and because of the great variety of local conditions, the formulation of decrees in these cases presents problems of considerable complexity. On reargument, the consideration of appropriate relief was necessarily subordinated to the primary question—the constitutionality of segregation in public education. We have now announced that such segregation is a denial of the equal protection of the laws.

IMPLEMENTATION DECISION (1955)

These cases were decided on May 17, 1954. The opinions of that date, declaring the fundamental principle that racial discrimination in public education is unconstitutional, are incorporated herein by reference. All provisions of federal, state, or local law requiring or permitting such discrimination must yield to this principle. There remains for consideration the manner in which relief is to be accorded.

Because these cases arose under different local conditions and their disposition will involve a variety of local problems, we requested further argument on the question of relief. In view of the nationwide importance of the decision, we invited the Attorney General of the United States and the Attorneys General of all states requiring or permitting racial discrimination in public education to present their views on that question. The parties, the United States, and the States of Florida, North Carolina, Arkansas, Oklahoma, Maryland, and Texas filed briefs and participated in the oral argument.

These presentations were informative and helpful to the Court in its consideration of the complexities arising from the transition to a system of public education freed of racial discrimination. The presentations also demonstrated that substantial steps to eliminate racial discrimination in public schools have already been taken, not only in some of the communites in which these cases arose, but in some of the states appearing as *amici curiae,* and in other states as well. Substantial progress has been made in the District of Columbia and in the communities in Kansas and Delaware involved in this litigation. The defendants in the cases coming to us from South Carolina and Virginia are awaiting the decision of this Court concerning relief.

Full implementation of these constitutional principles may require solution of varied local school problems. School authorities have the primary responsibility for elucidating, assessing, and solving these problems; courts will have to consider whether the action of school authorities constitutes good faith implementation of the governing constitutional principles. Because of their proximity to local conditions and the possible need for further hearings, the courts which originally heard these cases can best perform this judicial appraisal. Accordingly, we believe it appropriate to remand the cases to those courts.

In fashioning and effectuating the decrees, the courts will be guided by equitable principles. Traditionally, equity has been characterized by a practical flexibility in shaping its remedies and by a facility for adjusting and reconciling public and private needs. These cases call for the exercise of these traditional attributes of equity power. At stake is the personal interest of the plaintiffs in admission to public schools as soon as practicable on a nondiscriminatory basis. To effectuate this interest may call for elimination of a variety of obstacles in making the transition to school systems operated in accordance with the constitutional principles set forth in our May 17, 1954, decision. Courts of equity may properly take into account the public interest in the elimination of such obstacles in a systematic and effective manner. But it should go without saying that the vitality of these constitutional principles cannot be allowed to yield simply because of disagreement with them.

While giving weight to these public and private considerations, the courts will require that the defendants make a prompt and reasonable start toward full compliance with our May 17, 1954, ruling.

Once such a start has been made, the courts may find that additional time is necessary to carry out the ruling in an effective manner. The burden rests upon the defendants to establish that such time is necessary in the public interest and is consistent with good faith compliance at the earliest practicable date. To that end, the courts may consider problems related to administration, arising from the physical condition of the school plant, the school transportation system, personnel, revision of school districts and attendance areas into compact units to achieve a system of determining admission to the public schools on a nonracial basis, and revision of local laws and regulations which may be necessary in solving the foregoing problems. They will also consider the adequacy of any plans the defendants may propose to meet these problems and to effectuate a transition to a racially nondiscriminatory school system. During this period of transition, the courts will retain jurisdiction of these cases.

The judgments below . . . are accordingly . . . remanded [to the lower courts] to take such proceedings and enter such orders and decrees consistent with this opinion as are necessary and proper to admit to public schools on a racially nondiscriminatory basis with all deliberate speed the parties to these cases. . . . ■

From Unanimous Opinion, Brown v. Board of
Education of Topeka, *1954.*

• JUSTICE WILLIAM O. DOUGLAS

These are suits by Virginia residents to have declared unconstitutional Virginia's poll tax. The three-judge District Court, feeling bound by our decision in *Breedlove* v. *Suttles* [1937] . . . dismissed the complaint. . . The cases came here on appeal and we noted probable jurisdiction.

While the right to vote in Federal elections is conferred by Art. 1, Section 2, of the Constitution, the right to vote in state elections is nowhere expressly mentioned. It is argued that the right to vote in state elections is implicit, particularly by reason of the First Amendment, and that it may not constitutionally be conditioned upon the payment of a tax or fee. We do not stop to canvass the relation between voting and political expression. For it is enough to say that once the franchise is granted to the electorate, lines may not be drawn which are inconsistent with the equal protection clause of the Fourteenth Amendment.

That is to say the right of suffrage "is subject to the imposition of state standards which are not discriminatory and which do not contravene any restriction that Congress, acting pursuant to its Constitutional power, has imposed." (*Lassiter* v. *Northampton Education Board,* 360 U.S. 45, 51.)

We were speaking there of a state literacy test which we sustained, warning that the result would be different if a literacy test, fair on its face, were used to discriminate against a class. But the Lassiter case does not govern the result here, because, unlike a poll tax, the "ability to read and write . . . has some relation to standards designed to promote intelligent use of the ballot."

We conclude that a state violates the equal protection clause of the Fourteenth Amendment whenever it makes the affluence of the voter or payment of any fee an electoral standard. Voter qualifications have no relation to wealth nor to paying or not paying this or any other tax. Our cases demonstrate that the equal protection clause of the Fourteenth Amendment restrains the States from fixing voter qualifications which invidiously discriminate. Thus without questioning the power of a State to impose reasonable residence restrictions on the availability of the ballot, we held in *Carrington* v. *Rash,* 380 U.S. 89, that a State may not deny the opportunity to vote to a bona fide resident merely because he is a member of the armed services. "By forbidding a soldier ever to controvert the presumption of nonresidence, the Texas Constitution imposes an invidious discrimination in violation of the Fourteenth Amendment."

Previously we had said that neither homesite nor occupation "affords a permissible basis for distinguishing between qualified voters within the State." *Gray* v. *Sanders,* 372 U.S. 368, 380. We think the same must be true of requirements of wealth or affluence or payment of a fee.

Long ago in *Yick Wo* v. *Hopkins,* the Court referred to "the political franchise of voting" as a "fundamental political right, because preservative of all rights." Recently in *Reynolds* v. *Sims,* we said, "Undoubtedly, the right of suffrage is a fundamental matter in a free and democratic society. Especially since the right to exercise the franchise in a free and unimpaired manner is preservative of other basic civil and political rights, any alleged infringement of the right of citizens to vote must be carefully and meticulously scrutinized." There we were considering charges that voters in one part of the State had greater representation per person in the State Legislature than voters in another part of the State. We concluded:

"A citizen, a qualified voter, is no more nor no less so because he lives in the city or on the farm. This is the clear and strong command of our Constitution's equal protection clause. This is an essential part of the concept of a government of laws and not of men. This is at the heart of Lincoln's vision of 'government of the people, by the people, for the people.'"

We say the same whether the citizen, otherwise qualified to vote, has $1.50 in his pocket or nothing at all, pays the fee or fails to pay it. The principle that denies the State the right to dilute a citizen's vote on account of his economic status or other such factors by analogy bars a system which excludes those unable to pay a fee to vote or who fail to pay.

It is argued that a State may exact fees from citizens for many different kinds of licenses; that if it can demand from all an equal fee for a driver's license, it can demand from all an equal poll tax for voting. But we must remember that the interest of the State, when it comes to voting, is limited to the power to fix qualifications. Wealth, like race, creed or color, is not germane to one's ability to participate intelligently in electoral process. Lines drawn on the basis of wealth or property, like those of race, are traditionally disfavored. To introduce wealth or payment of a fee as a measure of voter's qualifications is to introduce a capricious or irrelevant factor. The degree of the discrimination is irrelevant.

From Majority Opinion (six to three), Virginia Voters Cases, *holding the Virginia poll tax unconstitutional, March 24, 1966.*

5
PRESIDENTIAL STATEMENTS ON LAW AND EQUALITY

Dwight D. Eisenhower
John F. Kennedy
Lyndon B. Johnson

• EDITOR'S NOTE

Encouraged by the momentous 1954 Supreme Court decision in *Brown* v. *Board of Education*, Negroes made efforts to enroll in hitherto segregated southern schools. White southerners resisted, in many instances with ugly and organized violence. In states like Alabama, Arkansas, and Mississippi, the governors mobilized armed forces to prevent Negro students from entering formerly all-white schools. The federal government, determined to carry out the law of the land, called out military force. The three statements that follow here illustrate the new—and continuing—national policy in support of the equality of all citizens.

• DWIGHT D. EISENHOWER

I want to make several things very clear in connection with the disgraceful occurrences of today at Central High School in the city of Little Rock. They are:

1. The Federal law and orders of a United States District Court implementing that law cannot be flouted with impunity by any individual or any mob of extremists.

2. I will use the full power of the United States, including whatever force may be necessary, to prevent any obstruction of the law and to carry out the orders of the Federal court.

3. Of course, every right-thinking citizen will hope that the American sense of justice and fair play will prevail in this case. It will be a sad day for this country—both at home and abroad—if school children can safely attend their classes only under the protection of armed guards.

4. I repeat my expressed confidence that the citizens of Little Rock and of Arkansas will respect the law and will not countenance violations of law and order by extremists. ∎

From statement in connection with his Proclamation against the Arkansas National Guard's preventing Negro students from enrolling in Little Rock's Central High School, September 23, 1957.

• JOHN F. KENNEDY

Good evening, my fellow citizens:

The orders of the court in the case of *Meredith* v. *Fair* are beginning to be carried out.

Mr. James Meredith is now in residence on the campus of the University of Mississippi. This has been accomplished thus far without the use of the National Guard or other troops, and it is to be hoped that the law-enforcement officers of the State of Mississippi and the Federal marshals will continue to be sufficient in the future.

All students, members of the faculty and public officials in both Mississippi and the nation will be able, it is hoped, to return to their normal activities with full confidence in the integrity of American law.

This is as it should be, for our nation is founded on the principle that observance of the law is the eternal safeguard of liberty and defiance of the law is the surest road to tyranny.

The law which we obey includes the final rulings of the courts as well as the enactments of our legislative bodies. Even among law-abiding men few laws are universally loved.

But they are uniformly respected and not resisted.

Americans are free, in short, to disagree with the law, but not to disobey it. For in a government of laws and not of men, no man, however prominent or powerful, and no mob, however unruly or boisterous, is entitled to defy a court of law.

If this country should ever reach the point where any man or group of men, by force or threat of force, could long deny the commands of our court and our Constitution, then no law would stand free from doubt, no judge would be sure of his writ and no citizen would be safe from his neighbors.

In this case in which the United States Government was not until recently involved, Mr. Meredith brought a private suit in Federal Court against those who were excluding him from the university. A series of Federal Courts, all the way to the Supreme Court, repeatedly ordered Mr. Meredith's admission to the university.

When those orders were defied and those who sought to implement them threatened with arrest and violence, the United States Court of Appeals, consisting of Chief Tuttle of Georgia, Judge Hutcheson of Texas, Judge Rives of Alabama, Judge Jones of Florida, Judge Brown of Texas, Judge Wisdom of Louisiana, Judge Gewin of Alabama and Judge Bell of Georgia, made clear the fact that the enforcement of its order had become an obligation of the United States Government.

Even though this Government had not originally been a party to the case, my responsibility as President was therefore inescapable. I accept it.

My obligation under the Constitution and the statutes of the United States was and is to implement the orders of the courts with whatever means are necessary and with as little force and civil disorder as the circumstances permit.

It was for this reason that I federalized the Mississippi National Guard as the most appropriate instrument, should any be needed to preserve law and order while United States marshals carried out the orders of the court, and prepared to back them up with whatever other civil or military enforcement might have been required.

I deeply regret the fact that any action by the executive branch was necessary in this case. But all other avenues and alternatives including persuasion and conciliation, had been tried and exhausted.

Had the police powers of Mississippi been used to support the orders of the court instead of deliberately and unlawfully blocking them; had the University of Mississippi fulfilled its standard of excellence by quietly admitting this applicant in conformity with what so many other Southern state universities have done for so many years, a peaceable and sensible solution would have been possible without any Federal intervention.

This nation is proud of the many instances in which governors, educators, and everyday citizens from the South have shown to the world the gains that can be made by persuasion and goodwill in a society ruled by law.

Specifically, I would like to take this occasion to express the thanks of this nation to those Southerners who have contributed to the progress of our democratic development in the entrance of students regardless of race to such great institutions as the state-supported universities of Virginia, North Carolina, Georgia, Florida, Texas, Louisiana, Tennessee, Arkansas and Kentucky.

I recognize that the present period of transition and adjustment in our nation's Southland is a hard one for many people.

Neither Mississippi nor any other Southern state deserves to be charged with all the accumulated wrongs of the last 100 years of race relations to the extent that there has been failure. The responsibility for that failure must be shared by us all, by every state, by every citizen.

Mississippi and her univeristy, moreover, are noted for their courage, for their contribution of talent and thought to the affairs of this nation. This is the state of Lucius Lamar and many others who have placed the national good ahead of sectional interests.

This is the state which had four Medal of Honor winners in the Korean War alone. In fact, the Guard unit federalized this morning, early, is part of the 155th Infantry, one of the ten oldest regiments in the Union and one of the most decorated for sacrifice and bravery in six wars.

In 1945, a Mississippi sergeant, Jake Lindsay, was honored by an unusual joint session of the Congress.

I close therefore with this appeal to the students of the university—the people who are most concerned:

You have a great tradition to uphold; a tradition of honor and courage, won on the field of battle and on the gridiron, as well as the university campus.

You have a new opportunity to show that you are men of patriotism and integrity. For the most effective means of upholding the law is not the state policemen, or the marshals, or the National Guard. It is you.

It lies in your courage to accept those laws with which you disagree as well as those with which you agree.

The eyes of the nation and all the world are upon you and upon all of us. And the honor of your university—and state—are in the balance.

I am certain the great majority of the students will uphold that honor.

There is, in short, no reason why the books on this case cannot now be quickly and quietly closed in the manner directed by the court.

Let us preserve both the law and the peace, and then healing those wounds that are within, we can turn to the greater crises that are without and stand united as one people in our pledge to man's freedom.

Thank you, and good night. ■

From television address at the White House, September 31, 1962, in connection with mobilization of the National Guard to protect the Negro student, James Meredith, at the University of Mississippi.

• LYNDON B. JOHNSON

Good afternoon, ladies and gentlemen. This March week has brought a very deep and painful challenge to the unending search for American freedom.

That challenge is not yet over, but before it is ended every resource of this Government will be directed to insuring justice for all men of all races in Alabama and elsewhere in this land. That is the meaning of the oath that I swore before Almighty God when I took the office of the Presidency. That is what I believe in with all of my heart. That is what the people of this country demand.

Last Sunday a group of Negro Americans in Selma, Alabama, attempted peacefully to protest the denial of the most basic political right of all—the right to vote. They were attacked and some were brutally beaten.

From that moment until this we have acted effectively to protect the Constitutional rights of the citizens of Selma and to prevent further violence and lawlessness in this country wherever it occurs . . . .

But the final answer to this problem will be found not in armed confrontation but in the process of law. We have acted to bring this conflict from the streets to the courtroom. Your Government at my direction asked the Federal Court in Alabama to order the law officials of Alabama not to interfere with American citizens who are peacefully demonstrating for their Constitutional rights.

When the court has made its orders it must be obeyed.

The events of last Sunday cannot and will not be repeated. But the demonstrations in Selma have a much larger meaning. They are a protest against a deep and very unjust flaw in American democracy itself.

Ninety-five years ago our Constitution was amended to require that no American be denied the right to vote because of race or color. Almost a century later many Americans are kept from voting simply because they are Negroes.

Therefore this Monday I will send to the Congress a request for legislation to carry out the amendments of the Constitution. Wherever there is discrimination this law will strike down all restrictions used to deny the people the right to vote. . . .

This law is not an effort to punish or coerce anyone. Its object is one which no American in his heart can truly reject. It is to give all our people the right to choose their leaders. To deny this right, I think, is to deny democracy itself.

What happened in Selma was an American tragedy. The blows that were received, the blood that was shed, the life of the good man that was lost must strengthen the determination of each of us to bring full and equal and exact justice to all of our people.

This is not just the policy of your Government of your President. It is in the heart and the purpose and the meaning of America itself.

We all know how complex and how difficult it is to bring about basic social change in a democracy. But this complexity must not obscure the clear and simple moral issue.

It is wrong to do violence to peaceful citizens in the streets of their towns. It is wrong to deny Americans the right to vote. It is wrong to deny any person full equality because of the color of his skin.

The promise of America is a simple promise. Every person shall share in the blessings of this land. And they shall share on the basis of their merits as a person. They shall not be judged by their color or by their beliefs or by their religion or by where they were born or the neighborhood in which they live.

All my life I have seen America move closer toward that goal and every step of the way has brought in large opportunity and more happiness for all of our people. Those who do injustice are as surely the victims of their own acts as the people that they wrong.

They scar their own lives, and they scar the communities in which they live. By turning from hatred to understanding they can insure a richer and fuller life for themselves, as well as for their fellows.

For if we put aside disorder and violence, if we put aside hatred and lawlessness, we can provide for all our people great opportunity almost beyond our imagination. We will continue this battle of human dignity. We will apply all the resources of this great and powerful Government to this task.

We ask that all of our citizens unite in this hour of trial. We will not be moved by anyone or anything from the path of justice. . . . ■

From news conference at the White House, March 13, 1965, after the President's conference with Governor George C. Wallace in connection with violence against Negroes in Selma, Alabama.

PART V

FREEDOM OF COMMUNICATION — TO SPEAK, WRITE, AND PUBLISH

O f the freedoms, that of the mind is of first importance. All the other freedoms—for example, of voting, of worship, of association—must depend upon the antecedent right to speak, write, and print without fear of punishment by public authority. No other freedom, including the liberty to worship as one pleases, can exist where government hampers or denies independent expression of opinions or ideas. Indeed, the first act of any dictator is to forbid intellectual liberty and uncensored publication.

Freedom of the mind is something relatively modern. It did exist briefly, and somewhat sporadically, in ancient Greece and Rome. But as a rule, the practice which prevailed in Europe for nearly two thousand years was restraint on the human mind. This was true in the field of religion as well as politics. In both spheres, authoritarianism—that is to say, forcible imposition of dogmas and ideas even upon those who were reluctant to accept them—was the universal practice. Those who held different ideas, especially if they tried to utter them in public, were subjected to severe punishment.

The great struggle for the free mind began in the seventeenth century, mainly in England. There one of the most eloquent voices in favor of freedom of speech was that of the poet John Milton. His words, in attacking censorship of printing, echo through the ages: ". . . he who destroys a good book, kills reason itself, kills the image of God." Across the English Channel, in Holland, another seventeenth-century giant, Baruch Spinoza, calmly affirmed: ". . . every man should think what he likes and say what he thinks."

The battle for freedom of expression continued to be fought, in Western Europe and America, in the centuries that followed. Among the best-known champions of the free mind have been John Locke, Voltaire, Jean Jacques Rousseau, Thomas Jefferson, James Madison, John Stuart Mill, and the early Karl Marx.

1

GENERAL VIEWS

John Milton
Baruch Spinoza

• JOHN MILTON

I deny not but that it is of greatest concernment in the church and Commonwealth to have a vigilant eye how books demean themselves as well as men; and thereafter to confine, imprison, and do sharpest justice on them as malefactors: For books are not absolutely dead things, but do contain a potency of life in them[1] to be as active as that soul was whose progeny they are; nay, they do preserve as in a vial the purest efficacy and extraction of that living intellect that bred them. I know they are as lively, and as vigorously productive, as those fabulous dragon's teeth; and being sown up and down, may chance to spring up armed men. And yet, on the other hand, unless wariness be used, as good almost kill a man as kill a good book; who kills a man kills a reasonable creature, God's image; but he who destroys a good book, kills reason itself, kills the image of God, as it were in the eye. Many a man lives a burden to the earth; but a good book is the precious life-blood of a master spirit, embalmed and treasured up on purpose to a life beyond life. ■

From Areopagitica, *written in protest against an Act of Parliament establishing censorship over printing, 1644.*

• BARUCH (or BENEDICT) SPINOZA

If men's minds were as easily controlled as their tongues, every king would sit safely on his throne, and government by compulsion would cease; for every subject would shape his life according to the intentions of his rulers, and would esteem a thing true or false, good or evil, just or unjust, in obedience to their dictates. However . . . no man's mind can possibly lie wholly at the disposition of another, for no one can willingly transfer his natural right of free reason and judgment, or be compelled to do so.

---

[1] Compare Francis Bacon's Essay, "Of Studies" (1625): "Studies serve for delight, for ornament, and for ability . . . They perfect nature, and are perfected by experience . . . Some books are to be tasted, others to be swallowed, and some few to be chewed and digested."

For this reason government which attempts to control minds is accounted tyrannical, and it is considered an abuse of sovereignty and a usurpation of the rights of subjects to seek to prescribe what shall be accepted as true, or rejected as false, or what opinions should actuate men in their worship of God. All these questions fall within a man's natural right, which he cannot abdicate even with his own consent. . . .

However unlimited, therefore, the power of a sovereign may be, however implicitly it is trusted as the exponent of law and religion, it can never prevent men from forming judgments according to their intellect . . .

Since, therefore, no one can abdicate his freedom of judgment and feeling; since every man is by indefeasible natural right the master of his own thoughts, it follows that men, thinking in diverse and contradictory fashions, cannot, without disastrous results, be compelled to speak only according to the dictates of the supreme power. Not even the most experienced, to say nothing of the multitude, know how to keep silence. Men's common failing is to confide their plans to others, though there be need for secrecy, so that a government would be most harsh which deprived the individual of his freedom of saying and teaching what he thought . . . Still we cannot deny that authority may be as much injured by words as by actions. Hence, although the freedom we are discussing cannot be entirely denied to subjects, its unlimited concession would be most baneful; we must, therefore, now inquire, how far such freedom can and ought to be conceded without danger to the peace of the state, or the power of the rulers. . . .

The ultimate aim of government is not to rule, or restrain by fear, nor to exact obedience, but, contrariwise, to free every man from fear that he may live in all possible security; in other words, to strengthen his natural right to exist and work without injury to himself or others.

No, the object of government is not to change men from rational beings into beasts or puppets, but to enable them to develop their minds and bodies in security, and to employ their reason unshackled; neither showing hatred, anger or deceit, nor watched with the eyes of jealousy and injustice. In fact, the true aim of government is liberty.

Now we have seen that in forming a state the power of making laws must either be vested in the body of the citizens, or in a portion of them, or in one man. For, although men's free judgments are very diverse . . . and although complete unanimity of feeling and speech is out of the question, it is impossible to preserve peace unless individuals abdicate their right of acting entirely on their own judgment. Therefore, the individual justly cedes the right of free action, though not of free reason and judgment; no one can act against the authorities without danger to the state, though his feelings and judgment may be at variance therewith; he may even speak against them, provided that he does so from rational conviction, not from fraud, anger or hatred, and provided that he does not attempt to introduce any change on his private authority. . . .

An individual may declare and teach what he believes, without injury to the authority of his rulers, or to the public peace; namely, by leaving in their hands the entire power of legislation as it affects action, and by doing nothing against their laws, though he be compelled often to act in contradiction to what he believes, and openly feels, to be best.

Such a course can be taken without detriment to justice and dutifulness, nay, it is the one which a just and dutiful man would adopt. We have shown that justice is dependent on the laws of authorities . . . Therefore it is no less than undutiful for a man to act contrary to his country's laws, for if the practice became universal the ruin of states would necessarily follow. . . .

From the fundamental notions of a state, we have discovered how a man may exercise free judgment without detriment to the supreme power: from the same premises we can no less easily determine what opinions would be seditious. Evidently those which by their very nature nullify the compact by which the right of free action was ceded. For instance, a man who holds that the supreme power has no rights over him, or that promises ought not to be kept, or that everyone should live as he pleases . . . is seditious, not so much from his actual opinions and judgment, as from the deeds which they involve; for he who maintains such theories abrogates the contract which tacitly, or openly, he made with his rulers. Other opinions which do not involve acts violating the contract, such as revenge, anger, and the like, are not seditious, unless it be in some corrupt state, where superstitious and ambitious persons, unable to endure men of learning, are so popular with the multitude that their word is more valued than the law. . . .

If we hold to the principle that a man's loyalty to the state should be judged, like his loyalty to God, from his actions only—namely, from his charity toward his neighbors; we cannot doubt that the best government will allow freedom of philosophical speculation no less than of religious belief. I confess that from such freedom inconveniences may sometimes arise, but what question was ever settled so wisely that no abuses could possibly spring therefrom? . . . .

But let it be granted that freedom may be crushed, and men be so bound down that they do not dare to utter a whisper, save at the bidding of their rulers; nevertheless, this can never be carried to the pitch of making them think according to authority, so that the necessary consequences would be that men would daily be thinking one thing and saying another, to the corruption of good faith, that mainstay of government, and to the fostering of hateful flattery and perfidy. . . .

It is far from possible to impose uniformity of speech, for the more rulers strive to curtail freedom of speech the more obstinately are they resisted . . . Men, as generally constituted, are most prone to resent the branding as criminal of opinions which they believe to be true, and the proscription as wicked of that which inspires them with piety toward God and man; hence they are ready to forswear the laws and conspire against the authorities, thinking it not shameful but honorable to stir up seditions and perpetuate any sort of crime with this end in view. . . .

If governments are to retain a firm hold of authority and not be compelled to yield to agitators, it is imperative that freedom of judgment should be granted, so that men may live together in harmony, however diverse or even openly contradictory their opinions may be. We cannot doubt that such is the best system of government and open to the fewest objections, since it is the one most in harmony with human nature. In a democracy (the most natural form of government) everyone submits to the control of authority over his actions, but not over his judgment and reason; that is, seeing that all cannot think alike, the voice of the majority has the force of law, subject to repeal if circumstances bring about a change of opinion. In proportion as the power of free judgment is withheld we depart from the natural condition of mankind, and consequently the government becomes more tyrannical. . . .

I have thus shown: 1. That it is impossible to deprive men of the liberty of saying what they think. 2. That such liberty can be conceded to every man without injury to the rights and authority of the sovereign power, and that every man may retain it without injury to such rights, provided he does not presume upon it to the extent of introducing any new rights into the state, or acting in any way contrary to the existing laws. 3. That every man may enjoy this liberty without detriment to the public peace, and that no inconveniences arise therefrom which cannot easily be checked. 4. That every man may enjoy it without injury to his allegiance. 5. That laws dealing with speculative problems are entirely useless. 6. Lastly, that not only may such liberty be granted without prejudice to the public peace, to loyalty, and to the rights of rulers, but that it is even necessary for their preservation . . . Wherefore, the safest way for a state is to lay down the rule that religion is comprised solely in the exercise of charity and justice, and that the rights of rulers in sacred, no less than in secular matters, should merely have to do with actions, but that every man should think what he likes and say what he thinks. ■

From Tractatus Theologico-Politicus, *Chapter 20, 1670.*

2

FREEDOM OF OPINION AND OF THE PRESS

James Madison
Alexander Hamilton
Thomas Jefferson
Alexis de Tocqueville
William Ellery Channing
Karl Marx
John Stuart Mill
James Bryce

• JAMES MADISON

Public opinion sets bounds to every government, and is the real sovereign in every free one.

As there are cases where the public opinion must be obeyed by the government; so there are cases, where not being fixed, it may be influenced by the government. This distinction, if kept in view, would prevent or decide many debates on the respect due from the government to the sentiments of the people.

In proportion as government is influenced by opinion, it must be so, by whatever influences opinion. . . .

The larger a country, the less easy for its real opinion to be ascertained, and the less difficult to be counterfeited; when ascertained or presumed, the more respectable it is in the eyes of individuals. This is favorable to the authority of government. For the same reason, the more extensive a country, the more insignificant is each individual in his own eyes. This may be unfavorable to liberty.

Whatever facilitates a general intercourse of sentiments, as good roads, domestic commerce, a free press, and particularly a *circulation of newspapers through the entire body of the people,* and *Representatives going from, and returning among every part of them,* is equivalent to a contraction of territorial limits, and is favorable to liberty, where these may be too extensive. ■

From National Gazette, *December 19, 1791.*

• ALEXANDER HAMILTON

The liberty of the press consists, in my idea, in publishing the truth, from good motives and for justifiable ends, though it reflect on the government, on magistrates, or individuals. If it be not allowed, it excludes the privilege of canvassing men, and our rulers . . . To say that measures can be discussed, and that there shall be no bearing on those who are the authors of those measures, cannot be done. The very end and reason of discussion would be destroyed . . . It is essential to say, not only that the measure is bad and deleterious, but to hold up to the people who is the author, that, in this our free and elective government, he may be removed from the seat of power. If this is not to be done, then in vain will the voice of the people be raised against the inroads of tyranny. For, let a party but get into power, they may go on from step to step, and, in spite of canvassing their measures, fix themselves firmly in their seats, especially as they are never to be reproached for what they have done . . . But if . . . the power be allowed, the liberty for which I contend will operate as a salutary check. In speaking thus for the freedom of the press, I do not say there ought to be an unbridled license; or that the characters of men who are good will naturally tend eternally to support themselves. I do not stand here to say that no shackles are to be laid on this license. . . .

I contend for the liberty of publishing truth, with good motives, and for justifiable ends, even though it reflect on government, magistrates, or private persons. I contend for it under the restraint of our tribunals. . . .

It cannot be dangerous to government, though it may work partial difficulties. If it be not allowed, they will stand liable to encroachments on their rights. It is evident that if you cannot apply this mitigated doctrine, for which I speak, to the cases of libels here, you must forever remain ignorant of what your rulers do. I never can think this ought to be; I never did think the truth was a crime . . . my soul has ever abhorred the thought that a free man dared not speak the truth. . . .

If the doctrine for which we contend is true in regard to treason and murder, it is equally true in respect to libel. For there is the great danger. Never can tyranny be introduced into this country by arms; these can never get rid of a popular spirit of inquiry; the only way to crush it down is by a servile tribunal. It is only by the abuse of the forms of justice that we can be enslaved. An army never can do it. For ages it can never be attempted. The spirit of the country, with arms in their hands, and disciplined as a militia, would render it impossible. Every pretence that liberty can be thus invaded is idle declamation. It is not to be endangered by a few thousand of miserable, pitiful military. It is not thus that the liberty of this country is to be destroyed. It is to be subverted only by a pretence of adhering to all the forms of law, and yet by breaking down the substance of our liberties. ■

From speech before the court, in defense of Harry Croswell, editor of the Hudson, N.Y., Wasp, *accused of seditions libel, February 13, 1804.*

• THOMAS JEFFERSON

During this course of administration, and in order to disturb it, the artillery of the press has been levelled against us, charged with whatsoever its licentiousness could devise or dare. These abuses of an institution so important to freedom and science are deeply to be regretted, inasmuch as they tend to lessen its usefulness and to sap its safety. They might, indeed, have been corrected by the wholesome punishments reserved to and provided by the laws of the several States against falsehood and defamation, but public duties more urgent press on the time of public servants, and the offenders have therefore been left to find their punishment in the public indignation.

Nor was it uninteresting to the world that an experiment should be fairly and fully made, whether freedom of discussion, unaided by power, is not sufficient for the propagation and protection of truth—whether a government conducting itself in the true spirit of its constitution, with zeal and purity, and doing no act which it would be unwilling the whole world should witness, can be written down by falsehood and defamation. The experiment has been tried; you have witnessed the scene; our fellow-citizens looked on, cool and collected; they saw the latent source from which these outrages proceeded; they gathered around their public functionaries, and when the Constitution called them to the decision by suffrage, they pronounced their verdict, honorable to those who had served them and consolatory to the friend of man who believes that he may be trusted with the control of his own affairs.

No inference is here intended that the laws provided by the States against false and defamatory publications should not be enforced; he who has time renders a service to public morals and public tranquility in reforming these abuses by the salutary coercions of the law; but the experiment is noted to prove that, since truth and reason have maintained their ground against false opinions in league with false facts, the press, confined to truth, needs no other legal restraint; the public judgment will correct false reasonings and opinions on a full hearing of all parties; and no other definite line can be drawn between the inestimable liberty of the press and its demoralizing licentiousness. If there be still improprieties which this rule would not restrain, its supplement must be sought in the censorship of public opinion. ■

From Second Inaugural Address, March 4, 1805.

• THOMAS JEFFERSON

As to myself, conscious that there was not a *truth* on earth which I feared should be known, I have lent myself willingly as the subject of a great experiment, which was to prove that an administration, conducting itself with integrity and common understanding, cannot be battered down, even by the falsehoods of a licentious press, and consequently still less by the press, as restrained within the legal and wholesome limits of truth. This experiment was wanting for the world to demonstrate the falsehood of the pretext that freedom of the press is incompatible with orderly government. I have never therefore even contradicted the thousands of calumnies so industriously propagated against myself. But the fact being once established, that the press is impotent when it abandons itself to falsehood, I leave to others to restore it to its strength, by recalling it within the pale of truth. Within that it is a noble institution, equally the friend of science and of civil liberty. ■

From letter to Thomas Seymour, February 11, 1807.

• THOMAS JEFFERSON

In stating prudential rules for our government in society, I must not omit the important one of never entering into dispute or argument with another. I never saw an instance of one of two disputants convincing the other by argument. I have seen many, on their getting warm, becoming rude, and shooting one another. Conviction is the effect of our own dispassionate reasoning, either in solitude, or weighing within ourselves, dispassionately, what we hear from others . . . It was one of the rules which above all others, made Doctor Franklin the most amiable of men in society, "never to contradict anybody." If he was urged to announce an opinion, he did it rather by asking questions, as if for information, or by suggesting doubts.

When I hear another express an opinion which is not mine, I say to myself, he has a right to his opinion, as I to mine; why should I question it? His error does me no injury, and shall I become a Don Quixote, to bring all men by force of argument to one opinion? If a fact be mistated, it is probable he is gratified by a belief of it, & I have no right to deprive him of the gratification. If he wants information, he will ask for it, & then I will give it in measured terms; but if he still believes his own story, & shows a desire to dispute the fact with me, I hear him & say nothing. It is his affair, not mine, if he prefers error. ■

From letter to his grandson, Thomas Jefferson Randolph, November 24, 1808.

• THOMAS JEFFERSON

I am really mortified to be told that, *in the United States of America,* a fact like this[1] can become a subject of inquiry, and of criminal inquiry too, as an offence against religion; that a question about the

---

[1] The sale of a French book by Regnault de Bécourt, entitled *Sur la Création du Monde, ou Système d'Organisation Primitive* (1813), which led to the arrest of Philadelphia bookseller Nicholas Dufief on the charge of subversion and blasphemy. Dufief appealed to Jefferson, who had bought a copy of the book for two dollars. This letter is Jefferson's reply.

sale of a book can be carried before the civil magistrate. Is this then our freedom of religion? And are we to have a censor whose imprimatur shall say what we may buy? And who is thus to dogmatize religious opinions for our citizens? Whose foot is to be the measure to which ours are all to be cut or stretched? Is a priest to be our inquisitor, or shall a layman, simple as ourselves, set up his reason as the rule for what we are to read, and what we must believe? It is an insult to our citizens to question whether they are rational beings or not, and blasphemy against religion to suppose it cannot stand the test of truth and reason. If M.de Bécourt's book be false in its facts, disprove them; if false in its reasoning, refute it. But, for God's sake, let us freely hear both sides, if we choose. I know little of its contents, having barely glanced over here and there a passage, and over the table of contents. From this, the Newtonian philosophy seemed the chief object of attack, the issue of which might be trusted to the strength of the two combattants; Newton certainly not needing the auxiliary arm of the government, and still less the holy author of our religion, as to what in it concerns him. I though the work would be very innocent, and one which might be confided to the reason of any man; not likely to be much read if let alone, but, if persecuted, it will be generally read. Every man in the United States will think it a duty to buy a copy, in vindication of his right to buy, and to read what he pleases. ■

From letter to Nicholas Dufief, April 19, 1814.

• ALEXIS DE TOCQUEVILLE

Observe, too, that as the men who live in democratic societies are not connected with each other by any tie, each of them must be convinced individually; while in aristocratic society it is enough to convince a few—the rest follow. If Luther had lived in an age of equality, and had not had princes and potentates for his audience, he would perhaps have found it more difficult to change the aspect of Europe.

Not indeed that the men of democracies are naturally strongly persuaded of the certainty of their opinions, or are unwavering in belief; they frequently entertain doubts which no one, in their eyes, can remove. It sometimes happens at such times, that the human mind would willingly change its position; but as nothing urges or guides it forward, it oscillates to and fro without progressive motion.[1]

Even when the reliance of a democratic people has been won, it is still no easy matter to gain their attention. It is extremely difficult to obtain a hearing from men living in democracies, unless it be to speak to them of themselves. They do not attend to the things said to them, because they are always fully engrossed with the things they are doing. For indeed few men are idle in democratic nations; life is passed in the midst of noise and excitement, and men are so engaged in acting that little time remains to them for thinking. . . .

I think that it is extremely difficult to excite the enthusiasms of a democratic people for any theory which has not a palpable, direct, and immediate connection with the daily occupations of life: therefore, they will not easily forsake their old opinions; for it is enthusiasm which flings the minds of men out of the beaten track, and effects the great revolutions of the intellect as well as the great revolutions of the political world. . . .

If the influence of individuals is weak and hardly perceptible among such a people, the power exercised by the mass upon the mind of each individual is extremely great. . . .

In aristocracies men have often much greatness and strength of their own: when they find themselves at variance with the greater number of their fellow-countrymen, they withdraw to their own

---

[1] If I inquire what state of society is most favourable to the revolutions of the mind, I find that it occurs somewhere between the complete equality of the whole community and the absolute separation of ranks. Under a system of castes generations succeed each other without altering men's positions: some have nothing more, others nothing better, to hope for. The imagination slumbers amid this universal silence and stillness and the very idea of change fades from the human mind. When ranks have been abolished and social conditions are almost equalized, all men are in ceaseless excitement, but each of them stands alone, independent and weak . . . But between these two extremes of the history of nations is an intermediate period . . . when the conditions of men are not sufficiently settled for the mind to be lulled in torpor, when they are sufficiently unequal for men to exercise a vast power on the minds of one another, and when some few may modify the convictions of all. It is at such times that reformers start up, and new opinions suddenly change the face of the world. —Author's note.

circle, where they support and console themselves. Such is not the case in a democratic country; there, public favor seems as necessary as the air we breathe, and to live at variance with the multitude is, as it were, not to live. The multitude requires no laws to coerce those who think not like itself; public disapprobation is enough; a sense of their loneliness and impotence overtakes them and drives them to despair.

Whenever social conditions are equal, public opinion presses with enormous weight upon the mind of each individual; it surrounds, directs, and oppresses him; and this arises from the very constitution of society, much more than from its political laws. As men grow more alike, each man feels himself weaker in regard to all the rest; as he discerns nothing by which he is considerably raised above them, or distinguished from them, he mistrusts himself as soon as they assail him. Not only does he mistrust his strength, but he even doubts his right; and he is very near acknowledging that he is in the wrong, when the greater number of his countrymen assert that he is. The majority do not need to constrain him—they convince him. . . .

This circumstance is extraordinarily favorable to the stability of opinions. When an opinion has taken root among a democratic people, and established itself in the minds of the bulk of the community, it afterward subsists by itself and is maintained without effort, because no one attacks it. Those who at first rejected it as false, ultimately receive it as the general impression; and those who still dispute it in their hearts, conceal their dissent; they are careful not to engage in a dangerous and useless conflict.

It is true, that when the majority of a democratic people change their opinions, they may suddenly and arbitrarily effect strange revolutions in men's minds. But if their opinions do not change without much difficulty. . . . ■

From Democracy in America, *Part II, Chapter 21, 1835.*

• WILLIAM ELLERY CHANNING

Of all powers, the last to be entrusted to the multitude of men, is that of determining what questions shall be discussed. The greatest truths are often the most unpopular and exasperating; and were they to be denied discussion, till the many should be ready to accept them, they would never establish themselves in the general mind. The progress of society depends on nothing more, than on the exposure of time-honored abuses, which cannot be touched without offending multitudes, than on the promulgation of principles, which are in advance of public sentiment and practice, and which are constantly at war with the habits, prejudices, and immediate interests of large classes of the community . . . The multitude, if once allowed to dictate or proscribe subjects of discussion, would strike society with spiritual blindness, and death. The world is to be carried forward by truth, which at first offends, which wins its way by degrees, which the many hate and would rejoice to crush. The right of free discussion is therefore to be guarded by the friends of mankind, with peculiar jealousy. It is at once the most sacred, and the most endangered of all our rights. He who would rob his neighbor of it, should have a mark set on him as the worst enemy of freedom. ■

From "The Abolitionists," 1841.

• KARL MARX

We do not belong to those malcontents who even before the appearance of the latest Prussian Censorship Edict exclaim: *Timeo Danaos et dona ferentes.* [1] Rather, since a scrutiny of a law already passed is permitted in the new Instruction, even if it does not agree with the government, we will begin with such a scrutiny itself. *Censorship is official criticism*; its norms are critical norms, which, therefore, must not be withheld from criticism, a field to which they belong. . . .

For twenty-two years, illegal actions have been committed by an administration that controls the

---

[1] I fear the Greeks bearing gifts: Virgil, *Aeneas.*

highest interest of the citizens, *their minds,* an administration that, even more than the Roman censors ever did, regulates not only the behavior of the individual citizen but also even the behavior of the public mind . . .

But let us return to the Instruction.

"According to this law," that is, Article II, "censorship shall not obstruct any serious and moderate pursuit of truth, nor put undue compulsion on writers, nor hinder the unrestrained sale of books."

The pursuit of truth, which is not to be impeded by censorship, is qualified as *serious* and *moderate.* Both qualifications point not to the content of the pursuit, but rather to something that lies outside the content. At the outset, they divert from the pursuit of truth and bring into play an unknown third factor. If an inquiry must constantly keep in mind this third factor, an irritation supported by law, will it not lose sight of the truth? Is it not the first duty of the seeker after the truth to proceed directly at it, without glancing to the right or left? Do I not forget to speak about the substance if I must never forget to state it in a prescribed form?

Truth is as little moderate as is light, and against what is it to be moderated? Against oneself? *Verum index sui et falsi.*[2] Hence *against falsehood?*

When moderation shapes the character of the investigation, it is more a sign of shying away from the truth than from untruth. It is a drag on every step taken. *In an investigation, it is a prescription for fear of discovering the result,* a means of keeping one from the truth.

Furthermore, truth is universal. It does not belong to me, it belongs to all; it possesses me, I do not possess it. My *style* is my property; it is my spiritual individuality. *Le style c'est l'homme.* [Style is the man.] Indeed! The law permits me to write, only I am supposed to write in a style different from *mine!* I may show the profile of my mind, but first I must present it in *prescribed form.* What man of honor will not blush at this effrontery and prefer to hide his head under his toga? . . .

You admire the enchanting diversity, the inex-

haustible wealth, of nature. You do not demand that the rose smell like the violet. But the richest of all—the mind—is to exist only in one kind? I am humorous, but the law commands that I write seriously. I am daring, but the law commands that my style be modest. *Gray on gray* is to be the only permissible color of freedom. Every dewdrop that reflects the sun glitters in an inexhaustible play of colors, but the intellectual sun, in no matter how many individuals it may be refracted, may produce only one, only the *official color!* The essential form of the mind is brightness and light, and you want to make the shadow its only appropriate manifestation; it is only to be clad in black, and yet among flowers there are no black ones. The essence of the mind is *always the truth itself,* and what do you make its essence? *Moderation.* Only a scamp is moderate, says Geothe, and you want to turn the mind into such a scamp? Or if moderation is to be that moderation of genius of which Schiller speaks, then you must first transform all citizens and especially all censors into geniuses. . . .

Finally, all this proceeds from a completely topsy-turvy and abstract view of *truth.* All objects of literary activity are subsumed under the one general concept of "*truth.*" Even if we disregard the *subjective* aspect, namely, that one and the same object appears differently in different individuals and expresses its various sides in as many various intellects, should not the *character of the object* exert some influence, even the slightest, on the investigation? Not only the result, but also the way to it belongs to truth. The pursuit of truth must itself be true; the true investigation is the unfolded truth whose scattered parts are encompassed in the results. . . .

Or is this metaphysical torment unnecessary? Is *truth* to be understood in such a way that *it is what the government orders it to be,* and that any investigation is a superfluous and obnoxious third element which cannot be entirely rejected *for reasons of etiquette?* It almost seems so. For investigation is understood as being *a priori* in *opposition* to truth, and appears, therefore, with that suspicious official accompaniment of seriousness and modera-

---

[2] Truth is the test of itself and of falsehood: Spinoza, *Ethics.*

tion which a layman is supposed to display before a priest. . . .

Moderation and seriousness of the investigation —both the [old] Censorship Edict and the new Instruction contain this requirement; but the latter is satisfied with the decent form as little as it is with the content. The *tendency* has become the main criterion, indeed the pervading thought . . . Moreover, the new Instruction does not say what tendency consists of, but its significance can be seen from the following excerpt:

"It is an indispensable requirement that the tendency of the criticism of governmental measures be well-intentioned and not hateful and malevolent; and it must be demanded from the censor that he have good will and insight, enabling him to distinguish one from the other. The censor has to pay special attention to the form and tone of the language used and must not permit publication of writings if their tendency is harmful because of passion, violence, and presumptuousness."

Hence the writer is subject to the *most frightful terrorism,* to *jurisdiction based on suspicion.* Tendentious laws, laws without objective norms, are laws of terrorism, such as those created by Robespierre because of a national emergency and by Roman Emperors because of corruption of the state. Laws that make as their chief criteria, not the *action as such* but the *sentiment* of the acting person, are nothing but *positive sanctions of lawlessness.* It would be better to act like the Czar of Russia who had everybody's beard cut off by official Cossacks, than to make the intention in wearing a beard the criterion of cutting it off.

Only insofar as I *express* myself and enter the sphere of actuality, do I enter the legislator's sphere. As far as the law is concerned, I do not exist at all and am not subject to it, except in *my action.* It alone concerns the law . . . But a tendentious law does not punish me for what I do do, but for what I intend *apart* from any action. Hence it is an insult to the honor of the citizen, a hoax directed against my existence.

I can turn and twist as much as possible—action does not come into question. My existence is sus-

pect; my innermost being, my individuality, is considered to be *evil,* and *for this opinion* I am to be *punished.* The law does not penalize me for wrongs I commit, but for wrongs I do not commit. I am actually punished because my actions are *not illegal,* for in this way alone a mild and well-meaning judge is compelled to consider my *evil sentiment,* which I am so clever as not to bring out into the open.

Such a law is *no law of the state* for the *citizens,* but a *law of one party against another party.* The law of intentions abolishes the equality of citizens before the law. It is a law of division, not of unity, and all laws that divide are reactionary. It is not a law, but a *privilege.* One person may do what another may not, not because the latter lacks the objective capability for action, as does a child in regard to the drawing up of contracts, but rather because his opinions and his intentions are suspect. The *ethical state* subordinates the *view of the state* to its members, even if they *oppose an organ of the state,* or the government; but a society in which *one* organ thinks of itself as the only, exclusive possessor of political reason and political morality, a government that in principle opposes the people and assumes, therefore, *their political opposition* to be universal, the normal opinion, the evil conscience of a faction—such a government invents laws of intention, *laws of vengeance,* against an opinion that exists only in the members of the government themselves. Laws of intention are based on disloyalty, and on an unethical, materialistic view of the state. They are an indiscreet outry of a bad conscience. And how is such a law to be executed? Through means more outrageous than the law itself, through *spies,* or through *a priori* decisions to consider entire literary movements suspect, in which case one must discover to which movement an individual belongs. Just as in the law of intention, the *legal form contradicts the content,* and the government which promulgates it eagerly denounces the very thing it represents itself, namely, antistate opinion, so likewise it constitutes a topsy-turvy world of laws, which it measures with two yardsticks. What is law on the one side is lawlessness on the other. *Its laws become the opposite of what it proclaims to be law.*

The new Censorship Instruction is entangled in this dialectic. It is contradictory to make it the censors' duty to carry out the very thing that is condemned as being antistate when it takes place in the press. . . .

We are asked to behave lawfully and with respect for the law, but at the same time we are to honor institutions that make us lawless and replace law with arbitrariness. We are to acknowledge the principle of personality to such an extent that, despite the deficient institution of censorship, we trust the censor, and you violate the principle of personality so much that you judge, not the action but the opinion of the opinion of the action. You demand modesty, and you proceed from the enormous arrogance of making the civil servant a spy of the heart, an all-knowing person, a philosopher, a theologian, a politician, a Delphic oracle. On the one hand, you make it a duty to acknowledge arrogance, and, on the other hand, you forbid us arrogance. The essential arrogance consists in ascribing the perfection of a species to particular individuals. The censor is a particular individual, but the press constitutes the species. You recommend trust to us, but you lend lawful force to mistrust. You place so much confidence in political institutions that you make the weak mortal and the official into a saint, so that the impossible would be possible for him. But you distrust your political organism so much that you fear the isolated opinion of a private person; for you treat the press as a private person. You demand of the officials that they act impersonally, without anger, passion, narrow-mindedness, or human frailty. But the impersonal, the *idea,* you suspect to be full of personal intrigues and subjective vileness. The Instruction demands unlimited confidence in officialdom, but it proceeds from limitless distrust toward nonofficials. Why should we not repay with the same? Why should we not be suspicious of officialdom? Likewise as regards character. From the outset, an unprejudiced person would have more respect for the character of a public critic than for that of a secret one. . . .

The editors of the daily press, into which category all journalism falls, are to be completely irreproachable men. "Scientific competence" is stated to be the first guarantee of such complete irreproachableness. Not the slightest doubt is raised as to whether the censor possesses scientific competence to judge any sort of scientific competence. If it is true that Prussia has such a multitude of scientific geniuses who are known to the government —each city has at least one censor—why do not these encyclopedic brains appear as writers? If these officials, overwhelming in number, mighty by virtue of their science and their genius, would rise for once and crush those wretched writers who are active in one genre of writing only, and even there without officially tested qualifications, the confusions of the press could be terminated better than by censorship. Why do these clever men keep silent when, like the Roman geese, they could save the Capitol by their cackle? They must be men of too much modesty. The scientific world does not know them, but the government does.

And if those men are men such as no state could ever find, for never has a state known entire classes consisting of universal geniuses and polyhistorians, how much more gifted must be those who choose them! What secret science must the latter possess to be able to attest to the scientific qualifications of officials who are otherwise unknown to the republic of science! The higher we climb in this bureaucracy of intelligence, the more wondrous are the minds we meet. Practically speaking, for a state possessing such pillars of a perfect press, is it worth the effort to appoint these men guardians of a deficient press, to use the perfect as a means for debasing the imperfect?

The more censors you employ, the more chances of improvement you take away from the realm of the press. You remove healthy people from your army to make them physicians for the sick. . . .

Unfortunately, the Censorship Instruction interrupts our panegyric. Alongside the guarantee of scientific competence, one finds requirements of "rank and character." Rank and character!

Character, placed immediately after rank, seems to be almost a mere effluence of rank. Let us, above all, take a look at rank. . . .

The general requirement of scientific competence, how liberal! The special requirement of rank, how illiberal! Since scientific competence and character are very indefinite, while rank is, on the contrary, definite, why should we not conclude that logically and necessarily the indefinite will lean on the definite and find support and content there? Would it be a great mistake of the censor to interpret the Instruction as saying that the *external form* of scientific competence and of character, as they appear in the world, constitute *rank,* the more so since the censor's own rank assures him that this is the government's view? Without this interpretation, it is, to say the least, completely incomprehensible why scientific competence and character are not sufficient guarantees in themselves, and why rank is made a necessary third requirement. Since these requirements are seldom if ever combined, the censor is in a dilemma as to which to choose, for, after all, somebody has to edit newspapers and periodicals. In the absence of rank, scientific competence and character, because of their indefiniteness, can be a problem for the censor, since he must understandably wonder how such qualities can exist apart from rank. On the other hand, may the censor have doubts about character and science where rank is concerned? In such a case, he would place less confidence in the judgment of the state than in himself, while in the opposite case he would place more confidence in the writer than in the state. Should a censor be so tactless and so wrong-minded? This is not to be expected and it certainly was not expected. *Rank,* because it is the decisive criterion in *case of doubt,* is altogether the *absolutely decisive* one. . . .

"Equal caution must be applied in appointing the censor, so that the office of censorship is put in the hands of men of proven disposition and ability, who fully deserve the honorable confidence required. Such men must be right-thinking and at the same time keen-minded. . . ."

What rank and character are for the writer, proven loyalty is for the censor, since in him rank is assumed. More important is the fact that while *scientific competence* is required in the writer, only *ability, without further modification, is required in the censor. . . .*

All objective norms have been abandoned; the personal relationship is left, and the tact of the censor has to be called a guarantee. What, then, can the censor violate? Tact. And tactlessness is no crime. What is the writer threatened with? His existence. What state had ever made the existence of a whole class dependent on the tact of individual officials?

Let us say it again: *All objective norms have been abandoned.* For the writer, tendency is made the final content, commanded and prescribed, the object being a formless opinion. The tendency as subject, as opinion of the opinion, is the tact and the sole guide of the censor.

Although the censor's arbitrariness—and the justification of mere opinion is justification for arbitrariness—is concealed behind the semblance of concrete directives, the Instruction, on the other hand, clearly asserts the arbitariness of the *Supreme Censorship Office,* which is given complete confidence. This confidence placed in the director is the ultimate guarantee of the press. Thus the essence of censorship in general is based on a police state's arrogant conceit about its officials. The public's sense and good will is not trusted even with the simplest thing; but for the officials, even the impossible is to be possible.

This basic fault runs through all our institutions. Thus, for example, in criminal proceedings, judge, plaintiff, and defendant are united in *one person.* This combination is contrary to all the laws of psychology. But the official is above the psychological laws to which the public is subject. . . .

The censor, too, is plaintiff, defendant, and judge combined in one person; he is entrusted with the administration of the mind. The censor is *irresponsible.*

Censorship could acquire a provisional loyal character if it were subject to the regular courts, which, of course, is not possible so long as no objective censorship laws exist. But the worst possible way would be for the censorship also to be censored, by some director or supreme commission, for example.

Everything that was said about the relationship

between the press and the censorship applies also to the relationship between the censorship and some Supreme Censorship, even though an intermediary is shoved in between. It is the same relationship, placed on a higher level . . . Every point would require the same compulsion and the same reaction. The Supreme Censorship would again have to be censored in turn. To escape this vicious circle, one decides to be disloyal; lawlessness then begins on the third or ninety-ninth level. Because officialdom is hazily aware of this, it tries to raise the level of lawlessness to such a lofty sphere that it disappears from view, believing that it has vanished.

The real, *radical cure of the censorship* is its *abolition*. For it is a bad institution, and institutions are more powerful than men. . . .

Rara temporum felicitas, ubi quae velis sentire et quae sentias dicere licet.[3] ∎

From "Remarks on the Latest Prussian Censorship Instruction," in Anekdota zur neuesten deutschen Philosophie und Publicistik, *1843.*

• JOHN STUART MILL

The peculiar evil of silencing the expression of an opinion is, that it is robbing the human race; posterity as well as the existing generation; those who dissent from the opinion, still more than those who hold it. If the opinion is right, they are deprived of the opportunity of exchanging error for truth: if wrong, they lose, what is almost as great a benefit, the clearer perception and livelier impression of truth, produced by its collision with error.

It is necessary to consider separately these two hypotheses . . . We can never be sure that the opinion we are endeavouring to stifle is a false opinion; and if we were sure, stifling it would be an evil still.

First: the opinion which it is attempted to suppress by authority may possibly be true. Those who desire to suppress it, of course deny its truth; but they are not infallible. They have no authority to decide the question for all mankind, and exclude every other person from the means of judging. To refuse a hearing to an opinion, because they are sure that it is false, is to assume that *their* certainty is the same thing as *absolute* certainty. All silencing of discussion is an assumption of infallibility. . . .

Unfortunately for the good sense of mankind, the fact of their fallibility is far from carrying the weight in their practical judgment, which is always allowed to it in theory; for while everyone well knows himself to be fallible, few think it necessary to take any precautions against their own fallibility, or admit the supposition that any opinion, of which they feel very certain, may be one of the examples of the error to which they acknowledge themselves to be liable. Absolute princes, or others who are accustomed to unlimited deference, usually feel this complete confidence in their own opinions on nearly all subjects. People more happily situated, who sometimes hear their opinions disputed, and are not wholly unused to be set right when they are wrong, place the same unbounded reliance only on such of their opinions as are shared by all who surround them, or to whom they habitually defer: for in proportion to a man's want of confidence in his own solitary judgment, does he usually repose, with implicit trust, on the infallibility of "the world" in general. And the world, to each individual, means the part of it with which he comes in contact; his party, his sect, his church, his class of society . . . Nor is his faith in this collective authority at all shaken by his being aware that other ages, countries, sects, churches, classes, and parties have thought, and even now think, the exact reverse. He devolves upon his own world the responsibility of being in the right against the dissentient worlds of other people; and it never troubles him that mere accident has decided which of these numerous worlds is the object of his reliance, and that the same causes which make him a Churchman in London, would have made him a Buddhist or a Confucian in Pekin. Yet it is as evident in itself, as any amount of argument can make it, that ages are no more infallible than individuals; every age having held many opinions which subsequent ages have deemed not only false but absurd;

---

[3] How rare the fortunate times when you may think what you wish and say what you think: Tacitus.

and it is as certain that many opinions, now general, will be rejected by future ages, as it is that many, once general, are rejected by the present.

The objection likely to be made to this argument, would probably take some such form as the following. There is no greater assumption of infallibility in forbidding the propagation of error, than in any other thing which is done by public authority on its own judgment and responsibility. Judgment is given to men that they may use it. Because it may be used erroneously, are men to be told that they ought not to use it all? . . . If we were never to act on our opinions, because these opinions may be wrong, we should leave all our interests uncared for, and all our duties unperformed . . . Men, and governments, must act to the best of their ability. There is no such thing as absolute certainty, but there is assurance sufficient for human life. We may, and must, assume our opinion to be true for the guidance of our own conduct: and it is assuming no more when we forbid bad men to pervert society by the propagation of opinions which we regard as false and pernicious.

I answer, that it is assuming very much more. There is the greatest difference between presuming an opinion to be true, because, with every opportunity for contesting it, it has not been refuted, and assuming its truth for the purpose of not permitting its refutation. Complete liberty of contradicting and disproving our opinion, is the very condition which justifies us in assuming its truth for purposes of action; and on no other terms can a being with human faculties have any rational assurance of being right. . . .

In the present age—which has been described as "destitute of faith but terrified at scepticism"—in which people feel sure, not so much that their opinions are true, as that they should not know what to do without them—the claims of an opinion to be protected from public attack are rested not so much on its truth, as on its importance to society. There are, it is alleged, certain beliefs, so useful, not to say indispensable to well-being that it is as much the duty of governments to uphold those beliefs, as to protect any other of the interests of society . . . This mode of thinking makes the justification of restraints on discussion not a question of the truth of doc-

trines, but of their usefulness . . . But those who thus satisfy themselves, do not perceive that the assumption of infallibility is merely shifted from one point to another. The usefulness of an opinion is itself a matter of opinion: as disputable, as open to discussion, and requiring discussion as much, as the opinion itself . . . The truth of an opinion is part of its utility . . . There can be no fair discussion of the question of usefulness, when an argument so vital may be employed on one side, but not on the other. And in point of fact, when law or public feeling do not permit the truth of an opinion to be disputed, they are just as little tolerant of a denial of its usefulness. . . .

Aware of the impossibility of defending the use of punishment for restraining irreligious opinions . . . the enemies of religious freedom, when hard pressed, occasionally . . . say . . . that the persecutors of Christianity [under Marcus Aurelius] were in the right; that persecution is an ordeal through which truth ought to pass, and always passes successfully, legal penalties being, in the end, powerless against truth, though sometimes beneficially effective against mischievous errors. This is a form of the argument for religious intolerance, sufficiently remarkable not to be passed without notice.

A theory which maintains that truth may justifiably be persecuted because persecution cannot possibly do it any harm, cannot be charged with being intentionally hostile to the reception of new truths; but we cannot commend the generosity of its dealing with the persons to whom mankind are indebted for them. To discover to the world something which deeply concerns it, and of which it was previously ignorant; to prove to it that it had been mistaken on some vital point of temporal or spiritual interests, is as important a service as a human being can render to his fellow-creatures . . . That the authors of such splendid benefits should be requited by martyrdom; that their reward should be to be dealt with as the vilest of criminals, is not, upon this theory, a deplorable error and misfortune, for which humanity should mourn in sackcloth and ashes, but the normal and justifiable state of things. The propounder of a new truth, according to this doctrine, should stand . . . with a halter round his neck, to be instantly tightened if the public assembly did not, on hearing his reasons, then and there adopt his proposition. People who defend this mode of treating benefactors, cannot be supposed to set much value on the benefit. . . .

But, indeed, the dictum that truth always triumphs over persecution, is one of those pleasant falsehoods which men repeat after one another till they pass into commonplaces, but which all experiences refutes. History teems with instances of truth put down by persecution. If not suppressed for ever, it may be thrown back for centuries. To speak only of religious opinions: the Reformation broke out at least twenty times before Luther, and was put down. Arnold of Brescia was put down. Fra Dolcino was put down. Savonarola was put down. The Albigeois were put down. The Vaudois were put down. The Lollards were put down. The Hussites were put down. Even after the era of Luther, wherever persecution was persisted in, it was successful. In Spain, Italy, Flanders, the Austrian empire, Protestantism was rooted out: and, most likely, would have been so in England, had Queen Mary lived, or Queen Elizabeth died. Persecution has always succeeded, save where the heretics were too strong a party to be effectually persecuted. No reasonable person can doubt that Christianity might have been extirpated in the Roman Empire. It spread, and became predominant, because the persecutions were only occasional, lasting but a short time, and separated by long intervals of almost undisturbed propagandism. It is a piece of idle sentimentality that truth, merely as truth, has any inherent power denied to error, of prevailing against the dungeon and the stake. Men are not more zealous for truth than they often are for error, and a sufficient application of legal or even of social penalities will generally succeed in stopping the propagation of either. The real advantage which truth has, consists in this: that when an opinion is true, it may be extinguished once, twice or many times, but in the course of ages there will generally be found persons to rediscover it, until some one of its reappearances falls on a time when from favourable circumstances it escapes persecution until it has made such head as to withstand all subsequent attempts to suppress it. . . .

Let us now pass to the second division of the argument, and dismissing the supposition that any of the received opinions may be false, let us assume them to be true, and examine into the worth of the manner in which they are likely to be held, when their truth is not freely and openly canvassed. However unwillingly a person who has a strong opinion may admit the possibility that his opinion may be false, he ought to be moved by the consideration that however true it may be, if it be not fully, frequently, and fearlessly discussed, it will be held as a dead dogma, not a living truth. . . .

Such persons, if they can once get their creed taught from authority, naturally think that no good, and some harm, comes of its being allowed to be questioned. Where their influence prevails, they make it nearly impossible for the received opinion to be rejected wisely and considerately, though it may still be rejected rashly and ignorantly; for to shut out discussion entirely is seldom possible, and when it once gets in, beliefs not grounded on conviction are apt to give way before the slightest semblance of an argument . . . This is not the way truth ought to be held by a rational being. This is not knowing the truth. Truth, thus held, is but one superstition the more, accidentally clinging to the words which enunciate a truth. . . .

If, however, the mischievous operation of the absence of free discussion, when the received opinions are true, were confined to leaving men ignorant of the grounds of those opinions, it might be thought that this . . . is no moral evil, and does not affect the worth of the opinions . . . The fact, however, is, that not only the grounds of the opinion are forgotten in the absence of discussion, but too often the meaning of the opinion itself. The words which convey it, cease to suggest ideas, or suggest only a small portion of those they were originally employed to communicate. Instead of a vivid conception and a living belief, there remain only a few phrases retained by rote; or, if any part, the shell and husk only of the meaning is retained, the finer essence being lost. . . .

We have hitherto considered only two possibilities: that the received opinion may be false, and some other opinion, consequently, true; or that, the received opinion being true, a conflict with the opposite error is essential to a clear apprehension and deep feeling of its truth. But there is a commoner case than either of these; when the conflicting doctrines, instead of being one true and the other false, share the truth between them; and the nonconforming opinion is needed to supply the remainder of the truth, of which the received doctrine embodies only a part. Popular opinions . . . are often true, but seldom or never the whole truth. They are a part of the truth . . . but exaggerated, distorted, and disjoined from the truths by which they ought to be accompanied and limited. Heretical opinions, on the other hand, are generally some of these suppressed and neglected truths, bursting the bonds which kept them down, and either seeking reconciliation with the truth contained in the common opinion, or . . . setting themselves up, with similar exclusiveness, as the whole truth. The latter case is hitherto the most frequent, as in the human mind, one-sidedness has always been the rule, and many-sidedness the exception. Hence, even in revolutions of opinion, one part of the truth usually sets while the other rises. Even progress, which ought to superadd, for the most part only substitutes one partial and incomplete truth for another; improvement consisting chiefly in this, that the new fragment of truth is more wanted, more adapted to the needs of the time, than that which it displaces . . . Every opinion which embodies somewhat of the portion of truth which the common opinion omits, ought to be considered precious, with whatever amount of error and confusion that truth may be blended . . . As long as popular truth is one-sided, it is more desirable than otherwise that unpopular truth should have one-sided asserters too; such being usually the most energetic, and the most likely to compel reluctant attention to the fragment of wisdom which they proclaim as if it were the whole. . . .

In politics, again, it is almost a commonplace, that a party of order or stability, and a party of progress or reform, are both necessary elements of a healthy state of political life; until the one or the other shall have so enlarged its mental grasp as to be a party equally of order and of progress, knowning and dis-

tinguishing what is fit to be preserved from what ought to be swept away. Each of these modes of thinking derives its utility from the deficiencies of the other; but it is in a great measure the opposition of the other that keeps each within the limits of reason and sanity. Unless opinions favourable to democracy and to aristocracy, to property and to equality, to cooperation and to competition, to luxury and to abstinence, to sociality and individuality, to liberty and discipline, and all the other standing antagonisms of practical life, are expressed with equal freedom, and enforced and defended with equal talent and energy, there is no chance of both elements obtaining their due; one scale is sure to go up, and the other down. Truth, in the great practical concerns of life, is so much a question of the reconciling and combining of opposites, that very few have minds sufficiently capacious and impartial to make the adjustment with an approach to correctness, and it has to be made by the rough process of a struggle between combatants fighting under hostile banners. . . .

I do not pretend that the most unlimited use of the freedom of enunciating all possible opinions would put an end to the evils of religious or philosophical sectarianism. Every truth which men of narrow capacity are in earnest about, is sure to be asserted, inculcated, and in many ways even acted, as if no other truth existed in the world . . . But it is not on the impassioned partisan, it is on the calmer and more disinterested bystander, that this collision of opinions works its salutary effect. Not the violent conflict between parts of truth, but the quiet suppression of half of it, is the formidable evil: there is always hope when people are forced to listen to both sides; it is when they attend only to one that errors harden into prejudices, and truth itself ceases to have the effect of truth, by being exaggerated into falsehood . . . Truth has no chance but in proportion as every side of it, every opinion which embodies any fraction of the truth, not only finds advocates, but is so advocated as to be listened to.

We have now recognized the necessity to the mental well-being of mankind (on which all their other well-being depends) of freedom of opinion, and freedom of the expression of opinion, on four distinct grounds; which we will now briefly recapitulate.

First, if any opinion is compelled to silence, that opinion may, for aught we can certainly know, be true. To deny this is to assume our own infallibility.

Secondly, though the silenced opinion be an error, it may, and very commonly does, contain a portion of truth; and since the general or prevailing opinion on any subject is rarely or never the whole truth, it is only by the collision of adverse opinions that the remainder of the truth has any chance of being supplied.

Thirdly, even if the received opinion be not only true, but the whole truth; unless it is suffered to be, and actually is, vigorously and earnestly contested, it will, by most of those who receive it, be held in the manner of a prejudice, with little comprehension or feeling of its rational grounds. And not only this, but, fourthly, the meaning of the doctrine itself will be in danger of being lost or enfeebled, and deprived of its vital effect on the character and conduct: the dogma becoming a mere formal profession, inefficacious for good, but cumbering the ground, and preventing the growth of any real and heartfelt conviction, from reason or personal experience. ■

From On Liberty, *1859.*

• JAMES BRYCE

The obvious weakness of government by opinion is the difficulty of ascertaining it. Such is the din of voices that it is hard to say which cry prevails, which is welled by many, which only by a few throats. The organs of opinion seem almost as numerous as the people themselves, and they are all engaged in representing their own view as that of "the people." Like other valuable articles, genuine opinion is surrounded by counterfeits. The one positive test applicable is that of an election, and an election can at best do no more than test the division of opinion between two or three great parties, leaving subsidiary issues uncertain, while in many cases the result depends so much on the personal merits of the candidates as to render interpretation difficult. . . .

Thus the difficulty inherent in government by public opinion makes itself seriously felt. It can express desires, but has not the machinery for turning them into practical schemes. It can determine ends, but is less fit to examine and select means. . . .

Public opinion is slow and clumsy in grappling with large practical problems. It looks at them, talks incessantly about them, complains of Congress for not solving them, is distressed that they do not solve themselves. But they remain unsolved. Vital decisions have usually hung fire longer than they would have been likely to do in European countries. . . .

The long-suffering tolerance of public opinion towards incompetence and misconduct in officials and public men generally, is a feature which has struck recent European observers . . . We may attribute it partly to the good nature of the people, which makes them over-lenient to nearly all criminals, partly to the preoccupation with their private affairs of the most energetic and useful men, who therefore cannot spare time to unearth abuses and get rid of offenders, partly to an indifference induced by a sort of fatalistic sentiment. This sentiment acts in two ways. Being optimistic, it disposes each man to believe that things will come out right whether he "takes hold" himself or not, and that it is therefore no great matter whether a particular Ring or Boss is suppressed. And in making each individual man feel his insignificance, it disposes him to leave to the multitude the task of setting right what is everyone else's business just as much as his own. . . .

The enormous force of public opinion is a danger to the people themselves, as well as their leaders. It no longer makes them tyrannical. But it fills them with an undue confidence in their wisdom, their virtue, and their freedom. It may be thought that a nation which uses freedom well can hardly have too much freedom; yet even such a nation may be too much inclined to think freedom an absolute and all-sufficient good, to seek truth only in the voice of the majority, to mistake prosperity for greatness. . . .

Public opinion is a sort of atmosphere, fresh, keen, and full of sunlight, like that of the American cities, and this sunlight kills many of those noxious germs which are hatched where politicians congregate . . . Selfishness, injustice, cruelty, tricks, and jobs of all sorts shun the light; to expose them is to defeat them . . . So long as the opinion of a nation is sound, the main lines of its policy cannot go far wrong, whatever waste of time and money may be incurred in carrying them out. . . .

Opinion declares itself legally through elections. But opinion is at work at other times also, and has other methods of declaring itself. It secures full discussion of issues of policy and of the characters of men. It suffers nothing to be concealed. It listens patiently to all the arguments that are addressed to it . . . Thus a democracy governing itself through a constantly active public opinion, and not solely by its intermittent mechanism of elections, tends to become patient, tolerant, reasonable, and is more likely to be unembittered and unvexed by class divisions. ∎

From The American Commonwealth, *Part III,*
Chapter 57, 1888.

3

SUPREME COURT OPINIONS ON THE PRESS AND FREEDOM OF DISCUSSION

The "Clear and Present Danger" Doctrine
Justice Oliver Wendell Holmes

The "Test of Truth" Doctrine
Justice Oliver Wendell Holmes

Advocacy of Revolution
Justice Edward T. Sanford
Justice Louis D. Brandeis

Advocacy of Communism
Chief Justice Charles Evans Hughes
Chief Justice Frederick M. Vinson
Justice Hugo L. Black

• EDITOR'S NOTE

In modern times, wars and radical movements have created special conditions in the realm of free speech. Fundamentally, the question is what, if any, limits may or should be imposed upon the expression of unpopular ideas or on the public advocacy of dangerous policies. There is no problem in regard to subversive *action*: that is unequivocally punishable. But the line between expression of opinion and advocacy of a cause is, indeed, delicate and not easily measurable by legal yardsticks.

Did a democratic government have a right or duty to punish the propagators of subversive, or deemed subversive, *opinions* in time of war and crisis? If the expression of opinions distasteful to the great majority was forbidden in the name of national security or patriotism, what became of the free speech guarantee embodied in the First Amendment? On the other hand, did not a democratic government have a right, in self-defense, to protect itself against subversive ideas in periods of national danger? Which of the two was the paramount right?

Answers to these questions are not always clear, even in the minds of the justices of the Supreme Court who have had to grapple with them. Oliver Wendell Holmes seems to have reversed himself on the subject within the same year, voting for conviction in the Schenck case and for acquittal in Abrams. The opinions of the justices in the cases that follow, and the reasoning behind their decisions, are fascinating examples not only of the democratic process but also of the molding of the ideas and assumptions underlying the philosophy of freedom.

• JUSTICE OLIVER WENDELL HOLMES

This is an indictment in three counts. The first charges a conspiracy to violate the Espionage Act of June 15, 1917 . . . by causing and attempting to cause insubordination, etc., in the military and naval forces of the United States, and to obstruct the recruiting and enlistment service of the United States, when the United States was at war with the German Empire, to wit, that the defendants wilfully conspired to have printed and circulated to men . . . [in the] military service . . . a document to cause such insubordination and obstruction. . . .

Schenck personally attended to the printing [of the leaflet against conscription] . . . No reasonable man could doubt that the defendant Schenck was largely instrumental in sending the circulars about. . . .

The document in question upon its first printed side recited the first section of the Thirteenth Amendment,[1] said that the idea embodied in it was violated by the Conscription Act and that a conscript is little better than a convict. In impassioned language it intimated that conscription was despotism in its worst form and a monstrous wrong against humanity in the interest of Wall Street's chosen few . . . Of course the document would not have been sent unless it had been intended to have some effect, and we do not see what effect it could be expected to have upon persons subject to the draft except to influence them to obstruct the carrying of it out. . . .

But it is said, suppose that that was the tendency of this circular, it is protected by the First Amendment to the Constitution. . . . We admit that in many places and in ordinary times the defendants in saying all that was said in the circular would have been within their constitutional rights. But the character of every act depe   upon the circumstances in which it is done. The most stringent protection of free speech would not protect a man in falsely shouting fire in a theatre and causing a panic. It does not even protect a man from an injunction uttering words that may have all the effect of force. The question in every case is whether the words used are used in such circumstances and are of such a nature as to create a clear and present danger that they will bring about the substantive evils that Congress has a right to prevent. It is a question of prox-

imity and degree. When a nation is at war many things that might be said in time of peace are such a hindrance to its effort that their utterance will not be endured so long as men fight and that no court could regard them as protected by any constitutional right. It seems to be admitted that if an actual obstruction of the recruiting service were proved, liability for words that produced that effect might be enforced. The statute of 1917 . . . punishes conspiracies to obstruct as well as actual obstruction. If the act (speaking, or circulating a paper), its tendency and the intent with which it is done, are the same, we perceive no ground for saying that success alone warrants making the act a crime. . . .

Judgments *affirmed.* ■

From Majority Opinion, Schenck v. United States, 1919.

• JUSTICE OLIVER WENDELL HOLMES

This indictment is founded wholly upon the publication of two leaflets which I shall describe in a moment. The first count charges a conspiracy pending the war with Germany to publish abusive language about the form of government of the United States, laying the preparation and publishing of the first leaflet as overt acts. The second count charges a conspiracy pending the war to publish language intended to bring the form of government into contempt, laying the preparation and publishing of the two leaflets as overt acts. The third count alleges a conspiracy to encourage resistance to the United States in the same war and to attempt to effectuate the purpose by publishing the same leaflets. The fourth count lays a conspiracy to incite curtailment of production of things necessary to the prosecution of the war and to attempt to accomplish it by publishing the second leaflet to which I have referred.

The other leaflet, headed "Workers—Wake Up," with abusive language says that America together with the Allies will march for Russia to help the Czecho-Slovaks in their struggle against the Bolsheviki, and that this time the hypocrites shall not fool the Russian emigrants and friends of Russia in

---

[1] Article XIII, Section 1: "Neither slavery nor involuntary servitude, except as a punishment for crime whereof the party shall have been duly convicted, shall exist within the United States, or any place subject to their jurisdiction."

America. It tells the Russian emigrants that they now must spit in the face of false military propaganda by which their sympathy and help to the prosecution of the war have been called forth and says that with the money they have lent or are going to lend "they will make bullets not only for the Germans but also for the Workers' Soviets of Russia," and further, "Workers in the ammunition factories, you are producing bullets, bayonets, cannon, to murder not only the Germans but also your dearest, best, who are in Russia fighting for freedom." It then appeals to the same Russian emigrants at some length not to consent to the "inquisitionary expedition to Russia," and says that the destruction of the Russian revolution is "the politics of the march on Russia." The leaflet winds up by saying "Workers, our reply to this barbaric intervention has to be a general strike!" and after a few words on the spirit of revolution, exhortations not to be afraid, and some usual tall talk, ends "Woe unto those who will be in the way of progress. Let solidarity live! The Rebels."

No argument seems to me necessary to show that these pronunciamentos in no way attack the form of government of the United States, or that they do not support either of the first two counts. What little I have to say about the third count may be postponed until I have considered the fourth. With regard to that it seems too plain to be denied that the suggestion to workers in ammunition factories that they are producing bullets to murder their dearest, and the further advocacy of a general strike, both in the second leaflet, do urge curtailment of production of things necessary to the prosecution of the war within the meaning of the Act of May 16, 1918 . . . amending §3 of the earlier Act of 1917. But to make the conduct criminal that statute requires that it should be "with intent by such curtailment to cripple or hinder the United States in the prosecution of the war." It seems to me that no such intent is proved.

I am aware of course that the word intent as vaguely used in ordinary legal discussion means no more than knowledge at the time of the act that the consequences said to be intended will ensue. Even less than that will satisfy the general principle of civil and criminal liability. A man may have to pay damages, may be sent to prison, at common law might be hanged, if at the time of his act he knew facts from which common experience showed that the consequences would follow, whether he individually could foresee them or not. But, when words are used exactly, a deed is not done with intent to produce a consequence unless that consequence is the aim of the deed. It may be obvious, and obvious to the actor, that the consequence will follow, and he may be liable for it even if he forgets it, but he does not do the act with intent to produce it unless the aim to produce it is the proximate motive of the specific act, although there may be some deeper motive behind.

It seems to me that this statute must be taken to use its words in a strict and accurate sense. They would be absurd in any other. A patriot might think that we were wasting money on aeroplanes, or making more cannon of a certain kind than we needed, and might advocate curtailment with success, yet even if it turned out that the curtailment hindered and was thought by other minds to have been obviously likely to hinder the United States in the prosecution of the war, no one would hold such conduct a crime. I admit that my illustration does not answer all that might be said but it is enough to show what I think and to let me pass to a more important aspect of the case. I refer to the First Amendment to the Constitution that Congress shall make no law abridging the freedom of speech.

I never have seen any reason to doubt that the questions of law that alone were before this Court in the cases of Schenck, Frohwerk and Debs were rightly decided. I do not doubt for a moment that by the same reasoning that would justify punishing persuasion to murder, the United States constitutionally may punish speech that produces or is intended to produce a clear and imminent danger that it will bring about forthwith certain substantive evils that the United States constitutionally may seek to prevent. The power undoubtedly is greater in time of war than in time of peace because war opens dangers that do not exist at other times.

But as against dangers peculiar to war, as against others, the principle of the right to free speech is always the same. It is only the present danger of immediate evil or an intent to bring it about that warrants Congress in setting a limit to the expression of opinion where private rights are not concerned. Congress certainly cannot forbid all effort to change the mind of the country. Now nobody can suppose that the surreptitious publishing of a silly leaflet by an unknown man, without more, would present any immediate danger that its opinions would hinder the success of the Government arms or have any appreciable tendency to do so. Publishing these opinions for the very purpose of obstructing, however, might indicate a greater danger and at any rate would have the quality of an attempt. So I assume that the second leaflet, if published for the purpose alleged in the fourth count, might be punishable. But it seems pretty clear to me that nothing less than that would bring these papers within the scope of this law.

An actual intent in the sense that I have explained is necessary to constitute an attempt, where a further act of the same individual is required to complete the substantive crime, for reasons given in *Swift & Co.* v. *United States,* 196 U.S. 375, 396. It is necessary where the success of the attempt depends upon others, because if that intent is not present the actor's aim may be accomplished without bringing about the evils sought to be checked. An intent to prevent interference with the revolution in Russia might have been satisfied without any hindrance to carrying on the war in which we were engaged.

I do not see how anyone can find the intent required by the statute in any of the defendants' words. The second leaflet is the only one that affords even a foundation for the charge, and there, without invoking the hatred of German militarism expressed in the former one, it is evident from the beginning to the end that the only object of the paper is to help Russia and to stop American intervention there against the popular government—not to impede the United States in the war that it was carrying on. To say that two phrases taken literally might import a suggestion of conduct that would have interference with the war as an indirect and probably undesired effect seems to me by no means enough to show an attempt to produce that effect.

I return for a moment to the third count. That charges an intent to provoke resistance to the United States in its war with Germany. Taking the clause in the statute that deals with that in connection with the other elaborate provisions of the Act, I think that resistance to the United States means some forcible act of opposition to some proceeding of the United States in pursuance of the war. I think the intent must be the specific intent that I have described and for the reasons that I have given. I think that no such intent was proved or existed in fact. I also think that there is no hint at resistance to the United States as I construe the phrase.

In this case sentences of twenty years' imprisonment have been imposed for the publishing of two leaflets that I believe the defendants had as much right to publish as the Government has to publish the Constitution of the United States now vainly invoked by them. Even if I am technically wrong and enough can be squeezed from these poor and puny anonymities to turn the color of legal litmus paper— I will add, even if what I think the necessary intent were shown—the most nominal punishment seems to me all that possibly could be inflicted, unless the defendants are to be made to suffer not for what the indictment alleges but for the creed that they avow—a creed that I believe to be the creed of ignorance and immaturity when honestly held, as I see no reason to doubt that it was held here, but which, although made the subject of examination at the trial, no one has a right even to consider in dealing with the charges before the Court.

Persecution for the expression of opinions seems to me perfectly logical. If you have no doubt of your premises or your power and want a certain result with all your heart you naturally express your wishes in law and sweep away all opposition. To allow opposition by speech seems to indicate that you think speech impotent, as when a man says that he has squared the circle, or that you do not care wholeheartedly for the result, or that you doubt either your power or your premises.

But when men have realized that time has upset many fighting faiths, they may come to believe even more than they believe the very foundations of their own conduct that the ultimate good desired is better reached by free trade in ideas—that the best test of truth is the power of the thought to get itself accepted in the competition of the market, and that truth is the only ground upon which their wishes safely can be carried out. That, at any rate, is the theory of our Constitution. It is an experiment, as all life is an experiment. Every year if not every day we have to wager our salvation upon some prophecy based upon imperfect knowledge. While that experiment is part of our system I think that we should be eternally vigilant against attempts to check the expressions of opinions that we loathe and believe to be fraught with death, unless they so imminently threaten immediate interference with the lawful and pressing purposes of the law that an immediate check is required to save the country.

I wholly disagree with the argument of the Government that the First Amendment left the common law as to seditious libel in force. History seems to me against the notion. I had conceived that the United States through many years had shown its repentance for the Sedition Act of 1798 by repaying fines that it imposed. Only the emergency that makes it immediately dangeous to leave the correction of evil counsels to time warrants making any exception to the sweeping command, "Congress shall make no law . . . abridging the freedom of speech." Of course I am speaking only of expressions of opinion and exhortations, which were all that were uttered here, but I regret that I cannot put into more impressive words my belief that in their conviction upon this indictment the defendants were deprived of their rights under the Constitution of the United States. ■

From Dissenting Opinion, Abrams *v.* United States, *1919.*

• JUSTICE EDWARD T. SANFORD

Benjamin Gitlow was indicted in the Supreme Court of New York, with three others, for the statutory crime of criminal anarchy . . . He was separately tried, convicted, and sentenced to imprisonment. The judgment was affirmed by the Appellate Division and by the Court of Appeals . . . The case is here on writ of error to the Supreme Court, to which the record was remitted. . . .

The contention here is that the statute, by its terms and as applied in this case, is repugnant to the due process clause of the Fourteenth Amendment. . . .

The indictment was in two counts. The first charged that the defendant had advocated, advised and taught the duty, necessity and propriety of overthrowing and overturning organized government by force, violence and unlawful means, by certain writings therein set forth entitled "The Left Wing Manifesto"; the second that he had printed, published and knowingly circulated and distributed a certain paper called "The Revolutionary Age," containing the writings set forth in the first count advocating, advising and teaching the doctrine that organized government should be overthrown by force, violence and unlawful means. . . .

The court . . . charged the jury, in substance, that they must determine what was the intent, purpose and fair meaning of the Manifesto; that its words must be taken in their ordinary meaning, as they would be understood by people whom it might reach; that a mere statement or analysis of social and economic facts and historical incidents, in the nature of an essay, accompanied by prophecy as to the future course of events, but with no teaching, advice or advocacy of action, would not constitute the advocacy, advice or teaching of a doctrine for the overthrow of government within the meaning of the statute; that a mere statement that unlawful acts might accomplish such a purpose would be insufficient, unless there was a teaching, advising and advocacy of employing such unlawful acts for the purpose of overthrowing government; and that if the jury had a reasonable doubt that the Manifesto did teach, advocate or advise the duty, necessity or propriety of using unlawful means for the overthrowing of organized government, the defendant was entitled to an acquittal. . . .

The sole contention here is, essentially, that as there was no evidence of any concrete result flowing from the publication of the Manifesto or of circumstances showing the likelihood of such result, the statute as construed and applied by the trial court penalizes the mere utterance, as such, of "doctrine" having no quality of incitement, without regard either to the circumstances of its utterance or to the likelihood of unlawful sequences; and that, as the exercise of the right of free expression with relation to government is only punishable "in circumstances involving likelihood of substantive evil," the statute contravenes the due process clause of the Fourteenth Amendment. The argument in support of this contention rests primarily upon the following propositions: 1st, That the "liberty" protected by the Fourteenth Amendment includes the liberty of speech and of the press; and 2nd, That while liberty of expression "is not absolute," it may be restrained "only in circumstances where its exercise bears a causal relation with some substantive evil, consummated, attempted or likely," and as the statute "takes no account of circumstances," it unduly restrains this liberty and is therefore unconstitutional.

The precise question presented, and the only question which we can consider under this writ of error, then, is whether the statute, as construed and applied in this case by the state courts, deprived the defendant of his liberty of expression in violation of the due process clause of the Fourteenth Amendment.

The statute does not penalize the utterance or publication of abstract "doctrine" or academic discussion having no quality of incitement to any concrete action. It is not aimed against mere historical or philosophical essays. It does not restrain the advocacy of changes in the form of government by constitutional and lawful means. What it prohibits is language advocating, advising or teaching the overthrow of organized government by unlawful means. These words imply urging to action. Advocacy is defined in the Century Dictionary as: "1. The act of pleading for, supporting, or recommending; active espousal." It is not the abstract "doctrine" of overthrowing organized government by unlawful means which is denounced by the statute, but the advocacy of action for the accomplishment of that purpose. It was so construed and applied by the trial judge, who specifically charged the jury that: "A mere grouping of historical events and a prophetic deduction from them would neither

constitute advocacy, advice or teaching of a doctrine for the overthrow of government by force, violence or unlawful means. [And] if it were a mere essay on the subject, as suggested by counsel, based upon deductions from alleged historical events, with no teaching, advice or advocacy of action, it would not constitute a violation of the statute. . . ."

The Manifesto, plainly, is neither the statement of abstract doctrine nor, as suggested by counsel, mere prediction that industrial disturbances and revolutionary mass strikes will result spontaneously in an inevitable process of evolution in the economic system. It advocates and urges in fervent language mass action which shall progressively foment industrial disturbances and through political mass strikes and revolutionary mass action overthrow and destroy organized parliamentary government. It concludes with a call to action in these words: "The proletariat revolution and the Communist reconstruction of society—*the struggle for these*—is now indispensable . . . The Communist International calls the proletariat of the world to the final struggle!" This is not the expression of philosophical abstraction, the mere prediction of future events; it is the language of direct incitement.

The means advocated for bringing about the destruction of organized parliamentary government, namely, mass industrial revolts usurping the functions of municipal government, political mass strikes directed against the parliamentary state, and revolutionary mass action for its final destruction, necessarily imply the use of force and violence, and in their essential nature are inherently unlawful in a constitutional government of law and order. That the jury were warranted in finding that the Manifesto advocated not merely the abstract doctrine of overthrowing organized government by force, violence and unlawful means, but action to that end, is clear.

For present purposes we may and do assume that freedom of speech and of the press—which are protected by the First Amendment from abridgment by Congress—are among the fundamental personal rights and "liberties" protected by the due process clause of the Fourteenth Amendment from impairment by the States. . . .

It is a fundamental principle, long established, that the freedom of speech and of the press which is secured by the Constitution, does not confer an absolute right to speak or publish, without responsibility, whatever one may choose, or an unrestricted and unbridled license that gives immunity for every possible use of language and prevents the punishment of those who abuse this freedom . . . Reasonably limited, it was said by Story in the passage cited, this freedom is an inestimable privilege in a free government; without such limitation, it might become the scourge of the republic.

That a State in the exercise of its police power may punish those who abuse this freedom by utterances inimical to the public welfare, tending to corrupt public morals, incite to crime, or disturb the public peace, is not open to question. . . .

And, for yet more imperative reasons, a State may punish utterances endangering the foundations of organized government and threatening its overthrow by unlawful means. These imperil its own existence as a constitutional State. Freedom of speech and press, said Story . . . does not protect disturbances to the public peace or the attempt to subvert the government. It does not protect publications or teachings which tend to subvert or imperil the government or to impede or hinder it in the performance of its governmental duties . . . It does not protect publications prompting the overthrow of government by force: the punishment of those who publish articles which tend to destroy organized society being essential to the security of freedom and the stability of the State . . . And a State may penalize utterances which openly advocate the overthrow of the representative and constitutional form of government of the United States and the several States, by violence or other unlawful means . . . In short, this freedom does not deprive a State of the primary and essential right of self preservation: which, so long as human governments endure, they cannot be denied. . . .

By enacting the present statute the State has determined, through its legislative body, that utterances advocating the overthrow of organized government by force, violence and unlawful means, are so inimical to the general welfare and involve such danger of substantive evil that they may be penalized in the exercise of its police power. That determination must be given great weight. Every presumption is to be indulged in favor of the validity of the statute . . . That utterances inciting to the overthrow of organized government by unlawful means, present a sufficient danger of substantive evil to bring their punishment within the range of legislative discretion, is clear. Such utterances, by their very nature, involve danger to the public peace and to the security of the State. They threaten breaches of the peace and ultimate revolution. And the immediate danger is none the less real and substantial, because the effect of a given utterance cannot be accurately foreseen. The State cannot reasonably be required to measure the danger from every such utterance in the nice balance of a jeweler's scale. A single revolutionary spark may kindle a fire that, smouldering for a time, may burst into a sweeping and destructive conflagration. It cannot be said that the State is acting arbitrarily or unreasonably when in the exercise of its judgment as to the measures necessary to protect the public peace and safety, it seeks to extinguish the spark without waiting until it has enkindled the flame or blazed into the conflagration. It cannot reasonably be required to defer the adoption of measures for its own peace and safety until the revolutionary utterances lead to actual disturbances of the public peace or imminent and immediate danger of its own destruction; but it may, in the exercise of its judgment, suppress the threatened danger in its incipiency. . . .

We cannot hold that the present statute is an arbitrary or unreasonable exercise of the police power of the State unwarrantably infringing the freedom of speech or press; and we must and do sustain its constitutionality. . . . ∎

From Majority Opinion, Gitlow *v.* New York, *1925.*

• JUSTICE LOUIS D. BRANDEIS

The right of free speech, the right to teach and the right of assembly are, of course, fundamental rights . . . These may not be denied or abridged.

But, although the rights of free speech and assembly are fundamental, they are not in their nature absolute. Their exercise is subject to restriction, if the particular restriction proposed is required in order to protect the State from destruction or from serious injury, political, economic or moral. That the necessity which is essential to a valid restriction does not exist unless speech would produce, or is intended to produce, a clear and imminent danger of some substantive evil which the State constitutionally may seek to prevent has been settled. . . .

It is said to be the function of the legislature to determine whether at a particular time and under the particular circumstances the formation of, or assembly with, a society organized to advocate criminal syndicalism constitutes a clear and present danger of substantive evil; and that by enacting the law here in question the legislature of California determined that question in the affirmative . . . The legislature must obviously decide, in the first instance, whether a danger exists which calls for a particular protective measure. But where a statute is valid only in case certain conditions exist, the enactment of the statute cannot alone establish the facts which are essential to its validity. Prohibitory legislation has repeatedly been held invalid, because unnecessary, where the denial of liberty involved was that of engaging in a particular business. The power of the courts to strike down an offending law is no less when the interests involved are not property rights, but the fundamental personal rights of free speech and assembly.

This Court has not yet fixed the standard by which to determine when a danger shall be deemed clear; how remote the danger may be and yet be deemed present; and what degree of evil shall be deemed sufficiently substantial to justify resort to abridgement of free speech and assembly as the means of protection. To reach sound conclusions on these matters, we must bear in mind why a State is, ordinarily, denied the power to prohibit dissemination of social, economic and political doctrine which a vast majority of its citizens believes to be false and fraught with evil consequence.

Those who won our independence believed that the final end of the State was to make men free to develop their faculties; and that in its government the deliberative forces should prevail over the arbitrary. They valued liberty both as an end and as a means. They believed liberty to be the secret of happiness and courage to be the secret of liberty. They believed that freedom to think as you will and to speak as you think are means indispensable to the discovery and spread of political truth; that without free speech and assembly discussion would be futile; that with them, discussion affords ordinarily adequate protection against the dissemination of noxious doctrine; that the greatest menace to freedom is an inert people; that public discussion is a political duty; and that this should be a fundamental principle of the American government. They recognized the risks to which all human institutions are subject. But they knew that order cannot be secured merely through fear of punishment for its infraction; that it is hazardous to discourage thought, hope and imagination; that fear breeds repression; that repression breeds hate; that hates menaces stable government; that the path of safety lies in the opportunity to discuss freely supposed grievances and proposed remedies; and that the fitting remedy for evil counsels is good ones. Believing in the power of reason as applied through public discussion, they eschewed silence coerced by law—the argument of force in its worst form. Recognizing the occasional tyrannies of governing majorities, they amended the Constitution so that free speech and assembly should be guaranteed.

Fear of serious injury cannot alone justify suppression of free speech and assembly. Men feared witches and burnt women. It is the function of speech to free men from the bondage of irrational fears. To justify suppression of free speech there must be reasonable ground to fear that serious evil will result if free speech is practiced. There must be reasonable ground to believe that the danger apprehended is imminent. There must be reasonable ground to believe that the evil to be prevented is a serious one. Every denunciation of existing law tends in some measure to increase the probability that there will be violation of it. Condonation of a breach enhances the probability. Expressions of approval add to the probability. Propagation of the criminal state of mind by teaching syndicalism increases it. Advocacy of law-breaking heightens it still further. But even advocacy of violation, however reprehensible morally, is not a justification for denying free speech where the advocacy falls short of incitement and there is nothing to indicate that the advocacy would be immediately acted on. The wide difference between advocacy and incitement, between preparation and attempt, between assembling and conspiracy, must be borne in mind. In order to support a finding of clear and present danger it must be shown either that immediate serious violence was to be expected or was advocated, or that the past conduct furnished reason to believe that such advocacy was then contemplated.

Those who won our independence by revolution were no cowards. They did not fear political change. They did not exalt order at the cost of liberty. To courageous, self-reliant men, with confidence in the power of free and fearless reasoning applied through the processes of popular government, no danger flowing from speech can be deemed clear and present, unless the incidence of the evil apprehended is so imminent that it may befall before there is opportunity for full discussion. If there be time to expose through discussion the falsehood and fallacies, to avert the evil by the processes of education, the remedy to be applied is more speech, not enforced silence. Only an emergency can justify repression. Such must be the rule if authority is to be reconciled with freedom. Such, in my opinion, is the command of the Constitution. It is therefore always open to Americans to challenge a law abridging free speech and assembly by showing that there was no emergency justifying it.

Moreover, even imminent danger cannot justify resort to prohibition of these functions essential to effective democracy, unless the evil apprehended is relatively serious. Prohibition of free speech and assembly is a measure so stringent that it would be inappropriate as the means for averting a relatively trivial harm to society. A police measure may be unconstitutional merely because the remedy, although effective as means of protection, is unduly harsh or oppressive. Thus, a State might, in the exercise of its police power, make any trespass upon the land of another a crime, regardless of the results or of the intent or purpose of the trespasser. It might, also, punish at attempt, a conspiracy, or an incitement to commit the trespass. But it is hardly conceivable that this Court would hold constitutional a statute which punished as a felony the mere voluntary assembly with a society formed to teach that pedestrians had the moral right to cross unenclosed, unposted, waste lands and to advocate their doing so, even if there was imminent danger that advocacy would lead to trespass. The fact that speech is likely to result in some violence or in destruction of property is not enough to justify its suppression. There must be the probability of serious injury to the State. Among free men, the deterrents ordinarily to be applied to prevent crime are education and punishment for violations of the law, not abridgment of the rights of free speech and assembly. ■

From Concurring Opinion, Whitney v. California,
1927.

• CHIEF JUSTICE CHARLES EVANS HUGHES

Appellant, Dirk De Jonge, was indicted in Multnomah County, Oregon, for violation of the Criminal Syndicalism Law of that State. The act defines "criminal syndicalism" as "the doctrine which advocates crime, physical violence, sabotage or any unlawful acts or methods as a means of accomplishing or effecting industrial or political change or revolution.". . .

The stipulation, after setting forth the charging part of the indictment, recites in substance the following:

That on July 27, 1934, there was held in Portland a meeting which had been advertised by . . . the Communist party . . . that the meeting was open to the public . . . that the defendant De Jonge, the second speaker, was a member of the Communist party . . . that in his talk he protested against conditions in the county jail . . . that he discussed the reason for the raids on the Communist headquarters and and workers' halls and offices . . . that while the meeting was still in progress it was raided by the police; that the meeting was conducted in an orderly manner; that the defendant and several others . . . were arrested by the police. . . .

On the theory that this was a charge that criminal syndicalism and sabotage were advocated at the meeting in question, defendant moved for acquittal insisting that the evidence was insufficient to warrant his conviction. The trial court denied his motion and error in this respect was assigned on appeal.

The Supreme Court of the State put aside the contention by ruling that the indictment did not charge that criminal syndicalism or sabotage was advocated at the meeting described in the evidence, either by the defendant or by anyone else. . . .

"What the indictment does charge . . . is that the defendant presided at, conducted and assisted in conducting an assemblage of persons, organization, society and group, to wit, the Communist party, which . . . was unlawfully teaching and advocating . . . the doctrine of criminal syndicalism and sabotage."

In this view, lack of sufficient evidence as to illegal advocacy or action at the meeting became immaterial. Having limited the charge to defendant's participation in a meeting called by the Communist party, the State Court sustained the conviction upon that basis regardless of what was said or done at the meeting.

We must take this indictment as thus construed. Conviction upon a charge not made would be sheer denial of due process. It thus appears that, while defendant was a member of the Communist party, he was not indicted for participating in its organization, or for joining it, or for soliciting members or for distributing its literature. He was not charged with teaching or advocating criminal syndicalism or sabotage or any unlawful acts, either at the meeting or elsewhere.

He was accordingly deprived of the benefit of evidence as to the orderly and lawful conduct of the meeting and that it was not called or used for the advocacy of criminal syndicalism or sabotage or any unlawful action. His sole offense, as charged, and for which he was convicted and sentenced to imprisonment for seven years, was that he had assisted in the conduct of a public meeting, albeit otherwise lawful, which was held under the auspices of the Communist party.

The broad reach of the statute as thus applied is plain . . . A like fate might have attended any speaker, although not a member [of the Communist party] who "assisted in the conduct" of the meeting. However innocuous the object of the meeting, however lawful the subjects and tenor of the addresses, however reasonable and timely the discussion, all those assisting in the conduct of the meeting would be subject to imprisonment as felons if the meeting were held by the Communist party. . . .

Thus if the Communist party had called a public meeting in Portland to discuss the tariff, or the foreign policy of the government, or taxation, or relief, or candidacies for the offices of President, members of Congress, Governor or State legislators, every speaker who assisted in the conduct of the meeting would be equally guilty with the defendant in this case, upon the charge as here defined and sustained. . . .

While the States are entitled to protect themselves from the abuse of the privileges of our institutions . . . none . . . go to the length of sustaining such a curtailment of the right of free speech and assembly as the Oregon statute demands in its present application.

Freedom of speech and of the press are fundamental rights which are safeguarded by the due process clause of the Fourteenth Amendment of the Federal Constitution. The right of peaceable assembly is a right cognate to those of free speech and free press and is equally fundamental.

As this court said in *United States* v. *Cruikshank,* "The very idea of a government, republican in form, implies a right on the part of its citizens to meet peaceably for consultation in respect to public affairs and to petition for a redress of grievances."

The First Amendment of the Federal Constitution expressly guarantees that right against abridgment by Congress . . . For the right is one that cannot be denied without violating those fundamental principles of liberty and justice which lie at the base of all civil and political institutions, principles which the Fourteenth Amendment embodies in the general terms of its due process clause.

These rights may be abused by using speech or press or assembly in order to incite to violence and crime. The people, through their Legislatures, may protect themselves against that abuse. But the legislative intervention can find constitutional justification only by dealing with the abuse. The rights themselves must not be curtailed.

The greater the importance of safeguarding the community from incitements to the overthrow of our institutions by force and violence, the more imperative is the need to preserve inviolate the constitutional rights of free speech, free press and free assembly in order to maintain the opportunity for free political discussion, to the end that government may be responsive to the will of the people and that changes, if desired, may be obtained by peaceful means. Therein lies the security of the republic, the very foundation of constitutional government.

It follows from these considerations that, consistently with the Federal Constitution, peaceable assembly for lawful discussion cannot be made a crime. The holding of meetings for peaceable political action cannot be proscribed. Those who assist in the conduct of such meetings cannot be branded as criminals on that score. The question . . . is not as to the auspices under which the meeting is held, but as to its purpose. . . .

We are not called upon to review the findings of the State court as to the objectives of the Communist party. Notwithstanding those objectives, the defendant still enjoyed his personal right of free speech and to take part in a peaceable assembly having a lawful purpose, although called by that party. The defendant was none the less entitled to discuss the public issues of the day . . . to seek redress of alleged grievances. That was of the essence of his guaranteed personal liberty.

We hold that the Oregon statute as applied to the particular charge as defined by the State court is repugnant to the due process clause of the Fourteenth Amendment. The judgment of conviction is reversed and the cause is remanded for further proceedings not inconsistent with this opinion. It is so ordered. ■

Majority Opinion, De Jonge v. Oregon, 1937.

• EDITOR'S NOTE

In 1948, eleven Communist leaders were indicted and after a nine-month trial were found guilty of violating the Alien Registration Act (Smith Act) of 1940. The charge against them was advocacy of the overthrow of the government by force. They appealed to the Supreme Court on the ground that the Smith Act violated the First and Fifth Amendments which guarantee freedom of speech. In the following decision, Chief Justice Vinson, following Justice Holmes's doctrine of "clear and present danger," upheld the constitutionality of the Smith Act.

• CHIEF JUSTICE FREDERICK M. VINSON

Petitioners were indicted in July, 1948, for violation of the conspiracy provisions of the Smith Act . . . We granted certiorari . . . limited to the following two questions: (1) Whether either par. 2 or 3 of the Smith Act, inherently or as construed and applied in the instant case, violates the First Amendment and other provisions of the Bill of Rights; (2) whether either par. 2 or par. 3 of the Act, inherently or as construed and applied in the instant case, violates the First and Fifth Amendments because of indefiniteness.

The indictment charted the petitioners with wilfully and knowingly conspiring (1) to organize as the Communist Party of the United States of America a society, group and assembly of persons who teach and advocate the overthrow and destruction of the Government of the United States by force and violence, and (2) knowingly and wilfully to advocate and teach the duty and necessity of overthrowing and destroying the Government of the United States. . . .

The obvious purpose of the statute [Smith Act] is to protect existing Government, not from change by peaceable, lawful and constitutional means, but from change by violence, revolution and terrorism. That it is within the *power* of the Congress to protect the Government of the United States from armed rebellion is a proposition which requires little discussion. Whatever theoretical merit there may be to the argument that there is a "right" to rebellion against dictatorial governments is without force where the existing structure of the government provides for peaceful and orderly change. We reject any principle of governmental helplessness in the face of preparation for revolution, which principle carried to its logical conclusion must lead to anarchy. No one could conceive that it is not within the power of Congress to prohibit acts intended to overthrow the Government by force and violence. The question with which we are concerned here is not whether Congress has such *power,* but whether the *means* which it has employed conflict with the First and Fifth Amendments to the Constitution.

One of the bases for the contention that the means which Congress has employed are invalid takes the form of an attack on the face of the statute on the grounds that by its terms it prohibits academic discussion of the merits of Marxism-Leninism, that it stifles ideas and is contrary to all concepts of a free speech and a free press. . . .

The very language of the Smith Act negates the interpretation which petitioners would have us impose on that Act. It is directed at advocacy, not discussion. Thus, the trial judge properly charged the jury that they could not convict if they found that petitioners did "no more than pursue peaceful studies and discussions or teaching and advocacy in the realm of ideas." He further charged that it was not unlawful "to conduct in an American college or university a course explaining the philosophical theories set forth in the books which have been placed in evidence." Such a charge is in strict accord with the statutory language, and illustrates the meaning to be placed on those words. Congress did not intend to

eradicate the free discussion of political theories, to destroy the traditional rights of Americans to discuss and evaluate ideas without fear of governmental sanction. Rather Congress was concerned with the very kind of activity in which the evidence showed these petitioners engaged.

But although the statute is not directed at the hypothetical cases which petitioners have conjured, its application in this case has resulted in convictions for the teaching and advocacy of the overthrow of the Government by force and violence, which, even though coupled with the intent to accomplish that overthrow, contains an element of speech. For this reason, we must pay special heed to the demands of the First Amendment marking out the boundaries of speech.

. . . the basis of the First Amendment is the hypothesis that speech can rebut speech, propaganda will answer propaganda, free debate of ideas will result in the wisest governmental policies. It is for this reason that this Court has recognized the inherent value of free discourse. An analysis of the leading cases in this Court which have involved direct limitations on speech, however, will demonstrate that both the majority of the Court and the dissenters in particular cases have recognized that this is not an unlimited, unqualified right, but that the societal value of speech must, on occasion, be subordinated to other values and considerations.

No important case involving free speech was decided by this Court prior to *Schenck* v. *United States* . . . Indeed, the summary treatment accorded an argument based upon an individual's claim that the First Amendment protected certain utterances indicates that the Court at earlier dates placed no unique emphasis upon that right. It was not until the classic dictum of Justice Holmes in the Schenck case that speech per se received that emphasis in a majority opinion. . . .

Speech is not an absolute, above and beyond control by the legislature when its judgment, subject to review here, is that certain kinds of speech are so undesirable as to warrant criminal sanction. Nothing is more certain in modern society than the principle that there are no absolutes, that a name, a phrase, a standard has meaning only when associated with the considerations which gave birth to the nomenclature . . . To those who would paralyze our Government in the face of impending threat by encasing it in a semantic straitjacket we must reply that all concepts are relative.

In this case we are squarely presented with the application of the "clear and present danger" test, and must decide what that phrase imports. We first note that many of the cases in which this Court has reversed convictions by use of this or similar tests have been based on the fact that the interest which the State was attempting to protect was itself too insubstantial to warrant restriction of speech . . . Overthrow of the Government by force and violence is certainly a substantial enough interest for the Government to limit speech. Indeed, this is the ultimate value of any society, for if a society cannot protect its very structure from armed internal attack, it must follow that no subordinate value can be protected. If, then, this interest may be protected, the literal problem which is presented is what has been meant by the use of the phrase "clear and present danger" of the utterances bringing about the evil within the power of Congress to punish.

Obviously, the words cannot mean that before the Government may act, it must wait until the putsch is about to be executed, the plans have been laid and the signal is awaited. If the Government is aware that a group aiming at its overthrow is attempting to indoctrinate its members and to commit them to a course whereby they will strike when the leaders feel the circumstances permit, action by the Government is required . . . In the instant case the trial judge charged the jury that they could not convict unless they found that petitioners intended to overthrow the Government "as speedily as circumstances would permit." This does not mean, and could not properly mean, that they would not strike until there was certainty of success. What was meant was that the revolutionists would strike when they thought the time was ripe. We must therefore reject the contention that success or probability of success is the criterion.

The situation with which Justices Holmes and Brandeis were concerned in Gitlow was a comparatively isolated event, bearing little relation in their minds to any substantial threat to the safety of the community . . . They were not confronted with any situation comparable to the instant one—the development of an apparatus designed and dedicated to the overthrow of the Government, in the context of world crisis after crisis.

Chief Judge Learned Hand, writing for the majority below [the Court of Appeals], interpreted the phrase as follows: "In each case (courts) must ask whether the gravity of the 'evil,' discounted by its improbability, justifies such invasion of free speech as is necessary to avoid the danger." . . . We adopt this statement of the rule. As articulated by Chief Judge Hand, it is as succinct and inclusive as any other we might devise at this time. It takes into consideration those factors which we deem relevant, and relates their significances. More we cannot expect from words.

Likewise, we are in accord with the court below, which affirmed the trial court's finding that the requisite danger existed. The mere fact that from the period 1945 to 1948 petitioners' activities did not result in an attempt to overthrow the Government by force and violence is of course no answer to the fact that there was a group that was ready to make the attempt. The formation by petitioners of such a highly organized conspiracy, with rigidly disciplined members subject to call when the leaders, these petitioners, felt that the time had come for action, coupled with the inflammable nature of world conditions, similar uprisings in other countries, and the touch-and-go nature of our relations with countries with whom petitioners were in the very least ideologically attuned, convince us that their convictions were justified on this score. And this analysis disposes of the contention that a conspiracy to advocate, as distinguished from the advocacy itself, cannot be constitutionally restrained, because it comprises only the preparation . . . It is the existence of the conspiracy which creates the danger. If the ingredients of the reaction are present, we cannot bind the Government to wait until the catalyst is added.

We hold that II2(a)(1), 2(a)(3) and 3 of the Smith Act do not inherently, or as construed or applied in the instant case, violate the First Amendment and other provisions of the Bill of Rights, or the First and Fifth Amendments because of indefiniteness. Petitioners intended to overthrow the Government of the United States as speedily as the circumstances would permit. Their conspiracy to organize the Communist Party and to teach and advocate the overthrow of the Government of the United States by force and violence created a "clear and present danger" of an attempt to overthrow the Government by force and violence. They were properly and constitutionally convicted for violation of the Smith Act. The judgments of conviction are *Affirmed.* ■

> *From Opinion of the Court,* Dennis *v.*
> United States, *1951.*

• JUSTICE HUGO L. BLACK

At the outset I want to emphasize what the crime involved in this case is, and what it is not. These petitioners were not charged with an attempt to overthrow the Government. They were not charged with overt acts of any kind designed to overthrow the Government. They were not even charged with saying anything or writing anything designed to overthrow the Government. The charge was that they agreed to assemble and to talk and publish certain ideas at a later date: The indictment is that they conspired to organize the Communist Party and to use speech or newspapers and other publications in the future to teach and advocate the forcible overthrow of the Government. No matter how it is worded, this is a virulent form of prior censorship of speech and press, which I believe the First Amendment forbids. I would hold I3 of the Smith Act authorizing this prior restraint unconstitutional on its face and as applied.

But let us assume, contrary to all constitutional ideas of fair criminal procedure, that petitioners although not indicted for the crime of actual advocacy may be punished for it. Even on this radical assump-

tion, the other opinions in this case show that the only way to affirm these convictions is to repudiate directly or indirectly the established "clear and present danger" rule. This the Court does in a way which greatly restricts the protections afforded by the First Amendment. The opinions for affirmance indicate that the chief reason for jettisoning the rule is the expressed fear that advocacy of Communist doctrine endangers the safety of the Republic. Undoubtedly, a governmental policy of unfettered communication of ideas does entail dangers. To the Founders of this Nation, however, the benefits derived from free expression were worth the risk. They embodied this philosophy in the First Amendment's command that "Congress shall make no law . . . abridging the freedom of speech, or of the press . . ." I have always believed that the First Amendment is the keystone of our Government, that the freedoms it guarantees provide the best insurance against destruction of all freedom. At least as to speech in the realm of public matters, I believe that the "clear and present danger" test does not "mark the furthermost constitutional boundaries of protected expression" but does "no more than recognize a minimum compulsion of the Bill of Rights." . . .

So long as this Court exercises the power of judicial review of legislation, I cannot agree that the First Amendment permits us to sustain laws suppressing freedom of speech and press on the basis of Congress' or our own notions of mere "reasonableness." Such a doctrine waters down the First Amendment so that it amounts to little more than an admonition to Congress. The Amendment as so construed, is not likely to protect any but those "safe" or orthodox views which rarely need its protection. . . .

. . . few will protest the conviction of these Communist petitioners. There is hope, however, that in calmer times, when present pressures, passions and fears subside, this or some later Court will restore the First Amendment liberties to the high preferred place where they belong in a free society. ■

> *From Dissenting Opinion,* Dennis *v.*
> United States, *1951.*

PART VI

FREEDOM OF RELIGION— CONSCIENCE AND TOLERATION

The modern struggle for freedom in the Western world, which led to the introduction and development of democracy, began in the area of religion. This was inevitable, since the churches imposed, or made continuous efforts to impose, their domination upon Western civilization from its very beginnings. To assert freedom, including religious freedom, it was essential to break the absolute monopoly which churches wielded in matters of the mind and spirit—a protracted and painful process which began with the Reformation in the sixteenth century and continued for the next three centuries, and more. Those who engaged in the gigantic battle realized quite early that freedom of religion was the first of all freedoms. If that could be won, the other freedoms would follow.

The ecclesiastical monopoly over the mind and soul of Western man had its beginnings with Emperor Constantine I's conversion to Christianity early in the fourth century, when he made it, in effect, the official religion. Constantine's nephew, the Emperor Julian (denigrated as "the Apostate"), made an effort to re-establish Rome's traditional tolerance in the field of religion. His Edict of Toleration, issued in 362 A.D., was almost Jeffersonian. But Julian's successors asserted and proclaimed the opposite principle, that of religious intolerance. This era may be said to have begun with Emperor Theodosius I, whose edict of 380 A.D. became the foundation stone of the church-state alliance.

Thereafter the process of intolerance, and the forcible imposition of dogmas everywhere, continued relentlessly. The alliance between religion and government—a "loathsome combination," as Jefferson called it—resulted in more than a millennium of violence, bigotry, cruelty, and turbulence. Clergymen and policemen allied to support each other's position of power and privilege. An all-pervasive atmosphere of intolerance branded all intellectual and spiritual independence as heresy. "Heretics" were officially subject to persecution, harassment, and obloquy. Often they were physically extirpated. In the thirteenth century, in southern France, about one million Albigensians—a pre-Protestant sect—were exterminated in a crusade waged in the name of God. Later, the Inquisition, tacitly or actively supported by government, claimed countless other victims.

European man was never altogether passive in the face of combined religious-political tyranny. There was resistance, much of it sporadic, as exemplified by the fourteenth century's John Wycliffe in England and John Hus in Bohemia. The unabated struggle for freedom of conscience, in which such champions of genius as Voltaire and Rousseau were engaged, did not, however, begin to meet with substantial success until the eighteenth century. In this the Americans led the practical way with their constitutional separation of church and state— an epoch-making event in the history of the growth of freedom.

1

TOLERATION

Theodosius I
Valentinian III
Act of Parliament, 1534
Elizabeth I
Pope Julius II

• EDITOR'S NOTE

The root of the church-state alliance goes back to the Emperor Theodosius I, who, in his Edict, *"Cunctos Populos,"* issued in 380 A.D., decreed:

It is our desire that all the various nations which are subject to our clemency and moderation, should continue in the profession of that religion which was delivered to the Romans by the divine Apostle Peter . . . According to the Apostolic teaching and the doctrine of the Holy Spirit, let us believe the one deity of the Father, the Son and the Holy Spirit, in equal majesty and in a Holy Trinity. We authorize the followers of this law to assume the title of Catholic Christians; but as for the others, since, in our judgment, they are foolish madmen, we decree that they shall be branded with the ignominious name of heretics, and shall not presume to give to their conventicles the name of churches. They will suffer in the first place the chastisement which our authority, in accordance with the will of Heaven, shall decide to inflict.

The establishment of papal supremacy traces to the Emperor Valentinian III, who decreed in an Edict of the year 445 A.D.:

We are convinced that the only defense for us and for our Empire is in the favor of the God of heaven: and in order to deserve this favor it is our first care to support the Christian faith . . . Therefore, inasmuch as the pre-eminence of the Apostolic See is assured by the merit of St. Peter, the first of the bishops, by the leading position of the city of Rome and also by the authority of the Holy Synod, let not presumption strive to attempt anything contrary to the authority of that See. For the peace of the church will only then be everywhere preserved when the whole body acknowledge its ruler . . . We decree, by a perpetual edict, that nothing shall be attempted by the Gallican bishops, or by those of any other province, contrary to the ancient custom, without the authority of the venerable Pope of the Eternal City. But whatsoever the authority of the Apostolic See has enacted, or shall enact, let that be held as law for all. So that if any bishop summoned before the people of Rome shall neglect to attend, let him be compelled to appear by the governor of the province.

In England, the supremacy of the king over the Church of England was enacted by Parliament in 1534 (*Statutes of the Realm,* III, 492), during the reign of Henry VIII:

Albeit the King's Majesty rightfully is and ought to be the supreme head of the Church of England, so is recognized by the clergy of this realm in the Convocations, yet nevertheless for corroboration and confirmation thereof . . . and to repress and extirpate all errors, heresies, and other enormities and abuses . . . be it enacted by authority of this present Parliament, that the king our sovereign Lord, his heirs and successors, kings of this realm, shall be taken, accepted, and reputed the only supreme head on earth of the Church of England, called *Anglicana Ecclesia;* and shall have and enjoy, annexed and united to the imperial crown of this realm, as well the title and style thereof, as all honours, dignities, pre-eminences, jurisdictions, privileges, authorities, immunities, profits, and commodities to the said dignity of supreme head of the same Church belonging and appertaining; and that our said sovereign lord, his heirs and successors . . . shall have full power and authority . . . to visit, repress, redress, reform, order, correct, restrain, and amend all such errors, heresies, abuses, offences, contempts, and enormities, whatsoever they be, which by any manner spiritual authority or jurisdiction ought or may lawfully be reformed, repressed, ordered, redressed, corrected, restrained, or amended, most to the pleasure of Almighty God, the increase of virtue in Christ's religion, and for the conservation of the peace, unity, and tranquillity of this realm; any usage, custom, foreign law, foreign authority, prescription, or any other thing or things to the contrary thereof notwithstanding.

This absolute royal power over religion was further reinforced by Queen Elizabeth I, who in 1594 decreed:

For the preventing and avoiding . . . the wicked and dangerous practices of seditious sectaries and disloyal persons; be it enacted by the Queen's most excellent majesty, and by the lords spiritual and temporal, and the Commons . . . that if any person or persons above sixteen years, which shall obstinately refused to repair to some church, chapel, or usual place of common prayer, to hear divine service established by Her Majesty's laws and statutes . . . and shall forbear to do the same by the space of a month next after, without lawful cause, shall . . . by printing, writing, or express words or speeches, advisedly and purposely practice or go about to move or persuade any of Her Majesty's subjects . . . to deny, withstand, and impugn Her Majesty's power and authority in causes ecclesiastical . . . then every such person so offending . . . and being thereof lawfully convicted, shall be committed to prison, there to remain without bail or mainprize, until they shall conform and yield themselves to come to some church, chapel, or usual place of common prayer, and hear divine service, according to Her Majesty's laws and statutes aforesaid, and to make such open submission and declaration of their said conformity, as hereafter in this Act is declared and appointed.

This assertion of absolute governmental authority in matters of religion and faith—which meant general control over thought and opinion—led to conflict in England and ultimately resulted in the emigration of Puritans and other dissenters to America. It was this "great struggle" over religious liberty, John Adams said, "that peopled America."

The extension of religious intolerance to the Southern Hemisphere of the New World was aided by the Bull which Pope Julius II issued on July 28, 1508, granting the kings of Spain power over religion in the Americas:

Julius, bishop, servant of the servants of God. We, presiding by divine choice, although unworthily, over the government of the Universal Church, do concede voluntarily to the Catholic kings principally those things that augment their honor and glory, and contribute effectively to the benefit and security of their dominions . . . In view of the fact that the said Ferdinand [King of Aragon and of Sicily] . . . and our most cherished daughter in Christ, Juana, queen of the same kingdoms [Castile and León] . . . wish that no church, monastery, or pious place be erected or founded either in the islands and lands already possessed [in New Spain], or in those subsequently acquired, without their express consent and that of their successors; and considering that since it is convenient to those kings that the persons who preside over churches and monasteries be faithful and acceptable to them, they desire that they be conceded the right of patronage and of presentation of qualified persons for both the metropolitan and cathedral churches already erected, or to be created in the future, and for all the other ecclesiastical benefices . . . We, appreciating that these privileges increase the honor, beauty and security of those islands, and also of the said kingdoms . . . by these presents were conceded with apostolic authority . . . to the said Ferdinand and Juana, and to the future kings of Castile and León, that nobody without their consent can construct or build in the above mentioned islands, now possessed or to be possessed, large churches; and we concede the right of patronage and presenting qualified persons to cathedral churches, monasteries, *dignidades,* collegiates, and other ecclesiastical benefices and pious places . . . Nobody should deign to infringe on or act contrary to this concession, and if anyone attempts to do so, let him know that he will incur the indignation of God Almighty and of the blessed apostles Peter and Paul.

2

LIBERTARIAN VIEWS

• THE LOLLARDS

That king and bishop in one person, prelate and judge in temporal causes . . . puts any kingdom beyond good rule. This conclusion is clearly proved because the temporal and spiritual are two halves of the entire Holy Church. And so he who has applied himself to one should not meddle with the other, for no one can serve two masters. It seems that hermaphrodite or ambidexter would be good names for such men . . . A corollary is that we, the procurators of God in this behalf, do petition before Parliament that all curates, as well superior as inferior, be fully excused and should occupy themselves with their own charge and no other. ■

From Lollard Conclusions, No. 6, 1394. This is one of the earliest recorded pleas for the separation of church and state in England. The Lollards were followers of the reformer John Wycliff, in fourteenth-century England.

• SIR THOMAS MORE

There are several sorts of religions, not only in different parts of the island [Utopia], but even in every town; some worshiping the sun, others the moon, or one of the planets: some worship such men as have been eminent in former times for virtue, or glory, not only as ordinary deities, but as the supreme God: yet the greater and wiser sort of them worship none of these, but adore one eternal, invisible, infinite, and incomprehensible Deity; as a being that is far above all our apprehensions, that is spread over the whole universe, not by his bulk, but by his power and virtue; him they call the Father of All. . . .

Those among them that have not received our religion [Christianity], do not fright any from it, and use none ill that goes over to it; so that all the while I was there, one man only was punished on this occasion. He being newly baptized, did, notwithstanding all that we could say to the contrary, dispute publicly concerning the Christian religion with more zeal than discretion; and with so much heat, that he not only preferred our worship to theirs, but condemned all their rites as profane; and cried out against all that adhered to them, as impious and sacrilegious persons, that were to be damned to everlasting burning. Upon his having frequently preached in this manner, he was seized, and after trial he was condemned to banishment, not for having disparaged their religion, but for his inflaming the people to sedition: for this is one of their most ancient laws, that no man ought to be punished for his religion. At the first constitution of their government, Utopus having understood that before his coming among them the old inhabitants had been engaged in great quarrels concerning religion, by which they were so divided among themselves, that he found it an easy thing to conquer them, since instead of uniting their forces against him, every different party in religion fought by themselves; after he had subdued them, he made a law that every man might be of what religion he pleased, and might endeavor to draw others to it by the force of argument, and by amicable and modest ways, but without bitterness against those of other opinions; but that he ought to use no other force but that of persuasion, and was neither to mix with it reproaches nor violence; and such as did otherwise were to be condemned to banishment or slavery.

This law was made by Utopus, not only for preserving the public peace, which he saw suffered much by daily contentions and irreconcilable heats, but because he thought the interest of religion itself required it. He judged it not fit to determine anything rashly, and seemed to doubt whether those different forms of religion might not all come from God, who might inspire men in a different manner, and be pleased with this variety; he therefore thought it indecent and foolish for any man to threaten and terrify another to make him believe what did not appear to him to be true. And supposing that only one religion was really true, and the rest false, he imagined that the native force of truth would at last break forth and shine bright, if supported only by the strength of argument, and attended to with a gentle and unprejudiced mind; while on the other hand, if such debates were carried on with violence and tumults, as the most wicked are always the most obstinate, so the best and most holy religion might be choked with superstition, as corn is with briars and thorns; he therefore left men wholly to their liberty, that they might be free to believe as they should see cause. . . . ■

From Utopia, *1516.*

• MARTIN LUTHER

The Romanists have, with great adroitness, drawn three walls around themselves, with which they have hitherto protected themselves, so that no one could reform them, whereby all Christendom has fallen terribly.

Firstly . . . they have affirmed and maintained that the temporal power has no jurisdiction over them, but, on the contrary, that the spiritual power is above the temporal.

Secondly, if it were proposed to admonish them with the Scriptures, they objected that no one may interpret the Scriptures but the Pope.

Thirdly, if they are threatened with a council, they pretend that no one may call a council but the Pope.

Thus they have secretly stolen our three rods, so that they may be unpunished, and entrenched themselves behind these three walls, to act with all the wickedness and malice which we now witness. . . .

Let us, in the first place, attack the first wall:

It has been devised that the Pope, bishops, priests, and monks are called the *spiritual estate*; princes, lords, artificers, and peasants are the *temporal estate.* This is an artful lie and hypocritical device, but let no one be made afraid by it, and that for this reason: that all Christians are truly of the spiritual estate, and there is no difference among them, save of office alone . . . for baptism, Gospel, and faith, these alone make spiritual and Christian people.

As for the unction by a Pope or a bishop, tonsure, ordination, consecration, and clothes differing from those of laymen—all this may make a hypocrite or an anointed puppet, but never a Christian or a spiritual man. Thus we are all consecrated as priests by baptism. . . .

Therefore a priest should be nothing in Christendom but a functionary; as long as he holds his office, he has precedence of others; if he is deprived of it, he is a peasant or a citizen like the rest. . . .

It follows, then, that between laymen and priests, princes and bishops, or, as they call it, between spiritual and temporal persons, the only real difference is one of office and function, and not of estate. . . .

Now see what a Christian doctrine is this: that the temporal authority is not above the clergy, and may not punish it. This is as if one were to say the hand may not help, though the eye is in grievous suffering. Is it not unnatural, not to say unChristian, that one member may not help another, or guard it against harm? . . I say, forasmuch as the temporal power has been ordained by God for the punishment of the bad and the protection of the good, therefore we must let it do its duty throughout the whole Christian body, without respect of persons, whether it strike Popes, bishops, priests, monks, nuns, or whoever it may be. . . .

The second wall is even more tottering and weak: that they alone pretend to be considered masters of the Scriptures, although they learn nothing of them all their life. They assume authority, and juggle before us with impudent words, saying that the Pope cannot err in matters of faith, whether he be evil or good, albeit they cannot prove it by a single letter. That is why the canon law contains so many heretical and un-Christian, nay, unnatural laws. . . .

Therefore it is a wickedly devised fable—and they cannot quote a single letter to confirm it—that it is for the Pope alone to interpret the Scriptures or to confirm the interpretation of them. They have assumed the authority of their own selves. And though they say that this authority was given to St. Peter when the keys were given to him, it is plain enough that the keys were not given to St. Peter alone, but to the whole community. Besides, the keys were not ordained for doctrine or authority, but for sin, to bind or loose; and

what they claim besides this from the keys is mere invention. . . .

The third wall falls of itself, as soon as the first two have fallen. . . .

When need requires, and the Pope is a cause of offense to Christendom, in these cases whoever can best do so, as a faithful member of the whole body, must do what he can to procure a true free council. This no one can do so well as the temporal authorities, especially since they are fellow-Christians. . . .

As for their boasts of their authority, that no one must oppose it, this is idle talk. No one in Christendom has any authority to do harm, or to forbid others to prevent harm being done. There is no authority in the Chruch but for reformation. Therefore if the Pope wished to use his power to prevent the calling of a free council, so as to prevent the reformation of the Church, we must not respect him or his power; and if he should begin to excommunicate and fulminate, we must despise this as the doings of a madman, and, trusting in God, excommunicate and repel him as best we may. . . .

And now I hope the false, lying specter will be laid with which the Romanists have long terrified and stupefied our consciences. And it will be seen that, like all the rest of us, they are subject to the temporal sword; that they have no authority to interpret the Scriptures by force without skill; and that they have no power to prevent a council, or to pledge it in accordance with their pleasure, or to bind it beforehand, and deprive it of its freedom; and that if they do this, they are verily of the fellowship of Antichrist and the devil, and have nothing of Christ but the name. ■

From To the Christian Nobility of the German Nation, *1520. This pamphlet was the opening gun in the Reformation.*

• JOHN PYM

The greatest liberty of the kingdom is religion; thereby we are freed from spiritual evils, and no impositions are so grievous as those that are laid upon the soul. The next great liberty is justice, whereby we are preserved from injuries in our persons and estates . . . The third great liberty consists in the power and privilege of parliaments. ■

From speech in the Short Parliament,
April 17, 1640.

• ROGER WILLIAMS

First, That the blood of so many hundred thousand soules of Protestants and Papists, spilt in the Wars of present and former Ages, for their respective Consciences, is not required nor accepted by Jesus Christ the Prince of Peace.

Secondly, Pregnant Scriptures and Arguments are throughout the Worke proposed against the Doctrine of persecution for cause of Conscience.

Thirdly, Satisfactorie Answers are given to Scriptures, and objections produced by Mr. Calvin, Beza, Mr. Cotton, and the Ministers of the New English (urches and others former and later, tending to prove the Doctrine of persecution for cause of Conscience.

Fourthly, The Doctrine of persecution for cause of Conscience, is proved guilty of all the blood of the Soules crying for vengeance under the Altar.

Fifthly, All Civill States with their Officers of justice in their respective constitutions and administrations are proved essentially Civill, and therefore not Judges, Governours or Defendours of the Spirituall or Christian state and Worship.

Sixthly, It is the will and command of God that (since the comming of his Sonne the Lord Jesus) a permission of the most Paganish, Jewish, Turkish, or Antichristian consciences and worships bee granted to all men in all Nations and Countries: and they are onely to bee fought against with that Sword which is only (in Soule matters) able to conquer, to wit, the Sword of God's Spirit, the Word of God.

Seventhly, The state of the Land of Israel, the Kings and people thereof in Peace & War, is proved figurative and ceremoniall, and no patterne nor president for any Kingdome or civill state in the world to follow.

Eighthly, God requireth not an uniformity of Religion to be inacted and inforced in any civill state; which inforced uniformity (sooner or later) is the greatest occasion of civill Warre, ravishing of conscience, persecution of Christ Jesus in his servants, and of the hypocrisie and destruction of millions of souls.[1]

Ninthly, In holding an inforced uniformity of Religion in a civill state, wee must necessarily disclaime our desires and hopes of the Jewes conversion to Christ.

Tenthly, An inforced uniformity of Religion throughout a Nation or civill state, confounds the Civill and Religious, denies the principles of Christianity and civility, and that Jesus Christ is come in the Flesh.

Eleventhly, The permission of other consciences and worships then a state professeth, only can (according to God) procure a firme and lasting peace (good assurance being taken according to the wisdome of the civill state for uniformity of civill obedience from all sorts).

Twelfthly, lastly, true civility and Christianity may both flourish in a state or Kingdome, notwithstanding the permission of divers and contrary consciences, either of Jew or Gentile. ■

From the preface of The Bloudy Tenent of Persecution for Cause of Conscience, *1644.*

• ROBERT BARCLAY

Since God hath assumed to himself the power and dominion of the conscience, who alone can rightly instruct and govern it, therefore it is not lawful for

---

[1] Compare this to the statement, which may be considered official theological doctrine, by Thomas Aquinas in *Summa Theologica* (1267–73), Book II, Art. 3:

"I reply that, with regard to heretics, two considerations are to be kept in mind: 1, on their side, and 2, on the side of the Church.

"1. There is the sin, whereby they deserve not only to be separated from the Church by excommunication, but also to be shut off from the world by death. For it is a much more serious matter to corrupt faith, through which comes the soul's life, than to forge money, through which temporal life is supported. . . .

"2. But on the side of the Church there is mercy, with a view to the conversion of them that are in error . . . If he be found still stubborn, the Church . . . takes thought for the safety of others, by separating him from the Church by sentence of excommunication; and, further, leaves him to the secular court, to be exterminated from the world by death."

any whatsoever, by virtue of any authority or principality they bear in the government of this world, to force the consciences of others . . . provided always, that no man, under the pretence of conscience, prejudice his neighbour in his life or estate; or do anything destructive to, or inconsistent with, human society; in which case the law is for the transgressor, and justice to be administered upon all, without respect of persons.

Seeing the chief end of all religion is to redeem man from the spirit and vain conversation of this world, and to lead into inward communion with God . . . therefore all the vain customs and habits thereof, both in word and deed, are to be rejected and forsaken; such as the taking off the hat to a man, bowing and cringings of the body, and such other salutations of that kind, with all the foolish and superstitious formalities attending them. ∎

From Propositions Regarding the Quaker Faith,
Propositions XIV and XV, 1678

• DAVID HUME

The success which Gardiner,[1] from his cautious and prudent conduct, had met with in governing the Parliament and engaging them to concur both in the Spanish match [Catholic Queen Mary's marriage to Philip II of Spain, in 1554] and in the reestablishment of the ancient religion [Catholicism] . . . had so raised his character for wisdom and policy that his opinion was received as an oracle in the council . . . Cardinal Pole[2] himself, though more beloved on account of his virtue and candor . . . had not equal weight in public deliberations . . . A very important question was frequently debated before the queen [Mary] and council by these two ecclesiastics: whether the laws lately revived against heretics should be put in execution, or should only be employed to restrain by terror the bold attempts of these zealots. Pole was very sincere in his religious principles; and . . . he was seriously persuaded of the Catholic doctrines, and thought that no consideration of human policy ought ever to come in competition with such important interests. Gardiner, on the contrary, had always made his religion subservient to his schemes of safety or advancement; and by his unlimited complaisance to Henry [VIII] he had shown that . . . he was sufficiently disposed to make a sacrifice of his principles to the established theology. This was the well-known character of these two counsellors; yet such is the prevalance of temper above system that the benevolent disposition of Pole led him to advise a toleration of the heretical tenets which he highly blamed; while the severe manners of Gardiner inclined him to support by persecution that religion which, at the bottom, he regarded with great indifference . . . We shall relate . . . the topics by which each side supported, or might have supported, their scheme of policy [in the matter of persecution]. . . .

The practice of persecution, said the defenders of Pole's opinion, is the scandal of all religion; and the theological animosity so fierce and violent, far from being an argument of men's conviction in their opposite sects, is a certain proof that they have never reached any serious persuasion with regard to these remote and sublime subjects. Even those who are the most impatient of contradiction in other controversies are mild and moderate in comparison of polemical divines . . . But while men zealously maintain what they neither clearly comprehend nor entirely believe, they are shaken in their imagined faith by the opposite persuasion, or even doubts, of other men, and vent on their antagonists that impatience which is the natural result of so disagreeable a state of the understanding. They then easily embrace any pretence for representing opponents as impious and profane; and if they can also find a color for connecting this violence with the interests of civil government, they can no longer be restrained from giving uncontrolled scope to ven-

---

[1] Stephen Gardiner (*ca.* 1493–1555), English bishop and lord chancellor, supported Henry VIII in his break with Rome but was nevertheless a "thorough opponent of the Reformation" in matters of doctrine.

[2] Reginad Pole (1500–1558), Archbishop of Canterbury (1556–58), remained Catholic after Henry VIII broke with Catholicism, and went to live in Rome. After Queen Mary ascended the English throne (1553) and reestablished Catholicism, Cardinal Pole was sent as papal legate to England, where he vainly urged religious moderation upon Mary, whose brief reign, marked by violent persecutions, earned her the epithet of "Bloody Mary."

geance and resentment. But surely never enterprise was more unfortunate than that of founding persecution upon policy, or endeavoring, for the sake of peace, to settle an entire uniformity of opinion in questions which, of all others, are least subjected to the criterion of human reason . . . It may not, inde ' appear difficult to check, by a steady severity, the first beginnings of controversy; but besides that this policy exposes forever the people to all the abject terrors of superstition, and the magistrate to the endless encroachments of ecclesiastics, it also renders men so delicate that they can never endure to hear of opposition; and they will some time pay dearly for that false tranquillity in which they have been so long indulged. As healthful bodies are ruined by too nice a regimen, and are thereby rendered incapable of bearing the unavoidable incidents of human life, a people who never were allowed to imagine that their principles could be contested fly out into the most outrageous violence when any event (and such events are common) produces a faction among their clergy, and gives rise to any differences in tenet or opinion. But whatever may be said in favor of suppressing, by persecution, the first beginnings of heresy, no solid argument can be alleged for extending severity towards multitudes, or endeavoring, by capital punishments, to extirpate an opinion which has diffused itself among men of every rank and station. Besides the extreme barbarity of such an attempt, it commonly proves ineffectual to the purpose intended, and serves only to make men more obstinate in their persuasion, and to increase the number of their proselytes. The melancholy with which the fear of death, torture, and persecution inspires the sectaries is the proper disposition for fostering religious zeal: the prospect of eternal rewards, when brought near, overpowers the dread of temporal punishments; the glory of martyrdom stimulates all the more furious zealots, especially the leaders and preachers. Where a violent animosity is excited by oppression, men naturally pass from hating the persons of their tyrants to a more violent abhorrence of their doctrines; and the spectators, moved with pity towards the supposed martyrs, are easily seduced to embrace those

principles which can inspire men with a constancy that appears almost supernatural. Open the door to toleration, mutual hatred relaxes among the sectaries; their attachment to their particular modes of religion decays; the common occupations and pleasures of life succeed to the acrimony of disputation, and the same man who, in other circumstances, would have braved flames and tortures is induced to change his sect from the smallest prospect of favor and advancement, or even from the frivolous hope of becoming more fashionable in his principles. . . .

Though these arguments appear entirely satisfactory, yet such is the subtlety of human wit that Gardiner and the other enemies to toleration were not reduced to silence; and they still found topics on which to maintain the controversy. The doctrine, said they, of liberty of conscience is founded on the most flagrant impiety, and supposes such an indifference among all religions, such an obscurity in theological doctrines, as to render the church and magistrate incapable of distinguishing with certainty the dictates of Heaven from the mere fictions of human imagination. If the Divinity reveals principles to mankind, he will surely give a criterion by which they may be ascertained; and a prince who knowingly allows these principles to be perverted or adulterated is infinitely more criminal than if he gave permission for the vending of poison, under the shape of food, to all his subjects. Persecution may, indeed, seem better calculated to make hypocrites than converts; but experience teaches us that the habits of hypocrisy often turn into reality; and the children, at least, ignorant of the dissimulation of their parents, may happily be educated in more orthodox tenets. It is absurd, in opposition to considerations of such unspeakable importance, to plead the temporal and frivolous interests of civil society . . . Where sects arise whose fundamental principle on all sides is to execrate, and abhor, and damn, and extirpate each other, what choice has the magistrate left but to take part, and, by rendering one sect entirely prevalent, restore, at least for a time, the public tranquillity? The political body, being here sickly, must not be treated as if it were in a state of sound health; and an affected neutrality in the prince, or even a cool preference, may serve only to encourage the hopes of all the sects, and keep alive their animosity. The Protestants, far from tolerating the religion of their ancestors [Catholicism], regard it as an impious and detestable idolatry; and . . . when they were entirely masters, they enacted very severe, though not capital, punishments against all exercise of the Catholic worship, and even against such as barely abstained from their profane rites and sacraments. Nor are instances wanting of their endeavors to secure an imagined orthodoxy by the most rigorous executions: Calvin has burned Servetus at Geneva; Cranmer brought Arians[1] and Anabaptists to the stake; and if persecution of any kind be admitted, the most bloody and violent will surely be allowed the most justifiable, as the most effectual. Imprisonments, fines, confiscations, whippings, serve only to irritate the sects, without disabling them from resistance; but the stake, the wheel, and the gibbet must soon terminate in the extirpation or banishment of all the heretics inclined to give disturbance, and in the entire silence and submission of the rest.

The arguments of Gardiner, being more agreeable to the cruel bigotry of Mary and Philip, were better received; and though Pole pleaded . . . the scheme of toleration was entirely rejected. It was determined to let loose the laws in their full vigor against the reformed religion; and England was soon filled with scenes of horror, which have ever since rendered the Catholic religion the object of general detestation, and which prove that no human depravity can equal revenge and cruelty covered with the mantle of religion. ■

From The History of England, from the Invasion of Julius Caesar to the Revolution in 1688, *Vol. III, Chapter 37, 1759.*

---

[1] Arius (*ca.* 256–336 A.D.) was an Alexandrian priest who taught the doctrine that God had created a Son, the first creature, who was not equal with the Father and not eternal.

• THOMAS BABINGTON MACAULAY

My honourable friend, the Member for the University of Oxford, began his speech by declaring that he had no intention of calling in question the principles of religious liberty. He utterly disclaims persecution, that is to say, persecution as defined by himself. It would, in his opinion, be persecution to hang a Jew, or to flay him, or to draw his teeth, or to imprison, or to fine him . . . But is is not persecution, says my honourable friend, to exclude any individual or any class from office; for nobody has a right to office . . . He who obtains an office obtains it, not as a matter of right, but as a matter of favour . . . There are in the United Kingdom five and twenty million Christians without places; and, if they do not complain, why should five and twenty thousand Jews complain of being in the same case? . . .

Now, surely my honourable friend cannot have considered to what conclusions his reasoning leads. Those conclusions are so monstrous that he would, I am certain, shrink from them. Does he really mean that it would not be wrong in the legislature to enact that no man should be a judge unless he weighed twelve stone, or that no man should sit in Parliament unless he were six feet high? . . .

My honourable friend has appealed to us as Christians. Let me then ask him how he understands that great commandment which comprises the law and the prophets. Can we be said to do unto others as we would that they should do unto us if we wantonly inflict on them even the smallest pain? As Christians, surely we are bound to consider, first, whether, by excluding the Jews from all public trust, we give them pain; and, secondly, whether it be necessary to give that pain in order to avert some greater evil. That by excluding them from public trust we inflict pain on them my honourable friend will not dispute. . . .

But where, he says, are you to stop, if once you admit into the House of Commons people who deny the authority of the Gospels? Will you let in a Mussulman? Will you let in a Parsee? Will you let in a

Hindoo, who worships a lump of stone with seven heads? I will answer my honourable friend's question by another. Where does he mean to stop? Is he ready to roast unbelievers at slow fires? . . . Once admit that we are bound to inflict pain on a man because he is not of our religion; and where are you to stop? . . . When once you enter on a course of persecution, I defy you to find any reason for making a halt till you have reached the extreme point. . . .

In truth, those persecutors who use the rack and the stake have much to say for themselves. They are convinced that their end is good; and it must be admitted that they employ means which are not unlikely to attain the end. Religious dissent has repeatedly been put down by sanguinary persecution. In that way the Albigensians were put down. In that way Protestantism was suppressed in Spain and Italy, so that it has never since reared its head. But I defy anybody to produce an instance in which disabilities such as we are now considering have produced any other effect than that of making the sufferers angry and obstinate. My honourable friend should either persecute to some purpose, or not persecute at all.

He dislikes the word persecution, I know. He will not admit that the Jews are persecuted. And yet I am confident that he would rather be sent to the King's Bench Prison for three months, or be fined a hundred pounds, than be subject to the disabilities under which the Jews lie. How can he then say that to impose such disabilities is not persecution and that to fine and imprison is persecution? All his reasoning consists in drawing arbitrary lines. What he does not wish to inflict he calls persecution. What he does wish to inflict he will not call persecution. What he takes from the Jews he calls political power. What he is too good-natured to take from the Jews he will not call political power. The Jew must not sit in Parliament: but he may be the proprietor of all the ten-pound houses in a borough. . . .

All the rest of the system is of a piece. The Jew may be a juryman, but not a judge. He may decide issues of fact, but not issues of law. He may give a hundred thousand pounds damages; but he may

not in the most trivial case grant a new trial. He may rule the money-market: he may influence the exchanges: he may be summoned to congresses of Emperors and Kings. . . .

It has been said that it would be monstrous to see a Jew judge try a man for blasphemy. In my opinion it is monstrous to see any judge try a man for blasphemy under the present law. But, if the law on that subject were in a sound state, I do not see why a conscientious Jew might not try a blasphemer. Every man, I think, ought to be at liberty to discuss the evidences of religion; but no man ought to be at liberty to force on the unwilling ears and eyes of others sounds and sights which must cause annoyance and irritation. . . .

These, Sir, are the principles on which I would frame the law of blasphemy; and if the law were so framed, I am at a loss to understand why a Jew might not enforce it as well as a Christian. I am not a Roman Catholic; but if I were a judge at Malta, I should have no scruple about punishing a bigoted Protestant who should burn the Pope in effigy before the eyes of thousands of Roman Catholics. I am not a Mussulman; but if I were a judge in India, I should have no scruple about punishing a Christian who should pollute a mosque. Why, then, should I doubt that a Jew, raised by his ability, learning, and integrity to the judicial bench, would deal properly with any person who, in a Christian country, should insult the Christian religion? . . .

It reminds that one of the arguments against this motion is that the Jews are an unsocial people, that they draw close to each other, and stand aloof from strangers. Really, Sir, it is amusing to compare the manner in which the question of Catholic emancipation was argued formerly by some gentlemen with the manner in which the question of Jew emancipation is argued by the same gentlemen now. When the question was about Catholic emancipation, the cry was, "See how restless, how versatile, how encroaching, how insinuating, is the spirit of the Church of Rome. See how her priests compass earth and sea to make one proselyte, how indefatigably they toil, how attentively they study the weak and strong parts of every character, how skillfully they employ literature, arts, sciences, as engines for the propagation of their faith . . . Will you give power to the members of a Church so busy, so aggressive, so insatiable?" . . .

The truth is, that bigotry will never want a pretence. Whatever the sect be which it is proposed to tolerate, the peculiarities of that sect will, for the time, be pronounced by intolerant men to be the most odious and dangerous that can be conceived. As to the Jews, that they are unsocial as respects religion is true; and so much the better: for, surely, as Christians, we cannot wish that they should bestir themselves to pervert us from our own faith. But that the Jews would be unsocial members of the civil community, if the civil community did its duty by them, has never been proved. . . .

Another charge has been brought against the Jews . . . . The honourable Member for Oldham [William Cobbett] tells us that the Jews are naturally a mean race, a sordid race, a money-getting race; that they are averse to all honourable callings; that they neither sow nor reap; that they have neither flocks nor herds; that usury is the only pursuit for which they are fit; that they are destitute of all elevated and amiable sentiments.

Such, Sir, has in every age been the reasoning of bigots. They never fail to plead in justification of persecution the vices which persecution has engendered. . . . We treat them [the Jews] as slaves, and wonder that they do not regard us as brethren. We drive them to mean occupations, and then reproach them for not embracing honourable professions. We long forbade them to possess land; and we complain that they chiefly occupy themselves in trade. We shut them out from all the paths of ambition; and then we despise them for taking refuge in avarice. During many ages we have, in all our dealings with them, abused our immense superiority of force; and then we are disgusted because they have recourse to that cunning which is the natural and universal defence of the weak against the violence of the strong.

But were they always a mere money-changing, money-getting, money-hoarding race? Nobody knows better than my honourable friend the Member for

the University of Oxford that there is nothing in their national character which unfits them for the highest duties of citizens. He knows that, in the infancy of civilisation, when our island was as savage as New Guinea, when letters and arts were still unknown to Athens, when scarcely a thatched hut stood on what was afterwards the site of Rome, this condemned people had their fenced cities and cedar palaces, their splendid Temple, their fleets of merchant ships, their schools of sacred learning, their great statesmen and soldiers, their natural philosophers, their historians and their poets. What nation ever contended more manfully against overwhelming odds for its independence and religion? What nation ever, in its last agonies, gave such signal proofs of what may be accomplished by a brave despair? And if, in the course of many centuries, the oppressed descendants of warriors and sages have degenerated from the qualities of their fathers, if, while excluded from the blessings of law, and bowed under the yoke of slavery, they have contracted some of the vices of outlaws and of slaves, shall we consider this as matter of reproach to them? Shall we not rather consider it as matter of shame and remorse to ourselves?

Let us do justice to them. Let us open to them the door of the House of Commons. Let us open to them every career in which ability and energy can be displayed. Till we have done this, let us not presume to say that there is no genius among the countrymen of Isaiah, no heroism among the descendants of the Maccabees. . . . ∎

From speech in the House of Commons, April 17, 1883, supporting a "Bill for the Removal of Jewish Disabilities." The bill was in the form of a resolution stating "that it is expedient to remove all civil disabilities at present existing with respect to His Majesty's subjects professing the Jewish religion, with the like exceptions as are provided with respect to His Majesty's subjects professing the Roman Catholic religion." The resolution was passed, but it was not until 1860 that discriminations against Jews were finally removed.

3

VIEWS OF THE AMERICAN FOUNDING FATHERS

Benjamin Franklin
James Madison
Samuel Adams
Thomas Jefferson
George Washington
Thomas Paine
John Adams

• BENJAMIN FRANKLIN

My mother grieves, that one of her sons is an Arian, another an Arminian.[1] What an Arminian or an Arian is, I cannot say that I very well know. The truth is, I make such distinctions very little my study. I think vital religion has always suffered when orthodoxy is more regarded than virtue; and the Scriptures assure me, that at the last day we shall not be examined what we *thought*, but what we *did*; and our recommendation will not be, that we said, *Lord! Lord!* but that we did good to our fellow creatures. See Matthew XXV. ∎

From letter to his father, Josiah Franklin,
April 13 1738.

• BENJAMIN FRANKLIN

1. And it came to pass after these things, that Abraham sat in the door of his tent, about the going down of the sun.

2. And behold a man, bent with age, coming from the way of the wilderness, leaning on a staff.

3. And Abraham arose and met him, and said unto him, Turn in, I pray thee, and wash thy feet, and tarry all night, and thou shalt arise early in the morning, and go on thy way.

4. But the man said, Nay, for I will abide under this tree.

5. And Abraham pressed him greatly; so he turned, and they went into the tent; and Abraham baked unleavened bread, and they did eat.

6. And Abraham saw that the man blessed not God, he said unto him, Wherefore dost thou not worship the most high God, Creator of heaven and earth?

7. And the man answered and said, I do not worship thy God, neither do I call upon his name; for I have made to myself a god, which abideth always in mine house, and provideth me with all things.

8. And Abraham's zeal was kindled against the

---

[1] Jacobus Arminius (1560–1609) was a liberal Dutch theologian who opposed the Calvinist doctrine of predestination.

man, and he arose and fell upon him, and drove him forth with blows into the wilderness.

9. And God called unto Abraham, saying, Abraham, where is the stranger?

10. And Abraham answered and said, Lord, he would not worship thee, neither would he call upon thy name; therefore have I driven him out from before my face into the wilderness.

11. And God said, Have I borne with him these hundred and ninety and eight years, and nourished him, and cloathed him, notwithstanding his rebellion against me; and couldst not thou, who are thyself a sinner, bear with him one night?

12. And Abraham said, Let not the anger of the Lord wax hot against his servant; lo, I have sinned; lo, I have sinned; forgive me, I pray thee.

13. And Abraham arose, and went forth into the wilderness, and sought diligently for the man, and found him, and returned with him to the tent; and when he had entreated him kindly, he sent him away on the morrow with gifts.

14. And God spake again unto Abraham, saying, For this thy sin shall thy seed be afflicted four hundred years in a strange land;

15. But for thy repentance will I deliver them; and they shall come forth with power and with gladness of heart, and with much substance. ■

From Parable Against Persecution, *1774.*

• JAMES MADISON

I have indeed as good an atmosphere at home as the climate will allow; but have nothing to brag of as to the state and liberty of my country. Poverty and luxury prevail among all sorts; pride, ignorance, and knavery among the priesthood, and vice and wickedness among the laity. This is bad enough, but it is not the worst I have to tell you. That diabolical, hell-conceived principle of persecution rages among some; and to their eternal infamy, the clergy can furnish their quota of imps for such business. This vexes me the worst of anything whatever. There are at this time in the adjacent country not less than five or six well-meaning men in close jail

for publishing their religious sentiments, which in the main are very orthodox. I have neither patience to hear, talk, or think of anything relative to this matter; for I have squabbled and scolded, abused and ridiculed, so long about it to little purpose, that I am without common patience. So I must beg you to pity me, and pray for liberty of conscience to all. ■

From letter to William Bradford, Jr., January 24,
1774.

• SAMUEL ADAMS

Freedom of thought and the right of private judgment, in matters of conscience, driven from every corner of the earth, direct their course to this happy country as their last asylum. Let us cherish the noble guests, and shelter them under the wings of an universal toleration. Be this the seat of unbounded religious freedom. She will bring with her in her train industry, wisdom, and commerce. She thrives most when left to shoot forth in her natural luxuriance. ■

From speech in the State House, Philadelphia,
August 1, 1776.

• THOMAS JEFFERSON

How far does the duty of toleration extend? 1. No church is bound by the duty of toleration to retain within her bosom obstinate offenders against her laws. 2. We have no right to prejudice another in his civil enjoyments because he is of another church. If any man err from the right way, it is his own misfortune, no injury to thee; nor therefore art thou to punish him in the things of this life because thou supposest he will be miserable in that which is to come, on the contrary, according to the spirit of the Gospel, charity, bounty, liberality is due to him.

Each church being free, no one can have jurisdiction over another; no, not even when the civil magistrate joins it. It neither acquires the right of the sword by the magistrate's coming to it, nor does it lose the rights of instruction or excommunication by his going from it. It cannot by the accession of any new member acquire jurisdiction over those who do not accede. He brings only himself, having no power to bring others.

Suppose for instance two churches, one of Arminians another of Calvinists in Constantinople. Has either any right over the other? Will it be said the orthodox one has? Every church is to itself orthodox, to others erroneous or heretical.

No man complains of his neighbor for ill management of his affairs, for an error in sowing his land, or marrying his daughter, for consuming his substance in taverns, pulling down building, etc. In all these he has his liberty; but if he do not frequent the church, or there conform to ceremonies, there is an immediate uproar.

The care of every man's soul belongs to himself. But what if he neglect the care of it? Well, what if he neglect the care of his health or estate, which more nearly relate to the state. Will the magistrate make a law that he shall not be poor or sick? Laws provide against injury from others; but not from ourselves. God himself will not save men against their wills. . . .

If the magistrate command me to bring my commodity to a publick store house, I bring it because he can indemnify me if he erred & I thereby lose it; but what idemnification can he give me for the kingdom of heaven?

I cannot give up my guidance to the magistrate; because he knows no more of the way to heaven than I do & is less concerned to direct me right than I am to go right. . . .

Why have Christians been distinguished above all people who have ever lived, for persecutions? Is it because it is the genius of their religion? No, its genius is the reverse. It is the refusing *toleration* to those of a different opinion which has produced all the bustles & wars on account of religion. It was the misfortune of mankind that during the darker centuries the Christian priests following their ambition & avarice combining with the magistrate to divide the spoils of the people, could establish the notion that schismatics

might be ousted of their possessions & destroyed. This notion we have not yet cleared ourselves from. In this case no wonder the oppressed should rebel, & they will continue to rebel & raise disturbance until their civil rights are fully restored to them & all partial distinctions, exclusions & incapacitations removed. ■

From "Notes on Religion," October, 1776.

• THOMAS JEFFERSON

Our rulers can have authority over such natural rights, only as we have submitted to them. The rights of conscience we never submitted, we could not submit. We are answerable for them to our God. The legitimate powers of government extend to such acts only as are injurious to others. But it does me no injury for my neighbor to say there are twenty gods, or no God. It neither picks my pocket nor breaks my leg. If it be said his testimony in a court of justice cannot be relied on, reject it then, and be the stigma on him. Constraint may make him worse by making him a hypocrite, but it will never make him a truer man. It may fix him obstinately in his errors, but will not cure them.

Reason and free inquiry are the only effectual agents against error. Give a loose to them, they will support the true religion by bringing every false one to their tribunal, to the test of their investigation. They are the natural enemies of error, and of error only. Had not the Roman government permitted free inquiry, Christianity could never have been introduced. Had not free inquiry been indulged, at the era of the Reformation, the corruptions of Christianity could not have been purged away. If it be restrained now, the present corruptions will be protected, and new ones encouraged.

Was the government to prescribe to us our medicine and diet, our bodies would be in such keeping as our souls are now. Thus in France the emetic was once forbidden as a medicine, and the potato as an article of food. Government is just as fallible, too, when it fixes systems in physics. Galileo was sent to the Inquisition for affirming that the earth was a sphere; the government had declared it to be as flat as a trencher, and Galileo was obliged to abjure his error. This error, however, at length prevailed, the earth became a globe, and Descartes declared it was whirled round its axis by a vortex. The government in which he lived was wise enough to see that this was no question of civil jurisdiction, or we should all have been involved by authority in vortices. In fact, the vortices have been exploded, and the Newtonian principle of gravitation is now more firmly established, on the basis of reason, than it would be were the government to step in and make it an article of faith. Reason and experiment have been indulged, and error has fled before them.

It is error alone which needs the support of government. Truth can stand by itself. Subject opinion to coercion; whom will you make your inquisitors? Fallible men; men governed by bad passions, by private as well as public reasons. And why subject it to coercion? To produce uniformity. But is uniformity of opinion desirable? No more than of face and stature. Introduce the bed of Procrustes then, and as there is danger that the large men may beat the small, make us all of a size, by lopping the former and stretching the latter.

Difference of opinion is advantageous in religion. The several sects perform the office of a *censor morum* over each other. Is uniformity attainable? Millions of innocent men, women and children since the introduction of Christianity, have been burnt, tortured, fined, imprisoned; yet we have not advanced one inch towards uniformity. What has been the effect of coercion? To make one half the world fools, and the other half hypocrites. To support roguery and error all over the earth.

Let us reflect that it is inhabited by a thousand millions of people. That these profess probably a thousand different systems of religion. That ours is but one of that thousand. That if there be but one right, and ours that one, we should wish to see the 999 wandering sects gathered into the fold of truth. But against such a majority we cannot effect this by force. Reason and persuasion are the only practicable instruments. To make way for these, free inquiry must be indulged; and how can we wish others to indulge it while we refuse it ourselves.

But every state, says an inquisitor, has established some religion. No two, say I, have established the same. Is this a proof of the infallibility of establishments? Our sister states of Pennsylvania and New York, however, have long subsisted without any establishment at all. The experiment was new and doubtful when they made it. It has answered beyond conception. They flourish infinitely. Religion is well supported; of various kinds, indeed, but all good enough; all sufficient to preserve peace and order: or if a sect arises whose tenets would subvert morals, good sense has fair play, and reasons and laughs it out of doors, without suffering the state to be troubled by it. They do not hang more malefactors than we do. They are not more disturbed with religious dissensions. On the contrary, their harmony is unparallelled, and can be ascribed to nothing but their unbounded tolerance . . . They have made the happy discovery, that the way to silence religious disputes, is to take no notice of them.

Let us, too, give this experiment fair play, and get rid, while we may, of those tyrannical laws. It is true we are as yet secured against them by the spirit of the times. I doubt whether the people of this country would suffer an execution for heresy, or a three years imprisonment for not comprehending the mysteries of the trinity. But is the spirit of the people an infallible, permanent reliance? Is it government? . . . The spirit of the times may alter, will alter. Our rulers will become corrupt, our people careless. A single zealot may commence persecutor, and better men be his victims. It can never be too often repeated, that the time for fixing every essential right on a legal basis is while our rulers are honest, and ourselves united. ■

From Notes on Virginia, *Query XVII, 1782.*

• GEORGE WASHINGTON

Every man conducting himself as a good citizen, and being accountable to God alone for his religious opinions, ought to be protected in worshipping the Deity according to the dictates of his own conscience . . . If I could have entertained the slightest apprehension that the Constitution framed in the Convention, where I had the honor to preside, might possibly endanger the religious rights of any ecclesiastical Society, certainly I would never have placed my signature to it; if I could now conceive that the general Government might ever be so administered as to render liberty of conscience insecure, I beg you will be persuaded that no one would be more zealous than myself to establish effectual barriers against the horrors of spiritual tyranny, and every species of religious persecution . . . Be assured, Gentlemen, that I entertain a proper sense of your fervent supplications to God for my temporal and eternal happiness. ■

*From letter to the United Baptist Churches of
Virginia, May, 1789*

• GEORGE WASHINGTON

Gentlemen:

While I receive with much satisfaction, your address replete with expressions of affection and esteem; I rejoice in the opportunity of assuring you, that I shall always retain a grateful remembrance of the cordial welcome I experienced in my visit to Newport, from all classes of Citizens.

The reflection on the days of difficulty and danger which are past is rendered the more sweet, from a consciousness that they are succeeded by days of uncommon prosperity and security. If we have wisdom to make the best use of the advantages with which we are now favored, we cannot fail, under the just administration of a good Government, to become a great and happy people.

The Citizens of the United States of America have a right to applaud themselves for having given to mankind examples of an enlarged and liberal policy: a policy worthy of imitation. All possess alike liberty of conscience and immunities of citizenship. It is now no more that toleration is spoken of,[1] as if it was by the indulgence of one class of people,

that another enjoyed the exercise of their inherent natural rights. For happily the Government of the United States, which gives to bigotry no sanction, to persecution no assistance, requires only that they who live under its protection, should demean themselves as good citizens, in giving it on all occasions their effectual support.

It would be inconsistent with the frankness of my character not to avow that I am pleased with your favorable opinion of my administration, and fervent wishes for my felicity. May the Children of the Stock of Abraham, who dwell in this land, continue to merit and enjoy the good will of the other inhabitants; while every one shall sit in safety under his own vine and fig tree, and there shall be none to make him afraid. May the father of all mercies scatter light and not darkness in our paths, and make us all in our several vocations useful here, and in his own due time and way everlastingly happy. ■

*From letter to the Hebrew Congregation in
Newport, Rhode Island, August, 1790.*

• THOMAS PAINE

The French Constitution hath abolished or renounced *toleration,* and *intolerance* also, and hath established UNIVERSAL RIGHT OF CONSCIENCE.

Toleration is not the *opposite* of intoleration, but is the *counterfeit* of it. Both are despotisms. The one assumes to itself the right of withholding liberty of conscience, and the other of granting it. The one is the Pope, armed with fire and faggot, and the other is the Pope selling or granting indulgences. The former is church and state, and the latter is church and traffic.

But toleration may be viewed in a much stronger

---

[1] A similar idea was developed by Emperor Joseph II of Austria, in a letter he wrote to Gottfried van Swieten in the "Fanaticism shall in future be known in my states only by the contempt I have for it; nobody shall any longer be exposed to hardships on account of his creed; no man shall be compelled in future to profess the religion of

the State, if it be contrary to his persuasion and if he have other ideas of the right way of insuring blessedness. In future my empire shall not be the scene of abominable intolerance . . . Tolerance is an effect of that beneficent increase of knowledge which now enlightens Europe, and which is owing to philosophy and the efforts of great men; it is a convincing proof of the improvement of the human mind, which has boldly reopened a road through the dominions of superstition, which was trodden centuries ago by Zoroaster and Confucius, and which, fortunately for mankind, has now become the highway of monarchs." See Saul K. Padover, *The Revolutionary Emperor: Joseph II* (1934), Ch. III.

light. Man worships not himself, but his Maker: and the liberty of conscience which he claims, is not for the service of himself, but of his God. . . .

Toleration, therefore, places itself not between man and man, nor between church and church, nor between one denomination of religion and another, but between God and man. . . .

Who, then, are thou, vain dust and ashes! by whatever name thou art called, whether a king, a bishop, a church or a state, a parliament or anything else, that obtrudest thine insignificance between the soul of man and his Maker? Mind thine own concerns. . . .

With respect to what are called denominations of religion, if everyone is left to judge of his own religion, there is no such thing as a religion that is wrong; but if they are to judge of each other's religion, there is no such thing as a religion that is right. . . .

But with respect to religion itself, without regard to names, and as directing itself from the universal family of mankind to the divine object of all adoration, *it is man bringing to his Maker the fruits of his heart*; and though these fruits may differ from each other like the fruits of the earth, the grateful tribute of every one is accepted. . . .

All religions are in their nature mild and benign, and united with principles of morality . . . Like everything else, they had their beginning; and they proceeded by persuasion, exhortation, and example. How then is it that they lose their native mildness, and become morose and intolerant?

It proceeds from the connection [church and state] which Mr. Burke recommends. By engendering the church with the state, a sort of mule-animal, capable only of destroying, and not of breeding up, is produced, called, *The Church established by Law*. It is a stranger, even from its birth to any parent mother on which it is begotten, and whom in time it kicks out and destroys. . . .

The Inquisition in Spain does not proceed from the religion originally professed, but from this mule-animal, engendered between the church and the state. . . .

Persecution is not an original feature in *any*

religion; but it is always the strongly marked feature of all law-religions, or religions established by law. Take away the law-establishment, and every religion reassumes its original benignity. In America, a Catholic priest is a good citizen, a good character, and a good neighbour; an Episcopal minister is of the same description; and this proceeds, independently of the men, from there being no law-establishment in America. ■

From The Rights of Man, *Part I, 1791.*

• THOMAS JEFFERSON

I thank you for the discourse on the consecration of the Synagogue in your city [Mill Street Synagogue, in New York], with which you have been pleased to favor me. I have read it with pleasure and instruction, having learnt from it some valuable facts in Jewish history which I did not know before. Your sect by its sufferings has furnished a remarkable proof of the universal spirit of religious intolerance inherent in every sect, disclaimed by all while feeble, and practiced by all when in power. Our laws have applied the only antidote to this vice, protecting our religious, as they do our civil rights, by putting all on an equal footing. But more remains to be done, for although we are free by the law, we are not so in practice; public opinion erects itself into an Inquisition, and exercises its office with as much fanaticism as fans the flames of an auto-da-fé.

The prejudice still scowling on your section of our religion, although the elder one,[1] cannot be unfelt by yourselves; it is to be hoped that individual dispositions will at length mould themselves to the model of the law, and consider the moral basis, on which all our religions rest, as the rallying point which unites them in a common interest; while the peculiar dogmas branching from it are the exclusive concern of the respective sects embracing them, and

---

[1] Jefferson expressed a similar view in his letter to Joseph Marx in 1820: "[I have] ever felt regreat at seeing a sect, the parent and basis of all those of Christendom, singled out by all of them for a persecution and oppression which proved they have profited nothing from the benevolent doctrines of him whom they profess to make the model of their principle and practice."

no rightful subject of notice to any other; public opinion needs reformation on that point, which would have the further happy effect of doing away with the hypocritical maxim of *"intus et lubet, foris ut moris"* ["love for the insider, death for the outsider"]. Nothing, I think, would be so likely to effect this, as to your sect particularly, as the more careful attention to education, which you recommend, and which, placing its members on the equal and commanding benches of science,[2] will exhibit them as equal objects of respect and favor. I salute you with great respect and esteem. ■

From letter to Mordecai Manuel Noah, editor of the New York National Advocate, *May 28, 1818.*

• JOHN ADAMS

Sir: Accept my best thanks for your polite and obliging favour of the 24th, and especially for the discourse inclosed. I know not when I have read a more liberal or more elegant composition.

You have not extended your ideas of the right of private judgment and the liberty of conscience, both in religion and philosophy farther than I do. Mine are limited only by morals and propriety.

I have had occasion to be acquainted with several gentlemen of your nation, and to transact business with some of them, whom I found to be men of as liberal minds, as much honor, probity, generosity and good breeding, as any I have known in any sect of religion or philosophy.

I wish your nation may be admitted to all privileges of citizens in every country of the world. This country has done much. I wish it may do more; and annul every narrow idea in religion, government, and commerce. Let the wits joke; the philosophers sneer! What then? It has pleased the Providence of the "first cause," the universal cause, that Abraham

should give religion, not only to Hebrews, but to Christians and Mahometans, the greatest part of the modern civilized world.[1] ■

From letter to Mordecai Manuel Noah, July 13, 1818, on the occasion of the consecration of the New York Synagogue.

• JAMES MADISON

The history of the Jews must forever be interesting. The modern part of it is, at the same time so little generally known, that every ray of light on the subject has its value.

Among the features peculiar to the Political system of the United States, is the perfect equality of rights which it secures to every religious sect. And it is particularly pleasing to observe in the good citizenship of such as have been most distrusted and oppressed elsewhere, a happy illustration of the safety & success of this experiment of a just & benignant policy. Equal laws protecting equal rights, are found as they ought to be presumed, the best guarantee of loyalty & love of country; as well as best calculated to cherish that mutual respect & good will among Citizens of every religious denomination which are necessary to social harmony and most favorable to the advancement of truth. The account you give of the Jews of your Congregation [in Savannah, Georgia] brings them fully within the scope of these observations.

From letter to Jacob de la Motta, August, 1820.

---

[2] Jefferson used the same expression in a letter written to Jacob de la Motta in 1820: "It excites in[me] the gratifying reflection that [my] country has been the first to prove to the world two truths, the most salutary to human society, that man can govern himself, and that religious freedom is the most effectual anodyne against religious dissension. . . . [I am] happy in the restoration, of the Jews particularly, to their social rights, and hope they will be seen taking their seats on the benches of science, as preparatory to their doing the same at the board of government."

[1] Adams wrote in a letter to Thomas Jefferson:
"In spite of Bolingbroke and Voltaire, I will insist that the Hebrews have done more to civilize men than any other nation. If I were an atheist, and believed in blind eternal fate, I should still believe that fate had ordained the Jews to be the most essential instrument for civilizing the nations. If I were an atheist of the other sect, who believe or pretend to believe that all is ordered by chance, I should believe that chance had ordered the Jews to preserve and propagate to all mankind the doctrine of a supreme, intelligent, wise, almighty sovereign of the universe, which I believe to be the great essential principle of all morality, and consequently of all civilization."

4

CHURCH AND STATE SEPARATION IN THE UNITED STATES

James Madison
Thomas Jefferson
Ulysses S. Grant
Thomas Bayard
Alfred E. Smith
John F. Kennedy

• EDITOR'S NOTE

In the United States, the separation of church and state was established by the First Amendment to the Federal Constitution, which, together with the other nine Amendments—the Bill of Rights—went into effect on December 15, 1791. In regard to religion, the key words of the First Amendment are: "Congress shall make no law respecting an establishment of religion, or prohibiting the free exercise thereof. . . ."

• JAMES MADISON

Is a Bill of Rights a security for religion? . . . If there were a majority of one sect, a Bill of Rights would be a poor protection for liberty. Happily for the states, they enjoy the utmost freedom of religion. This freedom arises from that multiplicity of sects, which pervades America, and which is the best and only security for religious liberty. For where there is such a variety of sects, there cannot be a majority of any one sect to oppress and persecute the rest. Fortunately for this commonwealth [Virginia], a majority of the people are decidedly against any exclusive establishment—I believe it to be so in the other states. There is not a shadow of right in the general government to intermeddle with religion. Its least interference with it, would be a most flagrant usurpation. I can appeal to my uniform conduct on this subject, that I have warmly supported religious freedom . . . The United States abound in such a variety of sects, that it is a strong security against religious persecution, and it is sufficient to authorize a conclusion, that no one sect will ever be able to outnumber or depress the rest. ■

From speech in the Virginia Ratification Convention, June 12, 1788.

• THOMAS JEFFERSON

Believing with you that religion is a matter which lies solely between man and his God, that he owes account to none other for his faith or his worship, that the legislative powers of government reach actions only, and not opinions, I contemplate with sovereign reverence that act of the whole American people which declared that their legislature should "make no law respecting an establishment of religion, or prohibiting the free exercise thereof," thus building a wall of separation between church and State.[1] Adhering to this expression of the supreme will of the nation in behalf of the rights of conscience, I shall see with sincere satisfaction the progress of those sentiments which tend to restore to man all his natural rights, convinced he has no natural rights in opposition to his social duties. ■

From letter of reply to the Danbury, Conn., Baptist Association, January 1, 1802.

• THOMAS JEFFERSON

I consider the government of the United States as interdicted by the Constitution from intermeddling with religious institutions, their doctrines, discipline, or exercises. This results not only from the provision that no law shall be made respecting the establishment or free exercise, of religion, but from that also which reserves to the States the powers not delegated to the United States . . . I do not believe it is for the interest of religion to invite the civil magistrate to direct its exercises, its discipline, or its doctrines . . . Fasting & prayer are religious exercises. The enjoining them an act of discipline. Every religious society has a right to determine for itself the times for these exercises, & the objects proper for them, according to their own particular tenets; and this right can never be safer than in their own hands, where the Constitution has deposited them. . . .

Every one must act according to the dictates of his own reason, & mine tells me that civil powers alone have been given to the President of the United States and no authority to direct the religious exercises of his constituents. ■

From letter to the Reverend Samuel Miller (refusing to recommend a day of fasting and prayer), January 23, 1808.

• JAMES MADISON

Having examined and considered the bill entitled "An Act incorporating the Protestant Episcopal Church in the town of Alexandria, in the District of Columbia," I now return the bill to the House of Representatives, in which it originated, with the following objections:

Because the bill exceeds the rightful authority to which governments are limited by the essential distinction between civil and religious functions, and violates in particular the article of the Constitution of the United States which declares that "Congress shall make no law respecting a religious establishment." The bill enacts into and establishes by law sundry rules and proceedings relative purely to the organization and polity of the church incorporated, and comprehending even the election and removal of the minister of the same, so that no change could be made therein by the particular society or by the general church of which it is a member, and whose authority it recognizes. This particular church, therefore, would so far be a religious establishment by law, a legal force and sanction being given to certain articles in its constitution and administration. Nor can it be considered that the articles thus established are to be taken as the descriptive criteria only of the corporate identity of the society, inasmuch as this identity must depend on other characteristics, as the regulations established are in general unessential and alterable according to the principles and canons by which churches of that denominations govern themselves, and as the injunctions and prohibitions contained in the regulations would be enforced by . . . the local law.

Because the bill vests in the said incorporated

---

[1] Jefferson wrote to Levi Lincoln, his Attorney General, on January 1, 1802: "Averse to receive addresses, yet unable to prevent them, I have generally endeavored to turn them to some account, by making them the occasion, by way of answer, of sowing useful truths and principles among the people, which might germinate and become rooted among their political tenets. The Baptist address, now enclosed, admits of a condemnation of the alliance between Church and State, under the authority of the Constitution. It furnishes an occasion, too, which I have long wished to find, of saying why I do not proclaim fastings and thanksgivings, as my predecessors did."

church an authority to provide for the support of the poor and the education of poor children of the same, an authority which, being altogether superfluous if the provision is to be the result of pious charity, would be a precedent for giving to religious societies as such a legal agency in carrying into effect a public and civil duty.[1] ■

From Veto Message to the U. S. House of Representatives, February 21, 1811.

• THOMAS JEFFERSON

Of publishing a book on religion, my dear Sir, I never had an idea. I should as soon think of writing for the reformation of Bedlam, as of the world of religious sects. Of these there must be, at least, ten thousand, every individual of every one of which believes all wrong but his own. To undertake to bring them all right, would be like undertaking, single-handed, to fell the forests of America. . . .

Government, as well as religion, has furnished its schisms, its persecutions, and its devices for fattening idleness on the earnings of the people. It has its hierarchy of emperors, kings, princes, and nobles, as that has of popes, cardinals, archbishops, bishops, and priests. In short, cannibals are not to be found in the wilds of America only, but are revelling on the blood every living people. Turning, then, from this loathsome combination of Church and State, and weeping over the follies of our fellow men, who yield themselves the willing dupes and drudges of these mountebanks, I consider reformation and redress as desperate, and abandon them to the Quixotism of more enthusiastic minds. ■

From letter to the Reverend Charles Clay, January 29, 1815.

---

[1] On February 28, 1811, President Madison vetoed another bill on the same grounds — that it violated the constitutional separation of church and state: "Because the bill in reserving a certain parcel of land of the United States for the use of said Baptist Church [in Salem, in the Mississippi Territory] comprises a principle and precedent for the appropriation of funds of the United States for the use and support of religious societies, contrary to the article of the Constitution which declares that 'Congress shall make no law respecting a religious establishment.'"

• JAMES MADISON

Whilst I was honored with the Executive Trust [the Presidency] I found it necessary on more than one occasion to follow the example of predecessors. But I was always careful to make the Proclamation absolutely indiscriminate, and merely recommendatory; or rather mere *designations* of a day, on which all who thought proper might *unite* in consecrating it to religious purposes, according to their own faith & forms. In this sense, I presume you reserve to the Government a right to *appoint* particular days for religious worship throughout the State, without any penal sanction *enforcing* the worship.

I know not what may be the way of thinking on this subject in Louisiana. I should suppose the Catholic portion of the people, at least, as a small & even unpopular sect in the U. S., would rally, as they did in Virginia when religious liberty was a Legislative topic, to its broadest principle.

Notwithstanding the general progress made within the two last centuries in favor of this branch of liberty, & the full establishment of it, in some parts of our Country, there remains in others a strong bias towards the old error, that without some sort of alliance or coalition between Government & Religion neither can be duly supported. Such indeed is the tendency to such a coalition, and such its corrupting influence on both the parties, that the danger cannot be too carefully guarded against. And in a Government of opinion, like ours, the only effectual guard must be found in the soundness and stability of the general opinion on the subject. Every new & successful example therefore of a perfect separation between ecclesiastical and civil matters, is of importance. And I have no doubt that every new example, will succeed, as every past one has done, in showing that religion & Government will both exist in greater purity, the less they are mixed together.

It was the belief of all sects at one time that the establishment of Religion by law, was right & necessary; that the true religion ought to be established in exclusion of every other; and that the only question to be decided was which was the true religion. The example of Holland proved that a toleration of sects, dissenting from the established sect, was safe & even useful. The example of the Colonies, now States, which rejected religious establishments altogether, proved that all sects might be safely & advantageously put on a footing of equal & entire freedom ... We are teaching the world the great truth that Governments do better without Kings & Nobles than with them. The merit will be doubled by the other lesson that Religion flourishes in greater purity, without than with the aid of Government. ■

From letter to Edward Livingston, July 10, 1822.

• ULYSSES S. GRANT

... I would also call your attention to the importance of correcting an evil that, if permitted to continue, will probably lead to great trouble in our land before the close of the nineteenth century. It is the accumulation of vast amounts of untaxed church property.

In 1850, I believe, the church property of the United States which paid no taxes, municipal or State, amounted to about $83,000,000. In 1860 the amount had doubled; in 1875 it is about $1,000,000,000. By 1900, without check, it is safe to say this property will reach a sum exceeding $3,000,000,000. So vast a sum, receiving all the protection and benefits of Government without bearing its proportion of the burdens and expenses of the same, will not be looked upon acquiescently by those who have to pay the taxes. In a growing country, where real estate enhances so rapidly with time, as in the United States, there is scarcely a limit that may be acquired by corporations, religious or otherwise, if allowed to retain real estate without taxation. The contemplation of so vast a property as here alluded to, without taxation, may lead to sequestration without constitutional authority and through blood.

I would suggest the taxation of all property equal-ly, whether church or corporation, exempting only the last resting place of the dead and possibly, with proper restrictions, church edifices. ■

From Seventh Annual Message to Congress, December 7, 1875.

• ALFRED E. SMITH

Let me make myself perfectly clear. I do not want any Catholic in the United States of America to vote for me on the sixth of November [1928] because I am a Catholic. If any Catholic in this country believes that the welfare, the well-being, the prosperity, the growth and the expansion of the United States is best conserved and best promoted by the election of Hoover, I want him to vote for Hoover and not for me.

But, on the other hand, I have the right to say that any citizen of this country who believes I can promote its welfare, that I am capable of steering the ship of state safely through the next four years, and then votes against me because of my religion, he is not a real, pure, genuine American. ■

From speech during Smith's campaign for the Presidency, in Oklahoma City, September 20, 1928.

• JOHN F. KENNEDY

I believe in an America where the separation of church and state is absolute—where no Catholic prelate would tell the President (should he be a Catholic) how to act and no Protestant minister would tell his parishioners for whom to vote—where no church or church school is granted any public funds or political preference—and where no man is denied public office merely because his religion differs from the President who might appoint him or the people who might elect him.

I believe in an America that is officially neither Catholic, Protestant nor Jewish—where no public official either requests or accepts instructions on public policy from the Pope, the National Council of Churches or any other ecclesiastical source—where no religious body seeks to impose its will directly or indirectly upon the general populace or the public acts of its officials—and where religious liberty is so indivisible that an act against one church is treated as an act against all.

For while this year it may be a Catholic against whom the finger of suspicion is pointed, in other years it has been, and may someday be again, a Jew, or a Quaker, or a Unitarian, or a Baptist. It was Virginia's harassment of Baptist preachers, for example, that led to Jefferson's statute of religious freedom. Today, I may be the victim—but tomorrow it may be you—until the whole fabric of our harmonious society is ripped apart at a time of great national peril.

Finally, I believe in an America where religious intolerance will someday end—where all men and all churches are treated as equal, where every man has the same right to attend or not to attend the church of his choice, where there is no Catholic vote, no anti-Catholic vote, no bloc voting of any kind, and where Catholics, Protestants and Jews, both the lay and the pastoral level, will refrain from those attitudes of disdain and division which have so often marred their works in the past, and promote instead the American ideal of brotherhood.

That is the kind of America in which I believe. And it represents the kind of Presidency in which I believe—a great office that must be neither humbled by making it the instrument of any religious group, nor tarnished by arbitrarily withholding it—its occupancy—from the members of any religious group. I believe in a President whose views on religion are his own private affair, neither imposed upon him by the nation nor imposed by the nation upon him as a condition to holding that office.

I would not look with favor upon a President working to subvert the First Amendment's guarantee of religious liberty (nor would our system of checks and balances permit him to do so). And neither do I look with favor upon those who would work to subvert Article VI of the Constitution by requiring a religious test—even by indirection—for if they disagree with that safeguard, they should be openly working to repeal it.

I want a Chief Executive whose public acts are responsible to all and obligated to none—who can attend any ceremony, service or dinner his office may appropriately require him to fulfill—and whose fulfillment of his Presidential office is not limited or conditioned by any religious oath, ritual or obligation. . . .

I ask you tonight to follow in that tradition, to judge me on the basis of fourteen years in the Congress—on my declared stands against an ambassador to the Vatican, against unconstitutional aid to parochial schools, and against any boycott of the public schools (which I attended myself)—instead of judging me on the basis of these pamphlets and publications we have all seen that carefully select quotations out of context from the statements of Catholic Church leaders, usually in other countries, frequently in other centuries, and rarely relevant to any situation here. . . .

I do not consider these other quotations binding upon my public acts—why should you? But let me say, with respect to other countries, that I am wholly opposed to the state being used by any religious group, Catholic or Protestant, to compel, prohibit or persecute the free exercise of any other religion. And that goes for any persecution at any time, by anyone, in any country.

And I hope that you and I condemn with equal fervor those nations which deny their Presidency to Protestants and those which deny it to Catholics. And rather than cite the misdeeds of those who differ, I would also cite the record of the Catholic Church in such nations as France and Ireland—and the independence of such statesmen as de Gaulle and Adenauer.

But let me stress again that these are my views—for, contrary to common newspaper usage, I am not the Catholic candidate for President. I am the Democratic party's candidate for President, who happens also to be a Catholic.

I do not speak for my church on public matters—and the church does not speak for me.

Whatever issue may come before me as President,

if I should be elected—on birth control, divorce, censorship, gambling, or any other subject—I will make my decision in accordance with these views, in accordance with what my conscience tells me to be in the national interest, and without regard to outside religious pressure or dictate. And no power or threat of punishment could cause me to decide otherwise.

But if the time should ever come—and I do not concede any conflict to be remotely possible—when my office would require me to either violate my conscience, or violate the national interest, then I would resign the office, and I hope any other conscientious public servant would do likewise. . . . ■

From speech to the Greater Houston Ministerial Association, Houston, Texas, September 12, 1960.

5

RELIGION
IN THE SCHOOLS

Thomas Jefferson
Horace Mann
Ulysses S. Grant

• THOMAS JEFFERSON

In the . . . report of the [University of Virginia] Commissioners of 1818, it was stated by them that in conformity with the principles of our constitution, which places all sects of religion on an equal footing, with the jealousies of the different sects in guarding that equality from encroachment or surprise, and with the sentiments of the Legislature in favor of freedom of religion, manifested on former occasions, they had not proposed that any professorship of divinity should be established in the University; that provision, however, was made for giving instruction in the Hebrew, Greek, and Latin languages, the depositories of the originals and of the earliest and most respected authorities of the faith of every sect; and for courses of ethical lectures, developing those moral obligations in which all sects agree; that proceeding thus far without offence to the constitution, they had left at this point to every sect to take into their own hands the office of further instruction in the peculiar tenets of each.

It was not, however, to be understood that instruction in religious opinions and duties was meant to be precluded by the public authorities, as indifferent to the interests of society. On the contrary, the relations which exist between man and his Maker, and the duties resulting from those relations, are the most interesting and important to every human being, and the most incumbent on his study and investigation. The want of instruction in the various creeds of religious faith existing among our citizens, presents therefore a chasm in a general institution of the useful sciences. But it was thought that this want, and the intrustment to each society of instruction in its own doctrines, were evils of less danger than a permission to the public authorities to dictate modes or principles of religious instruction[1]—or

---

[1] A similar idea was expressed by James Madison, then a commissioner of the University of Virginia, in a letter to Edward Everett, March 19, 1823: "A university with sectarian professorships becomes, of course, a sectarian monopoly; with professorships of rival sects, it would be an arena of theological gladiators. Without any such professorships it may incur, for a time at least, the imputation of irreligious tendencies, if not designs. The last difficulty was thought more manageable than either of the others."

than opportunities furnished them of giving countenance or ascendency to any one sect over another. A remedy, however, has been suggested of promising aspect, which, while it excludes the public authorities from the dominion of religious freedom, would give to the sectarian schools of divinity the full benefit of the public provisions made for instruction in the other branches of science . . . It has, therefore, been in contemplation, and suggested by some pious individuals . . . to establish their religious schools on the confines of the University, so as to give their students ready and convenient access and attendance on the scientific lectures of the University . . . To such propositions the Visitors are disposed to lend a willing ear . . . but always understanding that these schools shall be independent of the University and of each other. . . . ■

From Annual Report, as Rector of the University of Virginia, October 7, 1822.

• HORACE MANN

I can, then, confess myself second to no one in the depth and sincerity of my convictions and desires respecting the necessity and universality . . . of a religious education for the young . . . But the question still remains, How shall so momentous an object be pursued? . . . Shall we do, as has almost universally been done ever since the unhallowed union between Church and State under Constantine—shall we seek to educate the community religiously through the use of the most irreligious means? . . .

All the schemes ever devised by governments to secure the prevalence and permanence of religion among the people . . . are substantially resolvable into two systems. One of these systems holds the regulation and control of the religious belief of the people to be one of the functions of government, like the command of the army or the navy, or the establishment of courts, or the collection of revenues. According to the other system, religious belief is a matter of individual and parental concern; and, while the government furnishes all practicable facilities for the independent formation of that belief, it exercises no authority to prescribe, or coercion to enforce it. The former is the system, which, with very few exceptions, has prevailed throughout Christendom for fifteen hundred years. Our own government is almost a solitary example among the nations of the earth, where freedom of opinion, and the inviolability of conscience, have been even theoretically recognized by law.

The argument in behalf of a government-established religion, at the time when it was first used, was not without its plausibility; but the principle, once admitted, drew after it a train of the most appalling consequences. If religion is absolutely essential to the stability of the State as well as to the present and future happiness of the subject, why, it was naturally asked, should not the government enforce it? And, if government is to enforce religion, it follows, as a necessary consequence, that it must define it . . . And again: if government begins to define religion, it must define what it is not, as well as what it is; and, while it upholds whatever is included in the definition, it must suppress and abolish whatever is excluded from it . . . Both in regard to matters of form and of substance, all recusancy must be subdued, either by the deprivation of civil rights, or by positive inflictions; for the laws of man, not possessing, like the laws of God, a self-executing power, must be accompanied by some effective sanction, or they will not be obeyed. If a light penalty proves inadequate, a heavier one must follow—the loss of civil privileges by disfranchisement, or of religious hopes by excommunication. If the nonconformist feels himself, by the aid of a higher power, to be secure against threats of future perdition, the civil magistrate has terrible resources at command in this life—imprisonment, scourging, the rack, the fagot, death. Should it ever be said that these are excessive punishments for exercising freedom of thought . . . the answer is always ready, that nothing is so terrible as the heresy that draws after it the endless wrath of the Omnipotent. . . .

So when the news of the Massacre of St. Bartholomew's [in France, on August 23–24, 1572]—on which occasion thirty thousand men, women, and children were butchered at the stroke of a signal-bell—reached Rome, the pope and his cardinals ordained a thanksgiving, that all true believers might rejoice together at so glorious an event, and that God might be honored for the pious hearts that designed, and the benevolent hands that executed, so Christian a deed. . . .

In all the persecutions and oppressions ever committed in the name of religion, one point has been unwarrantably assumed; namely, *that the faith of their authors was certainly and infallibly the true faith.* With the fewest exceptions, the advocates of all the myriad conflicting creeds that have ever been promulgated have held substantially the same language: "*Our* faith we know to be true. For its truth, we have the evidence of our reason and our conscience; we have the Word of God in our hands, and we have the Spirit of God in our hearts, testifying to its truth." The answer to this claim is almost too obvious to be mentioned. The advocates of hundreds and thousands of hostile creeds have placed themselves upon the same ground. Each has claimed the same proof from reason and conscience, the same external revelation from God, and the same inward light of his Spirit. But if truth be *one* . . .; if God be its author; and if the voice of God be not more dissonant than the tongues of Babel—then, at least, all but one of the different forms of faith ever promulgated by human authority . . . cannot have emanated from the Fountain of all truth. These faiths must have been more or less erroneous. The believers in them must have been more or less mistaken. . . .

Did the history of mankind show that there has been the most of virtue and piety in those nations where religion has been most rigorously enforced by law, the advocates of ecclesiastical domination would have a powerful argument in favor of their measures of coercion; but the united and universal voice of history, observation, and experience, gives the argument to the other side. Nor is this surprising. Weak and fallible as human reason is, it was too much to expect that any mere man, even though aided by the light of a written revelation, would

ever fathom the whole counsels of the Omnipotent and the Eternal . . . The easily acquired but awful power possessed by those who were acknowledged to be the chosen expounders of the divine will tempted men to set up a false claim to be the depositories of his communication with them . . . Those who were supposed able to determine the destiny of the soul in the next world came easily to control opinion, conduct, and fortune in this. Hence they established themselves as a third power—a power between the creature and the Creator—not to facilitate the direct communion between man and his Maker, but to supersede it. They claimed to carry on the intercourse between heaven and earth as merchants carry on commerce between distant nations, where the parties to the interchange never meet each other. The consequence soon was, that this celestial commerce degenerated into the basest and most mercenary traffic. The favors of heaven were bought and sold like goods in the market-place. . . .

Among the infinite errors and enormities resulting from systems of religion devised by man, and enforced by the terrors of human government, have been those dreadful reactions which have abjured all religion, spurned its obligations, and voted the Deity into non-existence. This extreme is, if possible, more fatal than that by which it was produced. Between these extremes, philanthropic and godly men have sought to find a medium, which should avoid both the evils of ecclesiastical tyranny and the greater evils of atheism. And this medium has at length been supposed to be found. It is promulgated in the great principle, that government should do all that it can to facilitate the acquisition of religious truth, but shall leave the decision of the question, what religious truth is, to the arbitrament, without human appeal to each man's reason and conscience; in other words, that government shall never, by the infliction of pains and penalties, or by the privation of rights or immunities, call such decision either into prejudgment or into review. The formula in which the constitution of Massachusetts expresses it is in these words: "All religious sects and denominations demeaning themselves peaceably and as good citizens shall be equally under the protection of law; and no subordination of one sect or denomination to another shall ever be established by law."

The great truth recognized and expressed in these few words of our constitution is one which it has cost centuries of struggle and of suffering, and the shedding of rivers of blood, to obtain. . . .

For any human government, then, to attempt to coerce and predetermine the religious opinions of children by law, and contrary to the will of their parents, is unspeakably more criminal than the usurpation of such control over the opinions of men. The latter is treason against truth; but the former is sacrilege. . . .

If, then, a government would recognize and protect the rights of religious freedom, it must abstain from subjugating the capacities of its children to any legal standard of religious faith with as great fidelity as it abstains from controlling the opinions of men. It must meet the unquestionable fact, that the old spirit of religious domination is adopting new measures to accomplish its work—measures which, if successful, will be as fatal to the liberties of mankind as those which were practised in bygone days of violence and terror. These new measures are aimed at children instead of men. They propose to supersede the necessity of subduing free thought *in the mind of the adult*, by forestalling the development of any capacity of free thought *in the mind of the child.* They expect to find it easier to subdue the free agency of children by binding them in fetters of bigotry than to subdue the free agency of men by binding them in fetters of iron. For this purpose, some are attempting to deprive children of their right to labor, and, of course, of their daily bread, unless they will attend a government school, and receive its sectarian instruction. Some are attempting to withhold all means even of secular education from the poor, and thus punish them with ignorance, unless, with the secular knowledge which they desire, they will accept theological knowledge which they condemn. Others still are striving to break down all free public-school systems where they exist, and to prevent their establishment where they do not exist, in the hope, that, on the downfall of these, their system will succeed. The sovereign antidote against these machinations is free schools for all, and the right of every parent to determine the religious education of his children. ▪

From Twelfth Annual Report of the Secretary of the Board of Education of Massachusetts, 1848.

• ULYSSES S. GRANT

As this will be the last annual message which I shall have the honor of transmitting to Congress before my successor is chosen, I will repeat or recapitulate the questions which I deem of vital importance which may be legislated upon and settled at this session:

First. That the States shall be required to afford the opportunity of a good common-school education to every child within their limits.

Second. No sectarian tenets shall ever be taught in any school supported in whole or in part by the State, nation, or by the proceeds of any tax levied upon any community. . . .

Third. Declare church and state forever separate and distinct, but each free within their proper spheres; and that all church property shall bear its own proportion of taxation. ▪

From Seventh Annual Message to Congress, December 7, 1875.

6

U.S. SUPREME COURT OPINIONS

• EDITOR'S NOTE

From a Constitutional and legal point of view, it may be said that the whole development of spiritual and intellectual freedom in the United States has pivoted on the First Amendment, particularly in regard to religion. Here the role of the United States Supreme Court has been crucial, and often also controversial.

The Court's interpretations of the words and intent of the First Amendment have helped to shape the climate of American freedom. Over the years, the Court has been called upon to interpret not only the meaning of the keystone phrase, "*establishment* of religion," but also the whole role of religion in American public life. It has had to deal with such religion-related subjects as oaths of office, religious teaching in the schools, governmental assistance to parochial schools, and compulsory prayers in classrooms.

The Supreme Court opinions, including dissenting opinions, presented here illuminate the area under discussion. They also show how basic ideas affecting freedom are painfully arrived at, by thoughtful but fallible men, through the democratic process of open discussion.

• JUSTICE FELIX FRANKFURTER

A grave responsibility confronts this Court whenever in course of litigation it must reconcile the conflicting claims of liberty and authority. But when the liberty invoked is liberty of conscience, and the authority is authority to safeguard the nation's fellowship, judicial conscience is put to its severest test. Of such a nature is the present controversy.

Lillian Gobitis, aged twelve, and her brother William, aged ten, were expelled from the public schools of Minersville, Pennsylvania, for refusing to salute the national flag as part of a daily school exercise. The local Board of Education required both teachers and pupils to participate in this ceremony. The ceremony is a familiar one. The right hand is placed on the breast and the following pledge recited in unison: "I pledge allegiance to my flag . . ." While the words are spoken, teachers and pupils extend their right hands in salute to the flag. The Gobitis family are affiliated with "Jehovah's Witnesses," for whom the Bible as the Word of God is the supreme authority. The children had been brought up conscientiously to believe that such a gesture of respect for the flag was forbidden by command of Scripture.

The Gobitis children were of an age for which Pennsylvania makes school attendance compulsory. Thus they were denied a free education and their parents had to put them into private schools. To be relieved of the financial burden thereby entailed, their father, on behalf of the children and in his own behalf, brought this suit. He sought to enjoin the authorities from continuing to exact participation in the flag-salute ceremony as a condition of his children's attendance at the Minersville school. After trial of the issues, Judge Maris gave relief in the District Court on the basis of a thoughtful opinion; his decree was affirmed by the Circuit Court of Appeals. Since this decision ran counter to several per curiam dispositions of this Court, we granted certiorari to give the matter full reconsideration. By their able submissions, the Committee on the Bill of Rights of the American Bar Association and the American Civil Liberties Union, as friends of the Court, have helped us to our conclusion.

We must decide whether the requirement of participation in such a ceremony, exacted from a child who refuses upon sincere religious grounds, infringes without due process of law the liberty guaranteed by the Fourteenth Amendment. . . .

Centuries of strife over the erection of particular dogmas as exclusive or all-comprehending faiths led to the inclusion of a guarantee for religious freedom in the Bill of Rights. The First Amendment, and the Fourteenth through its absorption of the First, sought to guard against repetition of those bitter religious struggles by prohibiting the establishment of a state religion and by securing to every sect the free exercise of its faith. So pervasive is the acceptance of this precious right that its scope is brought

into question, as here, only when the conscience of individuals collides with the felt necessities of society.

Certainly the affirmative pursuit of one's convictions about the ultimate mystery of the universe and man's relation to it is placed beyond the reach of law. Government may not interfere with organized or individual expression of belief or disbelief. Propagation of belief—or even of disbelief—in the supernatural is protected, whether in church or chapel, mosque or synagogue, tabernacle or meeting-house. Likewise the Constitution assures generous immunity to the individual from imposition of penalties for offending, in the course of his own religious activities, the religious views of others, be they a minority or those who are dominant in government.

But the manifold character of man's relations may bring his concept of religious duty into conflict with the secular interests of his fellow-men. When does the constitutional guarantee compel exemption from doing what society thinks necessary for the promotion of some great common end, or from a penalty for conduct which appears dangerous to the general good? To state the problem is to recall the truth that no single principle can answer all of life's complexities. The right to freedom of religious belief, however dissident and however obnoxious to the cherished beliefs of others—even of a majority—is itself the denial of an absolute. But to affirm that the freedom to follow conscience has itself no limits in the life of a society would deny that very plurality of principles which, as a matter of history, underlies protection of religious toleration. Our present task, then, as so often the case with courts, is to reconcile two rights in order to prevent either from destroying the other. But, because in safeguarding conscience we are dealing with interests so subtle and so dear, every possible leeway should be given to the claims of religious faith.

In the judicial enforcement of religious freedom we are concerned with a historic concept. The religious liberty which the Constitution protects has never excluded legislation of general scope not directed against doctrinal loyalties of particular sects. Judicial nullification of legislation cannot be justified by attributing to the framers of the Bill of Rights views for which there is no historic warrant. Conscientious scruples have not, in the course of the long struggle for religious toleration, relieved the individual from obedience to a general law not aimed at the promotion or restriction of religious beliefs. The mere possession of religious convictions which contradict the relevant concerns of a political society does not relieve the citizens from the discharge of political responsibilities. The necessity for this adjustment has again and again been recognized. In a number of situations the exertion of political authority has been sustained, while basic considerations of religious freedom have been left inviolate. . . . In all these cases the general laws in question, upheld in their application to those who refused obedience from religious conviction, were manifestations of specific powers of government deemed by the legislature essential to secure and maintain the orderly, tranquil, and free society without which religious toleration itself is unattainable. Nor does the freedom of speech assured by Due Process move in a more absolute circle of immunity than that enjoyed by religious freedom. Even if it were assumed that freedom of speech goes beyond the historic concept of full opportunity to utter and to disseminate views, however heretical or offensive to dominant opinion, and includes freedom from conveying what may be deemed and implied but rejected affirmation, the question remains whether school children, like the Gobitis children, must be excused from conduct required of all of the other children in the promotion of national cohesion. We are dealing with an interest inferior to none in the hierarchy of legal values. National unity is the basis of national security. To deny the legislature the right to select appropriate means for its attainment presents a totally different order of problem from that of the propriety of subordinating the possible ugliness of littered streets to the free expression of opinion through distribution of handbills.

Situations like the present are phases of the profoundest problem confronting a democracy—the problem which Lincoln cast in memorable dilemma. "Must a government of necessity be too strong for the liberties of its people, or too weak to maintain its own existence?" No mere textual reading or logical talisman can solve the dilemma. And when the issue demands judicial determination, it is not the personal notion of judges of what wise adjustment requires which must prevail.

Unlike the instances we have cited, the case before us is not concerned with an exertion of legislative power for the promotion of some specific need or interest of secular society . . . The ultimate foundation of a free society is the binding tie of cohesive sentiment. Such a sentiment is fostered by all those agencies of the mind and spirit which may serve to gather up the traditions of a people, transmit them from generation to generation, and thereby create that continuity of a treasured common life which constitutes a civilization. . . .

The case before us must be viewed as though the legislature of Pennsylvania had itself formally directed the flag-salute for the children of Minersville; had made no exemption for children whose parents were possessed of conscientious scruples like those of the Gobitis family . . . The precise issue, then, for us to decide is whether the legislatures of the various states and the authorities in a thousand counties and school districts of this country are barred from determining the appropriateness of various means to evoke that unifying sentiment without which there can ultimately be no liberties, civil or religious. To stigmatize legislative judgment in providing for this universal gesture of respect for the symbol of our national life in the setting of the common school as a lawless inroad on that freedom of conscience which the Constitution protects, would amount to no less than the pronouncement of pedagogical and psychological dogma in a field where courts possess no marked and certainly no controlling competence. The influences which help toward a common feeling for the common country are manifold. Some may seem harsh and others no doubt are foolish. Surely, however, the end is legitimate . . . It mocks reason and denies our whole history to find in the allowance of a requirement to salute our flag on fitting occasions the seeds of sanction for obeisance to a leader. . . . *Reversed.* ■

*From Majority Opinion, Minersville School
District* v. *Gobitis, 1940.*

• JUSTICE HARLAN F. STONE

The guaranties of civil liberty are but guaranties of freedom of the human mind and spirit and of reasonable freedom and opportunity to express them. They presuppose the right of the individual to hold such opinions as he will and to give them reasonably free expression, and his freedom, and that of the state as well, to teach and persuade others by the communication of ideas. The very essence of the liberty which they guaranty is the freedom of the individual from compulsion as to what he shall think and what he shall say, at least where the compulsion is to bear false witness to his religion. If these guaranties are to have any meaning they must, I think, be deemed to withhold from the state any authority to compel belief or the expression of it where that expression violates religious convictions, whatever may be the legislative view of the desirability of such compulsion.

History teaches us that there have been but few infringements of personal liberty by the state which have not been justified, as they are here, in the name of righteousness and the public good, and few which have not been directed, as they are now, at politically helpless minorities. The framers were not unaware that under the system which they created most governmental curtailments of personal liberty would have the support of a legislative judgment that the public interest would be better served by its curtailment than by its constitutional protection. I cannot conceive that in prescribing, as limitations upon the powers of government, the freedom of the mind and spirit secured by the explicit guaranties of freedom of speech and religion, they intended or rightly could have left any latitude for a legislative judgment that the compulsory expression of belief which violates religious convictions would better serve the public interest than their protection. The Constitution may well elicit expressions of loyalty to it and to the government which it created, but it does not command such expressions or otherwise give any indication that compulsory expressions of loyalty play any such part in our scheme of government as to override the constitutional protection of freedom of speech and religion. And while such expressions of loyalty, when voluntarily given, may promote national unity, it is quite another matter to say that their own and their parents' religious convictions can be regarded as playing so important a part in our national unity as to leave local school boards free to exact it despite the constitutional guarantee of freedom of religion. The very terms of the Bill of Rights preclude, it seems to me, any reconciliation of such compulsions with the constitutional guaranties by a legislative declaration that they are more important to the public welfare than the Bill of Rights.

But even if this view be rejected and it is considered that there is some scope for the determination by legislatures whether the citizen shall be compelled to give public expression of such sentiments contrary to his religion, I am not persuaded that we should refrain from passing upon the legislative judgment "as long as the remedial channels of the democratic process remain open and unobstructed." This seems to me no less than the surrender of the constitutional protection of the liberty of small minorities to the popular will. We have previously pointed to the importance of a searching judicial inquiry into the legislative judgment in situations where prejudice against discrete and insular minorities may tend to curtail the operation of those political processes ordinarily to be relied on to protect minorities. And until now we have not hesitated similarly to scrutinize legislation restricting the civil liberty of racial and religious minorities although no political process was affected. Here we have such a small minority entertaining in good faith a religious belief, which is such a departure from the usual course of human conduct, that most persons are disposed to regard it with little toleration or concern. In such circumstances careful scrutiny of legislative efforts to secure conformity of belief and opinion by a compulsory affirmation of the desired belief, is especially needful if civil rights are to receive any protection. Tested by this standard, I am not prepared to say that the right of this small and helpless minority, including children having a strong religious conviction, whether they understand its nature or not, to refrain from an expression obnoxious to their religion, is to be overborne by the interest of the state in maintaining discipline in the schools.

The Constitution expresses more than the conviction of the people that democratic processes must be preserved at all costs. It is also an expression of faith and a command that freedom of mind and spirit must be preserved, which government must obey, if it is to adhere to that justice and moderation without which no free government can exist. For this reason it would seem that legislation which operates to repress the religious freedom of small minorities, which is admittedly within the scope of the protection of the Bill of Rights, must at least be subject to the same judicial scrutiny as legislation which we have recently held to infringe the constitutional liberty of religious and racial minorities.

With such scrutiny I cannot say that the inconveniences which may attend some sensible adjustment of school discipline in order that the religious convictions of these children may be spared, presents a problem so momentous or pressing as to outweigh the freedom from compulsory violation of religious faith which has been thought worthy of constitutional protection. ■

From Dissenting Opinion, Minersville School District v. *Gobitis, 1940.*

• EDITOR'S NOTE

As a result of the *Gobitis* case, the West Virginia State Board of Education ordered that saluting the flag be made compulsory in the public schools. Members of the Jehovah's Witnesses sued in the U. S. District Court to prevent enforcement of this order against their children. They won the case in the District Court, whereupon the Board of Education appealed to the United States Supreme Court. In the opinions given below, the Supreme Court upheld the lower court, reversing its earlier stand in the *Gobitis* case.

• JUSTICE ROBERT H. JACKSON

This case calls upon us to reconsider a precedent decision, as the Court throughout its history often has been required to do. Before turning to the Gobitis case, however, it is desirable to notice certain characteristics by which this controversy is distinguished.

The freedom asserted by these respondents does not bring them into collision with rights asserted by any other individual . . . The refusal of these persons to participate in the ceremony does not interfere with or deny rights of others to do so. Nor is there any question in this case that their behavior is peaceable and orderly. The sole conflict is between authority and rights of the individual. The State asserts power to condition access to public education on making a prescribed sign and profession and at the same time to coerce attendance by punishing both parent and child. The latter stand on a right of self-determination in matters that touch individual opinion and personal attitude. . . .

There is no doubt that, in connection with the pledges, the flag-salute is a form of utterance. Symbolism is a primitive but effective way of communicating ideas. The use of an emblem or flag to symbolize some system, idea, institution, or personality, is a short cut from mind to mind. . . .

Whether the First Amendment to the Constitution will permit officials to order observance of ritual of this nature does not depend upon whether as a voluntary exercise we would think it to be good, bad or merely innocuous. Any credo of nationalism is likely to include what some disapprove or to omit what others think essential . . . If official power exists to coerce acceptance of any patriotic creed, what it shall contain cannot be decided by courts. . . .

Nor does the issue as we see it turn on one's possession of particular religious views, or the sincerity with which they are held. . . . It is not necessary to inquire whether nonconformist beliefs will exempt from the duty to salute unless we first find power to make the salute a legal duty.

The Gobitis decision, however, *assumed,* as did the argument in that case and in this, that power exists in the State to impose the flag-salute discipline upon school children in general. The Court only examined and rejected a claim based on religious beliefs of immunity from an unquestioned general rule. The question which underlies the flag-salute controversy is whether such a ceremony so touching matters of opinion and political attitude may be imposed upon the individual by official authority under powers committed to any political organization under our Constitution. We examine rather than assume existence of this power and, against the broader definition of issues in this case, re-examine specific grounds assigned for the Gobitis decision. . . .

The very purpose of a Bill of Rights was to withdraw certain subjects from the vicissitudes of political controversy, to place them beyond the reach of majorities and officials and to establish them as legal principles to be applied by the courts. One's right to life, liberty, and property, to free speech, a free press, freedom of worship and assembly, and other fundamental rights may not be submitted to vote; they depend on the outcome of no elections. . . . They are susceptible of restriction only to prevent grave and immediate danger to interests which the state may lawfully protect. It is important to note that while it is the Fourteenth Amendment which bears directly upon the State it is the more specific limiting principles of the First Amendment that finally govern this case.

Nor does our duty to apply the Bill of Rights to assertions of official authority depend upon our possession of marked competence in the field where the invasion of rights occurs. True, the task of translating the majestic generalities of the Bill of Rights, conceived as part of the pattern of liberal government in the eighteenth century, into concrete restraints on officials dealing with the problems of the twentieth century, is one to disturb self-confidence . . . But we act in these matters not by authority of our competence but by force of our commissions. We cannot, because of modest estimates of our competence in such specialties as public education, withhold the judgment that history authenticates as the function of this Court when liberty is infringed.

Lastly, and this is the very heart of the Gobitis opinion, it reasons that "National unity is the basis of national security," that the authorities have "the right to select appropriate means for its attainment,"

and hence reaches the conclusion that such compulsory measures toward "national unity" are constitutional. Upon the verity of this assumption depends our answer in this case.

National unity as an end which officials may foster by persuasion and example is not in question. The problem is whether under our Constitution, compulsion as here employed is a permissible means for its achievement.

Struggles to coerce uniformity of sentiment in support of some end thought essential to their time and country have been waged by many good as well as by evil men. Nationalism is a relatively recent phenomenon but at other times and places the ends have been racial or territorial security, support of a dynasty or regime, and particular plans for saving souls. As first and moderate methods to attain unity have failed, those bent on its accomplishment must resort to an ever increasing severity. As governmental pressure toward unity becomes greater, so strife becomes more bitter as to whose unity it shall be. Probably no deeper division of our people could proceed from any provocation than from finding it necessary to choose what doctrine and whose program public educational officials shall compel youth to unite in embracing. Ultimate futility of such attempts to compel coherence is the lesson of every such effort from the Roman drive to stamp out Christianity as a disturber of its pagan unity, the Inquisition, as a means to religious and dynastic unity, the Siberian exiles as a means to Russian unity, down to the fast failing efforts of our present totalitarian enemies. Those who begin coercive elimination of dissent soon find themselves exterminating dissenters. Compulsory unification of opinion achieves only the unanimity of the graveyard.

It seems trite but necessary to say that the First Amendment to our Constitution was designed to avoid these ends by avoiding these beginnings. There is no mysticism in the American concept of the State or of the nature or origin of its authority. We set up government by consent of the governed, and the Bill of Rights denies those in power any legal opportunity to coerce that consent. Authority here is to be controlled by public opinion, not public opinion by authority. . . .

If there is any fixed star in our constitutional constellation, it is that no official, high or petty, can prescribe what shall be orthodox in politics, nationalism, religion, or other matters of opinion or force citizens to confess by word or act their faith therein. If there are any circumstances which permit an exception, they do not now occur to us.

We think the action of the local authorities in compelling the flag-salute and pledge transcends constitutional limitations on their power and invades the sphere of intellect and spirit which it is the purpose of the First Amendment to our Constitution to reserve from all official control.

The decision of this Court in *Minersville School District* v. *Gobitis* and the holdings of those few per curiam decisions which preceded and foreshadowed it are overruled, and the judgment enjoining enforcement of the West Virginia Regulation is *affirmed.* ∎

From Majority Opinion, West Virginia State Board of Education *v.* Barnette, *1943.*

• JUSTICE HUGO L. BLACK *and* JUSTICE WILLIAM O. DOUGLAS

No well-ordered society can leave to the individuals an absolute right to make final decisions, unassailable to the State, as to everything they will or will not do. The First Amendment does not go so far. Religious faiths, honestly held, do not free individuals from responsibility to conduct themselves obediently to laws which are either imperatively necessary to protect society as a whole from grave and pressingly imminent dangers or which, without any general prohibition, merely regulate time, place or manner of religious activity. Decision as to the constitutionality of particular laws which strike at the substance of religious tenets and practices must be made by this Court. The duty is a solemn one, and in meeting it we cannot say that failure, because of religious scruples, to assume a particular physical position and to repeat the words of a patriotic formula creates a grave danger to the nation. Such a statutory exaction is a form of test oath, and the test oath has always been abhorrent in the United States.

Words uttered under coercion are proof of loyalty to nothing but self-interest. Love of country must spring from willing hearts and free minds inspired by a fair administration of wise laws enacted by the people's elected representatives within the bounds of express constitutional prohibitions. These laws must, to be consistent with the First Amendment, permit the widest toleration of conflicting viewpoints consistent with a society of free men.

Neither our domestic tranquility in peace nor our martial effort in war depend on compelling little children to participate in a ceremony which ends in nothing for them but a fear of spiritual condemnation. If, as we think, their fears are groundless, time and reason are the proper antidotes for their errors. ∎

From Concurring Opinion, West Virginia State Board of Education *v.* Barnette, *1943.*

• JUSTICE FRANK MURPHY

A reluctance to interfere with considered state action, the fact that the end sought is a desirable one, the emotion aroused by the flag as a symbol for which we have fought and are now fighting again— all of these are understandable. But there is before us the right of freedom to believe, freedom to worship one's Maker according to the dictates of one's conscience, a right which the Constitution specifically shelters. Reflection has convinced me that as a judge I have no loftier duty or responsibility than to uphold that spiritual freedom to its farthest reaches.

The right of freedom of thought and of religion as guaranteed by the Consittution against State action includes both the right to speak freely and the right to refrain from speaking at all, except in so far as essential operations of government may require it for the preservation of an orderly society—as in the case of compulsion to give evidence in court. Without wishing to disparage the purposes and intentions of those who hope to inculcate sentiments of loyalty and patriotism by requiring a declaration of allegiance as a feature of public education, or unduly belittle the benefits that may accrue therefrom, I am impelled to conclude that such a requirement is not essential to the maintenance of effective government and orderly society. To many it is deeply distasteful to join in a public chorus of affirmation of private belief. By some, including the members of this sect, it is apparently regarded as incompatible with a primary religious obligation, therefore a restriction on religious freedom. Official compulsion to affirm what is contrary to one's religious beliefs is the antithesis of freedom of worship which, it is well to recall, was achieved in this country only after what Jefferson characterized as the "severest contests in which I have ever been engaged."

I am unable to agree that the benefits that may accrue to society from the compulsory flag-salute are sufficiently definite and tangible to justify the invasion of freedom and privacy that is entailed or to compensate for a restraint on the freedom of the individual to be vocal or silent according to his conscience or personal inclination. . . . Any spark of love for country which may be generated in a child or his associates by forcing him to make what is to him an empty gesture and recite words wrung from him contrary to his religious beliefs is overshadowed by the desirability of preserving freedom of conscience to the full. It is in that freedom and the example of persuasion, not in force and compulsion, that the real unity of America lies. ∎

From Concurring Opinion, West Virginia State Board of Education *v.* Barnette, *1943.*

• JUSTICE FELIX FRANKFURTER

Conscientious scruples, all would admit, cannot stand against every legislative compulsion to do positive acts in conflict with such scruples. We have been told that such compulsions override religious scruples only as to major concerns of the state. But the determination of what is major and what is minor itself raises questions of policy. For the way in which men equally guided by reason appraise importance goes to the very heart of policy. Judges should be very diffident in setting their judgment against that of a state in determining what is and what is

not a major concern, what means are appropriate to proper ends, and what is the total social cost in striking the balance of imponderables.

What one can say with assurance is that the history out of which grew constitutional provisions for religious equality, and the writings of the great exponents of religious freedom—Jefferson, Madison, John Adams, Benjamin Franklin—are totally wanting in justification for a claim by dissidents of exceptional immunity from civic measures of general applicability, measures not in fact disguised assaults upon such dissident views. The great leaders of the American Revolution were determined to remove political support from every religious establishment. They put on an equality the different religious sects —Episcopalians, Presbyterians, Catholics, Baptists, Methodists, Quakers, Huguenots—which as dissenters, had been under the heel of the various orthodoxies that prevailed in different colonies. So far as the state was concerned, there was to be neither orthodoxy nor heterodoxy. And so Jefferson and those who followed him wrote guarantees of religious freedom into our Constitution.[1] Religious minorities as well as religious majorities were to be equal in the eyes of the political state. But Jefferson and the others also knew that minorities may disrupt society. It never would have occurred to them to write into the Constitution the subordination of the general civil authority of the state to sectarian scruples.

The constitutional protection of religious freedom terminated disabilities, it did not create new privileges. It gave religious equality, not civil immunity. Its essence is freedom from conformity to religious dogma, not freedom from conformity to law because of religious dogma. Religious loyalties may be exercised without hindrance from the state, and the state may not exercise that which except by leave of religious loyalties is within the domain of temporal power. Otherwise each individual could set up his own censor against obedience to laws conscientiously deemed for the public good by those whose business it is to make laws.

---

[1] Actually Jefferson had little to do with the Federal Constitution. He did, however, draft the "Bill for Establishing Religious Freedom in Virginia."

The prohibition against any religious establishment by the government placed denominations on an equal footing—it assured freedom from support by the government to any mode of worship and the freedom of individuals to support any mode of worship. Any person may therefore believe or disbelieve what he pleases. He may practice what he will in his own house of worship or publicly within the limits of public order. But the lawmaking authority is not circumscribed by the variety of religious beliefs, otherwise the constitutional guaranty would not be a protection of the free exercise of religion but a denial of the exercise of legislation.

The essence of the religious freedom guaranteed by our Constitution is therefore this: no religion shall either receive the state's support or incur its hostility. Religion is outside the sphere of political government. This does not mean that all matters on which religious organizations or beliefs may pronounce are outside the sphere of government. Were this so, instead of the separation of church and state, there would be the subordination of the state on any matter deemed within the sovereignty of the religious conscience. Much that is the concern of temporal authority affects the spiritual interests of men. But it is not enough to strike down a nondiscriminatory law that it may hurt or offend some dissident view. It would be too easy to cite numerous prohibitions and injunctions to which laws run counter if the variant interpretaions of the Bible were made the tests of the obedience to law. The validity of secular laws cannot be measured by their conformity to religious doctrines. It is only in a theocratic state that ecclesiastical doctrines measure legal right or wrong.

An act compelling profession of allegiance to a religion, no matter how subtly or tenuously promoted, is bad. But an act promoting good citizenship and national allegiance is within the domain of governmental authority and is therefore to be judged by the same considerations of power and of constitutionality as those involved in the many claims of immunity from civil obedience because of religious scruples.

That claims are pressed on behalf of sincere religious convictions does not of itself establish their constitutional validity. Nor does waving the banner of religious freedom relieve us from examining the power we are asked to deny the states. Otherwise the doctrine of separation of church and state, so cardinal in the history of this nation and for the liberty of our people, would mean not the disestablishment of a state church but the establishment of all churches and of all religious groups. . . . ■

From Dissenting Opinion, West Virginia State Board of Education *v.* Barnett, *1943.*

• JUSTICE HUGO L. BLACK

A New Jersey statute authorizes its local school districts to make rules and contracts for the transportation of children to and from schools . . . Part of this money was for the payment of transportation of some children in the community to Catholic parochial schools . . .

The appellant, in his capacity as a district taxpayer, filed suit in a State court challenging the right of the Board [of Education] to reimburse parents of parochial school students. He contended that the statute and the resolution passed pursuant to it violated both the State and the Federal Constitution. . . .

The New Jersey statute is challenged as a "law respecting an establishment of religion." The First Amendment, as made applicable to the states by the Fourteenth, *Murdock* v. *Pennsylvania,* 319 U.S. 105, commands that a state "shall make no law respecting an establishment of religion, or prohibiting the free exercise thereof. . . ." These words of the First Amendment reflected in the minds of early Americans a vivid mental picture of conditions and practices which they fervently wished to stamp out in order to preserve liberty for themselves and for their posterity. Doubtless their goal has not been entirely reached; but so far has the Nation moved toward it that the expression "law respecting an establishment of religion," probably does not so vividly remind present-day Americans of the evils, fears and political problems that caused that expression to be written into our Bill of Rights. Whether this New Jersey law is one respecting an "establishment of religion" requires an understanding of the meaning of that language, particularly with respect to the imposition of taxes. Once again, therefore, it is not inappropriate briefly to review the background and environment of the period in which that constitutional language was fashioned and adopted.

A large proportion of the early settlers of this country came here from Europe to escape the bondage of laws which compelled them to support and attend government-favored churches. The centuries immediately before and contemporaneous with the colonization of America had been filled with turmoil, civil strife, and persecutions, generated in large part by established sects determined to maintain their absolute political and religious supremacy. With the power of government supporting them, at various times and places, Catholics had persecuted Protestants, Protestants had persecuted Catholics, Protestants sects had persecuted other Protestant sects, Catholics of one shade of belief had persecuted Catholics of another shade of belief, and all of these had from time to time persecuted Jews. In efforts to enforce loyalty to whatever religious group happened to be on top and in league with the government of a particular time and place, men and women had been fined, cast in jail, cruelly tortured, and killed. Among the offenses for which these punishments had been inflicted were such things as speaking disrespectfully of the views of ministers of government-established churches, nonattendance at those churches, expressions of nonbelief in their doctrines, and failure to pay taxes and tithes to support them.

These practices of the old world were transplanted to and began to thrive in the soil of the new America. The very charters granted by the English Crown to the individuals and companies designated to make the laws which would control the destinies of the colonials authorized these individuals and companies to erect religious establishments which all, whether believers or nonbelievers, would be required to support and attend. An exercise of this authority was accompanied by a repetition of many of the old-world practices and persecutions. Catholics found themselves hounded and proscribed because of their faith; Quakers who followed their conscience went to jail; Baptists were peculiarly obnoxious to certain dominant Protestant sects; men and women of varied faiths who happened to be in a minority in a particular locality were persecuted because they steadfastly persisted in worshipping God only as their own consciences dictated. And all of these dissenters were compelled to pay tithes and taxes to support government-sponsored churches whose ministers preached inflammatory sermons designed to strengthen and consolidate the established faith by generating a burning hatred against dissenters.

These practices became so commonplace as to shock the freedom-loving colonials into a feeling of abhorrence. The imposition of taxes to pay ministers' salaries and to build and maintain churches and church property aroused their indignation. It was these feelings which found expression in the First Amendment. No one locality and no one group throughout the Colonies can rightly be given entire credit for having aroused the sentiment that culminated in adoption of the Bill of Rights' provisions embracing religious liberty. But Virginia, where the established church had achieved a dominant influence in political affairs and where many excesses attracted wide public attention, provided a great stimulus and able leadership for the movement. The people there, as elsewhere, reached the conviction that individual religious liberty could be achieved best under a government which was stripped of all power to tax, to support, or otherwise to assist any or all religions, or to interfere with the beliefs of any religious individual or group.

The movement toward this end reached its dramatic climax in Virginia in 1785–86 when the Virginia legislative body was about to renew Virginia's tax levy for the support of the established church. Thomas Jefferson and James Madison led the fight against this tax. Madison wrote his great Memorial and Remonstrance against the law. In it, he eloquently argued that a true religion did not need the support of law; that no person, either believer or nonbeliever, should be taxed to support a religious institution of any kind; that the best interest of a society required that the minds of men always be wholly free; and that cruel persecutions were the inevitable result of government-established religions. Madison's Remonstrance received strong support throughout Virginia, and the Assembly postponed consideration of the proposed tax measure until its next session. When the proposal came up for consideration at that session, it not only died in committee, but the Assembly enacted the famous "Virginia Bill for Religious Liberty" originally written by Thomas Jefferson. . . .

This court has previously recognized that the provisions of the First Amendment, in the drafting and adoption of which Madison and Jefferson played such leading roles, had the same objective and were intended to provide the same protection against governmental intrusion on religious liberty as the Virginia statute. . . . Prior to the adoption of the Fourteenth Amendment, the First Amendment did not apply as a restraint against the states. Most of them did soon provide similar constitutional protections for religious liberty. But some states persisted for about half a century in imposing restraints upon the free exercise of religion and in discriminating against particular religious groups. In recent years, so far as the provision against the establishment of a religion is concerned, the question has most frequently arisen in connection with proposed state aid to church schools and efforts to carry on religious teachings in the public schools in accordance with the tenets of a particular sect. Some churches have either sought or accepted state financial support for their schools. Here again the efforts to obtain state aid or acceptance of it have not been limited to any one particular faith. The state courts, in the main, have remained faithful to the language of their own constitutional provisions designed to protect religious freedom and to separate religions and governments. Their decisions, however, show the difficulty in drawing the line between tax legislation which provides funds for the welfare of the general public and that which is designed to support institutions which teach religion.

The meaning and scope of the First Amendment,

preventing establishment of religion or prohibiting the free exercise thereof, in the light of its history and the evils it was designed forever to suppress, have been several times elaborated by the decisions of this Court prior to the application of the First Amendment to the states by the Fourteenth. The broad meaning given the Amendment by these earlier cases has been accepted by this Court in its decisions concerning an individual's religious freedom rendered since the Fourteenth Amendment was interpreted to make the prohibitions of the First applicable to state action abridging religious freedom. There is every reason to give the same application and broad interpretation to the "establishment of religion" clause. The interrelation of these complementary clauses was well summarized in a statement of the Court of Appeals of South Carolina . . . "The structure of our government has, for the preservation of civil liberty, rescued the temporal institutions from religious interference. On the other hand, it has secured religious liberty from the invasion of the civil authority."

The "establishment of religion" clause of the First Amendment means at least this: Neither a state nor the Federal Government can set up a church. Neither can pass laws which aid one religion, aid all religions, or prefer one religion over another. Neither can force nor influence a person to go to or to remain away from church against his will or force him to profess a belief or disbelief in any religion. No person can be punished for entertaining or professing religious beliefs or disbeliefs, for church attendance or nonattendance. No tax in any amount, large or small, can be levied to support any religious activities or institutions, whatever they may be called, or whatever form they may adopt to teach or practice religion. Neither a state nor the Federal Government can, openly or secretly, participate in the affairs of any religious organizations or groups and vice versa. In the words of Jefferson, the clause against establishment of religion by law was intended to erect "a wall of separation between church and State.". . .

We must consider the New Jersey statute in accordance with the foregoing limitations imposed by the First Amendment . . . New Jersey cannot consistently with the "establishment of religion" clause of the First Amendment contribute tax-raised funds to the support of an institution which teaches the tenets and faith of any church. On the other hand, other language of the amendment commands that New Jersey cannot hamper its citizens in the free exercise of their own religion. Consequently, it cannot exclude individual Catholics, Lutherans, Mohammedans, Baptists, Jews, Methodists, Nonbelievers, Presbyterians, or the members of any other faith, *because of their faith, or lack of it,* from receiving the benefits of public welfare legislation. While we do not mean to intimate that a state could not provide transportation only to children attending public schools, we must be careful, in protecting the citizens of New Jersey against state-established churches, to be sure that we do not inadvertently prohibit New Jersey from extending its general State law benefits to all its citizens without regard to their religious belief.

Measured by these standards, we cannot say that the First Amendment prohibits New Jersey from spending tax-raised funds to pay the bus fares of parochial school pupils as a part of a general program under which it pays the fares of pupils attending public and other schools. It is undoubtedly true that children are helped to get to church schools. There is even a possibility that some of the children might not be sent to the church schools if the parents were compelled to pay their children's bus fares out of their own pockets . . . The same possibility exists where the State requires a local transit company to provide reduced fares to school children . . . Moreover, state-paid policemen, detailed to protect children going to and from church schools . . . would serve much the same purpose and accomplish much the same result as State provisions intended to guarantee free transportation of a kind which the State deems to be best for the school children's welfare . . . But such is obviously not the purpose of the First Amendment. That Amendment requires the State to be a neutral in its relations with groups of religious believers and nonbelievers; it does not require the State to be their adversary. State power

is no more to be used so as to handicap religions, than it is to favor them.

This Court has said that parents may, in the discharge of their duty under State compulsory education laws, send their children to a religious rather than a public school . . . It appears that these parochial schools meet New Jersey's requirements. The State contributes no money to the schools. It does not support them. Its legislation, as applied, does no more than provide a general program to help parents get their children, regardless of their religion, safely and expeditiously to and from accredited schools.

The First Amendment has erected a wall between church and State. That wall must be kept high and impregnable. We could not approve the slightest breach. New Jersey has not breached it here. *Affirmed.* ■

From Majority Opinion, Everson v. Board of Education, *1947.*

• JUSTICE ROBERT H. JACKSON

It is of no importance in this situation whether the beneficiary of this expenditure of tax-raised funds is primarily the parochial school and incidentally the pupil, or whether the aid is directly bestowed on the pupil with indirect benefits to the school. The state cannot maintain a Church and it can no more tax its citizens to furnish free carriage to those who attend a Church. The prohibition against establishment of religion cannot be circumvented by a subsidy, bonus or reimbursement of expense to individuals for receiving religious instruction and indoctrination . . .

Of course, the state may pay out tax-raised funds to relieve pauperism, but it may not under our Constitution do so to induce or reward piety. It may spend funds to secure old age against want, but it may not spend funds to secure religion against skepticism. It may compensate individuals for loss of employment, but it cannot compensate them for adherence to a creed.

It seems to me that the basic fallacy in the Court's reasoning, which accounts for its failure to apply the principles it avows, is in ignoring the essentially religious test by which beneficiaries of this expenditure are selected. A policeman protects a Catholic, of course—but not because he is a Catholic; it is because he is a man and a member of our society. The fireman protects the Church school—but not because it is a Church school; it is because it is property, part of the assets of our society. Neither the fireman nor the policeman has to ask before he renders aid "Is this man or building identified with the Catholic Church?" . . . I agree that this Court has left, and always should leave to each state, great latitude in deciding for itself, in the light of its own conditions, what shall be public purposes in the scheme of things. It may socialize utilities and economic enterprises and make taxpayers' business out of what conventionally had been private business. It may make public business of individual welfare, health, education, entertainment or security. But it cannot make public business of religious worship or instruction, or of attendance at religious institutions of any character . . .

This policy of our Federal Constitution has never been wholly pleasing to most religious groups. They all are quick to invoke its protection; they all are irked when they feel its restraints . . .

But we cannot have it both ways. Religious teaching cannot be a private affair when the state seeks to impose regulations which infringe on it indirectly, and a public affair when it comes to taxing citizens of one faith to aid another, or those of no faith to aid at all. If these principles seem harsh in prohibiting aid to Catholic education, it must not be forgotten that it is the same Constitution that alone assures Catholics the right to maintain these schools at all when predominant local sentiment would forbid them . . . Nor should I think that those who have done so well without this aid would want to see this separation between Church and State broken down. If the state may aid these religious schools, it may therefore regulate them. Many groups have sought aid from tax funds only to find that it carried political controls with it. ∎

From Dissenting Opinion, Everson *v.* Board of Education, *1947.*

• JUSTICE HUGO BLACK

This case relates to the power of a state to utilize its tax-supported public school system in aid of religious instruction insofar as that power may be restricted by the First and Fourteenth Amendments to the Federal Constitution.

The appellant, Vashti McCollum, began this action for mandamus against the Champaign Board of Education in the Circuit Court of Champaign County, Illinois. Her asserted interest was that of a resident and taxpayer of Champaign and of a parent whose child was then enrolled in the Champaign public schools. Illinois has a compulsory education law which, with exceptions, requires parents to send their children, aged seven to sixteen, to its tax-supported public schools where the children are to remain in attendance during the hours when the schools are regularly in session. Parents who violate this law commit a misdemeanor punishable by fine unless the children attend private or parochial schools which meet educational standards fixed by the State. District boards of education are given general supervisory powers over the use of the public school buildings within the school districts.

Appellant's petition for mandamus alleged that religious teachers, employed by private religious groups, were permitted to come weekly into the school buildings during the regular hours set apart for secular teaching, and then and there for a period of thirty minutes substitute their religious teaching for the secular education provided under the compulsory education law. The petitioner charged that this joint public-school religious-group program violated the First and Fourteenth Amendments to the United States Constitution. . . .

Although there are disputes between the parties as to various inferences that may or may not properly be drawn from the evidence concerning the religious program, the following facts are shown by the record without dispute. In 1940 interested members of the Jewish, Roman Catholic, and a few of the Protestant faiths formed a voluntary association called the Champaign Council on Religious Education. They obtained permission from the Board of Education to offer classes in religious instruction to public school pupils in grades four to nine inclusive. Classes were made up of pupils whose parents signed printed cards requesting that their children be permitted to attend; they were held weekly, thirty minutes for the lower grades, forty-five minutes for the higher. The council employed the religious teachers at no expense to the school authorities, but the instructors were subject to the approval and supervision of the superintendent of schools. The classes were taught in three separate religious groups by Protestant teachers, Catholic priests, and a Jewish rabbi, although for the past several years there have apparently been no classes instructed in the Jewish religion. Classes were conducted in the regular classrooms of the school building. Students who did not choose to take the religious instruction were not released from public school duties; they were required to leave their classrooms and go to some other place in the school building for pursuit of their secular studies. On the other hand, students who were released from secular study for the religious instructions were required to be present at the religious classes. Reports of their presence or absence were to be made to their secular teachers.

The foregoing facts, without reference to others that appear in the record, show the use of tax-supported property for religious instruction and the close cooperation between the school authorities and the religious council in promoting religious education. The operation of the state's compulsory education system thus assists and is integrated with the program of religious instruction carried on by separate religious sects. Pupils compelled by law to go to school for secular education are released in part from their legal duty upon the condition that they attend the religious classes. This is beyond all question a utilization of the tax-established and tax-supported public school system to aid religious groups to spread their faith. And it falls squarely under the ban of the First Amendment (made applicable to the States by the Fourteenth) as we interpreted it in *Everson* v. *Board of Education*. There we said: "Neither a state nor the Federal Govern-

ment can set up a church. Neither can pass laws which aid one religion, aid all religions, or prefer one religion over another. Neither can force nor influence a person to go to or to remain away from church against his will or force him to profess a belief or disbelief in any religion. No person can be punished for entertaining or professing religious beliefs or disbeliefs, for church attendance or non-attendance. No tax in any amount, large or small, can be levied to support any religious activities or institutions, whatever they may be called, or whatever form they may adopt to teach or practice religion. Neither a state nor the Federal Government can, openly or secretly, participate in the affairs of any religious organizations or groups, and vice versa. In the words of Jefferson, the clause against establishment of religion by law was intended to erect 'a wall of separation between Church and State.'" The majority in the Everson case, and the minority as shown by quotations from the dissenting views agreed that the First Amendment's language, properly interpreted, had erected a wall of separation between Church and State. They disagreed as to the facts shown by the record and as to the proper application of the First Amendment's language to those facts.

Recognizing that the Illinois program is barred by the First and Fourteenth Amendments if we adhere to the views expressed both by the majority and the minority in the Everson case, counsel for the respondents challenge those views as dicta and urge that we reconsider and repudiate them. They argue that historically the First Amendment was intended to forbid only government preference of one religion over another, not an impartial governmental assistance of all religions. In addition they ask that we distinguish or overrule our holding in the Everson case that the Fourteenth Amendment made the "establishment of religion" clause of the First Amendment applicable as a prohibition against the States. After giving full consideration to the arguments presented we are unable to accept either of these contentions.

To hold that a state cannot consistently with the First and Fourteenth Amendments utilize its public school system to aid any or all religious faiths or sects in the dissemination of their doctrines and ideals does not, as counsel urge, manifest a governmental hostility to religions or religious teachings. A manifestation of such hostility would be at war with our national tradition as embodied in the First Amendment's guaranty of the free exercise of religion. For the First Amendment rests upon the premise that both religion and government can best work to achieve their lofty aims if each is left free from the other within its respective sphere. Or, as we said in the Everson case, the First Amendment has erected a wall between Church and State which must be kept high and impregnable.

Here not only are the State's tax-supported public school buildings used for the dissemination of religious doctrines. The State also affords sectarian groups an invaluable aid in that it helps to provide pupils for their religious classes through use of the State's compulsory public school machinery. This is not separation of Church and State.

The cause is reversed and remanded to the State Supreme Court for proceedings not inconsistent with this opinion. ■

From Majority Opinion, McCollum *v.* Board of Education, *1948.*

• JUSTICE FELIX FRANKFURTER

It is pertinent to remind that the establishment of this principle of Separation in the field of education was not due to any decline in the religious beliefs of the people. Horace Mann was a devout Christian, and the deep religious feeling of James Madison is stamped upon the Remonstrance. The secular public school did not imply indifference to the basic role of religion in the life of the people, nor rejection of religious education as a means of fostering it. The claims of religion were not minimized by refusing to make the public school agencies of their assertion. The nonsectarian or secular public school was the means of reconciling freedom in general with religious freedom. The sharp confinement of the public schools to secular education

was a recognition of the need of a democratic society to educate its children, in so far as the State undertook to do so, in an atmosphere free from pressures in a realm in which pressures are most resisted and where conflicts are most easily and most bitterly engendered. Designed to serve as perhaps the most powerful agency for promoting cohesion among a heterogeneous democratic people, the public school must keep scrupulously free from entanglement in the strife of sects. The preservation of the community from divisive conflicts, of Government from irreconcilable pressures by religious groups, of religion from censorship and coercion however subtly exercised, requires strict confinement of the State to instruction other than religious, leaving to the individual's church and home, indoctrination in the faith of his choice. . . .

Separation means separation, not something less. Jefferson's metaphor in describing the relation between Church and State speaks of a "wall of separation," not of a fine line easily overstepped. The public school is at once the symbol of our democracy and the most pervasive means for promoting our common destiny. In no activity of the State is it more vital to keep out divisive forces than in its schools, to avoid confusing, not to say fusing, what the Constitution sought to keep strictly apart. "The great American principle of eternal separation"— Elihu Root's phrase bears repetition—is one of the vital reliances of our constitutional system for assuring unities among our people stronger than our diversities. It is the Court's duty to enforce this principle in its full integrity.

We renew our conviction that "we have staked the very existence of our country on the faith that complete separation between the state and religion is best for the state and best for religion.". . . If nowhere else, in the relation between Church and State, "good fences make good neighbors." ■

From Concurring Opinion, McCollum *v.* Board of Education, *1948.*

• JUSTICE WILLIAM O. DOUGLAS

New York City has a program which permits its public schools to release students during the school day so that they may leave the school buildings and school grounds and go to religious centers for religious instruction or devotional exercises. A student is released on written request of his parents. Those not released stay in the classrooms. The churches make weekly reports to the schools, sending a list of children who have been released from public school but who have not reported for religious instruction.

This "released time" program involves neither religious instruction in public school classrooms nor the expenditure of public funds. All costs, including the application blanks, are paid by the religious organizations. The case is therefore unlike *McCollum* v. *Board of Education* . . . which involved a "released time" program from Illinois. In that case the classrooms were turned over to religious instuctors. We accordingly held that the program violated the First Amendment which (by reason of the Fourteenth Amendment) prohibits the states from establishing religion or prohibiting its free exercise.

Appellants, who are taxpayers and residents of New York City and whose children attend its public schools, challenge the present law, contending it is in essence no different from the one involved in the McCollum case. Their argument, stated elaborately in various ways, reduces itself to this: the weight and influence of the school is put behind a program for religious instruction; public school teachers police it, keeping tab on students who are released; the classroom activities come to a halt while the students who are released for religious instruction are on leave; the school is a crutch on which the churches are leaning for support in their religious training; without the cooperation of the schools this "released time" program, like the one in the McCollum case, would be futile and ineffective. The New York Court of Appeals sustained the law against this claim of unconstitutionality. . . .

Our problem reduces itself to whether New York by this system has either prohibited the "free exercise" of religion or has made a law "respecting an establishment of religion" within the meaning of the First Amendment.

It takes obtuse reasoning to inject any issue of the "free exercise" of religion into the present case. No one is forced to go to the religious classroom and no religious exercise or instruction is brought to the classrooms of the public schools. A student need not take religious instruction. He is left to his own desires as to the manner or time of his religious devotions, if any.

There is a suggestion that the system involves the use of coercion to get public school students into religious classrooms. There is no evidence in the record before us that supports that conclusion. The present record indeed tells us that the school authorities are neutral in this regard and do no more than release students whose parents so request. If in fact coercion were used, if it were established that any one or more teachers were using their office to persuade or force students to take the religious instruction, a wholly different case would be presented. Hence we put aside that claim of coercion both as respects the "free exercise" of religion and "an establishment of religion" within the meaning of the First Amendment.

Moreover, apart from that claim of coercion, we do not see how New York by this type of "released time" program has made a law respecting an establishment of religion within the meaning of the First Amendment. There is much talk of the separation of Church and State in the history of the Bill of Rights and in the decisions clustering around the First Amendment . . . There cannot be the slightest doubt that the First Amendment reflects the philosophy that Church and State should be separated. And so far as interference with the "free exercise" of religion and an "establishment" of religion are concerned, the separation must be complete and unequivocal. The First Amendment within the scope of its coverage permits no exception; the prohibition is absolute. The First Amendment, however, does not say that in every and all respects there shall be a separation of Church and State. Rather, it studiously defines the manner, the specific ways, in which there shall be no concert or union or dependency one on the other. That is the common sense of the matter. Otherwise the state and religion would be aliens to each other—hostile, suspicious, and even unfriendly. Churches could not be required to pay even property taxes. Municipalities would not be permitted to render police or fire protection to religious groups. Policemen who helped parishioners into their places of worship would violate the Constitution. Prayers in our legislative halls; the appeals to the Almighty in the messages of the Chief Executive; the proclamation making Thanksgiving Day a holiday; "so help me God" in our courtroom oaths—these and all other references to the Almighty that run through our laws, our public rituals, our ceremonies would be flouting the First Amendment. A fastidious atheist or agnostic could even object to the supplication with which the Court opens each session: "God save the United States and this Honorable Court."

We would have to press the concept of separation of Church and State to these extremes to condemn the present law on constitutional grounds. The nullification of this law would have wide and profound effects. A Catholic student applies to his teacher for permission to leave the school during hours on a Holy Day of Obligation to attend a mass. A Jewish student asks his teacher for permission to be excused for Yom Kippur. A Protestant wants the afternoon off for a family baptismal ceremony. In each case the teacher requires parental consent in writing. In each case the teacher, in order to make sure the student is not a truant, goes further and requires a report from the priest, the rabbi, or the minister. The teacher in other words cooperates in a religious program to the extent of making it possible for her students to participate in it. Whether she does it occasionally for a few students, regularly for one, or pursuant to a systemized program designed to further the religious needs of all the stufents does not alter the character of the act.

We are a religious people whose institutions presuppose a Supreme Being. We guarantee the freedom to worship as one chooses. We make room for as wide a variety of beliefs and creeds as the spiritual needs of man deem necessary. We sponsor an attitude on the part of government that shows no partiality to any one group and that lets each flourish according to the zeal of its adherents and the appeal of its dogma. When the state encourages religious instruction or cooperates with religious authorities by adjusting the schedule of public events to sectarian needs, it follows the best of our traditions. For then it respects the religious nature of our people and accommodates the public service to their spiritual needs. To hold that it may not would be to find in the Constitution a requirement that the government show a callous indifference to religious groups. That would be preferring those who believe in no religion over those who do believe. Government may not finance religious groups nor undertake religious instruction nor blend secular and sectarian education nor use secular institutions to force one or some religion on any person. But we find no constitutional requirement which makes it necessary for government to be hostile to religion and to throw its weight against efforts to widen the effective scope of religious influence. The government must be neutral when it comes to competition between sects. It may not thrust any sect on any person. It may not make a religious observance compulsory. It may not coerce anyone to attend church, to observe a religious holiday, or to take religious instruction. But it can close its doors or suspend its operations as to those who want to repair to their religious sanctuary for worship or instruction. No more than that is undertaken here.

This program may be unwise and improvident from an educational or a community viewpoint. That appeal is made to us on a theory, previously advanced, that each case must be decided on the basis of "our own prepossessions." . . . Our individual preferences, however, are not the constitutional standard. The constitutional standard is the separation of Church and State. The problem, like many problems in constitutional law, is one of degree. . . .

In the McCollum case the classrooms were used for religious instruction and the force of the public school was used to promote that instruction. Here, as we have said, the public schools do no more than accommodate their schedules to a program of outside religious instruction. We follow the McCollum case. But we cannot expand it to cover the present released time program unless separation of Church and State means that public instituions can make no adjustments of their schedules to accommodate the religious needs of the people. We cannot read into the Bill of Rights such a philosophy of hostility to religion. *Affirmed.* ■

From Majority Opinion, Zorach v. Clauson, *1952.*

• JUSTICE HUGO L. BLACK

I see no significant difference between the invalid Illinois system and that of New York here sustained. Except for the use of the school buildings in Illinois, there is no difference between the systems which I consider even worthy of mention . . . As we attempted to make categorically clear, the McCollum decision would have been the same if the religious classes had not been held in the school buildings. . . .

McCollum thus held that Illinois could not constitutionally manipulate the compelled classroom hours of its compulsory school machinery so as to channel children into sectarian classes. Yet that is exactly what the Court holds New York can do.

I am aware that our McCollum decision on separation of Church and State has been subjected to a most searching examination throughout the country. Probably few opinions from this Court in recent years have attracted more attention or stirred wider debate. Our insistence on "a wall between Church and State which must be kept high and impregnable" has seemed to some a correct exposition of the philosophy and a true interpretation of the language of the First Amendment to which we should strictly adhere. With equal conviction and sincerity, others have thought the McCollum decision fundamentally wrong and have pledged continuous warfare against it. The opinions in the court below and the briefs here reflect these diverse viewpoints. In dissenting

today, I mean to do more than give routine approval to our McCollum decision. I mean also to reaffirm my faith in the fundamental philosophy expressed in McCollum and *Everson* v. *Board of Education,* 330 U.S. 1. That reaffirmance can be brief because of the exhaustive opinions in those recent cases. . . .

The Court's validation of the New York system rests in part on its statement that Americans are "a religious people whose institutions presuppose a Supreme Being." This was at least as true when the First Amendment was adopted; and it was just as true when eight Justices of this Court invalidated the released time system in McCollum on the premise that a state can no more "aid all religions" than it can aid one. It was precisely because eighteenth-century Americans were a religious people divided into many fighting sects that we were given the constitutional mandate to keep Church and State completely separate . . . The First Amendment was therefore to insure that no one powerful sect or combination of sects could use political or governmental power to punish dissenters whom they could not convert to their faith. Now as then, it is only by wholly isolating the state from the religious sphere and compelling it to be completely neutral, that the freedom of each and every denomination and of all nonbelievers can be maintained. It is this neutrality the Court abandons today when it treats New York's coercive system as a program which *merely* "encourages religious instruction or cooperates with religious authorities." The abandonment is all the more dangerous to liberty because of the Court's legal exaltation of the orthodox and its derogation of unbelievers.

Under our system of religious freedom, people have gone to their religious sanctuaries not because they feared the law but because they loved their God. The choice of all has been as free as the choice of those who answered the call to worship moved only by the music of the old Sunday morning church bells. The spiritual mind of man has thus been free to believe, disbelieve, or doubt, without repression, great or small, by the heavy hand of government. Statutes authorizing such repression have been stricken. Before today, our judicial opinions have refrained from drawing invidious distinctions between those who believe in no religion and those who do believe. The First Amendment has lost much if the religious follower and the atheist are no longer to be judicially regarded as entitled to equal justice under law.

State help to religion injects political and party prejudices into a holy field. It too often substitutes force for prayer, hate for love, and persecution for persuasion. Government should not be allowed under cover of the soft euphemism of "cooperation," to steal into the sacred area of religious choice. ■

From Dissenting Opinion, Zorach v. Clauson, *1952.*

• JUSTICE ROBERT H. JACKSON

This released time program is founded upon a use of the State's power of coercion, which, for me, determines its unconstitutionality. . . .

The greater effectiveness of this system over voluntary attendance after school hours is due to the truant officer who, if the youngster fails to go to the Church school, dogs him back to the public schoolroom. Here schooling is more or less suspended during the "released time" so the nonreligious attendants will not forge ahead of the churchgoing absentees. But it serves as a temporary jail for a pupil who will not go to Church. It takes more subtlety of mind than I possess to deny that this is governmental constraint in support of religion. It is as unconstitutional, in my view, when exerted by indirection as when exercised forthrightly.

As one whose children, as a matter of free choice, have been sent to privately supported Church schools, I may challenge the Court's suggestion that opposition to this plan can only be antireligious, atheistic, or agnostic. My evangelistic brethren confuse an objection to compulsion with an objection to religion. It is possible to hold a faith with enough confidence to believe that what should be rendered to God does not need to be decided and collected by Caesar.

The day that this country ceases to be free for irreligion it will cease to be free for religion—except for the sect that can win political power. The same epithetical jurisprudence used by the Court today to beat down those who oppose pressuring children into some religion can devise as good epithets tomorrow against those who object to pressuring them into a favored religion. And, after all, if we concede to the State power and wisdom to single out "duly constituted religious" bodies as exclusive alternatives for compulsory secular instruction, it would be logical to also uphold the power and wisdom to choose the true faith among those "duly constituted." We start down a rough road when we begin to mix compulsory public education with compulsory godliness. . . .

The wall which the Court was professing to erect between Church and State has become even more warped and twisted than I expected. Today's judgment will be more interesting to students of psychology and of the judicial processes than to students of constitutional law. ■

From Dissenting Opinion, Zorach v. Clauson, *1952.*

• EDITOR'S NOTE

Article VI of the Constitution requires that an "Oath or Affirmation" be taken by all American government officials, including members of the federal and state legislatures. At the same time, the Article prohibits any religious test for public office —thus guaranteeing the right of any citizen, regardless of whether he is affiliated with any church or not, to hold any government position. The words of this clause, of crucial importance in the practices of freedom, read: "but no religious Test shall ever be required as a Qualification to any Office or public Trust under the United States."

As a rule, the state constitutions have followed the federal. There have been, however, some variations potentially dangerous to religious freedom. One such qualification was in the constitution of Maryland—calling for a "declaration of belief in the existence of God" as a requirement for public office—which was declared unconstitutional in the significant case that follows here.

• JUSTICE HUGO L. BLACK

Article 37 of the Declaration of Rights of the Maryland Constitution provides: "(N)o religious test ought ever to be required as a qualification for any office of profit or trust in this State, other than a declaration of belief in the existence of God. . . ." The appellant Torcaso was appointed to the office of Notary Public by the Governor of Maryland but was refused a commission to serve because he would not declare his belief in God. He then brought this action in a Maryland Circuit Court to compel issuance of his commission, charging that the State's requirement that he declare this belief violated "the First and Fourteenth Amendments to the Constitution of the United States. . . ."

There is, and can be, no dispute about the purpose or effect of the Maryland Declaration of Rights requirement before us—it sets up a religious test which was designed to and, if valid, does bar every person who refuses to declare a belief in God from holding a public "office of profit or trust" in Maryland. The power and authority of the State of Maryland thus is put on the side of one particular sort of believers—those who are willing to say they believe in "the existence of God." It is true that there is much historical precedent for such laws. Indeed, it was largely to escape religious test oaths and declarations that a great many of the early colonists left Europe and came here hoping to worship in their own way. It soon developed, however, that many of those who had fled to escape religious test oaths turned out to be perfectly willing, when they had the power to do so, to force dissenters from their faith to take test oaths in conformity with that faith.

This brought on a host of laws in the new Colonies imposing burdens and disabilities of various kinds upon varied beliefs depending largely upon what group happened to be politically strong enough to legislate in favor of its own beliefs. The effect of all this was the formal or practical "establishment" of particular religious faiths in most of the Colonies, with consequent burdens imposed on the free exercise of the faiths of nonfavored believers.

There were, however, wise and far-seeing men in the Colonies—too many to mention—who spoke out against test oaths and all the philosophy of intolerance behind them. One of these, it so happens, was George Calvert (the first Lord Baltimore), who took a most important part in the original establishment of the Colony of Maryland. He was a Catholic and had, for this reason, felt compelled by his conscience to refuse to take the Oath of Supremacy in England at the cost of resigning from high governmental office. He again refused to take that oath when it was demanded by the Council of the Colony of Virginia, and as a result he was denied settlement in that Colony. A recent historian of the early period of Maryland's life has said that it was Calvert's hope and purpose to establish in Maryland a colonial government free from the religious persecutions he had known—one "securely beyond the reach of oaths. . . ."

When our Constitution was adopted, the desire to put the people "securely beyond the reach" of religious test oaths brought about the inclusion in Article VI of that document of a provision that "no religious Test shall ever be required as a Qualification to any Office or public Trust under the United States. . . ." Not satisfied, however, with Article VI and other guarantees in the original Constitution, the First Congress proposed and the states very shortly thereafter adopted our Bill of Rights, including the First Amendment. That Amendment broke new constitutional ground in the protection it sought to afford to freedom of religion, speech, press, petition and assembly. . . .

In *Cantwell* v. *Connecticut* we said: "The First Amendment declares that Congress shall make no law respecting an establishment of religion or prohibiting the free exercise thereof. The Fourteenth Amendment has rendered the legislatures of the states as incompetent as Congress to enact such laws. . . . Thus the Amendment embraces two concepts—freedom to believe and freedom to act. The first is absolute but, in the nature of things, the second cannot be."[1]

Later we decided *Everson* v. *Board of Education,* and said . . . "The 'establishment of religion' clause of the First Amendment means at least this: Neither a state nor the Federal Government can set up a church. Neither can pass laws which aid one religion, aid all religions, or prefer one religion over another. Neither can force nor influence a person to go to or to remain away from church against his will or force him to profess a belief or disbelief in any religion. No person can be punished for entertaining or professing religious beliefs or disbeliefs, for church attendance or nonattendance. No tax in any amount, large or small, can be levied to support any religious activities or institutions, whatever they may be called, or whatever form they may adopt to teach or practice religion. Neither a state nor the Federal Government can, openly or secretly, participate in the affairs of any religious organizations or groups and vice versa. In the words of Jefferson, the clause against establishment of religion by law was intended to erect 'a wall of separation between church and State.'"

We repeat and again reaffirm that neither a State nor the Federal Government can constitutionally force a person "to profess a belief or disbelief in any religion." Neither can constitutionally pass laws nor impose requirements which aid all religions as against nonbelievers, and neither can aid those religions based on a belief in the existence of God as against those religions founded on different beliefs.

In upholding the State's religious test for public office the highest court of Maryland said: "The petitioner is not compelled to believe or disbelieve, under threat of punishment or other compulsion. True, unless he makes the declaration of belief he

---

[1].The Opinion of the Court in *Cantwell* v. *Connecticut* (1940), was written by Justice Owen J. Roberts.

cannot hold public office in Maryland, but he is not compelled to hold office."

The fact, however, that a person is not compelled to hold public office cannot possibly be an excuse for barring him from office by state imposed criteria forbidden by the Constitution. . . .

This Maryland religious test for public office unconstitutionally invades the appellant's freedom of belief and religion and therefore cannot be enforced against him. *Reversed and Remanded.* ∎

From Unanimous Opinion of the Court,
Torcaso v. Watkins, *1961.*

• JUSTICE HUGO L. BLACK

The respondent board of education of Union Free School District No. 9, New Hyde Park, N.Y., acting in its official capacity under state law, directed the school district's principal to cause the following prayer to be said aloud by each class in the presence of a teacher at the beginning of each school day: "Almighty God, we acknowledge our dependence upon Thee, and we beg Thy blessings upon us, our parents, our teachers, and our country."

This daily procedure was adopted on the recommendation of the State Board of Regents, a governmental agency created by the State Constitution to which the New York Legislature has granted broad supervisory, executive, and legislative powers over the state's public school system.

These state officials composed the prayer which they recommended and published as a part of their "statement on moral and spiritual training in the schools," saying: "We believe that this statement will be subscribed to by all men and women of goodwill, and we call upon all of them to aid in giving life to our program."

Shortly after the practice of reciting the Regents' prayer was adopted by the school district, the parents of ten pupils brought this action in a New York State court insisting that use of this official prayer in the public schools was contrary to the beliefs, religions, or religious practices of both themselves and their children.

Among other things, these parents challenged the constitutionality of both the state law authorizing the school districts ordering the recitation of this particular prayer, on the ground that these actions of official governmental agencies violate that part of the First Amendment of the Federal Constitution which commands that "Congress shall make no law respecting an establishment of religion"—a command which was "made applicable to the State of New York by the Fourteenth Amendment of the said Constitution."

The New York Court of Appeals, over the dissent of Judges Dye and Fuld, sustained an order of the lower state courts which had upheld the power of New York to use the Regents' prayer as a part of the daily procedures of its public schools so long as the schools did not compel any pupil to join in the prayer over his or her parents' objection. We granted certiorari to review this important decision involving rights protected by the First and Fourteenth Amendments.

We think that by using its public school system to encourage recitation of the Regents' prayer, the State of New York has adopted a practice wholly inconsistent with the establishment clause. There can, of course, be no doubt that New York's program of daily classroom invocation of God's blessings as prescribed in the Regents' prayer is a religious activity. It is a solemn avowal of divine faith and supplication for the blessings of the Almighty. The nature of such a prayer has always been religious, none of the respondents has denied this and the trial court expressly so found:

"The religious nature of prayer was recognized by Jefferson and has been concurred in by theological writers, the United States Supreme Court and state courts and administrative officials, including New York's commissioner of education. A committee of the New York Legislature has agreed.

"The Board of Regents as amicus curiae, the respondents and intervenors all concede the religious nature of prayer, but seek to distinguish this prayer because it is based on our spiritual heritage."

The petitioners contend, among other things, that the state laws requiring or permitting use of the Regents' prayer must be struck down as violation of the establishment clause because that prayer was composed by governmental officials as a part of a governmental program to further religious beliefs.

For this reason, petitioners argue, the state's use of the Regents' prayer in its public school system breaches the constitutional wall of separation between church and state.

We agree with that contention since we think that the constitutional prohibition against laws respecting an establishment of religion must at least mean that in this country it is no part of the business of government to compose official prayers for any group of the American people to recite as part of a religious program carried on by government.

It is a matter of history that this very practice of establishing governmentally composed prayers for religious services was one of the reasons which caused many of our early colonists to leave England and seek religious freedom in America. The Book of Common Prayer, which was created under governmental direction and which was Approved by Acts of Parliament in 1548 and 1549, set out in minute detail the accepted form and content of prayer and other religious ceremonies to be used in the established, tax-supported Church of England. The controversies over the Book and what should be its content repeatedly threatened to disrupt the peace of that country as the accepted forms of prayer in the established church changed with the views of the particular ruler that happened to be in control at the time. Powerful groups representing some of the varying religious views of the people struggled among themselves to impress their particular views upon the government and obtain amendments of the Book more suitable to their respective notions of how religious services should be conducted in order that the official religious establishment would advance their particular religious beliefs.

Other groups, lacking the necessary political power to influence the government on the matter, decided to leave England and its established church and seek freedom in America from England's governmentally ordained and supported religion.

It is an unfortunate fact of history that when

some of the very groups which had most strenuously opposed the established Church of England found themselves sufficiently in control of colonial governments in this country to write their own prayers into law, they passed laws making their own religion the official religion of their respective colonies. Indeed, as late as the time of the Revolutionary War, there were established churches in at least eight of the thirteen former colonies and established religions in four of the other five. But the successful revolution against English political domination was shortly followed by intense opposition to the practice of establishing religion by law. This opposition crystallized rapidly into an effective political case in Virginia where the minority religious groups such as Presbyterians, Lutherans, Quakers and Baptists had gained such strength that the adherents to the established Episcopal church were actually a minority themselves.

In 1785-1786, those opposed to the established church, led by James Madison and Thomas Jefferson, who though themselves not members of any of these dissenting religious groups, opposed all religious establishments by law on grounds of principle, obtained the enactment of the famous "Virginia bill for religious liberty" by which all religious groups were placed on an equal footing so far as the state was concerned. Similar though less far-reaching legislation was being considered and passed in other states.

By the time of the adoption of the Constitution, our history shows that there was a widespread awareness among many Americans of the dangers of a union of church and state. These people knew, some of them from bitter personal experience, that one of the greatest dangers to the freedom of the individual to worship in his own way lay in the government's placing its official stamp of approval upon one particular kind of prayer or one particular form of religious services. They knew the anguish, hardship, and bitter strife that could come when zealous religious groups struggled with one another to obtain the government's stamp of approval from each king, queen, or protector that came to temporary power.

The Constitution was intended to avert a part of this danger by leaving the government of this country in the hands of the people rather than in the hands of any monarch. But this safeguard was not enough. Our founders were no more willing to let the content of their prayers and their privilege of praying whenever they pleased be influenced by the ballot box than they were to let these vital matters of personal conscience depend upon the succession of monarchs.

The First Amendment was added to the Constitution to stand as a guarantee that neither the power nor the prestige of the Federal Government would be used to control, support or influence the kinds of prayer the American people can say—that the people's religions must not be subjected to the pressures of government for change each time a new political administration is elected to office.

Under that amendment's prohibition against governmental establishment of religion, as reinforced by the provisions of the Fourteenth Amendment, government in this country, be it state or federal, is without power to prescribe by law any particular form of prayer which is to be used as an official prayer in carrying on any program of governmentally sponsored religious activity.

There can be no doubt that New York's state prayer program officially establishes the religious beliefs embodied in the Regents' prayer. The respondents' argument to the contrary, which is largely based upon the contention that the Regents' prayer is "nondenominational" and the fact that "the program, as modified and approved by state courts, does not require all pupils to recite the prayer but permits those who wish to do so to remain silent or be excused from the room," ignores the essential nature of the program's constitutional defects.

Neither the fact that the prayer may be denominationally neutral, nor the fact that its observance on the part of the students is voluntary, can serve to free it from the limitations of the establishment clause, as it might from the free exercise clause, of the First Amendment, both of which are operative against the states by virtue of the Fourteenth Amendment.

Although these two clauses may, in certain instances, overlap, they forbid two quite different kinds of governmental encroachment upon religious freedom. The establishment clause, unlike the free exercise clause, does not depend upon any showing of direct governmental compulsion and is violated by the enactment of laws which establish an official religion whether those laws operate directly to coerce nonobserving individuals or not. This is not to say, of course, that laws officially prescribing a particular form of religious worship do not involve coercion of such individuals. When the power, prestige and financial support of government is placed behind a particular religious belief, the indirect coercive pressure upon religious minorities to conform to the prevailing officially approved religion is plain.

But the purposes underlying the establishment clause go much further than that. Its first and most immediate purpose rested on the belief that a union of government and religion tends to destroy government and to degrade religion. The history of governmentally established religion, both in England and in this country, showed that whenever government had allied itself with one particular form of religion, the inevitable result had been that it had incurred the hatred, disrespect and even contempt of those who held contrary beliefs. That same history showed that many people had lost their respect for any religion that had relied upon the support of government to spread its faith.

The establishment clause thus stands as an expression of principle on the part of the founders of our Constitution that religion is too personal, too sacred, too holy, to permit its "unhallowed perversion" by a civil magistrate.

Another purpose of the establishment clause rested upon an awareness of the historical fact that governmentally established religions and religious persecutions go hand in hand. The founders knew that only a few years after the Book of Common Prayer became the only accepted form of religious services in the established Church of England, an Act of Uniformity was passed to compel all Englishmen to attend those services and to make it a criminal offense to conduct or attend religious gatherings of any other kind—a law which was consistently flouted by dissenting religious groups in England and which contributed to widespread persecutions of people like John Bunyan who persisted in holding "unlawful (religious) meetings . . . to the great disturbance and distraction of the good subjects of this Kingdom. . . ." And they knew that similar persecutions had received the sanction of a law in several of the colonies in this country soon after the establishment of official religions in those colonies.

It was in large part to get completely away from this sort of systematic religious persecution that the founders brought into being our nation, our Constitution, and our Bill of Rights with its prohibition against any governmental establishment of religion. The New York laws officially prescribing the Regents' prayer are inconsistent with both the purposes of the establishment clause and with the establishment clause itself.

It has been argued that to apply the Constitution in such a way as to prohibit state laws respecting an establishment of religious services in public schools is to indicate a hostility toward religion or toward prayer. Nothing, of course, could be more wrong. The history of man is inseparable from the history of religion. And perhaps it is not too much to say that since the beginning of that history many people have devoutly believed that "More things are wrought by prayer than this world dreams of." It was doubtless largely due to men who believed this that there grew up a sentiment that caused men to leave the cross-currents of officially established state religions and religious persecution in Europe and come to this country filled with the hope that they could find a place in which they could pray when they pleased to the God of their faith in the language they chose.

And there were men of this same faith in the power of prayer who led the fight for adoption of our Constitution and also for our Bill of Rights with the very guarantees of religious freedom that forbid the sort of governmental activity which New York has attempted here. These men knew that the First Amendment, which tried to put an end to governmental control of religion and of prayer, was not written to destroy either. They knew rather that it was written to quiet well-justified fears which nearly all of them felt arising out of an awareness that governments of the past had shackled men's tongues to make them speak only the religious thoughts that government wanted them to speak and to pray only to the God that government wanted them to pray to.

It is neither sacrilegious nor antireligious to say that each separate government in this country should stay out of the business of writing or sanctioning official prayers and leave that purely religious function to the people themselves and to those the people choose to look to for religious guidance.

It is true that New York's establishment of its Regents' prayer as an officially approved religious doctrine of that State does not amount to a total establishment of one particular religious sect to the exclusion of all others—that, indeed, the governmental endorsement of that prayer seems relatively insignificant when compared to the governmental encroachments upon religion which were commonplace 200 years ago. To those who may subscribe to the view that because the Regents' official prayer is so brief and general there can be no danger to religious freedom in its governmental establishment, however, it may be appropriate to say in the words of James Madison, the author of the First Amendment:

"It is proper to take alarm at the first experiment on our liberties . . . Who does not see that the same authority which can establish Christianity, in exclusion of all other religions, may establish with the same ease any particular sect of Christians, in exclusion of all other sects? That the same authority which can force a citizen to contribute three pence only of his property for the support of any one may force him to conform to any other establishment in all cases whatsoever?"

The judgment of the Court of Appeals of New York is reversed and the cause remanded for further proceedings not inconsistent with this opinion. ■

From Majority Opinion, Engel *v.* Vitale, *1962.*

• JUSTICE WILLIAM O. DOUGLAS

It is customary in deciding a constitutional question to treat it in its narrowest form. Yet at times the setting of the question gives it a form and content which no abstract treatment could do. The point for decision is whether the Government can constitutionally finance a religious exercise. Our system at the Federal and state levels is presently honeycombed with such financing. Nevertheless, I think it is an unconstitutional undertaking whatever form it takes.

First, a word as to what this case does not involve.

Plainly, our Bill of Rights would not permit a state or the Federal Government to adopt an official prayer and penalize anyone who would not utter it. This, however, is not that case, for there is no element of compulsion or coercion in New York's regulation requiring that public schools be opened each day with the following prayer:

Almighty God, we acknowledge our dependence upon Thee,

And we beg Thy blessings upon us, our parents, our teachers and our country.

The prayer is said upon the commencement of the school day, immediately following the Pledge of Allegiance to the Flag. The prayer is said aloud in the presence of a teacher, who either leads the recitation or selects a student to do so. No student, however, is compelled to take part.

The respondents have adopted a regulation which provides that "neither teachers nor any school authority shall comment on participation or nonparticipation . . . nor suggest or request that any posture or language be used or dress be worn or be not used or not worn." Provision is also made for excusing children, upon written request of a parent or guardian, from the saying of the prayer or from the room in which the prayer is said. A letter implementing and explaining this regulation has been sent to each taxpayer and parent in the school district.

As I read this regulation, a child is free to stand or not to stand, to recite or not recite, without fear of reprisal or even comment by the teacher or any other school officials.

In short, the only one who need utter the prayer is the teacher; and no teacher is complaining of it. Students can stand mute or even leave the classroom, if they desire.

McCollum v. *Board of Education* does not decide this case. It involved the use of public school facilities for religious education of students. Students either had to attend religious instruction or "go to some other place in the school building for pursuit of their secular studies . . . Reports of their presence or absence were to be made to their secular teachers." The influence of the teaching staff was therefore brought to bear on the student body, to support the instilling of religious principles. In the present case, school facilities are used to say the prayer and the teaching staff is employed to lead the pupils in it. There is, however, no effort at indoctrination and no attempt at exposition. Prayers of course may be so long and of such a character as to amount to an attempt at the religious instruction that was denied the public schools by the McCollum case. But New York's prayer is of a character that does not involve any element of proselytizing as in the McCollum case.

The question presented by this case is therefore an extremely narrow one. It is whether New York oversteps the bounds when it finances a religious exercise.

What New York does on the opening of its public schools is what we do when we open court. Our marshal has from the beginning announced the convening of the court and then added "God save the United States and this honorable court." That utterance is a supplication, a prayer in which we, the judges, are free to join, but which we need not recite any more than the students need recite the New York prayer.

What New York does on the opening of its public schools is what each House of Congress does at the opening of each day's business. Rev. Frederick B. Harris is Chaplain of the Senate; Rev. Bernard Braskamp is Chaplain of the House. Guest chaplains of various denominations also officiate.

In New York the teacher who leads in prayer is on the public payroll; and the time she takes seems minuscule as compared with the salaries appropriat-

ed by State Legislatures and Congress for chaplains to conduct prayers in the legislative halls. Only a bare fraction of the teacher's time is given to reciting this short 22-word prayer, about the same amount of time that our marshal spends announcing the opening of our sessions and offering a prayer for this court. Yet for me the principle is the same, no matter how briefly the prayer is said, for in each of the instances given the person praying is a public official on the public payroll, performing a religious exercise in a governmental institution. It is said that the element of coercion is inherent in the giving of this prayer. If that is true here, it is also true of the prayer with which this court is convened, and with those that open the Congress. Few adults, let alone children, would leave our courtroom or the Senate or the House while those prayers are being given. Every such audience is in a sense a "captive" audience.

At the same time I cannot say that to authorize this prayer is to establish a religion in the strictly historic meaning of those words. A religion is not established in the usual sense merely by letting those who choose to do so say the prayer that the public school teacher leads. Yet once Government finances a religious exercise it inserts a divisive influence into our communities. The New York court said that the prayer given does not conform to all of the tenets of the Jewish, Unitarian, and Ethical Culture groups. One of the petitioners is an agnostic. . . .

The First Amendment leaves the Government in a position not of hostility to religion but of neutrality. The philosophy is that the atheist or agnostic— the nonbeliever—is entitled to go his own way.

The philosophy is that if Government interferes in matters spiritual, it will be a divisive force. The First Amendment teaches that a Government neutral in the field of religion better serves all religious interests.

My problem today would be uncomplicated but for *Everson* v. *Board of Education,* which allowed taxpayers' money to be used to pay "the bus fares of parochial school pupils as a part of a general program under which "the fares of pupils attending public and other schools" are also paid. The Everson case seems in retrospect to be out of line with the

First Amendment. Its result is appealing, as it allows aid to be given to needy children. Yet by the same token, public funds could be used to satisfy other needs of children in parochial schools—lunches, books, and tuition being obvious examples. Mr. Justice Rutledge stated in dissent what I think is durable First Amendment philosophy:

"The reasons underlying the amendment's policy have not vanished with time or diminished in force. Now as when it was adopted the price of religious freedom is double. It is that the church and religion shall live both within and upon that freedom. There cannot be freedom of religion, safeguarded by the state, and intervention by the church or its agencies in the state's domain or dependency on its largesse. Madison's Remonstrance, Par. 6, 8. The great condition of religious liberty is that it be maintained free from sustenance, as also from other interferences, by the state. For when it comes to rest upon that secular foundation it vanishes with the resting. Ib., Par. 7, 8. Public money devoted to payment of religious costs, educational or other, brings the quest for more. It brings too the struggle of sect against sect for the larger share or for any.

"Here one by numbers alone will benefit most, there another. That is precisely the history of societies which have had an established religion and dissident groups. Ib., Par. 8, 11. It is the very thing Jefferson and Madison experienced and sought to guard against, whether in its blunt or in its more screened forms. Ibid. The end of such strife cannot be other than to destroy the cherished liberty. The dominating group will achieve the dominant benefit; or all will embroil the state in their dissensions, Ib. Par. 11." Ib., pp. 53–54.

What New York does with this prayer is a break with that tradition. I therefore join the court in reversing the judgment below. ∎

From Concurring Opinion, Engel v. Vitale, 1962.

• JUSTICE POTTER STEWART

A local school board in New York has provided that those pupils who wish to do so may join in a brief prayer at the beginning of each school day, acknowl-

edging their dependence upon God and asking His blessing upon them and upon their parents, their teachers, and their country. The court today decides that in permitting this brief nondenominational prayer the school board has violated the Constitution of the United States. I think this decision is wrong.

The court does not hold, nor could it, that New York has interfered with the free exercise of anybody's religion. For the state courts have made clear that those who object to reciting the prayer must be entirely free of any compulsion to do so, including any "embarrassment and pressures." . . . But the court says that in permitting school children to say this simple prayer, the New York authorities have established "an official religion."

With all respect, I think the court has misapplied a great constitutional principle. I cannot see how an "official religion" is established by letting those who want to say a prayer say it. On the contrary, I think that to deny the wish of these school children to join in reciting this prayer is to deny them the opportunity of sharing in the spiritual heritage of our nation.

The court's historical review of the quarrels over the Book of Common Prayer in England throws no light for me on the issue before us in this case. England had then and has now an established church. Equally unenlightening, I think, is the history of the early establishment and later rejection of an official church in our own states. For we deal here not with the establishment of a state church, which would, of course, be constitutionally impermissible, but with whether school children who want to begin their day by joining in prayer must be prohibited from doing so. Moreover, I think that the court's task in this as in all areas of constitutional adjudication, is not responsibly aided by the uncritical invocation of metaphors like the "wall of separation," a phrase nowhere to be found in the Constitution. What is relevant to the issue here is not the history of an established church in sixteenth-century England or in eighteenth-century America, but the history of the religious traditions of our people, reflected in countless practices of the institutions and officials of our Government.

At the opening of each day's session of this court we stand, while on of our officials invokes the protection of God. Since the days of John Marshall our crier has said, "God save the United States and this honorable court." Both the Senate and the House of Representatives open their daily sessions with prayer. Each of our Presidents, from George Washington to John F. Kennedy, has upon assuming his office asked the protection and help of God.

The court today says that the State and Federal Governments are without constitutional power to prescribe any particular form of words to be recited by any group of the American people on any subject touching religion. The third stanza of "The Star-Spangled Banner," made our national anthem by Act of Congress in 1931, contains these verses:

Blest with victory and peace,
May the Heav'n rescued land
Praise the pow'r that hath made and pre-
    served us a nation!
Then conquer we must,
When our cause it is just,
And this be our motto "In God is our
    trust."

In 1954 Congress added a phrase to the Pledge of Allegiance to the Flag so that it now contains the words "one nation under God, indivisible, with liberty and justice for all." In 1952 Congress enacted legislation calling upon the President each year to proclaim a national day of prayer. Since 1865 the words "in God we trust" have been impressed on our coins.

Countless similar examples could be listed, but there is no need to belabor the obvious. It was all summed up by this Court just ten years ago in a single sentence: "We are a religious people whose institutions presuppose a Supreme Being." *Zorach v. Clauson,* 343 U.S. 306, 313.

I do not believe that this court, or the Congress, or the President has by the actions and practices I have mentioned established an "official religion" in violation of the Constitution. And I do not believe the State of New York has done so in this case. What each has done has been to recognize and to follow the deeply entrenched and highly cherished spiritual traditions of our nation—traditions which come down to us from those who almost two hundred years ago avowed their "firm reliance on the protection of divine providence" when they proclaimed the freedom and independence of this brave new world.

I dissent. ■

From Dissenting Opinion, Engel *v.* Vitale, *1962.*

PART VII

WHO SHALL VOTE –
PROPERTIED
WHITE MEN
OR EVERYBODY ?

U ntil modern times, the right to vote—obviously a crucial element in democracy—was everywhere hedged in by many qualifications and requirements. In the American colonies, which enjoyed a large measure of self-government, the suffrage was restricted to a relatively small group of white males. The privilege of voting, and the concomitant one of officeholding, were confined to those who owned a certain amount of land (freeholds), or personal property, or who paid taxes. There were also certain religious requirements, such as a Christian oath of office, which barred Jews, Quakers, and non-affiliates. This was forbidden by the Constitution and finally outlawed by the U. S. Supreme Court.

Even after the Constitution went into effect in 1789, the suffrage remained limited. Some of the constitutions of the original thirteen states continued to list varying restrictions on the right to vote or to hold office.

The new states of the West tended toward fewer restrictions. With the exception of Ohio, Louisiana, and Mississippi (which required the paying of taxes for the right to vote), the Western states entered the Union with universal white man-hood suffrage. Possibly under the impetus of the egalitarianism of these frontiersmen, the disfranchised white men in the East (anywhere from one-third to one-half of the adult males) began a prolonged struggle for the right to vote without property or tax-paying qualifications.

This drive for the abolition of restrictions on the suffrage went on for years. It met with success, but slowly, as this record shows: Vermont entered the Union in 1791 without any bars to male voting, Georgia abolished restrictions (on whites) in 1798, Maryland in 1809, South Carolina in 1810, Kentucky in 1812, New York in 1826, Massachusetts in the 1830s, Rhode Island in 1842, Connecticut in 1845, North Carolina in 1868, Delaware in 1897, and Pennsylvania in 1933.

In 1920, after almost three-quarters of a century of effort and agitation, the Nineteenth Amendment extended the suf-frage to women.

The one remaining obstacle to universal suffrage in the United States has been the restriction on Negro voting, prac-ticed nearly everywhere in the South. Of the many techniques used to deprive blacks of their right to vote, the poll tax and the literacy test have been the most effective. In Alabama, for example, the poll (or head) tax was cumulative, so that before a person could vote he had to pay up the taxes he had missed between the ages of twenty-one and forty-five—a total of $36. Impoverished rural Negroes (as well as poor whites) could not afford to pay any such sum for the privilege of casting their ballot. The Twenty-fourth Amendment to the Federal Consti-tution, ratified January 23, 1964, eliminated the poll tax throughout the nation.

But literacy tests, combined with various forms of intimida-tion, long prevailed and made it virtually impossible for most Negroes to vote. Black applicants for voter registration were asked such questions as these: "If no national candidate for Vice President receives a majority of the electoral vote, how is a Vice President chosen? In such cases how many votes must a person receive to become Vice President?" "Name two things which the states are forbidden to do by the United States Constitution." "How many votes must a person receive in order to become President if the election is decided by the United States House of Representatives?"

Questions of this kind were obviously a hurdle that southern Negroes, many of them with hardly more than a sixth-grade education, could not overcome. Nor, of course, could most whites, had they been similarly questioned. But such tactics are now being fought in the courts as a violation of the recent Civil Rights Acts.

When Negroes finally win the right to vote freely and without contrived obstacles throughout the South, as they are bound to do, universal suffrage will truly prevail in the United States.

1
DISCUSSION IN THE CONSTITUTIONAL CONVENTION, 1787

Oliver Ellsworth
George Mason
Pierce Butler
John Dickinson
Gouverneur Morris
James Madison
Benjamin Franklin
John Francis Mercer
John Rutledge
Nathaniel Gorham
Charles Pinckney
Charles Cotesworth Pinckney
Elbridge Gerry
Rufus King
Luther Martin
James Wilson
John Langdon

• EDITOR'S NOTE

The Constitutional Convention of 1787 discussed the question of the suffrage at length, but left the decision in regard to voting qualifications to the individual states,[1] rather than the federal government. The debates on the subject are given below.

• THE CONSTITUTIONAL CONVENTION

AUGUST 7

MR. [OLIVER] ELLSWORTH thought the qualifications of the electors stood on the most proper footing. The right of suffrage was a tender point and strongly guarded by most of the state constitutions. The people will not readily subscribe to the national Constitution if it should subject them to be disfranchised. The states are the best judges of the circumstances and temper of their own people.

MR. [GEORGE] MASON: The force of habit is certainly not attended to by those gentlemen who wish for innovations on this point. Eight or nine states have extended the right of suffrage beyond the freeholders. What will the people there say if they should be disfranchised? A power to alter the qualifications would be a dangerous power in the hands of the legislature.

MR. [PIERCE] BUTLER: There is no right of which the people are more jealous than that of suffrage. Abridgments of it tend to the same revolution as in Holland where they have at length thrown all power into the hands of the senates, who fill up vacancies themselves and form a rank of aristocracy.

MR. [JOHN] DICKINSON had a very different idea of the tendency of vesting the right of suffrage in the freeholders of the country. He considered them as the best guardians of liberty and the restriction of the right to them as a necessary defence

---

[1] As provided in Article I, Section 2, of the Constitution: "The House of Representatives shall be composed of members chosen every second year by the people of the several states, and *the electors* [voters] *in each state shall have the qualifications requisite for electors of the most numerous* branch of the state legislature." (Italics added.)

against the dangerous influence of those multitudes without property and without principle with which our country, like all others, will in time abound. As to the unpopularity of the innovation, it was in his opinion chimerical. The great mass of our citizens is composed at this time of freeholders and will be pleased with it.

MR. ELLSWORTH: How shall the freehold be defined? Ought not every man who pays a tax to vote for the representative who is to levy and dispose of his money? Shall the wealthy merchants and manufacturers who will bear a full share of the public burdens not be allowed a voice in the imposition of them? Taxation and representation ought to go together.

MR. GOUVERNEUR MORRIS: He had long learned not to be the dupe of words. The sound of aristocracy, therefore, had no effect upon him. It was the thing, not the name, to which he was opposed, and one of his principal objections to the Consitution as it is now before us is that it threatens the country with an aristocracy. The aristocracy will grow out of the House of Representatives. Give the votes to people who have no property and they will sell them to the rich, who will be able to buy them. We should not confine our attention to the present moment. The time is not distant when this country will abound with mechanics and manufacturers who will receive their bread from their employers. Will such men be the secure and faithful guardians of liberty? Will they be the impregnable barrier against aristocracy? He was as little duped by the association of the words "taxation and representation." The man who does not give his vote freely is not represented. It is the man who dictates the vote. Children do not vote. Why? Because they want prudence, because they have no will of their own. The ignorant and the dependent can be as little trusted with the public interest. He did not conceive the difficulty of defining "freeholders" to be insuperable, still less that the restriction could be unpopular. Nine-tenths of the people are at present freeholders, and these will certainly be pleased with it. As to merchants and others, if they have wealth, and value the right, they can acquire it. If not, they don't deserve it.

MR. MASON: We all feel too strongly the remains of ancient prejudices and view things too much through a British medium. A freehold is the qualification in England, and hence it is imagined to be the only proper one. The true idea in his opinion was that every man having evidence of attachment to, and permanent common interest with, the society ought to share in all its rights and privileges. Was this qualification restrained to freeholders? Does no other kind of property but land evidence a common interest in the proprietor? Does nothing besides property mark a permanent attachment? Ought the merchant, the moneyed man, the parent of a number of children, whose fortunes are to be pursued in his own country, to be viewed as suspicious characters and unworthy to be trusted with the common rights of their fellow citizens?

MR. [JAMES] MADISON: The right of suffrage is certainly one of the fundamental articles of republican government and ought not to be left to be regulated by the legislature. A gradual abridgment of this right has been the mode in which aristocracies have been built on the ruins of popular forms. Whether the constitutional qualification ought to be a freehold would with him depend much on the probable reception such a change would meet with in the states where the right was now exercised by every description of people. In several of the states, a freehold was now the qualification. Viewing the subject in its merits alone, the freeholders of the country would be the safest depositories of republican liberty. In future times, a great majority of the people will not only be without land, but any other sort of property. These will either combine under the influence of their common situation—in which case the rights of property and the public liberty will not be secure in their hands—or what is more probable, they will become the tools of opulence and ambition—in which case there will be equal danger on another side. The example of England has been misconceived (by Col. Mason). A very small proportion of the representatives are there chosen by freeholders. The greatest part are chosen by the cities and boroughs, in many of which the qualification of suffrage is as low as it is in any one of the United States, and it was in the boroughs and cities, rather than the counties, that bribery most prevailed and the influence of the crown on elections was most dangerously exerted.

DR. [BENJAMIN] FRANKLIN: It is of great consequence that we should not depress the virtue and public spirit of our common people, of which they displayed a great deal during the war and which contributed principally to the favorable issue of it. He related the honorable refusal of the American seamen, who were carried in great numbers into the British prisons during the war, to redeem themselves from misery or to seek their fortunes by entering on board the ships of the enemies to their country, contrasting their patriotism with a contemporary instance in which the British seamen made prisoners by the Americans readily entered on the ships of the latter on being promised a share of the prizes that might be made out of their own country. This proceeded, he said, from the different manner in which the common people were treated in America and Great Britain. He did not think that the elected had any right, in any case, to narrow the privileges of the electors. He quoted as arbitrary the British statute setting forth the danger of tumultuous meetings and under that pretext narrowing the right of suffrage to persons having freeholds of a certain value, observing that this statute was soon followed by another under the succeeding Parliament subjecting the people who had no votes to peculiar labors and hardships. He was persuaded, also, that such a restriction as was proposed would give great uneasiness in the populous states. The sons of a substantial farmer, not being themselves freeholders, would not be pleased at being disfranchised, and there are a great many persons of that description.

MR. [JOHN FRANCIS] MERCER: The Constitution is objectionable in many points, but in none more than the present. He objected to the footing on which the qualification was put, but particularly to the mode of election by the people. The people cannot know and judge of the characters of candidates. The worst possible choice will be made. He quoted the case of the Senate in Virginia as an example in point. The people in towns can unite their votes in favor of one favorite and by that means always prevail over the people of the country, who, being dispersed, will scatter their votes among a variety of candidates.

MR. [JOHN] RUTLEDGE thought the idea of restraining the right of suffrage to the freeholders a very unadvised one. It would create division among the people and make enemies of all those who should be excluded. ■

AUGUST 8

In convention, Article 4, Section 1, being under consideration, Mr. Mercer expressed his dislike of the whole plan and his opinion that it never could succeed.

MR. [NATHANIEL] GORHAM: He had never seen any inconvenience from allowing such as were not freeholders to vote, though it had long been tried. The elections in Philadelphia, New York, and Boston, where the merchants and mechanics vote, are at least as good as those made by freeholders only. The case in England was not accurately stated yesterday (by Mr. Madison). The cities and large towns are not the seat of crown influence and corruption. These prevail in the boroughs, and not on account of the right which those who are not freeholders have to vote, but of the smallness of the number who vote. The people have been long accustomed to this right in various parts of America and will never allow it to be abridged. We must consult their rooted prejudices if we expect their concurrence in our propositions.

MR. MERCER did not object so much to an election by the people at large, including such as were not freeholders, as to their being left to make their choice without any guidance. He hinted that candidates ought to be nominated by the state legislatures.

On the question for agreeing to Article 4, Section 1, it passed. ■

AUGUST 26

MR. MASON moved, "That the Committe of Detail be instructed to receive a clause, requiring certain qualifications of landed property, and citizenship of the United States, in members of the national legislature, and disqualifying persons having unsettled accounts with, or being indebted to, the United States, from being members of the national legislature."

He observed that persons of the latter descriptions had frequently got into the state legislatures in order to promote laws that might shelter their delinquencies and that this evil had crept into Congress if report was to be regarded.

MR. [CHARLES] PINCKNEY seconded the motion.

MR. GOUVERNEUR MORRIS: If qualifications are proper, he would prefer them in the electors rather than the elected. As to debtors of the United States, they are but few. As to persons having unsettled accounts, he believed them to be pretty many. He thought, however, that such a discrimination would be both odious and useless and, in many instances, unjust and cruel. The delay of settlement had been more the fault of the public than of the individual. What will be done with those patriotic citizens who have lent money or services or property to their country without having been yet able to obtain a liquidation of their claims? Are they to be excluded?

MR. GORHAM was for leaving to the legislature the providing against such abuses as had been mentioned.

MR. MASON mentioned the parliamentary qualifications adopted in the reign of Queen Anne, which, he said, had met with universal approbation.

MR. MADISON had witnessed the zeal of men having accounts with the public to get into the legislature for sinister purposes. He thought, however, that if any precaution were taken for excluding them, the one proposed by Col. Mason ought to be remodeled. It might be well to limit the exclusion to persons who had received money from the public and had not accounted for it.

MR. GOUVERNEUR MORRIS: It was a precept of great antiquity, as well as of high authority, that we should not be righteous overmuch. He thought we ought to be equally on our guard against being wise overmuch. The proposed regulation would enable the government to exclude particular persons from office as long as they pleased. He mentioned the case of the Commander-in-Chief's presenting his account

for secret services, which, he said, was so moderate that everyone was astonished at it and so simple that no doubt could arise on it. Yet, had the auditor been disposed to delay the settlement, how easily he might have effected it, and how cruel would it be in such a case to keep a distinguished and meritorious citizen under a temporary disability and disfranchisement. He mentioned this case merely to illustrate the objectionable nature of the proposition. He was opposed to such minutious regulations in a constitution. The parliamentary qualifications quoted by Col. Mason had been disregarded in practice and were but a scheme of the landed against the moneyed interest.

MR. PINCKNEY and GEN. [CHARLES COTESWORTH] PINCKNEY moved to insert by way of amendment the words "judiciary and executive," so as to extend the qualifications to those departments, which was agreed to unanimously.

MR. [ELBRIDGE] GERRY thought the inconvenience of excluding a few worthy individuals, who might be public debtors or have unsettled accounts ought not to be put in the scale against the public advantages of the regulation, and that the motion did not go far enough.

MR. [RUFUS] KING observed that there might be great danger in requiring landed property as a qualification, since it might exclude the moneyed interest whose aids may be essential, in particular emergencies, to the public safety.

MR. DICKINSON was against any recital of qualifications in the Constitution. It was impossible to make a complete one, and a partial one would by implication tie up the hands of the legislature from supplying the omissions. The best defense lay in the freeholders, who were to elect the legislature. Whilst this resource should remain pure, the public interest would be safe. If it ever should be corrupt, no little expedients would repel the danger. He doubted the policy of interweaving into a republican constitution a veneration for wealth. He had always understood that a veneration for poverty and virtue were the objects of republican encouragement. It seemed improper that any man of merit should be subjected to disabilities in a republic, where merit was understood to form the great title to public trust, honors, and rewards.

MR. GERRY: If property be one object government, provisions to secure it cannot be improper.

MR. MADISON moved to strike out the word "landed" before the word "qualifications." If the proposition should be agreed to, he wished the committee to be at liberty to report the best criterion they could devise. Landed possessions were no certain evidence of real wealth. Many enjoyed them to a great extent who were more in debt than they were worth. The unjust laws of the states had proceeded more from this class of men than any others. It had often happened that men who had acquired landed property on credit got into the legislatures with a view of promoting an unjust protection against their creditors. In the next place, if a small quantity of land should be made the standard, it would be no security; if a large one, it would exclude the proper representatives of those classes of citizens who were not landholders. It was politic as well as just that the interests and rights of every class should be duly represented and understood in the public councils. It was a provision everywhere established that the country should be divided into districts and representatives taken from each, in order that the legislative assembly might equally understand and sympathize with the rights of the people in every part of the community. It was not less proper that every class of citizens should have an opportunity of making its rights be felt and understood in the public councils. The three principal classes into which our citizens were divisible were the landed, the commercial, and the manufacturing. The second and third class bear, as yet, a small proportion to the first. The proportion, however, will daily increase. We see in the populous countries of Europe now what we shall be hereafter. These classes understand much less of each other's interests and affairs than men of the same class inhabiting different districts. It is particularly requisite, therefore, that the interests of one or two of them should not be left entirely to the care or impartiality of the third. This must be the case if landed qualifications should be required; few of the mercantile

and scarcely any of the manufacturing class choosing, whilst they continue in business, to turn any part of their stock into landed property. For these reasons he wished, it it were possible, that some other criterion than the mere possession of land should be devised. He concurred with Mr. Gouverner Morris in thinking that qualifications in the electors would be much more effectual than in the elected. The former discriminate between real and ostensible property in the latter, but he was aware of the difficulty of forming any uniform standard that would suit the different circumstances and opinions prevailing in the different states.

MR. GOUVERNEUR MORRIS seconded the motion.

Motion for striking out "landed" approved, 10 to 1.

MR. MASON'S proposition as to "qualification of property and citizenship" approved, 8 to 3.

The second part, for disqualifying debtors and person having unsettled accounts, being under consideration, Mr. Carroll moved to strike out "having unsettled accounts."

MR. GORHAM seconded the motion, observing that it would put the commercial and manufacturing part of the people on a worse footing than others, as they would be most likely to have dealings with the public.

MR. [LUTHER] MARTIN: If these words should be struck out and the remaining words concerning debtors retained, it will be (to) the interest of the latter class to keep their accounts unsettled as long as possible.

MR. [JAMES] WILSON was for striking them out. They put too much power in the hands of the auditors, who might combine with rivals in delaying settlements in order to prolong the disqualifications of particular men. We should consider that we are providing a constitution for future generations and not merely for the peculiar circumstances of the moment. The time has been and will again be when the public safety may depend on the voluntary aids of individuals, which will necessarily open accounts with the public, and when such accounts will be a characteristic of patriotism. Besides, a partial enumeration of cases will disable the legislature from disqualifying odious and dangerous characters.

MR. [JOHN] LANGDON was for striking out the whole clause for the reasons given by Mr. Wilson. So many exclusions, he thought, too, would render the system unacceptable to the people.

MR. GERRY: If the arguments used today were to prevail, we might have a legislature composed of public debtors, pensioners, placemen, and contractors. He thought the proposed disqualifications would be pleasing to the people. They will be considered as a security against unnecessary or undue burdens being imposed on them.

He moved to add "pensioners" to the disqualified characters, which was disapproved, 7 to 3; North Carolina remained divided on the issue.

MR. GOUVERNEUR MORRIS: The last clause relating to public debtors will exclude every importing merchant. Revenue will be drawn, it is foreseen, as much as possible from trade. Duties, of course, will be bonded and the merchants will remain debtors to the public. He repeated that it had not been so much the fault of individuals as of the public that transactions between them had not been more generally liquidated and adjusted. At all events, to draw from our short and scanty experience rules that are to operate through succeeding ages does not savor much of real wisdom.

The question for striking out "persons having unsettled accounts with the United States" approved, 9 to 2.

MR. ELLSWORTH was for disagreeing to the remainder of the clause disqualifying public debtors and for leaving to the wisdom of the legislature and the virtue of the citizens, the task of providing against such evils. Is the smallest as well as the largest debtor to be excluded? Then every arrear of taxes will disqualify. Besides, how is it to be known to the people when they elect, who are or are not public debtors? The exclusion of pensioners and placemen in England is founded on a consideration not existing here. As persons of that sort are dependent on the crown, they tend to increase its influence.

MR. PINCKNEY said he was at first a friend to the proposition for the sake of the clause relating to qualifications of property, but he disliked the exclusion of public debtors. It went too far. It would exclude persons who had purchased confiscated property or should purchase western territory of the public, and might be some obstacle to the sale of the latter.

Question for agreeing to the clause disqualifying public debtors defeated, 9 to 2.   ■

From Records of the Constitutional Convention, 1787.

2
PERSONS OR PROPERTY?

Alexander Hamilton *or* James Madison
James Madison
Thomas Jeffersosn
Daniel Webster

• EDITOR'S NOTE

The Federal Constitution, as shaped in 1787, did not guarantee the suffrage to any citizen. Voting regulations and provisions were left to the states. But after the Civil War two amendments, the Fourteenth and Fifteenth, forbade the states to deny or abridge the privileges of citizenship, including the right to vote, on account of race, color, or previous condition of servitude. Subsequently, the Nineteenth Amendment extended the suffrage to women.

• ALEXANDER HAMILTON *or* JAMES MADISON

We have hitherto proceeded on the idea that representation related to persons only, and not at all to property. But is it a just idea? Government is instituted no less for protection of the property, than of the persons, or individuals. The one as well as the other, therefore, may be considered as represented by those who are charged with the government. Upon this principle it is, that in several of the States, and particularly in the State of New York, one branch of the government is intended more especially to be the guardian of property, and is accordingly elected by that part of the society which is most interested in this object of government. In the Federal Constitution, this policy does not prevail. The rights of property are committed into the same hands with the personal rights. Some attention ought, therefore, to be paid to property in the choice of those hands.[1] ■

From The Federalist, *No. 54, February 12, 1788.*

---

[1] Compare this with John Locke's classic formulation of the purpose of government, in his *Two Treatises of Government* (1690): "The great and chief end, therefore, of men's uniting into common wealths, and putting themselves under government, is the preservation of their property. . . . Absolute arbitrary power, or governing without settled standing laws, can neither of them consist with the ends of society and government, which men would not quit the freedom of the state of nature for, and tie themselves up under, were it not to preserve their lives, liberties, and fortunes; and by stated rules of right and property to secure their peace and quiet. . . . The supreme power cannot take from any man any part of his property without his own consent. For the preservation of property . . . [is] the end of government, and that for which men enter into society. . . ."

• ALEXANDER HAMILTON *or* JAMES MADISON

The third charge against the House of Representatives is, that it will be taken from that class of citizens which will have least sympathy with the mass of the people, and be most likely to aim at an ambitious sacrifice of the many to the aggrandizement of the few.

Of all the objections which have been framed against the Federal Constitution, this is perhaps the most extraordinary. . . .

Who are to be the electors of the federal representatives? Not the rich, more than the poor; not the learned, more than the ignorant; not the haughty heirs of distinguished names, more than the humble sons of obscurity and unpropitious fortune. The electors are to be the great body of the people of the United States. They are to be the same who exercise the right in every State of electing the corresponding branch of the legislature of the State.

Who are to be the objects of popular choice? Every citizen whose merit may recommend him to the esteem and confidence of his country. No qualification of wealth, of birth, of religious faith, or of civil profession is permitted to fetter the judgment or disappoint the inclination of the people. . . .

Were the objection to be read by one who had not seen the mode prescribed by the Constitution for the choice of representatives, he could suppose nothing less than that some unreasonable qualification of property was annexed to the right of suffrage; or that the right of eligibility was limited to persons of particular families or fortunes; or at least that the mode prescribed by the State constitutions was, in some respect or other, very grossly departed from. We have seen how far such a supposition would err, as to the two first points. Nor would it, in fact, be less erroneous as to the last. The only difference discoverable between the two cases is, that each representative of the United States will be elected by five or six thousand citizens; whilst in the individual States, the election of a representative is left to about as many hundreds. Will it be pretended that this difference is sufficient to justify an attachment to the State governments, and an abhorrence to the Federal government? If this be the point on which the objection turns, it deserves to be examined.

Is it supported by reason? This cannot be said, without maintaining that five or six thousand citizens are less capable of choosing a fit representative, or more liable to be corrupted by an unfit one, than five or six hundred. Reason, on the contrary, assures us, that as in so great a number a fit representative would be most likely to be found, so the choice would be less likely to be diverted from him by the intrigues of the ambitious or the bribes of the rich. ∎

From The Federalist, *No. 57, February 19, 1788.*

• JAMES MADISON

This term ["property"] in its particular application means "that domination which one man claims and exercises over the external things of the world, in exclusion of every other individual."

In its larger and juster meaning, it embraces everything to which a man may attach a value and have a right; and which leaves to everyone else the like advantage.

In the former sense, a man's land, or merchandise, or money is called his property.

In the latter sense, a man has property in his opinions and the free communication of them.

He has a property of peculiar value in his religious opinions, and in the profession and practice dictated by them.

He has property very dear to him in the safety and liberty of his person.

He has an equal property in the free use of his faculties and free choice of the objects on which to employ them.

In a word, as a man is said to have a right to his property, he may be equally said to have a property in his rights.

Where an excess of power prevails, property of no sort is duly respected. No man is safe in his opinions, his person, his faculties or his possessions.

Where there is an excess of liberty, the effect is the same, tho from an opposite cause.

Government is instituted to protect property of

every sort; as well that which lies in the various rights of individuals, as that which the term particularly expresses. This being the end of government, that alone is a just government, which impartially secures to every man, whatever is his own. . . .

Conscience is the most sacred of all property; other property depending in part on positive law, the exercise of that, being a natural and inalienable right. To guard a man's house as his castle, to pay public and enforce private debts with the most exact faith, can give no title to invade a man's conscience which is more sacred than his castle. . . .

That is not a just government, nor is property secure under it, where the property which a man has in his personal safety and personal liberty, is violated by arbitrary seizures of one class of citizens for the service of the rest. A magistrate issuing warrants to a press gang, would be in his proper functions in Turkey or Indostan, under appellations proverbial of the most compleat despotism.

That is not a just government, nor is property secure under it, where arbitrary restrictions, exemptions, and monopolies deny to part of its citizens that free use of their faculties, and free choice of their occupations, which not only constitute their property in the general sense of the word; but are the means of acquiring property strictly so called. . . .

A just security to property is not afforded by that government under which unusual taxes oppress one species of property and reward another species; where arbitrary taxes invade the domestic sanctuaries of the rich, and excessive taxes grind the faces of the poor; where the keenness and competitions of want are deemed an insufficient spur to labor, and taxes are again applied by an unfeeling policy, as another spur; in violation of that sacred property, which Heaven, in decreeing man to earn his bread by the sweat of his brow, kindly reserved to him, in the small repose that could be spared from the supply of his necessities.

If there be a government then which prides itself on maintaining the inviolability of property; which provides that none shall be taken directly even for public use without indemnification to the owner, and yet directly violates the property which indi-

viduals have in their opinions, their religion, their persons, and their faculties; nay more, which indirectly violates their property, in their actual possessions; in the labor that acquires their daily subsistence, and in the hallowed remnant of time which ought to relieve their fatigues and soothe their cares, the inference will have been anticipated, that such a government is not a pattern for the United States.

If the United States mean to obtain or deserve the full praise due to wise and just governments, they will equally respect the rights of property, and the property in rights. ■

From the National Gazette, *March 29, 1792.*

• THOMAS JEFFERSON

When the constitution of Virginia was formed I was in attendance at Congress. Had I been here I should probably have proposed a general suffrage; because my opinion has always been in favor of it. Still I find very honest men who, thinking the possession of some property necessary to give due independence of mind, are for restraining the elective franchise to property.[1] I believe we may lessen the danger of buying and selling votes, by making the number of voters too great for any means of purchase: I may further say that I have not observed men's honesty to increase with their riches.[2] ■

From letter to Jeremiah Moor, August 14, 1800.

---

[1] Jefferson himself partly incorporated this view in a draft of a constitution for Virginia which he sketched out in June, 1776: "All male persons of full age and sane mind having a freehold estate [one fourth of an acre] in land in any town, or in [twenty-five] acres of land in the country, and all persons resident in the colony who shall have paid scot and lot to government the last [two years] shall have right to give their vote in the election of their respective representatives. And every person so qualified capable of being elected; provided he shall have given no bribe either directly or indirectly to any elector. . . ."

[2] Jefferson wrote in his *Notes on Virginia* (1782), Query XIV: "The government of Great Britain has been corrupted, because but one man in ten has a right to vote for members of parliament. . . . It has been thought that corruption is restrained by confining the right of suffrage to a few of the wealthier of the people; but it would be more effectually restrained by an extension of that right to such numbers as would bid defiance to the means of corruption."

• DANIEL WEBSTER

It seems to me to be plain, that in the absence of military force, political power naturally and necessarily goes into the hands which hold the property. . . .

It would seem, then, to be the part of political wisdom to found government on property; and to establish such distribution of property, by the laws which regulate its transmission and alienation, as to interest the great majority of society in the protection of government. This is, I imagine, the true theory and the actual practice of our republican institutions. With property divided, as we have it, no other government than that of a republic could be maintained, even were we foolish enough to desire it. There is reason, therefore, to expect a long continuance of our systems. Party and passion, doubtless, may prevail at times, and much temporary mischief be done. Even modes and forms may be changed, and perhaps to the worse. But a great revolution, in regard to property, must take place, before our governments can be moved from their republican basis, unless they be violently struck off by military power. The people possess the property, more emphatically than it could ever be said of the people of any other country, and they can have no interest to overturn a government which protects that property by equal laws.

If the nature of our institutions be to found government on property, and that it should look to those who hold property for its protection, it is entirely just that property should have its due weight and consideration, in political arrangements. Life, and personal liberty, are, no doubt, to be protected by law; but property is also to be protected by law, and is the fund out of which the means for protecting life and liberty are usually furnished. We have no experience that teaches us, that any other rights are safe, where property is not safe. Confiscation and plunder are generally in revolutionary commotions not far before banishment, imprisonment and death. It would be monstrous to give even the name of government, to any association, in which the rights of property should not be competently secured. The disastrous revolutions which the world has witnessed, those political thunderstorms, and earthquakes which have overthrown the pillars of society from their very deepest foundations, have been revolutions against property. . . .

The English revolution of 1688 was a revolution in favor of property, as well as of other rights. It was brought about by the men of property, for their security; and our own immortal revolution was undertaken, not to shake or plunder property, but to protect it. The acts of which the country complained, were such as violated rights of property. An immense majority of all those who had an interest in the soil were in favor of the revolution; and they carried it through, looking to its results for the security of their possessions. It was the property of the frugal yeomanry of New England, hard earned, but freely given, that enabled her to act her proper part, and perform her full duty, in achieving the independence of the country. . .

I will beg leave to ask, sir, whether property may not be said to deserve this portion of respect and power in the government? It pays, at this moment, I think, five-sixths of all the public taxes—one-sixth only being raised on persons. Not only, sir, do these taxes support those burdens, which all governments require, but we have, in New England, from early times holden property to be subject to another great public use—I mean the support of schools. . . .

Does any history show property more beneficently applied? Did any government ever subject the property of those who have estates, to a burden, for a purpose more favorable to the poor, or more useful to the whole community? Sir, property and the power which the law exercises over it, for the purpose of instruction, is the basis of the system. It is entitled to the respect and protection of government, because, in a very vital respect, it aids and sustains government . . . If we take away from the towns the power of assessing taxes on property, will the school houses remain open? If we deny to the poor, the benefit which they now derive from the property of the rich, will their children remain on their farms, or will they not, rather, be in the streets, in idleness and in vice? . . . ■

From speech in Massachusetts Constitutional Convention, 1820.

• JAMES MADISON

The right of suffrage is a fundamental article in Republican Constitutions. The regulation of it is, at the same time, a task of peculiar delicacy. Allow the right exclusively to property, and the rights of persons may be oppressed. The feudal polity alone sufficiently proves it. Extend it equally to all, and the rights of property or the claims of justice may be overruled by a majority without property, or interested in measures of injustice. . . .

In civilized communities, property as well as personal rights is an essential object of the laws, which encourage industry by securing the enjoyment of its fruits. . . .

In a just & a free Government, therefore, the rights both of property and of persons ought to be effectually guarded. Will the former be so in case of a universal and equal suffrage? Will the latter be so in case of a suffrage confined to the holders of property?

As the holders of property have at stake all the other rights common to those without property, they may be the more restrained from infringing, as well as the less tempted to infringe the rights of the latter. It is nevertheless certain, that there are various ways in which the rich may oppress the poor; in which property may oppress liberty . . . It is necessary that the poor should have a defence against the danger.

On the other hand, the danger to the holders of property cannot be disguised, if they be undefended against a majority without property. Bodies of men are not less swayed by interest than individuals, and are less controlled by the dread of reproach and the other motives felt by individuals. Hence the ability of the rights of property, and of the impartiality of laws affecting it, to be violated by Legislative majorities having an interest real or supposed in the injustice: Hence agrarian laws, and other levelling schemes: Hence the cancelling or evading of debts, and other violations of contracts. We must not shut our eyes to the nature of man, nor to the light of experience. Who would rely on a fair decision from three individuals if two had an interest in the case opposed to the rights of the third? . . .

The United States have a precious advantage also in the actual distribution of property, particularly the landed property; and in the universal hope of acquiring property . . . There may be at present a majority of the Nation, who are even freeholders, or the heirs, or aspirants to freeholds . . . Whenever the majority shall be without landed or other equivalent property and without the means or hope of acquiring it, what is to secure the rights of property against the danger from an equality and universality of suffrage, vesting complete power over property in hands without a share in it? . . .

These reflections suggest the expediency of such a modification of Government as would give security to the part of the Society having most at stake and being most exposed to danger. Three modifications present themselves.

1. Confining the right of suffrage to freeholders, and to such as hold an equivalent property . . . The objection to this regulation is obvious. It violates the vital principle of free Government, that those who are to be bound by laws, ought to have a voice in making them . . . The regulation would be as unpropitious also as it would be unjust. It would engage the numerical and physical force in a constant struggle against the public authority; unless kept down by a standing army fatal to all parties.

2. Confining the right of suffrage for one Branch [of the legislature] to the holders of property, and for the other Branch to those without property. This arrangement . . . has an aspect of equality and fairness. But it would not be in fact either equal or fair, because the rights to be defended would be unequal, being on one side those of property as well as of persons, and on the other those of persons only. The temptation also to encroach . . . would be felt more strongly on one side than on the other. It would be more likely to beget an abuse of the Legislative Negative [veto] in extorting concessions at the expense of property . . . The division of the State into the two Classes, with distinct and independent organs of power, and without any intermingled agency whatever, might lead to contests and antipathies not dissimilar to those between the Patricians and Plebeians at Rome.

3. Confining the right of electing one Branch of

the Legislature to freeholders, and admitting all others to a common right with holders of property, in electing the other Branch. This would give a defensive power to holders of property, and to the class also without property . . . without depriving them in the mean time of a participation in the public Councils . . . And if no exact and safe equilibrium can be introduced, it is more reasonable that a preponderating weight should be allowed to the greater interest than to the lesser. Experience also can decide how far the practice in this case would correspond with the theory. . . .

4. Should experience or public opinion require an equal and universal suffrage for each branch of the Government, such as prevails generally in the United States, a resource favorable to the rights of landed and other property, when its possessors become the minority, may be found in an enlargement of the Election Districts for one branch of the Legislature, and an extension of its period of service. Large districts are manifestly favorable to the election of persons of general respectability, and of probable attachment to the rights of property . . . And although an ambitious candidate, of personal distinction, might occasionally recommend himself to popular choice by espousing a popular though unjust object, it might rarely happen to many districts at the same time. The tendency of a longer period of service would be, to render the Body more stable in its policy, and more capable of stemming popular currents taking a wrong direction, till reason and justice could regain their ascendancy.

5. Should even such a modification as the last be deemed inadmissible, and universal suffrage and very short periods of election within contracted spheres be required for each branch of the Government, the security for the holders of property when the minority, can only be derived from the ordinary influence possessed by property, and the superior information incident to its holders; from the popular sense of justice enlightened and enlarged by a diffusive education; and from the difficulty of combining and effectuating unjust purposes throughout an extensive country. . . .

Under every view of the subject, it seems indis-

pensable that the mass of citizens should not be without a voice, in making the laws which they are to obey, in choosing the magistrates, who are to administer them, and if the only alternative be between an equal and universal right of suffrage for each branch of the Government and a confinement of the *entire* right to a part of the citizens, it is better that those having the greater interest at stake, namely that of property and persons both, should be deprived of half their share in the Government, than that those having the lesser interest, that of personal rights only, should be deprived of the whole. ■

From "Note to Speech on the Right of Suffrage,"
1821.

3

DEBATE IN THE NEW YORK CONSTITUTIONAL CONVENTION, 1821

John Cramer
James Kent

• JOHN CRAMER

But it has been said, that the landed interest of this state, bears more than its equal proportion of the burthens of taxation. This, sir, I deny. All property, real and personal, is equally taxed, and bears its just proportion of the public burthens; but, sir, is not life and liberty dearer than property, and common to all, and entitled to equal protection. No, sir. That gentleman appeared to be impressed with the idea, that the *turf* is of all things the most sacred, and that for its security, you must have thirty-two grave turf senators from the soil, in that Sanctum Sanctorum, the Senate chamber, and then all your rights will be safe. No matter whether they possess intelligence, if they are selected by your rich landholders, all is well. But it is alleged by gentlemen, who have spoken on that side of the house, that the poor are a degraded class of beings, have no will of their own, and would not exercise this high prerogative with independence and sound discretion if entrusted with it: and, therefore, it would be unwise to trust them with ballots. This, sir, is unfounded: for more integrity and more patriotism are generally found in the laboring class of the community than in the higher orders. These are the men, who add to the substantial wealth of the nation, in peace. These are the men, who constitute your defence in war . . . And we are told, that these men, because they have no property, are not to be trusted at the ballot boxes! Men, who in defence of their liberties, and to protect the property of this country, have hazarded their lives; and who, to shield your wives and children from savage brutality, have faced the destructive cannon, and breasted the pointed steel? All this they could be trusted to do. They could, without apprehension, be permitted to handle their muskets, bayonets, powder and balls; but, say the gentlemen, it will not answer to trust them with tickets at the ballot boxes.

I would admonish gentlemen of this committee, to reflect, whom they are about to exclude from the right of suffrage, if the amendment under consideration should prevail. They will exclude your honest industrious mechanics, and many farmers, for many there are, who do not own the soil which they till. And what for? . . . Not because they are not virtuous, not because they are not meritorious; but, sir, because they are poor and dependent, and can have no will of their own, and will vote as the man who feeds them and clothes them may direct . . . I know of no men in this country, who are not dependent. The rich man is as much dependent upon the poor man for his labor, as the poor man is upon the rich for his wages. I know of no men, who are more dependent upon others for their bread and raiment, than the judges of your Supreme Court are upon the legislature, and who will pretend that this destroys their independence, or makes them subservient to the views of the legislature. Let us not, sir, disgrace ourselves in the eyes of the world, by expressing such degrading opinions of our fellow citizens. Let us grant universal suffrage, for after all, it is upon the virtue and intelligence of the people that the stability of your government must rest. Let us not brand this Constitution with any odious distinctions as to property. ■

From speech in the New York State Constitutional Convention, 1821.

• JAMES KENT

The Senate has hitherto been elected by the farmers of the state—by the free and independent lords of the soil, worth at least $250 in freehold estate, over and above all debts charged thereon. The governor has been chosen by the same electors, and we have hitherto elected citizens of elevated rank and character. Our assembly has been chosen by freeholders, possessing a freehold of the value of $50, or by persons renting a tenement of the yearly value of $5, and who have been rated and actually paid taxes to the state. By the report before us, we propose to annihilate, at one stroke, all those property distinctions and to bow before the idol of universal suffrage. That extreme democratic principle, when applied to the legislative and executive departments of government, has been regarded with terror, by the wise men of every age, because in every European republic, ancient and modern, in which it has been tried, it has terminated disastrously, and been productive of corruption, injustice, violence, and tyranny. And dare we flatter ourselves that we are a peculiar people, who can run the career of history, exempted from the passions which have disturbed and corrupted the rest of mankind? If we are like other races of men, with similar follies and vices, then I greatly fear that our posterity will have reason to deplore in sackcloth and ashes, the delusion of the day. . . .

The apprehended danger from the experiment of universal suffrage applied to the whole legislative department, is no dream of the imagination. It is too mighty an excitement for the moral constitution of men to endure. The tendency of universal suffrage, is to jeopardize the rights of property, and the principles of liberty, and the history of every age proves it; there is a tendency in the poor to covet and to share the plunder of the rich; in the debtor to relax or avoid the obligation of contracts; in the majority to tyrannize over the minority, and trample down their rights; in the indolent and the profligate, to cast the whole burdens of society upon the industrious and the virtuous; and there is a tendency in wicked and ambitious men, to inflame these combustible materials. It requires a vigilant government, and a firm administration of justice, to counteract that tendency . . . Who can undertake to calculate with any precision, how many millions of people, this great state will contain in the course of this and the next century . . . ? The disproportion between the men of property, and the men of no property, will be in every society in a ratio to its commerce, wealth, and population. We are no longer to remain plain and simple republics of farmers, like the New England colonists, or the Dutch settlements on the Hudson. We are fast becoming a great nation, with great commerce, manufactures, population, wealth, luxuries, and with the vices and miseries that they engender. One seventh of the population of the city of Paris at this day subsists on charity, and one third of the inhabitants of that city die in the hospitals; what would become of such a city with universal suffrage? France has upwards of four, and England upwards of five millions of manufacturing and commercial laborers without property. Could these kingdoms sustain the weight of universal suffrage? The radicals in England, with the force of that mighty engine, would at once sweep away the property, the laws, and the liberties of that island like a deluge.

The growth of the city of New York is enough to startle and awaken those who are pursuing the *ignis fatuus* of universal suffrage. . . .

It is rapidly swelling into the unwieldy population, and with the burdensome pauperism, of an European metropolis. New York is destined to become the future London of America; and in less than a century, that city, with the operation of universal suffrage, and under skillful direction, will govern this state.

The notion that every man that works a day on the road, or serves an idle hour in the militia, is entitled as of right to an equal participation in the whole power of the government, is most unreasonable, and has no foundation in justice . . . Society is an association for the protection of property as well as of life, and the individual who contributes only one cent to the common stock, ought not to have the same power and influence in directing the property concerns of the partnership, as he who contributes his thousands. He will not have the same inducements to care, and diligence, and fidelity. . . .

Liberty, rightly understood, is an inestimable blessing, but liberty without wisdom, and without justice, is no better than wild and savage licentiousness. The danger which we have hereafter to apprehend, is not the want, but the abuse, of liberty. We have to apprehend the oppression of minorities, and a disposition to encroach on private right—to disturb chartered privileges—and to weaken, degrade, and overawe the administration of justice; we have to apprehend the establishment of unequal, and consequently, unjust systems of taxation, and all the mischiefs of a crude and mutable legislation. A stable Senate, exempted from the influence of universal suffrage, will powerfully check these dangerous propensities. . . .

We are destined to become a great manufacturing as well as commercial state . . . Large manufacturing and mechanical establishments can act in an instant with the unity and efficacy of disciplined troops. It is against such combinations, among others, that I think we ought to give to the freeholders, or those who have interest in land, one branch of the legislature for their asylum and their comfort. Universal suffrage, once granted, is granted forever, and never can be recalled. There is no retrograde step in the rear of democracy. However mischievous the precedent may be in its consequences, or however fatal in its effects, universal suffrage never can be recalled or checked, but by the strength of the bayonet. We stand, therefore, at this moment, on the brink of fate, on the very edge of the precipice. If we let go our present hold of the Senate, we commit our proudest hopes and our most precious interests to the waves. ■

From speech in the New York State Constitutional Convention, 1821.

4

DEBATE IN THE VIRGINIA CONSTITUTIONAL CONVENTION, 1829–30

Abel Parker Upshur
Non-Freeholders of Richmond
Mr. Trezvant

• ABEL PARKER UPSHUR

What, Sir, are the constituent elements of society? Persons *and* property. What are subjects of legislation? Persons *and property.* Was there ever a society seen on earth, which consisted only of men, women and children? The very idea of society, carries with it the idea of property, as its necessary and inseparable attendant. History cannot show any form of the social compact, at any time, or in any place, in which property did not enter as a constituent element, nor one in which that element did not enjoy protection in a greater or less degree . . . Society cannot exist without property; it constitutes the full half of its being. Take away all protection from property, and our next business is to cut each other's throats. All experience proves this. The safety of men depends on the safety of property . . . And shall it not then be protected? Sir, your government cannot move an inch without property. . . .

The obligations of man in his social state are twofold; to bear arms, and to pay taxes for the support of Government. The obligation to bear arms, results from the duty which society owes him, to protect his rights of person. The society which protects me, I am bound to protect in return. The obligation to pay taxes, results from the protection extended to property. . . . Here, then, is the plain agreement between Government on the one hand, and the tax-paying citizen on the other. It is an agreement which results, of necessity, from the social compact . . .

If men enter into the social compact upon unequal terms; if one man brings into the partnership, his rights of person alone, and another brings into it, equal rights of person and all the rights of property beside, can they be said to have an equal interest in the common stock? Shall not he who has most at stake; who has, not only a *greater* interest, but a *peculiar* interest in society, possess an authority proportioned to that interest, and adequate to its protection? . . .

Why do you not admit a pauper to vote? He is a person, he counts one in your numerical majority. In rights strictly personal, he has as much interest in the Government as any other citizen. He is liable to commit the same offences, and to become exposed to the same punishments as the rich man. When then, shall he not vote? Because, thereby, he would receive an influence over property; and all who own it, feel it to be unsafe, to put the power of controlling it, into the hands of those who are not the owners. If you go on population alone, as the basis of representation, you will be obliged to the length of giving the elective franchise to every human being over twenty-one years; yes, and under twenty-one years, on whom your penal laws take effect; an experiment, which has met with nothing but utter and disastrous failure, wherever it has been tried. No, Mr. Chairman: Let us be consistent. Let us openly acknowledge the truth; let us boldly take the bull by the horns, and incorporate this influence of property as a leading principle in our Constitution. ■

From speech, Proceedings and Debates of the Virginia Constitutional Convention, 1829–30.

• THE NON-FREEHOLDERS OF RICHMOND

The Memorial of the Non-Freeholders of the City of Richmond respectfully addressed to the Convention, now assembled to deliberate on amendments to the State Constitution, 1829.

Your memorialists, as their designation imports, belong to that class of citizens, who, not having the good fortune to possess a certain portion of land, are, for that cause only, debarred from the enjoyment of the right of suffrage. Experience has but too clearly evinced, what, indeed, reason had always foretold, by how frail a tenure they hold every other right, who are denied this, the highest prerogative of freemen. The want of it has afforded both the pretext and the means of excluding the entire class, to which your memorialists belong, from all participation in the recent election of the body they now respectfully address. Comprising a very large part, probably a majority of male citizens of mature age, they have been passed by, like aliens or slaves, as if

destitute of interest, or unworthy of a voice, in measures involving their future political destiny; whilst the freeholders, sole possessors, under the existing Constitution, of the elective franchise, have, upon the strength of that possession alone, asserted and maintained in themselves, the exclusive power of new-modelling the fundamental laws of the State: in other words, have seized upon the sovereign authority. . . .

To that privilege [the suffrage], they respectfully contend, they are entitled equally with its present possessors. Many are bold enough to deny their title. None can show a better. It rests upon no subtle or abstruse reasoning; but upon grounds simple in their character, intelligible to the plainest capacity, and such as appeal to the heart, as well as the understanding, of all who comprehend and duly appreciate the principles of free Government. Among the doctrines inculcated in the great charter handed down to us, as a declaration of the rights pertaining to the good people of Virginia and their posterity [the Virginia Bill of Rights] . . . we are taught:

"That all men are by nature equally free and independent, and have certain inherent rights . . . namely, the enjoyment of life and liberty, with the means of acquiring and possessing property, and pursuing and obtaining happiness and safety . . . That all men . . . have a right of suffrage, and cannot be taxed, or deprived of their property, without due consent, or that of their representatives, nor bound by any law, to which they have not, in like manner, assented. . . ."

How do the principles thus proclaimed, accord with the existing regulation of suffrage? A regulation, which, instead of the equality nature ordains, creates an odious distinction between members of the same community; robs of all share, in the enactment of the laws, a large portion of the citizens, bound by them, and whose blood and treasure are pledged to maintain them, and vests in a favored class, not in consideration of their public services, but of their private possessions, the highest of all privileges. ■

From Proceedings and Debates of the Virginia Constitutional Convention of 1829–30.

• MR. TREZVANT

What is the question under consideration? The object of the amendment is to abolish the present modification of the Right of Suffrage, and to substitute in its place, one entirely new to us. When a people undertake to make a change in their political institutions, affecting the foundation of Government, it behooves them to proceed with the utmost caution and circumspection. . . .

This Government has existed for more than fifty years, and under it, the people have enjoyed happiness and contentment. There are, it is true, occasional clamors arising from local causes and prejudices, and not from any real defects in the form of Government; and I hope this amendment will not be adopted to allay such complaints. . . .

We are called upon to substitute for the Freehold Suffrage, that which, if it be not Universal Suffrage, falls but little short of it. It is proposed that those who are twenty-one years of age, who bear arms, and have resided twelve months in the county in which they propose to vote, should have this right, and the adoption of the principle amounts in effect, to what I call Universal Suffrage. I was told by one gentleman . . . that the adoption of this measure would add to the number of voters in the State more than 60,000, the present number being somewhat more than 40,000. Thus, the power of the Government is to be transferred from the hands of the 40,000, who have the deepest interest at stake, to the 60,000, who have comparatively but little interest.

It is no idle chimera of the brain, that the possession of land furnishes the strongest evidence of permanent, common interest with, and attachment to, the community. Much has been already said by gentlemen on both sides, demonstrating the powerful influence of local attachment upon the conduct of man, and I cannot be made to comprehend how that passion could be more effectually brought into action, than by a consciousness of the fact, that he is the owner of the spot which he can emphatically call his home. It is upon this foundation I wish to place the Right of Suffrage. This is the best general standard which can be resorted to for the purpose of determining whether the persons to be invested with the Right of Suffrage are such persons as could be, consistently with the safety and well-being of the community, entrusted with the exercise of that right. ■

From speech, Proceedings and Debates of the Virginia Constitutional Convention of 1829-30.

5

WOMAN SUFFRAGE

Margaret Fuller
Wendell Phillips
George William Curtis
Walt Whitman
Susan B. Anthony
Justice Morrison Remick Waite
Louis D. Brandeis
Woodrow Wilson

• EDITOR'S NOTE

Under the stimulus of suffrage leaders—among them Susan B. Anthony, Carrie Chapman Catt, Elizabeth Cady Stanton, and Lucy Stone— women gradually but steadily gained the right to vote in many states. By 1919 fifteen states had granted full and twenty states partial woman suffrage. Between 1878 and 1919 suffrage amendments were introduced in every Congress, but failed to pass.

In May and June, 1919, the United States House of Representatives and Senate finally adopted the Nineteenth Amendment. After ratification by three-fourths (thirty-six) of the states, it came into force on August 26, 1920. The Nineteenth Amendment reads: "The right of citizens of the United States to vote shall not be denied or abridged by the United States or by any State on account of sex." ∎

• MARGARET FULLER

It is not the transient breath of poetic incense that women want; each can receive that from a lover. It is not life-long sway; it needs but to become a coquette, a shrew, or a good cook to be sure of that. It is not money, nor notoriety, nor the badges of authority that men have appropriated to themselves. If demands, made in their behalf, lay stress on any of these particulars, those who make them have not searched deeply into the need. It is for that which at once includes these and precludes them; which would not be forbidden power, lest there be temptation to steal and misuse it; which would not have the mind perverted by flattery from a worthiness of esteem. It if for that which is the birthright of every being capable to receive it—the freedom, the religious, the intelligent freedom of the universe, to use its means; to learn its secret as far as nature has enabled them, with God alone for their guide and their judge.

Ye cannot believe it, men; but the only reason why women ever assume what is more appropriate to you is because you prevent them from finding out what is fit for themselves. Were they free, were they wise fully to develop the strength and beauty of woman, they would never wish to be men, or man-like. The well-instructed moon flies not from her orbit to seize on the glories of her partner. No; for she knows that one law rules, one heaven contains, one universe replies to them alike. It is with women as with the slave—

> Vor dem Sklaven, wenn er die Kette bricht,
> Vor dem frein Menschen erzittert
>   nicht."[1]   ■

From Woman in the Nineteenth Century, *1845.*

• WENDELL PHILLIPS

In every great reform, the majority have always said to the claimant, no matter what he claimed, "You are not fit for such a privilege." Luther asked of the Pope liberty for the masses to read the Bible. The reply was that it would not be safe to trust the common people with the word of God. "Let them try!" said the great reformer. . . .

Woman stands now at the same door. She says, "You tell me I have no intellect: give me a chance. You tell me I shall only embarrass politics: let me try. The only reply is the same stale argument that said to the Jews of Europe. 'You are fit only to make money: you are not fit for the ranks of the army or the halls of Parliament.'" How cogent the eloquent appeal of Macaulay—"What right have we to take this question for granted? Throw open the doors of this House of Commons, throw open the ranks of the imperial army, before you deny eloquence to the countrymen of Isaiah or valor to the descendants of the Maccabees." It is the same now with us. Throw open the doors of Congress, throw open those courthouses, throw wide open the doors of your colleges, and give to the sisters of the Motts and the Somervilles the same opportunities for culture that men have, and let the result

prove what their capacity and intellect really are. When, I say, woman has enjoyed, for as many centuries as we have the aid of books, the discipline of life, and the stimulus of fame, it will be time to begin the discussion of these questions—"What is the intellect of woman?" "Is it equal to that of man?" Till then, all such discussion is mere beating of the air. . . .

The mightiest intellects of the race, from Plato down to the present time, some of the rarest minds of Germany, France, and England, have successively yielded their assent to the fact that woman is, not perhaps identically, but equally, endowed with man in all intellectual capabilities. It is generally the second-rate men doubt—doubt, perhaps, because they fear a fair field. . . .

We do not attempt to settle what shall be the profession, education, or employment of woman. We have not that presumption. What we ask is simply this—what all other classes have asked before: Leave it to woman to choose for herself her profession, her education, and her sphere . . . All that woman asks through this movement is to be allowed to prove what she can do.   ■

From Woman's Rights, *1851.*

• GEORGE WILLIAM CURTIS

I wish to know, sir, and I ask in the name of the political justice and consistency of this State, why it is that half of the adult population, as vitally interested in good government as the other half, who own property, manage estates, and pay taxes, who discharge all the duties of good citizens and are perfectly intelligent and capable, are absolutely deprived of political power, and classed with lunatics and felons. The boy will become a man and a voter; the lunatic may emerge from the cloud and resume his rights; the idiot, plastic under the tender hand of modern science, may be moulded into a full citizen; the criminal whose hand still drips with the blood of his country and of liberty may be pardoned and restored. But no age, no wisdom, no

---

[1] This may be freely translated as: "Tremble not before the slave who breaks his chain any more than you would before the free man."

peculiar fitness, no public service, no effort, no desire can remove from women this enormous and extraordinary disability. Upon what reasonable grounds does it rest? Upon none whatever. It is contrary to natural justice, to the acknowledged and traditional principles of the American government, and to the most enlightened political philosophy. . . .

Or shall I be told that women, if not numerically counted at the polls, do yet exert an immense influence upon politics, and do not really need the ballot? If this argument were seriously urged, I should suffer my eyes to rove through this chamber and they would show the many honorable gentlemen of reputed political influence. May they, therefore, be properly and justly disfranchised? I ask the honorable chairman of the committee whether he thinks that a citizen should have no vote because he has influence? What gives influence? Ability, intelligence, honesty. Are these to be excluded from the polls? Is it only stupidity, ignorance, and rascality which ought to possess political power? . . .

But I shall be told, in the language of the report of the committee, that the proposition is openly at war with the distribution of functions and duties between the sexes. Translated into English, Mr. Chairman, this means that it is unwomanly to vote. Well, sir, I know that at the very mention of the political rights of women there arises in many minds a dreadful vision of a mighty exodus of the whole female world, in bloomers and spectacles, from the nursery and kitchen to the polls. It seems to be thought that if women practically took part in politics, the home would instantly be left a howling wilderness of cradles and a chaos of undarned stockings and buttonless shirts. But how is it with men? Do they desert their workshops, their plows and offices, to pass their time at the polls? Is it a credit to a man to be called a professional politician? The pursuits of men in the world, to which they are directed by the natural aptitude of sex and to which they must devote their lives, are as foreign from political functions as those of women. To take an extreme case. There is nothing more incompatible with political duties in cooking and taking care of children than there is in digging ditches or making shoes or in any other necessary employment, while in every superior interest of society growing out of the family the stake of women is not less than men, and their knowledge is greater. . . .

When the committee declare that voting is at war with the distribution of functions between the sexes, what do they mean? Are not women as much interested in good government as men? Has the mother less at stake in equal laws honestly administered than the father? There is fraud in the legislature; there is corruption in the courts; there are hospitals and tenement-houses and prisons; there are gambling houses and billiard-rooms and brothels; there are grog-shops at every corner, and I know not what enormous proportion of crime in the State proceeds from them; there are forty thousand drunkards in the State and their hundreds of thousands of children. All these things are subjects of legislation, and under the exclusive legislation of men; the crime associated with all these things becomes vast and complicated; have the wives and mothers and sisters of New York less vital interest in them, less practical knowledge of them and their proper treatment, than the husbands and fathers? No man is so insane as to pretend it. Is there then any natural incapacity in women to understand politics? It is not asserted. Are they lacking in the necessary intelligence? But the moment that you erect a standard of intelligence which is sufficient to exclude women as a sex, that moment most of their amiable fellow-citizens in trousers would be disfranchised. It it that they ought not to go to public political meetings? But we earnestly invite them. Or that they should not go to the polls? Some polls, I allow, in the larger cities, are dirty and dangerous places, and those it is the duty of the police to reform. But no decent man wishes to vote in a grog-shop, or to have his head broken while he is doing it; while the mere act of dropping a ballot in a box is about the simplest, shortest, and cleanest that can be done. ■

From speech in the New York Constitutional Convention, 1867.

• WALT WHITMAN

Democracy, in silence, biding its time, ponders its own ideals, not of literature and art only—not of men only, but of women. The idea of the women of America, (extricated from this daze, this fossil and unhealthy air which hangs about the word *lady*), develop'd, raised to become the robust equals, workers, and, it may be, even practical and political deciders with the men—greater than man, we may admit, through their divine maternity, always their towering, emblematical attribute—but great, at any rate, as man, in all departments; or, rather, capable of being so, soon as they realize it, and can bring themselves to give up toys and fictions, and launch forth, as men do, amid real, independent, stormy life. ■

From Democratic Vistas, *1871.*

• SUSAN B. ANTHONY

For any state to make sex a qualification that must ever result in the disfranchisement of one entire half of the people is to pass a bill of attainder, or an *ex post facto* law, and is therefore a violation of the supreme law of the land. By it the blessings of liberty are forever withheld from women and their female posterity. To them this government has no just powers derived from the consent of the governed. To them, this government is not a democracy. It is not a republic. It is an odious aristocracy; a hateful oligarchy of sex; the most hateful aristocracy ever established on the face of the globe; an oligarchy of wealth, where the rich govern the poor. An oligarchy of learning, where the educated govern the ignorant, or even an oligarchy of race, where the Saxon rules the African, might be endured; but this oligarchy of sex, which makes father, brothers, husband, sons, the oligarchs over the mother and sisters, the wife and daughters of every household— which ordains all men sovereigns, all women subjects, carries dissension, discord and rebellion into every home of the nation.

Webster, Worcester and Bouvier all define a citizen to be a person in the United States, entitled to vote and hold office.

The only question left to be settled now is: Are women persons? And I hardly believe any of our opponents will have the hardihood to say they are not. Being persons, then, women are citizens; and no state has a right to make any law, or to enforce any old law, that shall abridge their privileges or immunities. Hence, every discrimination against women in the Constitution and laws of the several states is today null and void, precisely as in every one against Negroes. ■

From speech in 1873, after she was arrested and fined ($100) for voting in the presidential election of 1872.

• JUSTICE MORRISON REMICK WAITE

The question is presented in this case, whether, since the adoption of the Fourteenth Amendment, a woman, who is a citizen of the United States and of the State of Missouri, is a voter in that State, notwithstanding the provision of the Constitution and laws of the State, which confine the right of suffrage to men alone. . . .

It is contended that the provisions of the Constitution and laws of the State of Missouri, which confine the right of suffrage and registration therefor to men, are in violation of the Constitution of the United States, and therefore void. The argument is, that as a woman, born or naturalized in the United States and subject to the jurisdiction thereof, is a citizen of the United States and of the State in which she resides, she has the right of suffrage as one of the privileges and immunities of her citizenship, which the State cannot by its laws or constitution abridge.

There is no doubt that women may be citizens. They are persons, and by the Fourteenth Amendment "all persons born or naturalized in the United States and subject to the jurisdiction thereof" are expressly declared to be "citizens of the United States and of the State wherein they reside. . . ."

Sex has never been made one of the elements of citizenship in the United States. In this respect men have never had an advantage over women. The same laws precisely apply to both. The Fourteenth Amendment did not affect the citizenship of women any more than it did of men. . . .

If the right of suffrage is one of the necessary privileges of a citizen of the United States, then the constitution and laws of Missouri confining it to men are in violation of the Constitution of the United States, as amended, and consequently void. The direct question is, therefore, presented whether all citizens are necessarily voters.

The Constitution does not define the privileges and immunities of citizens. For that definition we must look elsewhere. In this case we need not determine what they are, but only whether suffrage is necessarily one of them.

It certainly is nowhere made so in express terms. The United States has no voters in the States of its own creation. The elective officers of the United States are all elected directly or indirectly by State voters. . . .

The [Fourteenth] Amendment did not add to the privileges and immunities of a citizen. It simply furnished an additional guaranty for the protection of such as he already had. No new voters were necessarily made by it.

It is clear, therefore, we think, that the Constitution has not added the right of suffrage to the privileges and immunities of citizenship as they existed at the time it was adopted. This makes it proper to inquire whether suffrage was coextensive with the citizenship of the States at the time of its adoption. If it was, then it may with force be argued that suffrage was one of the rights which belonged to citizenship, and in the enjoyment of which every citizen must be protected. But if it was not, the contrary may with propriety be assumed.

When the Federal Constitution was adopted, all the States, with the exception of Rhode Island and Connecticut, had constitutions of their own. . . . Upon an examination of those constitutions we find that in no State were all citizens permitted to vote. . . .

It is true that the United States guarantees to every State a republican form of government. . . . No particular government is designated as republican, neither is the exact form to be guaranteed. . . .

All the States had governments when the Constitution was adopted. In all the people participated to some extent, through their representatives elected in the manner specially provided. These governments the Constitution did not change. They were accepted precisely as they were. . . . Thus we have unmistakable evidence of what was republican in form, within the meaning of that term as employed in the Constitution.

As we have seen, all the citizens of the States were not invested with the right of suffrage. In all, save perhaps New Jersey, this right was only bestowed upon men and not upon all of them. Under these circumstances it is certainly now too late to contend that a government is not republican, within the meaning of this guaranty in the Constitution, because women are not made voters. . . .

Certainly if the courts can consider any question settled, this is one. For nearly ninety years the people have acted upon the idea that the Constitution, when it conferred citizenship, did not necessarily confer the right of suffrage. . . .

Being unanimously of the opinion that the Constitution of the United States does not confer the right of suffrage upon anyone, and that the constitutions and laws of the several States which commit that important trust to men alone are not necessarily void, we affirm the judgment. ■

From U. S. Supreme Court Unanimous Opinion,
Minor *v.* Happersett, *1875.*

• LOUIS D. BRANDEIS

As years have passed I have been more and more impressed with the difficulty and complexity of social, economic, and political problems and also with the power of society to solve them; but I am convinced that for their solution we must look to the many, not to the few. We need all the people, women as well as men. In the democracy which is to solve them we must have not a part of society but the whole. The insight that women have shown into problems which men did not and perhaps could not understand has convinced me not only that women should have the ballot, but that we need them to have it. This is especially the case because these problems will have to be solved largely through collective action in which legislation is necessary. ■

From Address at National Congress of Charities and Correction, Boston, June 14, 1911.

• WOODROW WILSON

The whole nature of our political questions has been altered. They have ceased to be legal questions. They have more and more become social questions, questions with regard to the relations of human beings to one another ... As these questions have assumed greater and greater prominence, the movement which this association [Woman Suffrage] represents has gathered cumulative force ... It means something that has not only come to stay, but has come with conquering power. ...

It is going to prevail ... It is not merely because the women are discontented. It is because the women have seen visions of duty, and that is something which we not only cannot resist, but ... we do not wish to resist. ...

I have come to suggest, among other things, that when the forces of nature are steadily working and the tide is rising to meet the moon, you need not be afraid that it will not come to its flood. We feel the tide; we rejoice in the strength of it; and we shall not quarrel in the long run as to the method of it. Because, when you are working with masses of men and organized bodies of opinion, you have got to carry the organized body along. The whole art and practice of government consists, not in moving individuals, but in moving masses. It is all very well to run ahead and beckon, but, after all, you have got to wait for the body to follow. I have not come to ask you to be patient, because you have been, but I have come to congratulate you that there was a

force behind you that will beyond any peradventure be triumphant, and for which you can afford a little while to wait. ■

From Address at Woman Suffrage Convention, Atlantic City, September 8, 1916.

• WOODROW WILSON

I regard the concurrence of the Senate in the Constitutional amendment proposing the extension of the suffrage to women as vitally essential to the successful prosecution of the great war of humanity [World War I] in which we are engaged ... It is my duty to win the war and to ask you to remove every obstacle that stands in the way of winning it. ...

This is a peoples' war and the peoples' thinking constitutes its atmosphere and morale, not the predilections of the drawing room or the political considerations of the caucus. If we be indeed democrats and wish to lead the world to democracy, we can ask other peoples to accept in proof of our sincerity and our ability to lead them whither they wish to be led nothing less persuasive and convincing than our actions. Verification must be forthcoming ... And in this case verification is asked for ... It is asked for by the anxious, expectant, suffering peoples with whom we are dealing and who are willing to put their destinies in some measure in our hands ... Through many, many channels I have been made aware that the plain, struggling, workaday folk are thinking upon whom the chief terror and suffering of this tragic war falls. They are looking to the great, powerful, famous Democracy of the West to lead them to the new day for which they have so long waited; and they think, in their logical simplicity, that democracy means that women shall play their part in affairs alongside men and upon an equal footing with them. If we reject measures like this ... they will cease to follow or to trust us. ...

Are we alone to refuse to learn the lesson? Are we alone to ask and take the utmost that our women can give—service and sacrifice of every kind—and still say we do not see what title that gives them to

stand by our sides in the guidance of the affairs of
their nation and ours? We have made partners of the
women in this war; shall we admit them only to a
partnership of suffering and sacrifice and toil and
not to a partnership of privilege and right? . . .

The women of America are too noble and too intelligent and too devoted to be slackers whether you
give or withhold this thing that is mere justice; but
I know the magic it will work in their thoughts and
spirits if you give it to them. I propose it as I would
propose to admit soldiers to the suffrage, the men
fighting in the field for our liberties and the liberties of the world, were they excluded. . . .

I tell you plainly that this measure which I urge
upon you is vital to the winning of the war and to
the energies alike of preparation and of battle.

And not the winning of the war only. It is vital
to the right solution of the great problems which we
must settle . . . when the war is over. We shall
need them in our vision of affairs,[1] as we have never
needed them before, the sympathy and insight and
clear moral instinct of the women of the world . . .
We shall need their moral sense to preserve what is
right and fine and worthy in our system of life as
well as to discover just what it is that ought to be
purified and reformed. Without their counsellings
we shall be only half wise. . . . ■

*From Address to the Senate urging the adoption
of a Woman Suffrage Resolution (which the
House had already adopted), September 30, 1918.*

---

[1]. Until the Wilson era, most American political leaders continued to
agree with the statement made by Jefferson, an ardent believer in
human rights in general, in a letter to his Secretary of the Treasury,
Albert Gallatin, January 13, 1807: "The appointment of a woman to
office is an innovation for which the public is not prepared, nor am I."

6

POLITICAL PARTICIPATION

Thomas Jefferson
Francis Hall
Woodrow Wilson
Lyndon B. Johnson

• THOMAS JEFFERSON

In every government on earth is some trace of human weakness, some germ of corruption and degeneracy, which cunning will discover, and wickedness insensibly open, cultivate and improve. Every government degenerates when trusted to the rulers of the people alone. The people themselves therefore are its only safe depositories. And to render them safe, their minds must be improved to a certain degree. This indeed is not all that is necessary, though it be essentially necessary. An amendment of our constitution must here come in aid of the public education. The influence over government must be shared among all the people. If every individual which composes their mass participates of the ultimate authority, the government will be safe; because the corrupting the whole mass will exceed any private resources of wealth; and public ones cannot be provided but by levies on the people. In this case every man would have to pay his own price. The government of Great Britain has been corrupted, because but one man in ten has a right to vote for members of parliament. The sellers of the government, get nine-tenths of their price clear. It has been thought that corruption is restrained by confining the right of suffrage to a few of the wealthier of the people; but it would be more effectually restrained by an extension of that right to such numbers as would bid defiance to the means of corruption. ■

From Notes on Virginia, *Query XIV, 1782.*

• FRANCIS HALL

Mr. Jefferson . . . seemed to consider much of the freedom and happiness of America to rise from local circumstances: "Our population," he observed, "has an elasticity, by which it would fly off from oppressive taxation . . ." Their ingenuity in mechanical inventions, agricultural improvements, and that mass of general information to be found among Americans of all ranks and conditions he ascribed to that ease of circumstances which afforded them leisure to cultivate their minds, after the cultivation of their lands was completed . . . Another cause, Mr. Jefferson observed, might be discovered in the many court and county meetings, which brought men frequently together on public business, and thus gave them habits, both of thinking and of expressing their thoughts on subjects, which in other countries are confined to the . . . privileged few. ■

From Travels in Canada and the United States in 1816 and 1817, *1818.*

• WOODROW WILSON

It is harder for democracy to organize administration than for monarchy . . . We have enthroned public opinion . . . The very fact that we have realized popular rule in its fullness has made the task of *organizing* that rule just so much the more difficult. In order to make any advance at all we must instruct and persuade a multitudinous monarch called public opinion—a much less feasible undertaking than to influence a single monarch called a king. An individual sovereign will adopt a simple plan and carry it out directly; he will have but one opinion, and he will embody that one opinion in one command. But this other sovereign, the people, will have a score of differing opinions. They can agree upon nothing simple: advance must be made through compromise, by a compounding of differences, by a trimming of plans and a suppression of too straightforward principles. . . .

In government, as in virtue, the hardest of hard things is to make progress. Formerly the reason for this was that the single person who was sovereign was generally either selfish, ignorant, timid, or a fool—albeit there was now and again one who was wise. Nowadays the reason is that the many, the people, who are sovereign have no single ear which one can approach, and are selfish, ignorant, timid, stubborn, or foolish, with the selfishnesses, the ignorances, the stubbornnesses, the timidities, or the follies of several thousand persons—albeit there are hundreds who are wise. Once the advantage of the

reformer was that the sovereign's mind had a definite locality, that it was contained in one man's head, and that consequently it could be gotten at . . . Now, on the contrary, the reformer is bewildered by the fact that the sovereign's mind has no definite locality, but is contained in a voting majority of several million heads. . . .

Wherever regard for public opinion is a first principle of government, practical reform must be slow and all reform must be full of compromises. For wherever public opinion exists it must rule. This is now an axiom half the world over, and will presently come to be believed even in Russia. Whoever would effect a change in a modern constitutional government must first educate his fellow-citizens to want *some* change . . . He must first make public opinion willing to listen and then see to it that it listen to the right things. He must stir it up to search for an opinion, and then manage to put the right opinion in its way.

The first step is no less difficult than the second. With opinions, possession is more than nine points of the law. It is next to impossible to dislodge them. . . .

The bulk of mankind is rigidly unphilosophical, and nowadays the bulk of mankind votes. A truth must become not only plain but also commonplace before it will be seen by the people who go to their work very early in the morning. . . .

And where is this unphilosophical bulk of mankind more multifarious in its composition than in the United States? To know the public mind of this country, one must know the mind, not of Americans of the older stock only, but also of Irishmen, of Germans, of Negroes. In order to get a footing for new doctrine, one must influence minds cast in every mould of race, minds inheriting every bias of environment, warped by the histories of a score of different nations, warmed or chilled, closed or expanded, by almost every climate of the globe. . . .

What part shall public opinion take in the conduct of administration? The right answer seems to be that public opinion shall play the part of authoritative critic. . . .

Our success is made doubtful by that besetting

error of ours, the error of trying to do too much by vote. Self-government does not consist in having a hand in everything, any more than housekeeping consists necessarily in cooking dinner with one's own hands. The cook must be trusted with a large discretion as to the management of the fires and the ovens . . . In trying to instruct our own public opinion, we are dealing with a pupil apt to think itself quite sufficiently instructed beforehand.

The problem is to make public opinion efficient without suffering it to be meddlesome. Directly exercised, in the oversight of the daily details and in the choice of the daily means of government, public criticism is of course a clumsy nuisance, a rustic handling of delicate machinery. But as superintending the greater forces of formative policy alike in politics and administration, public criticism is altogether safe and beneficent, altogether indispensable. . . . ■

From article in Political Science Quarterly, *June, 1887.*

• LYNDON B. JOHNSON

Public participation in the processes of government is the essence of democracy. Public confidence in those processes strengthens democracy.

No Government can long survive which does not fuse the public will to the institutions which serve it. The American system has endured for almost two centuries because the people have involved themselves in the work of their Government, with full faith in the meaning of that involvement.

But Government itself has the continuing obligation—second to no other—to keep the machinery of public participation functioning smoothly and to improve it where necessary so that democracy remains a vital and vibrant institution.

It is in the spirit of that obligation that I send this message to the Congress today. I propose a five-point program to:

—Reform our campaign financing laws to assure full disclosure of contributions and expenses, to place realistic limits on contributions, and to re-

move the meaningless and ineffective ceilings on campaign expenditures.

—Provide a system of public financing for Presidential election campaigns.

—Broaden the base of public support for election campaigns, by exploring ways to encourage and stimulate small contributions.

—Close the loopholes in the Federal laws regulating lobbying.

—Assure the right to vote for millions of Americans who change their residences.

In our democracy, politics is the instrument which sustains our institutions and keeps them strong and free.

The laws which govern political activity should be constantly reviewed—and reshaped when necessary—to preserve the essential health and vitality of the political process which is so fundamental to our way of life. . . .

A sweeping overhaul of the laws governing election campaigns should no longer be delayed.

Basic reform—with an emphasis on clear and straightforward disclosure—is essential to insure public confidence and involvement in the political process. On the cornerstone of disclosure we can build toward further reform—by charting new ways to broaden the base of financial support for candidates and parties in election campaigns. . . .

Complete disclosure will open to public view where campaign money comes from and how it is spent. Such disclosure will help dispel the growth of public skepticism which surrounds the present methods of financing political campaigns. . . .

To insure full disclosure, I recomment that:

Every candidate, including those for the Presidency and Vice Presidency, and every committee, state, interstate, and national, that supports a candidate for federal office be required to report on every contribution, loan and expense item over $100.

Primaries and convention nomination contests be brought within the disclosure laws.

Closely related to full disclosure—the basic step in any election reform—is another equally demanding task. It requires that we make political financing more democratic by recognizing that great wealth—in reality or appearance—could be used to achieve undue political influence. . . .

I recommend that a $5,000 limit be placed on the total amount that could come from any individual, his wife or minor children, to the campaign of any candidate.

With full disclosure and an effective ceiling on contributions we can move forward to cure another defect in our election campaign laws—the artificial limits on campaign expenditures.

Under present law, for example:

National political committees can raise and spend no more than $3 million. But the law does not limit the number of national committees.

Senate candidates are limited to expenses of $24,000 and House candidates to $5,000. But the law does not limit the number of committees that can spend and raise money on the candidate's behalf.

These legal ceilings on expenditures were enacted many years ago, when the potential of radio in a campaign was virtually unknown and when television did not exist. They are totally unrealistic and inadequate. They have led to the endless proliferation of political committees.

I therefore recommend a repeal of the present arbitrary limits on the total expenditures of candidates for federal office. . . .

Democracy rests on the voice of the people. Whatever blunts the clear expression of that voice is a threat to democratic government. In this century one phenomenon in particular poses such a threat—the soaring costs of political campaigns.

Historically, candidates for public office in this country have always relied upon private contributions to finance their campaigns.

But in the last few decades, technology—which has changed so much of our national life—has modified the nature of political campaigning as well. Radio, television, and the airplane have brought sweeping new dimensions and costs to the concept of political candidacy.

In many ways these changes have worked to the decided advantage of the American people. They have served to bring the candidates and the issues before virtually every voting citizen. They have contributed immeasurably to the political education of the nation.

In another way, however, they have worked to the opposite effect by increasing the costs of campaigning to spectacular proportions. Costs of such magnitude can have serious consequences for our democracy:

—More and more, men and women of limited means may refrain from running for public office. . . .

—Increases in the size of individual contributions create uneasiness in the minds of the public. . . . It erodes public confidence in the democratic order.

—The necessity of acquiring substantial funds to finance campaigns diverts a candidate's attention from his public obligations and detracts from his energetic exposition of the issues.

—The growing importance of large contributions serves to deter the search for small ones, and thus effectively narrows the base of financial support. This is exactly the opposite of what a democratic society should strive to achieve. . . .

The election of a President is the highest expression of the free choice of the American people. It is the most visible level of politics—and also the most expensive.

For their free choice to be exercised wisely, the people must be fully informed about the opposing candidates and issues. To achieve this, candidates and parties must have the funds to bring their platforms and programs to the people.

Yet, as we have seen, the costs of campaigning are skyrocketing. This imposes extreme and heavy financial burdens on party and candidate alike, creating a potential for danger—the possibility that men of great wealth could achieve undue political influence through large contributions. . . .

I make these eleven recommendations to improve and strengthen the Presidential Election Campaign Fund Act:

1. Funds to finance Presidential campaigns should be provided by direct Congressional appropri-

ation, rather than determined by individual tax check-offs. . . .

2. The funds should be used only for expenses which are needed to bring the issues before the public. . . .

3. Private contributions for major parties could not be used for those items of expense to which public funds could be applied. . . .

4. A "major party" should be defined as one which received 25 percent or more of the popular votes cast in the last election. . . .

5. A "minor party" should be defined as one which received between 5 and 25 percent of the popular votes cast in the current election. . . .

6. A "minor party" should be eligible for reimbursement promptly following an election [50 cents per vote cast]. . . .

7. The percentage of federal funds received by a major or minor party which could be used in any one state should be limited to 140 percent of the percentage the population of that state bears to the population of the country. . . .

8. The Comptroller General should be required to make a full report to the Congress as soon as practicable after each Presidential election. . . .

9. The Comptroller General should be given clear authority to audit the expenses of Presidential campaigns. . . .

10. To bring greater wisdom and experience to the administration of the act, the Comptroller General's special Advisory Board on the Presidential Election Campaign Fund should be expanded from seven to eleven members. . . .

11. Criminal penalties should be applied for the willful misuse of payments received under the Act by any person with custody of the funds. . . .

These recommendations represent my thoughts on the issues at stake. I believe they highlight the problems in an area so new and complex that there is little experience in our national life to guide us. . . .

Full disclosure can serve the integrity of government in another important area—the regulation of lobbying.

Lobbying dates back to the earliest days of our Republic. It is based on the constitutionally guaranteed right of the people to petition their elected representatives for a redress of grievances.

Yet to realize the American ideal of Government, our elected representatives must be able to evaluate the varied pressures to which they are regularly subjected. In 1946 Congress responded to this need by enacting the Federal Regulation of Lobbying Act. Its purpose was not to curtail lobbying but to regulate it through disclosure. For the first time, individuals and groups who directly attempted to influence legislation were required to register.

More than twenty years of experience with the Act have highlighted its flaws. Through loopholes in the law, immune from its registration provisions, have passed some of the most powerful, best financed and best organized lobbies. . . .

The Congress has properly taken the initiative to meet this problem. Two months ago, the Senate passed S.355 by a decisive vote. In that measure, Federal regulation of lobbying has been strengthened by:

—Supplanting the "principal purpose" test with the broader test of "substantial purpose," thus extending the reach of the Act by a wider definition of those required to register.

—Transferring the responsibility for administration of the law from the Clerk of the House and the Secretary of the Senate to the Comptroller General.

I strongly endorse the Senate's action in strengthening regulation of lobbying as an important step toward better Government, and I urge the House to take similar action. . . .

Voting is the first duty of democracy. H. G. Wells called it, "Democracy's ceremonial, its feast, its great function."

This Nation has already assured that no man can legally be denied the right to vote because of the color of his skin or his economic condition. But we find that millions of Americans are still disenfranchised—because they have moved their residence from one locality to another.

Mobility is one of the attributes of a free society, and increasingly a chief characteristic of our Nation in the twentieth century. More American citizens than ever before move in search of new jobs and better opportunities.

For a mobile society, election laws which impose unduly long residence requirements are obsolete. They serve only to create a new class of disenfranchised Americans . . . Almost half the states, for example, through laws a century old require a citizen to be a resident a full twelve months before he can vote even in a Presidential election.

These requirements diminish democracy. The people's rights to travel freely from State to State is constitutionally protected. The exercise of that right should not imperil the loss of another constitutionally protected right—the right to vote.

I propose the Residency Voting Act of 1967 which provides that a citizen, otherwise qualified to vote under the laws of the state, may not be denied his vote in a Presidential election if he becomes a resident of the state by the first day of September preceding the election.

CONCLUSION

Seventy years ago, the great American historian Frederick Jackson Turner wrote these words:

"Behind institutions, behind constitutional forms and modifications, lie the vital forces that call these organs into life and shape them to meet changing conditions. The peculiarity of American institutions is in the fact that they have been compelled to adapt themselves to the changes of an expanding people. . . ."

This represents a valid exposition of the vitality of our democratic process as it has endured for almost two hundred years.

Over those two centuries Presidents and Congresses have strengthened that process as changing circumstances presented the clear need to do so. History has spared few generations that continuing obligation.

Today, that obligation poses for us the requirement—and the opportunity as well—to bring new strength to the processes which underlie our free institutions.

It is in keeping with this obligation that I submit the proposals in this Message. ■

From Message to Congress, May 25, 1967.

$$\overline{7}$$

THE RIGHTS OF BLACKS

U.S. Commission on Civil Rights

• EDITOR'S NOTE

Just after the Civil War, during Reconstruction, Congress passed the Fourteenth and Fifteenth Amendments, designed to guarantee the Negro's right to vote.

Section 1 of the Fourteenth Amendment (declared in force on July 28, 1868) read: "All persons born or naturalized in the United States, and subject to the jurisdiction thereof, are citizens of the United States and of the State wherein they reside. No State shall make or enforce any law which shall abridge the privileges or immunities of citizens of the United States; nor shall any State deprive any person of life, liberty, or property without due process of law; nor deny to any person within its jurisdiction the equal protection of the law." The Fifteenth Amendment (in force March 30, 1870) was more specific: "The right of the citizens of the United States to vote shall not be denied or abridged by the United States or by any State, on account of race, color, or previous condition of servitude." Despite these Amendments, however, the rights of Negroes, particularly the right to vote, were consistently violated. This was true mainly, but not exclusively, in the South.

The Supreme Court decision in *Brown* v. *Board of Education of Topeka* (1954), a landmark in American democracy, affected the whole movement for Negro rights. It supplied those who struggle for Negro equality with a broad legal and constitutional base that had been lacking hitherto. It gave powerful impetus to the "Negro revolution" that was on the way all over the country—a revolution for democracy, aimed at achieving equality not only in education but also in voting, housing, jobs, and other opportunities long denied to Negroes.

In 1957 Congress passed the first civil rights act since the Reconstruction Amendments. The law provided for the establishment of a Commission on Civil Rights to promote the right to vote, mainly in the South. Three years later, in 1960, another act was passed to strengthen the law of 1957. It called for penalties for those who obstructed federal court decisions in regard to voting; for the preservation of federal election records; and for the education of children residing on Federal property (families of members of the armed forces, etc.) if local schools were not available to them.

These acts too were insufficient to guarantee Negro equality. The times and the needs called for much more extensive and effective legislation. This was provided in the Civil Rights Act of 1964, the most far-reaching enactment of its kind in American history. It was passed, after a long Southern filibuster, by majorities of more than two to one in both the House of Representatives and the Senate. The majorities were supplied by Democrats (mostly non-Southern) and Republicans. The Act was signed by President Lyndon B. Johnson on July 2, 1964.

The Act of 1964 has eleven sections, or titles.

Title I—*Voting Rights:* reinforces the government's authority under the Acts of 1957 and 1960.

Title II—*Places of Public Accommodation:* forbids discrimination in places of public accommodation, defined as including hotels, motels, eating places, gasoline stations, theatres, sports arenas, etc.

Title III—*Public Facilities:* prohibits racial discrimination in state-supported facilities, such as libraries and parks.

Title IV—*School Desegregation:* offers assistance to schools carrying out desegregation and empowers the U.S. Attorney General to sue in federal courts to end segregation where it exists, provided the victims cannot do so themselves.

Title V—*Civil Rights Commission:* extends its life for four years and authorizes it to collect information about segregation or fraud in Federal elections.

Title VI—*Federally Aided Programs:* aims to stop spending public funds on programs practicing racial discrimination.

Title VII—*Equal Employment Opportunity:* bars racial discrimination in job hiring.

Title VIII—*Registration and Voting Data:* directs the Secretary of Commerce to gather such statistics as to race.

Title IX—*Legal Procedures:* empowers the federal government to move civil rights cases from state to federal courts and the attorney general to intervene in private suits connected with a denial of equality because of race, color, religion, or national origin.

Title X—*Community Relations Service:* establishes this Service to help local communities voluntarily to solve problems and disputes arising out of the public accommodation provisions (Title II).

Title XI—*Jury Trial:* guarantees jury trial for those who violate court orders under Titles II through VII.

The Civil Rights Act of 1964—long overdue as a matter of simple justice—may be regarded as a Magna Carta for blacks and others suffering from discrimination. President Johnson said of it: "This Civil Rights Act is a challenge to all of us to go to work in our communities and our States, in our homes and in our hearts, to eliminate the last vestiges of injustice in our beloved America." ■

• U. S. COMMISSION ON CIVIL RIGHTS

CIVIL RIGHTS, 1961

In war and peace the American people have met challenge after challenge with vigor and resourcefulness. Perhaps the most persistent challenge is the one to which this Commission addresses itself in this report—the challenge of civil rights.

The Republic began with an obvious inconsistency between its precepts of liberty and the fact of slavery. The words of the Declaration of Independence were clear: "We hold these truths to be self-evident, that all men are created equal, that they are endowed by their Creator with certain unalienable rights, that among these are Life, Liberty, and the Pursuit of Happiness. That to secure these rights, Governments are instituted among Men, deriving their just powers from the consent of the governed."

Equally clear was the fact that Negroes were not free. The great American experiment in self-government began for white people only.

The inconsistency between the Nation's principles and its practices has diminished over the years. Constitutional amendments, court decisions, acts of Congress, Executive orders, administrative rulings, State and local legislation, the work of private agencies, efforts by Negroes and other minority groups —all these have helped remove many of the barriers to full citizenship for all.

The gains have been considerable. As the second term of this Commission draws to a close, it can report that more persons than ever before are exercising more fully their rights as citizens of the United States. The American people are increasingly aware that professions of belief in the dignity of man have meaning only if they are realized by all people in all aspects of life. The gap between the promise of liberty and its fulfillment is narrower today than it has ever been.

Yet a gap remains. In the changing world of 1961 it seems wide and deep, and the demand to close it is more urgent than ever. Perhaps this is because the closer we come to the achievement of our ideals, the more obvious and galling is the remaining disparity. Partly, too, events in a rapidly changing world have put a new focus on the way in which the United States puts it principles into practice. The emergence of new nonwhite nations in Africa and Asia does not make an inequity any more unjust. It may, however, make remedial action more urgent.

The report that follows attempts to measure the remaining gap between the American promise and its fulfillment; to tell of progress that has been made, and to suggest approaches for what remains to be done.

This report principally concerns the civil rights problems of Negroes. Mexican-Americans, Puerto Ricans, Indians, and other minorities to some extent still suffer inequalities and deprivation. But Negroes are our largest minority group, and their rights are denied more often in more respects and in more places than are those of any other group. Of all minorities, Negroes seem most closely bound to the history and conscience of America. Their struggle has become symbolic. By measuring the extent to which they enjoy civil rights, we may measure our respect for freedom. To the extent that this Nation can successfully resolve its racial problems, it lends hope to afflicted minorities and troubled majorities everywhere. For this Nation is concerned not just with the civil rights of a particular minority. It is concerned with human rights for all men everywhere. . . .

The two years since the Commission submitted its first report have brought dynamic changes in civil rights at all levels of government. These are some of the milestones of progress on the national level:

In 1960 Congress passed the second Civil Rights Act since 1875, strengthening the measures available to the Federal Government for dealing with such matters as discriminatory denials of the right to vote, obstruction of Federal court orders, and bombing or other desecration of schools and churches.

Through the courts the Federal Government acted energetically to secure the constitutional rights of its citizens against invasion by the States: it brought suits to protect the right of Negroes to vote without discrimination or coercion on account of race in fifteen counties in Alabama, Louisiana, Georgia, Mississippi, and Tennessee; in New Orleans it intervened in a school desegregation suit to protect its courts and its citizens against State defiance of the law of the land; in Montgomery, Ala., it sued to protect the right of Americans to travel freely among the States, without distinction or obstruction because of their race; again in New Orleans, and in Montgomery, it sued to end segregation in airport facilities built in part with Federal funds; in Jackson, Miss., it intervened in a suit to restrain arrests of persons seeking unsegregated service in bus terminals; in Biloxi, Miss., it brought suit to assure that a public beach constructed with funds from the National Government would be available to all the public without racial discrimination.

With the creation of the President's Committee on Equal Employment Opportunity in 1961, the executive branch of the Federal Government took a major step to achieve the national policy that there shall be no discrimination on grounds of race, color, creed, or national origin, either in employment by the Government itself, or in employment created by funds dispensed from the National Treasury.

The President of the United States publicly affirmed his support of the Supreme Court's decision that segregated public schools were forbidden by the Constitution.

The Supreme Court, followed by the lower Federal courts, has firmly upheld constitutional and statutory commands against discrimination in this period:

It held in 1961 that a State could not redraw municipal boundary lines on racial grounds.

In 1961 it held that the operation of a private restaurant in space leased from a public agency was State action within the meaning of the Fourteenth Amendment; and that the facility, therefore, could not be operated on a discriminatory basis.

In 1960 it held that Congress had forbidden racial segregation in services provided for interstate travelers even if the services are not provided directly by an interstate carrier itself.

Also in 1960 it upheld the 1957 Civil Rights Act against constitutional attack.

State and local governments also took important steps:

Twenty-three State laws aimed at preventing racial or religious discrimination in such areas as housing, employment, and public accommodations were enacted or strengthened—not only in Northern and Western States but in border States such as Kentucky, West Virginia, Delaware, Missouri, and Kansas.

In the deeper South, Georgia followed the example of Virginia in abandoning massive resistance to the requirements of the Constitution regarding public education. The first public educational institution in Georgia—the University of Georgia—was successfully desegregated with only temporary difficulty, and preparations were made for the orderly advent of desegregation in the Atlanta public schools. Thus, all but three States (Alabama, Mississippi, and South Carolina) had made at least some progress toward the constitutional operation of public schools and colleges. A handful of school districts in the South passed quietly and without difficulty from segregation into a program of compliance with the Constitution.

With or without lawsuits, public libraries, parks, and recreation facilities were successfully desegregated in a number of southern cities.

Perhaps the most important events of the period, however, were brought about by private citizens:

On February 1, 1960, four freshmen students from the North Carolina Agricultural & Technical College entered a variety store in Greensboro, made several purchases, then sat down at the lunch counter and ordered coffee. They were refused service because they were Negroes, but they remained in their seats until the store closed. Thus began the sit-in movement, a movement of protest mainly by Negro youth. It spread rapidly through the South and even to some places in the North, manifesting itself as well in other forms of peaceful protest— kneel-ins, stand-ins, wade-ins, and more recently and spectacularly in the "Freedom Rides." This protest movement has aroused widespread interest and strong feelings. Although doubts of its wisdom and concern as to its methods are genuinely felt by many, there can be no question that its moral impetus is strong, that it expresses a profound and widespread demand for faster realization of equal opportunity for Negroes, or that it will continue until the issues raised by its demands have been resolved.

Partly as a result of the sit-ins, there has been a marked change, for the most part unpublicized and without drama, in many southern cities. Racial barriers have been removed not only in areas where the law of the land supported the claim for equal treatment—as in publicly operated facilities and interstate transportation terminals—but also in many areas of private concern where no legal compulsion has been held to exist. By the close of 1960, for instance, variety store chains had opened lunch counters in 112 southern and border cities to Negro patrons.

Equally important has been the growing awareness among thoughtful southern white leaders of the dimensions of civil rights problems. James J. Kilpatrick, a Virginian, editor of the *Richmond News-Leader,* and one of the earliest proponents of massive resistance to school desegregation, spoke for many when he said: "What I am groping to say is that many a southerner is seeing now, and hearing now. Aspects of segregation that once were his nonconcern now trouble his spirit uncomfortably: Sit-ins. Segregated libraries. Certain job discrimination. Genuinely unequal schools in some areas. The Negro as citizen, as a political being possessed of equal rights, never had existed in the white southerner's past as he begins to exist now. The familiar black faces, seen through new glasses, are startlingly unfamiliar. A sense of the Negro point of view, totally unrecognized before, stirs uneasily in the conscious mind. . . ."

That Mr. Kilpatrick spoke for many responsible white southerners is confirmed by their effective efforts in such vital spots as Little Rock, Atlanta, and New Orleans to keep public schools open, even if it meant desegregation. A number of church and other organizations throughout the South have decried the immorality of all forms of racial discrimination.

In the North and West as well, private groups have become increasingly active in expressing by action as well as words a belief in equal treatment regardless of race, creed, or ancestry. . . .

Despite this progress, however, the Nation still faces substantial and urgent problems in civil rights. It is with these that the Commission, by virtue of its statutory directive, has been principally concerned. Among the major civil rights problems discussed in the report that follows are these:

In some 100 counties in eight Southern States there is reason to believe that Negro citizens are prevented—by outright discrimination or by fear of physical violence or economic reprisal—from exercising the right to vote.

There are many places throughout the country where, though citizens may vote freely, their votes are seriously diluted by unequal electoral districting, or malapportionment.

There are many counties in the South where a substantial Negro population not only has no voice in government, but suffers extensive deprivation—legal, economic, educational, and social.

There are still some places in the Nation where the fear of racial violence clouds the atmosphere. There is reason to hope that the worst form of such violence—lynching—has disappeared; no incidents have occurred during the last two years. Still, mob violence has erupted several times in response to the campaign for recognition of Negro rights—in Jacksonville, Fla., and New Orleans, La.; in Anniston, Montgomery, and Birmingham, Ala.; in Chicago, Ill.

Unlawful violence by the police remains in 1961 not a regional but a national shame.

In public education there still are three States—Alabama, Mississippi, and South Carolina—where not one public school or college conforms with the constitutional requirements enumerated by the Supreme Court seven years ago. In May 1961, 2,062 of the 2,837 biracial school districts in the seventeen Southern and border States remained totally segregated.

Perhaps even more serious is the threat posed by a new southern strategy of avoiding the full impact of constitutional commands by withdrawing the State from public education.

One Southern State, Louisiana, not only set itself in defiance of constitutional requirements in public education, but attempted to "interpose" its authority against the Federal Constitution, and obstruct the processes of the National Government. Its legislature passed no fewer than fifty-six laws for these purposes—twenty-five of which were struck down quickly by the Federal courts. Other Louisiana laws, all part of a "segregation package" were intended to diminish Negro voting; to inhibit protest demonstrations; to deprive thousands of children, mainly Negro, of welfare assistance.

A Federal court decision in 1961 brought to the Nation's attention the fact that unconstitutional inequality in public education is not confined to Southern States. Such inequalities in public educational systems seem to exist in many cities throughout the Nation.

Unemployment in the recent recession, hitting Negroes more than twice as hard as others, underlined the fact that they are by and large confined to the least skilled, worst paid, most insecure occupations; that they are most vulnerable to cyclical and structural unemployment and least prepared to share in, or contribute to, the economic progress of the Nation.

Although racial segregation in the Armed Forces of the United States officially ended six years ago, it continues in some parts of the Reserves and the National Guard.

Much of the housing market remains closed in 1961 to millions of Americans because of their race, their religion, or their ancestry; and partly in consequence millions are confined to substandard housing in slums.

In spite of repeated commitments to the principle that benefits created by the funds of all the people shall be available to all without regard to race, religion, or national ancestry, the Federal Government continues in some programs to give indirect support to discriminatory practices in higher education, in training programs, in employment agencies and opportunities, in public facilities such as libraries, and in housing.

THE RIGHT TO VOTE

An essential feature of our form of government is the right of the citizen to participate in the governmental process. The political philosophy of the Declaration of Independence is that governments derive their just powers from the consent of the governed; and the right to a voice in the selection of officers of government on the part of all citizens is important, not only as a means of insuring that government shall have the strength of popular support, but also as a means of securing to the individual citizen proper consideration of his rights by those in power.

The freedom of a democratic system is not that its people are free of law, but that they are free to make and enforce their own law through elected representatives. It follows that freedom to vote is the cornerstone of democracy.

One of the glories of America has been the constant expansion of the suffrage. As the Commission pointed out in its *1959 Report,* this evolutionary experience marks an effort to achieve something very close to government by all the people. Yet the Commission also pointed out in 1959 that "many Americans . . . are denied the franchise because of race. . . . There exists here a striking gap between our principles and our everyday practices." Today, two years later, this gap has not been closed.

Virtually no one publicly defends racial discrimination at the polls. The Supreme Court has held it unconstitutional. Congress has outlawed it. Yet it persists. In some States there is an effort to restrict Negro suffrage.

If "the disfranchised can never speak with the same force as those who are able to vote," it follows that they are apt to suffer in other ways. The Commission's studies indicate that this is in fact the case; deprivations of the right to vote tend to go hand in hand with other deprivations. Indeed this is tacitly recognized by many organizations that oppose the Supreme Court's school desegregation decisions — for an important thrust of their effort has been to restrict Negro suffrage. It may not necessarily follow that freedom to vote automatically assures full enjoyment of all other rights, but it is clearly a helpful tool for securing them. As a Negro witness put it at the Commission's Louisiana hearing: "So, you see, we have nobody to represent us, on the jury, school board office, the State legislature, nowhere. All the laws are being passed we have no voice in, whether it is for us or against us, and I don't think you can find many that is for us." . . .

In the election of candidates for State and local offices the suffrage may be conferred or withheld by each State according to its own standards, but even in such elections, States are not wholly unrestricted. Two provisions of the Constitution, the Fifteenth and Nineteenth Amendments, explicitly apply to the States as well as to the Federal Government — to say nothing of the Fourteenth Amendment which forbids discrimination by the States. Therefore, in the making and administration of suffrage qualifications for State and local, as well as

Federal elections, no State may discriminate upon grounds of race, color, or previous condition of servitude, nor upon grounds of sex. Thus it is sometimes said, that, if otherwise qualified, one has a right not to be discriminated against by reason of race or sex.

With respect to the election of candidates for the Congress—both the House of Representatives and the Senate—the Constitution leaves to the States the decision as to who may vote, but no State may prescribe qualifications for electors of Members of Congress different from those it prescribes for electors of the most numerous branch of its own legislature. Of course, neither the States nor the Federal Government can discriminate against Negroes who are otherwise qualified to vote for Members of Congress. Furthermore, although the basic power to fix qualifications for the electors of Senators and Congressmen is left to the States (as is the actual conduct of elections), the Constitution gives the Congress a paramount power to regulate "the times, places, and manner of holding elections for Senators and Representatives."

The significance of the distinction between the vote in State and local elections and the vote in congressional elections lies not in whether the voter is subject to racial discrimination—the Fifteenth Amendment prohibits such discrimination in all elections—but in the scope of Federal protective power. The provisions of the Fifteenth Amendment, pursuant to which the Congress may legislate and courts may intervene to prevent exclusions from State and local elections or racial grounds, are cast in the form of limitations upon governmental action. The purely private acts of individuals therefore are beyond the reach of this amendment and legislation enacted pursuant thereto. On the other hand, private individuals (as well as persons clothed with governmental authority) who act to deprive *anyone* of the right to vote for Members of the Congress, are amenable to Federal legislative authority by virtue of the "times, places, and manner" and "necessary and proper" clauses of the Constitution.

In the election of candidates for the offices of President and Vice President, still another situation prevails. First, although popular election of the Executives has long been the practice in every State, no election at all is required. For the Constitution provides that: "Each State shall appoint, in such manner as the legislature thereof may direct, a number of electors . . . ," and the term "appoint" here is used as "conveying the broadest power of determination." Hence, although such a course at the present time seems politically improbable, popular election of Executives could be eliminated by State legislation. As a matter of history, electors for the Executives have at one time or another been chosen by State legislatures without popular votes in at least sixteen States. But, although popular elections of the Executive could be wholly eliminated by State legislation, it seems clear that however electors are "appointed," all Federal constitutional and legislative safeguards apply. Thus, assuming popular elections, the vote for Federal Executive officers may not be denied or abridged on grounds of race, color, or sex by action of either private persons or persons clothed with governmental authority.

If, then, the Federal law grants no absolute right to vote, it does give an immunity, or freedom, from voting restraints based on race. And this immunity is applicable to the whole electoral process including primaries, with respect to all public officials whether local, State, or national.

Such, then, is the nature of the "right" to vote with which the Commission is here concerned. Its importance cannot be overemphasized. Its impairment is inconsistent with our democratic system. Its protection by legislative, executive, and judicial action at all levels of government must be a matter of prime concern to every American.

FEDERAL LEGISLATION

On March 30, 1870, the Fifteenth Amendment was officially declared in effect. It provides: "The right of citizens of the United States to vote shall not be denied or abridged by the United States or by any State on account of race, color, or previous condition of servitude."

Shortly thereafter Congress passed a law embodying that amendment's command: "All citizens of the

United States who are otherwise qualified by law to vote at any election by the people in any State, Territory, district, county, city, parish, township, school district, municipality, or other territorial subdivision shall be entitled and allowed to vote at all such elections, without distinction of race, color, or previous condition of servitude; any constitution, law, custom, usage, or regulation of any State or Territory, or by or under its authority, to the contrary notwithstanding."

While the Supreme Court has long since struck down much Reconstruction legislation as unconstitutional, this provision survives as section 1971(a) of title 42 of the United States Code, a cornerstone of Federal legislation to protect the right to vote.

But this section merely declared a right. It provided no legal remedy. And other relevant Reconstruction legislation has proved difficult to apply, or depends on private initiative. Until the passage of the Civil Rights Act of 1957, therefore, the Federal Government could do little to combat discriminatory denials of the right to vote. The 1957 act, and its successor act in 1960, opened the way to more direct and effective Federal action to protect the fundamental right of participation in government.

For 70 years, the Federal Government relied almost solely on two sections of the U.S. Criminal Code to prevent discrimination in voting. Both were Reconstruction measures.

Section 241 of the U.S. Criminal Code penalizes conspiracies to "injure, oppress, threaten, or intimidate any citizen in the free exercise or enjoyment of any right . . . secured . . . by the Constitution or laws of the United States. . . ." This provision applies to actions by either State officials or private persons that interfere with voting in Federal elections, and apparently to discrimination by State officials in State and local elections as well. The other criminal provision, now section 242 of the United States Code, prohibits action "under color of law"— i.e., by State officials or persons acting in concert with them which interferes with "rights . . . secured or protected by the Constitution or laws of the United States," including the right not to be discriminated against on grounds of race or color.

Section 241 was involved in the 1884 case of *Ex parte Yarbrough* where the Supreme Court declared that the right to vote in Federal elections arose from the Federal Constitution, and was therefore subject to protection by Federal legislation. This was true, said the Court, despite the fact that State laws prescribe the qualifications of electors. Both sections were involved in *United States* v. *Classic,* in 1941, where the Supreme Court first held that the guarantees of the Constitution cover primary as well as general elections.

In 1939 Congress enacted, as part of the Hatch Act, another criminal provision, protecting the right to vote: This provision sets penalties for whoever intimidates, threatens, coerces, or attempts to intimidate, threaten, or coerce, any other person for the purpose of interfering with the right of such other person to vote. This provision is clearly broad enough to include discrimination on grounds of race, but by its terms is applicable only to Federal elections. It does not appear to have been used.

Before 1957, in addition to these criminal remedies, three provisions of Federal law laid a basis for civil suits for injunction or damages regarding discriminatory denials of the right to vote. One (now sec. 1971(a) of title 42), quoted above, condemned racial discrimination in both State and Federal elections. While this did not in itself provide for civil actions, two other sections did—sections 1983 and 1985 of title 42 of the United States Code. Section 1983 (much like sec. 242 of the Criminal Code) allows suits against persons acting "under color of any statute, ordinance, regulation, custom or usage," to deprive citizens of rights secured by the Constitution and laws of the United States. The injured party can sue for injunctive relief or damages. This section, together with section 1971(a), which declared the right to be free of discrimination, was involved in a number of landmark cases—among others, *Nixon* v. *Herndon, Smith* v. *Allwright,* and *Rice* v. *Elmore,* which defined the right to be free of racial discrimination in primary, as well as general elections. The other pertinent provision of the Federal statutes, section 1985, authorizes actions for damages (but not injunctions) against private persons (as well as those acting under color of law) who conspire to prevent another from voting in a Federal election. Section 1985, which, unlike section 1983, does not apply to State elections, has been little used.

These provisions set the framework for a series of important cases expanding and defining the Federal right to vote—but they were weak. Most of these cases were civil, not criminal. The Federal Government was empowered only to bring criminal cases, and the criminal statutes were unwieldy and difficult to apply. Civil cases, with their flexible remedies and relative ease of proof, could be brought only by private persons, who are not always able to bear the expense and difficulty involved in long and complicated litigation. . . .

THE CIVIL RIGHTS ACT OF 1957

By the Civil Rights Act of 1957, Congress wrought a major change. It authorized the Federal Government to bring civil actions for injunctive relief where discrimination denied or threatened the right to vote. This was done by adding a new subsection (c) to section 1971 (quoted above), giving the Attorney General power to institute civil suits when the rights declared in that section were in jeopardy. The 1957 act added another provision, subsection (b) to the statute, forbidding intimidation, threats, and coercion for the purpose of interfering with the right to vote in Federal elections. Subsection (b) is similar to the criminal provision of the Hatch Act, except that it explicitly mentions primary, as well as general elections, and provides a basis for civil suits by both private persons and the Attorney General to seek civil relief.

Other provisions of the 1957 act gave the Federal district courts jurisdiction of such civil proceedings without a requirement that State administrative or other remedies first be exhausted; provided for contempt proceedings in the event of disobedience of court orders under the section; and, by authorizing the appointment of an additional Assistant Attorney General, led to raising the Department of Justice's Civil Rights Section to the status of a full division. The 1957 act also created this Commission.

Two years after the passage of the 1957 Civil Rights Act, when this Commission issued its first report in September of 1959, the results of the act in the field of voting seemed disappointing. The Commission noted that discriminatory denials of the vote were serious and widespread. The Civil Rights Division had instituted only three actions under the new section 1971(c), and none had yet been successful. In one case, because the registrars against whom the suit was brought had previously resigned from office, a court had held that there was no one the Federal Government could sue. In another case the district court had held the 1957 act unconstitutional, and the Supreme Court had not yet settled this question.

As a result the Commission made several recommendations for strengthening the Federal laws intended to deal with discrimination in the electoral process: that Federal law should place an affirmative duty on registrars to perform their duties; that a Federal law require that State registration and voting records be preserved for a period of five years and that these records be subject to public inspection—this recommendation was based on the Commission's finding that "lack of uniform provision for the preservation and public inspection of all records pertaining to registration and voting hampers and impedes investigation of alleged denials of the right to vote. . . ."; and that provisions be made for the appointment of Federal officers to replace State and local registration officials when the latter were shown to be acting in a discriminatory fashion.

The Civil Rights Act of 1960 reflected in part all three of these recommendations as well as the Commission's findings which supported them.

THE CIVIL RIGHTS ACT OF 1960

The 1960 act took care of the problem of resigning registrars which had hampered the application of the 1957 act. This was done not by imposing an affirmative duty on the registrars, as the Commission had recommended, but by amending the 1957 law to provide that in suits brought under section 1971 (a) and (c), "the act or practice shall also be deemed that of the State and the State may be joined as a party defendant and, if, prior to the institution of such proceeding, such official has resigned or has been relieved of his office and no successor has assumed such office, the proceeding may be instituted against the State."

Another provision of the 1960 act, Title III, declared voting records public and required their preservation for a period of twenty-two months following any general or special election. (The Commission had recommended a five-year preservation period.) The most significant feature of this "records-demand" law is that the Attorney General may secure such records upon request for "inspection, reproduction and copying. . . ." Unlike ordinary judicial discovery procedures, Title III gives the Attorney General access to records before a suit has been filed. Thus it may help him to decide which cases warrant prosecution, and also to gather evidence for suits that are ultimately filed.

The most significant provision of the 1960 act, however, appears to lie in Title VI, providing for Federal voting referees. Like the Commission's registrar proposal, the voting referee provision of the 1960 act was designed to relieve all citizens in the area affected from discriminatory denials of the right to vote. To this end, both of the remedies called for temporary replacement of local registration officials by Federal officers whose duty it would be to place registration and voting upon a nondiscriminatory basis in the area where such discrimination had been common practice. The Commission recommended that such officers be appointed by the executive; the Administration preferred a judicial rather than an administrative approach. The latter view prevailed.

Title VI is a significant legislative breakthrough, but it is a long way from providing equal access to the ballot. The machinery for appointing a Federal referee is formidable. It consists of four steps:

First, the Government has to file a suit under section 1971 (a) and (c) and obtain a court finding that a "person has been deprived on account of race or color" of the right to vote.

Second, the court must find that "such deprivation was or is pursuant to a pattern or practice."

Third, for at least a year after such a finding, any person in the area of the race found to be discriminated against may apply for an order declaring him qualified to vote. To get such an order he must prove: "(1) he is qualified under State law to vote, and (2) he has since such finding by the court been (a) deprived of or denied under color of law the opportunity to register to vote or otherwise to qualify to vote, or (b) found not qualified to vote by any person acting under color of law."

Fourth, the court may hear the applicants itself, or it may, at its discretion, appoint referees from among qualified voters in the district to rule on the applications. Such referees have "all the powers conferred upon a master by rule 53(c) of the Federal Rules of Civil Procedure."

At the hearing (which must be held within ten days of application) the referee or the court accepts the applicant's statement under oath as to age, residence, and prior efforts to register. If State law requires a literacy test, the referee or court administers it. The referee, if one is appointed, then reports his determination to the court and the court requires the U.S. Attorney General to send a copy of his report to the State attorney general and any other party to the suit. Since the referee (or the court, if no referee has been appointed) has been in effect applying the State's voter qualification laws, this allows the State the opportunity to show that the applicant is in fact not qualified.

If the State does file an exception to the order, it must support its objection with public records or sworn documents, or memoranda of law. This provision militates against willful delay. The exceptions may be determined by the court, or "if the due and speedy administration of justice requires, they may be referred to the voting referee to determine in accordance with procedure prescribed by the court." After the issues thus raised have been resolved (or ten days after the State was notified of the referee's report, if no exceptions were filed), the court issues an order declaring, if appropriate, that certain named persons are qualified and entitled to vote. This order is transmitted to "the appropriate election officers," who are thus drawn within the court's power to punish for contempt if they disregard the order. Also, "the court, or at its discretion the voting referee, shall issue to each applicant so declared qualified a certificate identifying the holder thereof as a person so qualified."

Title VI also allows for provisional voting where applications for orders are not determined by election day, but if an application is filed less than twenty days before an election, the court has discretion to grant or deny provisional voting.

Title VI, then, does not become a weapon against discriminatory denials of the vote until a suit filed in the "affected area" has resulted in a finding that such discrimination has actually occurred, and a further finding that such discrimination "was or is pursuant to a pattern or practice." After a finding of a pattern or practice has been entered, the court may itself receive applications for orders to qualify voters or it may appoint a referee to do so. The court also retains, however, the discretion to employ whatever additional remedy lies within its power as a court of equity. "This subsection shall in no way be construed as a limitation upon the existing powers of the court."

These are the principal tools now available to the Federal Government in protecting the right to vote against discrimination on grounds of race: Section 1971(a), prohibiting discrimination in all elections; 1971(b), prohibiting threats, intimidation, and coercion in connection with Federal elections; 1971(c), authorizing suits by the United States in connection with (a) or (b), and providing as well the voting referee machinery; and Title III of the 1960 act, requiring the preservation of voting records and allowing the Attorney General to inspect them.

CONCLUSIONS

The right to vote without distinctions of race or color—the promise of the Fifteenth Amendment—continues to suffer abridgment. Investigations, hearings, and studies conducted by the Commission since its *1959 Report* indicate, however, that discriminatory disfranchisement is confined to certain parts of the country—indeed that it does not exist in forty-two States. But in about 100 counties in Ala-

bama, Florida, Georgia, Louisiana, Mississippi, North Carolina, South Carolina, and Tennessee, there has been evidence, in varying degree, of discriminatory disfranchisement.

Efforts to deny the right to vote take many forms: economic reprisals as in Fayette and Haywood Counties, Tenn.; discriminatory purges of Negroes from the registration rolls as in Washington, Ouachita, and Bienville Parishes, La.; and restrictive voter qualification laws as in Mississippi and Louisiana. The most prevalent form of discrimination, however, occurs in arbitrary registration procedures. On this the Commission's Louisiana hearing produced detailed testimony and documentation.

The hearing showed that Negroes in eleven Louisiana parishes have encountered a variety of procedural obstacles to registration: a requirement, not equally applied to whites, that they fill out their application forms with unusual precision; that they secure registered voters to vouch for their identity (a difficult requirement in parishes where few or no Negroes are registered to vote); that they give a "reasonable" interpretation of a provision of the Constitution; that they defer to white persons who want to register ahead of them; that they submit to exasperating delays. It can be said, in general, that Negroes exercise their right to vote at the discretion of registrars.

Commission studies indicate that many other pressures have been brought to bear against Negro electors in Louisiana—by citizens councils and by the State legislature itself. The latter, acting through agencies like the Joint Legislative Committee, has actively encouraged registration officials to discriminate against Negro applicants. More directly it has sponsored an amendment to the State constitution and enacted a number of statutes—a "segregation law package"—plainly designed to encourage further discriminatory disfranchisement.

Despite this, certain trends are encouraging. It should not be forgotten that systematic disfranchisement is a problem in only eight of fifty States; and that after seventy years of no civil rights legislation, Congress passed the Civil Rights Act of 1957 and 1960. Before these acts the only possibility of Federal court remedy was under Reconstruction legislation, which was clear as to rights, but inadequate as to remedies.

The Civil Rights Act of 1957, which elevated the Civil Rights Section in the Department of Justice to a Division, and created this Commission, gave the Federal Government power to bring civil actions for injunctive relief where discrimination denied or threatened the right to vote. After extended litigation concerning the constitutionality of the Civil Rights Act of 1957, the Federal Government has secured injunctions against discriminatory registration practices in Terrell County, Ga., and Macon County, Ala. It obtained a court order restoring 1,377 Negroes to the registration rolls in Washington Parish, La. In addition, it has tried suits in Bienville Parish, La., and Bullock County, Ala.; these are awaiting decision. Other voting suits have been filed in East Carroll and Ouachita Parishes, La.; Dallas and Montgomery Counties, Ala.; and Forrest, Clarke, Walthall, and Jefferson Davis Counties, Miss.

Under provisions of the 1957 act prohibiting threats, intimidation, and coercion of voters in Federal elections, the Government brought suits to end economic boycotts against Negro voters in Fayette and Haywood Counties, Tenn., and East Carroll Parish, La. It obtained temporary injunctions in the Tennessee suits and stipulated an agreement in the East Carroll suit.

The Civil Rights Act of 1960 strengthened the 1957 act. It provided that States, as well as registrars, may be sued for discriminatory voting practices. Under Title III, the 1960 act required the preservation of voting records, and empowered the U.S. Attorney General to inspect them. Also, title VI of this act introduced for the first time the possibility of Federal voting referees to see that persons who have been improperly disfranchised are in fact registered, where a court finds a "pattern or practice" of discrimination. In fact, only one court has found such a "pattern or practice," and in that case chose not to appoint referees. But ever since the enactment of the referee provision, the Government has succeeded in obtaining broad and detailed

decrees—decrees which, assuming continuing court surveillance over compliance, may well be as effective as the voting referees themselves. Under the records-inspection provision of the 1960 act the Federal Government has made demand for the inspection and copying of registration records in twenty-six southern counties. Suits necessitated by refusals ended in favor of the Government, and since their disposition it has obtained voluntary compliance with demands for records in eighteen of the twenty-six counties involved.

Thus the new Federal laws concerned with discriminatory denials of the right to vote have been vigorously and effectively invoked. But litigation is necessarily a long, hard, and expensive process, affecting one county at a time; and much remains to be done before the right to vote is secure against discrimination in every part of the Nation.

Statistics showing registration and voting by race are valuable adjuncts of any study of discrimination in the suffrage. Unfortunately, they are not available for every State and county. Such data as are available show significant variations in Negro registration. In at least 129 counties in ten Southern States where Negroes constitute more than 5 percent of the voting-age population, less than 10 percent of those ostensibly eligible are in fact registered. In twenty-three counties in five of these States, no Negroes are registered, although similarly populated counties in each of these same States have large Negro registration. Statistics also show that in all but the border States of Delaware, Maryland, and West Virginia, there appears to be an inverse correlation between concentration of Negro population and Negro registration. Such figures often suggest racial discrimination, though they are only a starting, not a concluding point in any study of deprivations of the right to vote. (The succeeding part of this report analyzes in depth the status of civil rights in a group of counties where statistics suggest discrimination in the franchise.)

Connected with racial discrimination, but also raising constitutional questions of their own, are the related problems of gerrymander and malapportionment. Efforts by the State of Alabama to gerrymander Negro voters out of Tuskegee, Ala., were struck down by the Supreme Court as violating the Fifteenth Amendment. Malapportionment, or unequal distribution of voters among electoral districts, is nationwide, diluting the votes of millions of citizens. Disfranchisement on racial grounds in some areas exaggerates the inequalities produced by malapportionment, and each inequity makes the other more difficult of solution.

So in 1961 the franchise is denied entirely to some because of race and diluted for many others. The promise of the Constitution is not yet fulfilled. ■

From Voting: 1961 Commission on Civil Rights
Report *(U.S. Government Printing Office).*

PART VIII

MIRROR
FOR AMERICANS

A special self-consciousness has been one of the characteristics of American civilization. Quite early in their history Americans began to view themselves as somehow different from their British, or other European, progenitors. The difference could be found in their general behavior as well as viewpoint. "The American," wrote de Crèvecoeur, one of the early analysts of the American scene, "is a new man, who acts on new principles."

The American self-image, a product of the wide spaces and generous resources of the New World, has been a compound of optimism and universalism. Despite touches of naïveté and even of arrogance, the American self-view has, nevertheless, been rooted in a genuine belief in the goodness of life and the possibilities of human progress.

George Washington, upon being inaugurated first President of what was then a weak and backward country of only about 3,000,000 people, made the astonishing claim that the "sacred fire of liberty" and of republicanism were "staked" on the

American experiment in self government. Walt Whitman sang triumphantly that the "American programme" was not merely for the United States, but "for universal man." Woodrow Wilson made it universally known that the mission of the United States was to "make the world safe for democracy." Franklin D. Roosevelt proclaimed the Four Freedoms as applicable "everywhere in the world."

The American self-image has continued to be what it has been for a long time, a vital element in the country's sense of mission and of destiny.

1

THE AMERICAN SELF-IMAGE

Benjamin Franklin
J. Hector St. John de Crèvecoeur
George Washington
James Monroe
William Henry Harrison
Walt Whitman
Abraham Lincoln
Ralph Waldo Emerson
Woodrow Wilson
Franklin D. Roosevelt
Harold L. Ickes
Wendell L. Willkie
Lyndon B. Johnson

• BENJAMIN FRANKLIN

Many Persons in Europe, having directly or by Letters, express'd to the Writer of this, who is well acquainted with North America, their Desire of transporting and establishing themselves in that Country; but who appear to have formed, thro' Ignorance, mistaken Ideas and Expectations of what is to be obtained there; he thinks it may be useful, and prevent inconvenient, expensive, and fruitless Removals and Voyages of improper Persons, if he gives some clearer and truer Notions of that part of the World, than appear to have hitherto prevailed.

He finds it is imagined by Numbers, that the Inhabitants of North America are rich, capable of rewarding, and dispos'd to reward, all sorts of Ingenuity; that they are at the same time ignorant of all the Sciences, and, consequently, that Strangers, possessing Talents in the Belles-Lettres, fine Arts, etc., must be highly esteemed, and so well paid, as to become easily rich themselves; that there are also abundance of profitable Offices to be disposed of, which the Natives are not qualified to fill; and that, having few Persons of Family among them, Strangers of Birth must be greatly respected, and of course easily obtain the best of those Offices, which will make all their Fortunes; that the Governments too, to encourage Emigrations from Europe, not only pay the Expence of personal Transportation, but give Lands gratis to Strangers, with Negroes to work for them, Utensils of Husbandry, and Stocks of Cattle. These are all wild Imaginations; and those who go to America with Expectations founded upon them will surely find themselves disappointed.

The Truth is, that though there are in that Country few People so miserable as the poor of Europe, there are also very few that in Europe would be called rich; it is rather a general happy Mediocrity that prevails. There are few great Proprietors of the Soil, and few Tenants; most People cultivate their own Lands, or follow some Handicraft or Merchandise; very few are rich enough to live idly upon their Rents or Incomes, or to pay the high Prices given in Europe for Paintings, Statues, Architecture, and the other Works of Art, that are more curious than useful. Hence the natural Geniuses, that have arisen in America with such Talents, have uniformly quitted that Country for Europe, where they can be more suitably rewarded. It is true, that Letters and Mathematical Knowledge are in Esteem there, but they are at the same time more common than is apprehended; there being already existing nine Colleges or Universities . . . all furnish'd with learned Professors; besides a number of smaller Academies; these educate many of their Youth in the Languages, and those Sciences that qualify men for the Professions of Divinity, Law, or Physick. Strangers indeed are by no means excluded from exercising those Professions; and the quick Increase of Inhabitants everywhere gives them a Chance of Employ, which they have in common with the Natives. Of civil Offices, or Employments, there are few; no superfluous Ones, as in Europe; and it is a Rule establish'd in some of the States, that no Office should be so profitable as to make it desirable.

These Ideas prevailing more or less in all the United States, it cannot be worth any Man's while, who has a means of Living at home, to expatriate himself, in hopes of obtaining a profitable civil Office in America; and, as to military Offices, they are at an End with the War, the Armies being disbanded. Much less is it advisable for a Person to go thither, who has no other Quality to recommend him but his Birth. In Europe it has indeed its Value; but it is a Commodity that cannot be carried to a worse Market than that of America, where people do not inquire concerning a Stranger, *What is he?* but, *What can he do?* If he has any useful Art, he is welcome; and if he exercises it, and behaves well, he will be respected by all that know him; but a mere Man of Quality, who, on that Account, wants to live upon the Public, by some Office or Salary, will be despis'd and disregarded. The Husbandman is in honor there, and even the Mechanic, because their Employments are useful. The People have a saying, that God Almighty is himself a Mechanic, the greatest in the Universe; and he is respected and admired more for the Variety, Ingenuity, and Utility of his Handyworks, than for the Antiquity of his Family. . . .

With regard to Encouragements for Strangers from Government, they are really only what are derived from good Laws and Liberty. Strangers are welcome, because there is room enough for them all, and therefore the old Inhabitants are not jealous of them; the Laws protect them sufficiently, so that they have no need of the Patronage of the Great Men; and everyone will enjoy securely the Profits of his Industry. But if he does not bring a Fortune with him, he must work and be industrious to live. One or two Years' residence gives him all the Rights of a Citizen . . . In short, America is the Land of Labour, and by no means what the English call *Lubberland,* and the French *Pays de Cocagne,* where the streets are said to be pav'd with half-peck Loaves, the Houses til'd with Pancakes, and where the Fowls fly about ready roasted, crying, *Come eat me!* ■
From "Information to Those Who Would Remove to America," 1782.

• J. HECTOR ST. JOHN DE CRÈVECOEUR

It [America] is not composed, as in Europe, of great lords who possess everything, and of a herd of people who have nothing. Here are no aristocratical families, no courts, no kings, no bishops, no ecclesiastical dominion, no invisible power giving to a few a very visible one, no great manufacturers employing thousands, no great refinements of luxury. The rich and the poor are not so far removed from each other as they are in Europe. Some few towns excepted, we are all tillers of the earth, from Nova Scotia to West Florida. We are a people of cultivators, scattered over an immense territory, communicating with each other by means of good roads and navigable rivers, united by the silken bands of mild government, all respecting the laws, without dreading their power, because they are equitable. We are all animated with the spirit of an industry which is unfettered and unrestrained, because each person works for himself. If he travels through our rural districts, he views not the hostile castle and the haughty mansion contrasted with the clay-built hut and the miserable cabin, where cattle and men help to keep each other warm, and dwell in meanness, smoke, and indigence. A pleasing uniformity of decent competence appears throughout our habitations. The meanest of our loghouses is a dry and comfortable habitation. Lawyer or merchant are the fairest titles our towns afford: that of a farmer is the only appellation of the rural inhabitants of our country . . . There, on a Sunday, he [the traveller] sees a congregation of respectable farmers and their wives, all clad in neat homespun, well mounted, or riding in their own humble wagons. There is not among them an esquire, saving the unlettered magistrate. There he sees a parson as simple as his flock, a farmer who does not riot on the labor of others. We have no princes, for whom we toil, starve, and bleed. We are the most perfect society now existing in the world. Here man is free as he ought to be; nor is this pleasing equality so transitory as many others are. Many ages will not see the shores of our great lakes replenished with inland nations, nor the unknown bounds of North America entirely peopled. Who can tell how far it extends? Who can tell the millions of men whom it will feed and contain? For no European foot has, as yet, travelled half the extent of this mighty continent.

The next wish of this traveller will be, to know whence came all these people? They are a mixture of English, Scotch, Irish, French, Dutch, Germans, and Swedes. From this promiscuous breed, that race, now called Americans, have risen. The Eastern provinces must indeed be excepted as being the unmixed descendants of Englishmen. I have heard many wish that they had been more intermixed also. . . .

In this great American asylum, the poor of Europe have by some means met together, and in consequence of various causes. To what purpose should they ask one another what countrymen they are? Alas, two-thirds of them had no country. Can a wretch, who wanders about, who works and starves, whose life is a continual scene of sore affliction or pinching penury; can that man call England or any other kingdom his country? A country that had no bread for him; whose fields procured him no har-vest; who met with nothing but the frowns of the rich, the severity of the laws, with jails and punishments: who owned not a single foot of the extensive surface of this planet? No! Urged by a variety of motives here they came. Everything has tended to regenerate them. New laws, a new mode of living, a new social system. Here they are become men. In Europe they were as so many useless plants, wanting vegetative mould and refreshing showers. They withered, and were mowed down by want, hunger, and war; but now, by the power of transplantation, like all other plants, they have taken root and flourished! Formerly they were not numbered in any civil lists of their country, except in those of the poor: here they rank as citizens. By what invisible power has this surprising metamorphosis been performed? By that of the laws and that of their industry. The laws, the indulgent laws, protect them as they arrive, stamping on them the symbol of adoption: they receive ample rewards for their labors: these accumulated rewards procure them lands: those lands confer on them the title of free men, and to that title every benefit is affixed which men can possibly require. This is the great operation daily performed by our laws. . . .

What then is the American, this new man? He is neither an European, nor the descendant of an European: hence that strange mixture of blood, which you will find in no other country. I could point out to you a family, whose grandfather was an Englishman, whose wife was Dutch, whose son married a French woman, and whose present four sons have now four wives of different nations. He is an American, who, leaving behind him all his ancient prejudices and manners, receives new ones from the new mode of life he has embraced, the new government he obeys, and the new rank he holds. He becomes an American by being received in the broad lap of our great *alma mater.* Here individuals of all nations are melted into a new race of men, whose labors and posterity will one day cause great changes in the world. Americans are the western pilgrims, who are carrying along with them the great mass of arts, sciences, vigor, and industry, which began long since in the East. They will finish the great circle. The Americans were once scattered all over Europe. Here they are incorporated into one of the finest systems of population which has ever appeared, and which will hereafter become distinct by the power of the different climates they inhabit. The American ought therefore to love this country much better than that in which either he or his forefathers were born. Here the rewards of his industry follow, with equal steps, the progress of his labor . . . Here religion demands but little of him; a small voluntary salary to the minister, and gratitude to God: can he refuse these? The American is a new man, who acts on new principles; he must therefore entertain new ideas and form new opinions. ■

From Letters from an American Farmer, *1782.*

• GEORGE WASHINGTON

The foundation of our national policy will be laid in the pure and immutable principles of private morality, and the preeminence of free government . . . I dwell on this prospect with every satisfaction which an ardent love for my country can inspire, since there is no truth more thoroughly established than that there exists in the economy and course of nature an indissoluble union between virtue and happiness; between duty and advantage; between the genuine maxims of an honest and magnanimous policy and the solid rewards of public prosperity and felicity; since we ought to be no less persuaded that the propitious smiles of Heaven can never be expected on a nation that disregards the eternal rules of order and right which Heaven itself has ordained; and since the preservation of the sacred fire of liberty and the destiny of the republican model of government are justly considered, perhaps, as *deeply,* as *finally,* staked on the experiment intrusted to the hands of the American people.[1] ■

From First Inaugural Address, April 30, 1789.

---

[1]Lazare Carnot (French General and President of the Directory) remarked in a speech in the National Assembly, in 1802: "It is not from the character of their government that great republics have lacked stability; it is because, having been born in the breasts of storms, it is always in a state of exaltation that they are established. Only one re-

• JAMES MONROE

From the commencement of our Revolution to the present day almost forty years have elapsed. Through this whole term the Government has been what may emphatically be called self-government. And what has been the effect? To whatever object we turn our attention, whether it relates to our foreign or domestic concerns, we find abundant cause to felicitate ourselves in the excellence of our institutions. . . .

Under this Constitution our commerce has been wisely regulated with foreign nations and between the States; new States have been admitted into our Union; our territory has been enlarged by fair and honorable treaty . . . the States, respectively protected by the National Government under a mild, parental system against foreign dangers, and enjoying within their separate spheres, by a wise partition of power, a just proportion of the sovereignty, have improved their police, extended their settlements, and attained a strength and maturity which are the best proofs of wholesome laws well administered. And if we look to the condition of individuals what a proud spectacle does it exhibit! On whom has oppression fallen in any quarter of our Union? Who has been deprived of any right of person or property? Who restrained from offering his vows in the mode which he prefers to the Divine Author of his being? It is well known that all these blessings have been enjoyed in their fullest extent; and I add with peculiar satisfaction that there has been no example of a capital punishment being inflicted on anyone for the crime of high treason. . . .

Such, then, is the happy Government under which we live—a Government adequate to every purpose for which the social compact is formed; a Government elective in all its branches, under which every citizen may by his merit obtain the highest trust recognized by the Constitution; which contains within it no cause of discord, none to

---

public was the labor of philosophy, organized calmly. That republic, the United States of America, full of wisdom and of strength, exhibits this phenomenon, and each day their prosperity shows an increase which astonishes other nations. Thus it was reserved for the New World to teach the Old that existence is possible and peaceable under the rule of liberty and equality."

put at variance one portion of the community with another; a Government which protects every citizen in the full enjoyment of his rights, and is able to protect the nation against injustice from foreign powers. . . .

In explaining my sentiments on this subject it may be asked, What raised us to the present happy state? . . . The Government has been in the hands of the people. To the people, therefore, and to the faithful and able depositories of their trust is the credit due. Had the people of the United States been educated in different principles, had they been less intelligent, less independent, or less virtuous, can it be believed that we should have maintained the same steady and consistent career or been blessed with the same success? . . . It is only when the people become ignorant and corrupt, when they degenerate into a populace, that they are incapable of exercising the sovereignty. Usurpation is then an easy attainment, and an usurper soon found. The people themselves become the willing instruments of their own debasement and ruin. Let us, then, look to the great cause, and endeavor to preserve it in full force. Let us by all wise and constitutional measures promote intelligence among the people as the best means of preserving our liberties. ■

From First Inaugural Address, March 4, 1817.

• WILLIAM HENRY HARRISON

The broad foundation upon which our Constitution rests being the people . . . it can be assigned to none of the great divisions of government but to that of democracy. If such is its theory, those who are called upon to administer it must recognize as its leading principle the duty of shaping their measures so as to produce the greatest good to the greatest number. But . . . if we would compare the sovereignty acknowledged to exist in the mass of our people with the power claimed by other sovereignties, even by those which have been considered most purely democratic, we shall find a most essential difference. All others lay claim to power limited only by their own will. The majority of our citizens, on the con-

trary, possess a sovereignty with an amount of power precisely equal to that which has been granted to them by the parties to the national compact, and nothing beyond. We admit of no government by divine right, believing that so far as power is concerned the Beneficent Creator has made no distinction amongst men; that all are upon an equality, and that the only legitimate right to govern is an express grant of power from the governed. The Constitution of the United States is the instrument containing this grant of power to the several departments composing the Government. ■

From Inaugural Address, March 4, 1841.

• WALT WHITMAN

America does not repel the past, or what the past has produced under its forms, or amid other politics, or the idea of castes or the old religions—accepts the lessons with calmness . . . is not impatient because the slough still sticks to opinions and manners and literature, while the life which served its requirements has passed into the new life of the new forms—perceives that the corpse is slowly borne from the eating and sleeping rooms of the house—perceives that it waits a little while in the door—that it was fittest for its days—that its action has descended to the stalwart and well-shaped heir who approaches—and that he shall be fittest for his days.

The Americans of all nations at any time upon the earth, have probably the fullest poetical nature. The United States themselves are essentially the greatest poem. In the history of the earth hitherto, the largest and most stirring appear tame and orderly to their ampler largeness and stir. Here at last is something in the doings of man that corresponds with the broadcast doings of the day and night. Here is action untied from strings, necessarily blind to particulars and details, magnificently moving in masses. Here is the hospitality which forever indicates heroes. Here the performance, disdaining the trivial, unapproach'd in the tremendous audacity of its crowds and groupings, and the push of its perspective, spreads with crampless and flowing breadth, and showers its prolific and splendid extravagance. One sees it must indeed own the riches of the summer and winter, and need never be bankrupt while corn grows from the ground, or the orchards drop apples, or the bays contain fish, or men beget children upon women.

Other states indicate themselves in their deputies —but the genius of the United States is not best or most in its executives or legislatures, nor in its ambassadors or authors, or colleges or churches or parlors, nor even in its newspapers or inventors— but always most in the common people, south, north, west, east, in all its States, through all its mighty amplitude. The largeness of the nation, however, were monstrous without a corresponding largeness and generosity of the spirit of the citizen. Not swarming states, nor streets and steamships, nor prosperous business, nor farms, nor capital, nor learning, may suffice for the ideal of man—nor suffice the poet. No reminiscences may suffice either. A live nation can always cut a deep mark, and can have the best authority the cheapest—namely, from its own soul. This is the sum of the profitable uses of individuals or states, and of present action and grandeur, and of the subjects of poets. (As if it were necessary to trot back generation after generation to the eastern records! As if the beauty and sacredness of the demonstrable must fall behind that of the mythical! As if men do not make their mark out of any times! As if the opening of the western continent by discovery, and what has transpired in North and South America, were less than the small theatre of the antique, or the aimless sleep-walking of the middle ages!) The pride of the United States leaves the wealth and finesse of the cities, and all returns of commerce and agriculture, and all the magnitude of geography or shows of exterior victory, to enjoy the sight and realization of full-sized men, or one full-sized man unconquerable and simple. ■

From Preface to the first edition of Leaves of Grass, *1855.*

• WALT WHITMAN

1

By blue Ontario's shore,
As I mused of these warlike days and of
  peace return'd, and the dead that return
  no more,
A Phantom gigantic, superb, with stern
  visage accosted me,
Chant me the poem, it said, *that comes from
  the soul of*
America, chant me the carol of victory,
And strike up the marches of Libertad,
  marches more powerful yet,
And sing me before you go the song of the
  throes of Democracy.
(Democracy, the destin'd conqueror, yet
  treacherous lip-smiles everywhere,
And death and infidelity at every step.)

2

A Nation announcing itself,
I myself make the only growth by which I
  can be appreciated,
I reject none, accept all, then reproduce all
  in my own forms.
A breed whose proof is in time and deeds,
What we are we are, nativity is answer
  enough to objections,
We wield ourselves as a weapon is wielded,
We are powerful and tremendous in our-
  selves,
We are executive in ourselves, we are
  sufficient in the variety of ourselves,
We are the most beautiful to ourselves and
  in ourselves,
We stand self-pois'd in the middle, branch-
  ing thence over the world,
From Missouri, Nebraska, or Kansas, laugh-
  ing attacks to scorn. . . .

5

Ages, precedents, have long been accumu-
  lating undirected materials,
America brings builders, and brings it own styles.

The immortal poets of Asia and Europe have
   done their work and pass'd to other spheres,
A work remains, the work of surpassing all
   they have done.
America, curious toward foreign characters,
   stands by its own at all hazards,
Stands removed, spacious, composite, sound,
   initiates the true use of precedents,
Does not repel them or the past or what
   they have produced under their forms,
Takes the lesson with calmness, perceives
   the corpse slowly borne from the house,
Perceives that it waits a little while in the
   door, that it was fittest for its days,
That its life has descended to the stalwart
   and well-shaped heir who approaches,
And that he shall be fittest for his days.
Any period one nation must lead,
One land must be the promise and reliance
   of the future.
These States are the amplest poem,
Here is not merely a nation but a teeming
   Nation of nations,
Here the doings of men correspond with the
   broadcast doings of the day and night.
Here is what moves in magnificent masses
   careless of particulars,
Here are the roughs, beards, friendliness,
   combativeness, the soul loves,
Here the flowing trains, here the crowds,
   equality, diversity, the soul loves. . . .

8

Others take finish, but the Republic is ever
   constructive and ever keeps vista,
Others adorn the past, but you 0 days of
   the present, I adorn you.
0 days of the future I believe in you—I
   isolate myself for your sake.
0 America because you build for mankind
   I build for you. . . .

9

I listened to the Phantom by Ontario's
   shore,
I heard the voice arising demanding bards,

By them all native and grand, by them alone
   can these States be fused into the compact
   organism of a Nation.
To hold men together by paper and seal or
   by compulsion is no account,
That only holds men together which aggre-
   gates all in a living principle, as the hold
   of the limbs of the body or the fibres of
   plants.
Of all races and eras these States with veins
   full of poetical stuff most needs poets, and
   are to have the greatest, and use them the
   greatest,
Their Presidents shall not be their common
   referee so much as their poets shall. . . .

12

Are you he who would assume a place to
   teach or be a poet here in the States?
The place is august, the terms obdurate.
Who would assume to teach here may well
   prepare himself body and mind,
He may well survey, ponder, arm, fortify,
   harden, make lithe himself,
He shall surely be question'd beforehand by
   me with many and stern questions.
Who are you indeed who would talk or sing
   to America?
Have you studied out the land, its idioms
   and men?
Have you learn'd the physiology, phrenol-
   ogy, politics, geography, pride, freedom,
   friendship of the land? its substratums
   and objects?
Have you consider'd the organic compact
   of the first day of the first year of Independence, sign'd by the Commissioners,
   ratified by the States, and read by Washington at the head of the army?
Have you possess'd yourself of the Federal
   Constitution?
Do you see who have left all feudal processes and poems behind them, and
   assumed the poems and processes of
   Democracy?
Are you faithful to things? do you teach

what the land and sea, the bodies of men,
womanhood, amativeness, heroic angers,
teach? . . .

15

I swear I begin to see the meaning of these
    things,
It is not the earth, it is not America who is
    so great,
It is I who am great or to be great, it is You
    up there, or any one,
It is to walk rapidly through civilisations,
    governments, theories,
Through poems, pageants, shows to form
    individuals.
Underneath all, individuals,
I swear nothing is good to me now that
    ignores individuals,
The American compact is altogether with
    individuals,
The only government is that which makes
    minute of individuals,
The whole theory of the universe is directed
    unerringly to one single individual—
    namely to You. . . .

17

O I see flashing that this America is only
    you and me,
Its power, weapons, testimony, are you and
    me,
Its crimes, lies, thefts, defections, are you
    and me,
Its Congress is you and me, the officers,
    capitols, armies, ships, are you and me.
Its endless gestations of new States are you
    and me,
The war (that war so bloody and grim, the
    war I will henceforth forget), was you
    and me,
Natural and artificial are you and me,
Freedom, language, poems, employments,
    are you and me,
Past, present, future, are you and me.

    From "By Blue Ontario's Shore," 1856.

• ABRAHAM LINCOLN

In their [the Founding Fathers'] enlightened belief nothing stamped with the Divine image and likeness was sent into the world to be trodden on and degraded and imbruted by its fellows. They grasped not only the whole race of man then living, but they reached forward and seized upon the farthest posterity. They erected a beacon to guide their children, and their children's children, and the countless myriads who should inhabit the earth in other ages. Wise statesmen as they were, they knew the tendency of prosperity to breed tyrants, and so they established these great self-evident truths, that when in the distant future some man, some faction, some interest, should set up the doctrine that none but rich men, or none but white men, or none but Anglo-Saxon white men, were entitled to life, liberty and the pursuit of happiness, their posterity might look up again to the Declaration of Independence and take courage to renew the battle which their fathers began, so that truth and justice and mercy and all the humane and Christian virtues might not be extinguished from the land, so that no man would hereafter dare to limit and circumscribe the great principles on which the temple of liberty was being built. ■

    From speech at Lewiston, Ill., August 17, 1858.

• ABRAHAM LINCOLN

This country, with its institutions, belongs to the people who inhabit it. Whenever they shall grow weary of the existing Government, they can exercise their *constitutional* right of amending it or their *revolutionary* right to dismember or overthrow it. I cannot be ignorant of the fact that many worthy and patriotic citizens are desirous of having the National Constitution amended. While I make no recommendation of amendments, I fully recognize the rightful authority of the people over the whole subject, to be exercised in either of the modes prescribed in the instrument itself; and I should, under existing circumstances, favor rather than oppose a fair opportunity being afforded the people to act upon it. I will venture to add that to me the convention mode seems preferable, in that it allows amendments to originate with the people themselves, instead of only permitting them to take or reject propositions originated by others. . . .

The Chief Magistrate derives all his authority from the people, and they have conferred none upon him to fix terms for the separation of the States. The people themselves can do this if also they choose, but the Executive as such has nothing to do with it. His duty is to administer the present Government as it came to his hands and to transmit it unimpaired by him to his successor.

Why should there not be a patient confidence in the ultimate justice of the people? Is there any better or equal hope in the world? In our present differences, is either party without faith of being in the right? If the Almighty Ruler of Nations, with His eternal truth and justice, be on your side of the North, or on yours of the South, that truth and that justice will surely prevail by the judgment of this great tribunal of the American people. ■

From First Inaugural Address, March 4, 1861.

• RALPH WALDO EMERSON

The word of the Lord by night
To the watching Pilgrims came,
As they sat by the seaside,
And filled their hearts with flame.

God said, I am tired of kings,
I suffer them no more;
Up to my ear the morning brings
The outrage of the poor.

Think ye I made this ball
A field of havoc and war,
Where tyrants great and tyrants small
Might harry the weak and poor?

My angel—his name is Freedom—
Choose him to be your king;
He shall cut pathways east and west,
And fend you with his wing.

Lo! I uncover the land
Which I hid of old time in the West,
As the sculptor uncovers the statue
When he has wrought his best;

I show Columbia, of the rocks
Which dip their foot in the seas,
And soar to the air-borne flocks
Of clouds, and the boreal fleece.

I will divide my goods;
Call in the wretch and slave:
None shall rule but the humble,
And none but Toil shall have.

I will have never a noble,
No lineage counted great;
Fishers and choppers and ploughmen
Shall constitute a state.
Go, cut down trees in the forest,
And trim the straightest boughs;
Cut down trees in the forest,
And build me a wooden house.

Call the people together,
The young men and the sires,
The digger in the harvest field,
Hireling, and him that hires;

And here in a pine state-house
They shall choose men to rule
In every needful faculty,
In church, and state, and school.

From "Boston Hymn," read in Music Hall,
Boston, January 1, 1863.

• ABRAHAM LINCOLN

Fourscore and seven years ago our fathers brought forth on this continent a new nation, conceived in liberty, and dedicated to the proposition that all men are created equal.

Now we are engaged in a great civil war, testing whether that nation, or any nation so conceived and so dedicated, can long endure. We are met on a great battlefield of that war. We have come to dedicate a portion of that field as a final resting-place for those who here gave their lives that that nation might live. It is altogether fitting and proper that we should do this.

But in a larger sense, we cannot dedicate—we cannot consecrate—we cannot hallow—this ground. The brave men, living and dead, who struggled here, have consecrated it far above our poor power to add or detract. The world will little note nor long remember what we say here, but it can never forget what they did here. It is for us, the living, rather, to be dedicated here to the unfinished work which they who fought here have thus far so nobly advanced. It is rather for us to be here dedicated to the great task remaining before us—that from these honored dead we take increased devotion to that cause for which they gave the last full measure of devotion; that we here highly resolve that these dead shall not have died in vain; that this nation, under God, shall have a new birth of freedom; and that government of the people, by the people, for the people, shall not perish from the earth.[1] ∎

Address at Gettysburg, Pa.,
November 19, 1863.

• WALT WHITMAN

Their politics the United States have, in my opinion, with all their faults, already substantially establish'd, for good, on their own native, sound, long-vista'd principles, never to be overturn'd, offering a sure basis for all the rest. With that, their future religious forms, sociology, literature, teachers, schools, costumes, etc., are of course to make a compact whole, uniform, on tallying principles. For how can we remain, divided, contradicting ourselves, this way? I say we can only attain harmony and stability by consulting ensemble and the ethic purports, and faithfully building upon them. For the New World,

---

[1]In the Preface of John Wycliffe's English translation of the Bible (1382) it is stated:

"This Bible is for the government of the people, by the people, and for the people." Thomas Cooper, in *Some Information Respecting America* (1795), referred to "Government of the people and for the people."

indeed, after two grand stages of preparation-strata, I perceive that now a third stage, being ready for (and without which the other two were useless), with unmistakable signs appears. The First stage was the planning and putting on record the political foundation rights of immense masses of people —indeed all people—in the organization of republican National, State, and municipal governments, all constructed with reference to each, and each to all. This is the American programme, not for classes, but for universal man, and is embodied in the compacts of the Declaration of Independence, and . . . the Federal Constitution—and in the State governments, with all their interiors, and with general suffrage. . . . The Second stage relates to material prosperity, wealth, produce, labor-saving machines, iron, cotton, local, State and continental railways, intercommunication and trade with all lands, steamships, mining, general employment, organization of great cities, cheap appliances for comfort, numberless technical schools, books, newspapers, a currency for money circulation, etc. The Third stage, rising out of the previous ones, to make them and all illustrious, I, now, for one, promulge, announcing a native expression-spirit, getting into form, adult, and through mentality, for these States, self-contain'd, different from others, more expansive, more rich and free, to be evidenced by original authors and poets to come, by American personalities, plenty of them, male and female, traversing the States, none excepted—and by native superber tableaux and growths of language, songs, operas, orations, lectures, architecture—and by a sublime and serious Religious Democracy sternly taking command, dissolving the old, sloughing off surfaces, and from its own interior and vital principles, reconstructing, democratizing society. ∎

From Democratic Vistas, *1871.*

• WOODROW WILSON

There has been a change of government . . . It means much more than the mere success of a party. The success of a party means little except when the Nation is using that party for a large and definite purpose. No one can mistake the purpose for which the Nation now seeks to use the Democratic Party. . . .

We have built up, moreover, a great system of government, which has stood through a long age as in many respects a model for those who seek to set liberty upon foundations that will endure against fortuitous change, against storm and accident. Our life contains every great thing, and contains it in rich abundance.

But the evil has come with the good, and much fine gold has been corroded. With riches has come inexcusable waste. We have squandered a great part of what we might have used, and have not stopped to conserve the exceeding bounty of nature . . . We have been proud of our industrial achievements, but we have not hitherto stopped thoughtfully enough to count the human cost, the cost of lives snuffed out, of energies overtaxed and broken, the fearful physical and spiritual cost to the men and women and children upon whom the dead weight and burden of it all has fallen pitilessly . . .

At last a vision has been vouchsafed us of our life as a whole. We see the bad with the good, the debased and decadent with the sound and vital. With this vision we approach new affairs. Our duty is to cleanse, to reconsider, to restore, to correct the evil without impairing the good, to purify and humanize every process of our common life . . . There has been something crude and heartless and unfeeling in our haste to succeed and be great. Our thought has been "Let every man look out for himself, let every generation look out for itself," while we reared giant machinery which made it impossible that any but those who stood at the levers of control should have a chance to look out for themselves. . . .

We have come now to the sober second thought. The scales of heedlessness have fallen from our eyes. We have made up our minds to square every process of our national life again with the standards we so proudly set up at the beginning and have always carried at our hearts. Our work is a work of restoration. . . .

Nor have we studied and perfected the means by which government may be put at the service of humanity, in safeguarding the health of the Nation, the health of its men and its women and its children, as well as their rights in the struggle for existence. This is no sentimental duty. The firm basis of government is justice, not pity. These are matters of justice. There can be no equality of opportunity, the first essential of justice in the body politic, if men and women and children be not shielded in their lives, their very vitality, from the consequences of great industrial and social processes which they cannot alter, control, or singly cope with. Society must see to it that it does not itself crush or weaken or damage its own constituent parts. The first duty of law is to keep sound the society it serves. Sanitary laws, pure food laws, and laws determining conditions of labor which individuals are powerless to determine for themselves are intimate parts of the very business of justice and legal efficiency. . . .

This is the high enterprise of the new day: To lift everything that concerns our life as a Nation to the light that shines from the hearthfire of every man's conscience and vision of the right . . . We shall restore, not destroy. We shall deal with our economic system as it is and as it may be modified, not as it might be if we had a clean sheet of paper to write upon; and step by step we shall make it what it should be . . . Justice, and only justice, shall always be our motto. ■

From First Inaugural Address, March 4, 1913.

• FRANKLIN D. ROOSEVELT

When four years ago we met to inaugurate a President, the Republic, single-minded in anxiety, stood in spirit here. We dedicated ourselves to the fulfillment of a vision—to speed the time when there would be for all the people that security and peace essential to the pursuit of happiness. We of the Republic pledged ourselves to drive from the temple of our ancient faith those who had profaned it; to end by action, tireless and unafraid, the stagnation and despair of that day. We did those first things first.

Our covenant with ourselves did not stop there. Instinctively we recognized a deeper need—the need to find through government the instrument of our united purpose to solve for the individual the ever-rising problems of a complex civilization. Repeated attempts at their solution without the aid of government had left us baffled and bewildered. For, without that aid, we had been unable to create those moral controls over the services of science which are necessary to make science a useful servant instead of a ruthless master of mankind. To do this we knew that we must find practical controls over blind economic forces and blindly selfish men.

We of the Republic sensed the truth that democratic government has innate capacity to protect its people against disasters once considered inevitable, to solve problems once considered unsolvable. We would not admit that we could not find a way to master economic epidemics just as, after centuries of fatalistic suffering, we had found a way to master epidemics of disease. We refused to leave the problems of our common welfare to be solved by the winds of chance and the hurricanes of disaster.

In this we Americans were discovering no wholly new truth; we were writing a new chapter in our book of self-government.

This year marks the one hundred and fiftieth anniversary of the Constitutional Convention which made us a nation. At that Convention our forefathers found the way out of the chaos which followed the Revolutionary War; they created a strong government with powers of united action sufficient then and now to solve problems utterly beyond individual or local solution. A century and a half ago they established the Federal Government in order to promote the general welfare and secure the blessings of liberty to the American people.

Today we invoke those same powers of government to achieve the same objectives.

Four years of new experience have not belied our historic instinct. They hold out the clear hope that government within communities, government within the separate States, and government of the United States can do the things the time requires, without yielding its democracy. Our tasks in the last four years did not force democracy to take a holiday.

Nearly all of us recognize that as intricacies of human relationships increase, so power to govern them also must increase—power to stop evil; power to do good. The essential democracy of our Nation and the safety of our people depend not upon the absence of power, but upon lodging it with those whom the people can change or continue at stated intervals through an honest and free system of elections. The Constitution of 1787 did not make our democracy impotent.

In fact, in these last four years, we have made the exercise of all power more democratic; for we have begun to bring private autocratic powers into their proper subordination to the public's government. The legend that they are invincible—above and beyond the processes of a democracy—has been shattered. They have been challenged and beaten. . . .

Among men of good will, science and democracy together offer an ever richer life and ever larger satisfaction to the individual. With this change in our moral climate and our rediscovered ability to improve our economic order, we have set our feet upon the road of enduring progress. . . .

I see a great nation, upon a great continent, blessed with a great wealth of natural resources . . . I see a United States which can demonstrate that, under democratic methods of government, national wealth can be translated into a spreading volume of human comforts hitherto unknown, and the lowest standard of living can be raised far above the level of mere subsistence.

But here is the challenge to our democracy: In this nation I see tens of millions of its citizens—a substantial part of its whole population—who at this very moment are denied the greater part of what the very lowest standards of today call the necessities of life.

I see millions of familes trying to live on incomes so meager that the pall of family disaster hangs over them day by day.

I see millions whose daily lives in city and on farm continue under conditions labeled indecent by a so-called polite society half a century ago.

I see millions denied education, recreation, and the opportunity to better their lot and the lot of their children.

I see millions lacking the means to buy the products of farm and factory and by their poverty denying work and productiveness to many other millions.

I see one-third of a nation ill-housed, ill-clad, ill-nourished.

It is not in despair that I paint you that picture. I paint it for you in hope—because the Nation, seeing and understanding the injustice in it, proposes to paint it out. We are determined to make every American citizen the subject of his country's interest and concern; and we will never regard any faithful law-abiding group within our borders as superfluous. . . .

If I know aught of the spirit and purpose of our Nation, we will not listen to Comfort, Opportunism, and Timidity. We will carry on. . . . ■

From Second Inaugural Address, January 20, 1937.

• HAROLD L. ICKES

What constitutes an American? Not color nor race nor religion. Not the pedigree of his family nor the place of his birth. Not the coincidence of his citizenship. Not his social status nor his bank account. Not his trade nor his profession. An American is one who loves justice and believes in the dignity of man. An American is one who will fight for his freedom and that of his neighbor. An American is one who will sacrifice property, ease and security in order that he and his children may retain the rights of free men. An American is one in whose heart is engraved the immortal second sentence of the Declaration of Independence.

Americans have always known how to fight for their rights and their way of life. Americans are not afraid to fight. They fight joyously in a just cause. ■

From address at "I Am an American Day" rally, New York City, May 18, 1941.

• WENDELL L. WILLKIE

American liberty means, of course, certain governmental processes. It means the right of men to vote in free election for public officials of their own choice, responsive to their will; it means, of course, the right of men to have their differences determined in courts undominated by government and the powerful.

It means, of course, the right of freedom of religion and freedom of speech and freedom from another thing that has come into the world with the cruelty of totalitarianism—the freedom from espionage, the freedom from interference with one's private life and one's daily doings and one's daily habits.

But American liberty means much more than that. American liberty is a religion. It is a thing of the spirit. It is an aspiration on the part of people for not alone a free life but a better life; and so I say to you people of the world . . . the American people will reach out, will give their utmost to see that this precious thing we call liberty shall not disappear from the world, either in Europe or in Asia or in America. ■

From radio address, July 4, 1941.

• LYNDON B. JOHNSON

My fellow countrymen: On this occasion, the oath I have taken before you—and before God—is not mine alone, but ours together. We are one nation and one people. Our fate as a nation and our future as a people rests not upon one citizen but upon all citizens. That is the majesty and the meaning of this moment.

For every generation, there is a destiny. For some, history decides. For this generation, the choice must be our own.

Even now, a rocket moves toward Mars. It reminds us that the world will not be the same for our children, or even ourselves in a short span of years. The next man to stand here will look out on a scene that is different from our own, because ours is a time of change—rapid and fantastic change, baring the secrets of nature, multiplying the nations, placing in uncertain hands new weapons for mastery and destruction, shaking old values and uprooting old ways.

Our destiny in the midst of change will rest on the unchanged character of our people, and on their faith.

They came here—the exile and the stranger, brave but frightened—to find a place where a man could be his own man.

They made a covenant with this land. Conceived in justice, written in liberty, bound in union, it was meant one day to inspire the hopes of all mankind, and it binds us still. If we keep its terms, we shall flourish.

First, justice was the promise that all who made the journey would share in the fruits of the land.

In a land of great wealth, families must not live in hopeless poverty. In a land rich in harvest, children just must not go hungry. In a land of healing miracles, neighbors must not suffer and die untended. In a great land of learning and scholars, young people must be taught to read and write.

For more than thirty years that I have served this nation, I have believed that this injustice to our people—this waste of our resources—was our real enemy. For thirty years or more, with the resources I have had, I have vigilantly fought against it. I have learned, and I know that it will not surrender easily.

But change has given us new weapons. Before this generation of Americans is finished, this enemy will not only retreat—it will be conquered.

Justice requires us to remember—when any citizen denies his fellow, saying, "His color is not mine," or "His beliefs are strange and different"— in that moment he betrays America, though his forebears created this nation.

Liberty was the second article of our covenant. It was self-government. It was our Bill of Rights. But it was more. America would be a place where each man could be proud to be himself—stretching his talents, rejoicing in his work, important in the life of his neighbors and his nation.

This has become more difficult in a world where change and growth seem to tower beyond the control, and even the judgment of men. We must work to provide the knowledge and the surroundings which can enlarge the possibilities of every citizen.

The American covenant called on us to help show the way for the liberation of man. And that is today our goal. Thus, if as a nation there is much outside our control, as a people no stranger is outside our hope.

Change has brought new meaning to that old mission. We can never again stand aside prideful in isolation. Terrific dangers and troubles that we once called "foreign" now constantly live among us. If American lives must end, and American treasure be spilled, in countries that we barely know, then that is the price that change has demanded of conviction and of our enduring covenant.

Think of our world as it looks from that rocket that's heading toward Mars. It is like a child's globe, hanging in space, the continents stuck to its side like colored maps. We are all fellow passengers on a dot of earth. And each of us, in the span of time, has really only a moment among our companions.

How incredible it is that in this fragile existence we should hate and destroy one another. There are possibilities enough for all who will abandon mastery over others to pursue mastery over nature. There is world enough for all to seek their happiness in their own way.

And our nation's course is abundantly clear. We aspire to nothing that belongs to others. We seek no dominion over our fellow man, but man's dominion over tyranny and misery.

But more is required. Men want to be part of a common enterprise—a cause greater than themselves. And each of us must find a way to advance the purpose of the nation, and thus find new purpose for ourselves. Without this, we will simply become a nation of strangers.

The third article is union. To those who were small and few against the wilderness, the success of liberty demanded the strength of the Union. Two centuries of change have made this true again.

No longer need capitalist and worker, farmer and clerk, city and countryside, struggle to divide our bounty. By working shoulder to shoulder together we can increase the bounty of all.

We have discovered that every child who learns, and every man who finds work, and every sick body that's made whole—like a candle added to an altar—brightens the hope of all the faithful.

So let us reject any among us who seek to reopen old wounds and rekindle old hatreds. They stand in the way of a seeking nation.

Let us now join reason to faith, and action to experience, to transform our unity of interest into a unity of purpose. For the hour and the day and the time are here to achieve progress without strife, to achieve change without hatred; not without difference of opinion, but without the deep and abiding divisions which scarred the Union for generations.

Under this covenant of justice, liberty and union, we have become a nation; prosperous, great and mighty. And we have kept our freedom.

But we have no promise from God that our greatness will endure. We have been allowed by Him to seek greatness with the sweat of our hands and the strength of our spirit.

I do not believe that the Great Society is the ordered, changeless and sterile battalion of the ants.

It is the excitement of becoming—always becoming, trying, probing, falling, resting and trying again—but always trying and always gaining.

In each generation—with toil and tears—we have had to earn our heritage again.

If we fail now, then we will have forgotten in abundance what we learned in hardship; that democracy rests on faith, that freedom asks more than it gives and the judgment of God is harshest on those who are most favored.

If we succeed, it will not be because of what we have, but it will be because of what we are; not because of what we own, but rather because of what we believe.

For we are a nation of believers. Underneath the clamor of building and the rush of our day's pursuits, we are believers in justice and liberty and union, and in our own Union. We believe that every man must some day be free. And we believe in ourselves.

And that is the mistake that our enemies have always made. In my lifetime—in depression and in war—they have awaited our defeat. Each time, from the secret places of the American heart, came forth the faith that they could not see or that they could not even imagine. It brought us victory. And it will again.

For this is what America is all about. It is the uncrossed desert and the unclimbed ridge. It is the star that is not reached and the harvest that's sleeping in the unplowed ground.

Is our world gone? We say farewell. Is a new world coming? We welcome it—and we will bend it to the hopes of man.

And to those trusted public servants and to my family and those close friends of mine who have followed me down a long winding road and to all the people of this Union and the world I will repeat today what I said on that sorrowful day in November . . . I will lead and I will do the best I can.

But you—you must look within your own hearts to the old promises and to the old dream. They will lead you best of all.

For myself, I ask only in the words of an ancient leader: "Give me now wisdom and knowledge, that I may go out and come in before these people: for who can judge this thy people, that is so great?" ■

From Inaugural Address, January 20, 1965.

2

CRIES FOR JUSTICE, PEACE, AND FREEDOM

• TECUMSEH

It is TRUE I am a Shawanee. My forefathers were warriors. Their son is a warrior. From them I only take my existence; from my tribe I take nothing. I am the maker of my own fortune; and oh! that I could make that of my red people, and of my country, as great as the conceptions of my mind, when I think of the Spirit that rules the universe. I would not then come to Governor Harrison, to ask him to tear the treaty and to obliterate the landmark; but I would say to him: Sir, you have liberty to return to your own country. The being within, communing with past ages, tells me that once, nor until lately, there was no white man on this continent. That it then all belonged to red men, children of the same parents, placed on it by the Great Spirit that made them, to keep it, to traverse it, to enjoy its productions, and to fill it with the same race. Once a happy race. Since made miserable by the white people, who are never contented, but always encroaching. The way, and the only way, to check and to stop this evil, is for all the red men to unite in claiming a common and equal right in the land, as it was at first, and should be yet; for it never was divided, but belongs to all for the use of each. That no part has a right to sell, even to each other, much less to strangers; those who want all, and will not do with less.

The white people have no right to take the land from the Indians, because they had it first; it is theirs. They may sell, but all must join. Any sale not made by all is not valid. The late sale is bad. It was made by a part only. Part do not know how to sell. It requires all to make a bargain for all. All red men have equal rights to the unoccupied land. The right of occupancy is as good in one place as in another. There cannot be two occupations in the same place. The first excludes all others. It is not so in hunting or traveling; for there the same ground will serve many, as they may follow each other all day; but the camp is stationary, and that is occupancy. It belongs to the first who sits down on his blanket or skins which he has thrown upon the ground; and till he leaves it no other has a right. ■

From Address to Governor William Henry Harrison, Vincennes, Ind., 1810.

• RALPH WALDO EMERSON

Sir:

The seat you fill places you in a relation of credit and nearness to every citizen. By right and natural position, every citizen is your friend. Before any acts contrary to his own judgment or interest have repelled the affections of any man, each may look with trust and living anticipation to your government. Each has the highest right to call your attention to such subjects as are of a public nature and properly belong to the chief magistrate; and the good magistrate will feel a joy in meeting such confidence. In this belief and at the instance of a few of my friends and neighbors, I crave of your patience a short hearing for their sentiments and my own: and the circumstance that my name will be utterly unknown to you will only give the fairer chance to your equitable construction of what I have to say.

Sir, my communication respects the sinister rumors that fill this part of the country concerning the Cherokee people. The interest always felt in the aboriginal population—an interest naturally growing as that decays—has been heightened in regard to this tribe. Even in our distant State some good rumor of their worth and civility has arrived. We have learned with joy their improvement in the social arts. We have read their newspapers. We have seen some of them in our schools and colleges. In common with the great body of the American people, we have witnessed with sympathy the painful labors of these red men to redeem their own race from the doom of eternal inferiority, and to borrow and domesticate in the tribe the arts and customs of the Caucasian race. And notwithstanding the unaccountable apathy with which of late years the Indians have been sometimes abandoned to their enemies, it is not to be doubted that it is the good pleasure and the understanding of all humane persons in the republic, of the men and the matrons sitting in the thriving independent families all over the land, that they shall be duly cared for; that they shall taste justice and love from all to whom we have delegated the office of dealing with them.

The newspapers now inform us that, in December, 1835, a treaty contracting for the exchange of all the Cherokee territory was pretended to be made by an agent on the part of the United States with some persons appearing on the part of the Cherokees; that the fact afterwards transpired that these deputies did by no means represent the will of the nation; and that, out of eighteen thousand souls composing the nation, fifteen thousand six hundred and sixty-eight have protested against the so-called treaty. It now appears that the government of the United States choose to hold the Cherokees to this sham treaty, and are proceeding to execute the same. Almost the entire Cherokee nation stand up and say, "This is not our act. Behold us. Here are we. Do not mistake that handful of deserters for us"; and the American President and the Cabinet, the Senate and the House of Representatives, neither hear these men nor see them, and are contracting to put this active nation into carts and boats, and drag them over mountains and rivers to a wilderness at a vast distance beyond the Mississippi. And a paper purporting to be an army-order fixes a month from this day as the hour for this doleful removal.

In the name of God, sir, we ask you if this be so. Do the newspapers rightly inform us? Men and women with pale and perplexed faces meet one another in the streets and churches here, and ask if this be so. We have inquired if this be a gross misrepresentation from the party opposed to the government and anxious to blacken it with the people. We have looked in the newspapers of different parties, and find a horrid confirmation of the tale. We are slow to believe it. We hoped the Indians were misinformed, and that their remonstrance was premature, and will turn out to be a needless act of terror.

The piety, the principle that is left in the United States—if only in its coarsest form, a regard to the speech of men—forbid us to entertain it as a fact. Such a dereliction of all faith and virtue, such a denial of justice, and such deafness to screams for mercy were never heard of in times of peace and in the dealing of a nation with its own allies and wards, since the earth was made. Sir, does this government think that the people of the United States are become savage and mad? From their mind are the sentiments of love and a good nature wiped clean out? The soul of man, the justice, the mercy that is the heart's heart in all men, from Maine to Georgia, does abhor this business.

In speaking thus the sentiments of my neighbors and my own, perhaps I overstep the bounds of decorum. But would it not be a higher indecorum coldly to argue a matter like this? We only state the fact that a crime is projected that confounds our understandings by its magnitude—a crime that really deprives us as well as the Cherokees of a country; for how could we call the conspiracy that should crush these poor Indians our government, or the land that was cursed by their parting and dying imprecations our country, any more? You, sir, will bring down that renowned chair in which you sit into infamy if your seal is set to this instrument of perfidy; and the name of this nation, hitherto the sweet omen of religion and liberty, will stink to the world.

You will not do us the injustice of connecting this remonstrance with any sectional and party feeling. It is in our hearts the simplest commandment of brotherly love. We will not have this great and solemn claim upon national and human justice huddled aside under the flimsy plea of its being a party-act. Sir, to us the questions upon which the government and the people have been agitated during the past year, touching the prostration of the currency and of trade, seem but motes in comparison. These hard times, it is true, have brought the discussion home to every farmhouse and poor man's house in this town; but it is the chirping of grasshoppers beside the immortal question whether justice shall be done by the race of civilized to the race of savage man—whether all the attributes of reason, of civility, of justice, and even of mercy, shall be put off by the American people, and so vast an outrage upon the Cherokee nation and upon nature shall be consummated.

One circumstance lessens the reluctance with which I intrude at this time on your attention my conviction that the government ought to be admonished of a new historical fact, which the discussion of this question has disclosed, namely, that there exists in a great part of the Northern people a gloomy diffidence in the *moral* character of the government.

On the broaching of this question, a general expression of despondency, of disbelief that any good will accrue from a remonstrance on an act of fraud and robbery, appeared in those men to whom we naturally turn for aid and counsel. Will the American government steal? Will it lie? Will it kill? we ask triumphantly. Our counsellors and old statesmen here say that ten years ago they would have staked their life on the affirmation that the proposed Indian measures could not be executed; that the unanimous cry would put them down. And now the steps of this crime follow each other so fast, at such fatally quick time, that the millions of virtuous citizens, whose agents the government are, have no place to interpose, and must shut their eyes until the last howl and wailing of these tormented villages and tribes shall afflict the ear of the world.

I will not hide from you, as an indication of the alarming distrust, that a letter addressed as mine is, and suggesting to the mind of the executive the plain obligations of man, has a burlesque character in the apprehensions of some of my friends. I, sir, will not beforehand treat you with the contumely of this distrust. I will at least state to you this fact, and show you how plain and humane people, whose love would be honor, regard the policy of the government, and what injurious inferences they draw as to the minds of the governors. A man with your experience in affairs must have seen cause to appreciate the futility of opposition to the moral sentiment. However feeble the sufferer and however great the oppressor, it is in the nature of things that the blow should recoil upon the aggressor. For God is in the sentiment, and it cannot be withstood. The potentate and the people perish before it; but with it, and as its executor, they are omnipotent.

I write thus, sir, to inform you of the state of mind these Indian tidings have awakened here, and to pray with one voice more that you, whose hands are strong with the delegated power of fifteen millions of men, will avert with that might the terrific injury which threatens the Cherokee tribe.

With great respect, sir, I am your fellow citizen, *Ralph Waldo Emerson* ■

From letter to President Martin Van Buren, April 23, 1838.

• DOROTHEA LYNDE DIX

I come to present the strong claims of suffering humanity. I come to place before the Legislature of Massachusetts the condition of the miserable, the desolate, the outcast. I come as the advocate of helpless, forgotten, insane, and idiotic men and women . . . of beings wretched in our prisons, and more wretched in our almshouses. . . .

I proceed, gentlemen, briefly to call your attention to the present state of insane persons confined within this Commonwealth, in cages, closets, cellars, stalls, pens! Chained, naked, beaten with rods, and lashed into obedience. . . .

Men of Massachusetts, I beg, I implore, I demand pity and protection for these of my suffering, outraged sex. Fathers, husbands, brothers, I would supplicate you for this boon . . . Lay off the armor of local strife and political opposition; here and now, for once, forgetful of the earthly and perishable, come up . . . with one heart and one mind to works of righteousness and just judgment. . . .

Gentlemen, I commit you to this sacred cause. . . . ■

From Memorial to the Legislature of Massachusetts, January, 1843.

• JOHN BROWN

I have, may it please the Court, a few words to say.

In the first place, I deny everything but what I have all along admitted: of a design on my part to free slaves. I intended certainly to have made a clean thing of that matter, as I did last winter, when I went into Missouri and there took slaves without the snapping of a gun on either side, moving them through the country, and finally leaving them in Canada. I designed to have done the same thing again on a larger scale. That was all I intended. I never did intend murder, or treason, or the destruction of property, or to excite or incite slaves to rebellion, or to make insurrection.

I have another objection, and that is that it is unjust that I should suffer such a penalty. Had I interfered in the manner which I admit, and which I admit has been fairly proved—for I admire the truthfulness and candor of the greater portion of the witnesses who have testified in this case—had I so interfered in behalf of the rich, the powerful, the intelligent, the so-called great, or in behalf of any of their friends, either father, mother, brother, sister, wife or children, or any of that class, and suffered and sacrificed what I have in this interference, it would have been all right. Every man in this Court would have deemed it an act worthy of reward rather than punishment.

This Court acknowledges, too, as I suppose, the validity of the law of God. I see a book kissed, which I suppose to be the Bible, or at least the New Testament, which teaches me that all things whatsoever I would that men should do to me, I should do even so to them. It teaches me, further, to remember them that are in bonds as bound with them. I endeavored to act up to that instruction. I say I am yet too young to understand that God is any respecter of persons. I believe that to have interfered as I have done, as I have always freely admitted I have done, in behalf of His despised poor, I did no wrong, but right. Now, if it is deemed necessary that I should forfeit my life for the furtherance of the ends of justice, and mingle my blood further with the blood of my children and with the blood of millions in this slave country whose rights are disregarded by wicked, cruel, and unjust enactments, I say, let it be done.

Let me say one word further. I feel entirely satisfied with the treatment I have received on my trial. Considering all the circumstances, it has been more generous than I expected. But I feel no consciousness of guilt. I have stated from the first what was my intention, and what was not. I never had any design against the liberty of any person, nor any disposition to commit treason or incite slaves to rebel or make any general insurrection. I never encouraged any man to do so, but always discouraged any idea of that kind.

Let me say, also, in regard to the statements made by some of those who were connected with me, I hear it has been stated by some of them that I have induced them to join me. But the contrary is true. I do not say this to injure them, but as regretting their weakness. Not one but joined me of his own accord, and the greater part at their own expense. A number of them I never saw, and never had a word of conversation with, till the day they came to me, and that was for the purpose I have stated.

Now, I have done. ■

From speech to the court, November 2, 1859, on being sentenced to death.

• WILLIAM LLOYD GARRISON

God forbid that we should any longer continue the accomplices of thieves and robbers, of men-stealers and women-whippers! We must join together in the name of freedom. As for the Union—where is it and what is it? In one-half of it no man can exercise freedom of speech or the press—no man can utter the words of Washington, of Jefferson, of Patrick Henry—except at the peril of his life; and Northern men are everywhere hunted and driven from the South if they are supposed to cherish the sentiment of freedom in their bosoms. We are living under an awful despotism—that of a brutal slave oligarchy. And they threaten to leave us if we do not continue to do their evil work, as we have hitherto done it, and go down in the dust before them! Would to heaven they would go! It would only be the paupers clearing out from the town, would it not? But no, they do not mean to go; they mean to cling to you, and they mean to subdue you. But will you be subdued? I tell you our work is the dissolution of this slavery-cursed Union, if we would have a fragment of our liberties left to us! Surely between freemen, who believe in exact justice and impartial liberty, and slaveholders, who are for cleaving down all human rights at a blow, it is not possible there should be any Union whatever. "How can two walk togeth-

er except they be agreed?" The slaveholder with his hands dripping in blood—will I make a compact with him? The man who plunders cradles—will I say to him, "Brother, let us walk together in unity"? The man who, to gratify his lust or his anger, scourges woman with the lash till the soil is red with her blood—will I say to him, "Give me your hand; let us form a glorious Union"? No, never—never! There can be no union between us: "What concord hath Christ with Belial?" What union has freedom with slavery? Let us tell the inexorable and remorseless tyrants of the South that their conditions hitherto imposed upon us, whereby we are morally responsible for the existence of slavery, are horribly inhuman and wicked, and we cannot carry them out for the sake of their evil company.

By the dissolution of the Union we shall give the finishing blow to the slave system; and then God will make it possible for us to form a true, vital, enduring, all-embracing Union, from the Atlantic to the Pacific—one God to be worshipped, one Savior to be revered, one policy to be carried out—freedom everywhere to all the people, without regard to complexion or race—and the blessing of God resting upon us all! I want to see that glorious day! ■

From speech delivered in Boston on the day John Brown was hanged, December 2, 1859, in tribute to Brown.

• EUGENE V. DEBS

Your Honor, years ago I recognized my kinship with all living beings, and I made up my mind that I was not one bit better than the meanest of earth. I said then, I say now, that while there is a lower class, I am in it; while there is a criminal element, I am of it; while there is a soul in prison, I am not free.

If the law under which I have been convicted is a good law,[1] then there is no reason why sentence should not be pronounced upon me. I listened to all that was said in this court in support and justification of this law, but my mind remains unchanged. I look upon it as a despotic enactment in flagrant con-

---

[1] The Espionage Act of June 15, 1917.

flict with democratic principles and with the spirit of free institutions.

Your Honor, I have stated in this court that I am opposed to the form of our present Government; that I am opposed to the social system in which we live; that I believe in the change of both—but by perfectly peaceable and orderly means.

I believe, Your Honor, in common with all Socialists, that this nation ought to own and control its industries. I believe, as all Socialists do, that all things that are jointly needed and used ought to be jointly owned—that industry, the basis of life, instead of being the private property of the few and operated for their enrichment, ought to be the common property of all, democratically administered in the interest of all.

I have been accused, Your Honor, of being an enemy of the soldier. I hope I am laying no flattering unction to my soul when I say that I don't believe the soldier has a more sympathetic friend than I am. If I had my way there would be no soldiers. But I realize the sacrifice they are making, Your Honor. I can think of them. I can feel for them. I can sympathize with them. That is one of the reasons why I have been doing what little has been in my power to bring about a condition of affairs in this country worthy of the sacrifices they have made and that they are now making in its behalf.

Your Honor, I wish to make acknowledgment of my thanks to the counsel for the defense. They have not only defended me with exceptional legal ability, but with a personal attachment and devotion to which I am deeply sensible, and which I can never forget.

Your Honor, I ask no mercy. I plead for no immunity. I realize that finally the right must prevail. I never more clearly comprehended than now the great struggle between the powers of greed on the one hand and upon the other the rising hosts of freedom.

I can see the dawn of a better day of humanity. The people are awakening. In due course of time they will come to their own.

When the mariner, sailing over tropic seas, looks for relief from his weary watch, he turns his eyes toward the Southern Cross, burning luridly above the tempest-tossed ocean. As the midnight approaches, the Southern Cross begins to bend, and the whirling worlds change their places, and with starry finger-points the Almighty marks the passage of time upon the dial of the universe, and though no bell may beat the glad tidings, the lookout knows that the midnight is passing—that relief and rest are close at hand.

Let the people take heart and hope everywhere, for the cross is bending, the midnight is passing, and joy cometh with the morning.

Your Honor, I thank you, and I thank all of this court for their courtesy, for their kindness, which I shall remember always.

I am prepared to receive sentence. ■

From speech before the court, Chicago, Ill., in September, 1918, upon being sentenced to jail.

• FRANKLIN D. ROOSEVELT

This is preeminently the time to speak the truth, the whole truth, frankly and boldly. Nor need we shrink from honestly facing conditions in our country today. This great Nation will endure as it has endured, will revive and will prosper. So, first of all, let me assert my firm belief that the only thing we have to fear is fear itself—nameless, unreasoning, unjustified terror which paralyzes needed efforts to convert retreat into advance. In every dark hour of our national life a leadership of frankness and vigor has met with that understanding and support of the people themselves which is essential to victory. I am convinced that you will again give that support to leadership in these critical days. . . .

Plenty is at our doorstep, but a generous use of it languishes in the very sight of the supply. Primarily this is because the rulers of the exchange of mankind's goods have failed, through their own stubbornness and their own incompetence, have admitted their failure, and abdicated. Practices of the unscrupulous money changers stand indicted in the court of public opinion, rejected by the hearts and minds of men.

True they have tried, but their efforts have been cast in the pattern of an outworn tradition . . . They know only the rules of a generation of self-seekers. They have no vision, and when there is no vision the people perish.

The money changers have fled from their high seats in the temple of our civilization. We may now restore that temple to the ancient truths. The measure of the restoration lies in the extent to which we apply social values more noble than mere monetary profit.

Happiness lies not in the mere possession of money; it lies in the joy of achievement, in the thrill of creative effort. The joy and moral stimulation of work no longer must be forgotten in the mad chase of evanescent profits. . . .

Restoration calls, however, not for changes in ethics alone. This Nation asks for action, and action now. . . .

Action in this image and to this end is feasible under the form of government which we have inherited from our ancestors. Our Constitution is so simple and practical that it is possible always to meet extraordinary needs by changes in emphasis and arrangement without loss of essential form. That is why our constitutional system has proved itself the most superbly enduring political mechanism the modern world has produced. It has met every stress of vast expansion of territory, of foreign wars, of bitter internal strife, of world relations. . . .

We do not distrust the future of essential democracy. The people of the United States have not failed. In their need they have registered a mandate that they want direct, vigorous action. They have asked for discipline and direction under leadership. They have made me the present instrument of their wishes. In the spirit of the gift I take it. ■

From First Inaugural Address, March 4, 1933.

• FRANKLIN D. ROOSEVELT

We must be the great arsenal of democracy. For us this is an emergency as serious as war itself. We must apply ourselves to our task with the same resolution, the same sense of urgency, the same spirit of patriotism and sacrifice as we would show were we at war.

We have furnished the British great material support and we will furnish far more in the future.

There will be no "bottlenecks" in our determination to aid Great Britain. No dictator, no combination of dictators, will weaken that determination by threats of how they will construe that determination.

The British have received invaluable military support from the heroic Greek Army and from the forces of all the governments in exile. Their strength is growing. It is the strength of men and women who value their freedom more highly than they value their lives.

I believe that the Axis powers are not going to win this war. I base that belief on the latest and best of information.

We have no excuse for defeatism. We have every good reason for hope—hope for peace, yes, and hope for the defense of our civilization and for the building of a better civilization in the future.

I have the profound conviction that the American people are now determined to put forth a mightier effort than they have ever yet made to increase our production of all the implements of defense, to meet the threat to our democratic faith.

As President of the United States, I call for that national effort. I call for it in the name of this nation which we love and honor and which we are privileged and proud to serve. I call upon our people with absolute confidence that our common cause will greatly succeed. ■

From radio address from the White House,
December 29, 1940.

• MARTIN LUTHER KING, JR.

My dear and abiding friend Ralph Abernathy, to all of the distinguished Americans seated here on the rostrum, my friends and co-workers of the state of Alabama, and to all of the freedom-loving people who have assembled here this afternoon, from all over our nation and from all over the world:

Last Sunday more than eight thousand of us started on a mighty walk from Selma, Alabama. We have walked through desolate valleys and across the trying hills. We have walked on the meandering highways and rested our bodies on rocky byways. Some of our faces are burned from the outpouring of the sweltering sun. Some have literally stepped in the mud. We have been drenched by the rain. Our bodies are tired, our feet are somewhat sore. But today as I stand before you and think back over that great march, I can say as Sister Pollack has said, the seventy year old Negro woman who lived in this community during the bus boycott and one day she was asked, while walking, if she didn't want to ride and when she answered "No," the person said, "Well, aren't you tired?" With her ungrammatical profundity she said, "My feets is tired but my soul is rested." That's right. And in a real sense this afternoon we can say that our feet are tired but our souls are rested.

They told us that we wouldn't get here. And there were those who said that we would get here only over their dead bodies. But all the world today knows that we are here and we are standing before the forces of power in the state of Alabama, saying "We ain't going to let nobody turn us around."

Now it is not an accident, one of the great marches of American history should terminate in Montgomery, Alabama. Just ten years ago in this very city, a new philosophy was born of the Negro struggle. Montgomery was the first city in the South in which the entire Negro community united and squarely faced its age-old oppressor. Out of this struggle more than bus segregation was won. A new idea, more powerful than guns or clubs, was born. Negroes took it and carried it across the South in epic battles. And electrified the nation and the world. Yet strangely the climactic conflicts always were fought and won on Alabama soil. After Montgomery's, heroic confrontations loomed up in Mississippi, Arkansas, Georgia, and elsewhere. But not until the philosophy of segregation was challenged in Birmingham did the conscience of America begin to bleed. White America was profoundly aroused by Birmingham, because it witnessed a whole community of Negroes facing terror and brutality with majestic scorn and heroic courage. From the wells of its democratic spirit, the nation finally forced Congress to write legislation in the hope that it would eradicate the stain of Birmingham.

The Civil Rights Act of 1964 gave Negroes some part of their rightful dignity. But without the vote, it was dignity without strength. Once more the method of nonviolent resistance was unsheathed from its scabbard and once again an entire community was mobilized to confront the adversary. And again the brutality of the dying orders swept across the land. Yes, Selma, Alabama, became a shining moment in the conscience of Man. If the worst in American life lurked in dark streets, the best of American instincts arose passionately from across the nation to overcome it. There never was a moment in American history more honorable and more inspiring than the pilgrimage of clergymen and laymen of every race and faith, pouring into Selma to face danger at the side of its embattled Negroes. The confrontation of good and evil compressed in the tiny community of Selma generated a massive power, turned the whole nation to a new course. A President born in the South had the sensitivity to feel the will of the country, and in an address that will live in history, one of the most passionate pleas for human rights ever made by the President of our nation, he pledged the might of the federal government to cast off the centuries-old blight. President Johnson rightly praised the courage of the Negro for awakening the conscience of the nation. On our part we must pay our profound respects to the white Americans who cherish their democratic traditions over the ugly customs and privileges of generations; to come forth boldly to join hands with us, from Montgomery to Birmingham, from Birmingham to Selma, from Selma back to Montgomery. The trail wound in a circle long and often bloody. Yet it has become a highway up from darkness. Alabama has tried to nurture and defend evil, but evil is choking to death in the dusty roads and streets of this state. So I stand before you this afternoon with the conviction that segregation is on its deathbed in Alabama, and the only thing I'm certain about is I'm positive that segregationists and [Governor] Wallace will make the funeral.

Our whole campaign in Alabama has been centered on the rights of old. In focusing the attention of the nation and the world today on the flagrant denial of the right to vote, we are exposing the very origin, the root cause of racial segregation in the Southland. Racial segregation as a way of life did not come about as the natural result of hatred between the races immediately after the Civil War. There were no laws segregating the races then. As the noted historian C. Vann Woodward, in his book *The Strange Career of Jim Crow,* clearly points out, the segregation of the races was really a political stratagem employed by the emerging bourbon interests in the South, to keep the southern masses divided and southern labor the cheapest in the land. You see, it was a simple thing to keep the poor white masses working for mere starvation wages in the years that followed the Civil War. Why, if a poor white plantation or mill worker became dissatisfied with his low wages, the plantation or mill owner would merely threaten to fire him and hire a former Negro slave and pay him even less. Thus the southern wage level was kept almost unbearably low.

Toward the end of the Reconstruction era, something very significant happened: there developed what was known as the Populist movement. The leaders of this movement began awakening the poor white masses and the former Negro slaves to the fact that they were being fleeced by the emerging bourbon interests. Not only that but they began uniting the Negro and white masses into a voting bloc that threatened to drive the bourbon interests from the command post of political power in the South. To meet this threat the southern aristocracy began immediately to engineer the development of a segregated society. I want you to follow me through here, because this is very important—to see the roots of racism and the denial of the right to vote. Through their control of mass media, they revised the doctrine of white supremacy, they saturated the thinking of the poor white masses with it. Thus clouding their minds to the real issue involved in the Populist movement, they then directed the placement on the books of the South of laws that made it a crime for Negroes and whites to come together as equals at any level. And that did it. And that crippled and eventually destroyed the Populist movement of the nineteenth century.

If it may be said of the slavery era that the white man took the world and gave the Negro Jesus, then it may be said of the Reconstruction era that the southern aristocracy took the world and gave the poor white man Jim Crow. He gave him Jim Crow and when his wrinkled stomach cried out for the food that his empty pockets could not provide, he ate Jim Crow, the psychological bird that told him that no matter how bad off he was, at least he was a white man better than the black man. He ate Jim Crow and when his undernourished children cried out for the necessities and his low wages could not provide, he showed them the Jim Crow signs on the buses and in the stores, on the streets and in the public buildings, and his children too learned to feed upon Jim Crow, their last outposts of psychological oblivion.

And thus the threat of the free exercise of the ballot by the Negro and white masses alike resulted in the establishment of a segregated society. They've segregated southern money from the poor whites. They've segregated southern mores from the rich whites. They've segregated southern churches from Christianity. They've segregated southern minds from honest thinking. And they've segregated the Negro from everything. Guess what happened? The Negro and white masses of the South threatened to unite, and built a great society. A society of justice where none would prey upon weakness of others. A society of plenty where greed and poverty would be done away with. A society of brotherhood where every man would respect the dignity and worth of human personality.

We've come a long way since that travesty of justice was perpetrated upon the American mind. James Weldon Johnson put it eloquently. He said, "We have come over a way that with tears has been watered. We have come treading our paths through the blood of the slaughtered. Out of the gloomy past, till now we stand at last where the white gleam of our bright star has cast."

Today I want to tell the city of Selma, today I want to say to the state of Alabama, today I want to say to the people of America, and the nations of the world, that we are not about to turn around. We are on the move now. Yes, we are on the move and no wave of racism can stop us. We are on the move now. And the burning of our churches will not deter us. We are on the move now. The bombing of our homes will not persuade us. We are on the move now. The beating and killing of our clergymen and young people will not divert us. We are on the move now. The word of the release of their known murderers will not discourage us. We are on the move now. Like an idea whose time has come. Not even the marching of mighty armies can halt us. We are moving to the land of freedom. Let us therefore continue our time for our march to the realization of the American dream. Let us march on segregated housing, until every ghetto of social and economic depression is dissolved and Negroes and whites live side by side in decent, safe, and sanitary houses. Let us march on segregated schools, until every vestige of segregated and inferior education becomes a thing of the past. And Negroes and whites study side by side in the socially healing context of the classrooms. Let us march on poverty until no American parent has to skip a meal so that his children may eat. March on poverty until no starved man walks the streets of our cities and towns, in search of jobs that do not exist. Let us march on poverty until wrinkled stomachs in Mississippi are filled, and the idle industries of Appalachia are realized, and revitalized. And broken lives in sweltering ghettoes are mended and remolded. Let us march on ballot boxes. March on ballot boxes until race bigots disappear from the political arena. Let us march on ballot boxes until the misdeeds of bloodthirsty mobs are transformed into the calculated good deeds of orderly citizens. Let us march on ballot boxes until the Wallaces of our nation tremble away in silence. Let us march on ballot boxes until we send to our city councils, state legislature, and the United States Congress men who will not fear to do justly, love mercy and walk humbly with thy God. Let us march on ballot boxes until brotherhood becomes more than a meaningless word in an opening prayer, but the order of the day on every legislative agenda. Let us march on ballot boxes until all over Alabama God's children will be able to walk the earth in de-

cency and honor. There is nothing wrong with marching in this sense. The Bible tells us that the mighty men of Joshua merely walked about the walled city of Jericho, and the barriers for freedom came tumbling down. I like that old Negro spiritual, "Joshua Fit the Battle of Jericho," in its simple yet colorful depiction of that great moment in Biblical history. It tells us that Joshua fit the battle of Jericho, Joshua fit the battle of Jericho, and the walls come tumbling down. Up to the walls of Jericho they marched with spear in hand. "Go blow them ram horns," Joshua cried, "across the battle lands and in my hand." These words I have given you just as they were given us by the unknown long dead dark-skinned originators—some now-long-gone black bard that sweeps to posterity these words in ungrammatical form.

For all of us today, the battle is in our hands. We can answer with creative nonviolence the call to higher ground, which the new direction of our struggle summons us. The road ahead is not altogether a smooth one. There are no broad highways that lead us easily and inevitably to quick solutions. We must keep going.

In the glow of the lamplight on my desk a few nights ago, I gazed again upon the wonderous minds of our times, full of hope and promises of the future. And I smiled to see in the newspaper photographs of nearly a decade ago—the faces so bright, and so solemn—of our valiant heroes, the people of Montgomery. To this list may be added the names of all those who had fought and, yes, died in the nonviolent army of our day: Medgar Evers, three civil rights workers in Mississippi last summer, William Moore, as had already been mentioned, The Reverend James Reem, Jimmy Lee Jackson, four little girls in the Church of God in Birmingham on Sunday morning. In spite of this, we most go on and be sure that they did not die in vain. The patter of their feet as they walked through Jim Crow barriers in the great stride toward freedom, and the thunder of the marching men of Johnson as the world rocks beneath their trail.

My people, my people, listen. The battle is in our hands. The battle is in our hands in Mississippi, and

Alabama, and all over the United States. And I know there is a cry today in Alabama. We see it in numerous editorials—"When will Martin Luther King, SCLC, SNCC, and all these civil rights agitators, and all of the white clergymen and labor leaders, and students and others get out of our community and let Alabama return to normal?" I have a message that I would like to leave with Alabama this evening. That is exactly what we don't want, and we will not allow it to happen. We know that it was normalcy in Marion that led to the brutal murder of Jimmy Lee Jackson. It was normalcy in Birmingham that led to the murder on Sunday morning of four beautiful, unoffending, innocent girls. It was normalcy on Highway Eighty that led state troopers to use tear gas and horses and billy clubs against unarmed human beings who were simply marching for justice. It was normalcy by a café in Selma, Alabama, that led to the brutal beating of Reverend Jay Greer. It is normalcy all over our country which leaves the Negro perishing all along the island of poverty, in the midst of a vast ocean of material prosperity. It is normalcy all over Alabama that prevents the Negro from becoming a registered voter.

No, we will not allow Alabama to return to normalcy. The only normalcy that we will settle for is the normalcy that recognizes the dignity and worth of all of God's children. The only normalcy that we will settle for is the normalcy that allows judgment to run down like waters and righteousness like a mighty stream. The only normalcy that we will settle for is the normalcy of brotherhood, the normalcy of true peace. The normalcy of justice. And so as we go away this afternoon, let us go away more than ever before committed to this struggle, and committed to nonviolence.

I must admit to you there are still some difficult days ahead. We are still in for a season of suffering in many of the black-belt counties of Alabama, and many areas of Mississippi, many areas of Louisiana. I must admit to you there are still jail cells waiting for us, dark and difficult moments. But we will go on with the faith that nonviolence and its power can transform dark yesterdays into bright tomorrows. We will be able to change all of these conditions.

And so I plead with you this afternoon as we go ahead. Remain committed to nonviolence. Our aim must never be to defeat and humiliate the white man, but to win his friendship and understanding. We must come to see that the end we seek is a society at peace with itself, a society that can live with its conscience. That will be a day not of the white man, not of the black man, that will be the day of man as man.

I know you are asking today, "How long will it take?" Somebody's asking, "How long will prejudice blind the visions of men? Darken their understanding and drive right out wisdom from a sacred throne?" Somebody's asking, "When will wounded justice lying prostrate on the streets of Selma, Birmingham, and communities all over the South be lifted from this dust of shame, to reign supreme among the children of men?" Somebody's asking, "When will the radiant star of hope be plunged against the nocturnal bosom of this lonely night? Put from weary souls the chains of fear and the manacles of death? How long will justice be crucified, and truth buried?"

I come to say to you this afternoon, however difficult the moment, however frustrating the hour, it will not be long. Because truth crushed to earth will rise again.

How long? Not long. Because no lie can live forever. How long? Not long. Because you shall reap what you sow. How long? Not long. Truth forever on the scaffold, wrong forever on the throne. Yet that scaffold sways the future. And behind the dim unknown standeth God within the shadow, keeping watch above his own. How long? Not long. Because the arm of the moral universe is long, but it bends toward justice. How long? Not long. Because mine eyes have seen the glory of the coming of the lord. He's trampling out the vintage where the grapes of wrath are stored. He has loosed the fateful lightning of his terrible swift sword, his truth is marching on. He has sounded forth the trumpet that shall never call retreat. He is sifting out the hearts of men before his judgment seat. Oh, be swift my soul to answer him, be jubilant my feet, our God is marching on. Glory hallelujah, glory hallelujah. Glory hallelujah, glory hallelujah, his truth is marching on! ∎

"How Long? Not Long," address on the steps of the Alabama Capitol in Montgomery, March 25, 1965.

3

AMERICA'S MISSION

Theodore Roosevelt
Woodrow Wilson
Franklin D. Roosevelt
Dwight D. Eisenhower
John F. Kennedy

• THEODORE ROOSEVELT

Our relations with the other powers of the world are important; but still more important are our relations among ourselves. Such growth in wealth, in population, and in power as this nation has seen during the century and a quarter of its national life is inevitably accompanied by a like growth in the problems which are ever before every nation that rises to greatness. Power invariably means both responsibility and danger. Our forefathers faced certain perils which we have outgrown. We now face other perils, the very existence of which it was impossible that they should foresee. Modern life is both complex and intense, and the tremendous changes wrought by the extraordinary industrial development of the last half century are felt in every fiber of our social and political being. Never before have men tried so vast and formidable an experiment as that of administering the affairs of a continent under the forms of a democratic republic. The conditions which have told for our marvelous material well-being, which have developed to a very high degree our energy, self-reliance, and individual initiative, have also brought the care and anxiety inseparable from the accumulation of great wealth in industrial centers. Upon the success of our experiment much depends, not only as regards our own welfare, but as regards the welfare of mankind. If we fail, the cause of free self-government throughout the world will rock to its foundations, and therefore our responsibility is heavy, to ourselves, to the world as it is today, and to the generations yet unborn. There is no good reason why we should fear the future, but there is every reason why we should face it seriously. . . .

We know that self-government is difficult. We know that no people needs such high traits of character as that people which seeks to govern its affairs aright through the freely expressed will of the freemen who compose it. But we have faith that we shall not prove false to the memories of the men of the mighty past. They did their work, they left us the splendid heritage we now enjoy. We in our turn have an assured confidence that we shall be able to leave this heritage unwasted and enlarged to our children and our children's children. ■

From Inaugural Address, March 4, 1905.

• WOODROW WILSON

Great democracies are not belligerent. They do not seek or desire war. Their thought is of individual liberty and of the free labor that supports life and the uncensored thought that quickens it. Conquest and dominion are not in our reckoning, or agreeable to our principles. But just because we demand unmolested development and the undisturbed government of our own lives upon our own principles of right and liberty, we resent, from whatever quarter it may come, the aggression we ourselves will not practice. We insist upon security in prosecuting our self-chosen lines of national development. We do more than that. We demand it also for others. We do not confine our enthusiasm for individual liberty and free national development to the incidents and movements of affairs which affect only ourselves. We feel it wherever there is a people that tries to walk in these difficult paths of independence and right. From the first we have made common cause with all partisans of liberty on this side of the sea. . . . ■

From Third Annual Message to Congress, December 7, 1915.

• WOODROW WILSON

This nation was created to be the mediator of peace because it draws its blood from every civilized stock in the world and is ready by sympathy and understanding to understand the peoples of the world, their interests, their rights, their hopes, their destiny. America is the only nation in the world that has that equipment. Every other nation is set in the mold of a particular breeding. We are set in no mold at all. Every other nation has certain prepossessions

which run back through all the ramifications of an ancient history. We have nothing of the kind. We know what all peoples are thinking, and yet we, by a fine alchemy of our own, combine that thinking into an American plan and an American purpose. America is the only nation which can sympathetically lead the world in organizing peace. ■

From letter to a Jackson Day dinner, January 8, 1920.

• WOODROW WILSON

This is the mission ["faith that right makes might"] upon which democracy came into the world. Democracy is an assertion of the right of the individual to live and to be treated justly as against any attempt on the part of any combination of individuals to make laws which will overburden him or which will destroy his equality among his fellows in the matter of right or privilege, and I think we all realize that the day has come when democracy is being put upon its final test. The old world is just now suffering from a wanton rejection of the principle of democracy and a substitution of the principle of autocracy as asserted in the name but without the authority and sanction of the multitude. This is the time of all others when democracy should prove its purity and its spiritual power to prevail. It is surely the manifest destiny of the United States to lead in the attempt to make this spirit prevail. ■

From Eighth Annual Message to Congress (not delivered in person), December 7, 1920.

• FRANKLIN D. ROOSEVELT

Democracy is still the hope of the world. If we in our generation can continue its successful applications in the Americas it will spread and supersede other methods by which men are governed and which seem to most of us to run counter to our ideals of human liberty and human progress.

Three centuries of history, three centuries sowed

the seeds which grew into our nations; the fourth century saw those nations become equal and free and brought us to a common system of constitutional government; the fifth century is giving to us a common meeting ground of mutual help and understanding. Our hemisphere has at last come of age. We are here assembled to show its unity to the world. We took from our ancestors a great dream. We here offer it back as a great unified reality.

And finally, in expressing our faith of the Western World, let us affirm:

That we maintain and defend the democratic form of constitutional representative government.

That through such government we can more greatly provide a wider distribution of culture, of education, of thought and of free expression.

That through it we can obtain a greater security of life for our citizens and a more equal opportunity for them to prosper.

That through it we can best foster commerce and the exchange of art and science between nations; that through it we can avoid the rivalry of armament, avert hatred and encourage good will and true justice.

And that through it we offer hope for peace and a more abundant life to the peoples of the whole world.

But this faith, this faith of the Western World will not be complete if we fail to affirm our faith in God. In the whole history of mankind, far back into the dim past before man knew how to record thoughts or events, the human race has been distinguished from other forms of life by the existence —the fact—of religion. Periodic attempts to deny God have always come and will always come to naught.

In the constitutions and in the practice of our nations is the right of freedom of religion. But this ideal, these words presuppose a belief and a trust in God.

The faith of the Americas, therefore, lies in the spirit. The system, the sisterhood of the Americas is impregnable so long as her nations maintain that spirit.

In that faith and spirit we will have peace over the Western World. In that faith and spirit we will all watch and guard our hemisphere. In that faith and spirit may we also, with God's help, offer hope to our brethren overseas. ∎

From Address, Buenos Aires, December 1, 1936.

• DWIGHT D. EISENHOWER

At such a time in history, we who are free must proclaim anew our faith. . . .

This faith rules our whole way of life. It decrees that we, the people, elect leaders not to rule but to serve. It asserts that we have the right to choice of our own work and to the reward of our own toil. It inspires the initiative that makes our productivity the wonder of the world. . . .

The enemies of this faith know no god but force, no devotion but its use. They tutor men in treason. They feed upon the hunger of others. Whatever defies them, they torture, especially the truth.

Here, then, is joined no argument between slightly differing philosophies. This conflict strikes directly at the faith of our fathers and the lives of our sons. No principle or treasure that we hold, from the spiritual knowledge of our free schools and churches to the creative magic of free labor and capital, nothing lies safely beyond the reach of this struggle.

Freedom is pitted against slavery; lightness against the dark.

The faith we hold belongs not to us alone but to the free of all the world. This common bond binds the grower of rice in Burma and the planter of wheat in Iowa, the shepherd in southern Italy and the mountaineer in the Andes. ∎

From First Inaugural Address, January 20, 1953.

• JOHN F. KENNEDY

We observe today, not a victory of party but a celebration of freedom—symbolizing an end as well as a beginning—signifying renewal as well as change. For I have sworn before an Almighty God the same solemn oath our forebears prescribed nearly a century and three-quarters ago.

The world is very different now. For man holds in his mortal hands the power to abolish all forms of human poverty and all forms of human life. And yet the same revolutionary beliefs for which our forebears fought are still at issue around the globe —the belief that the rights of man come not from the generosity of the state but from the hand of God.

We dare not forget today that we are the heirs of that first revolution. Let the word go forth from this time and place, to friend and foe alike, that the torch has been passed to a new generation of Americans—born in this century, tempered by war, disciplined by a hard and bitter peace, proud of our ancient heritage—and unwilling to witness or permit the slow undoing of those human rights to which this nation has always been committed, and to which we are committed today at home and around the world.

Let every nation know, whether it wishes us well or ill, that we shall pay any price, bear any burden, meet any hardship, support any friend, oppose any foe to assure the survival and the success of liberty.

This much we pledge . . .

In the long history of the world, only a few generations have been granted the role of defending freedom in its hour of maximum danger. I do not shrink from this responsibility—I welcome it. I do not believe that any of us would exchange places with any other people or any other generation. The energy, the faith, the devotion which we bring to this endeavor will light our country and all who serve it— and the glow from that fire can truly light the world.

And so, my fellow Americans: ask not what your country can do for you—ask what you can do for your country.

My fellow citizens of the world: ask not what America will do for you, but what together we can do for the freedom of man. ■

From Inaugural Address, January 20, 1961.

• JOHN F. KENNEDY

We are not against any man—or any nation—or any system—except as it is hostile to freedom. Nor am I here to present a new military doctrine bearing any one name or aimed at any one area. I am here to promote the freedom doctrine.

The great battleground for the defense and expansion of freedom today is the whole southern half of the globe—Asia, Latin America, Africa and the Middle East—the lands of the rising peoples. Their revolution is the greatest in human history. They seek an end to injustice, tyranny and exploitation. . . .

The adversaries of freedom did not create the revolution; nor did they create the conditions which compel it. But they are seeking to ride the crest of its wave—to capture it for them . . .

I stress the strength of our economy because it is essential to the strength of our nation. And what is true in our case is true in the case of other countries. Their strength in the struggle for freedom depends on the strength of their economic and their social progress. We would be badly mistaken to consider their problems in military terms alone.

For no amount of arms and armies can help stabilize those governments which are unable or unwilling to achieve social and economic reform and development. Military pacts cannot help nations whose social injustice and economic chaos invite insurgency and penetration and subversion. The most skillful counter-guerrilla efforts cannot succeed where the local population is too caught up in its own misery to be concerned about the advance of communism. ■

From Address to Congress, May 25, 1961.

PART IX

MILESTONES
ON THE ROAD
TO FREEDOM

DECLARATIONS AND DOCUMENTS

• ROMAN EDICTS OF TOLERATION OF CHRISTIANS

We therefore . . . are pleased to grant indulgence to these men, allowing Christians the right to exist again and to set up their places of worship; provided always that they do not offend against public order . . . In return for this indulgence of ours it will be the duty of Christians to pray to God for our recovery, for the public weal and for their own; that the state may be preserved from danger on every side, and that they themselves may dwell safely in their homes. ■

From Edict of Emperor Galerius, on his deathbed, 311 A.D.

We decided that the things that are of profit to all mankind, the worship of God, ought rightly to be our first and chiefest care, and that it was a right that Christians and all others should have freedom to follow the kind of religion they favored . . . We therefore announce that, notwithstanding any provisions concerning the Christians in our former instructions, all who choose that religion are to be permitted to continue therein, without any let or hindrance, and are not to be in any way troubled or molested. Note that at the same time all others are to be allowed the free and unrestricted practice of their religions; for it accords with the good order of the realm and the peacefulness of our times that each should have freedom to worship God after his own choice. ■

From order issued by Emperors Constantine I and Licinius, confirming Galerius' Edict, March, 313 A.D.

We allow none . . . to be dragged to the altars unwillingly . . . It is therefore my pleasure to announce and publish to all the people by this edict, that they must not abet the seditions of the clergy . . . They may hold their meetings, if they wish, and

offer prayers according to their established use . . . And for the future let the people live in harmony. Let no one . . . do wrong to another . . . Men should be taught and won over by reason, not by blows, insults and corporal punishments. I therefore most earnestly admonish the adherents of the true religion [Roman] not to injure or insult the Galileans [Christians] in any way, either by physical attack or by reproaches. Those who are in the wrong in matters of supreme importance are objects of pity rather than of hate. ■

From order issued by Emperor Julian, the so-called "Apostate," in 362 A.D.

• THE MAGNA CARTA

Ch. 1   We have granted also, and given to all the Freemen of our realm, for us and for our heirs forever, those liberties underwritten; to have and to hold, to them and their heirs for ever. . . .

Ch. 9   The City of London shall have all the old liberties and customs which it hath been used to have. Moreover, we will and grant that all other cities and boroughs, towns, and the Barons of the Five Ports, and all other ports, shall have all their liberties and free customs.

Ch. 11   Common Pleas shall not follow our Court, but shall be holden in some place certain.

Ch. 31   No constable, or other bailiff of ours, shall take corn or other chattels of any man, unless he presently gives him money for it.

Ch. 33   No sheriff or bailiff of ours, or any other, shall take horses or carts of any Freeman for transportation, unless with the consent of that freeman.

Ch. 38   No bailiff shall, upon his own unsupported complaint, put anyone to his "law," without credible witnesses brought for this purpose.

Ch. 39   No Freeman shall be taken, or imprisoned, or disseised of his freehold, or liberties, or free customs, or be outlawed, or exiled, or any otherwise destroyed, nor will we pass upon him, nor condemn him, but by lawful judgment of his peers, or by the law of the land. We will sell to no man, we will not deny or defer to any man, either justice or right.

Ch. 63 (final) Wherefore it is our will, and we firmly enjoin, that the English Church be free, and that the men in our kingdom have and hold all the aforesaid liberties, rights, and concessions, well and peaceably, freely and quietly, full and wholly, for themselves and their heirs, of us and our heirs, in all respects and in all places for ever, as is aforesaid. ■

Granted to the English barons by King John, at Runnymede, June 15, 1215. Although it was later repudiated by the King, Magna Carta has remained the basis of English liberties and the foundation of constitutional supremacy over monarchy. The excerpts here are somewhat modernized. The original did not contain any titles or chapter headings.

• THE DUTCH DECLARATION OF INDEPENDENCE

THE STATES GENERAL OF THE UNITED PROVINCES OF THE LOW COUNTRIES, TO ALL WHOM IT MAY CONCERN, DO BY THESE PRESENTS SEND GREETING:

As it is apparent to all that a prince is constituted by God to be ruler of a people, to defend them from oppression and violence as the shepherd his sheep; and whereas God did not create the people slaves to their prince, to obey his commands, whether right or wrong, but rather the prince for the sake of the subjects (without which he could be no prince), to govern them according to equity, to love and support them as a father his children or a shepherd his flock, and even at the hazard of life to defend and preserve them. And when he does not behave thus, but, on the contrary, oppresses them, seeking opportunities to infringe their ancient customs and privileges, exacting from them slavish compliance, then he is no longer a prince, but a tyrant, and the subjects are to consider him in no other view. And

particularly when this is done deliberately, unauthorized by the states, they may not only disallow his authority, but legally proceed to the choice of another prince for their defense. This is the only method left for subjects whose humble petitions and remonstrances could never soften their prince or dissuade him from his tyrannical proceedings; and this is what the law of nature dictates for the defense of liberty, which we ought to transmit to posterity, even at the hazard of our lives. And this we have seen done frequently in several countries upon the like occasion, whereof there are notorious instances, and more justifiable in our land, which has been always governed according to their ancient privileges, which are expressed in the oath taken by the prince at his admission to the government; for most of the Provinces receive their prince upon certain conditions, which he swears to maintain, which, if the prince violates, he is no longer sovereign.

Now thus it was that the king of Spain after the demise of the emperor, his father, Charles the Fifth, of the glorious memory (of whom he received all these provinces), forgetting the services done by the subjects of these countries, both to his father and himself . . . did rather hearken to the counsel of those Spaniards about him, who had conceived a secret hatred to this land and to its liberty, because they could not enjoy posts of honor and high employments here under the states as they did in Naples, Sicily, Milan and the Indies, and other countries under the king's dominion. Thus allured by the riches of the said provinces, wherewith many of them were well acquainted, the said counsellors, I say, or the principal of them, frequently remonstrated to the king that it was more for his majesty's reputation and grandeur to subdue the Low Countries a second time, and to make himself absolute (by which they mean to tyrannize at pleasure), than to govern according to the restrictions he had accepted, and at his admission sworn to observe. From that time forward the king of Spain, following these evil counsellors, sought by all means possible to reduce this country (stripping them of their ancient privileges) to slavery, under the government of Spaniards, having first, under the mask of religion, endeavored to settle new bishops in the largest and principal cities, endowing and incorporating them with the richest abbeys, assigning to each bishop nine canons to assist him as counsellors, three whereof should superintend the Inquisition. By this incorporation the said bishops (who might be strangers as well as natives) would have had the first place and vote in the assembly of the states, and always the prince's creatures at devotion; and by the addition of the said canons he would have introduced the Spanish Inquisition, which has been always as dreadful and detested in these provinces as the worst of slavery . . . But, notwithstanding the many remonstrances made to the king both by the provinces and particular towns, in writing as well as by some principal lords by word of mouth . . . And, although the king had by fair words given them grounds to hope that their request should be complied with, yet by his letters he ordered the contrary, soon after expressly commanding, upon pain of his displeasure, to admit the new bishops immediately, and put them in possession of their bishoprics and incorporated abbeys, to hold the court of the Inquisition in the places where it had been before, to obey and follow the decrees and ordinances of the Council of Trent, which in many articles are destructive of the privilege of the country. This being come to the knowledge of the people gave just occasion to great uneasiness and clamor among them, and lessened that good affection they had always borne toward the king and his predecessors. And, especially, seeing that he did not only seek to tyrannize over their persons and estates, but also over their consciences, for which they believed themselves accountable to God only. Upon this occasion the chief of the nobility in compassion to the poor people, in the year 1566, exhibited a certain remonstrance in form of a petition, humbly praying, in order to appease them and prevent public disturbances, that it would please his majesty (by showing clemency due from a good prince to his people) to soften the said points, and especially with regard to the rigorous Inquisition, and capital punishments for matters of religion. And to inform the king of this affair in a more solemn manner, and to represent to him how

necessary it was for the peace and prosperity of the public to remove the aforesaid innovations, and moderate the severity of his declarations published concerning divine worship, the Marquis de Berghen, and the aforesaid Baron of Montigny had been sent, at the request of the said lady regent [the Duchess of Parma; governess of the Low Countries], the council of state, and of the states-general, as ambassadors to Spain, where the king, instead of giving them audience, and redressing the grievances they had complained of . . . did, by the advice of Spanish council, declare all those who were concerned in preparing the said remonstrance to be rebels, and guilty of high treason, and to be punished with death, and confiscation of their estates; and, what is more (thinking himself well assured of reducing these countries under absolute tyranny of the army of the Duke of Alva), did soon after imprison and put to death the said lords the ambassadors, and confiscated their estates, contrary to the law of nations, which has been always religiously observed even among the most tyrannical and barbarous princes.

And, although the said disturbances, which in the year 1566 happened on the aforementioned occasion, were now appeased by the governess and her ministers, and many friends to liberty were either banished or subdued, in so much that the king had not any show of reason to use arms and violences, and further oppress this country, yet for these causes and reasons, long time before sought by the council of Spain (as appears by intercepted letters from the Spanish ambassador, Alana, then in France, writ to the Duchess of Parma), to annul all the privileges of this country, and govern it tyrannically at pleasure as in the Indies; and in their new conquests he has, at the instigation of the council of Spain, showing the little regard he had for his people (so contrary to the duty which a good prince owes to his subjects), sent the Duke of Alva with a powerful army to oppress this land, who for his inhuman cruelties is looked upon as one of its greatest enemies, accompanied with counsellors too like himself . . . The said duke, immediately after his arrival (though a stranger, and no way related to the royal family), declared that he had a captain-general's commission, and soon after that of governor of these provinces, contrary to all its ancient customs and privileges; and . . . he immediately garrisoned the principal towns and castles, and caused fortresses and citadels to be built in the great cities to awe them into subjection, and very courteously sent for the chief of nobility in the king's name, under pretense of taking their advice, and to employ them in the service of their country. And those who believed his letters were seized and carried out of Brabant, contrary to law, where they were imprisoned and prosecuted as criminals before him who had no right, nor could be a competent judge; and at last he, without hearing their defense at large, sentenced them to death, which was publicly and ignominiously executed. The others, better acquainted with Spanish hypocrisy, residing in foreign countries, were declared outlaws, and had their estates confiscated . . . besides a great number of other gentlemen and substantial citizens, some of whom were executed, and others banished so that their estates might be confiscated, plaguing the other honest inhabitants, not only by the injuries done to their wives, children and estates by the Spanish soldiers lodged in their houses, as also by diverse contributions, which they were forced to pay toward building citadels and new fortifications of towns even to their own ruin, besides the taxes of the hundredth, twentieth, and tenth penny, to pay for both the foreign armies and those raised in the country, to be employed against their fellow citizens and against those who at the hazard of their lives defended their liberties.

In order to impoverish the subjects, and to incapacitate them to hinder his design, and that he might with more ease execute the instructions received in Spain, to treat these countries as new conquests, he began to alter the course of justice after the Spanish mode, directly contrary to our privileges; and, imagining at last he had nothing more to fear, he endeavored by main force to settle a tax called the tenth penny on merchandise and manufacturing, to the total ruin of these countries, the prosperity of which depends upon a flourishing trade, notwithstanding frequent remonstrances, not by a single Province only, but by all of them united . . . All these considerations give us more than sufficient reason to renounce the King of Spain, and seek some other powerful and more gracious prince to take us under his protection. . . .

So, having no hope of reconciliation, and finding no other remedy, we have, agreeable to the law of nature in our own defense, and for maintaining the rights, privileges, and liberties of our countrymen, wives, and children, and latest posterity from being enslaved by the Spaniards, been constrained to renounce allegiance to the King of Spain, and pursue such methods as appear to us most likely to secure our ancient liberties and privileges.

Know all men by these presents that, being reduced to the last extremity, as above mentioned, we have unanimously and deliberately declared, and do by these presents declare, that the King of Spain has forfeited, *ipso jure,* all hereditary right to the sovereignty of those countries, and are determined from henceforward not to acknowledge his sovereignty or jurisdiction, nor any act of his relating to the domains of the Low Countries, nor make use of his name as prince, nor suffer others to do it. In consequence whereof we also declare all officers, judges, lords, gentlemen, vassals, and all other inhabitants of this country of what condition or quality soever, to be henceforth discharged from all oaths and obligations whatsoever made to the King of Spain as sovereign of those countries. . . .

Moreover, we order and command that from henceforth no money coined shall be stamped with the name, title, or arms of the King of Spain in any of these United Provinces, but that all new gold and silver pieces, with their halfs and quarters, shall only bear such impressions as the states shall direct. We order likewise and command the president and other lords of the privy council, and all other chancellors, presidents, accountants-general, and to others in all the chambers of accounts respectively in these said countries, and likewise to all other judges and officers, as we hold them discharged from henceforth of their oath made to the King of Spain, pursuant to the tenor of their commission, that they shall take a new oath to the states of that country on whose jurisdiction they depend. . . .

We further command the president and members of the privy council, chancellor of the Duchy of Brabant . . . of Guelders . . . of Zutphen . . . of Holland . . . of Zeeland . . . of Friese . . . of Mechelen . . . of Utrecht, and to all other justiciaries and officers whom it may concern . . . to cause this our ordinance to be published and proclaimed throughout their respective jurisdictions . . . And to cause our said ordinance to be observed inviolably . . . And, for better maintaining all and every article hereof, we give to all and every one of you, by express command, full power and authority. In witness whereof we have hereunto set our hands and seals, dated in our assembly at The Hague, the six and twentieth day of July, 1581, endorsed by the orders of the states-general, and signed, J. De Asseliers. ■

This 1581 declaration against Spain led to a prolonged struggle, which finally ended in Dutch independence by the truce of 1609, confirmed by the Treaty of Westphalia in 1648. The importance of this unusual document lies in its formulation of the revolutionary idea that rulers are responsible to the people and can be overthrown by the people if they violate established rights. These ideas were echoed in the American Declaration of Independence almost two centuries later. Jefferson's document, while more concise and more brilliantly formulated, contains many of the same ideas and grievances as the Dutch Declaration of Independence.

• THE EDICT OF NANTES

To leave no occasion for trouble or differences among our subjects: We permit those of the so-called Reformed Religion [Huguenots] to live and abide in all the towns and districts of this our realm . . . free from inquisition, molestation or compulsion to do anything in the way of religion, against their conscience. . . .

We most expressly forbid to those of this religion

the practice thereof . . . except in the places permitted and granted by this edict. The practice of this religion is forbidden in our court and suite, in our domains beyond the mountains, in our city of Paris, or within five leagues thereof . . . Books concerning this religion are not to be printed and exposed for sale save in towns and districts where the public practice of the said religion is allowed.

No distinction is to be made with regard to this religion, in the reception of pupils for education in universities, colleges and schools, nor in the reception of the sick and needy into hospitals, almshouses or public charities.

Members of this religion are capable of holding any office or position in this realm. . . . ■

From the edict granted by Henry IV of France, April 15, 1598. Even though it was an act of limited toleration, it marked a milestone in European freedom. The Edict of Nantes was revoked by Louis XIV on October 18, 1685, which resulted in an irreparable weakening of France.

• THE MAYFLOWER COMPACT

In the name of God, Amen. We, whose names are underwritten, the loyal subjects of our dread sovereigne Lord, King James, by the grace of God, of Great Britaine, France, and Ireland king, defender of the faith, etc., having undertaken, for the glory of God, and advancement of the Christian faith, and honour of our king and country, a voyage to plant the first colony in the Northerne parts of Virginia, doe, by these presents solemnly and mutually in the presence of God, and one of another, covenant and combine ourselves together into a civill body politick, for our better ordering and preservation and furtherance of the ends aforesaid; and by virtue hereof to enacte, constitute, and frame such just and equall laws, ordinances, acts, constitutions, and offices, from time to time, as shall be thought most meete and convenient for the generall good of the Colonie unto which we promise all due submission and obedience. In witness whereof we have hereunder subscribed our names at Cap-Codd the 11. of November, in the year of the raigne of our sovereigne lord, King James, of England, France, and Ireland, the eighteenth, and of Scotland the fiftie-fourth. Anno. Dom. 1620. ∎

Made in 1620. The text here is from William Bradford, History of Plymouth Plantation, 1856.

• THE FUNDAMENTAL ORDERS OF CONNECTICUT

Forasmuch as it hath pleased the Almighty God by the wise disposition of His divine prudence so to order and dispose of things that we the inhabitants and residents of Windsor, Hartford and Wethersfield are now cohabiting and dwelling in and upon the River of Connecticut and the lands thereunto adjoining; and well knowing where a people are gathered together the word of God requires that to maintain the peace and union of such a people there should be an orderly and decent government established according to God, to order and dispose of the affairs of the people at all seasons as occasion shall require, do therefore associate and convene ourselves to be as one Public State or Commonwealth; and do, for ourselves and our successors, and such as shall be adjoined to us at any time hereafter, enter into combination and confederation together, to maintain and preserve the liberty and purity of the Gospel of our Lord Jesus which we now profess, as also the discipline of the churches, which according to the truth of the said Gospel is now practised among us; as also in our civil affairs to be guided and governed according to such laws, rules, orders and decrees as shall be made, ordered and decreed, as followeth:—

1. It is ordered, sentenced and decreed, that there shall be yearly two general assemblies or courts, one on the second Thursday in April, the other on the second Thursday in September, following; the first shall be called the Court of Election, wherein shall be yearly officers as shall be found requisite: whereof one to be chosen governor for the year ensuing and until another be chosen, and no other magistrate to be chosen for more than one year; provided always there be six chosen besides the governor; which being chosen and sworn according to

an oath recorded for that purpose shall have power to administer justice according to the laws here established, and for want thereof according to the rule of the word of God; which choice shall be made by all that are admitted freeman and have taken the oath of fidelity, and cohabitate within this jurisdiction (having been admitted inhabitants by the major part of the town in which they live), or the major part of such as shall be then present.

2. It is ordered, sentenced and decreed, that the election of the aforesaid magistrates shall be on this manner: Every person present and qualified for choice shall bring in (to the person deputed to receive them) one single paper with the name of him written in whom he desires to have governor, and he that hath the greatest number of papers shall be governor for that year. And the rest of the magistrates or public officers to be chosen in this manner: The secretary for the time being shall first read the names of all that are to be put in choice and then shall severally nominate them distinctly, and every one that would have the person nominated to be chosen shall bring in one single paper written upon, and he that would not have him chosen shall bring in a blank: and every one that hath more written papers than blanks shall be a magistrate for that year; which papers shall be received and told by one or more that shall be then chosen by the court and sworn to be faithful therein; but in case there should not be six chosen as aforesaid, besides the governor, out of those which are nominated, then he or they which have the most written papers shall be a magistrate or magistrates for the ensuing year, to make up the aforesaid number.

3. It is ordered, sentenced and decreed, that the secretary shall not nominate any person, nor shall any person be chosen newly into the magistracy which was not propounded in some general court before, to be nominated the next election; and to that end it shall be lawful for each of the towns aforesaid by their deputies to nominate any who they conceive fit to be put to election; and the court may add so many more as they judge requisite.

4. It is ordered, sentenced and decreed that no person be chosen governor above once in two years, and that the governor be always a member of some

approved congregation, and formerly of the magistracy within this jurisdiction; and all the magistrates freemen of this commonwealth: and that no magistrate or other public officer shall execute any part of his or their office before they are severally sworn, which shall be done in the face of the court if they be present, and in case of absence by some deputed for that purpose.

5. It is ordered, sentenced and decreed, that to the aforesaid court of election the several towns shall send their deputies, and when the elections are ended they may proceed in any public service as at other courts. Also the other general court in September shall be for making of laws, and any other public occasion, which concerns the good of the commonwealth.

6. It is ordered, sentenced and decreed, that the governor shall, either by himself or by the secretary, send out summons to the constables of every town for the calling of these two standing courts, one month at least before their several times: and also if the governor require, upon a shorter notice, giving sufficient grounds for it to the deputies when they meet, or else be questioned for the same; and if the governor and major part of magistrates shall either neglect or refuse to call the two general standing courts or either of them, as also at other times when the occasion of the commonwealth require, and the greatest part of the magistrates see cause upon any special occasion to call a general court, they may give order to the secretary so to do: if then it be either denied or neglected the said freemen or the freemen thereof, or the major part of them, shall petition to them so to do; if then it be either denied or neglected the said freemen or the major part of them shall have power to give orders to the constables of the several towns to do the same, and so may meet together, and choose to themselves a moderator, and may proceed to do any act of power, which any other general court may.

7. It is ordered, sentenced and decreed that after there are warrants given out for any of the said general courts, the constable or constables of each town shall forthwith give notice distinctly to the inhabitants of the same, in some public assembly or by going or sending from house to house, that a place and time by him or them limited and set, they meet and assemble themselves together to elect and choose certain deputies to be at the general court then following to agitate the affairs of the commonwealth; which said deputies shall be chosen by all that are admitted inhabitants in the several towns and have taken the oath of fidelity; provided that none be chosen a deputy for any general court who is not a freeman of this commonwealth.

The aforesaid deputies shall be chosen in manner following: Every person that is present and qualified as before expressed, shall bring the names of such, written in several papers, as they desire to have chosen for that employment, and these three or four, more or less, being the number agreed on to be chosen for that time, that have greatest number of papers written for them shall be deputies for that court; whose names shall be endorsed on the back side of the warrant and returned into the court, with the constable or constables' hand unto the same.

8. It is ordered, sentenced and decreed, that Windsor, Hartford and Wethersfield shall have power, each town, to send four of their freemen as deputies to every general court; and whatsoever towns shall be hereafter added to this jurisdiction, they shall send so many deputies as the court shall judge meet, a reasonable proportion to the number of freemen that are in said towns being to be attended therein; which deputies shall have the power of the whole town to give their votes and allowance to all such laws and orders as may be for the public good, and unto which the said towns are to be bound.

9. It is ordered and decreed, that the deputies thus chosen shall have power and liberty to appoint a time and a place of meeting together before any general court to advise and consult of all such things as may concern the good of the public, as also to examine their own elections, whether according to their order, and if they or the greatest part of them find any election to be illegal, they may exclude such for the present from their meeting, and return the same and their reasons to the court; and if it prove

true, the court may fine the party or parties so intruding and the town, if they see cause, and give out a warrant to have a new election in a legal way, either in part or in whole. Also the said deputies shall have power to fine any that shall be disorderly at their meetings, or for not coming in due time or place according to appointment; and they may return the said fines into the court if it be refused to be paid, and the treasurer to take notice of it, and to enter or levy the same as he doth other fines.

10. It is ordered, sentenced and decreed, that every general court, except such as through neglect of the governor and the greatest part of magistrates the freeman themselves do call, shall consist of the governor, or some one chosen to moderate the court, and four other magistrates at least, with the major part of the deputies of the several towns legally chosen; and in case the freemen or larger part of them, through neglect or refusal of the governor and larger part of the magistrates, shall call a court, it shall consist of the larger part of freemen that are present or their deputies, with a moderator chosen by them; in which said general courts shall consist of the supreme power of the Commonwealth, and they only shall have power to make laws or repeal them, to grant levies, to admit of freemen, dispose of lands undisposed of, to several towns or persons, and also shall have power to call either court or magistrate or any other person whatsoever into question for any misdemeanor, and may for just causes displace or deal otherwise according to the nature of the offence; and also may deal in any other matter that concerns the good of this commonwealth, except election of magistrates, which shall be done by the whole body of freemen.

In which court the governor or moderator shall have power to order the court to give liberty of speech, and silence unseasonable and disorderly speakings, to put all things to vote, and in case the vote be equal, to have the casting vote. But none of these courts shall be adjourned or dissolved without the consent of the major part of the court.

11. It is ordered, sentenced and decreed, that when any general court upon the occasions of the commonwealth have agreed upon any sum or sums of money to be levied upon the several towns within this jurisdiction, that a committee be chosen to set out and appoint what shall be the proportion of every town to pay of the said levy, provided the committees be made up of an equal number out of each town.

14th January, 1638, the 11 orders aforesaid are voted.

THE OATH OF THE GOVERNOR, FOR THE PRESENT.

I, ... , being now chosen to be governor within this jurisdiction, for the year ensuing, and until a new one be chosen, do swear by the great and dreadful name of the everlasting God, to promote the public good and peace of the same, according to the best of my skill; as also will maintain all lawful privileges of the commonwealth; as also that all wholesome laws that are or shall be made by lawful authority here established, be duly executed; and will further the execution of justice according to the rule of God's word; so help me God, in the name of the Lord Jesus Christ.

THE OATH OF THE MAGISTRATE, FOR THE PRESENT.

I, ... , being chosen a magistrate within this jurisdiction for the year ensuing, do swear by the great and dreadful name of the everlasting God, to promote the public good and peace of the same, according to the best of my skill, and that I will maintain all the lawful privileges thereof according to my understanding, as also assist in the execution of all such wholesome laws as are made or shall be made by lawful authority here establish, and will further the execution of justice for the time aforesaid according to the righteous rule of God's word; so help me God, etc. ■

Drafted in 1638, and adopted in 1639 under the leadership of the democratic clergyman Thomas Hooker. The Fundamental Orders *is believed to be the first written constitution for popular government made by the people themselves. It became a model for other American state constitutions.*

• THE MASSACHUSETTS "BODY OF LIBERTIES"

No mans life shall be taken away, no mans honour or good name shall be stayned, no mans person shall be arrested, restrayned, banished, dismembred, nor any ways punished, no man shall be deprived of his wife or children, no mans goods or estate shall be taken away from him, nor any way indammaged under Colour of law, of Courtenance of Authoritie, unless it be by virtue or equitie of some expresse law of the Country warranting the same, established by a general Court and sufficiently published. . . . ◼

Drafted by Nathaniel Ward, adopted by the Massachusetts General Court, 1641.

• THE INSTRUMENT OF GOVERNMENT

The government of the Commonwealth of England, Scotland, and Ireland, and the dominions thereunto belonging.

I. That the supreme legislative authority of the Commonwealth of England, Scotland, and Ireland, and the dominions thereunto belonging, shall be and reside in one person, and the people assembled in Parliament; the style of which person shall be the Lord Protector of the Commonwealth of England, Scotland, and Ireland.

II. That the exercise of the chief magistracy and the administration of the government over the said countries and dominions, and the people thereof, shall be in the Lord Protector, assisted with a council, the number whereof shall not exceed twenty-one, nor be less than thirteen.

III. That all writs, processes, commissions, patents, grants, and other things, which now run in the name and style of the keepers of the liberty of England by authority of Parliament, shall run in the name and style of the Lord Protector, from whom, for the future, shall be derived all magistracy and honours in these three nations; and have the power of pardons (except in case of murders and treason) and benefit of all forfeitures for the public use; and shall govern the said countries and dominions in all things by the advice of the council, and according to these presents and the laws.

IV. That the Lord Protector, the Parliament sitting, shall dispose and order the militia and forces, both by sea and land, for the peace and good of the three nations, by consent of Parliament; and that the Lord Protector, with the advice and consent of the major part of the council, shall dispose and order the militia for the ends aforesaid in the intervals of Parliament.

V. That the Lord Protector, by the advice aforesaid, shall direct in all things concerning the keeping and holding of a good correspondency with foreign kings, princes, and states; and also, with the consent of the major part of the council, have the power of war and peace.

VI. That the laws shall not be altered, suspended, abrogated, or repealed, nor any new law made, nor any tax, charge, or imposition laid upon the people, but by common consent in Parliament, save only as is expressed in the thirtieth article.

VII. That there shall be a Parliament summoned to meet at Westminster upon the third day of September, 1654, and that successively a Parliament shall be summoned once in every third year, to be accounted from the dissolution of the present Parliament.

VIII. That neither the Parliament to be next summoned, nor any successive Parliaments, shall, during the time of five months, to be accounted from the day of their first meeting, be adjourned, prorogued, or dissolved, without their own consent.

IX. That as well the next as all other successive Parliaments, shall be summoned and elected in manner hereafter expressed; that is to say, the persons to be chosen within England, Wales, the Isles of Jersey, Guernsey, and the town of Berwick-upon-Tweed, to sit and serve in Parliament, shall be, and not exceed, the number of four hundred. The persons to be chosen within Scotland to sit and serve in Parliament, shall be, and not exceed, the number of thirty; and the persons to be chosen to sit in Parliament for Ireland shall be, and not exceed, the number of thirty.

X. That the persons to be elected to sit in Parliament from time to time, for the several counties of England, Wales, the Isles of Jersey and Guernsey, and the town of Berwick-upon-Tweed, and all places within the same respectively, shall be according to the proportions and numbers hereafter expressed: that is to say,

Bedfordshire, 5; Bedford Town, 1; Berkshire, 5; Abingdon, 1; Reading, 1; Buckinghamshire, 5; Buckingham Town, 1; Aylesbury, 1; Wycomb, 1; Cambridgeshire, 4; Cambridge Town, 1; Cambridge University, 1; Isle of Ely, 2; Cheshire, 4; Chester, 1; Cornwall, 8; Launceston, 1; Truro, 1; Penryn, 1; East Looe and West Looe, 1; Cumberland, 2; Carlisle, 1; Derbyshire, 4; Derby Town, 1; Devonshire, 11; Exeter, 2; Plymouth, 2; Clifton, Dartmouth, Hardness, 1; Totnes, 1; Barnstable, 1; Tiverton, 1; Honiton, 1; Dorsetshire, 6; Dorchester, 1; Weymouth and Melcomb-Regis, 1; Lyme-Regis, 1; Poole, 1; Durham, 2; City of Durham, 1; Essex, 13; Malden, 1; Colchester, 2; Gloucestershire, 5; Gloucester, 2; Tewkesbury, 1; Cirencester, 1; Herefordshire, 4; Hereford, 1; Leominster, 1; Hertfordshire, 5; St. Alban's, 1; Hertford, 1; Huntingdonshire, 3; Huntingdon, 1; Kent, 11; Canterbury, 2; Rochester, 1; Maidstone, 1; Dover, 1; Sandwich, 1; Queenborough, 1; Lancashire, 4; Preston, 1; Lancaster, 1; Liverpool, 1; Manchester, 1; Leicestershire, 4; Leicester, 2; Lincolnshire, 10; Lincoln, 2; Boston, 1; Grantham, 1; Stamford, 1; Great Grimsby, 1; Middlesex, 4; London, 6; Westminster, 2; Monmouthshire, 3; Norfolk, 10; Norwich, 2; Lynn-Regis, 2; Great Yarmouth, 2; Northamptonshire, 6; Peterborough, 1; Northampton, 1; Nottinghamshire, 4; Nottingham, 2; Northumberland, 3; Newcastle-upon-Tyne, 1; Berwick, 1; Oxfordshire, 5; Oxford City, 1; Oxford University, 1; Woodstock, 1; Ruthlandshire, 2; Shropshire, 4; Shrewsbury, 2; Bridgnorth, 1; Ludlow, 1; Staffordshire, 3; Lichfield, 1; Stafford, 1; Newcastle-under-Lyme, 1; Somersetshire, 11; Bristol, 2; Taunton, 2; Bath, 1; Wells, 1; Bridgwater, 1; Southamptonshire, 8; Winchester, 1; Southampton, 1; Portsmouth, 1;

Isle of Wight, 2; Andover, 1; Suffolk, 10; Ipswich, 2; Bury St. Edmunds, 2; Dunwich, 1; Sudbury, 1; Surrey, 6; Southwark, 2; Guildford, 1; Reigate, 1; Sussex, 9; Chichester, 1; Lewes, 1; East Grinstead, 1; Arundel, 1; Rye, 1; Westmoreland, 2; Warwickshire, 4; Coventry, 2; Warwick, 1; Wiltshire, 10; New Sarum, 2; Marlborough, 1; Devizes, 1; Worcestershire, 5; Worcester, 2.

YORKSHIRE.—West Riding, 6; East Riding, 4; North Riding, 4; City of York, 2; Kingston-upon-Hull, 1; Beverley, 1; Scarborough, 1; Richmond, 1; Leeds, 1; Halifax, 1.

WALES.—Anglesey, 2; Brecknockshire, 2; Cardiganshire, 2; Carmarthenshire, 2; Carnarvonshire, 2; Denbighshire, 2; Flintshire, 2; Glamorganshire, 2; Cardiff, 1; Merionethshire, 1; Montgomeryshire, 2; Pembrokeshire, 2; Haverfordwest, 1; Radnorshire, 2.

The distribution of the persons to be chosen for Scotland and Ireland, and the several counties, cities, and places therein, shall be according to such proportions and number as shall be agreed upon and declared by the Lord Protector and the major part of the council, before the sending forth writs of summons for the next Parliament.

XI. That the summons to Parliament shall be by writ under the Great Seal of England, directed to the sheriffs of the several and respective counties, with such alteration as may suit with the present government, to be made by the Lord Protector and his council, which the Chancellor, Keeper, or Commissioners of the Great Seal shall seal, issue, and send abroad by warrant from the Lord Protector. If the Lord Protector shall not give warrent for issuing of writs of summons for the next Parliament, before the first of June, 1654, or for the Triennial Parliaments, before the first day of August in every third year, to be accounted as aforesaid; that then the Chancellor, Keeper, or Commissioners of the Great Seal for the time being, shall, without any warrant or direction, within seven days after the said first day of June, 1654, seal, issue, and send abroad writs of summons (changing therein what is to be changed as aforesaid) to the several and respective sheriffs of England, Scotland, and Ireland, for summoning the Parliament to meet at Westminster, the third day of September next; and shall likewise, within seven days after the said first day of August, in every third year, to be accounted from the dissolution of the precedent Parliament, seal, issue, and send forth abroad several writs of summons (changing therein what is to be changed) as aforesaid, for summoning the Parliament to meet at Westminster the sixth of November in that third year. That the said several and respective sheriffs, shall, within ten days after the receipt of such writ as aforesaid, cause the same to be proclaimed and published in every market-town within his county upon the market-days thereof, between twelve and three of the clock; and shall then also publish and declare the certain day of the week and month, for choosing members to serve in Parliament for the body of the said county, according to the tenor of the said writ, which shall be upon Wednesday five weeks after the date of the writ; and shall likewise declare the place where the election shall be made: for which purpose he shall appoint the most convenient place for the whole county to meet in; and shall send precepts for elections to be made in all and every city, town, borough, or place within his county, where elections are to be made by virtue of these presents, to the Mayor, Sheriff, or other head officer of such city, town, borough, or place, within three days after the receipt of such writ and writs; which the said Mayors, Sheriffs, and officers respectively are to make publication of, and of the certain day for such elections to be made in the said city, town, or place aforesaid, and to cause elections to be made accordingly.

XII. That at the day and place of elections, the Sheriff of each county, and the said Mayors, Sheriffs, Bailiffs, and other head officers within their cities, towns boroughs, and places respectively, shall take view of the said elections, and shall make return into the chancery within twenty days after the said elections, of the persons elected by the greater number of electors, under their hands and seals, between him on the one part, and the electors on the other part; wherein shall be contained, that the persons elected shall not have power to alter the government as it is hereby settled in one single person and a Parliament.

XIII. That the Sheriff, who shall wittingly and willingly make any false return, or neglect his duty, shall incur the penalty of 2000 marks of lawful English money; the one moiety to the Lord Protector, and the other moiety to such person as will sue for the same.

XIV. That all and every person and persons, who have aided, advised, assisted, or abetted in any war against the Parliament, since the first day of January 1641 (unless they have been since in the service of the Parliament, and given signal testimony of their good affection thereunto) shall be disabled and incapable to be elected, or to give any vote in the election of any members to serve in the next Parliament, or in the three succeeding Triennial Parliaments.

XV. That all such, who have advised, assisted, or abetted the rebellion of Ireland, shall be disabled and incapable for ever to be elected, or give any vote in the election of any member to serve in Parliament; as also all such who do or shall profess the Roman Catholic religion.

XVI. That all votes and elections given or made contrary, or not according to these qualifications, shall be null and void; and if any person, who is hereby made incapable, shall give his vote for election of members to serve in Parliament, such person shall lose and forfeit one full year's value of his real estate, and one full third part of his personal estate; one moiety thereof to the Lord Protector, and the other moiety to him or them who shall sue for the same.

XVII. That the persons who shall be elected to serve in Parliament, shall be such (and no other than such) as are persons of known integrity, fearing God, and of good conversation, and being of the age of twenty-one years.

XVIII. That all and every person and persons seised or possessed to his own use, of any estate, real or personal, to the value of £200, and not within the aforesaid exceptions, shall be capable to elect members to serve in Parliament for counties.

XIX. That the Chancellor, Keeper, or Commissioners of the Great Seal, shall be sworn before they enter into their offices, truly and faithfully to issue forth, and send abroad, writs of summons to Parliament, at the times and in the manner before expressed: and in case of neglect or failure to issue and send abroad writs accordingly, he or they shall for every such offence be guilty of high treason, and suffer the pains and penalties thereof.

XX. That in case writs be not issued out, as is before expressed, but that there be a neglect therein, fifteen days after the time wherein the same ought to be issued out by the Chancellor, Keeper, or Commissioners of the Great Seal; that then the Parliament shall, as often as such failure shall happen, assemble and be held at Westminster, in the usual place, at the times prefixed, in manner and by the means hereafter expressed; that is to say, that the sheriffs of the several and respective counties, sheriffdoms, cities, boroughs, and places aforesaid, within England, Wales, Scotland, and Ireland, the Chancellor, Masters, and Scholars of the Universities of Oxford and Cambridge, and the Mayor and Bailiffs of the borough of Berwick-upon-Tweed and other places aforesaid respectively, shall at the several courts and places to be appointed as aforesaid, within thirty days after the said fifteen days, cause such members to be chosen for their said several and respective counties, sheriffdoms, universities, cities, boroughs, and places aforesaid, by such persons, and in such manner as if several and respective writs of summons to Parliament under the Great Seal had issued and been awarded according to the tenor aforesaid: that if the sheriff, or other persons authorized, shall neglect his or their duty herein, that all and every such sheriff and person authorized as aforesaid, so neglecting his or their duty, shall, for every such offence, be guilty of high treason, and shall suffer the pains and penalties thereof.

XXI. That the clerk, called the clerk of the Commonwealth in Chancery for the time being, and all others, who shall afterwards execute that office, to whom the returns shall be made, shall for the next Parliament, and the two succeeding Triennial Parliaments, the next day after such return, certify the names of the several persons so returned, and of the places for which he and they were chosen respectively, unto the Council; who shall peruse the said returns, and examine whether the persons so elected and returned be such as is agreeable to the qualifications, and not disabled to be elected: and that every person and persons being so duly elected, and being approved of by the major part of the Council to be persons not disabled, but qualified as aforesaid, shall be esteemed a member of Parliament, and be admitted to sit in Parliament, and not otherwise.

XXII. That the persons so chosen and assembled in manner aforesaid, or any sixty of them, shall be, and be deemed the Parliament of England, Scotland, and Ireland; and the supreme legislative power to be and reside in the Lord Protector and such Parliament, in manner herein expressed.

XXIII. That the Lord Protector, with the advice of the major part of the Council, shall at any other time than is before expressed, when the necessities of the State shall require it, summon Parliaments in manner before expressed, which shall not be adjourned, prorogued, or dissolved without their own consent, during the first three months of their sitting. And in case of future war with any foreign State, a Parliament shall be forthwith summoned for their advice concerning the same.

XXIV. That all Bills agreed unto by the Parliament, shall be presented to the Lord Protector for his consent; and in case he shall not give his consent thereto within twenty days after they shall be presented to him, or give satisfaction to the Parliament within the time limited, that then, upon declaration of the Parliament that the Lord Protector hath not consented nor given satisfaction, such Bills shall pass into and become laws, although he shall not give his consent thereunto; provided such Bills contain nothing in them contrary to the matters contained in these presents.

XXV. That Henry Lawrence, Esq., &c. . . . or any seven of them, shall be a Council for the purposes expressed in this writing; and upon the death or other removal of any of them, the Parliament shall nominate six persons of ability, integrity, and fearing God, for every one that is dead or removed; out of which the major part of the Council shall elect two, and present them to the Lord Protector, of which he shall elect one; and in case the Parliament shall not nominate within twenty days after notice given unto them thereof, the major part of the Council shall nominate three as aforesaid to the Lord Protector, who out of them shall supply the vacancy; and until this choice be made, the remaining part of the Council shall execute as fully in all things, as if their number were full. And in case of corruption, or other miscarriage in any of the Council in their trust, the Parliament shall appoint seven of their number, and the Council six, who, together with the Lord Chancellor, Lord Keeper, or Commissioners of the Great Seal for the time being, shall have power to hear and determine such corruption and miscarriage, and to award and inflict punishment, as the nature of the offense shall deserve, which punishment shall not be pardoned or remitted by the Lord Protector; and, in the interval of Parlaments, the major part of the Council, with the consent of the Lord Protector, may, for corruption or other miscarriage as aforesaid, suspend any of their number from the exercise of their trust, if they shall find it just, until the matter shall be heard and examined as aforesaid.

XXVI. That the Lord Protector and the major part of the Council aforesaid may, at any time before the meeting of the next Parliament, add to the Council such persons as they shall think fit, provided the number of the Council be not made thereby to exceed twenty-one, and the quorum to be proportioned accordingly by the Lord Protector and the major part of the Council.

XXVII. That a constant yearly revenue shall be raised, settled, and established for maintaining of 10,000 horse and dragoons, and 20,000 foot, in England, Scotland and Ireland, for the defence and security thereof, and also for a convenient number of ships for guarding of the seas; besides £200,000 per annum for defraying the other necessary charges of administration of justice, and other expenses of the Government, which revenue shall be raised by the customs, and such other ways and means as shall be agreed upon by the Lord Protector and the Coun-

cil, and shall not be taken away or diminished, nor the way agreed upon for raising the same altered, but by the consent of the Lord Protector and the Parliament.

XXVIII. That the said yearly revenue shall be paid into the public treasury, and shall be issued out for the uses aforesaid.

XXIX. That in case there shall not be cause hereafter to keep up so great a defence both at land or sea, but that there be an abatement made thereof, the money which will be saved thereby shall remain in bank for the public service, and not be employed to any other use but by consent of Parliament, or, in the intervals of Parliament, by the Lord Protector and major part of the Council.

XXX. That the raising of money for defraying the charge of the present extraordinary forces, both at sea and land, in respect of the present wars, shall be by consent of Parliament, and not otherwise: save only that the Lord Protector, with the consent of the major part of the Council, for preventing the disorders and dangers which might otherwise fall out both by sea and land, shall have power, until the meeting of the first Parliament, to raise money for the purposes aforesaid; and also to make laws and ordinances for the peace and welfare of these nations where it shall be necessary, which shall be binding and in force, until order shall be taken in Parliament concerning the same.

XXXI. That the lands, tenements, rents, royalties, jurisdictions and hereditaments which remain yet unsold or undisposed of, by Act or Ordinance of Parliament, belonging to the Commonwealth (except the forests and chases, and the honours and manors belonging to the same; the lands of the rebels in Ireland, lying in the four counties of Dublin, Cork, Kildare, and Carlow; the lands forfeited by the people of Scotland in the late wars, and also the lands of Papists and delinquents in England who have not yet compounded), shall be vested in the Lord Protector, to hold, to him and his successors, Lords Protectors of these nations, and shall not be alienated but by consent in Parliament. And all debts, fines, issues, amercements, penalties and profits, certain and casual, due to the Keepers of the liberties of England by authority of Parliament, shall be due to the Lord Protector, and be payable into his public receipt, and shall be recovered and prosecuted in his name.

XXXII. That the office of Lord Protector over these nations shall be elective and not hereditary; and upon the death of the Lord Protector, another fit person shall be forthwith elected to succeed him in the Government; which election shall be by the Council, who, immediately upon the death of the Lord Protector, shall assemble in the Chamber where they usually sit in Council; and, having given notice to all their members of the cause of their assembling, shall, being thirteen at least present, proceed to the election; and, before they depart the said Chamber, shall elect a fit person to succeed in the Government, and forthwith cause proclamation thereof to be made in all the three nations as shall be requisite; and the person that they, or the major part of them, shall elect as aforesaid, shall be, and shall be taken to be, Lord Protector over these nations of England, Scotland and Ireland, and the dominions thereto belonging. Provided that none of the children of the late King, nor any of his line or family, be elected to be Lord Protector or other Chief Magistrate over these nations, or any of the dominions thereto belonging. And until the aforesaid election be past, the Council shall take care of the Government, and administer in all things as fully as the Lord Protector, or the Lord Protector and Council are enabled to do.

XXXIII. That Oliver Cromwell, Captain-General of the forces of England, Scotland and Ireland, shall be, and is hereby declared to be, Lord Protector of the Commonwealth of England, Scotland and Ireland, and the dominions thereto belonging, for his life.

XXXIV. That the Chancellor, Keeper or Commissioners of the Great Seal, the Treasurer, Admiral, Chief Governors of Ireland and Scotland, and the Chief Justices of both the Benches, shall be chosen by the approbation of Parliament; and, in the intervals of Parliament, by the approbation of the major part of the Council, to be afterwards approved by the Parliament.

XXXV. That the Christian religion, as contained in the Scriptures, be held forth and recommended as the public profession of these nations; and that, as soon as may be, a provision, less subject to scruple and contention, and more certain than the present, be made for the encouragement and maintenance of able and painful teachers, for the instructing the people, and for discovery and confutation of error, hereby, and whatever is contrary to sound doctrine; and until such provision be made, the present maintenance shall not be taken away or impeached.

XXXVI. That to the public profession held forth none shall be compelled by penalties or otherwise; but that endeavours be used to win them by sound doctrine and the example of a good conversation.

XXXVII. That such as profess faith in God by Jesus Christ (though differing in judgment from the doctrine, worship or discipline publicly held forth) shall not be restrained from, but shall be protected in, the profession of the faith and exercise of their religion; so as they abuse not this liberty to the civil injury of others and to the actual disturbance of the public peace on their parts: provided this liberty be not extended to Popery or Prelacy, nor to such as, under the profession of Christ, hold forth and practice licentiousness.

XXXVIII. That all laws, statutes and ordinances, and clauses in any law, statute or ordinance to the contrary of the aforesaid liberty, shall be esteemed as null and void.

XXXIX. That the Acts and Ordinances of Parliament made for the sale or other disposition of the lands, rents and hereditaments of the late King, Queen, and Prince, of Archbishops and Bishops, &c., Deans and Chapters, the lands of delinquents and forest-lands, or any of them, or of any other lands, tenements, rents and hereditaments belonging to the Commonwealth, shall nowise be impeached or made invalid, but shall remain good and firm; and that the securities given by Act and Ordinance of Parliament for any sum or sums of money, by any of the said lands, the excise, or any other public revenue; and also the securities given by the public faith of the nation, and the engagement of the public faith for satisfaction of debts and damages, shall remain firm and good, and not be made void and invalid upon any pretence whatsoever.

XL. That the Articles given to or made with the enemy, and afterwards confirmed by Parliament, shall be performed and made good to the persons concerned therein; and that such appeals as were depending in the last Parliament for relief concerning bills of sale of delinquent's estates, may be heard and determined the next Parliament, any thing in this writing or otherwise to the contrary notwithstanding.

XLI. That every successive Lord Protector over these nations shall take and subscribe a solemn oath, in the presence of the Council, and such others as they shall call to them, that he will seek the peace, quiet and welfare of these nations, cause law and justice to be equally administered; and that he will not violate or infringe the matters and things contained in this writing, and in all other things will, to his power and to the best of his understanding, govern these nations according to the laws, statutes and customs thereof.

XLII. That each person of the Council shall, before they enter upon their trust, take and subscribe an oath, that they will be true and faithful in their trust, according to the best of their knowledge; and that in the election of every successive Lord Protector they shall proceed therein impartially, and do nothing therein for any promise, fear, favour or reward. ∎

Adopted by Cromwell and his officers, December 16, 1653, as the basis of Cromwell's office of Lord Protector.

• THE ENGLISH BILL OF RIGHTS

Whereas the Lords Spiritual and Temporal, and Commons, assembled at Westminster, lawfully, fully, and freely representing all the estates of the people of this realm, did . . . present unto their Majesties . . . a certain declaration in writing . . . in the words following . . .

Whereas the late King James II . . . did endeavour to subvert and extirpate the Protestant religion, and the laws and liberties of this kingdom. . . .

All of which are utterly and directly contrary to the known laws and statutes, and freedom of this realm. . . .

And thereupon the said Lords Spiritual and Temporal, and Commons . . . being now assembled in a full and free representation of this nation . . . do in the first place (as their ancestors in like case have usually done), for the vindicating and asserting their ancient rights and liberties, declare:

1. That the pretended power of suspending of laws or the execution of laws by regal authority without consent of Parliament is illegal.

2. That the pretended power of dispensing with laws . . . as it hath been assumed . . . of late, is illegal.

3. That the commission for electing the late court . . . for ecclesiastical causes, and all other commissions and courts of like nature, are illegal and pernicious.

4. That levying money for or to the use of the Crown . . . without grant of Parliament . . . is illegal.

5. That it is the right of the subject to petition the king. . . .

6. That the raising or keeping a standing army within the kingdom in time of peace, unless it be with consent of Parliament, is against the law.

7. That the subjects which are Protestants may have arms for their defence suitable to their condition, and as allowed by law.

8. That elections of members of Parliament ought to be free.

9. That the freedom of speech, and debates or proceedings in Parliament, ought not to be impeached or questioned in any court or place out of Parliament.

10. That excessive bail ought not be required, nor excessive fines imposed; nor cruel and unusual punishment inflicted.

11. That jurors ought to be duly impanelled and returned, and jurors which pass upon men in trials for high treason ought to be freeholders.

12. That all grants and promises of fines and forfeitures of particular persons before conviction are illegal and void.

13. And that for redress of all grievances, and for the amending, strengthening, and preserving of the laws, Parliaments ought to be held frequently. ∎

From the bill declared on February 13, 1689, and accepted by William III (of Orange) when he was invited to become King of England.

• THE PENNSYLVANIA CHARTER OF PRIVILEGES

WILLIAM PENN, Proprietary and Governor of the Province of *Pensilvania* and Territories thereunto belonging, To all to whom these Presents shall come, sendeth Greeting. WHEREAS King CHARLES *the Second,* by His Letters Patents, under the Great Seal of England . . . was graciously pleased to give and grant unto me, and my Heirs and Assigns for ever, this Province of *Pensilvania,* with divers great Powers and Jurisdictions for the well Government thereof. . . .

KNOW YE THEREFORE, That for the further well-being and good Government of the said Province, and Territories; and in Pursuance of the Rights and Powers before-mentioned, I the said *William Penn* do declare, grant and confirm, unto all the Freemen, Planters and Adventurers, and other Inhabitants of this Province and Territories, these following Liberties, Franchises and Privileges, so far as in me lieth, to be held, enjoyed and kept, by the Freemen, Planters and Adventurers, and other Inhabitants of and in the said Province and Territories thereunto annexed.

FIRST

BECAUSE no People can be truly happy, though under the greatest enjoyment of Civil Liberties, if abridged of the Freedom of their Consciences, as to their Religious Profession and Worship: And Almighty God being the only Lord of Conscience, Father of Lights and Spirits; and the Author as well as Object of all divine Knowledge, Faith and Worship, who only doth enlighten the Minds, and persuade and convince the Understandings of People, I do hereby grant and declare, That no Person or Persons, inhabiting this Province or Territories, who shall confess and acknowledge *One* Almighty God, the Creator, Upholder and Ruler of the World; and profess him or themselves obliged to live quietly under the Civil Government, shall be in any Case molested or prejudiced, in his or their Person or Estate, because of his or their conscientious Persuasion or Practice, nor be compelled to frequent or maintain any religious Worship, Place or Ministry, contrary to his or their Mind, or to do or suffer any other Act or Thing, contrary to their religious Persuasion . . .

AND no Act, Law or Ordinance whatsoever, shall at any Time hereafter, be made or done, to alter, change or diminish the Form or Effect of this Charter, or of any Part or Clause therein, contrary to the true Intent and Meaning thereof, without the Consent of the Governor for the time being, and six parts of seven of the Assembly met.

BUT because the Happiness of Mankind depends so much upon the enjoying of Liberty of their Consciences as aforesaid, I do hereby solemnly declare, promise and grant, for me, my Heirs and Assigns, That the *First* Article of this Charter relating to Liberty of Conscience, and every Part and Clause therein, according to the true Intent and Meaning thereof, shall be kept and remain, without any Alteration, inviolably forever. . . . ∎

From the document granted by William Penn, October 28, 1701.

• THE COLONIAL DECLARATION OF RIGHTS

The members of this congress, sincerely devoted, with the warmest sentiments of affection and duty to his majesty's person and government, inviolably attached to the present happy establishment of the protestant succession, and with minds deeply impressed by a sense of the present and impending misfortunes of the British colonies on this continent; having considered as maturely as time will permit, the circumstances of the said colonies, esteem it our indispensable duty to make the following declarations of our humble opinion, respecting the most essential rights and liberties of the colonists, and of the grievances under which they labour, by reason of several late acts of parliament.

1. That his majesty's subjects in these colonies, owe the same allegiance to the crown of Great Britain, that is owing from his subjects born within the realm, and all due subordination to that august body the parliament of Great Britain.

2. That his majesty's liege subjects in these colonies, are entitled to all the inherent rights and liberties of his natural born subjects, within the kingdom of Great Britain.

3. That it is inseparably essential to the freedom of a people, and the undoubted right of Englishmen, that no taxes be imposed on them but with their own consent, given personally, or by their representatives.

4. That the people of these colonies are not, and, from their local circumstances, cannot be, represented in the House of Commons in Great Britain.

5. That the only representatives of the people of these colonies, are persons chosen therein by themselves; and that no taxes ever have been, or can be constitutionally imposed on them, but by their respective legislatures.

6. That all supplies to the crown being free gifts of the people, it is unreasonable and inconsistent with the principles and spirit of the British constitution, for the people of Great Britain to grant to his majesty the property of the colonists.

7. That trial by jury, is the inherent and invaluable right of every British subject in these colonies.

8. That the late act of parliament, entitled, an act for granting and applying certain stamp duties, and other duties, in the British colonies and plantations in America, &c., by imposing taxes on the inhabitants of these colonies, and the said act, and several other acts, by extending the jurisdiction of the courts of admiralty beyond its ancient limits, have a manifest tendency to subvert the rights and liberties of the colonists.

9. That the duties imposed by several late acts of parliament, from the peculiar circumstances of these colonies, will be extremely burdensome and grievous; and from the scarcity of specie, the payment of them absolutely impracticable.

10. That as the profits of the trade of these colonies ultimately center in Great Britain, to pay for the manufactures which they are obliged to take from thence, they eventually contribute very largely to all supplies granted there to the crown.

11. That the restrictions imposed by several late acts of parliament on the trade of these colonies, will render them unable to purchase the manufactures of Great Britain.

12. That the increase, prosperity and happiness of these colonies, depend on the full and free enjoyments of their rights and liberties, and an intercourse with Great Britain mutually affectionate and advantageous.

13. That it is the right of the British subjects in these colonies, to petition the king, or either house of parliament.

Lastly, That it is the indispensable duty of these colonies, to the best of sovereigns, to the mother country, and to themselves, to endeavour by a loyal and dutiful address to his majesty, and humble applications to both houses of parliament, to procure the repeal of the act for granting and applying certain stamp duties, of all clauses of any other acts of parliament whereby the jurisdiction of the admiralty is extended as aforesaid, and of the other late acts for the restriction of American Commerce. ■

Adopted by delegates of nine American colonies, in New York, October 7, 1765, in protest against the British Parliament's Stamp Act of March, 1765.

• THE VIRGINIA BILL OF RIGHTS

A declaration or rights made by the representatives of the good people of Virginia, assembled in full and free convention, which rights do pertain to them and their posterity, as the basis and foundation of government.

That all men are by nature equally free and independent, and have certain inherent rights of which, when they enter into a state of society, they cannot, by any compact, deprive or divert their posterity; namely, the enjoyment of life and liberty, with the means of acquiring and possessing property, and pursuing and obtaining happiness and safety.

That all power is vested in, and consequently derived from, the people; that magistrates are their trustees and servants, and at all times amenable to them.

That government is, or ought to be instituted for the common benefit; protection, and security of the people, nation, or community; of all the various modes and forms of government, that is best which is capable of producing the greatest degree of happiness and safety, and is most effectually secured against the danger of maladministration; and that when any government shall be found inadequate or contrary to these purposes, a majority of the community hath an indubitable, inalienable, and indefeasible right to reform, alter, or abolish it, in such manner as shall be judged most conducive to the public weal.

That no man, or set of men, are entitled to exclusive or separate emoluments, or privileges from the community, but in consideration of public services; which, not being descendible, neither ought the offices of magistrate, legislator, or judge to be hereditary.

That the legislative and executive powers of the State should be separate and distinct from the judiciary; and that the members of the two first may be restrained from oppression, by feeling and participating the burdens of the people, they should, at fixed periods, be reduced to a private station, return into that body from which they were originally taken, and the vacancies be supplied by frequent, certain, and regular elections, in which all, or any part of the former members, to be again eligible or ineligible, as the laws shall direct. . . .

(SEC. 6) That elections of members to serve as representatives of the people, in assembly, ought to be free; and that all men, having sufficient evidence of permanent common interest with, and attachment to, the community, have the right of suffrage, and cannot be taxed or deprived of their property for public uses, without their own consent, or that of their representatives so elected, nor bound by any law to which they have not, in like manner, assented for the public good.

(SEC. 7) That all power of suspending laws, or the execution of laws, by any authority without consent of the representatives of the people, is injurious to their rights, and ought not to be exercised.

(SEC. 8) That in all capital or criminal prosecutions a man hath a right to demand the cause and nature of his accusation, to be confronted with the accusers and witnesses, to call for evidence in his favor, and to a speedy trial by an impartial jury of twelve men of his vicinage, without whose unanimous consent he cannot be found guilty; nor can he be compelled to give evidence against himself; that no man be deprived of his liberty, except by the law of the land or the judgement of his peers.

(SEC. 9) That excessive bail ought not to be required, nor excessive fines imposed, nor cruel and unusual punishments inflicted.

(SEC. 10) That general warrants, whereby an officer or messenger may be commanded to search suspected places without evidence of a fact committed, or to seize any person or persons not named, or whose offence is not particularly described and supported by evidence, are grievous and oppressive, and ought not to be granted.

(SEC. 11) That in controversies respecting property, and in suits between man and man, the ancient trial by jury is preferable to any other, and ought to be held sacred.

(SEC. 12) That the freedom of the press is one of the great bulwarks of liberty, and can never be restrained but by despotic governments.

(SEC. 13) That a well-regulated militia, composed of the body of the people trained to arms, is the proper, natural, and safe defence of a free State; that standing armies, in time of peace, should be avoided as dangerous to liberty; and that in all cases the military should be under strict subordination to, and governed by, the civil power.

(SEC. 14) That the people have a right to uniform government; and, therefore, that no government separate from, or independent of the government of Virginia, ought to be erected or established within the limits thereof.

(SEC. 15) That no free government, or the blessings of liberty, can be preserved to any people, but by a firm adherence to justice, moderation, temperance, frugality, and virtue, and by frequent recurrence to fundamental principles.

That religion, or the duty which we owe to our Creator, and the manner of discharging it, can be directed only by reason and conviction, not by force or violence; and therefore all men are equally entitled to the free exercise of religion, according to the dictates of conscience; and that it is the mutual duty of all to practise Christian forbearance, love, and charity towards each other. ■

From document drafted by George Mason,
adopted June 12, 1776.

• THE DECLARATION OF INDEPENDENCE

A DECLARATION BY THE REPRESENTATIVES OF THE UNITED STATES OF AMERICA, IN GENERAL CONGRESS ASSEMBLED

When in the Course of human events, it becomes necessary for one people to dissolve the political bands which have connected them with another, and to assume among the powers of the earth, the separate and equal station to which the Laws of Nature and of Nature's God entitle them, a decent respect to the opinions of mankind requires that they should declare the causes which impel them to the separation.

We hold these truths to be self-evident, that all men are created equal, that they are endowed by

their Creator with certain unalienable Rights, that among these are Life, Liberty and the pursuit of Happiness. That to secure these rights, Governments are instituted among Men, deriving their just powers from the consent of the governed. That whenever any Form of Government becomes destructive of these ends, it is the Right of the People to alter or to abolish it, and to institute new Government, laying its foundation on such principles and organizing its powers in such form, as to them shall seem most likely to effect their Safety and Happiness. Prudence, indeed, will dictate that Governments long established should not be changed for light and transient causes, and accordingly, all experience hath shewn, that mankind are more disposed to suffer, while evils are sufferable, than to right themselves by abolishing the forms to which they are accustomed. But when a long train of abuses and usurpations, pursuing invariably the same Object, evinces a design to reduce them under absolute Despotism, it is their right, it is their duty, to throw off such Government, and to provide new Guards for their future security. Such has been the patient sufferance of these Colonies; and such is now the necessity which constrains them to expunge their former systems of government. The history of the present King of Great Britain is a history of unremitting injuries and usurpations, all having in direct object the establishment of an absolute tyranny over these states. To prove this let facts be submitted to a candid world.

He has refused his assent to laws the most wholesome and necessary for the public good.

He has forbidden his governors to pass laws of immediate and pressing importance, unless suspended in their operation till his assent should be obtained, and when so suspended, he has utterly neglected to attend to them.

He has refused to pass other laws for the accommodation of large districts of people, unless those people would relinquish the right of representation in the legislature, a right inestimable to them, and formidable to tyrants only.

He has called together legislative bodies at places unusual, uncomfortable, and distant from the depository of the public records, for the sole purpose of fatiguing them into compliance with his measures.

He has dissolved representative houses repeatedly and continually for opposing with manly firmness his invasions on the right of the people.

He has refused for a long time after such dissolutions to cause others to be elected whereby the legislative powers incapable of annihilation have returned to the people at large for their exercise, the state remaining in the meantime exposed to all the dangers of invasion from without and convulsions within.

He has endeavored to prevent the population of these states, for that purpose obstructing the laws for naturalization of foreigners, refusing to pass others to encourage their migrations hither, and raising the conditions of new appropriations of lands.

He has suffered the administration of justice totally to cease in some of these states, refusing his assent to laws for establishing judiciary powers.

He has made judges dependent on his will alone, for the tenure of their offices and the amount and payment of their salaries.

He has erected a multitude of new offices, and sent hither swarms of officers to harass our people and eat out their substance.

He has kept among us, in times of peace, standing armies without the consent of our legislatures.

He has affected to render the military independent of and superior to the civil power.

He has combined with others to subject us to a jurisdiction foreign to our constitutions and unacknowledged by our laws, giving his assent to their acts of pretended legislation, for quartering large bodies of armed troops among us; for protecting them, by a mock trial from punishment for any murders which they should commit on the inhabitants of these states; for cutting off our trade with all parts of the world; for imposing taxes on us without our consent; for depriving us in many cases of the benefits of trial by jury; for transporting us beyond seas to be tried for pretended offenses; for abolishing the free system of English laws in a neighboring

province, establishing therein an arbitrary government, and enlarging its boundaries so as to render it at once an example and fit instrument for introducing the same absolute rule into these colonies; for taking away our charters, abolishing our most valuable laws, and altering fundamentally the forms of our governments; for suspending our own legislatures and declaring themselves invested with power to legislate for us in all cases whatsoever.

He has abdicated government here by declaring us out of his protection, and waging war against us.

He has plundered our seas, ravaged our coasts, burnt our towns, and destroyed the lives of our people.

He is at this time transporting large armies of foreign mercenaries to complete the works of death, desolation, and tyranny, already begun with circumstances of cruelty and perfidy scarcely parallel in the most barbarous ages, and totally unworthy the head of a civilized nation.

He has endeavored to bring on the inhabitants of our frontiers the merciless Indian savages, whose known rule of warfare is an undistinguished destruction of all ages, sexes, and conditions of existence.

He has excited domestic insurrection among us, and has endeavoured to bring on the inhabitants of our frontiers, the merciless Indian savages, whose known rules of warfare, is an undistinguished destruction of all ages, sexes and conditions.

He has constrained our fellow citizens, taken captive on the high seas, to bear arms against their country, to become the executioners of their friends and brethren, or to fall themselves by their hands.

In every stage of these oppressions we have petitioned for redress in the most humble terms; our repeated petitions have been answered only by repeated injuries. A prince whose character is thus marked by every act which may define a tyrant is unfit to be the ruler of a people.

Nor have we been wanting in attentions to our British brethren. We have warned them from time to time of attempts by their legislature to extend an unwarrantable jurisdiction over us. We have reminded them of the circumstances of our emigration and settlement here. We have appealed to their native justice and magnanimity and we have conjured them by the ties of our common kindred to disavow these usurpations which would inevitably interrupt our connection and correspondence. They too have been deaf to the voice of justice and of consanguinity. We must therefore acquiesce in the necessity which denounces our separation and hold them, as we hold the rest of mankind, enemies in war, in peace friends.

We, therefore, the Representatives of the United States of America, in General Congress assembled, appealing to the Supreme Judge of the world for the rectitude of our intentions, do, in the name, and by authority of the good People of these Colonies, solemnly publish and declare, that these United Colonies are, and of right ought to be, free and independent states; that they are absolved from all allegiance to the British Crown, and that all political connection between them and the state of Great Britain, is and ought to be totally dissolved; and that as free and independent states, they have full power to levy war, conclude peace, contract alliances, establish commerce, and to do all other acts and things which independent states may of right do.

And for the support of this Declaration, with a firm reliance on the protection of divine Providence, we mutually pledge to each other our lives, our fortunes, and our sacred honor. ■

SIGNERS OF THE DECLARATION OF INDEPENDENCE: 1776

John Adams, *Massachusetts*
Samuel Adams, *Massachusetts*
Josiah Bartlett, *New Hampshire*
Carter Braxton, *Virginia*
Charles Carroll, *Maryland*
Samuel Chase, *Maryland*
Abraham Clark, *New Jersey*
George Clymer, *Pennsylvania*
William Ellery, *Rhode Island*
William Floyd, *New York*
Benjamin Franklin, *Pennsylvania*
Elbridge Gerry, *Massachusetts*

Button Gwinnett, *Georgia*
Lyman Hall, *Georgia*
John Hancock, *Massachusetts*
Benjamin Harrison, *Virginia*
John Hart, *New Jersey*
Joseph Hewes, *North Carolina*
Thomas Heyward, *South Carolina*
William Hooper, *North Carolina*
Stephen Hopkins, *Rhode Island*
Francis Hopkinson, *New Jersey*
Samuel Huntington, *Connecticut*
Thomas Jefferson, *Virginia*
Richard Henry Lee, *Virginia*
Francis Lightfoot Lee, *Virginia*
Francis Lewis, *New York*
Philip Livingston, *New York*
Thomas Lynch, *South Carolina*
Thomas McKean, *Delaware*
Arthur Middleton, *South Carolina*
John Morton, *Pennsylvania*
Thomas Nelson, *Virginia*
William Paca, *Maryland*
Robert Treat Paine, *Massachusetts*
John Penn, *North Carolina*
George Read, *Delaware*
Caesar Rodney, *Delaware*
George Ross, *Delaware*
Benjamin Rush, *Pennsylvania*
Edward Rutledge, *South Carolina*
Roger Sherman, *Connecticut*
James Smith, *Pennsylvania*
Richard Stockton, *New Jersey*
Thomas Stone, *Maryland*
George Taylor, *Pennsylvania*
Matthew Thornton, *New Hampshire*
George Walton, *Georgia*
William Whipple, *New Hampshire*
William Williams, *Connecticut*
James Wilson, *Pennsylvania*
John Witherspoon, *New Jersey*
Oliver Wolcott, *Connecticut*
George Wythe, *Virginia*

Engrossed copy; drafted by Thomas Jefferson in June, 1776, and adopted by the Continental Congress at Philadelphia, July 4, 1776

• BILL FOR THE MORE GENERAL DIFFUSION OF KNOWLEDGE

Whereas it appeareth that however certain forms of government are better calculated than others to protect individuals in the free exercise of their natural rights, and are at the same time themselves better guarded against degeneracy, yet experience hath shown, that even under the best forms, those entrusted with power have, in time, and by slow operations, perverted it into tyranny; and it is believed that the most effectual means of preventing this would be, to illuminate, as far as practicable, the minds of the people at large, and more especially to give them knowledge of those facts, which history exhibiteth, that, possessed thereby of the experience of other ages and countries, they may be enabled to know ambition under all its shapes, and prompt to exert their natural powers to defeat its purposes; and whereas it is generally true that people will be happiest whose laws are best, and are best administered, and that laws will be wisely formed, and honestly administered, in proportion as those who form and administer them are wise and honest; whence it becomes expedient for promoting the publick happiness that those persons, whom nature hath endowed with genius and virtue, should be rendered by liberal education worthy to receive, and able to guard the sacred deposit of the rights and liberties of their fellow citizens, and that they should be called to that charge without regard to wealth, birth or other accidental condition or circumstance; but the indigence of the greater number disabling them from so educating, at their own expence, those of their children whom nature hath fitly formed and disposed to become useful instruments for the public, it is better that such should be sought for and educated at the common expence of all, than that the happiness of all should be confided to the weak or wicked:

Be it therefore enacted by the General Assembly, that in every county within this commonwealth, there shall be chosen annually, by the electors qualified to vote for Delegates, three of the most honest and able of their county, to be called the Aldermen of the county. . . .

The said Aldermen . . . shall meet at the courthouse of their county, and proceed to divide their said county into hundreds . . . regulating the size of the said hundreds . . . so as that they may contain a convenient number of children to make up a school, and be of such convenient size that all the children within each hundred may daily attend the school to be established therein. . . .

The said Aldermen shall forthwith proceed to have a school-house built at the said place, and shall see that the same be kept in repair. . . .

At everyone of these schools shall be taught reading, writing, and common arithmetic, and the books which shall be used therein for instructing the children to read shall be such as will at the same time make them acquainted with Grecian, Roman, English and American history. At these schools all the free children, male and female, resident within the respective hundred, shall be entitled to receive tuition gratis, for the term of three years, and as much longer, at their private expence, as their parents, guardians or friends, shall think proper. ∎

From Jefferson's draft, completed in December, 1778; adopted by the Virginia Assembly in 1779.

• THE VIRGINIA BILL FOR ESTABLISHING RELIGIOUS FREEDOM

Well aware that Almighty God hath created the mind free; that all attempts to influence it by temporal punishments or burdens, or by civil incapacitations, tend only to beget habits of hypocrisy and meanness, and are a departure from the plan of the Holy Author of our religion, who being Lord both of body and mind, yet chose not to propagate it by coercion on either, as was in his Almighty power to do;

that the impious presumption of legislators and rulers, civil as well as ecclesiastical, who, being themselves but fallible and uninspired men have assumed dominion over the faith of others, setting up their own opinions and modes of thinking as the only true and infallible, and as such endeavoring to impose them on others, hath established and maintained false religions over the greatest part of the world, and through all time;

that to compel a man to furnish contributions of money for the propagation of opinions which he disbelieves, is sinful and tyrannical;

that even the forcing him to support this or that teacher of his own religious persuasion, is depriving him of the comfortable liberty of giving his contributions to the particular pastor whose morals he would make his pattern, and whose powers he feels most persuasive to righteousness, and is withdrawing from the ministry those temporal rewards, which proceeding from an approbation of their personal conduct, are an additional incitement to earnest and unremitting labors for the instruction of mankind;

that our civil rights have no dependence on our religious opinions, more than our opinions in physics or geometry;

that, therefore, the proscribing of any citizen as unworthy of the public confidence by laying upon him an incapacity of being called to the offices of trust and emolument, unless he profess or renounce this or that religious opinion, is depriving him injuriously of those privileges and advantages to which in common with his fellow citizens he has a natural right;

that it tends also to corrupt the principles of that very religion it is meant to encourage, by bribing, with a monopoly of worldly honors and emoluments, those who will externally profess and conform to it;

that though indeed these are criminal who do not withstand such temptation, yet neither are those innocent who lay the bait in their way;

that to suffer the civil magistrate to intrude his powers into the field of opinion and to restrain the profession or propagation of principles, on the supposition of their ill tendency, is a dangerous fallacy, which at once destroys all religious liberty, because he being of course judge of that tendency,

will make his opinions the rule of judgment, and approve or condemn the sentiments of others only as they shall square with or differ from his own;

that it is time enough for the rightful purposes of civil government, for its officers to interfere when principles break out into overt acts against peace and good order;

and finally, that truth is great and will prevail if left to herself, that she is the proper and sufficient antagonist to error, and has nothing to fear from the conflict, unless by human interposition disarmed of her natural weapons, free argument and debate, errors ceasing to be dangerous when it is permitted freely to contradict them.

Be it therefore enacted by the General Assembly:

That no man shall be compelled to frequent or support any religious worship place or ministry whatsoever, nor shall be enforced, restrained, molested, or burthened in his body or goods, nor shall otherwise suffer on account of his religious opinions or belief; but that all men shall be free to profess, and by argument to maintain, their opinions in matters of religion, and that the same shall in nowise diminish, enlarge or affect their civil capacities.

And though we well know that this Assembly, elected by the people for their ordinary purposes of legislation only, have no power to restrain the acts of succeeding Assemblies, constituted with powers equal to our own, and that therefore to declare this act to be irrevocable would be of no effect in law; yet we are free to declare, and do declare, that the rights hereby asserted are of the natural rights of mankind, and that if any act shall be hereafter passed to repeat the present or to narrow its operations, such act will be an infringement of natural right. ■

Drafted by Thomas Jefferson in 1779, passed by the Virginia Assembly in 1786.

• MEMORIAL AND REMONSTRANCE AGAINST RELIGIOUS ASSESSMENTS

TO THE HONORABLE GENERAL ASSEMBLY OF THE COMMONWEALTH OF VIRGINIA A MEMORIAL AND REMONSTRANCE [1]

We, the subscribers, citizens of the said Commonwealth having taken into serious consideration a Bill printed by order of the last Session of General Assembly, entitled "A Bill establishing a provision for Teachers of the Christian Religion," and conceiving that the same, if finally armed with the sanctions of a law, will be a dangerous abuse of power, are bound as faithful members of a free State, to remonstrate against it, and to declare the reasons by which we are determined. We remonstrate against the said Bill,

1. Because we hold it for a fundamental and undeniable truth, "that Religion or the duty which we owe to our Creator and the conviction, not by force or violence." The Religion then of every man must be left to the conviction and conscience of every man; and, it is the right of every man to exercise it as these may dictate. This right is in its nature an unalienable right. It is unalienable; because the opinions of men, depending only on the evidence contemplated by their own minds, cannot follow the dictates of other men: It is unalienable also; because what is here a right towards men, is a duty towards the Creator. It is the duty of every man to render to the Creator such homage, and such only as he believes to be acceptable to him. This duty is precedent both in order of time and degree of obligation, to the claims of Civil Society. Before any man can be considered as a member of Civil Society, he must be considered as a subject of the Governor of the Universe: And if a member of Civil Society, who enters into any subordinate Association, must always do it with a reservation of his duty to the general authority; much more must every man who becomes a member of any particular Civil Society, do it with a savings of his allegiance to the Universal Sovereign. We maintain therefore that in matters of Religion, no man's right is abridged by the institution of Civil Society, and that Religion is wholly exempt from its cognizance. True it is, that no other rule exists, by which any question which may divide a Society, can be ultimately determined, but the will of the majority; but it is also true, that the majority may trespass on the rights of the minority.

2. Because if religion be exempt from the authority of the Society at large, still less can it be subject to that of the Legislative Body. The latter are but the creatures and vicegerents of the former. Their jurisdiction is both derivative and limited: it is limited with regard to the co-ordinate departments, more necessarily is it limited with regard to the constituents. The preservation of a free government requires not merely, that the metes and bounds which separate each department of power may be invariably maintained; but more especially, that neither of them be suffered to overleap the great Barrier which defends the rights of the people. The Rulers who are guilty of such an encroachment, exceed the commission from which they derive their authority, and are Tyrants. The People who submit to it are governed by laws made neither by themselves, nor by an authority derived from them, and are slaves.

[1] Madison wrote to George Mason, July 14, 1826: "I have received, sir, your letter of the 6th instant, requesting such information as I may be able to give as to the origin of the document (Memorial and Remonstrance Against Religious Establishments), a copy of which was inclosed in it. The motive and manner of the request would entitle it to respect, if less easily complied with than by the following statement: During the session of the General Assembly 1784–5, a bill was introduced into the House of Delegates providing for the legal support of the teachers of the Christian religion, and being patronized by the most popular talents in the House, seemed likely to obtain a majority of votes. In order to arrest its progress, it was insisted, with success, that the bill should be postponed till the ensuing session, and in the mean time printed for public consideration, that the sense of the people might be the better called forth. Your highly distinguished ancestor, Col. Geo. Mason, Col. Geo. Nicholas also possessing much public weight, and some others, thought it advisable that a remonstrance against the bill should be prepared for general circulation and signature, and imposed on me the task of drawing up such a paper. This draught having received their sanction, a large number of printed copies were distributed, and so extensively signed by the people of every religious denomination, that at the ensuing session the projected measure was entirely frustrated; and under the influence of the public sentiment thus manifested, the celebrated bill "establishing religious freedom" enacted into a permanent barrier against future attempts on the rights of conscience, as declared in the great charter prefixed to the Constitution of the State."

3. Because it is proper to take alarm at the first experiment on our liberties. We hold this prudent jealousy to be the first duty of citizens, and one of [the] noblest characteristics of the late Revolution. The freemen of America did not wait till usurped power had strengthened itself by exercise, and entangled the question in precedents. They saw all the consequences in the principle, and they avoided the consequences by denying the principle. We revere this lesson too much, soon to forget it. Who does not see that the same authority which can establish Christianity, in exclusion of all other Religions, may establish with the same ease any particular sect of Christians, in exclusion of all other Sects? That the same authority which can force a citizen to contribute three pence only of his property for the support of any one establishment, may force him to conform to any other establishment in all cases whatsoever?

4. Because the bill violates that equality which ought to be the basis of every law and which is more indispensable, in proportion as the validity or expediency of any law is more liable to be impeached. If "all men are by nature equally free and independent," all men are to be considered as entering into Society on equal conditions; as relinquishing no more and therefore retaining no less, one than another of their natural rights. Above all are they to be considered as retaining an "equal title to the free exercise of Religion according to the dictates of conscience." Whilst we assert for ourselves a freedom to embrace, to profess and to observe the Religion which we believe to be of divine origin, we cannot deny an equal freedom to those whose minds have not yet yielded to the evidence which has convinced us. If this freedom be abused, it is an offence against God, not against man: To God, therefore, not to men, must an account of it be rendered. As the Bill violates equality by subjecting some to peculiar burdens; so it violates the same principle, by granting to others peculiar exemptions. Are the Quakers and Men[n]onists the only sects who think a compulsive support of their religions unnecessary and unwarrantable? Can their piety alone be intrusted

with the care of public worship? Ought their Religions to be endowed above all others, with extraordinary privileges, by which proselytes may be enticed from all others. We think too favorably of the justice and good sense of these denominations, to believe that they either covet pre-eminencies over their fellow citizens, or that they will be seduced by them, from the common opposition to the measure.

5. Because the bill implies either that the Civil Magistrate is a competent Judge of Religious truth; or that he may employ Religion as an engine of Civil policy. The first is an arrogant pretension falsified by the contradictory opinions of Rulers in all ages, and throughout the world: The second an unhallowed perversion of the means of salvation.

6. Because the establishment proposed by the Bill is not requisite for the support of the Christian Religion. To say that it is, is a contradiction to the Christian Religion itself; for every page of it disavows a dependence on the powers of this world: it is a contradiction to fact; for it is known that this Religion both existed and flourished, not only without the support of human laws, but in spite of every opposition from them; and not only during the period of miraculous aid, but long after it had been left to its own evidence, and the ordinary care of Providence: Nay, it is a contradiction in terms; for a Religion not invented by human policy, must have pre-existed and been supported, before it was established by human policy. It is moreover to weaken in those who profess this Religion a pious confidence in its innate excellence, and the patronage of its Author; and to foster in those who still reject it, a suspicion that its friends are too conscious of its fallacies to trust to its own merits.

7. Because experience witnesseth that ecclesiastical establishments, instead of maintaining the purity and efficacy of Religion, have had a contrary operation. During almost fifteen centuries, has the legal establishment of Christianity been on trial. What have been its fruits? More or less in all places, pride and indolence in the Clergy; ignorance and servility in the laity; in both, superstition, bigotry and persecution. Enquire of the Teachers of Christianity for

the ages in which it appeared in its greatest lustre; those of every sect, point to the ages prior to its incorporation with Civil policy. Propose a restoration of this primitive state in which its Teachers depended on the voluntary rewards of their flocks; many of them predict its downfall. On which side ought their testimony to have greatest weight, when for or when against their interest?

8. Because the establishment in question is not necessary for the support of Civil Government. If it be urged as necessary for the support of Civil Government only as it is a means of supporting Religion, and it be not necessary for the latter purpose, it cannot be necessary for the former. If Religion be not within cognizance of Civil Government, how can its legal establishment be said to be necessary to Civil Government? What influence in fact have ecclesiastical establishments had on Civil Society? In some instances they have been seen to erect a spiritual tyranny on the ruins of Civil authority; in many instances they have been seen upholding the thrones of political tyranny; in no instance have they been seen the guardians of the liberties of the people. Rulers who wished to subvert the public liberty, may have found an established clergy convenient auxiliaries. A just government, instituted to secure & perpetuate it, needs them not. Such a government will be best supported by protecting every citizen in the enjoyment of his Religion with the same equal hand which protects his person and his property; by neither invading the equal rights of any Sect, nor suffering any Sect to invade those of another.

9. Because the proposed establishment is a departure from that generous policy, which, offering an asylum to the persecuted and oppressed of every Nation and Religion, promised a lustre to our country, and an accession to the number of its citizens. What a melancholy mark is the Bill of sudden degeneracy? Instead of holding forth an asylum to the persecuted it is itself a signal of persecution. It degrades from the equal rank of Citizens all those whose opinions in Religion do not bend to those of the Legislative authority. Distant as it may be, in its present form, from the Inquisition it differs from it only in degree. The one is the first step, the other the last in the career of intolerance. The magnanimous sufferer under this cruel scourge in foreign Regions, must view the Bill as a Beacon on our Coast, warning him to seek some other haven, where liberty and philanthropy in their due extent may offer a more certain repose from his troubles.

10. Because, it will have a like tendency to banish our Citizens. The allurements presented by other situations are every day thinning their number. To superadd a fresh motive to emigration, by revoking the liberty which they now enjoy, would be the same species of folly which has dishonored and depopulated flourishing kingdoms.

11. Because it will destroy that moderation and harmony which the forbearance of our laws to intermeddle with Religion, has produced amongst its several sects. Torrents of blood have been spilt in the old world, by vain attempts of the secular arm to extinguish Religious discord, by proscribing all difference in Religious opinions. Time has at length revealed the true remedy. Every relaxation of narrow and rigorous policy, wherever it has been tried, has been found to assuage the disease. The American Theatre has exhibited proofs, that equal and compleat liberty, if it does not wholly eradicate it, sufficiently destroys its malignant influence on the health and prosperity of the State. If with the salutary effects of this system under our own eyes, we begin to contract the bonds of Religious freedom, we know no name that will too severely reproach our folly. At least let warning be taken at the first fruits of the threatened innovation. The very appearance of the Bill has transformed that "Christian forbearance; love and charity," which of late mutually prevailed, into animosities and jealousies, which may not soon be appeased. What mischiefs may not be dreaded should this enemy to the public quiet be armed with the force of a law?

12. Because the policy of the bill is adverse to the diffusion of the light of Christianity. The first wish of those who enjoy this precious gift, ought to be that it may be imparted to the whole race of mankind. Compare the number of those who have as yet

received it with the number still remaining under the dominion of false Religions; and how small is the former! Does the policy of the Bill tend to lessen the disproportion? No; it at once discourages those who are strangers to the light of [revelation] from coming into the Region of it; and countenances, by example, the nations who continue in darkness, in shutting out those who might convey it to them. Instead of levelling as far as possible, every obstacle to the victorious progress of truth, the Bill with an ignoble and unchristian timidity would circumscribe it, with a wall of defence, against the encroachments of error.

13. Because attempts to enforce by legal sanctions, acts obnoxious to so great a proportion of Citizens, tend to enervate the laws in general, and to slacken the bands of Society. If it be difficult to execute any law which is not generally deemed necessary or salutary, what must be the case where it is deemed invalid and dangerous? and what may be the effect of so striking an example of impotency in the Government, on its general authority.

14. Because a measure of such singular magnitude and delicacy ought not to be imposed, without the clearest evidence that it is called for by a majority of citizens: and no satisfactory method is yet proposed by which the voice of the majority in this case may be determined, or its influence secured. "The people of the respective counties are indeed requested to signify their opinion respecting the adoption of the Bill to the next Session of Assembly." But the representation must be made equal, before the voice either of the Representatives or of the Counties, will be that of the people. Our hope is that neither of the former will, after due consideration, espouse the dangerous principle of the Bill. Should the event disappoint us, it will still leave us in full confidence, that a fair appeal to the latter will reverse the sentence against our liberties.

15. Because, finally, "the equal right of every citizen to the free exercise of his Religion according to the dictates of conscience" is held by the same tenure with all our other rights. If we recur to its origin, it is equally the gift of nature; if we weigh

its importance, it cannot be less dear to us; if we consult the Declaration of those rights which pertain to the good people of Virginia, as the "basis and foundation of Government," it is enumerated with equal solemnity, or rather studied emphasis. Either then, we must say, that the will of the Legislature is the only measure of their authority; and that in the plenitude of this authority, they may sweep away all our fundamental rights; or, that they are bound to leave this particular right untouched and sacred: Either we must say, that they may controul the freedom of the press, may abolish the trial by jury, may swallow up the Executive and Judiciary Powers of the State; may that they may despoil us of our very right of suffrage, and erect themselves into an independent and hereditary assembly: or we must say, that they have no authority to enact into law the Bill under consideration. We the subscribers say, that the General Assembly of this Commonwealth have no such authority: And that no effort may be omitted on our part against so dangerous an usurpation, we oppose to it, this remonstrance; earnestly praying, as we are in duty bound, that the Supreme Lawgiver of the Universe, by illuminating those to whom it is addressed, may on the one hand, turn their councils from every act which would affront his holy prerogative, or violate the trust committed to them: and on the other, guide them into every measure which may be worthy of his blessing, may redound to their own praise, and may establish more firmly the liberties, the property, and the happiness of the Commonwealth. ■

Presented by James Madison to the Virginia Assembly, 1785.

• THE NORTHWEST ORDINANCE

ARTICLE I: No person, demeaning himself in a peaceable and orderly manner, shall ever be molested on account of his mode of worship or religious sentiments, in the said territory.

ARTICLE II: The inhabitants of the said territory shall always be entitled to the benefits of the writs of habeas corpus, and of the trial by jury; of a proportionate representation of the people in the legislature, and of judicial proceedings according to the course of the common law. All persons shall be bailable, unless for capital offences, where the proof shall be evident, or the presumption great. All fines shall be moderate; and no cruel or unusual punishments shall be inflicted. No man shall be deprived of his liberty or property, but by the judgment of his peers, or the law of the land, and, should the public exigencies make it necessary, for the common preservation, to take any person's property, or to demand his particular services, full compensation shall be made for the same. . . . ■

From the ordinance probably drafted by Nathan Dane and Rufus King, along the lines of Jefferson's preliminary ordinance of 1784. Enacted by the Congress of the Confederation, July 13, 1787.

• THE CONSTITUTION OF THE UNITED STATES

We the People of the United States, in order to form a more perfect Union, establish Justice, ensure Domestic Tranquillity, provide for the common Defence, promote the general Welfare, and secure the Blessings of Liberty to ourselves and our Posterity, do ordain and establish this CONSTITUTION for the United States of America.

ARTICLE I

SEC. 1. ALL legislative powers herein granted shall be vested in a Congress of the United States, which shall consist of a Senate and House of Representatives.

SEC. 2. The House of Representatives shall be composed of members chosen every second year by the people of the several states, and the electors in each state shall have the qualifications requisite for electors of the most numerous branch of the state legislature.

No person shall be a representative who shall not have attained to the age of 25 years, and been seven years a citizen of the United States, and who shall not, when elected, be an inhabitant of that state in which he shall be chosen.

Representatives and direct taxes shall be apportioned among the several states which may be included within this union, according to their respective numbers, which shall be determined by adding to the whole number of free persons,[1] including those bound to service for a term of years, and excluding Indians not taxed, three-fifths of all other persons.[2] The actual enumeration shall be made within three years after the first meeting of the Congress of the United States, and within every subsequent term of ten years, in such manner as they shall by law direct. The number of representatives shall not exceed one for every 30,000, but each state shall have at least one representative; and until such enumeration shall be made, the state of New-Hampshire shall be entitled to choose three, Massachusetts eight, Rhode-Island and Providence Plantations one, Connecticut five, New-York six, New-Jersey four, Pennsylvania eight, Delaware one, Maryland six, Virginia ten, North-Carolina five, South-Carolina five, and Georgia three.

When vacancies happen in the representation from any state, the executive authority thereof shall issue writs of election to fill such vacancies.

The House of Representatives shall choose their speaker and other officers; and shall have the sole power of impeachment.

SEC. 3. The Senate of the United States shall be composed of two senators from each state, chosen by the legislature thereof, for six years;[3] and each senator shall have one vote.

Immediately after they shall be assembled in consequence of the first election, they shall be divided as equally as may be into three classes. The seats of

---

[1] *"Which shall be determined . . . free persons"*—modified by the Fourteenth Amendment.

[2] *"Three-fifths . . . persons"*—superseded by the Fourteenth Amendment.

[3] *"The Senate . . . for six years"*—superseded by the Seventeenth Amendment.

the senators of the first class shall be vacated at the expiration of the second year, of the second class at the expiration of the fourth year, and of the third class at the expiration of the sixth year, so that one-third may be chosen every second year; and if vacancies happen by resignation, or otherwise, during the recess of the legislature of any state, the executive thereof may make temporary appointments until the next meeting of the legislature, which shall then fill such vacancies.[4]

No person shall be a senator who shall not have attained to the age of 30 years, and been nine years a citizen of the United States, and who shall not, when elected, be an inhabitant of that state for which he shall be chosen.

The vice-president of the United States shall be president of the Senate, but shall have no vote, unless they be equally divided.

The Senate shall choose their other officers, and also a president *pro tempore,* in the absence of the vice-president, or when he shall exercise the office of president of the United States.

The Senate shall have the sole power to try all impeachments. When sitting for that purpose, they shall be on oath or affirmation. When the president of the United States is tried, the chief justice shall preside: And no person shall be convicted without the concurrence of two-thirds of the members present.

Judgment in cases of impeachment shall not extend further than to removal from office, and disqualification to hold and enjoy any office of honour, trust or profit under the United States; but the party convicted shall nevertheless be liable and subject to indictment, trial, judgment and punishment, according to law.

SEC. 4. The times, places and manner of holding elections for senators and representatives, shall be prescribed in each state by the legislature thereof: But the Congress may at any time by law make or alter such regulations, except as to the places of choosing senators.

The Congress shall assemble at least once in every year, and such meeting shall be on the first Monday in December, unless they shall by law appoint a different day.[5]

SEC. 5. Each house shall be the judge of the elections, returns and qualifications of its own members, and a majority of each shall constitute a quorum to do business; but a smaller number may adjourn from day to day, and may be authorized to compel the attendance of absent members, in such manner, and under such penalties as each house may provide.

Each house may determine the rules of its proceedings, punish its members for disorderly behaviour, and, with the concurrence of two-thirds, expel a member.

Each house shall keep a journal of its proceedings, and from time to time publish the same, excepting such parts as may, in their judgment, require secrecy; and the yeas and nays of the members of either house on any question, shall, at the desire of one-fifth of those present, be entered on the journal.

Neither house, during the session of Congress, shall, without the consent of the other, adjourn for more than three days, nor to any other place than that in which the two houses shall be sitting.

SEC. 6. The senators and representatives shall receive a compensation for their services, to be ascertained by law, and paid out of the treasury of the United States. They shall in all cases, except treason, felony and breach of the peace, be privileged from arrest during their attendance at the session of their respective houses, and in going to and returning from the same; and for any speech or debate in either house, they shall not be questioned in any other place.

No senator or representative shall, during the time for which he was elected, be appointed to any civil office under the authority of the United States, which shall have been created, or the emoluments whereof shall have been increased during such time; and no person holding any office under the United

---

[4] *"And if vacancies . . . such vacancies"*—modified by the Seventeenth Amendment.

[5] *"The Congress . . . a different day"*—superseded by the Twentieth Amendment.

States, shall be a member of either house during his continuance in office.

SEC. 7. All bills for raising revenue shall originate in the House of Representatives; but the Senate may propose or concur with amendments as on other bills.

Every bill which shall have passed the House of Representatives and the Senate, shall, before it become a law, be presented to the president of the United States; if he approve, he shall sign it, but if not, he shall return it, with his objections, to that house in which it shall have originated, who shall enter the objections at large on their journal, and proceed to reconsider it. If after such reconsideration, two-thirds of that house shall agree to pass the bill, it shall be sent, together with the objections, to the other house, by which it shall likewise be reconsidered, and if approved by two-thirds of that house, it shall become a law. But in all such cases the votes of both houses shall be determined by yeas and nays, and the names of the persons voting for and against the bill shall be entered on the journal of each house respectively. If any bill shall not be returned by the president within ten days, (Sundays excepted) after it shall have been presented to him, the same shall be a law, in like manner as if he had signed it, unless the Congress by their adjournment prevent its return, in which case it shall not be a law.

Every order, resolution, or vote to which the concurrence of the Senate and House of Representatives may be necessary, (except on a question of adjournment) shall be presented to the president of the United States; and before the same shall take effect, shall be approved by him, or, being disapproved by him, shall be re-passed by two-thirds of the Senate and House of Representatives, according to the rules and limitations prescribed in the case of a bill.

SEC. 8. The Congress shall have power to lay and collect taxes, duties, imposts and excises, to pay the debts and provide for the common defence and general welfare of the United States; but all duties, imposts and excises shall be uniform throughout the United States:

To borrow money on the credit of the United States:

To regulate commerce with foreign nations, and among the several states, and with the Indian tribes:

To establish an uniform rule of naturalization, and uniform laws on the subject of bankruptcies throughout the United States:

To coin money, regulate the value thereof, and of foreign coin, and fix the standard of weights and measures:

To provide for the punishment of counterfeiting the securities and current coin of the United States:

To establish post-offices and post-roads:

To promote the progress of science and useful arts, by securing for limited times to authors and inventors the exclusive right to their respective writings and discoveries:

To constitute tribunals inferior to the supreme court:

To define and punish piracies and felonies committed on the high seas, and offences against the law of nations:

To declare war, grant letters of marque and reprisal, and make rules concerning captures on land and water:

To raise and support armies, but no appropriation of money to that use shall be for a longer term than two years:

To provide and maintain a navy:

To make rules for the government and regulation of the land and naval forces:

To provide for calling forth the militia to execute the laws of the union, suppress insurrections and repel invasions:

To provide for organizing, arming and disciplining the militia, and for governing such part of them as may be employed in the service of the United States, reserving to the states respectively, the appointment of the officers, and the authority of training the militia according to the discipline prescribed by Congress:

To exercise exclusive legislation in all cases whatsoever, over such district (not exceeding ten miles square) as may, by cession of particular states, and the acceptance of Congress, become the seat of the government of the United States, and to exercise like authority over all places purchased by the consent of the legislature of the state in which the same shall be, for the erection of forts, magazines, arsenals, dock-yards, and other needful buildings: And,

To make all laws which shall be necessary and proper for carrying into execution the foregoing powers, and all other powers vested by this constitution in the government of the United States, or in any department or officer thereof.

SEC. 9. The migration or importation of such persons as any of the states now existing shall think proper to admit, shall not be prohibited by the Congress prior to the year 1808, but a tax or duty may be imposed on such importations, not exceeding 10 dollars for each person.

The privilege of the writ of *habeas corpus* shall not be suspended, unless when in cases of rebellion or invasion the public safety may require it.

No bill of attainder or *ex post facto* law shall be passed.

No capitation, or other direct tax shall be laid unless in proportion to the *census* or enumeration herein before directed to be taken.[6]

No tax or duty shall be laid on articles exported from any state.

No preference shall be given by any regulation of commerce or revenue to the ports of one state or those of another: nor shall vessels bound to, or from one state, be obliged to enter, clear, or pay duties in another.

No money shall be drawn from the treasury but in consequence of appropriations made by law; and a regular statement and account of the receipts and expenditures of all public money shall be published from time to time.

No title of nobility shall be granted by the United States: And no person holding any office or profit or trust under them, shall, without the consent of the Congress, accept of any present, emolument, office, or title, of any kind whatever, from any king, prince or foreign state.

---

[6] *"No capitation . . . to be taken"*—modified by the Sixteenth Amendment.

SEC. 10. No state shall enter into any treaty, alliance, or confederation; grant letters of marque and reprisal; coin money; emit bills of credit; make any thing but gold and silver coin a tender in payment of debts; pass any bill of attainder, *ex post facto* law, or law impairing the obligation of contracts, or grant any title of nobility.

No state shall, without the consent of the Congress, lay any imposts or duties on imports or exports, except what may be absolutely necessary for executing its inspection laws; and the net produce of all duties and imposts, laid by any state on imports or exports, shall be for the use of the treasury of the United States; and all such laws shall be subject to the revision and control of the Congress.

No state shall, without the consent of Congress, lay any duty of tonnage, keep troops, or ships of war in time of peace, enter into any agreement or compact with another state, or with a foreign power, or engage in a war, unless actually invaded, or in such imminent danger as will not admit of delay.

ARTICLE II

SEC. 1. The executive power shall be vested in a president of the United States of America. He shall hold his office during the term of four years, and, together with the vice-president, chosen for the same term, be elected as follows:

Each state shall appoint, in such manner as the legislature thereof may direct, a number of electors, equal to the whole number of senators and representatives to which the state may be entitled in the Congress; but no senator or representative, or person holding an office of trust or profit under the United States, shall be appointed an elector.

The electors shall meet in their respective states, and vote by ballot for two persons, of whom one at least shall not be an inhabitant of the same state with themselves. And they shall make a list of all the persons voted for, and of the number of votes for each; which list they shall sign and certify, and transmit sealed to the seat of the government of the United States, directed to the president of the Senate. The president of the Senate shall, in the presence of the Senate and House of Representatives, open all the certificates and the votes shall then be counted. The person having the greatest number of votes shall be the president, if such number be a majority of the whole number of electors appointed; and if there be more than one who have such majority, and have an equal number of votes, then the House of Representatives shall immediately choose by ballot one of them for president; and if no person have a majority, then from the five highest on the list, the said House shall, in like manner, choose the president. But in choosing the president, the votes shall be taken by states, the representation from each state having one vote; a quorum for this purpose shall consist of a member or members from two-thirds of the states, and a majority of all the states shall be necessary to a choice. In every case, after the choice of the president, the person having the greatest number of votes of the electors shall be the vice-president. But if there should remain two or more who have equal votes, the Senate shall choose from them by ballot the vice-president.[7]

The Congress may determine the time of choosing the electors, and the day on which they shall give their votes; which day shall be the same throughout the United States.

No person except a natural born citizen, or a citizen of the United States, at the time of the adoption of this constitution, shall be eligible to the office of president; neither shall any person be eligible to that office, who shall not have attained to the age of 35 years, and been 14 years a resident within the United States.

In case of the removal of the president from office, or of his death, resignation, or inability to discharge the powers and duties of the said office, the same shall devolve on the vice-president, and the Congress may by law provide for the case of removal, death, resignation, or inability, both of the president and vice-president, declaring what officer shall then act as president, and such officer shall act accordingly, until the disability be removed, or a president shall be elected.

---

[7] *"The electors shall meet . . . the vice-president"*—superseded by the Twelfth Amendment, which is modified by the Twentieth.

The president shall, at stated times, receive for his services, a compensation, which shall neither be increased nor diminished during the period for which he shall have been elected, and he shall not receive within that period any other emolument from the United States, or any of them.

Before he enter on the execution of his office, he shall take the following oath or affirmation:

"I do solemnly swear (or affirm) that I will faithfully execute the office of president of the United States, and will to the best of my ability, preserve, protect and defend the constitution of the United States."

SEC. 2. The president shall be commander in chief of the army and navy of the United States, and of the militia of the several states, when called into the actual service of the United States; he may require the opinion, in writing, of the principal officer in each of the executive departments, upon any subject relating to the duties of their respective offices, and he shall have power to grant reprieves and pardons for offences against the United States, except in cases of impeachment.

He shall have power, by and with the advice and consent of the Senate, to make treaties, provided two-thirds of the senators present concur; and he shall nominate, and by and with the advice and consent of the Senate, shall appoint ambassadors, other public ministers and consuls, judges of the supreme court, and all other officers of the United States, whose appointments are not herein otherwise provided for, and which shall be established by law. But the Congress may by law vest the appointment of such inferior officers, as they think proper in the president alone, in the courts of law, or in the heads of departments.

The president shall have power to fill up all vacancies that may happen during the recess of the Senate, by granting commissions, which shall expire at the end of their next session.

SEC. 3. He shall, from time to time, give to the Congress information of the state of the union, and recommend to their consideration, such measures as he shall judge necessary and expedient; he may, on extraordinary occasions, convene both houses, or either of them, and in case of disagreement between them, with respect to the time of adjournment, he may adjourn them to such time as he shall think proper; he shall receive ambassadors and other public ministers; he shall take care that the laws be faithfully executed, and shall commission all the officers of the United States.

SEC. 4. The president, vice-president, and all civil officers of the United States shall be removed from office on impeachment for, and conviction of, treason, bribery, or other high crimes and misdemeanors.

ARTICLE III

SEC. 1. The judicial power of the United States, shall be vested in one supreme court, and in such inferior courts as the Congress may, from time to time, ordain and establish. The judges, both of the supreme and inferior courts, shall hold their offices during good behaviour, and shall, at stated times, receive for their services a compensation, which shall not be diminished during their continuance in office.

SEC. 2. The judicial power shall extend to all cases, in law and equity, arising under this constitution, the laws of the United States, and treaties made, or which shall be made under their authority; to all cases affecting ambassadors, other public ministers and consuls; to all cases of admiralty and maritime jurisdiction; to controversies to which the United States shall be a party: to controversies between two or more states, between a state and citizens of another state,[8] between citizens of different states, between citizens of the same state, claiming lands under grants of different states, and between a state, or the citizens thereof, and foreign states, citizens or subjects.

In all cases affecting ambassadors, other public ministers and consuls, and those in which a state shall be party, the supreme court shall have original jurisdiction. In all the other cases before-mentioned,

the supreme court shall have appellate jurisdiction, both as to law and fact, with such exceptions, and under such regulations as the Congress shall make.

The trial of all crimes, except in cases of impeachment, shall be by jury; and such trial shall be held in the state where the said crimes shall have been committed; but when not committed within any state, the trial shall be at such place or places as the Congress may by law have directed.

SEC. 3. Treason against the United States shall consist only in levying war against them, or in adhering to their enemies, giving them aid and comfort. No person shall be convicted of treason unless on the testimony of two witnesses to the same overt act, or on confession in open court.

The Congress shall have power to declare the punishment of treason, but no attainder of treason shall work corruption of blood, or forfeiture, except during the life of the person attainted.

ARTICLE IV

SEC. 1. Full faith and credit shall be given in each state to the public acts, records and judicial proceedings of every other state. And the Congress may by general laws prescribe the manner in which such acts, records and proceedings shall be proved, and the effect thereof.

SEC. 2. The citizens of each state shall be entitled to all privileges and immunities of citizens in the several states.

A person charged in any state with treason, felony, or other crime, who shall flee from justice, and be found in another state, shall, on demand of the executive authority of the state from which he fled, be delivered up, to be removed to the state having jurisdiction of the crime.

No person held to service or labour in one state, under the laws thereof, escaping into another, shall, in consequence of any law or regulation therein, be discharged from such service or labour, but shall be delivered up on claim of the party to whom such service or labour may be due.[9]

---

[8] *"Between a state . . . another state"*—limited by the Eleventh Amendment.

[9] *"No person . . . may be due"*—superseded by the Thirteenth Amendment in regard to slaves.

Sec. 3. New states may be admitted by the Congress into this union; but no new state shall be formed or erected within the jurisdiction of any other state, nor any state be formed by the junction of two or more states, or parts of states, without the consent of the legislatures of the states concerned, as well as of the Congress.

The Congress shall have power to dispose of and make all needful rules and regulations respecting the territory or other property belonging to the United States; and nothing in this constitution shall be so construed as to prejudice any claims of the United States, or of any particular state.

Sec. 4. The United States shall guarantee to every state in this union, a republican form of government, and shall protect each of them against invasion; and on application of the legislature, or of the executive (when the legislature cannot be convened), against domestic violence.

ARTICLE V

The Congress, whenever two-thirds of both houses shall deem it necessary, shall propose amendments to this constitution, or on the application of the legislatures of two-thirds of the several states, shall call a convention for proposing amendments, which, in either case, shall be valid to all intents and purposes, as part of this constitution, when ratified by the legislatures of three-fourths of the several states, or by conventions in three-fourths thereof, as the one or the other mode of ratification may be proposed by the Congress: Provided, that no amendment which may be made prior to the year 1808, shall in any manner affect the first and fourth clauses in the ninth section of the first article; and that no state, without its consent, shall be deprived of its equal suffrage in the Senate.

ARTICLE VI

All debts contracted and engagements entered into, before the adoption of this constitution, shall be as valid against the United States under this constitution, as under the confederation.

This constitution, and the laws of the United States which shall be made in pursuance thereof; and all treaties made, or which shall be made, under the authority of the United States, shall be the supreme law of the land; and the judges in every state shall be bound thereby, any thing in the constitution or laws of any state to the contrary notwithstanding.

The senators and representatives before-mentioned, and the members of the several state legislatures, and all executive and judicial officers, both of the United States and of the several states, shall be bound by oath or affirmation, to support this constitution; but no religious test shall ever be required as a qualification to any office or public trust under the United States.

ARTICLE VII

The ratification of the conventions of nine states, shall be sufficient for the establishment of this constitution between the states so ratifying the same.

DONE in convention, by the unanimous consent of the states present, the 17th day of September, in the year of our Lord 1787, and of the independence of the United States of America the 12th. In witness whereof we have hereunto subscribed our names.

GEORGE WASHINGTON, *President, And Deputy from Virginia.*

New-Hampshire,
John Langdon, Nicholas Gilman.

Massachusetts,
Nathaniel Gorham, Rufus King.

Connecticut,
William Samuel Johnson, Roger Sherman.

New-York,
Alexander Hamilton.

New-Jersey,
William Livingston, David Brearly, William Paterson, Jonathan Dayton.

Pennsylvania,
Benjamin Franklin, Thomas Mifflin, Robert

Morris, George Clymer, Thomas Fitzsimons, Jared Ingersoll, James Wilson, Gouverneur Morris.

Delaware,
George Read, Gunning Bedford, jun., John Dickinson, Richard Bassett, Jacob Broom.

Maryland,
James M'Henry, Daniel of St. Thomas Jenifer, Daniel Carroll.

Virginia,
John Blair, James Madison, jun.

North-Carolina,
William Blount, Richard Dobbs Spaight, Hugh Williamson.

South-Carolina,
John Rutledge, Charles Cotesworth Pinckney Charles Pinckney, Pierce Butler.

Georgia,
William Few, Abraham Baldwin.

Attest:
WILLIAM JACKSON, *Secretary.*

AMENDMENTS

ARTICLE I

Congress shall make no law respecting an establishment of religion, or prohibiting the free exercise thereof; or abridging the freedom of speech or of the press; or the right of the people peaceably to assemble, and to petition the government for a redress of grievances.

ARTICLE II

A well-regulated militia being necessary to the security of a free state, the right of the people to keep and bear arms shall not be infringed.

ARTICLE III

No soldier shall, in time of peace, be quartered in any house without the consent of the owner, nor in time of war but in a manner to be prescribed by law.

ARTICLE IV

The right of the people to be secure in their persons, houses, papers, and effects, against unreasonable searches and seizures, shall not be violated, and no warrants shall issue but upon probable cause, supported by oath or affirmation, and particularly describing the place to be searched, and the persons or things to be seized.

ARTICLE V

No person shall be held to answer for a capital or other infamous crime unless on a presentment or indictment of a grand jury, except in cases arising in the land or naval forces, or in the militia, when in actual service, in time of war or public danger; nor shall any person be subject for the same offence to be twice put in jeopardy of life or limb; nor shall be compelled in any criminal case to be a witness against himself, nor be deprived of life, liberty, or property, without due process of law; nor shall private property be taken for public use without just compensation.

ARTICLE VI

In all criminal prosecutions, the accused shall enjoy the right to a speedy and public trial, by an impartial jury of the state and district wherein the crime shall have been committed, which district shall have been previously ascertained by law, and to be informed of the nature and cause of the accusation; to be confronted with the witnesses against him; to have compulsory process for obtaining witnesses in his favor, and to have the assistance of counsel for his defence.

ARTICLE VII

In suits at common law, where the value in controversy shall exceed twenty dollars, the right of trial by jury shall be preserved, and no fact tried by a jury shall be otherwise reexamined in any court of the United States than according to the rules of the common law.

ARTICLE VIII

Excessive bail shall not be required, nor excessive

fines imposed, nor cruel and unusual punishments inflicted.

ARTICLE IX

The enumeration in the constitution of certain rights shall not be construed to deny or disparage others retained by the people.

ARTICLE X

The powers not delegated to the United States by the constitution, nor prohibited by it to the states, are reserved to the states respectively, or to the people.[10]

ARTICLE XI

The judicial power of the United States shall not be construed to extend to any suit in law or equity, commenced or prosecuted against one of the United States, by citizens of another state, or by citizens or subjects of any foreign state.

[Declared in force, January 8, 1798.]

ARTICLE XII

The electors shall meet in their respective states, and vote by ballot for president and vice-president, one of whom at least shall not be an inhabitant of the same state with themselves; they shall name in their ballots the person voted for as president, and in distinct ballots the person voted for as vice-president; and they shall make distinct lists of all persons voted for as president, and of all persons voted for as vice-president, and of the number of votes for each, which lists they shall sign and certify, and transmit, sealed, to the seat of the government of the United States directed to the president of the Senate; the president of the Senate shall, in the presence of the Senate and House of Representatives, open all the certificates, and the votes shall then be counted; the person having the greatest number of votes for president shall be the president, if such number be a majority of the whole number of electors appointed; and if no person have such majority, then from the persons having the highest numbers not exceeding

three, on the list of those voted for as president, the House of Representatives shall choose immediately, by ballot, the president. But in choosing the president, the votes shall be taken by states, the representation from each state having one vote; a quorum for this purpose shall consist of a member or members from two-thirds of the states, and a majority of all the states shall be necessary to a choice. And if the House of Representatives shall not choose a president, whenever the right of choice shall devolve upon them, before the fourth day of March next following, then the vice-president shall act as president, as in the case of the death or other constitutional disability of the president. The person having the greatest number of votes as vice-president shall be the vice-president, if such number be a majority of the whole number of electors appointed, and if no person have a majority, then from the two highest numbers on the list the Senate shall choose the vice-president; a quorum for the purpose shall consist of two-thirds of the whole number of senators, and a majority of the whole number shall be necessary to a choice. But no person constitutionally ineligible to the office of president shall be eligible to that of vice-president of the United States.

[Declared in force, September 25, 1804.]

ARTICLE XIII

Sec. 1. Neither slavery nor involuntary servitude, except as a punishment for crime whereof the party shall have been duly convicted, shall exist within the United States, or any place subject to their jurisdiction.

Sec. 2. Congress shall have power to enforce this article by appropriate legislation.

[Declared in force, December 18, 1865.]

ARTICLE XIV

Sec. 1. All persons born or naturalized in the United States, and subject to the jurisdiction thereof, are citizens of the United States and of the state wherein they reside. No state shall make or enforce any law which shall abridge the privileges or immunities of citizens of the United States; nor shall any state

---

[10] The first ten amendments, the Bill of Rights, were declared in force December 15, 1791, during the first session of Congress.

deprive any person of life, liberty, or property without due process of law; nor deny to any person within its jurisdiction the equal protection of the law.

Sec. 2. Representatives shall be apportioned among the several States according to their respective numbers, counting the whole number of persons in each state, excluding Indians not taxed. But when the right to vote at any election for the choice of electors for president and vice-president of the United States, representatives in Congress, the executive and judicial officers of a State, or the members of the legislature thereof, is denied to any of the male members of such state being of twenty-one years of age, and citizens of the United States, or in any way abridged, except for participation in rebellion or other crime, the basis of representation therein shall be reduced in the proportion which the number of such male citizens shall bear to the whole number of male citizens twenty-one years of age in such state.

Sec. 3. No person shall be a senator or representative in Congress, or elector of president and vice-president, or hold any office, civil or military, under the United States, or under any state, who, having previously taken an oath, as a member of Congress, or as an officer of the United States, or as a member of any state legislature, or as an executive or judicial officer of any state, to support the constitution of the United States, shall have engaged in insurrection or rebellion against the same, or given aid and comfort to the enemies thereof. But Congress may, by a vote of two-thirds of each House, remove such disability.

Sec. 4. The validity of the public debt of the United States, authorized by law, including debts incurred for payment of pensions and bounties for services in suppressing insurrection or rebellion, shall not be questioned. But neither the United States nor any state shall assume or pay any debt or obligation incurred in aid of insurrection or rebellion against the United States, or any claim for the loss or emancipation of any slave; but all such debts, obligations, and claims shall be held illegal and void.

Sec. 5. The Congress shall have power to enforce, by appropriate legislation, the provisions of this article.

[Declared in force, July 28, 1868.]

ARTICLE XV

Sec. 1. The right of citizens of the United States to vote shall not be denied or abridged by the United States or by any state on account of race, color, or previous condition of servitude.

Sec. 2. The Congress shall have power to enforce this article by appropriate legislation.

[Declared in force, March 30, 1870.]

ARTICLE XVI

The Congress shall have power to lay and collect taxes on incomes, from whatever source derived, without apportionment among the several States, and without regard to any census or enumeration.

[Declared in force, February 25, 1913.]

ARTICLE XVII

The Senate of the United States shall be composed of two senators from each state, elected by the people thereof for six years; and each senator shall have one vote. The electors in each state shall have the qualifications requisite for electors of the most numerous branch of the state legislatures.

When vacancies happen in the representation of any state in the senate, the executive authority of such state shall issue writs of election to fill such vacancies; provided, that the legislature of any state may empower the executive thereof to make temporary appointments until the people fill the vacancies by election as the legislature may direct.

This amendment shall not be so construed as to affect the election or term of any senator chosen before it becomes valid as part of the Constitution.

[Declared in force, May 31, 1913.]

ARTICLE XVIII

Sec. 1. After one year from the ratification of this article the manufacture, sale, or transportation of intoxicating liquors within, the importation thereof into, or exportation thereof from the United States and all territory subject to the jurisdiction thereof, for beverage purposes is hereby prohibited.

SEC. 2. The Congress and the several states shall have concurrent power to enforce this article by appropriate legislation.

SEC. 3. This article shall be inoperative unless it shall have been ratified as an amendment to the Constitution by the legislatures of the several states, as provided in the Constitution, within seven years from the date of submission hereof to the states by the Congress.

[Declared in force, January 29, 1919; repealed by Twenty-first Amendment.]

ARTICLE XIX

The right of citizens of the United States to vote shall not be denied or abridged by the United States or by any state on account of sex.

Congress shall have power to enforce this article by appropriate legislation.

[Declared in force, August 26, 1920.]

ARTICLE XX

SEC. 1. The terms of the President and Vice-President shall end at noon on the 20th day of January, and the terms of senators and representatives at noon on the 3rd day of January, of the years in which such terms would have ended if this article had not been ratified; and the terms of their successors shall then begin.

SEC. 2. The Congress shall assemble at least once in every year, and such meeting shall begin at noon on the 3rd day of January, unless they shall by law appoint a different day.

SEC. 3. If, at the time fixed for the beginning of the term of President, the President elect shall have died, the Vice-President elect shall become President. If a President shall not have been chosen before the time fixed for the beginning of his term, or if the President elect shall have failed to qualify, then the Vice-President elect shall act as President until a President shall have qualified; and the Congress may by law provide for the case wherein nei-

ther a President elect nor a Vice-President elect shall have qualified, declaring who shall then act as President, or the manner in which one who is to act shall be selected, and such person shall act accordingly until a President or Vice-President shall have qualified.

SEC. 4. The Congress may by law provide for the case of the death of any of the persons from whom the House of Representatives may choose a President, wherever the right of choice shall have devolved upon them, and for the case of the death of any of the persons from whom the Senate may choose a Vice-President, whenever the right of choice shall have devolved upon them.

SEC. 5. Sections 1 and 2 shall take effect on the 15th day of October following the ratification of this article.

SEC. 6. This article shall be inoperative unless it shall have been ratified as an amendment to the Constitution by the legislatures of three-fourths of the several states within seven years from the date of its submission.

[Declared in force, February 6, 1933.]

ARTICLE XXI

SEC. 1. The eighteenth article of amendment to the Constitution of the United States is hereby repealed.

SEC. 2. The transportation or importation into any state, territory, or possession of the United States, for delivery or use therein of intoxicating liquors, in violation of the laws thereof, is hereby prohibited.

SEC. 3. This article shall be inoperative unless it shall have been ratified as an amendment to the Constitution by conventions in the several states, as provided in the Constitution, within seven years from the date of the submission hereof to the states by the Congress.

[Declared in force, December 5, 1933.]

ARTICLE XXII

No person shall be elected to the office of the President more than twice, and no person who has held the office of President, or acted as President, for more than two years of a term to which some other person was elected President shall be elected to the office of the President more than once. But this Article shall not apply to any person holding the office of the President when this Article was proposed by the Congress, and shall not prevent any person who may be holding the office of President, or acting as President, during the term within which this Article becomes operative from holding the office of President or acting as President during the remainder of such term.

[Declared in force, February 26, 1951.]

ARTICLE XXIII

SEC. 1. The District constituting the seat of Government of the United States shall appoint in such manner as the Congress may direct:

A number of electors of President and Vice President equal to the whole number of Senators and Representatives in Congress to which the District would be entitled if it were a State, but in no event more than the least populous State; they shall be in addition to those appointed by the States, but they shall be considered for the purposes of the election of President and Vice President, to be electors appointed by a State; and they shall meet in the District and perform such duties as provided by the twelfth article of amendment.

SEC. 2. The Congress shall have power to enforce this article by appropriate legislation.

[Declared in force, April 3, 1961.]

ARTICLE XXIV

SEC. 1. The right of citizens of the United States to vote in any primary or other election for President or Vice President, for electors for President or Vice President, or for Senator or Representative in Congress, shall not be denied or abridged by the United States or any State by reason of failure to pay any poll tax or other tax.

SEC. 2. The Congress shall have the power to enforce this article by appropriate legislation.

[Declared in force, January 23, 1964.]

ARTICLE XXV

SEC. 1. In case of the removal of the President from office or his death or resignation, the Vice President shall become President.

SEC. 2. Whenever there is a vacancy in the office of the Vice President, the President shall nominate a Vice President who shall take the office upon confirmation by a majority vote of both houses of Congress.

SEC. 3. Whenever the President transmits to the President pro tempore of the Senate and the Speaker of the House of Representatives his written declaration that he is unable to discharge the powers and duties of his office, and until he transmits to them a written declaration to the contrary, such powers and duties shall be discharged by the Vice President as Acting President.

SEC. 4. Whenever the Vice President and a majority of either the principal officers of the executive departments or of such other body as Congress may by law provide, transmit to the President pro tempore of the Senate and the Speaker of the House of Representatives their written declaration that the President is unable to discharge the powers and duties of his office, the Vice President shall immediately assume the powers and duties of the office as Acting President.

Thereafter, when the President transmits to the President pro tempore of the Senate and the Speaker of the House of Representatives his written declaration that no inability exists, he shall resume the powers and duties of the office unless the Vice President and a majority of either the principal officers of the executive department or of such other body as Congress may by law provide, transmit within four days to the President pro tempore of the Senate and the Speaker of the House of Representatives their written declaration that the President is unable to discharge the powers and duties of his office. Thereupon Congress shall decide the issue, assembling within 48 hours for that purpose if not in session. If the Congress, within 21 days after receipt of the latter written declaration, or, if Congress is not in session, within 21 days after Congress is required to assemble, determines by two-thirds vote of both houses that the President is unable to discharge the powers and duties of his office, the Vice President shall continue to discharge the same as Acting President; otherwise, the President shall resume the powers and duties of his office.

[Declared in force 1967.]

• THE FRENCH DECLARATION OF THE RIGHTS OF MAN AND OF THE CITIZEN

The representatives of the people of France, formed into a National Assembly, considering that ignorance, neglect, or contempt of human rights, are the sole causes of public misfortunes and corruptions of government, have resolved to set forth in a solemn declaration these natural, imprescriptible, and inalienable rights, that this declaration being constantly present to the minds of the members of the body social, they may be ever kept attentive to their rights and their duties; that the acts of the legislative and executive powers of government, being capable of being every moment compared with the end of political institutions, may be more respected; and also, that the future claims of the citizens, being directed by simple and incontestable principles, may always tend to the maintenance of the Constitution and the general happiness.

For these reasons the National Assembly doth recognize and declare, in the presence of the Supreme Being, and with the hope of His blessing and favor, the following sacred rights of men and of citizens:

I. Men are born, and always continue, free and equal in respect of their rights. Civil distinctions, therefore, can be founded only on public utility.

II. The end of all political associations is the preservation of the natural and imprescriptible rights of man; and these rights are Liberty, Property, Security, and Resistance of Oppression.

III. The nation is essentially the source of all sovereignty; nor can any individual, or any body of men, be entitled to any authority which is not expressly derived from it.

IV. Political Liberty consists in the power of doing whatever does not injure another. The exercise of the natural rights of every man has no other limits than those which are necessary to secure to every other man the free exercise of the same rights; and these limits are determinable only by the law.

V. The law ought to prohibit only actions hurtful to society. What is not prohibited by the law should not be hindered; nor should anyone be compelled to do that which the law does not require.

VI. The law is an expression of the will of the community. All citizens have a right to concur, either personally or by their representatives, in its formation. It should be the same to all, whether it protects or punishes; and all being equal in its sight, are equally eligible to all honors, places, and employments, according to their different abilities, without any other distinction than that created by their virtues and talents.

VII. No man should be accused, arrested, or held in confinement, except in cases determined by the law, and according to the forms which it has prescribed. All who promote, solicit, execute, or cause to be executed, arbitrary orders, ought to be punished, and every citizen called upon, or apprehended by virtue of the law, ought immediately to obey, and renders himself culpable by resistance.

VIII. The law ought to impose no other penalties but such as are absolutely and evidently necessary; and no one ought to be punished, but in virtue of a law promulgated before the offense, and legally applied.

IX. Every man being presumed innocent till he has been convicted, whenever his detention becomes indispensable, all rigor to him, more than is necessary to secure his person, ought to be provided against by the law.

X. No man ought to be molested on account of his opinions, not even on account of his religious opinions, provided his avowal of them does not disturb the public order established by the law.

XI. The unrestrained communication of thoughts and opinions being one of the most precious rights of man, every citizen may speak, write, and publish freely, provided he is responsible for the abuse of this liberty, in cases determined by the law.

XII. A public force being necessary to give security to the rights of men and of citizens, that force is instituted for the benefit of the community and not for the particular benefit of the persons with whom it is intrusted.

XIII. A common contribution being necessary for the support of the public force, and for defraying the other expenses of government, it ought to be divided equally among the members of the community, according to their abilities.

XIV. Every citizen has a right, either by himself or his representative, to a free voice in determining the necessity of public contributions, the appropriations of them, and their amount, mode of assessment, and duration.

XV. Every community has a right to demand of all its agents an account of their conduct.

XVI. Every community in which a separation of powers and a security of rights is not provided for, wants a constitution.

XVII. The right to property being inviolable and sacred, no one ought to be deprived of it, except in cases of evident public necessity, legally ascertained, and on condition of a previous just indemnity. ∎

Passed by the National Assembly, at Paris, August, 1789.

• CHARTIST DOCUMENTS

PETITION, 1837

TO THE HONORABLE THE COMMONS OF GREAT BRITAIN AND IRELAND

The Petition of the undersigned Members of the Working Men's Association and others sheweth— That the only *rational use* of the institutions and laws of society is justly to protect, encourage, and support all that can be made to contribute *to the happiness of all the people.*

That, as the object to be obtained is mutual benefit, so ought the enactment of laws to be by mutual consent.

That obedience to laws can only be *justly enforced* on the certainty that those who are called on to obey them have had, either personally or by their representatives, the power to enact, amend, or repeal them.

That all those who are excluded from this share of political power are not justly included within the operation of the laws; to them the laws are only despotic enacments, and the legislative assembly from whom they emanate can only be considered parties to an unholy compact, devising plans and schemes for taxing and subjecting the many.

That the universal political right of every human being is superior and stands apart from all customs, forms, or ancient usage; a fundamental right not in the power of man to confer, or justly to deprive him of.

That to take away this sacred right from the *person* and to vest it in *property,* is a wilful perversion of justice and common sense, as the creation and security of property *are the consequences of society* —the great object of which is human happiness.

That any constitution or code of laws, formed in violation of men's political and social rights, are not rendered sacred by time nor sanctified by custom.

That the ignorance which originated, or permits their operation, forms no excuse for perpetuating the injustice; nor can aught but force or fraud sustain them, when any considerable number of people perceive and feel their degradation.

That the intent and object of your petitioners are to present such facts before your Honorable House as will serve to convince you and the country at large that you do not represent the people of these realms; and to appeal to your sense of right and justice as well as to every principle of honour, for directly making such legislative enactments as shall cause the mass of the people to be represented; with the view of securing *the greatest amount of happiness to all classes of society.*

Your Petitioners find, by returns ordered by your Honourable House, that the whole people of Great Britain and Ireland are about 24 millions, and that the males above 21 years of age are 6,023,752, who, in the opinion of your petitioners, are justly entitled to the elective right.

That according to S. Wortley's return (ordered by your Honourable House) the number of registered electors, who have the power to vote for members of Parliament, are only 839,519, and of this number only 8½ in 12 give their votes.

That on an analysis of the constituency of the United Kingdom, your petitioners find that 331 members (being a *majority* of your Honourable House) are returned by *one hundred and fifty-one thousand four hundred and ninety-two* registered electors!

That comparing the whole of the male population above the age of 21 with the 151,492 electors, it appears that 1–40 of them, or 1–160 of the entire population, have the power of passing all the laws in your Honourable House.

And your petitioners further find on investigation, that this majority of 331 members are composed of 163 Tories or Conservatives, 134 Whigs and Liberals, and only 34 who call themselves Radicals; and out of this limited number it is questionable whether 10 can be found who are truly the representatives of the wants and wishes of the producing classes.

Your petitioners also find that 15 members of your Honourable House are returned by electors under 200; 55 under 300; 90 under 400; 121 under 500; 150 under 600; 196 under 700; 214 under 800; 240 under 900; and 256 under 1,000; and that many of these constituencies are divided between two members.

They also find that your Honourable House, which is said to be exclusively the people's or the Commons House, contains *two hundred and five persons who are immediately or remotely related to the Peers of the Realm.*

Also that your Honourable House contains 1 marquess, 7 earls, 19 viscounts, 32 lords, 25 right honourables, 52 honourables, 63 baronets, 13 knights, 3 admirals, 7 lord-lieutenants, 42 deputy and vice-lieutenants, 1 general, 5 lieutenant-generals, 9 major-generals, 32 colonels, 33 lieutenant-colonels, 10 majors, 49 captains in army and navy, 10 lieutenants, 2 cornets, 58 barristers, 3 solicitors, 40 bankers, 33 East India proprietors, 13 West India proprietors, 52 place-men, 114 patrons of church livings having the patronage of 274 livings between them; the names of whom your petitioners can furnish at the request of your Honourable House.

Your peitioners therefore respectfully submit to your Honourable House that these facts afford abundant proofs that you do not represent the numbers or the interests of the millions; but that the persons composing it have interests for the most part foreign or directly opposed to the true interests of the great body of the people.

That perceiving the tremendous power you possess over the lives, liberty and labour of the unrepresented millions—perceiving the *military* and *civil forces* at your command—*the revenue* at your disposal—the *relief of the poor* in your hands—the *public press* in your power, by enactments expressly excluding the working classes alone—moreover, the power of delegating to others the whole control of the *monetary arrangements* of the Kingdom, by which the labouring classes may be silently plundered or suddenly suspended from employment—seeing all these elements of power wielded by your Honourable House as at present constituted, and fearing the consequences that may result if a thorough reform is not speedily had recourse to, your petitioners earnestly pray your Honourable House *to enact the following as the law of these realms,* with such other essential details as your Honourable House shall deem necessary:

A LAW FOR EQUALLY REPRESENTING THE PEOPLE OF GREAT BRTAIN AND IRELAND

Equal Representation

That the United Kingdom be divided into 200 electoral districts; dividing, as nearly as possible, an equal number of inhabitants; and that each district do send a representative to Parliament.

Universal Suffrage

That every person producing proof of his being 21 years of age, to the clerk of the parish in which he has resided six months, shall be entitled to have his name registered as a voter. That the time for registering in each year be from the 1st of January to the 1st of March.

Annual Parliaments

That a general election do take place on the 24th of June in each year, and that each vacancy be filled up a fortnight after it occurs. That the hours for voting be from six o-clock in the morning till six o'clock in the evening.

No Property Qualifications

That there shall be no property qualification for members; but on a requisition, signed by 200 voters, in favour of any candidate being presented to the clerk of the parish in which they reside, such candidate shall be put in nomination. And the list of all the candidates nominated throughout the district shall be stuck on the church door in every parish, to enable voters to judge of their qualification.

Vote by Ballot

That each voter must vote in the parish in which he resides. That each parish provide as many balloting boxes as there are candidates proposed in the district; and that a temporary place be fitted up in each parish church for the purpose of *secret voting.* And, on the day of election, as each voter passes orderly on to the ballot, he shall have given to him, by the officer in attendance, a balloting ball, which he shall drop into the box of his favourite candidate. At the close of the day the votes shall be counted, by the proper officers, and the numbers stuck on the church doors. The following day the clerk of the district and two examiners shall collect the votes of all the parishes throughout the district, and cause the name of the successful candidate to be posted in every parish of the district.

Sittings and Payments to Members

That the members do take their seats in Parliament on the first Monday in October next after their election, and continue their sittings every day (Sundays excepted) till the business of the sitting is terminated, but not later than the 1st of September. They shall meet every day (during the Session) for business at 10 o'clock in the morning, and adjourn at 4. And every member shall be paid quarterly out of the public treasury £400 a year. That all electoral officers shall be elected by universal suffrage.

By passing the foregoing as the law of the land, you will confer a great blessing on the people of England; and your petitioners, as in duty bound, will every pray. ■

Agreed Upon at the "Crown and Anchor" meeting in London, February 28, 1837. This Petition was the basis of The People's Charter, *drafted by William Lovett and Francis Place. Together with the* National Petition, *written by R. K. Douglas, with a list of 1,283,000 signatures, the* Charter *was submitted to Parliament, which rejected it, in 1839, 1842, and 1848. Subsequently, of course, the six demands of the Charter were accepted and became established democratic practice in England.*

PETITION AND PROTEST, 1854

Ernest Jones has started on another tour through the manufacturing districts, in order to agitate them in favor of the Charter. At Halifax, Bacup, and the other localities he has already visited, the following petition to the Parliament was adopted:

"To the Honorable the Commons of Great Britain and Ireland in Parliament assembled—The humble Petition of the Inhabitants of Bacup, in public meeting assembled, on Tuesday, the 30th day of July, 1854, showeth:

"That your petitioners have long and closely observed the conduct of the present Ministers of the Crown in their home and foreign policy, and are convinced from calm observation, that in both they are utterly undeserving the confidence of the country.

"That your petitioners feel convinced no domestic amelioration will take place, and no external vigor be displayed so long as such men remain at the helm of national affairs.

"Your petitioners therefore pray your honorable House to present an address to the throne to the effect that her Majesty may be pleased to discard her present advisers, and call to her assistance men more in harmony with the progressive spirit of the age, and better suited to the requirements of the times.

"And your petitioners will ever pray."

On Sunday a large meeting assembled at Dirpley Moor, Bacup, where the agitator delivered one of the most powerful speeches ever made by him, some extracts from which deserve a place in your journal:

"The time for action has at last arrived, and we are commencing now such a revival of Chartism in England as never yet succeeded on a pause of apathy. At last the hour is drawing nigh when we shall have the Charter. . . .

"Against the fall of wages you have struggled and struggled vainly; hunger led you to the breach; but poverty was your teacher, even as hunger was your drill-sergeant; and after every fresh fall you rose in intelligence and knowledge. At first combinations and strikes were your remedy. You sought to conquer by them—forgetting that, not having the means of working for yourselves, you had not the means of resisting the capitalist—whose purse sat very comfortably watching your belly—seeing which could stand out longest. You thought short time would do it, and were told that if each man worked two hours less, there would be two hours' work for those who had not worked at all. But you forgot that while you shortened the hours of labor one percent, monopoly increased machinery one hundred.

"You then flew to cooperation. You compassed a great truth—the salvation of labor must depend on cooperation—but you overlooked the means of insuring that salvation. If you manufacture, you require a market—if you have something to sell, you require somebody who wants to buy it—and you forgot that that somebody was not at hand. Cooperative manufacture starts—but where's the market? Where then are you to get the market? How can you make the poor rich, which alone can enable them to become purchasers of what cooperation manufacutres? By those British Californians, whose gold is on the surface of the soil, and tints the waving wheat field of the harvest. Look at your

feet—there, on the grassy banks whereon you sit—there, on the broad field whereon you stand—there lies liberty—there lies cooperation—there lies high wages—there lies prosperity and peace! In the fifteen millions of our public lands—the twenty-seven millions of our uncultivated British prairies here at home. A Greek fable says Hercules wrestled with the giant Antaeus, whose mother was the Earth, and threw him often—but every time he fell upon his mother's breast he gained fresh force, and bounded up more strong. Hercules, discovering this, lifted him up, and held him in the air till he had conquered him. Thus does the Hercules monopoly tear giant labor from its parent soil, and hold it by the grasp of competition, weak, powerless, and suspended, like Mahomet's tomb, 'twixt heaven and hell'—only much nearer to the latter place!

"But how to get the land? There are some men who tell you that political power is not needed for the purpose. Who are they who tell you so? Is it the leaders of ten per cent movements, and ten hours movements, and short time movements, and restriction on machinery movements, and burial club movements, and partnership movements, and benefit society movements, and church separation movements, and education movements, and municipal movements, and all the other movements besides? What a lot of 'movements,' and yet we have not *moved.* Not want political power? Why, these are the very men who go dancing around a political Tidd Pratt—or send whining deputations to a political Palmerston—or petition a political parliament, or wheedle around a political throne. Why, then it is political power we must go to after all, by their own showing. Only those men tell you to go to the political power of your *enemies,* and I tell you to go to a political power of your *own.* I lay down this sovereign truth:

"THE CHARTER IS THE UNIVERSAL REMEDY."

"What have we opposed to us? First, a coalition ministry. What does it mean? The leaders of factions not one of which can stand alone. Some dozen men, too weak to stand on their own legs, and so they lean against each other, and the whole lot of them can't make one proper man at last. That is a coalition. What have we besides? A Tory opposition that would kick them out but dare not, for it knows that it would be kicked out in turn; and then comes the deluge, in which Noah himself could not save class government. What have we else? A landed aristocracy, three-fourths of whose estates are mortgaged for above two-thirds of their value—a glorious power that to crush a people! Thirty-eight thousand bankrupt landlords, with 300,000 farmers, who groan beneath high rents, game laws and landlord tyranny. What have we more? A millocracy becoming bankrupt beneath the working of their own vile race of competition—who soon will not be able to keep their mills over their own heads. A precious power that to strike the pedestal of freedom from your feet! What remains? The working man and the shopkeeper. Often has it been endeavored to unite the two on the basis of a compromise. I for one have always opposed it, because a compromise of the franchise would only have strengthened the moneyed interest and perfected class legislation. But the time for that union has now come at last—and come without the need of compromise or treason. The retail shopkeepers are fast becoming democratic. It is said the way to a workingman's brain is through his belly. Aye! And the way to a shopkeeper's heart is through his pocket! For every shilling less he takes he gets a new idea. Insolvency is teaching him the truth. . . . Thus the moral force of our enemies is annihilated—and new allies are joining us. Their physical force is gone as well. The Czar's done that! In Ireland there are scarce 1,000 men. In England there is now no standing army. But there's the militia! Ah, the militia, of which the desertions are so immensely numerous, says the London *Times,* that the 'Hue and cry' is no longer enough, but special circulars are sent to every parish, to every place where the deserter ever lived, if but a week, to see if force and terror can drag him back. I wish the Government joy of their new force. Thus the field is clear—the people's opportunity has come. Do not suppose from this I mean violence. No! Far from it! *We mean a great peaceable moral movement.* But because *we* mean moral force, it does not follow our *enemies* should mean it *too.*

"England has begun to think and listen. As yet she is listening for the drums of Poland and the tramp of Hungary. As yet she is listening for the cries of Milan and the shouts of Paris! But amid the passing pause she is beginning to hear the beating of her own proud heart—and cries 'I also have a work to do—a foe to vanquish, and a field to conquer.'"

The chairman of the meeting adverted to the presence of the superintendent and other men of the police—trusting that no misrepresentations of what was said would be reported by those employed by government. Referring to his warning, Ernest Jones said:

"For my part, I don't care what they say—they may say what they choose. I go into agitation like a soldier into battle—taking my chance amid the balls that fly—to fall and perish, or to live and conquer; for I am a soldier of Democracy." ■

From dispatch by Karl Marx in the New-York Daily Tribune; *written August 8, published August 21, 1854.*

• THE SENECA FALLS DECLARATION

Resolved, That all laws which prevent woman from occupying such a station in society as her conscience shall dictate, or which place her in a position inferior to that of man, are contrary to the great precept of nature, and therefore of no force or authority.

Resolved, That woman is man's equal—was intended to be so by the Creator, and the highest good of the race demands that she should be recognized as such. . . .

Resolved, That inasmuch as man, while claiming for himself intellectual superiority, does accord to woman moral superiority, it is preeminently his duty to encourage her to speak and teach, as she has an opportunity, in all religious assembles. . . .

Resolved, That woman has too long rested satisfied in the circumscribed limits which corrupt customs and a perverted application of the Scriptures have marked out for her, and that it is time she should move in the enlarged sphere to which her great Creator has assigned her.

Resolved, That it is the duty of the women of this country to secure to themselves their sacred right to the elective franchise.

Resolved, That the equality of human rights results necessarily from the fact of the identity of the race in capabilities and responsibilities.

Resolved, That the speedy success of our cause depends upon the zealous and untiring efforts of both men and women, for the overthrow of the monopoly of the pulpit, and for the securing to women an equal participation with men in the various trades, professions, and commerce.

Resolved, therefore, That being invested by the Creator with the same capabilities, and the same consciousness of responsibility for their exercise, it is demonstrably the right and duty of woman, equally with man, to promote every righteous cause by every righteous means; and especially in regard to the great subjects of morals and religion, it is self-evidently her right to participate with her brother in teaching them, both in private and in public . . . and this being a self-evident truth growing out of the divinely implanted principles of human nature, any custom or authority adverse to it . . . is to be regarded as a self-evident falsehood, and at war with mankind. ■

From the Seneca Falls Declaration of Sentiments and Resolutions, July 19, 1848.

• THE MORRILL ACT

An Act donating Public Lands to the several States and Territories which may provide Colleges for the Benefit of Agriculture and Mechanic Arts.

Be it enacted . . . That there be granted to the several States . . . an amount of public land, to be apportioned to each State a quantity equal to thirty thousand acres for each senator and representative in Congress to which the States are respectively entitled. . . .

And be it further enacted, That the land aforesaid, after being surveyed, shall be apportioned to the several States in sections or subdivisions of sections, not less than one quarter of a section; and whenever there are public lands in a State subject to sale at private entry at one dollar and twenty-five cents per acre, the quantity to which said State shall be entitled shall be selected from such lands within the limits of such State. . . .

And be it further enacted, That all moneys derived from the sale of the lands aforesaid by the States . . . shall be invested in stocks of the United States, or of the States, or some other safe stocks, yielding not less than five per centum upon the par value of said stocks; and that the moneys so invested shall constitute a perpetual fund, the capital of which shall remain forever undiminished . . . and the interest of which shall be inviolably appropriated, by each State . . . to the endowment, support, and maintenance of at least one college where the leading object shall be, without excluding other scientific and classical studies, and including military tactics, to teach such branches of learning as are related to agriculture and mechanic arts, in such manner as the legislatures of the State may respectively prescribe, in order to promote the liberal and practical education of the industrial classes in the several pursuits and professions in life. ■

From the Morrill Act, passed by Congress July 2, 1862—perhaps the most important law for the advancement of education ever enacted in the United States. Under its provisions about thirteen million acres of the public domain were given by the federal government to the states for the establishment of mechanical and agricultural colleges—the so-called land-grant colleges—many of which became state universities.

• THE EMANCIPATION PROCLAMATION[1]

Now, therefore, I, Abraham Lincoln, President of the United States, by virtue of the power in me vested as commander-in-chief of the army and navy of the United States, in time of actual armed rebellion against the authority and government of the United States, and as a fit and necessary war measure for suppressing said rebellion, do . . . order and declare that all persons held as slaves within said designated States and parts of States are, and henceforward shall be, free; and that the Executive Government of the United States, including the military and naval authorities thereof, will recognize and maintain the freedom of said persons.

And I hereby enjoin upon the people so declared to be free to abstain from all violence, unless in necessary self-defense; and I recommend to them that, in all cases when allowed, they labor faithfully for reasonable wages.

And I further declare and make known that such persons of suitable condition will be received into the armed service of the United States to garrison forts, positions, stations, and other places, and to man vessels of all sorts in said service. And upon this act, sincerely believed to be an act of justice, warranted by the Constitution upon military necessity, I invoke the considerate judgment of mankind and the gracious favor of Almighty God. ∎

From President Lincoln's Proclamation issued at Washington, January 1, 1863.

• THE FOUR FREEDOMS

In the future days, which we seek to make secure, we look forward to a world founded upon four essential human freedoms.[1]

The first is freedom of speech and expression, everywhere in the world.

The second is freedom of every person to worship God in his own way, everywhere in the world.

The third is freedom from want, which, translated into world terms, means economic understandings which will secure to every nation a healthy peacetime life for its inhabitants, everywhere in the world.

The fourth is freedom from fear—which, translated into world terms, means a world-wide reduction of armaments to such a point and in such a thorough fashion that no nation will be in a position to commit an act of physical aggression against any neighbor—anywhere in the world.

This is no vision of a distant millennium. It is a definite basis for a kind of world attainable in our own time and generation. ∎

From President Franklin D. Roosevelt's Annual Message to Congress, January 6, 1941.

• THE CONSTITUTION OF JAPAN

We, the Japanese people, acting through our duly elected representatives in the National Diet, determined that we shall secure for ourselves and our posterity the fruits of peaceful cooperation with all nations and the blessings of liberty throughout this land, and resolved that never again shall we be visited with the horrors of war through the action of government, do proclaim that sovereign power resides with the people and do firmly establish this Constitution. Goverment is a sacred trust of the people, the authority for which is derived from the people, the powers of which are exercised by the

[1]On December 10, 1964, President Lyndon B. Johnson, in an address before the National Urban League community action assembly, said: "One of the Presidents that I admire most signed the Emancipation Proclamation 100 years ago. But emancipation was a proclamation and was not a fact. It shall be my purpose and it is my duty to make it a fact. Until every qualified person, regardless of the house where he worships or the state where he resides or the way he spells his name, or the color of his skin—until he has the right, unquestioned and unrestrained, to go in and cast his ballot in every precinct in this country, I am not going to be satified."

[1]In a Flag Day Address, June 14, 1942, President Roosevelt said: "The four freedoms of common humanity are as much elements of man's needs as air and sunlight, bread and salt. Deprive him of all these freedoms and he dies—deprive him of a part of them and a part of him withers."

representatives of the people, and the benefits of which are enjoyed by the people. This is a universal principle of mankind upon which this constitution is founded. We reject and revoke all constitutions, laws, ordinances, and rescripts in confict herewith.

We, the Japanese people, desire peace for all time and are deeply conscious of the high ideals controlling human relationship, and we have determined to preserve our security and existence, trusting in the justice and faith of the peace-loving peoples of the world. We desire to occupy an honored place in an international society striving for the preservation of peace, and the banishment of tyranny and slavery, oppression and intolerance for all time from the earth. We recognize that all peoples of the world have the right to live in peace, free from fear and want.

We believe that no nation is responsible to itself alone, but that laws of political morality are universal; and that obedience to such laws is incumbent upon all nations who would sustain their own sovereignty and justify their sovereign relationship with other nations.

We, the Japanese people, pledge our national honor to accomplish these high ideals and purposes with all our resources.

CHAPTER I
THE EMPEROR

ARTICLE 1. The Emperor shall be the symbol of the State and of the unity of the people, deriving his position from the will of the people with whom resides sovereign power.

ARTICLE 2. The Imperial Throne shall be dynastic and succeeded to in accordance with the Imperial House Law passed by the Diet.

ARTICLE 3. The advice and approval of the Cabinet shall be required for all acts of the Emperor in matters of state, and the Cabinet shall be responsible therefor.

ARTICLE 4. The Emperor shall perform only such acts in matters of state as are provided for in this Constitution and he shall not have powers related to government.

The Emperor may delegate the performance of his acts in matters of state as may be provided by law.

ARTICLE 5. When, in accordance with the Imperial House Law, a Regency is established, the Regent shall perform his acts in matters of state in the Emperor's name. In this case, paragraph one of the preceding article will be applicable.

ARTICLE 6. The Emperor shall appoint the Prime Minister as designated by the Diet.

The Emperor shall appoint the Chief Judge of the Supreme Court as designated by the Cabinet.

ARTICLE 7. The Emperor, with the advice and approval of the Cabinet, shall perform the following acts in matters of state on behalf of the people:

Promulgation of amendments of the constitution, laws, cabinet orders and treaties.

Convocation of the Diet.

Dissolution of the House of Representatives.

Proclamation of general election of members of the Diet.

Attestation of the appointment and dismissal of Ministers of State and other officials as provided for by law, and of full powers and credentials of Ambassadors and Ministers.

Attestation of general and special amnesty, commutation of punishment, reprieve, and restoration of rights.

Awarding of honors.

Attestation of instruments of ratification and other diplomatic documents as provided for by law.

Receiving foreign ambassadors and ministers.

Performance of ceremonial functions.

ARTICLE 8. No property can be given to, or received by, the Imperial House, nor can any gifts be made therefrom, without the authorization of the Diet.

CHAPTER II
RENUNCIATION OF WAR

ARTICLE 9. Aspiring sincerely to an international peace based on justice and order, the Japanese people forever renounce war as a sovereign right of the nation and the threat or use of force as means of settling international disputes.

In order to accomplish the aim of the preceding paragraph, land, sea, and air forces, as well as other war potential, will never be maintained. The right of belligerency of the state will not be recognized.

CHAPTER III
RIGHTS AND DUTIES OF THE PEOPLE

ARTICLE 10. The conditions necessary for being a Japanese national shall be determined by law.

ARTICLE 11. The people shall not be prevented from enjoying any of the fundamental human rights. These fundamental human rights guaranteed to the people by this Constitution shall be conferred upon the people of this and future generations as eternal and inviolate rights.

ARTICLE 12. The freedoms and rights guaranteed to the people by this Constitution shall be maintained by the constant endeavor of the people, who shall refrain from any abuse of these freedoms and rights and shall always be responsible for utilizing them for the public welfare.

ARTICLE 13. All of the people shall be respected as individuals. Their right to life, liberty, and the pursuit of happiness shall, to the extent that it does not interfere with the public welfare, be the supreme consideration in legislation and in other governmental affairs.

ARTICLE 14. All of the people are equal under the law and there shall be no discrimination in political, economic or social relations because of race, creed, sex, social status or family origin.

Peers and peerage shall not be recognized.

No privilege shall accompany any award of honor, decoration or any distinction, nor shall any such award be valid beyond the lifetime of the individual who now holds or hereafter may receive it.

ARTICLE 15. The people have the inalienable right to choose their public officials and to dismiss them.

All public officials are servants of the whole community and not of any group thereof.

Universal adult suffrage is guaranteed with regard to the election of public officials.

In all elections, secrecy of the ballot shall not be violated. A voter shall not be answerable, publicly or privately, for the choice he has made.

ARTICLE 16. Every person shall have the right of peaceful petition for the redress of damage, for the removal of public officials, for the enactment, repeal or amendment of laws, ordinances or regulations and for other matters; not shall any person be in any way discriminated against for sponsoring such a petition.

ARTICLE 17. Every person may sue for redress as provided by law from the State or a public entity, in case he has suffered damage through illegal act of any public official.

ARTICLE 18. No person shall be held in bondage of any kind. Involuntary servitude, except as punishment for crime, is prohibited.

ARTICLE 19. Freedom of thought and conscience shall not be violated.

ARTICLE 20. Freedom of religion is guaranteed to all. No religious organization shall receive any privileges from the State, nor exercise any political authority.

No person shall be compelled to take part in any religious act, celebration, rite or practice.

The State and its organs shall refrain from religious education or any other religious activity.

ARTICLE 21. Freedom of assembly and association as well as speech, press and all other forms of expression are guaranteed.

No censorship shall be maintained, nor shall the secrecy of any means of communication be violated.

ARTICLE 22. Every person shall have freedom to choose and change his residence and to choose his occupation to the extent that it does not interfere with the public welfare.

Freedom of all persons to move to a foreign country and to divest themselves of their nationality shall be inviolate.

ARTICLE 23. Academic freedom is guaranteed.

ARTICLE 24. Marriage shall be based only on the mutual consent of both sexes and it shall be maintained through mutual cooperation with the equal rights of husband and wife as a basis.

With regard to choice of spouse, property rights, inheritance, choice of domicile, divorce and other matters pertaining to marriage and the family, laws shall be enacted from the standpoint of individual dignity and the essential equality of the sexes.

ARTICLE 25. All people shall have the right to maintain the minimum standards of wholesome and cultured living.

In all spheres of life, the State shall use its endeavors for the promotion and extension of social welfare and security, and of public health.

ARTICLE 26. All people shall have the right to receive an equal education correspondent to their ability, as provided by law.

All people shall be obligated to have all boys and girls under their protection receive ordinary education as provided for by law. Such compulsory education shall be free.

ARTICLE 27. All people shall have the right and the obligation to work.

Standards for wages, hours, rest and other working conditions shall be fixed by law.

Children shall not be exploited.

ARTICLE 28. The right of workers to organize and to bargain and act collectively is guaranteed.

ARTICLE 29. The right to own or to hold property is inviolable.

Property rights shall be defined by law, in conformity with the public welfare.

Private property may be taken for public use upon just compensation therefor.

ARTICLE 30. The people shall be liable to taxation as provided by law.

ARTICLE 31. No person shall be deprived of life or liberty, nor shall any other criminal penalty be im-

posed, except according to procedure established by law.

ARTICLE 32. No person shall be denied the right of access to the courts.

ARTICLE 33. No person shall be apprehended except upon warrant issued by a competent judicial officer which specifies the offense with which the person is charged, unless he is apprehended, the offense being committed.

ARTICLE 34. No person shall be arrested or detained without being at once informed of the charges against him or without the immediate privilege of counsel; nor shall he be detained without adequate cause; and upon demand of any person such cause must be immediately shown in open court in his presence and the presence of his counsel.

ARTICLE 35. The right of all persons to be secure in their homes, papers and effects against entries, searches and seizures shall not be impaired except upon warrant issued for adequate cause and particularly describing the place to be searched and things to be seized, or except as provided by Article 33.

Each search or seizure shall be made upon separate warrant issued by a competent judicial officer.

ARTICLE 36. The infliction of torture by any public officer and cruel punishments are absolutely forbidden.

ARTICLE 37. In all criminal cases the accused shall enjoy the right to a speedy and public trial by an impartial tribunal.

He shall be permitted full opportunity to examine all witnesses, and he shall have the right of compulsory process for obtaining witnesses on his behalf at public expense.

At all times the accused shall have the assistance of competent counsel who shall, if the accused is unable to secure the same by his own efforts, be assigned to his use by the State.

ARTICLE 38. No person shall be compelled to testify against himself.

Confession made under compulsion, torture or

threat, or after prolonged arrest or detention shall not be admitted in evidence.

No person shall be convicted or punished in cases where the only proof against him is his own confession.

ARTICLE 39. No person shall be held criminally liable for an act which was lawful at the time it was committed, or of which he has been acquitted, nor shall he be placed in double jeopardy.

ARTICLE 40. Any person, in case he is acquitted after he has been arrested or detained, may sue the State for redress as provided by law.

CHAPTER IV
THE DIET

ARTICLE 41. The Diet shall be the highest organ of state power, and shall be the sole law-making organ of the State.

ARTICLE 42. The Diet shall consist of two Houses, namely the House of Representatives and the House, of Councillors.

ARTICLE 43. Both Houses shall consist of elected members, representative of all the people.

The number of the members of each House shall be fixed by law.

ARTICLE 44. The qualifications of members of both Houses and their electors shall be fixed by law. However, there shall be no discrimination because of race, creed, sex, social status, family origin, education, property or income.

ARTICLE 45. The term of office of members of the House of Representatives shall be four years. However, the term shall be terminated before the full term is up in case the House of Representatives is dissolved.

ARTICLE 46. The term of office of members of the House of Councillors shall be six years, and election for half the members shall take place every three years.

ARTICLE 47. Electoral districts, method of voting and other matters pertaining to the method of elec-

tion of members of both Houses shall be fixed by law.

ARTICLE 48. No person shall be permitted to be a member of both Houses simultaneously.

ARTICLE 49. Members of both Houses shall receive appropriate annual payment from the national treasury in accordance with law.

ARTICLE 50. Except in cases provided by law, members of both Houses shall be exempt from apprehension while the Diet is in session, and any members apprehended before the opening of the session shall be freed during the term of the session upon demand of the House.

ARTICLE 51. Members of both Houses shall not be held liable outside the House for speeches, debates or votes cast inside the House.

ARTICLE 52. An ordinary session of the Diet shall be convoked once per year.

ARTICLE 53. The Cabinet may determine to convoke extraordinary sessions of the Diet. When a quarter or more of the total members of either House makes the demand, the Cabinet must determine on such convocation.

ARTICLE 54. When the House of Representatives is dissolved, there must be a general election of members of the House of Representatives within forty (40) days from the date of dissolution, and the Diet must be convoked within thirty (30) days from the date of the election.

When the House of Representatives is dissolved, the House of Councillors is closed at the same time. However, the Cabinet may in time of national emergency convoke the House of Councillors in emergency session.

Measures taken at such session as mentioned in the proviso of the preceding paragraph shall be provisional and shall become null and void unless agreed to by the House of Representatives within a period of ten (10) days after the opening of the next session of the Diet.

ARTICLE 55. Each House shall judge disputes related to qualifications of its members. However, in order to deny a seat to any member, it is necessary to pass a resolution by a majority of two-thirds or more of the members present.

ARTICLE 56. Business cannot be transacted in either House unless one-third or more of total membership is present.

All matters shall be decided, in each House, by a majority of those present, except as elsewhere provided in the Constitution, and in case of a tie, the presiding officer shall decide the issue.

ARTICLE 57. Deliberation in each House shall be public. However, a secret meeting may be held where a majority of two-thirds or more of those members present passes a resolution therefor.

Each House shall keep a record of proceedings. This record shall be published and given general circulation, excepting such parts of proceedings of secret session as may be deemed to require secrecy.

Upon demand of one-fifth or more of the members present, votes of the members on any matter shall be recorded in the minutes.

ARTICLE 58. Each House shall select its own president and other officials.

Each House shall establish its rules pertaining to meetings, proceedings and internal discipline, and may punish members for disorderly conduct. However, in order to expel a member, a majority of two-thirds or more of those members present must pass a resolution thereon.

ARTICLE 59. A bill becomes a law on passage by both Houses, except as otherwise provided by the Constitution.

A bill which is passed by the House of Representatives, and upon which the House of Councillors makes a decision different from that of the House of Representatives, becomes a law when passed a second time by the House of Representatives by a majority of two-thirds or more of the members present.

The provision of the preceding paragraph does not preclude the House of Representatives from calling for the meeting of a joint committee of both Houses, provided for by law.

Failure by the House of Councillors to take final action within sixty (60) days after receipt of a bill passed by the House of Representatives, time in recess excepted, may be determined by the House of Representatives to constitute a rejection of the said bill by the House of Councillors.

ARTICLE 60. The budget must first be submitted to the House of Representatives.

Upon consideration of the budget, when the House of Councillors makes a decision different from that of the House of Representatives, and when no agreement can be reached even through a joint committee of both Houses, provided for by law, or in the case of failure by the House of Councillors to take final action within thirty (30) days, the period of recess excluded, after the receipt of the budget passed by the House of Representatives, the decision of the House of Representatives shall be the decision of the Diet.

ARTICLE 61. The second paragraph of the preceding article applies also to the Diet approval required for the conclusion of treaties.

ARTICLE 62. Each House may conduct investigations in relation to government, and may demand the presence and testimony of witnesses, and the production of records.

ARTICLE 63. The Prime Minister and other Ministers of State may, at any time, appear in either House for the purpose of speaking on bills, regardless of whether they are members of the House or not. They must appear when their presence is required in order to give answers or explanations.

ARTICLE 64. The Diet shall set up an impeachment court from among the members of both Houses for the purpose of trying those judges against whom removal proceedings have been instituted.

Matters relating to impeachment shall be provided by law.

CHAPTER V
THE CABINET

ARTICLE 65. Executive power shall be vested in the Cabinet.

ARTICLE 66. The Cabinet shall consist of the Prime Minister, who shall be its head, and other Ministers of State, as provided for by law.

The Prime Minister and other Ministers of State must be civilians.

The Cabinet, in the exercise of executive power, shall be collectively responsible to the Diet.

ARTICLE 67. The Prime Minister shall be designated from among the members of the Diet by a resolution of the Diet. This designation shall precede all other business.

If the House of Representatives and the House of Councillors disagree and if no agreement can be reached even through a joint committee of both Houses, provided for by law, or the House of Councillors fails to make designation within ten (10) days, exclusive of the period of recess, after the House of Representatives has made designation, the decision of the House of Representatives shall be the decision of the Diet.

ARTICLE 68. The Prime Minister shall appoint the Ministers of State. However, a majority of their number must be chosen from among the members of the Diet.

The Prime Minister may remove the Ministers of State as he chooses.

ARTICLE 69. If the House of Representatives passes a non-confidence resolution, or rejects a confidence resolution, the Cabinet shall resign en masse, unless the House of Representatives is dissolved within ten (10) days.

ARTICLE 70. When there is a vacancy in the post of Prime Minister, or upon the first convocation of the Diet after a general election of members of the House of Representatives, the Cabinet shall resign en masse.

ARTICLE 71. In the cases mentioned in the two preceding articles, the Cabinet shall continue its functions until the time when a new Prime Minister is appointed.

ARTICLE 72. The Prime Minister, representing the Cabinet, submits bills, reports on general national affairs and foreign relations to the Diet and exercises control and supervision over various administrative branches.

ARTICLE 73. The Cabinet, in addition to other general administrative functions, shall perform the following functions:

Administer the law faithfully; conduct affairs of state.

Manage foreign affairs.

Conclude treaties. However, it shall obtain prior or, depending on circumstances, subsequent approval of the Diet.

Administer the civil service, in accordance with standards established by law.

Prepare the budget, and present it to the Diet.

Enact cabinet orders in order to execute the provisions of this Constitution and of the law. However, it cannot include penal provisions in such cabinet orders unless authorized by such law.

Decide on general amnesty, special amnesty, commutation of punishment, reprieve, and restoration of rights.

ARTICLE 74. All laws and cabinet orders shall be signed by the competent Minister of State and countersigned by the Prime Minister.

ARTICLE 75. The Ministers of State, during their tenure of office, shall not be subject to legal action without the consent of the Prime Minister. However, the right to take that action is not impaired hereby.

CHAPTER VI
JUDICIARY

ARTICLE 76. The whole judicial power is vested in a Supreme Court and in such inferior courts as are established by law.

No extraordinary tribunal shall be established, nor shall any organ or agency of the Executive be given final judicial power.

All judges shall be independent in the exercise of their conscience and shall be bound only by this Constitution and the laws.

ARTICLE 77. The Supreme Court is vested with the rule-making power under which it determines the rules of procedure and of practice, and of matters relating to attorneys, the internal discipline of the courts and the administration of judicial affairs.

Public procurators shall be subject to the rule-making power of the Supreme Court.

The Supreme Court may delegate the power to make rules for inferior courts to such courts.

ARTICLE 78. Judges shall not be removed except by public impeachment unless judicially declared mentally or physically incompetent to perform official duties. No disciplinary action against judges shall be administered by any executive organ or agency.

ARTICLE 79. The Supreme Court shall consist of a Chief Judge and such number of judges as may be determined by law; all such judges excepting the Chief Judge shall be appointed by the Cabinet.

The appointment of the judges of the Supreme Court shall be reviewed by the people at the first general election of members of the House of Representatives following their appointment, and shall be reviewed again at the first general election of members of the House of Representatives after a lapse of ten (10) years, and in the same manner thereafter.

In cases mentioned in the foregoing paragraph, when the majority of the voters favors the dismissal of a judge, he shall be dismissed.

Matters pertaining to review shall be prescribed by law.

The judges of the Supreme Court shall be retired upon the attainment of the age as fixed by law.

All such judges shall receive, at regular stated intervals, adequate compensation which shall not be decreased during their terms of office.

ARTICLE 80. The judges of the inferior courts shall be appointed by the Cabinet from a list of persons nominated by the Supreme Court. All such judges shall hold office for a term of ten (10) years with privilege of reappointment, provided that they shall be retired upon the attainment of the age as fixed by law.

The judges of the inferior courts shall receive, at regular stated intervals, adequate compensation which shall not be decreased during their terms of office.

ARTICLE 81. The Supreme Court is the court of last resort with power to determine the constitutionality of any law, order, regulation or official act.

ARTICLE 82. Trials shall be conducted and judgment declared publicly.

Where a court unanimously determines publicity to be dangerous to public order or morals, a trial may be conducted privately, but trials of political offenses, offenses involving the press or cases wherein the rights of people as guaranteed in Chapter III of this Constitution are in question shall always be conducted publicly.

CHAPTER VII
FINANCE

ARTICLE 83. The power to administer national finances shall be exercised as the Diet shall determine.

ARTICLE 84. No new taxes shall be imposed or existing ones modified except by law or under such conditions as law may prescribe.

ARTICLE 85. No money shall be expended, nor shall the State obligate itself, except as authorized by the Diet.

ARTICLE 86. The Cabinet shall prepare and submit to the Diet for its consideration and decision a budget for each fiscal year.

ARTICLE 87. In order to provide for unforeseen deficiencies in the budget, a reserve fund may be authorized by the Diet to be expended upon the responsibility of the Cabinet.

The Cabinet must get subsequent approval of the Diet for all payments from the reserve fund.

ARTICLE 88. All property of the Imperial Household shall belong to the State. All expenses of the Imperial Household shall be appropriated by the Diet in the budget.

ARTICLE 89. No public money or other property shall be expended or appropriated for the use, benefit or maintenance of any religious institution or association, or for any charitable, educational or benevolent enterprises not under the control of public authority.

ARTICLE 90. Final accounts of the expenditures and revenues of the State shall be audited annually by a Board of Audit and submitted by the Cabinet to the Diet, together with the statement of audit, during the fiscal year immediately following the period covered.

The organization and competency of the Board of Audit shall be determined by law.

ARTICLE 91. At regular intervals and at least annually the Cabinet shall report to the Diet and the people on the state of national finances.

CHAPTER VIII
LOCAL SELF-GOVERNMENT

ARTICLE 92. Regulations concerning organization and operations of local public entities shall be fixed by law in accordance with the principle of local autonomy.

ARTICLE 93. The local public entities shall establish assemblies as their deliberative organs, in accordance with law.

The chief executive officers of all local public entities, the members of their assemblies, and such other local officials as may be determined by law shall be elected by direct popular vote within their several communities.

ARTICLE 94. Local public entities shall have the right to manage their property, affairs and administration and to enact their own regulations within law.

ARTICLE 95. A special law, applicable only to one local public entity, cannot be enacted by the Diet without the consent of the majority of the voters of the local public entity concerned, obtained in accordance with law.

CHAPTER IX
AMENDMENTS

ARTICLE 96. Amendments to this Constitution shall be initiated by the Diet, through a concurring vote of two-thirds or more of all the members of each House and shall thereupon be submitted to the people for ratification, which shall require the affirmative vote of a majority of all votes cast thereon, at a special referendum or at such election as the Diet shall specify.

Amendments when so ratified shall immediately be promulgated by the Emperor in the name of the people, as an integral part of this Constitution.

CHAPTER X
SUPREME LAW

ARTICLE 97. The fundamental human rights by this Constitution guaranteed to the people of Japan are fruits of the age-old struggle of man to be free; they have survived the many exacting tests for durability and are conferred upon this and future generations in trust, to be held for all time inviolate.

ARTICLE 98. This Constitution shall be the supreme law of the nation and no law, ordinance, imperial rescript or other act of government, or part thereof, contrary to the provisions hereof, shall have legal force or validity.

The treaties concluded by Japan and established laws of nations shall be faithfully observed.

ARTICLE 99. The Emperor or the Regent as well as Ministers of State, members of the Diet, judges, and all other public officials have the obligation to respect and uphold this Constitution.

CHAPTER XI
SUPPLEMENTARY PROVISIONS

ARTICLE 100. This Constitution shall be enforced as from the day when the period of six months will have elapsed counting from the day of its promulgation.

The enactment of laws necessary for the enforcement of this Constitution, the election of members of the House of Councillors and the procedure for the convocation of the Diet and other preparatory procedures necessary for the enforcement of this Constitution may be executed before the day prescribed in the preceding paragraph.

ARTICLE 101. If the House of Councillors is not constituted before the effective date of this Constitution, the House of Representatives shall function as the Diet until such time as the House of Councillors shall be constituted.

ARTICLE 102. The term of office for half the members of the House of Councillors serving in the first term under this Constitution shall be three years. Members falling under this category shall be determined in accordance with law.

ARTICLE 103. The Ministers of State, members of the House of Representatives and judges in office on the effective date of this Constitution, and all other public officials who occupy positions corresponding to such positions as are recognized by this Constitution shall not forfeit their positions automatically on account of the enforcement of this Constitution unless otherwise specified by law. When, however, successors are elected or appointed under the provisions of this Constitution, they shall forfeit their positions as a matter of course. ■

In effect 1947.

• THE UNITED NATIONS UNIVERSAL DECLARATION OF HUMAN RIGHTS

THE GENERAL ASSEMBLY

Proclaims this Universal Declaration of Human Rights as a common standard of achievement for all peoples and all nations, to the end that every individual and every organ of society, keeping this declaration constantly in mind, shall strive by teaching and education to promote respect for these rights and freedoms and by progressive measures, national and international, to secure their universal and effective recognition and observance, both among the people of Member States themselves and among the peoples of territories under their jurisdiction.

ARTICLE 1. All human beings are born free and equal in dignity and rights. They are endowed with reason and conscience and should act towards one another in a spirit of brotherhood.

ARTICLE 2. Everyone is entitled to all the rights and freedoms set forth in this Declaration, without distinction of any kind, such as race, colour, sex, language, religion, political or other opinion, national or social origin, property, birth, or other status.

Furthermore, no distinction shall be made on the basis of the political, jurisdictional, or international status of the country or territory to which a person belongs, whether it be an independent, trust, or non-self-governing territory or under any limitation of sovereignty.

ARTICLE 3. Everyone has the right to life, liberty, and security of person.

ARTICLE 4. No one shall be held in slavery or servitude; slavery and the slave trade shall be prohibited in all their forms.

ARTICLE 5. No one shall be subjected to torture or to cruel, inhuman, or degrading treatment or punishment.

ARTICLE 6. Everyone has the right to recognition everywhere as a person before the law.

ARTICLE 7. All are equal before the law and are entitled without any discrimination to equal protection of the law. All are entitled to equal protection against any discrimination in violation of this Declaration and against any incitement to such discrimination.

ARTICLE 8. Everyone has the right to an effective remedy by the competent national tribunals for acts violating the fundamental rights granted him by the Constitution or by law.

ARTICLE 9. No one shall be subjected to arbitrary arrest, detention, or exile.

ARTICLE 10. Everyone is entitled in full equality to a fair and public hearing by an independent and impartial tribunal, in the determination of his rights and obligations and of any criminal charge against him.

ARTICLE 11. 1. Everyone charged with a penal offence has the right to be presumed innocent until proved guilty according to law in a public trial at which he has had all the guarantees necessary for his defence. 2. No one shall be held guilty of any penal offence on account of any act or omission which did not constitute a penal offence, under national or international law, at the time when it was committed. Nor shall a heavier penalty be imposed than the one that was applicable at the time the penal offence was committed.

ARTICLE 12. No one shall be subjected to arbitrary interference with his privacy, family, home, or correspondence, nor to attacks upon his honour and reputation. Everyone has the right to the protection of the law against such interference or attacks.

ARTICLE 13. 1. Everyone has the right to freedom of movement and residence within the borders of each State. 2. Everyone has the right to leave any country, including his own, and to return to his country.

ARTICLE 14. 1. Everyone has the right to seek and to enjoy in other countries asylum from persecution. 2. This right may not be invoked in the case of prosecutions genuinely arising from non-political crimes or from acts contrary to the purposes and principles of the United Nations.

ARTICLE 15. 1. Everyone has the right to a nationality. 2. No one shall be arbitrarily deprived of his nationality nor denied the right to change his nationality.

ARTICLE 16. 1. Men and women of full age, without any limitation due to race, nationality, or religion, have the right to marry and to found a family. They are entitled to equal rights as to marriage, during marriage, and at its dissolution. 2. Marriage shall be entered into only with the free and full consent of the intending spouses. 3. The family is the natural and fundamental group unit of society and is entitled to protection by society and the State.

ARTICLE 17. 1. Everyone has the right to own property alone as well as in association with others. 2. No one shall be arbitrarily deprived of his property.

ARTICLE 18. Everyone has the right to freedom of thought, conscience, and religion; this right includes freedom to change his religion or belief, and freedom either alone or in community with others and in public or private, to manifest his religion or belief in teaching, practice, worship, and observance.

ARTICLE 19. Everyone has the right to freedom of opinion and expression, this right includes freedom to hold opinions without interference and to seek, receive, and impart information and ideas through any media and regardless of frontiers.

ARTICLE 20. 1. Everyone has the right to freedom of peaceful assembly and association. 2. No one may be compelled to belong to an association.

ARTICLE 21. 1. Everyone has the right to take part in the Government of his country, directly or through freely chosen representatives. 2. Everyone has the right of equal access to public service in his country. 3. The will of the people shall be the basis of the authority of Government; this will shall be expressed in periodic and genuine elections which shall be by universal and equal suffrage and shall be held by secret vote or by equivalent free voting procedures.

ARTICLE 22. Everyone, as a member of society, has the right to social security and is entitled to the realisation, through national effort and international co-operation and in accordance with the organisation and resources of each State, of the economic, social, and cultural rights indispensable for his dignity and the free development of his personality.

ARTICLE 23. 1. Everyone has the right to work, to free choice of employment, to just and favourable conditions of work, and to protection against unemployment. 2. Everyone, without any discrimination, has the right to equal pay for equal work. 3. Everyone who works has the right to just and favourable remuneration, insuring for himself and his family an existence worthy of human dignity, and supplemented, if necessary, by other means of social protection. 4. Everyone has the right to form and to join trade unions for the protection of his interests.

ARTICLE 24. Everyone has the right to rest and leisure, including reasonable limitation of working hours and periodic holidays with pay.

ARTICLE 25. 1. Everyone has the right to a standard of living adequate for the health and well-being of himself and of his family, including food, clothing, housing, and medical care and necessary social services, and the right to security in the event of unemployment, sickness disability, widowhood, old age, or other lack of livelihood in circumstances beyond his control. 2. Motherhood and childhood are entitled to special care and assistance. All children, whether born in or out of wedlock, shall enjoy the same social protection.

ARTICLE 26. 1. Everyone has the right to education. Education shall be free, at least in the elementary and fundamental stages. Elementary education shall be compulsory. Technical and professional education shall be made generally available, and higher education shall be equally accessible to all on the basis of merit. 2. Education shall be directed to the full development of the human personality and to the strengthening of respect for human rights and fundamental freedoms; it shall promote understanding, tolerance, and friendship among all nations, racial or religious groups, and shall further the activities of the United Nations for the maintenance of peace. 3. Parents have a prior right to choose the kind of education that shall be given to their children.

ARTICLE 27. 1. Everyone has the right freely to participate in the cultural life of the community, to enjoy the arts, and to share in scientific advancement and its benefits. 2. Everyone has the right to the protection of the moral and material interests resulting from any scientific, literary, or artistic production of which he is the author.

ARTICLE 28. Everyone is entitled to a social and international order in which the rights and freedoms set forth on this declaration can be fully realised.

ARTICLE 29. 1. Everyone has duties to the community in which alone the free and full development of his personality is possible. 2. In the exercise of his rights and freedoms, everyone shall be subject only to such limitations as are determined by law solely for the purpose of securing due recognition and respect for the rights and freedoms of others and of meeting the just requirements of morality, public order, and the general welfare in a democratic society. 3. These rights and freedoms may in no case be exercised contrary to the purposes and principles of the United Nations.

ARTICLE 30. Nothing in this Declaration may be interpreted as implying for any State, group, or person any right to engage in any activity or to perform any act aimed at the destruction of any of the rights and freedoms set forth herein. ◾

Adopted by the U.N. General Assembly,
December 6, 1948.

• THE GERMAN FEDERAL CONSTITUTION (BONN)

PREAMBLE

The German People in the *Laender* [provinces] of Baden, Bavaria, Bremen, Hamburg, Hesse, Lower Saxony, North Rhine-Westphalia, Rhineland-Palatinate, Schleswig-Holstein, Wuerttemberg-Baden and Wuerttemberg-Hohenzollern,

Conscious of its responsibility before God and men,

Animated by the resolve to preserve its national and political unity and to serve the peace of the world as an equal partner in a united Europe,

Desiring to give a new order to political life for a transitional period,

Has enacted, by virtue of its constituent power, this Basic Law of the Federal Republic of Germany.

It has also acted on behalf of those Germans to whom participation was denied.

The entire German people is called upon to achieve by free self-determination the unity and freedom of Germany.

I. BASIC RIGHTS

ARTICLE 1. 1. The dignity of man shall be inviolable. To respect and protect it shall be the duty of all state authority. 2. The German people therefore acknowledge inviolable and inalienable human rights as the basis of every community, of peace and of justice in the world. 3. The following basic rights shall bind the legislature, the executive and the judiciary as directly enforceable law.

ARTICLE 2. 1. Everyone shall have the right to the free development of his personality in so far as he does not violate the rights of others or offend against the constitutional order or the moral code. 2. Everyone shall have the right to life and to inviolability of his person. The freedom of the individual shall be inviolable. These rights may only be encroached upon pursuant to a law.

ARTICLE 3. 1. All persons shall be equal before the law. 2. Men and women shall have equal rights. 3. No one may be prejudiced or favored because of his sex, his parentage, his race, his language, his homeland and origin, his faith or his religious or political opinions.

ARTICLE 4. 1. Freedom of belief, of conscience, and freedom of creed, religious or ideological [*Weltanschaulich*], shall be inviolable. 2. The undisturbed practice of religion is guaranteed. 3. No one may be compelled against his conscience to render war service involving the use of arms. Details shall be regulated by a federal law.

ARTICLE 5. 1. Everyone shall have the right freely to express and disseminate his opinion by speech, writing and pictures and freely to inform himself from generally accessible sources. Freedom of the press and freedom of reporting by means of broadcasts and films are guaranteed. There shall be no censorship. 2. These rights are limited by the provisions of the general laws, the provisions of law for the protection of youth, and by the right to inviolability of personal honor. 3. Art and science, research and teaching shall be free. Freedom of teaching shall not absolve from loyalty to the constitution.

ARTICLE 6. 1. Marriage and family shall enjoy the special protection of the state. 2. The care and upbringing of children are a natural right of, and a duty primarily incumbent on, the parents. The national community shall watch over their endeavors in this respect. 3. Children may not be separated from their families against the will of the persons entitled to bring them up, except pursuant to a law, if those so entitled fail or the children are otherwise threatened with neglect. 4. Every mother shall be entitled to the protection and care of the community. 5. Illegitimate children shall be provided by legislation with the same opportunities for their physical and spiritual development and their place in society as are enjoyed by legitimate children.

ARTICLE 7. 1. The entire educational system shall be under the supervision of the state. 2. The persons entitled to bring up a child shall have the right to decide whether it shall receive religious instruction. 3. Religious instruction shall form part of the ordinary curriculum in state and municipal schools, except in secular [*bekenntnisfrei*] schools. Without prejudice to the state's right of supervision, religious instruction shall be given in accordance with the tenets of the religious communities. No teacher may be obliged against his will to give religious instruction. 4. The right to establish private schools is guaranteed. Private schools, as a substitute for state or municipal schools, shall require the approval of the state and shall be subject to the laws of the *Laender*. Such approval must be given if private schools are not inferior to the state or municipal schools in their educational aims, their facilities and the professional training of their teaching staff, and if segregation of pupils according to the means of the parents is not promoted thereby. Approval must be withheld if the economic and legal position of the teaching staff is not sufficiently assured. 5. A private elementary school shall be permitted only if the education authority finds that it serves a special pedagogic interest, or if, on the application of persons entitled to bring up children, it is to be established as an interdenominational or denominational or ideological [*Weltanschauung*] school and a state or municipal elementary school of this type does not exist in the commune [*Gemeinde*]. 6. Preparatory schools [*Vorschulen*] shall remain abolished.

ARTICLE 8. 1. All Germans shall have the right to assemble peaceably and unarmed without prior notification or permission. 2. With regard to open-air meetings this right may be restricted by or pursuant to a law.

ARTICLE 9. 1. All Germans shall have the right to form associations and societies. 2. Associations, the purposes or activities of which conflict with criminal laws or which are directed against the constitutional order or the concept of international understanding, are prohibited. 3. The right to form associations to safeguard and improve working and economic conditions is guaranteed to everyone and to all trades, occupations and professions. Agreements which restrict or seek to impair this right shall be null and void; measures directed to this end shall be illegal. Measures taken pursuant to Article 12a, to paragraphs 2 and 3 of Article 35, to paragraph 4 of Article 87a, or to Article 91, may not be directed against any industrial conflicts engaged in by associations within the meaning of the first sentence of this paragraph in order to safeguard and improve working and economic conditions.

ARTICLE 10. 1. Secrecy of mail, post and telecommunication shall be inviolable. 2. This right may be restricted only pursuant to a law. Such law may lay down that the person affected shall not be informed of any such restriction if it serves to protect the free democratic basic order or the existence or security of the Federation or a *Land,* and that recourse to the courts shall be replaced by a review of the case by bodies and auxiliary bodies appointed by Parliament.

ARTICLE 11. 1 All Germans shall enjoy freedom of movement throughout the federal territory. 2. This right may be restricted only by or pursuant to a law and only in cases in which an adequate basis of existence is lacking and special burdens would arise to the community as a result thereof, or in which such restriction is necessary to avert an imminent danger to the existence or the free democratic basic order of the Federation or a *Land,* to combat the danger of epidemics, to deal with natural disasters or particularly grave accidents, to protect young people from neglect or to prevent crime.

ARTICLE 12. 1. All Germans shall have the right freely to choose their trade, occupation, or profession, their place of work and their place of training. The practice of trades, occupations, and professions may be regulated by or pursuant to a law. 2. No specific occupation may be imposed on any person except within the framework of a traditional compulsory public service that applies generally and equally to all. 3. Forced labor may be imposed only on persons deprived of their liberty by court sentence.

ARTICLE 12a. 1. Men who have attained the age of eighteen years may be required to serve in the Armed Forces, in the Federal Border Police or in a Civil Defense organization. 2. A person who refuses, on grounds of conscience, to render war service involving the use of arms may be required to render a substitute service. The duration of such substitute service shall not exceed the duration of military service. Details shall be regulated by a law which shall not interfere with the freedom of conscience and must also provide for the possibility of a substitute service not connected with units of the Armed Forces or of the Federal Border Police. 3. Persons liable to military service who are not required to render service pursuant to paragraphs 1 or 2 of this Article may, when a state of defense [*Verteidigungsfall*] exists, be assigned by or pursuant to a law to specific occupations involving civilian services for defense purposes, including the protection of the civilian population; it shall, however, not be permissible to assign persons to an occupation subject to public law except for the purpose of discharging police functions or such other functions of public administration as can only be discharged by persons employed under public law. Persons may be assigned to occupations—as referred to in the first sentence of this paragraph—with the Armed Forces, including the supplying and servicing of the latter, or with public administrative authorities; assignments to occupations connected with supplying and servicing the civilian population shall not be permissible except in order to meet their vital requirements or to guarantee their safety. 4. If, while a state of defense exists, civilian service requirements in the civilian public health and medical system or in the stationary military hospital organization cannot be met on a voluntary basis, women between eighteen and fifty-five years of age may be assigned to such services by or pursuant to a law. They may on no account render service involving the use of arms. 5. During the time prior to the existence of any such state of defense, assignments under paragraph 3 of this Article may be effected only if the requirements of paragraph 1 of Article 80a are satisfied. It shall be admissible to require persons by or pursuant to a law to attend training courses in order to prepare them for the performance of such services in accordance with paragraph 3 of this Article as presuppose special knowledge or skills. To this extent, the first sentence of this paragraph shall not apply. 6. If, while a state of defense exists, the labor requirements for the purposes referred to in the second sentence of paragraph 3 of this Article cannot be met on a voluntary basis, the right of a German to give up the practice of his trade or occupation or profession, or his place of work, may be restricted by or pursuant to a law in order to meet these requirements. The first sentence of paragraph 5 of this Article shall apply *mutatis mutandis* prior to the existence of a state of defense.

ARTICLE 13. 1. The home shall be inviolable. 2. Searches may be ordered only by a judge or, in the event of danger in delay, by other organs as provided by law and may be carried out only in the form prescribed by law. 3. In all other respects, this inviolability may not be encroached upon or restricted except to avert a common danger or a mortal danger to individuals, or, pursuant to a law, to prevent imminent danger to public safety and order, especially to alleviate the housing shortage, to combat the danger of epidemics or to protect endangered juveniles.

ARTICLE 14. 1. Property and the right of inheritance are guaranteed. Their content and limits shall be determined by the laws. 2. Property imposes duties. Its use should also serve the public weal. 3. Expropriation shall be permitted only in the public weal. It may be effected only by or pursuant to a law which shall provide for the nature and extent of the compensation. Such compensation shall be determined by establishing an equitable balance between the public interest and the interests of those affected. In case of dispute regarding the amount of compensation, recourse may be had to the ordinary courts.

ARTICLE 15. Land, natural resources and means of production may for the purpose of socialization be transferred to public ownership or other forms of publicly controlled economy by a law which shall provide for the nature and extent of compensation. With respect to such compensation the third and fourth sentences of paragraph 3 of Article 14 shall apply *mutatis mutandis.*

ARTICLE 16. 1. No one may be deprived of his German citizenship. Loss of citizenship may arise only pursuant to a law, and against the will of the person affected only if such person does not thereby become stateless. 2. No German may be extradited to a foreign country. Persons persecuted on political grounds shall enjoy the right of asylum.

ARTICLE 17. Everyone shall have the right individually or jointly with others to address written requests or complaints to the appropriate agencies and to parliamentary bodies.

ARTICLE 17a*. 1. Laws concerning military service and substitute service may, by provisions applying to members of the Armed Forces and of substitute services during their period of military or substitute service, restrict the basic right freely to express and to disseminate opinions by speech, writing and pictures (first half-sentence of paragraph 1 of Article 5), the basic right of assembly (Article 8), and the right of petition (Article 17) in so far as this right permits the submission of requests or complaints jointly with others. 2. Laws for defense purposes including the protection of the civilian population may provide for the restriction of the basic rights of freedom of movement (Article 11) and inviolability of the home (Article 13).

ARTICLE 18. Whoever abuses freedom of expression of opinion, in particular freedom of the press (paragraph 1 of Article 5), freedom of teaching (paragraph 3 of Article 5), freedom of assembly (Article 8), freedom of association (Article 9), secrecy of mail, post and telecommunication (Article 10), property (Article 14), or the right of asylum (paragraph 2 of Article 16) in order to combat the free democratic basic order, shall forfeit these basic rights. Such forfeiture and the extent thereof shall be pronounced by the Federal Constitutional Court.

ARTICLE 19. 1. In so far as a basic right may, under this Basic Law, be restricted by or pursuant to a law, such law must apply generally and not solely to an individual case. Furthermore, such a law must name the basic right, indicating the Article concerned. 2. In no case may the essential content of a basic right be encroached upon. 3. The basic rights shall apply also to domestic juristic persons to the extent that the nature of such rights permits. 4. Should any person's right be violated by public authority, recourse to the court shall be open to him. If jurisdiction is not specified, recourse shall be to the ordinary courts. The second sentence of paragraph 2 of Article 10 shall not be affected by the provisions of this paragraph. ■

Part I, Basic Rights. In effect 1949.

*Inserted by federal law of 19 March 1956 (*Federal Law Gazette* I, p. 111).

• A CATHOLIC DECLARATION ON RELIGIOUS FREEDOM

ON THE RIGHT OF THE PERSON AND OF COMMUNITIES TO SOCIAL AND CIVIL FREEDOM IN MATTERS RELIGIOUS

1

A sense of the dignity of the human person has been impressing itself more and more deeply on the consciousness of contemporary man, and the demand is increasingly made that men should act on their own judgment, enjoying and making use of a responsible freedom, not driven by coercion but motivated by a sense of duty. The demand is likewise made that constitutional limits should be set to the powers of government, in order that there may be no. encroachment on the rightful freedom of the person and of associations.

This demand for freedom in human society chiefly regards the quest for the values proper to the human spirit. It regards, in the first place, the free exercise of religion in society. This Vatican Council takes careful note of these desires in the minds of men. It proposes to declare them to be greatly in accord with truth and justice. To this end, it searches into the sacred tradition and doctrine of the church—the treasury out of which the church continually brings forth new things that are in harmony with the things that are old.

First, the Council professes its belief that God Himself has made known to mankind the way in which men are to serve Him, and thus be saved in Christ and come to blessedness. We believe that this one true religion subsists in the Catholic and apostolic church, to which the Lord Jesus committed the duty of spreading it abroad among all men. Thus He spoke to the apostles: "Go, therefore, and make disciples of all nations, baptizing them in the name of the Father and of the Son and of the Holy Spirit, teaching them to observe all things whatsoever I have enjoined upon you" (Matthew XXVIII:19–20).

On their part, all men are bound to seek the truth,

especially in what concerns God and His church, and to embrace the truth they come to know, and to hold fast to it.

This Vatican Council likewise professes its belief that it is upon the human conscience that these obligations fall and exert their binding force. The truth cannot impose itself except by virtue of its own truth, as it makes its entrance into the mind at once quietly and with power.

Religious freedom, in turn, which men demand as necessary to fulfill their duty to worship God, had to do with immunity from coercion in civil society. Therefore it leaves untouched traditional Catholic doctrine on the moral duty of men and societies toward the true religion and toward the one church of Christ.

Over and above all this, the Council intends to develop the doctrine of recent Popes on the inviolable rights of the human person and the constitutional order of society.

2

This Vatican Council declares that the human person has a right to religious freedom. This freedom means that all men are to be immune from coercion on the part of individuals or of social groups and of any human power, in such ways that no one is to be forced to act in a manner contrary to his own beliefs, whether privately or publicly, whether alone or in association with others, within due limits.

The Council further declares that the right to religious freedom has its foundation in the very dignity of the human person as this dignity is known through the revealed word of God and by reason itself. This right of the human person to religious freedom is to be recognized in the constitutional law whereby society is governed and thus it is to become a civil right.

It is in accordance with their dignity as persons— that is, beings endowed with reason and free will and therefore privileged to bear personal responsibility—that all men should be at once impelled by nature and also bound by a moral obligation to seek the truth, especially religious truth. They are also bound to adhere to the truth, once it is known, and

to order their whole lives in accord with the demands of truth.

However, men cannot discharge these obligations in a manner in keeping with their own nature unless they enjoy immunity from external coercion as well as psychological freedom. Therefore the right to religious freedom has its foundation, not in the subjective disposition of the person, but in his very nature. In consequence, the right to this immunity continues to exist even in those who do not live up to their obligation of seeking the truth and adhering to it and the exercise of this right is not to be impeded, provided that just public order be observed.

Further light is shed on the subject if one considers that the highest norm of human life is the divine law—eternal, objective, and universal— whereby God orders, directs, and governs the entire universe and all the ways of the human community, by a plan conceived in wisdom and love. Man has been made by God to participate in this law, with the result that, under a gentle disposition of divine Providence, he can come to perceive ever more fully the truth that is unchanging.

3

Wherefore every man has the duty, and therefore the right, to seek the truth in matters religious, in order that he may with prudence form for himself right and true judgements of conscience, under use of all suitable means.

Truth, however, is to be sought after in a manner proper to the dignity of the human person and his social nature. The inquiry is to be free, carried on with the aid of teaching or instruction, communication and dialogue, in the course of which men explain to one another the truth they have discovered, or think they have discovered, in order thus to assist one another in the quest for truth.

Moreover, as the truth is discovered, it is by a personal assent that men are to adhere to it.

On his part, man perceives and acknowledges the imperatives of the divine law through the mediation of conscience. In all his activity a man is bound to follow his conscience, in order that he may come to God, the end and purpose of life. It follows that he is not to be forced to act in a manner contrary to his conscience.

Nor, on the other hand, is he to be restrained from acting in accordance with his conscience especially in matters religious. The reason is that the exercise of religion, of its very nature, consists before all else in those internal, voluntary, and free acts whereby man sets the course of his life directly toward God. No merely human power can either command or prohibit acts of this kind.

The social nature of man, however, itself requires that he should give external expression to his internal acts of religion: that he should share with others in matters religious: that he should profess his religion in community. Injury therefore is done to the human person and to the very order established by God for human life, if the free exercise of religion is denied in society, provided just public order is observed.

There is a further consideration. The religious acts whereby men, in private and in public and out of a sense of personal conviction, direct their lives to God transcend by their very nature the order of terrestrial and temporal affairs.

Government, therefore, ought indeed to take account of the religious life of the citizenry and show it favor, since the function of government is to make provision for the common welfare. However, it would clearly transgress the limits set to its power, were it to presume to command or inhibit acts that are religious.

4

The freedom or immunity from coercion in matters religious which is the endowment of persons as individuals is also to be recognized as their right when they act in community. Religious communities are a requirement of the social nature both of man and of religion itself.

Provided the just demands of public order are observed, religious communities rightfully claim freedom in order that they may govern themselves according to their own norms, honor the Supreme Being in public worship, assist their members in the practice of the religious life, strengthen them by instruction, and promote institutions in which they may join together for the purpose of ordering their own lives in accordance with their religious principles.

Religious communities also have the right not to be hindered, either by legal measures or by administrative action on the part of government, in the selection, training, appointment, and transferral of their own ministers in communicating with religious authorities and communities abroad in erecting buildings for religious purposes, and in the acquisition and use of suitable funds or properties.

Religious communities also have the right not to be hindered in their public teaching and witness to their faith, whether by the spoken or by the written word. However, in spreading religious faith and in introducing religious practices everyone ought at all times to refrain from any manner of action which might seem to carry a hint of coercion or of a kind of persuasion that would be dishonorable or unworthy, especially when dealing with poor or uneducated people. Such a manner of action would have to be considered an abuse of one's right and a violation of the right of others.

In addition, it comes within the meaning of religious freedom that religious communities should not be prohibited from freely undertaking to show the special value of their doctrine in what concerns the organization of society and the inspiration of the whole of human activity.

Finally, the solid nature of man and the very nature of religion afford the foundation of the right of men freely to hold meetings and to establish educational, cultural, charitable and social organizations, under the impulse of their own religious sense.

5

The family, since it is a society in its own original right, has the right freely to live its own domestic religious life under the guidance of parents. Parents, moreover, have the right to determine, in accordance with their own religious beliefs, the kind of religious education that their children are to receive.

Government, in consequence, must acknowledge the right of parents to make a genuinely free choice of schools and of other means of education, and the use of this freedom of choice is not to be made a reason for imposing unjust burdens on parents, whether directly or indirectly.

Besides, the rights of parents are violated if their children are forced to attend lessons or instruction which are not in agreement with their religious beliefs, or if a single system of education, from which all religious information is excluded, is imposed upon all.

6

Since the common welfare of society consists in the entirety of those conditions of social life under which men enjoy the possibility of achieving their own perfection in a certain fullness of measure and also with some relative ease, it chiefly consists in the protection of the rights, and in the performance of the duties, of the human person.

Therefore the care of the right to religious freedom devolves upon the whole citizenry, upon social groups, upon government, and upon the church and other religious communities, in virtue of the duty of all toward the common welfare, and in the manner proper to each.

The protection and promotion of the inviolable rights of man ranks among the essential duties of government. Therefore government is to assume the safeguard of the religious freedom of all its citizens, in an affective manner, by just laws and by other appropriate means.

Government is also to help create conditions favorable to the fostering of religious life, in order that the people may be truly enabled to exercise their religious rights and to fulfill their religious duties, and also in order that society itself may profit by the moral qualities of justice and peace which have their origin in men's faithfulness to God and to His holy will.

If, in view of peculiar circumstances obtaining among peoples, special civil recognition is given to one religious community in the constitutional order of society, it is at the same time imperative that the right of all citizens and religious communities to religious freedom should be recognized and made effective in practice.

Finally, government is to see to it that the equality of citizens before the law, which is itself an element of the common good, is never violated, whether openly or covertly, for religious reasons. Nor is there to be discrimination among citizens.

It follows that a wrong is done when government imposes upon its people, by force or fear or other means, the profession or repudiation of any religion, or when it hinders men from joining or leaving a religious community. All the more is it a violation of the will of God and of the sacred rights of the person and the family of nations, when force is brought to bear in any way in order to destroy or repress religion, either in the whole of mankind or in a particular country or in a definite community.

7

The right to religious freedom is exercised in human society: hence its exercise is subject to certain regulatory norms in the use of all freedoms the moral principle of personal and social responsibility is to be observed. In the exercise of their rights individual men and social groups are bound by the moral law to have respect both for the rights of others and for their own duties toward others and for the common welfare of all. Men are to deal with their fellows in justice and civility.

Furthermore, society has the right to defend itself against possible abuses committed on pretext of freedom of religion. It is the special duty of government to provide this protection. However, government is not to act in arbitrary fashion or in an unfair spirit of partisanship. Its action is to be controlled by juridical norms which are in conformity with the objective moral order.

These norms arise out of the need for effective safeguard of the rights of all citizens and for peaceful settlement of conflicts of rights, also out of the need for an adequate care of genuine public peace, which comes about when men live together in good order and in true justice: and finally out of the need for a proper guardianship of public morality.

These matters constitute the basic component of the common welfare: they are what is meant by public order. For the rest, the usages of society are to be the usages of freedom in their full range: that is, the freedom of man is to be respected as far as possible and is not to be curtailed except when and insofar as necessary.

8

Many pressures are brought to bear upon men of our day to the point where the danger arises lest they lose the possibility of acting on their own judgment. On the other hand, not a few can be found who seem inclined to use the name of freedom as the pretext for refusing to submit to authority and for making light of the duty of obedience.

Wherefore this Vatican Council urges everyone, especially those who are charged with the task of educating others, to do their utmost to form men who, on the one hand, will respect the moral order and be obedient to lawful authority, and, on the other hand, will be lovers of true freedom—men, in other words, who will come to decisions on their own judgment and in the light of truth, govern their activities with a sense of responsibility, and strive after what is true and right, willing always to join with others in cooperative effort.

Religious freedom therefore ought to have this further purpose and aim, namely, that men may come to act with greater responsibility in fulfilling their duties in community life.

RELIGIOUS FREEDOM IN THE LIGHT OF REVELATION

9

The declaration of this Vatican Council on the right of man to religious freedom has its foundation in the dignity of the person, whose exigencies have come to be more fully known to human reason through centuries of experience. What is more, this doctrine of freedom has roots in divine revelation, and for this reason Christians are bound to respect it all the more conscientiously.

Revelation does not indeed affirm in so many words the right of man to immunity from external coercion in matters religious. It does, however, disclose the dignity of the human person in its full dimensions: it gives evidence of the respect which Christ showed toward the freedom with which man is to fulfill his duty of belief in the word of God: and it gives us lessons in the spirit which disciples of such a master ought to adopt and continually follow.

Thus further light is cast upon the general principles upon which the doctrine of this declaration on religious freedom is based. In particular, religious freedom in society is entirely consonant with the freedom of the act of Christian faith.

10

It is one of the major tenets of Catholic doctrine that man's response to God in faith must be free: no one therefore is to be forced to embrace the Christian faith against his own will. This doctrine is contained in the word of God and it was constantly proclaimed by the fathers of the church. The act of faith is of its very nature a free act. Man, redeemed by Christ the Saviour and through Christ Jesus called to be God's adopted son, cannot give his adherence to God revealing Himself unless, under the drawing of the Father he offers to God the reasonable and free submission of faith.

It is therefore completely in accord with the nature of faith that in matters religious every manner of coercion on the part of men should be excluded. In consequence, the principle of religious freedom makes no small contribution to the creation of an environment in which men can without hindrance be invited to Christian faith, embrace it of their own free will, and profess it effectively in their whole manner of life.

11

God calls men to serve Him in spirit and in truth: hence they are bound in conscience but they stand under no compulsion. God has regard for the dignity of the human person whom He Himself created: man is to be guided by his own judgment and he is to enjoy freedom.

This truth appears at its height in Christ Jesus, in whom God manifested Himself and His ways with men. Christ is at once our Master and our Lord and also meek and humble of heart: in attracting and inviting His disciples He used patience. He wrought miracles to illuminate His teaching and to establish its truth: but His intention was to rouse faith in His hearers and to confirm them in faith, not to exert coercion upon them. He did indeed denounce the unbelief of some who listened to Him, but He left vengeance to God in expectation of the day of judgment.

When He sent His apostles into the world, He said to them: "He who believes and is baptized will be saved: he who does not believe will be condemned" (Mark XVI: 16). But He Himself, noting that cockle had been sown amid the wheat, gave orders that both should be allowed to grow until the harvest time, which will come at the end of the world. He refused to be a political messiah, ruling with force; He preferred to call Himself the son of man, who came to serve and to give his life as a ransom for the many (Mark X: 45). He showed Himself the perfect servant of God, who does not break the bruised reed or extinguish the smoking flax (Matthew XII: 20).

He acknowledged the power of government and its rights, when He commanded that tribute be given to Caesar: but He gave clear warning that the higher rights of God are to be kept inviolate: "Render to Caesar the things that are Caesar's and to God the things that are God's" (Matthew XXII: 21).

In the end, when He completed on the cross the work of redemption whereby He achieved salvation and true freedom for men, He brought His revelation to completion. For He bore witness to the truth, but He refused to impose the truth by force on those who spoke against it. Not by force of blows does His rule assert its claims. It is established by witnessing to the truth and by hearing the truth, and it extends its dominion by the love whereby Christ, lifted up on the cross, draws all men to Himself.

Taught by the word and example of Christ, the apostles followed the same way. From the very origins of the church the disciples of Christ strove to convert men to faith in Christ as the Lord—not,

however, by the use of coercion or devices unworthy of the gospel, but by the power, above all, of the word of God, steadfastly they proclaimed to all the plan of God our Saviour, who wills that all men should be saved and come to the acknowledgment of the truth (I Timothy II: 4).

At the same time, however, they showed respect for those of weaker stuff, even though they were in error, and thus they made it plain that each one of us is to render to God an account of himself (Romans XIV: 12). And for that reason is bound to obey his conscience. Like Christ himself, the apostles were unceasingly bent upon bearing witness to the truth of God, and they showed the fullest measure of boldness in speaking the word with confidence (Acts IV: 31) before the people and their rulers.

With a firm faith they held that the gospel is indeed the power of God unto salvation for all who believe. Therefore they rejected all carnal weapons. They followed the example of the gentleness and respectfulness of Christ and they preached the word of God in the full confidence that there was resident in this word itself a divine power able to destroy all the forces arrayed against God and bring men to faith in Christ and to his service.

As the Master, so too the apostles recognized legitimate civil authority. For there is no power except from God, the apostle teaches, and thereafter commands: Let everyone be subject to higher authorities . . .: he who resists authority resists God's ordinance (Romans XIII: 1-5). At the same time, however, they did not hesitate to speak out against governing powers which set themselves in opposition to the holy will of God: it is necessary to obey God rather than men (Acts V: 29). This is the way along which the martyrs and other faithful have walked through all ages and over all the earth.

12

In faithfulness therefore to the truth of the gospel, the church is following the way of Christ and the apostles when she recognizes, and gives support to, the principle of religious freedom as befitting the dignity of man and as being in accord with divine revelation.

Throughout the ages the church has kept safe and handed on the doctrine received from the Master and from the apostles. In the life of the people of God as it has made its pilgrim way through the vicissitudes of human history, there has at times appeared a way of acting that was hardly in accord with the spirit of the gospel or even opposed to it. Nevertheless, the doctrine of the church that no one is to be coerced into faith his always stood firm.

Thus the leaven of the gospel has long been about its quiet work in the minds of men, and to it is due in great measure the fact that in the course of time men have come more widely to recognize their dignity as persons, and the conviction has grown stronger that the person in society is to be kept free from all manner of coercion in matters religious.

13

Among the things that concern the good of the church and indeed the welfare of society here on earth—things therefore that are always and everywhere to be kept secure and defended against all injury—this certainly is pre-eminent, namely, that the church should enjoy that full measure of freedom which her care for the salvation of men requires.

This is a sacred freedom, because the only-begotten son endowed with it the church which He purchased with His blood. Indeed it is so much the property of the church that to act against it is to act against the will of God. The freedom of the church is the fundamental principle in what concerns the relations between the church and governments and the whole civil order.

In human society and the face of government the church claims freedom for herself in her character as a spiritual authority, established by Christ the Lord, upon which there rests, by divine mandate, the duty of going out into the whole world and preaching the gospel to every creature. The church also claims freedom for herself in her character as a society of men who have the right to live in society in accordance with the percepts of Christian faith.

In turn, where the principle of religious freedom is not only proclaimed in words or simply incorporated in law but also given sincere and practical application, there the church succeeds in achieving a stable situation of right as well as of fact and the independence which is necessary for the fulfillment of her divine mission.

This independence is precisely what the authorities of the church claim in society. At the same time, the Christian faithful, in common with all other men, possess the civil right not to be hindered in leading their lives in accordance with their conscience. Therefore a harmony exists between the freedom of the church and the religious freedom which is to be recognized as the right of all men and communities and sanctioned by constitutional law.

14

In order to be faithful to the divine command, teach all nations (Matthew XXVIII: 19-20), the Catholic Church must work with all urgency and concern that the word of God be spread abroad and glorified (II Thessalonians III: 1) ... Hence the church earnestly begs of its children that, first of all, supplications, prayers, petitions, acts of thanksgiving be made for all men ... for this is good and agreeable in the sight of God our Saviour, who wills that all men be saved and come to the knowledge of the truth (I Timothy II: 1-4).

In the formation of their consciences the Christian faithful ought carefully to attend to the sacred and certain doctrine of the Church. For the Church is, by the will of Christ, the teacher of the truth. It is her duty to give utterance to, and authoritatively to teach that truth which is Christ Himself, and also, to declare and confirm by her authority those principles of the moral order which have their origin in human nature itself.

Furthermore, let Christians walk in wisdom in the face of those outside, in the Holy Spirit, in unaffected love, in the word of truth (II Corinthians VI: 6-7), and let them be about their task of spreading the light of life with all confidence and apostolic courage, even to the shedding of their blood.

The disciple is bound by a grave obligation toward Christ his Master ever more fully to understand the truth received from Him, faithfully to proclaim it, never—be it understood—having recourse to means that are incompatible with the spirit of the Gospel.

At the same time, the charity of Christ urges him to love and have prudence and patience in his dealings with those who are in error or in ignorance with regard to the faith. All is to be taken into account—the Christian duty to Christ, the lifegiving word which must be proclaimed, and the rights of the human person, and the measure of grace granted by God through Christ to men, who are invited freely to accept and profess the faith.

15

The fact is that men of the present day want to be able freely to profess their religion in private and public; indeed religious freedom has already been declared to be a civil right in most constitutions; and it is solemnly recognized in international documents. The further fact is that forms of government still exist under which, even though freedom of religious worship receives constitutional recognition, the powers of government are engaged in the effort to deter citizens from the profession of religion and to make life very difficult and dangerous for religious communities.

This Council greets with joy the first of these two facts, as among the signs of the times. With sorrow, however, it denounces the other fact, as only to be deplored. The Council exhorts Catholics, and it directs a plea to all men, most carefully to consider how greatly necessary religious freedom is, especially in the present condition of the human family.

All nations are coming into even closer unity: men of different cultures and religions are being brought together in closer relationships: there is a growing consciousness of the personal responsibility that every man has. All this is evident. Consequently, in order that relationships of peace and harmony be established and maintained within the whole of mankind, it is necessary that religious freedom be everywhere provided with an effective constitutional guarantee and that respect be shown for the high duty and right of man freely to lead his religious life in society.

May the God and Father of all grant that the human family, through careful observance of the principle of religious freedom in society, may be brought by the grace of Christ and the power of the Holy Spirit to the sublime and unending and glorious freedom of the sons of God (Romans VIII: 21).

From declaration promulgated by Pope Paul VI and the Ecumenical Council of Bishops, Rome, December 7, 1965; This text translated by the North American Catholic Welfare Conference, appeared in the New York Times, *December 8, 1965.*

• THE CONSTITUTION OF THE STATE OF MONTANA

PREAMBLE

We the people of Montana grateful to God for the quiet beauty of our state, the grandeur of our mountains, the vastness of our plains, and desiring to improve the quality of life, equality of opportunity and to secure the blessings of liberty for this and future generations do ordain and establish this constitution.

ARTICLE I
COMPACT WITH THE UNITED STATES

All provisions of the enabling act of Congress (approved February 22, 1889, 25 Stat. 676), as amended and of Ordinance No. 1, appended to the Constitution of the state of Montana and approved February 22, 1889, including the agreement and declaration that all lands owned or held by any Indian or Indian tribes shall remain under the absolute jurisdiction and control of the Congress of the United States, continue in full force and effect until revoked by the consent of the United States and the people of Montana.

ARTICLE II
• DECLARATION OF RIGHTS
SECTION 1. POPULAR SOVEREIGNTY

All political power is vested in and derived from the people. All government of right originates with the people, is founded upon their will only, and is instituted solely for the good of the whole.

SECTION 2. SELF-GOVERNMENT

The people have the exclusive right of governing themselves as a free, sovereign, and independent state. They may alter or abolish the constitution and form of government whenever they deem it necessary.

SECTION 3. INALIENABLE RIGHTS

All persons are born free and have certain inalienable rights. They include the right to a clean and healthful environment and the rights of pursuing life's basic necessities, enjoying and defending their lives and liberties, acquiring, possessing and protecting property, and seeking their safety, health and happiness in all lawful ways. In enjoying these rights, all persons recognize corresponding responsibilities.

SECTION 4. INDIVIDUAL DIGNITY

The dignity of the human being is inviolable. No person shall be denied the equal protection of the laws. Neither the state nor any person, firm, corporation, or institution shall discriminate against any person in the exercise of his civil or political rights on account of race, color, sex, culture, social origin or condition, or political or religious ideas.

SECTION 5. FREEDOM OF RELIGION

The state shall make no law respecting an establishment of religion or prohibiting the free exercise thereof.

SECTION 6. FREEDOM OF ASSEMBLY

The people shall have the right peaceably to assemble, petition for redress or peaceably protest governmental action.

SECTION 7. FREEDOM OF SPEECH, EXPRESSION, AND PRESS

No law shall be passed impairing the freedom of speech or expression. Every person shall be free to speak or publish whatever he will on any subject, being responsible for all abuse of that liberty. In all suits and prosecutions for libel or slander the truth thereof may be given in evidence; and the jury, under the direction of the court, shall determine the law and the facts.

SECTION 8. RIGHT OF PARTICIPATION

The public has the right to expect governmental agencies to afford such reasonable opportunity for citizen participation in the operation of the agencies prior to the final decision as may be provided by law.

SECTION 9. RIGHT TO KNOW

No person shall be deprived of the right to examine documents or to observe the deliberations of all public bodies or agencies of state government and its subdivisions, except in cases in which the demand of individual privacy clearly exceeds the merits of public disclosure.

SECTION 10. RIGHT OF PRIVACY

The right of individual privacy is essential to the well-being of a free society and shall not be infringed without the showing of a compelling state interest.

SECTION 11. SEARCHES AND SEIZURES

The people shall be secure in their persons, papers, homes and effects from unreasonable searches and seizures. No warrant to search any place, or seize any person or thing shall issue without describing the place to be searched or the person or thing to be seized, or without probable cause, supported by oath or affirmation reduced to writing.

SECTION 12. RIGHT TO BEAR ARMS

The right of any person to keep or bear arms in defense of his own home, person, and property, or in aid of the civil power when thereto legally summoned, shall not be called in question, but nothing herein contained shall be held to permit the carrying of concealed weapons.

SECTION 13. RIGHT OF SUFFRAGE

All elections shall be free and open, and no power,

civil or military, shall at any time interfere to prevent the free exercise of the right of suffrage.

SECTION 14. ADULT RIGHTS

A person 18 years of age or older is an adult for all purposes.

SECTION 15. RIGHTS OF PERSONS NOT ADULTS

The rights of persons under 18 years of age shall include, but not be limited to, all the fundamental rights of this Article unless specifically precluded by laws which enhance the protection of such persons.

SECTION 16. THE ADMINISTRATION OF JUSTICE

Courts of justice shall be open to every person, and speedy remedy afforded for every injury of person, property, or character. No person shall be deprived of this full legal redress for injury incurred in employment for which another person may be liable except as to fellow employees and his immediate employer who hired him if such immediate employer provides coverage under the Workmen's Compensation Laws of this state. Right and justice shall be administered without sale, denial, or delay.

SECTION 17. DUE PROCESS OF LAW

No person shall be deprived of life, liberty, or property without due process of law.

SECTION 18. STATE SUBJECT TO SUIT

The state, counties, cities, towns, and all other local governmental entities shall have no immunity from suit for injury to a person or property. This provision shall apply only to causes of action arising after July 1, 1973.

SECTION 19. HABEAS CORPUS

The privilege of the writ of habeas corpus shall never be suspended.

SECTION 20. INITIATION OF PROCEEDINGS

(1) Criminal offenses within the jurisdiction of any court inferior to the district court shall be prosecuted by complaint. All criminal actions in district court, except those on appeal, shall be prosecuted either by information, after examination and commitment by a magistrate or after leave granted by the court, or by indictment without such examination, commitment or leave.

(2) A grand jury shall consist of eleven persons, of whom eight must concur to find an indictment. A grand jury shall be drawn and summoned only at the discretion and order of the district judge.

SECTION 21. BAIL

All persons shall be bailable by sufficient sureties, except for capital offenses, when the proof is evident or the presumption great.

SECTION 22. EXCESSIVE SANCTIONS

Excessive bail shall not be required, or excessive fines imposed, or cruel and unusual punishments inflicted.

SECTION 23. DETENTION

No person shall be imprisoned for the purpose of securing his testimony in any criminal proceeding longer than may be necessary in order to take his deposition. If he can give security for his appearance at the time of trial, he shall be discharged upon giving the same; if he cannot give security, his deposition shall be taken in the manner provided by law, and in the presence of the accused and his counsel, or without their presence, if they shall fail to attend the examination after reasonable notice of the time and place thereof.

SECTION 24. RIGHTS OF THE ACCUSED

In all criminal prosecutions the accused shall have the right to appear and defend in person and by counsel; to demand the nature and cause of the accusation; to meet the witnesses against him face to face; to have process to compel the attendance of witnesses in his behalf, and a speedy public trial by an impartial jury of the county or district in which the offense is alleged to have been committed, subject to the right of the state to have a change of venue for any of the causes for which the defendant may obtain the same.

SECTION 25. SELF-INCRIMINATION AND DOUBLE JEOPARDY

No person shall be compelled to testify against himself in a criminal proceeding. No person shall be again put in jeopardy for the same offense previously tried in any jurisdiction.

SECTION 26. TRIAL BY JURY

The right of trial by jury is secured to all and shall remain inviolate. But upon default of appearance or by consent of the parties expressed in such manner as the law may provide, all cases may be tried without a jury or before fewer than the number of jurors provided by law. In all civil actions, two-thirds of the jury may render a verdict, and a verdict so rendered shall have the same force and effect as if all had concurred therein. In all criminal actions, the verdict shall be unanimous.

SECTION 27. IMPRISONMENT FOR DEBT

No person shall be imprisoned for debt except in the manner provided by law, upon refusal to deliver up his estate for the benefit of his creditors, or in cases of tort, where there is strong presumption of fraud.

SECTION 28. RIGHTS OF THE CONVICTED

Laws for the punishment of crime shall be founded on the principles of prevention and reformation. Full rights are restored by termination of state supervision for any offense against the state.

SECTION 29. EMINENT DOMAIN

Private property shall not be taken or damaged for public use without just compensation to the full extent of the loss having been first made to or paid into court for the owner. In the event of litigation, just compensation shall include necessary expenses of litigation to be awarded by the court when the private property owner prevails.

SECTION 30. TREASON AND DESCENT OF ESTATES

Treason against the state shall consist only in levying war against it, or in adhering to its enemies, giving them aid and comfort; no person shall be convicted of treason except on the testimony of two witnesses to the same overt act, or on his confession in open court; no person shall be attainted of treason or felony by the legislature; no conviction shall cause the loss of property to the relatives or heirs of the convicted. The estates suicides shall descend or vest as in cases of natural death.

SECTION 31. EX POST FACTO, OBLIGATION OF CONTRACTS AND IRREVOCABLE PRIVILEGES

No ex post facto law nor any law impairing the obligation of contracts, or making any irrevocable grant of special privileges, franchises, or immunities, shall be passed by the legislature.

SECTION 32. CIVILIAN CONTROL OF THE MILITARY

The military shall always be in strict subordination to the civil power; no soldier shall in time of peace be quartered in any house without the consent of the owner, nor in time of war except in the manner provided by law.

SECTION 33. IMPORTATION OF ARMED PERSONS

No armed person or persons or armed body of men shall be brought into this state for the preservation of the peace, or the suppression of domestic violence, except upon the application of the legislature, or of the governor when the legislature cannot be convened.

SECTION 34. UNENUMERATED RIGHTS

The enumeration in this constitution of certain rights shall not be construed to deny, impair, or disparage others retained by the people.

SECTION 35. SERVICEMEN, SERVICEWOMEN, AND VETERANS

The people declare that Montana servicemen, servicewomen, and veterans may be given special considerations determined by the legislature.

ARTICLE III
• GENERAL GOVERNMENT

SECTION 1. SEPARATION OF POWERS

The power of the government of this state is divided into three distinct branches—legislative, executive, and judicial. No person or persons charged with the exercise of power properly belonging to one branch shall exercise any power properly belonging to either of the others, except as in this constitution expressly directed or permitted.

SECTION 2. CONTINUITY OF GOVERNMENT

The seat of government shall be in Helena, except during periods of emergency resulting from disasters or enemy attack. The legislature may enact laws to insure the continuity of government during a period of emergency without regard for other provisions of the constitution. They shall be effective only during the period of emergency that affects a particular office or governmental operation.

SECTION 3. OATH OF OFFICE

Members of the legislature and all executive, ministerial and judicial officers, shall take and subscribe the following oath or affirmation, before they enter upon the duties of their offices: "I do solemnly swear (or affirm) that I will support, protect and defend the constitution of the United States, and the constitution of the state of Montana, and that I will discharge the duties of my office with fidelity (so help me God)." No other oath, declaration, or test shall be required as a qualification for any office or public trust.

SECTION 4. INITIATIVE

(1) The people may enact laws by initiative on all matters except appropriations of money and local or special laws.

(2) Initiative petitions must contain the full text of the proposed measure, shall be signed by at least five percent of the qualified electors in each of at least one-third of the legislative representative districts and the total number of signers must be at least five percent of the total qualified electors of the state. Petitions shall be filed with the secretary of state at least three months prior to the election at which the measure will be voted upon.

(3) The sufficiency of the initiative petition shall not be questioned after the election is held.

SECTION 5. REFERENDUM

(1) The people may approve or reject by referendum any act of the legislature except an appropriation of money. A referendum shall be held either upon order by the legislature or upon petition signed by at least five percent of the qualified electors in each of at least one-third of the legislative representative districts. The total number of signers must be at least five percent of the qualified electors of the state. A referendum petition shall be filed with the secretary of state no later than six months after adjournment of the legislature which passed the act.

(2) An act referred to the people is in effect until suspended by petitions signed by at least 15 percent of the qualified electors in a majority of the legislative representative districts. If so suspended the act shall become operative only after it is approved at an election, the result of which has been determined and declared as provided by law.

SECTION 6. ELECTIONS

The people shall vote on initiative and referendum measures at the general election unless the legislature orders a special election.

SECTION 7. NUMBER OF ELECTORS.

The number of qualified electors required in each legislative representative district and in the state shall be determined by the number of votes cast for the office of governor in the preceding general election.

SECTION 8. PROHIBITION.

The provisions of this Article do not apply to Constitutional Revision, Article XIV.

SECTION 9. GAMBLING.

All forms of gambling, lotteries, and gift enterprises are prohibited.

ARTICLE IV
• SUFFRAGE AND ELECTIONS

SECTION 1. BALLOT

All elections by the people shall be by secret ballot.

SECTION 2. QUALIFIED ELECTOR

Any citizen of the United States 18 years of age or older who meets the registration and residence requirements provided by law is a qualified elector unless he is serving a sentence for a felony in a penal institution or is of unsound mind, as determined by a court.

SECTION 3. ELECTIONS

The legislature shall provide by law the requirements for residence, registration, absentee voting, and administration of elections. It may provide for a system of poll booth registration, and shall insure the purity of elections and guard against abuses of the electoral process.

SECTION 4. ELIGIBILITY FOR PUBLIC OFFICE

Any qualified elector is eligible to any public office except as otherwise provided in this constitution. The legislature may provide additional qualifications but no person convicted of a felony shall be eligible to hold office until his final discharge from state supervision.

SECTION 5. RESULT OF ELECTIONS

In all elections held by the people, the person or persons receiving the largest number of votes shall be declared elected.

SECTION 6. PRIVILEGE FROM ARREST

A qualified elector is privileged from arrest at polling places and in going to and returning therefrom, unless apprehended in the commission of a felony or a breach of the peace.

ARTICLE V
• THE LEGISLATURE

SECTION 1. POWER AND STRUCTURE

The legislative power is vested in a legislature consisting of a senate and a house of representatives. The people reserve to themselves the powers of initiative and referendum.

SECTION 2. SIZE

The size of the legislature shall be provided by law, but the senate shall not have more than 50 or fewer than 40 members and the house shall not have more than 100 or fewer than 80 members.

SECTION 3. ELECTION AND TERMS

A member of the house of representatives shall be elected for a term of two years and a member of the senate for a term of four years each to begin on a date provided by law. One-half of the senators shall be elected every two years.

SECTION 4. QUALIFICATIONS

A candidate for the legislature shall be a resident of the state for at least one year next preceding the general election. For six months next preceding the general election, he shall be a resident of the county if it contains one or more districts or of the district if it contains all or parts of more than one county.

SECTION 5. COMPENSATION

Each member of the legislature shall receive compensation for his services and allowances provided by law. No legislature may fix its own compensation.

SECTION 6. SESSIONS

The legislature shall be a continuous body for two-year periods beginning when newly elected members take office. Any business, bill, or resolution pending at adjournment of a session shall carry over with the same status to any other session of the legislature during the biennium. The legislature shall meet at least once a year in regular session of not more than 60 legislative days. Any legislature may increase the limit on the length of any subsequent session. The legislature may be convened in special sessions by the governor or at the written request of a majority of the members.

SECTION 7. VACANCIES

A vacancy in the legislature shall be filled by special election for the unexpired term unless otherwise provided by law.

SECTION 8. IMMUNITY

A member of the legislature is privileged from arrest during attendance at sessions of the legislature and in going to and returning therefrom, unless apprehended in the commission of a felony or a breach of the peace. He shall not be questioned in any other place for any speech or debate in the legislature.

SECTION 9. DISQUALIFICATION

No member of the legislature shall, during the term for which he shall have been elected, be appointed to any civil office under the state; and no member of congress, or other person holding an office (except notary public, or in the militia) under the United States or this state, shall be a member of the legislature during his continuance in office.

SECTION 10. ORGANIZATION AND PROCEDURE

(1) Each house shall judge the election and qualifications of its members. It may by law vest in the courts the power to try and determine contested elections. Each house shall choose its officers from among its members, keep a journal, and make rules for its proceedings. Each house may expel or punish a member for good cause shown with the concurrence of two-thirds of all its members.

(2) A majority of each house constitutes a quorum. A smaller number may adjourn from day to day and compel attendance of absent members.

(3) The sessions of the legislature and of the committee of the whole, all committee meetings, and all hearings shall be open to the public.

(4) The legislature may establish a legislative

council and other interim committees. The legislature shall establish a legislative post-audit committee which shall supervise post-auditing duties provided by law.

(5) Neither house shall, without the consent of the other, adjourn or recess for more than three days or to any place other than that in which the two houses are sitting.

SECTION 11. BILLS

(1) A law shall be passed by bill which shall not be so altered or amended on its passage through the legislature as to change its original purpose. No bill shall become law except by a vote of the majority of all members present and voting.

(2) Every vote of each member of the legislature on each substantive question in the legislature, in any committee, or in committee of the whole shall be recorded and made public. On final passage, the vote shall be taken by ayes and noes and the names entered on the journal.

(3) Each bill, except general appropriation bills and bills for the codification and general revision of the laws, shall contain only one subject, clearly expressed in its title. If any subject is embraced in any act and is not expressed in the title, only so much of the act not so expressed is void.

(4) A general appropriation bill shall contain only appropriations for the ordinary expenses of the legislative, executive, and judicial branches, for interest on the public debt, and for public schools. Every other appropriation shall be made by a separate bill, containing but one subject.

(5) No appropriation shall be made for religious, charitable, industrial, educational, or benevolent purposes to any private individual, private association, or private corporation not under control of the state.

(6) A law may be challenged on the ground of noncompliance with this section only within two years after its effective date.

SECTION 12. LOCAL AND SPECIAL LEGISLATION

The legislature shall not pass a special or local act when a general act is, or can be made, applicable.

SECTION 13. IMPEACHMENT

(1) The governor, executive officers, heads of state departments, judicial officers, and such other officers as may be provided by law are subject to impeachment, and upon conviction shall be removed from office. Other proceedings for removal from public office for cause may be provided by law.

(2) The legislature shall provide for the manner, procedure, and causes for impeachment and may select the senate as tribunal.

(3) Impeachment shall be brought only by a two-thirds vote of the house. The tribunal hearing the charges shall convict only by a vote of two-thirds or more of its members.

(4) Conviction shall extend only to removal from office, but the party, whether convicted or acquitted, shall also be liable to prosecution according to law.

SECTION 14. DISTRICTING AND APPORTIONMENT

(1) The state shall be divided into as many districts as there are members of the house, and each district shall elect one representative. Each senate district shall be composed of two adjoining house districts, and shall elect one senator. Each district shall consist of compact and contiguous territory. All districts shall be as nearly equal in population as is practicable.

(2) In the legislative session following ratification of this constitution and thereafter in each session preceding each federal population census, a commission of five citizens, none of whom may be public officials, shall be selected to prepare a plan for redistricting and reapportioning the state into legislative and congressional districts. The majority and minority leaders of each house shall each designate one commissioner. Within 20 days after their designation, the four commissioners shall select the fifth member, who shall serve as chairman of the commission. If the four members fail to select the fifth member within the time prescribed, a majority of the supreme court shall select him.

(3) The commission shall submit its plan to the legislature at the first regular session after its appointment or after the census figures are available. Within 30 days after submission, the legislature shall return the plan to the commission with its recommendations. Within 30 days thereafter the commission shall file its final plan with the secretary of state and it shall become law. The commission is then dissolved.

ARTICLE VI
• THE EXECUTIVE

SECTION 1. OFFICERS

(1) The executive branch includes a governor, lieutenant governor, secretary of state, attorney general, superintendent of public instruction, and auditor.

(2) Each holds office for a term of four years which begins on the first Monday of January next succeeding election, and until a successor is elected and qualified.

(3) Each shall reside at the seat of government, there keep the public records of his office, and perform such other duties as are provided in this constitution and by law.

SECTION 2. ELECTION

(1) The governor, lieutenant governor, secretary of state, attorney general, superintendent of public instruction, and auditor shall be elected by the qualified electors at a general election provided by law.

(2) Each candidate for governor shall file jointly with a candidate for lieutenant governor in primary elections, or so otherwise comply with nomination procedures provided by law that the offices of governor and lieutenant governor are voted upon together in primary and general elections.

SECTION 3. QUALIFICATIONS

(1) No person shall be eligible to the office of governor, lieutenant governor, secretary of state, attorney general, superintendent of public instruction, or auditor unless he is 25 years of age or older at the time of his election. In addition, each shall be a citizen of the United States who has resided within the state two years next preceding his election.

(2) Any person with the foregoing qualifications

is eligible to the office of attorney general if an attorney in good standing admitted to practice law in Montana who has engaged in the active practice thereof for at least five years before election.

(3) The superintendent of public instruction shall have such educational qualifications as are provided by law.

SECTION 4. DUTIES

(1) The executive power is vested in the governor who shall see that the laws are faithfully executed. He shall have such other duties as are provided in this constitution and by law.

(2) The lieutenant governor shall perform the duties provided by law and those delegated to him by the governor. No power specifically vested in the governor by this constitution may be delegated to the lieutenant governor.

(3) The secretary of state shall maintain official records of the executive branch and of the acts of the legislature, as provided by law. He shall keep the great seal of the state of Montana and perform any other duties provided by law.

(4) The attorney general is the legal officer of the state and shall have the duties and powers provided by law.

(5) The superintendent of public instruction and the auditor shall have such duties as are provided by law.

SECTION 5. COMPENSATION

(1) Officers of the executive branch shall receive salaries provided by law.

(2) During his term, no elected officer of the executive branch may hold another public office or receive compensation for services from any other governmental agency. He may be a candidate for any public office during his term.

SECTION 6. VACANCY IN OFFICE

(1) If the office of lieutenant governor becomes vacant by his succession to the office of governor, or by his death, resignation, or disability as determined by law, the governor shall appoint a qualified person to serve in that office for the remainder of the term. If both the elected governor and the elect-

ed lieutenant governor become unable to serve in the office of governor, succession to the respective offices shall be as provided by law for the period until the next general election. Then, a governor and lieutenant governor shall be elected to fill the remainder of the original term.

(2) If the office of secretary of state, attorney general, auditor, or superintendent of public instruction becomes vacant by death, resignation, or disability as determined by law, the governor shall appoint a qualified person to serve in that office until the next general election and until a successor is elected and qualified. The person elected to fill a vacancy shall hold the office until the expiration of the term for which his predecessor was elected.

SECTION 7. 20 DEPARTMENTS

All executive and administrative offices, boards, bureaus, commissions, agencies and instrumentalities of the executive branch (except for the office of governor, lieutenant governor, secretary of state, attorney general, superintendent of public instruction, and auditor) and their respective functions, powers, and duties, shall be allocated by law among not more than 20 principal departments so as to provide an orderly arrangement in the administrative organization of state government. Temporary commissions may be established by law and need not be allocated within a department.

SECTION 8. APPOINTING POWER

(1) The departments provided for in section 7 shall be under the supervision of the governor. Except as otherwise provided in this constitution or by law, each department shall be headed by a single executive appointed by the governor subject to confirmation by the senate to hold office until the end of the governor's term unless sooner removed by the governor.

(2) The governor shall appoint, subject to confirmation by the senate, all officers provided for in this constitution or by law whose appointment or election is not otherwise provided for. They shall hold office until the end of the governor's term unless sooner removed by the governor.

(3) If a vacancy occurs in any such office when the

legislature is not in session, the governor shall appoint a qualified person to discharge the duties thereof until the office is filled by appointment and confirmation.

(4) A person not confirmed by the senate for an office shall not, except at its request, be nominated again for that office at the same session, or be appointed to that office when the legislature is not in session.

SECTION 9. BUDGET AND MESSAGES

The governor shall at the beginning of each legislative session, and may at other times, give the legislature information and recommend measures he considers necessary. The governor shall submit to the legislature at a time fixed by law, a budget for the ensuing fiscal period setting forth in detail for all operating funds the proposed expenditures and estimated revenue of the state.

SECTION 10. VETO POWER

(1) Each bill passed by the legislature, except bills proposing amendments to the Montana constitution, bills ratifying proposed amendments to the United States constitution, resolutions, and initiative and referendum measures, shall be submitted to the governor for his signature. If he does not sign or veto the bill within five days after its delivery to him if the legislature is in session or within 25 days if the legislature is adjourned, it shall become law. The governor shall return a vetoed bill to the legislature with a statement of his reasons therefor.

(2) The governor may return any bill to the legislature with his recommendation for amendment. If the legislature passes the bill in accordance with the governor's recommendation, it shall again return the bill to the governor for his reconsideration. The governor shall not return a bill for amendment a second time.

(3) If after receipt of a veto message, two-thirds of the members present approve the bill, it shall become law.

(4) If the legislature is not in session when the governor vetoes a bill, he shall return the bill with his reasons therefor to the legislature as provided by law. The legislature may reconvene to reconsider any bill so vetoed.

(5) The governor may veto items in appropriation bills, and in such instances the procedure shall be the same as upon veto of an entire bill.

SECTION 11. SPECIAL SESSION

Whenever the governor considers it in the public interest, he may convene the legislature.

SECTION 12. PARDONS

The governor may grant reprieves, commutations and pardons, restore citizenship, and suspend and remit fines and forfeitures subject to procedures provided by law.

SECTION 13. MILITIA

(1) The governor is commander-in-chief of the militia forces of the state, except when they are in the actual service of the United States. He may call out any part or all of the forces to aid in the execution of the laws, suppress insurrection, repel invasion, or protect life and property in natural disasters.

(2) The militia forces shall consist of all able-bodied citizens of the state except those exempted by law.

SECTION 14. SUCCESSION

(1) If the governor-elect is disqualified or dies, the lieutenant governor-elect upon qualifying for the office shall become governor for the full term. If the governor-elect fails to assume office for any other reason, the lieutenant governor-elect upon qualifying as such shall serve as acting governor until the governor-elect is able to assume office, or until the office becomes vacant.

(2) The lieutenant governor shall serve as acting governor when so requested in writing by the governor. After the governor has been absent from the state for more than 45 consecutive days, the lieutenant governor shall serve as acting governor.

(3) He shall serve as acting governor when the governor is so disabled as to be unable to communicate to the lieutenant governor the fact of his inability to perform the duties of his office. The lieutenant governor shall continue to serve as acting

governor until the governor is able to resume the duties of his office.

(4) Whenever, at any other time, the lieutenant governor and attorney general transmit to the legislature their written declaration that the governor is unable to discharge the powers and duties of his office, the legislature shall convene to determine whether he is able to do so.

(5) If the legislature, within 21 days after convening, determines by two-thirds vote of its members that the governor is unable to discharge the powers and duties of his office, the lieutenant governor shall serve as acting governor. Thereafter, when the governor transmits to the legislature his written declaration that no inability exists, he shall resume the powers and duties of his office within 15 days, unless the legislature determines otherwise by two-thirds vote of its members. If the legislature so determines, the lieutenant governor shall continue to serve as acting governor.

(6) If the office of governor becomes vacant by reason of death, resignation, or disqualification, the lieutenant governor shall become governor for the remainder of the term, except as provided in this constitution.

(7) Additional succession to fill vacancies shall be provided by law.

(8) When there is a vacancy in the office of governor, the successor shall be the governor. The acting governor shall have the powers and duties of the office of governor only for the period during which he serves.

SECTION 15. INFORMATION FOR GOVERNOR

(1) The governor may require information in writing, under oath when required, from the officers of the executive branch upon any subject relating to the duties of their respective offices.

(2) He may require information in writing, under oath, from all officers and managers of state institutions.

(3) He may appoint a committee to investigate and report to him upon the condition of any executive office or state institution.

• ARTICLE VII
THE JUDICIARY

SECTION 1. JUDICIAL POWER

The judicial power of the state is vested in one supreme court, district courts, justice courts, and such other courts as may be provided by law.

SECTION 2. SUPREME COURT JURISDICTION

(1) The supreme court has appellate jurisdiction and may issue, hear, and determine writs appropriate thereto. It has original jurisdiction to issue, hear, and determine writs of habeas corpus and such other writs as may be provided by law.

(2) It has general supervisory control over all other courts.

(3) It may make rules governing appellate procedure, practice and procedure for all other courts, admission to the bar and the conduct of its members. Rules of procedure shall be subject to disapproval by the legislature in either of the two sessions following promulgation.

(4) Supreme court process shall extend to all parts of the state.

SECTION 3. SUPREME COURT ORGANIZATION

(1) The supreme court consists of one chief justice and four justices, but the legislature may increase the number of justices from four to six. A majority shall join in and pronounce decisions which must be in writing.

(2) A district judge shall be substituted for the chief justice or a justice in the event of disqualification or disability, and the opinion of the district judge sitting with the supreme court shall have the same effect as an opinion of a justice.

SECTION 4. DISTRICT COURT JURISDICTION

(1) The district court has original jurisdiction in all criminal cases amounting to felony and all civil matters and cases at law and in equity. It may issue all writs appropriate to its jurisdiction. It shall have

the power of naturalization and such additional jurisdiction as may be delegated by the laws of the United States or the state of Montana. Its process shall extend to all parts of the state.

(2) The district court shall hear appeals from inferior courts as trials anew unless otherwise provided by law. The legislature may provide for direct review by the district court of decisions of administrative agencies.

(3) Other courts may have jurisdiction of criminal cases not amounting to felony and such jurisdiction concurrent with that of the district court as may be provided by law.

SECTION 5. JUSTICES OF THE PEACE

(1) There shall be elected in each county at least one justice of the peace with qualifications, training, and monthly compensation provided by law. There shall be provided such facilities that they may perform their duties in dignified surroundings.

(2) Justice courts shall have such original jurisdiction as may be provided by law. They shall not have trial jurisdiction in any criminal case designated a felony except as examining courts.

(3) The legislature may provide for additional justices of the peace in each county.

SECTION 6. JUDICIAL DISTRICTS

(1) The legislature shall divide the state into judicial districts and provide for the number of judges in each district. Each district shall be formed of compact territory and be bounded by county lines.

(2) The legislature may change the number and boundaries of judicial districts and the number of judges in each district, but no change in boundaries or the number of districts or judges therein shall work a removal of any judge from office during the term for which he was elected or appointed.

(3) The chief justice may upon request of the district judge, assign district judges and other judges for temporary service from one district to another, and from one county to another.

SECTION 7. TERMS AND PAY

(1) All justices and judges shall be paid as provided

by law, but salaries shall not be diminished during terms of office.

(2) Terms of office shall be eight years for supreme court justices, six years for district court judges, four years for justices of the peace, and as provided by law for other judges.

(1) No change except in grammar.

(2) Supreme Court justice terms increased from six to eight years, district court judges from four to six and justices of the peace from two to four years.

SECTION 8. SELECTION

(1) The governor shall nominate a replacement from nominees selected in the manner provided by law for any vacancy in the office of supreme court justice or district court judge. If the governor fails to nominate within thirty days after receipt of nominees, the chief justice or acting chief justice shall make the nomination. Each nomination shall be confirmed by the senate, but a nomination made while the senate is not in session shall be effective as an appointment until the end of the next session. If the nomination is not confirmed, the office shall be vacant and another selection and nomination shall be made.

(2) If, at the first election after senate confirmation, and at the election before each succeeding term of office, any candidate other than the incumbent justice or district judge files for election to that office, the name of the incumbent shall be placed on the ballot. If there is no election contest for the office, the name of the incumbent shall nevertheless be placed on the general election ballot to allow voters of the state or district to approve or reject him. If an incumbent is rejected, another selection and nomination shall be made.

(3) If an incumbent does not run, there shall be an election for the office.

SECTION 9. QUALIFICATIONS

(1) A citizen of the United States who has resided in the state two years immediately before taking office is eligible to the office of supreme court justice or district court judge if admitted to the practice of law in Montana for at least five years prior to

the date of appointment or election. Qualifications and methods of selection of judges of other courts shall be provided by law.

(2) No supreme court justice or district court judge shall solicit or receive compensation in any form whatever on account of his office, except salary and actual necessary travel expense.

(3) Except as otherwise provided in this constitution, no supreme court justice or district court judge shall practice law during his term of office, engage in any other employment for which salary or fee is paid, or hold office in a political party.

(4) Supreme court justices shall reside within the state. Every other judge shall reside during his term of office in the district, county, township, precinct, city or town in which he is elected or appointed.

SECTION 10. FORFEITURE OF JUDICIAL POSITION

Any holder of a judicial position forfeits that position by either filing for an elective public office other than a judicial position or absenting himself from the state for more than 60 consecutive days.

SECTION 11. REMOVAL AND DISCIPLINE

(1) The legislature shall create a judicial standards commission consisting of five persons and provide for the appointment thereto of two district judges, one attorney, and two citizens who are neither judges nor attorneys.

(2) The commission shall investigate complaints, make rules implementing this section, and keep its proceedings confidential. It may subpoena witnesses and documents.

(3) Upon recommendation of the commission, the supreme court may:

(a) Retire any justice or judge for disability that seriously interferes with the performance of his duties and is or may become permanent; or

(b) Censure, suspend, or remove any justice or judge for willful misconduct in office, willful and persistent failure to perform his duties, or habitual intemperance.

• ARTICLE VIII
REVENUE AND FINANCE

SECTION 1. TAX PURPOSES

Taxes shall be levied by general laws for public purposes.

SECTION 2. TAX POWER INALIENABLE

The power to tax shall never be surrendered, suspended, or contracted away.

SECTION 3. PROPERTY TAX ADMINISTRATION

The state shall appraise, assess, and equalize the valuation of all property which is to be taxed in the manner provided by law.

SECTION 4. EQUAL VALUATION

All taxing jurisdictions shall use the assessed valuation of property established by the state.

SECTION 5. PROPERTY TAX EXEMPTIONS

(1) The legislature may exempt from taxation:

(a) Property of the United States, the state, counties, cities, towns, school districts, municipal corporations, and public libraries, but any private interest in such property may be taxed separately.

(b) Institutions of purely public charity, hospitals and places of burial not used or held for private or corporate profit, places for actual religious worship, and property used exclusively for educational purposes.

(c) Any other classes of property.

(2) The legislature may authorize creation of special improvement districts for capital improvements and the maintenance thereof. It may authorize the assessment of charges for such improvements and maintenance against tax exempt property directly benefited thereby.

SECTION 6. HIGHWAY REVENUE NONDIVERSION

(1) Revenue from gross vehicle weight fees and ex-

cise and license taxes (except general sales and use taxes) on gasoline, fuel, and other energy sources used to propel vehicles on public highways shall be used as authorized by the legislature, after deduction of statutory refunds and adjustments, solely for:

(a) Payment of obligations incurred for construction, reconstruction, repair, operation, and maintenance of public highways, streets, roads, and bridges.

(b) Payment of county, city, and town obligations on streets, roads, and bridges.

(c) Enforcement of highway safety, driver education, tourist promotion, and administrative collection costs.

(2) Such revenue may be appropriated for other purposes by a three-fifths vote of the members of each house of the legislature.

SECTION 7. TAX APPEALS

The legislature shall provide independent appeal procedures for taxpayer grievances about appraisals, assessments, equalization, and taxes. The legislature shall include a review procedure at the local government unit level.

SECTION 8. STATE DEBT

No state debt shall be created unless authorized by a two-thirds vote of the members of each house of the legislature or a majority of the electors voting thereon. No state debt shall be created to cover deficits incurred because appropriations exceeded anticipated revenue.

SECTION 9. BALANCED BUDGET

Appropriations by the legislature shall not exceed anticipated revenue.

SECTION 10. LOCAL GOVERNMENT DEBT

The legislature shall by law limit debts of counties, cities, towns, and all other local governmental entities.

SECTION 11. USE OF LOAN PROCEEDS

All money borrowed by or on behalf of the state or any county, town, or other local governmental entity shall be used only for purposes specified in the authorizing law.

SECTION 12. STRICT ACCOUNTABILITY

The legislature shall by law insure strict accountability of all revenue received and money spent by the state and counties, cities, towns, and all other local governmental entities.

SECTION 13. INVESTMENT OF PUBLIC FUNDS

(1) The legislature shall provide for a unified investment program for public funds and provide rules therefor, including supervision of investment of surplus funds of all counties, cities, towns, and other local governmental entities. Each fund forming a part of the unified investment program shall be separately identified. Except for monies contributed to retirement funds, no public funds shall be invested in private corporate capital stock. The investment program shall be audited at least annually and a report thereof submitted to the governor and legislature.

(2) The public school fund and the permanent funds of the Montana university system and all other state institutions of learning shall be safely and conservatively invested in:

(a) Public securities of the state, its subdivisions, local government units, and districts within the state, or

(b) Bonds of the United States or other securities fully guaranteed as to principal and interest by the United States, or

(c) Such other safe investments bearing a fixed rate of interest as may be provided by law.

SECTION 14. PROHIBITED PAYMENTS

Except for interest on the public debt, no money shall be paid out of the treasury unless upon an appropriation made by law and a warrant drawn by the proper officer in pursuance thereof.

• ARTICLE IX
ENVIRONMENT AND NATURAL RESOURCES

SECTION 1. PROTECTION AND IMPROVEMENT

(1) The state and each person shall maintain and improve a clean and healthful environment in Montana for present and future generations.

(2) The legislature shall provide for the administration and enforcement of this duty.

(3) The legislature shall provide adequate remedies for the protection of the environmental life support system from degradation and provide adequate remedies to prevent unreasonable depletion and degradation of natural resources.

SECTION 2. RECLAMATION

All lands disturbed by the taking of natural resources shall be reclaimed. The legislature shall provide effective requirements and standards for the reclamation of lands disturbed.

SECTION 3. WATER RIGHTS

(1) All existing rights to the use of any waters for any useful or beneficial purpose are hereby recognized and confirmed.

(2) The use of all water that is now or may hereafter be appropriated for sale, rent, distribution, or other beneficial use, the right of way over the lands of others for all ditches, drains, flumes, canals, and aqueducts necessarily used in connection therewith, and the sites for reservoirs necessary for collecting and storing water shall be held to be a public use.

(3) All surface, underground, flood, and atmospheric waters within the boundaries of the state are the property of the state for the use of its people and are subject to appropriation for beneficial uses as provided by law.

(4) The legislature shall provide for the adminis-

tration, control, and regulation of water rights and shall establish a system of centralized records, in addition to the present system of local records.

SECTION 4. CULTURAL RESOURCES

The legislature shall provide for the identification, acquisition, restoration, enhancement, preservation, and administration of scenic, historic, archeologic, scientific, cultural, and recreational areas, sites, records and objects, and for their use and enjoyment by the people.

• ARTICLE X
EDUCATION AND PUBLIC LANDS

SECTION 1. EDUCATIONAL GOALS AND DUTIES

(1) It is the goal of the people to establish a system of education which will develop the full educational potential of each person. Equality of educational opportunity is guaranteed to each person of the state.

(2) The state recognizes the distinct and unique cultural heritage of the American Indians and is committed in its educational goals to the preservation of their cultural integrity.

(3) The legislature shall provide a basic system of free quality public elementary and secondary schools. The legislature may provide such other educational institutions, public libraries, and educational programs as it deems desirable. It shall fund and distribute in an equitable manner to the school districts the state's share of the cost of the basic elementary and secondary school system.

SECTION 2. PUBLIC SCHOOL FUND

The public school fund of the state shall consist of:
(1) Proceeds from the school lands which have been or may hereafter be granted by the United States,

(2) Lands granted in lieu thereof,

(3) Lands given or granted by any person or corporation under any law or grant of the United States,

(4) All other grants of land or money made from the United States for general educational purposes or without special purpose,

(5) All interests in estates that escheat to the state,

(6) All unclaimed shares and dividends of any corporation incorporated in the state,

(7) All other grants, gifts, devises or bequests made to the state for general education purposes.

SECTION 3. PUBLIC SCHOOL FUND INVIOLATE

The public school fund shall forever remain inviolate, guaranteed by the state against loss or diversion.

SECTION 4. BOARD OF LAND COMMISSIONERS.

The governor, superintendent of public instruction, auditor, secretary of state, and attorney general constitute the board of land commissioners. It has the authority to direct, control, lease, exchange, and sell school lands and lands which have been or may be granted for the support and benefit of the various state educational institutions, under such regulations and restrictions as may be provided by law.

SECTION 5. PUBLIC SCHOOL FUND REVENUE

(1) Ninety-five percent of all the interest received on the public school fund and ninety-five percent of all rent received from the leasing of school lands and all other income from the public school fund shall be equitably apportioned annually to public elementary and secondary school districts as provided by law.

(2) The remaining five percent of all interest received on the public school fund, and the remaining five percent of all rent received from the leasing of school lands and all other income from the public school fund shall annually be added to the public school fund and become and forever remain an inseparable and inviolable part thereof.

SECTION 6. AID PROHIBITED TO SECTARIAN SCHOOLS.

(1) The legislature, counties, cities, towns, school districts, and public corporations shall not make any direct or indirect appropriation or payment from any public fund or monies, or any grant of lands or other property for any sectarian purpose or to aid any church, school, academy, seminary, college, university, or other literary or scientific institution, controlled in whole or part by any church, sect, or denomination.

(2) This section shall not apply to funds from federal sources provided to the state for the express purpose of distribution to non-public education.

SECTION 7. NON-DISCRIMINATION IN EDUCATION

No religious or partisan test or qualification shall be required of any teacher or student as a condition of admission into any public educational institution. Attendance shall not be required at any religious service. No sectarian tenets shall be advocated in any public educational institution of the state. No person shall be refused admission to any public educational institution on account of sex, race, creed, religion, political beliefs, or national origin.

SECTION 8. SCHOOL DISTRICT TRUSTEES

The supervision and control of schools in each school district shall be vested in a board of trustees to be elected as provided by law.

SECTION 9. BOARDS OF EDUCATION

(1) There is a state board of education composed of the board of regents of higher education and the board of public education. It is responsible for long-range planning, and for coordinating and evaluating policies and programs for the state's educational systems. It shall submit unified budget requests. A tie vote at any meeting may be broken by the governor, who is an ex officio member of each component board.

(2) (a) The government and control of the Mon-

tana university system is vested in a board of regents of higher education which shall have full power, responsibility, and authority to supervise, coordinate, manage and control the Montana university system and shall supervise and coordinate other public educational institutions assigned by law.

(b) The board consists of seven members appointed by the governor, and confirmed by the senate, to overlapping terms, as provided by law. The governor and superintendent of public instruction are ex officio non-voting members of the board.

(c) The board shall appoint a commissioner of higher education and prescribe his term and duties.

(d) The funds and appropriations under the control of the board of regents are subject to the same audit provisions as are all other state funds.

(3) (a) There is a board of public education to exercise general supervision over the public school system and such other public educational institutions as may be assigned by law. Other duties of the board shall be provided by law.

(b) The board consists of seven members appointed by the governor, and confirmed by the senate, to overlapping terms as provided by law. The governor, comissioner of higher education and state superintendent of public instruction shall be ex officio non-voting members of the board.

SECTION 10. STATE UNIVERSITY FUNDS

The funds of the Montana university system and of all other state institutions of learning, from whatever source accruing, shall forever remain inviolate and sacred to the purpose for which they were dedicated. The various funds shall be respectively invested under such regulations as may be provided by law, and shall be guaranteed by the state against loss or diversion. The interest from such invested funds, together with the rent from leased lands or properties, shall be devoted to the maintenance and perpetuation of the respective institutions.

SECTION 11. PUBLIC LAND TRUST, DISPOSITION

(1) All lands of the state that have been or may be granted by congress, or acquired by gift or grant or devise from any person or corporation, shall be public lands of the state. They shall be held in trust for the people, to be disposed of as hereafter provided, for the respective purposes for which they have been or may be granted, donated or devised.

(2) No such land or any estate or interest therein shall ever be disposed of except in pursuance of general laws providing for such disposition, or until the full market value of the estate or interest disposed of, to be ascertained in such manner as may be provided by law, has been paid or safely secured to the state.

(3) No land which the state holds by grant from the United States which prescribes the manner of disposal and minimum price shall be disposed of except in the manner and for at least the price prescribed without the consent of the United States.

(4) All public land shall be classified by the board of land commissioners in a manner provided by law. Any public land may be exchanged for other land, public or private, which is equal in value and, as closely as possible, equal in area.

• ARTICLE XI
LOCAL GOVERNMENT
SECTION 1. DEFINITION

The term "local government units" includes, but is not limited to, counties and incorporated cities and towns. Other local government units may be established by law.

SECTION 2. COUNTIES

The counties of the state are those that exist on the date of ratification of this constitution. No county boundary may be changed or county seat transferred until approved by a majority of those voting on the question in each county affected.

SECTION 3. FORMS OF GOVERNMENT

(1) The legislature shall provide methods for governing local government units and procedures for incorporating, classifying, merging, consolidating, and dissolving such units, and altering their bound-

aries. The legislature shall provide such optional or alternative forms of government that each unit or combination of units may adopt, amend, or abandon an optional or alternative form by a majority of those voting on the question.

(2) One optional form of county government includes, but is not limited to, the election of three county commissioners, a clerk and recorder, a clerk of district court, a county attorney, a sheriff, a treasurer, a surveyor, a county superintendent of schools, an assessor, a coroner, and a public administrator. The terms, qualifications, duties, and compensation of those offices shall be provided by law. The Board of county commissioners may consolidate two or more such offices. The Boards of two or more counties may provide for a joint office and for the election of one official to perform the duties of any such offices in those counties.

SECTION 4. GENERAL POWERS

(1) A local government unit without self-government powers has the following general powers:

(a) An incorporated city or town has the powers of a municipal corporation and legislative, administrative, and other powers provided or implied by law.

(b) A county has legislative, administrative, and other powers provided or implied by law.

(c) Other local government units have powers provided by law.

(2) The powers of incorporated cities and towns and counties shall be liberally construed.

SECTION 5. SELF-GOVERNMENT CHARTERS

(1) The legislature shall provide procedures permitting a local government unit or combination of units to frame, adopt, amend, revise, or abandon a self-government charter with the approval of a majority of those voting on the question. The procedures shall not require approval of a charter by a legislative body.

(2) If the legislature does not provide such procedures by July 1, 1975, they may be established by election either:

(a) Initiated by petition in the local government unit or combination of units; or

(b) Called by the governing body of the local government unit or combination of units.

(3) Charter provisions establishing executive, legislative, and administrative structure and organization are superior to statutory provisions.

SECTION 6. SELF-GOVERNMENT POWERS

A local government unit adopting a self-government charter may exercise any power not prohibited by this constitution, law, or charter. This grant of self-government powers may be extended to other local government units through optional forms of government provided for in section 3.

SECTION 7. INTERGOVERNMENTAL COOPERATION

(1) Unless prohibited by law or charter, a local government unit may

(a) cooperate in the exercise of any function, power, or responsibility with,

(b) share the services of any officer or facilities with,

(c) transfer or delegate any function, power, responsibility, or duty of any officer to one or more other local government units, school districts, the state, or the United States.

(2) The qualified electors of a local government unit may, by initiative or referendum, require it to do so.

SECTION 8. INITIATIVE AND REFERENDUM

The legislature shall extend the initiative and referendum powers reserved to the people by the constitution to the qualified electors of each local government unit.

SECTION 9. VOTER REVIEW OF LOCAL GOVERNMENT

(1) The legislature shall, within four years of the ratification of this constitution, provide procedures requiring each local government unit or combina-

tion of units to review its structure and submit one alternative form of government to the qualified electors at the next general or special election.

(2) The legislature shall require a review procedure once every ten years after the first election.

• ARTICLE XII
DEPARTMENTS AND INSTITUTIONS

SECTION 1. AGRICULTURE

(1) The legislature shall provide for a Department of Agriculture and enact laws and provide appropriations to protect, enhance, and develop all agriculture.

(2) Special levies may be made on livestock and on agricultural commodities for disease control and indemnification, predator control, and livestock and commodity inspection, protection, research, and promotion. Revenue derived shall be used solely for the purposes of the levies.

SECTION 2. LABOR

(1) The legislature shall provide for a Department of Labor and Industry, headed by a commissioner appointed by the governor and confirmed by the senate.

(2) A maximum period of 8 hours is a regular day's work, all industries and employment except agriculture and stocking. The legislature may change this maximum period to promote the general welfare.

SECTION 3. INSTITUTIONS AND ASSISTANCE

(1) The state shall establish and support institutions and facilities as the public good may require, including homes which may be necessary and desirable for the care of veterans.

(2) Persons committed to any such institutions shall retain all rights except those necessarily suspended as a condition of commitment. Suspended rights are restored upon termination of the state's responsibility.

(3) The legislature shall provide such economic assistance and social and rehabilitative services as may be necessary for those inhabitants who, by reason of age, infirmities, or misfortune may have need for the aid of society.

• ARTICLE XIII
GENERAL PROVISIONS

SECTION 1. NON-MUNICIPAL CORPORATIONS

(1) Corporate charters shall be granted, modified, or dissolved only pursuant to general law.

(2) The legislature shall provide protection and education for the people against harmful and unfair practices by either foreign or domestic corporations, individuals, or associations.

(3) The legislature shall pass no law retrospective in its operations which imposes on the people a new liability in respect to transactions or considerations already passed.

SECTION 2. CONSUMER COUNSEL

The legislature shall provide for an office of consumer counsel which shall have the duty of representing consumer interests in hearings before the public service commission or any other successor agency. The legislature shall provide for the funding of the office of consumer counsel by a special tax on the net income or gross revenues of regulated companies.

SECTION 3. SALARY COMMISSION

The legislature shall create a salary commission to recommend compensation for the judiciary and elected members of the legislative and executive branches.

SECTION 4. CODE OF ETHICS

The legislature shall provide a code of ethics prohibiting conflict between public duty and private interest for members of the legislature and all state and local officers and employees.

SECTION 5. EXEMPTION LAWS

The legislature shall enact liberal homestead and exemption laws.

SECTION 6. PERPETUITIES

No perpetuities shall be allowed except for charitable purposes.

• ARTICLE XIV
CONSTITUTIONAL REVISION

SECTION 1. CONSTITUTIONAL CONVENTION

The legislature, by an affirmative vote of two-thirds of all the members, whether one or more bodies, may at any time submit to the qualified electors the question of whether there shall be an unlimited convention to revise, alter, or amend this constitution.

SECTION 2. INITIATIVE FOR CONSTITUTIONAL CONVENTION

(1) The people may by initiative petition direct the secretary of state to submit to the qualified electors the question of whether there shall be an unlimited convention to revise, alter, or amend this constitution. The petition shall be signed by at least ten percent of the qualified electors of the state. That number shall include at least ten percent of the qualified electors in each of two-fifths of the legislative districts.

(2) The secretary of state shall certify the filing of the petition in his office and cause the question to be submitted at the next general election.

SECTION 3. PERIODIC SUBMISSION

If the question of holding a convention is not otherwise submitted during any period of 20 years, it shall be submitted as provided by law at the general election in the twentieth year following the last submission.

SECTION 4. CALL OF CONVENTION

If a majority of those voting on the question answer in the affirmative, the legislature shall provide for the calling thereof at its next session. The number of delegates to the convention shall be the same as that of the larger body of the legislature. The qualifications of delegates shall be the same as the highest qualifications required for election to the legislature. The legislature shall determine whether the delegates may be nominated on a partisan or a nonpartisan basis. They shall be elected at the same places and in the same districts as are the members of the legislative body determining the number of delegates.

SECTION 5. CONVENTION EXPENSES

The legislature shall, in the act calling the convention, designate the day, hour, and place of its meeting, and fix and provide for the pay of its members and officers and the necessary expenses of the convention.

SECTION 6. OATH, VACANCIES

Before proceeding, the delegates shall take the oath provided in this constitution. Vacancies occurring shall be filled in the manner provided for filling vacancies in the legislature if not otherwise provided by law.

SECTION 7. CONVENTION DUTIES

The convention shall meet after the election of the delegates and prepare such revisions, alterations, or amendments to the constitution as may be deemed necessary. They shall be submitted to the qualified electors for ratification or rejection as a whole or in separate articles or amendments as determined by the convention at an election appointed by the convention for that purpose not less than two months after adjournment. Unless so submitted and approved by a majority of the electors voting thereon, no such revision, alteration, or amendment shall take effect.

SECTION 8. AMENDMENT BY LEGISLATIVE REFERENDUM

Amendments to this constitution may be proposed by any member of the legislature. If adopted by an affirmative roll call vote of two-thirds of all the members thereof, whether one or more bodies, the proposed amendment shall be submitted to the qualified electors at the next general election. If approved by a majority of the electors voting thereon, the amendment shall become a part of this constitution on the first day of July after certification of the election returns unless the amendment provides otherwise.

SECTION 9. AMENDMENT BY INITIATIVE

(1) The people may also propose constitutional amendments by initiative. Petitions including the full text of the proposed amendment shall be signed by at least ten percent of the qualified electors of the state. That number shall include at least ten percent of the qualified electors in each of two-fifths of the legislative districts.

(2) The petitions shall be filed with the secretary of state. If the petitions are found to have been signed by the required number of electors, the secretary of state shall cause the amendment to be published as provided by law twice each month for two months previous to the next regular state-wide election.

(3) At that election, the proposed amendment shall be submitted to the qualified electors for approval or rejection. If approved by a majority voting thereon, it shall become a part of the constitution effective the first day of July following its approval, unless the amendment provides otherwise.

SECTION 10. PETITION SIGNERS

The number of qualified electors required for the filing of any petition provided for in this Article shall be determined by the number of votes cast for the office of governor in the preceding general election.

SECTION 11. SUBMISSION

If more than one amendment is submitted at the same election, each shall be so prepared and distinguished that it can be voted upon separately.

Passed, by a narrow margin, June 6, 1972

AUTHORS AND WORKS CITED

Acton, John Emerich, Lord — *Lectures on Modern History* (1906). Edited by John N. Figgis and R. V. Laurence. London: Macmillan, 1952. *History of Freedom and other Essays.* London: Macmillan and Co., Ltd., 1922. *Essays in the Liberal Interpretation of History.* Edited by William H. McNeill. Chicago: University of Chicago Press, 1967.

Adams, John — *Defense of the Constitutions of Government of the United States of America* (1787). 3 vols. New York: Adler, 1787. *The Works of John Adams.* Edited by Charles F. Adams. 10 vols. Boston: Little & Brown, 1850-1856. *Discourses on Davila* (1805). New York: Plenum Publishing Corp., 1969. *The Political Writings of John Adams:* Representative Selections. Edited by George A. Peck, Jr. New York: The Liberal Arts Press, 1954. *Correspondence of John Adams and Thomas Jefferson.* Edited by Paul Wilstach. New York: Bobbs Merrill Co., 1925.

Adams, Samuel — *The Writings of Samuel Adams.* Edited by Henry Alonzo Cushing. 4 vols. New York: Octagon Books, 1968. *Modern Eloquence.* Edited by Ashley H. Thorndike. Vol. 2. New York: Modern Eloquence Corporation, 1928.

Anthony, Susan B. — Harper, Ida Husted. *Life and Work of Susan B. Anthony* (1898). 3 vols. New York: Arno Press and the New York Times, 1969.

Antin, Mary — *The Promised Land* (1912). Boston: Houghton Mifflin Co., 1969.

Aquinas, Thomas — *Aquinas: Selected Political Writings.* Translated by A. P. D'Entrèves. (Blackwell's Political Texts) Oxford: Basil Blackwell & Mott, Ltd., 1959. *Selected Writings of St. Thomas Aquinas.* Translated by Robert P. Goodwin. New York: Bobbs Merrill Co., 1965. *Summa Theologicae.* 60 vols. New York: McGraw-Hill, 1964-. *The Political Ideas of St. Thomas Aquinas:* Representative Selections. Edited by Dino Bigongiari. New York: Hafner Publishing Co., 1953.

Aristotle — *Aristotle's Politics and Athenian Constitution.* Edited and translated by John Warrington. New York: E. P. Dutton & Co., 1959. *The Politics of Aristotle.* Translated and with notes by Ernest Barker. New York: Oxford University Press, 1962. (Also available in Viking and Penguin paperbacks and in The Modern Library.)

Bacon, Francis   *The Advancement of Learning* (1605). *Essays* (1625). *Essays, Advancement of Learning, New Atlantis and Other Pieces.* Edited by Richard F. Stone. New York: Odyssey Press, 1937. (*Essays* available in various other editions, including Oxford University Press and Everyman's Library.)

Bagehot, Walter   *The English Constitution* (1867). Ithaca, N.Y.: Cornell University Press, 1966. *Physics and Politics* (1867). New York: Alfred A. Knopf, 1948. *Collected Works of Walter Bagehot.* Edited by St. John-Stevas. 2 vols. Cambridge, Mass.: Harvard University Press, 1965.

Bakunin, Michael   *State and Anarchy* (1873). *Bakunin on Anarchy: Selected Works.* Edited and translated by Sam Dolgoff. New York: Alfred A. Knopf, 1972; Vintage Books, 1972.

Barclay, Robert   Propositions Regarding the Quaker Faith (1678). *Barclay's Apology in Modern English.* Edited by Dean Freiday. Privately published by Dean Freiday and Religious Society of Friends, Elberon, N.J.: 1967.

Black, Justice Hugo L.   *United States Reports.* Washington, D.C.: Government Printing Office: *Chambers* v. *Florida,* 1940, 309 U.S. 227; *Dennis* v. *U.S.,* 1951, 339 U.S. 162; *Engel* v. *Vitale,* 1962, 370 U.S. 421; *Everson* v. *Board of Education,* 1947, 330 U.S. 1; *McCollum* v. *Board of Education,* 1948, 333 U.S. 203; *Torcaso* v. *Watkins,* 1961, 367 U.S. 488; *Zorach* v. *Clauson,* 1952, 43 U.S. 306. *The Living U.S. Constitution.* Edited by Saul K. Padover. New York: New American Library, 1968.

Bossuet, Jacques   *Oeuvres complètes de Bossuet.* 43 vols. Versailles: J. A. Lebel, 1815-19.

Bradford, William   *History of Plymouth Plantation.* Edited by William T. Davis. New York: Barnes & Noble, Inc., 1959 (reprint of 1908 edition).

Brandeis, Louis   *United States Reports.* Washington, D.C.: Government Printing Office: *Whitney* v. *California,* 1927, 274 U.S. 357. *The Brandeis Guide to the Modern World.* Edited by A. Lief. Boston: Little Brown, 1941.

Brown, Justice Henry B.   *United States Reports.* Washington, D.C.: Government Printing Office: *Plessy* v. *Ferguson,* 1896, 163 U.S. 537.

Brown, John   *American Short Speeches.* Edited by Bower and Lucile F. Aly. New York: The Macmillan Company, 1968.

Bryce, James   *The American Commonwealth* (1888). 2 vols. New York: The Macmillan Company, 1893-95.

Burke, Edmund — *The Correspondence of Edmund Burke.* Edited by Thomas W. Copeland. 9 vols. Chicago: University of Chicago Press, 1958–63. *Reflections on the Revolution in France* (1790). Edited and with Introduction by Thomas H. D. Mahoney. New York: Liberal Arts Press, 1955. (Also available in Rinehart Editions, Dolphin, and Everyman's Library.)

Calhoun, John C. — *A Disquisition on Government* (1851). Edited by C. Gordon Post. New York: Liberal Arts Press, 1953.

Calvin, John — *Institutes of the Christian Religion* (1559). Translated by John Allen, revised by Benjamin Warfield. Presbyterian Board of Christian Education, 1928.

Carnot, Lazare — *Modern Eloquence.* Edited by Ashley H. Thorndike. Vol. 12. New York: Modern Eloquence Corporation, 1928.

Channing, William Ellery — *The Works of William E. Channing.* Boston: American Unitarian Association, 1856.

Constantine I — Holsapple, Lloyd B. *Constantine the Great.* New York: Sheed and Ward, 1942.

Cooper, James Fenimore — *The American Democrat* (1838). New York: Funk & Wagnalls, 1969. (Also available in a Penguin edition.)

Cramer, John — *Reports of the Proceedings and Debates of the Convention of 1821.* Nathaniel H. Carter & William Stone, Reporters. Albany, N.Y.: E. & E. Hosford, 1821.

Crévecoeur, J. Hector St. John de — *Letters from an American Farmer* (1782). Garden City, N.Y.: Doubleday, 1961. (Also available in Everyman's Library.)

Cromwell, Oliver — "The Instrument of Government" (1653).

Curtis, George William — *Proceedings and Debates of the Constitutional Convention of the State of New York, 1867-68.* Albany, N.Y.: Albion Wood, printer, 1868.

Debs, Eugene Victor — *Eugene V. Debs Speaks.* Edited by Jean Y. Tussey. New York: Pathfinder Press, 1970.

Dewey, John — *School and Society.* Chicago: University of Chicago Press, 1961.

Diderot, Denis — *Refutations de Helvetius* (c. 1774). *Selected Writings.* Edited by Lester G. Crocker, translated by Derek Coltman. New York: The Macmillan Company, 1966.

Dix, Dorothea Lynde — *Memorial to the Legislature of Massachusetts* (1843). Old South Leaflets, vol. 6, no. 148. Boston, 1904.

Douglas, Justice William O. *United States Reports.* Washington, D.C.: Government Printing Office: *Engel* v. *Vitale,* 1962, 370 U.S. 421; *Zorach* v. *Clauson,* 1952, 43 U.S. 306; *Harper* v. *Virginia Board of Elections,* 1966, 383 U.S. 663.

Eisenhower, Dwight D. *Selected Speeches of Dwight David Eisenhower.* Washington, D.C.: Government Printing Office, 1970.

Elizabeth I Act of 1594.

Emerson, Ralph Waldo *The Complete Writings of Ralph Waldo Emerson.* New York: William H. Wise & Co., 1875, 1929. (Selections from essays and poems are available in numerous paperback editions—Pyramid, Dover, Viking, and The Modern Library.)

Federalist, The *The Federalist.* Edited by Henry Cabot Lodge. New York: The Modern Library, 1941. (Many paperbacks containing some of the papers are available.)

Frankfurter, Justice Felix *United States Reports.* Washington, D.C.: Government Printing Office: *Minersville School District* v. *Gobitis,* 1940, 310 U.S. 586; *McCollum* v. *Board of Education,* 1948, 333 U.S. 203; *West Virginia State Board of Education* v. *Barnette,* 1943, 319 U.S. 624.

Franklin, Benjamin *Complete Works of Benjamin Franklin.* Edited by John Bigelow. 10 vols. New York: G. P. Putnam's Sons, 1887-88.

Fuller, Margaret *Woman in the Nineteenth Century* (1845) by [Sarah] Margaret Fuller Ossoli. Edited by Arthur B. Fuller with an Introduction by Horace Greely. New York: The Tribune Association, 1869.

Galerius Edict of Toleration, 311 A.D.

Garfield, James A. *The Presidents Speak: The Inaugural Addresses of the American Presidents from Washington to Nixon.* 3d ed. New York: Holt, Rinehart & Winston, 1969.

Garrison, William Lloyd *Modern Eloquence.* Edited by Ashley H. Thorndike. Vol. 13. New York: Modern Eloquence Corporation, 1928.

Godwin, Parke *Democracy, Constructive and Pacific* (1844). New York: J. Winchester, 1844.

Grant, Ulysses S. *A Compilation of the Messages and Papers of the Presidents, 1789-1897.* Washington, D.C.: Government Printing Office, 1896-1900.

Hall, Francis *Travels in Canada and the United States in 1816 and 1817.* Boston: Wells and Lilly, 1818.

Hamilton, Alexander	*The Mind of Alexander Hamilton.* Edited by Saul K. Padover. New York: Harper & Bros., 1958. *The Works of Alexander Hamilton.* Edited by Henry Cabot Lodge. New York: Putnam, 1904.
Harrison, William Henry	*The Presidents Speak: The Inaugural Addresses of the American Presidents from Washington to Nixon.* 3d ed. New York: Holt, Rinehart & Winston, 1969.
Helvétius, Claude Adrien	*A Treatise on Man* (1773). Translated with Notes by W. Hooper. New & rev. ed. Albion Press, 1910.
Henry IV	Edict of Nantes, April 15, 1598.
Hobbes, Thomas	*Leviathan.* Edited and with Introduction by John Plamenatz. New York and Cleveland: World, 1963. (Also available in various other editions, including Everyman's Library and Penguin Books.)
Holmes, Justice Oliver Wendell	*United States Reports.* Washington, D.C.: Government Printing Office: *Abrams* v. *U.S.,* 1919, 250 U.S. 616; *Schenck* v. *U.S.,* 1919, 249 U.S. 47.
Hoover, Herbert	*The Challenge to Liberty.* New York: Scribner, 1934.
Hughes, Chief Justice Charles Evans	*United States Reports.* Washington, D.C.: Government Printing Office: *De Jonge* v. *Oregon,* 1937, 299 U.S. 353.
Hume, David	*The History of England* (1759) Vol. III: The Invasion of Julius Caesar to the Revolution in 1688. Boston: Phillips, 1850–58.
Ickes, Harold L.	*A Treasury of Great American Speeches.* Selected by Charles Hurd, revised by Andrew Bauer. New York: Hawthorn Books, 1970.
Jackson, Andrew	*The Presidents Speak: The Inaugural Addresses of the American Presidents from Washington to Nixon.* 3d ed. New York: Holt, Rinehart & Winston. 1969.
Jackson, Justice Robert H.	*United States Reports.* Washington, D.C.: Government Printing Office: *Everson* v. *Board of Education,* 1947, 330 U.S. 1; *West Virginia Board of Education* v. *Barnette,* 1943, 319 U.S. 624; *Zorach* v. *Clauson,* 1952, 343 U.S. 306.
Jefferson, Thomas	*Notes on Virginia* (1782). Edited with Introduction by William Peden. Chapel Hill, N.C.: University of North Carolina Press, 1955. *The Complete Jefferson.* Containing His Major Writings. Published and Unpublished. Except His Letters. Edited by Saul K. Padover. New York: Duell, Sloan & Pearce, Inc., 1943. *A Jefferson Profile, as Revealed in His Letters.* Edited by Saul K. Padover. New York: The John Day

Co., 1956. Saul K. Padover, *Thomas Jefferson and the Foundations of American Freedom.* New York: D. Van Nostrand Co., 1965. *The Writings of Thomas Jefferson.* Edited by Saul K. Padover. New York: The Heritage Press, 1967. *Basic Writings of Thomas Jefferson.* Edited by Philip S. Foner. New York: Wiley Book Co., 1944. *The Life and Selected Writings of Thomas Jefferson.* Edited and with Introduction by Adrienne Koch and William Peden. New York: Random House, 1944. *The Writings of Thomas Jefferson.* Edited by A. A. Lipscomb and A. E. Bergh. 20 vols. Washington, D.C.: The Thomas Jefferson Memorial Assn. of the United States, 1903. *The Papers of Thomas Jefferson,* 55 vols. Princeton, N.J.: Princeton University Press, 1950-.

Johnson, Lyndon B. *The Presidents Speak: The Inaugural Addresses of the American Presidents from Washington to Nixon.* 3d ed. New York: Holt, Rinehart & Winston, 1969.

Julian, Emperor Edict for Religious Freedom, 363 A.D.

Julius II, Pope Papal Bull, July 28, 1508.

Kennedy, John F. *The Presidents Speak: The Inaugural Addresses of the American Presidents from Washington to Nixon.* 3d ed. New York: Holt, Rinehart & Winston, 1969.

Kent, James *Reports of the Proceedings and Debates of the Convention of 1821.* Nathaniel H. Carter & William Stone, Reporters. Albany, N.Y.: E. & E. Hosford, 1821.

King, Martin Luther Jr. Address In Montgomery, Alabama, March 25, 1965.

Lincoln, Abraham *Collected Works of Abraham Lincoln.* Edited by Roy P. Basler. The Abraham Lincoln Association. 8 vols. New Brunswick, N.J.: Rutgers University Press, 1953. *Complete Works of Abraham Lincoln.* Edited by John G. Nicolay and John Hay. 12 vols. New York: Tandy, 1905. *Abraham Lincoln's Speeches and Writings.* Edited by Roy P. Basler. New York and Cleveland: World, 1969.

Locke, John *Two Treatises of Government* (1690). Edited by Peter Laslett. Cambridge, England: Cambridge University Press, 1960. (The separate treatises are also available in various paperback editions.)

Lollards "The Twelve Conclusions The Lollards (1394)." *English Historical Review,* Vol. 22, pp. 292-304. London, 1907.

Luther, Martin *The Works of Martin Luther.* 6 vols. Philadelphia: Holman Company, 1915-32.

Macaulay, Thomas Babington	*Critical and Historical Essays* (1846). Selected by Hugh Trevor-Roper. New York: McGraw-Hill, 1965.
Madison, James	(For editions of *The Federalist*, see *Federalist, The.*) *The Presidents Speak: The Inaugural Addresses of the American Presidents from Washington to Nixon*, 3d ed. New York: Holt, Rinehart & Winston, 1969. *The Forging of American Federalism.* Edited by Saul K. Padover. New York: Harper & Row, 1953; Harper Torch Books, 1965.
Maine, Sir Henry	*Popular Government* London: J. Murray; 1885.
Mann, Horace	*The Republic and the School: The Education of Free Men.* Edited by Laurence A. Cremen. New York: Teachers College, Columbia University Press, 1957.
Marsiglio (Marsilius) of Padua	*Defensor Pacis. The Defender of Peace.* Translated with an Introduction by Alan Gewirth. New York: Columbia University Press, 1956. (A paperback edition is available in Harper Torch Books.)
Marx, Karl	*Anekdota zur neuesten deutschen Philosophie und Publicistik* (1843). *On the First International,* Translated by Saul K. Padover. Vol. III of the Karl Marx Library. New York: McGraw-Hill Book Co., 1973.
Mill, John Stuart	*Consideration on Representative Government.* Edited by Currin V. Shields. New York: Bobbs Merrill, 1958. (Also available in various other paperback editions.) *On Liberty.* Edited by Currin V. Shields. New York: Bobbs Merrill, 1958.
Milton, John	*The Complete Works of John Milton.* Edited by F. A. Patterson. New York: Columbia University Press, 1931–38.
Monroe, James	*The Presidents Speak: The Inaugural Addresses of the American Presidents from Washington to Nixon.* 3d ed. New York: Holt, Rinehart & Winston, 1969.
Montesquieu, Charles de Secondat, Baron de	*The Spirit of the Laws* (1748). Translated by Thomas Nugent. New York: Hafner Publishing Co., 1966.
More, Sir Thomas	*Utopia* (1516). Leeds, England: Scholar Press, 1966. (Also available in Penguin and Washington Square Press editions.) *Ideal Empires and Republics.* Edited by Charles Andrews. M. Walter Dunne, 1901. *The Complete Works of St. Thomas More.* Modernized series New Haven, Conn.: Yale University Press, 1961-.

Murphy, Justice Frank — *United States Reports.* Washington, D.C.: Government Printing Office: *West Virginia Board of Education* v. *Barnette,* 1943, 319 U.S. 624.

Paine, Thomas — *The Complete Writings of Thomas Paine.* Edited by Philip S. Foner. 2 vols. New York: Citadel Press, 1945. (Also available in Dutton and Penguin editions.) *The Life and Works of Thomas Paine.* Edited by William M. Van der Weyde. Thomas Paine National Historical Association, 1925.

Penn, William — Pennsylvania Charter of Privileges, 1701.

Phillips, Wendell — *Woman's Rights* (1851). *Speeches, Lectures and Letters.* Boston: Lee and Shepard, 1884.

Plutarch — *The Lives of the Noble Grecians and Romans.* Translated by John Dryden and revised by Arthur Hugh Clough. New York: The Modern Library, 1932. (There are various abridged versions available in paperback.)

Polybius — *The Histories.* Translated by W. R. Paton. Cambridge, Mass.: Harvard University Press, 1923.

Pufendorf, Samuel — *Of the Law of Nature and Nations* (1672). Translated by C. H. and W. A. Oldfather. Oxford, England: The Clarendon Press, 1934.

Pym, John — Speech, in Short Parliament, April 17, 1640. *The Kingdomes Manifestation.* London: B. H. and J. West, 1643.

Records of the Federal Convention of 1787 — Edited by M. Farrand, 1937. Condensed by Saul K. Padover in *To Secure These Blessings.* New York: Washington Square Press, 1962.

Roosevelt, Franklin D. — *The Presidents Speak: The Inaugural Addresses of the American Presidents from Washington to Nixon.* 3d ed. New York: Holt, Rinehart & Winston, 1969. *The Public Papers and Addresses of Franklin D. Roosevelt.* Edited by Samuel I. Rosenman. 9 vols. New York: Random House, 1938–1950. *Nothing to Fear:* Selected Addresses of Franklin D. Roosevelt, 1932–1945. Edited by B. D. Zevin. Boston: Houghton Mifflin, 1946.

Roosevelt, Theodore — *The Presidents Speak: The Inaugural Addresses of the American Presidents from Washington to Nixon.* 3d ed. New York: Holt, Rinehart & Winston, 1969.

Rousseau, Jean Jacques — *The Social Contract and Discourses.* Translated with Introduction by G. D. H. Cole. New York: Everyman's Library, 1950. (*A Discourse* is also available in a Washington Square

Press paperback edition, and *The Social Contract* is in Penguin, Washington Square Press, and Hafner paperbacks.) *Émile* (1762). New York: Everyman's Library, 1933. (*Émile* is also available in a Barron paperback edition.)

Sanford, Justice Edward T.   *United States Reports.* Washington, D.C.: Government Printing Office: *Gitlow* v. *New York,* 1925, 268 U.S. 652.

Sidney, Sir Algernon   *Discourse on Government* (1698). *Discourses.* Edited by J. Toland, 1763.

Smith, Alfred E.   *Campaign Addresses of Governor Alfred E. Smith, Democratic Candidate for President, 1928.* Washington, D.C.: The Democratic National Committee, 1929. *A Treasury of Great American Speeches.* Selected by Charles Hurd. Revised by Andrew Bauer. New York: Hawthorn Books, 1970.

Spinoza, Baruch (or Benedict)   *Tractatus-Theologico-Politicus* (1670). *The Chief Works of Benedict Spinoza.* Translated with Introduction by R. H. M. Elwes. New York: Dover, 1951.

Stewart, Justice Potter   *United States Reports.* Washington, D.C.: Government Printing Office: *Engel* v. *Vitale,* 1962, 370 U.S. 421.

Stone, Chief Justice Harlan F.   *United States Reports.* Washington, D.C.: Government Printing Office. *Minersville School District* v. *Gobitis,* 1940, 310 U.S. 586.

Taft, William Howard   *The Presidents Speak: The Inaugural Addresses of the American Presidents from Washington to Nixon.* 3d ed. New York: Holt, Rinehart & Winston, 1969.

Taylor, John   *An Inquiry into the Principles and Policy of the Government of the United States* (1814). New Haven: Yale University Press, 1950.

Tecumseh, Chief   *Modern Eloquence.* Edited by Ashley H. Thorndike. Vol. 15. New York: Modern Eloquence Corporation, 1928.

Theodosius I   Edict, "Cuntos Populos," 380 A.D.

Thucydides   *History of the Peloponnesian War.* Edited by Richard Livingstone. New York: Oxford University Press. 1943. (Also available in Penguin and Washington Square Press abridged editions.)

Tocqueville, Alexis de   *Democracy in America* (1835). Translated by Henry Reeves. Edited and revised by Francis Bowan. 2 vols. New York: Vintage Books, 1958. (Also available in other paperback editions, most abridged versions.)

Townshend   *Report of the Debates and Proceedings of the Convention for the Revision of the Constitution of the State of Ohio, 1850-51.* Columbus, Ohio: S. Medary, 1851.

Trezvant   *Proceedings and Debates of the Virginia Convention of 1829-30.* Winchester, Va.: S. H. Davis, 1830.

Truman, Harry S.   *The Presidents Speak: The Inaugural Addresses of the American Presidents from Washington to Nixon.* 3d ed. New York: Holt, Rinehart & Winston, 1969.

U.S. Commission on Civil Rights   *Voting: 1961 Commission on Civil Rights Report.* Washington, D.C.: U.S. Government Printing Office, 1961.

Upshur, Abel Parker   *Proceedings and Debates of the Virginia Convention of 1829-30.* Winchester, Va.: S. H. Davis.

Valentinian III   Edict, 445 A.D.

Vinson, Chief Justice Frederick M.   *United States Reports.* Washington, D.C.: Government Printing Office: *Dennis* v. *U.S.,* 1951, 341 U.S. 494.

Voltaire, F. M. Arouet de   *Philosophical Dictionary.* Edited and translated by Theodore Besterman. New York and London: Penguin Books, 1971.

Waite, Justice Morrison Remick   *United States Reports.* Washington, D.C.: Government Printing Office: *Minor* v. *Happersett,* 1875, 21 Wallace 162.

Ward, Nathaniel   Massachusetts "Body of Liberties," (1641). *The Earliest New England Code of Laws,* 1641. American History Leaflets. Edited by A. B. Hart and E. Channing. No. 25, Jan. 1896.

Warren, Chief Justice Earl   United States Reports. Washington, D.C.: Government Printing Office: *Brown* v. *Board of Education of Topeka.* 1954, 347 U.S. 483.

Washington, George   *The Washington Papers.* Edited and with Introduction by Saul K. Padover. New York: Harper & Bros., 1955; University Library, 1967.

Webster, Daniel   *Selected Speeches of Daniel Webster.* Introduction by A. J. George. Boston: D.C. Heath & Co., 1911. *The Works of Daniel Webster.* 6 vols. Boston: Little Brown, 1853.

Whitman, Walt   *Leaves of Grass and Selected Prose Poems.* Edited with Introduction by John Kouwenhoven. New York: Modern Library, 1950. (*Leaves of Grass* is also available in Viking Press, Norton, and other paperback editions.)

Williams, Roger   *The Bloody Tenent of Persecution for Cause of Conscience* (1644). Edited by Edward Bean Underhill for the Hanserd Knollys Society, 1848. *The Complete Writings of Roger Williams.* New York: Russell & Russell, 1963.

Willkie, Wendell L.   Radio Address, July 4, 1941.

Wilson, Woodrow   *President Wilson's State Papers and Messages.* Edited by Albert Shaw. New York: George H. Doran Co., 1917. *Wil-*

son's Ideals. Edited by Saul K. Padover. Washington, D.C.: American Council on Public Affairs, 1942. *Public Papers of Woodrow Wilson.* Edited by Ray Stannard Baker and William E. Dodd. 6 vols. New York: Harper & Bros., 1925–27.

Winthrop, John   *A Treasury of Great American Speeches.* Selected by Charles Hurd. Revised by Andrew Bauer. New rev. ed. New York: Hawthorn Books, 1970

Wise, John   *A Vindication of the Government of the New-England Churches* (1717). Facsimile edition with Introduction by Perry Miller. Gainesville, Fla.: Scholars Facsimiles and Reprints, 1958.

BIBLIOGRAPHY

The following list of readings, all too brief among the myriad of books available on the subject of democracy, may be helpful for a general orientation. For a more extensive bibliography, the reader is referred to Saul K. Padover's *The Meaning of Democracy* (1963), pp. 123–31; and R. S. Hoyt, "Recent Publications in the United States and Canada on the History of Representative Institutions before the French Revolution," in *Speculum* (1954), pp. 356–77.

Collections:

Blau, J. L.   *Cornerstones of Religious Freedom in America* (1949)

Coker, F. W.   *Democracy, Liberty, and Property* (1942)

Edman, I.   *Fountainheads of Freedom: The Growth of the Democratic Idea* (1941)

Mason, A. T.   *Free Government in the Making: Readings in American Political Thought* (1949)

Rhys, E.   *The Growth of Political Liberty: A Source Book of English History* (1942)

Padover, S. K.   *The World of the Founding Fathers: Their Basic Ideas on Freedom and Self-Government* (1960)

Pennock, J. R. and Chapman, J. W.   *Representation* (1968)

Histories:

Acton, Lord   *The History of Freedom and Other Essays* (1907)

Bury, J. B.   *A History of Freedom of Thought* (1913)

Croce, B.   *History as the Story of Liberty* (1941)

Glover, T. R.   *Democracy in the Ancient World* (1927)

Gooch, G. P.   *English Democratic Ideas in the Seventeenth Century* (rev. ed., 1927)

Jones, A. H. M.   *Athenian Democracy* (1958)

Larsen, J. O. A.   *Representative Government in Greek and Roman History* (1955)

Palmer, R. R.   *The Age of the Democratic Revolution* (1959 and 1964)

Schapiro, J. S.   *Liberalism: Its Meaning and History* (1958)

Talmon, J. L.   *The Rise of Totalitarian Democracy* (1960)

Thomson, D.   *The Democratic Ideal in France and England* (1940)

Theories and Interpretations:

Commager, H. S.	*Majority Rule and Minority Rights* (1950)
Dahl, R. A.	*A Preface to Democratic Theory* (1956)
Downs, A.	*An Economic Theory of Democracy* (1957)
Hallowell, J. H.	*The Moral Foundation of Democracy* (1954)
Hook, S.	*Political Power and Personal Freedom* (1959)
Laski, H.	*Liberty in the Modern State* (1930)
Lippmann, W.	*Essays in the Public Philosophy* (1955)
Lipset, S. M.	*Political Man: The Social Bases of Politics* (1960)
Locke, J.	*A Letter Concerning Toleration* (1689)
Mannheim, K.	*Freedom, Power and Democratic Planning* (1950)
Maritain, J.	*Christianity and Democracy* (1944)
Mayo, H. B.	*An Introduction to Democratic Theory* (1960)
Mill, John Stuart	*Utilitarianism, Liberty and Representative Government* (1863)
Niebuhr, R.	*The Children of Light and the Children of Darkness: A Vindication of Democracy and a Critique of its Traditional Defense* (1944)
Ortega y Gasset, J.	*Revolt of the Masses* (1932)
Padover, S. K.	*The Forging of American Federalism* (1965)
Pennock, J. R.	*Liberal Democracy: Its Merits and Prospects* (1950)
Plamenatz, J.	*Aspects of Human Equality* (1956)
Popper, K. R.	*The Open Society and Its Enemies* (1945)
Salvadori, M.	*Liberal Democracy* (1957)
Sartori, G.	*Democratic Theory* (1962)
Schumpeter, J.	*Capitalism, Socialism and Democracy* (1943)
Simon, Y.	*The Philosophy of Democratic Government* (1951)
Spitz, D.	*Democracy and the Challenge of Power* (1958)
Tawney, R. H.	*Equality* (1931)
Wootton, B.	*Freedom Under Planning* (1945)

Practices:

Cahn, E.	*The Predicament of Democratic Man* (1961)
Dahl, R. A.	*Who Governs: Democracy and Power in an American Community* (1961)
Dewey, J.	*Democracy and Education* (1916)

Dewey, J. *Liberalism and Social Action* (1935)

Gellhorn, W. *Individual Freedom and Governmental Restraint* (1956)

Hunter, Floyd *Community Power Structure* (1963)

Key, V. O. *Public Opinion and American Democracy* (1961)

Lakeman, E., and
Lambert, J. D. *Voting in Democracies* (1955)

Lasswell, H. D. *Democracy Through Public Opinion* (1941)

Lowry, R. P. *Who's Running This Town?* (1965)

Meiklejohn, A. *Free Speech and Its Relation to Self-Government* (1948)

Michels, R. *Political Parties: A Sociological Study of the Oligarchical Tendencies of Modern Democracy* (1949)

Ranney, A., and Kendall, W. *Democracy and the American Party System* (1956)

Warner, W. Lloyd *Democracy in Jonesville* (1949)

Williams, O. P., and Press, C. *Democracy in Urban America* (1964)

The American View and Experience:

Beard, C. A. *Economic Origins of Jeffersonian Democracy* (1915)

Chafee, Z. *Free Speech in the United States* (1942)

Commager, H. S. *The American Mind* (1950)

Curti, M. E. *Growth of American Thought* (1943)

Filler, L. *Crusaders for American Liberalism* (1940)

Gabriel, R. H. *The Course of Democratic Thought* (1941)

Goldman, E. *Rendezvous with Destiny* (1952)

Hartz, L. *The Liberal Tradition in America* (1955)

Hofstadter, R. *The American Political Tradition and the Men Who Made It* (1951)

Kornhauser, A., ed. *Problems of Power in American Democracy* (1957)

Padover, S. K. *The Genius of America* (1960)

Padover, S. K., ed. *Jefferson on Democracy* (1939)

Padover, S. K. *Thomas Jefferson and the Foundations of American Freedom* (1965)

Rossiter, C. *Seedtime of the Republic: The Origin of the American Tradition of Political Liberty* (1953)

Tocqueville, A. de *Democracy in America* (2 vols., 1958)

INDEX

A